The
Secret
Teachings
of
All Ages

READER'S EDITION

Phoenix

MANLY P. HALL

COLOR ILLUSTRATIONS BY J. AUGUSTUS KNAPP

JEREMY P. TARCHER/PENGUIN   a member of Penguin Group (USA) Inc.   *New York*

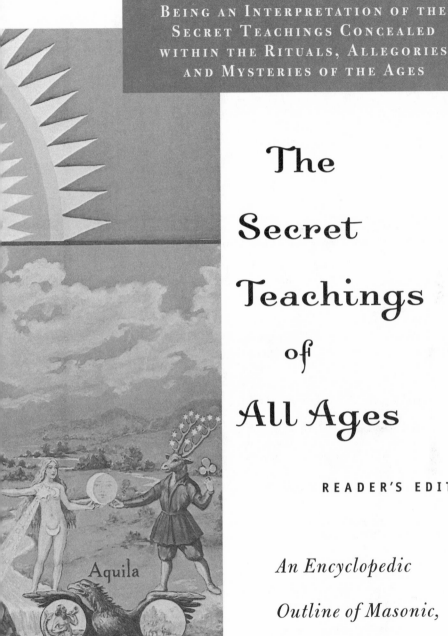

BEING AN INTERPRETATION OF THE
SECRET TEACHINGS CONCEALED
WITHIN THE RITUALS, ALLEGORIES
AND MYSTERIES OF THE AGES

The Secret Teachings of All Ages

READER'S EDITION

An Encyclopedic

Outline of Masonic,

Hermetic, Qabbalistic

and Rosicrucian

Symbolical Philosophy

Aquila

Jeremy P. Tarcher/Penguin
a member of
Penguin Group (USA) Inc.
375 Hudson Street
New York, NY 10014
www.penguin.com

First Trade Paperback Edition 2003

Library of Congress Cataloging-in-Publication Data

Hall, Manly Palmer, date.
    The secret teachings of all ages : an encyclopedic outline of Masonic, Hermetic,
    Qabbalistic and Rosicrucian symbolical philosophy : being an interpretation of the secret
    teachings concealed within the rituals, allegories and mysteries of all ages / by Manly P.
    Hall ; color illustrations by J. Augustus Knapp.—Reader's ed.
       p. cm.
    Originally published: Los Angeles, Calif.: Philosophical Research Society, 1928.
    Includes bibliographical references and index.
    ISBN 1-58542-250-9 (alk. paper)
    1. Occultism—History. 2. Symbolism. 3. Mysteries, Religious. 4. Secret societies.
    5. Freemasonry—Symbolism. 6. Hermetism. 7. Cabala. I. Title.
    BF1411.H3   2003   2003053721
    135'.4—dc21

Book design by Mauna Eichner

Printed in the United States of America

30 29 28 27 26 25 24 23

*This book is
dedicated to the
Rational Soul
of the World*

Contents

Preface to the Reader's Edition

hat you hold in your hands is a volume of the ages. Originally published in 1928 by the mystical scholar and sage Manly P. Hall (1901–1990), this book—like none before it and none that have followed—is a codex to the ideas and mysteries that resonate within the symbols, myths, and philosophies that have guided humankind since its earliest efforts at self-knowledge.

The Philosophical Research Society (www.prs.org) of Los Angeles has been the publisher of *The Secret Teachings of All Ages* since Mr. Hall founded the organization in 1934. Today, PRS continues to publish the original edition of the *Secret Teachings* and, through public lectures, research, publications, and the University of Philosophical Research, continues his legacy. With that legacy in mind, PRS has worked with Tarcher/Penguin to create this new "Reader's Edition" of Mr. Hall's classic work.

This edition brings a new level of accessibility to Mr. Hall's magisterial volume. The text is fully reset and the pages renumbered according to contemporary numerals, rather than the Roman numerals of the original edition. The original features fifty-four color plates by the artist J. Augustus Knapp and more than two hundred line drawings. This edition includes some of the finest of the color plates and approximately one hundred of the most pertinent line drawings.

Otherwise, the book is largely unaltered. It retains Mr. Hall's original index and—with the exception of small excisions for clarity and ease of use—features his complete unabridged text.

—OBADIAH S. HARRIS, PH.D.
President
Philosophical Research Society
April 1, 2003

Preface to the Diamond Jubilee Edition

n the occasion of the sixtieth anniversary of this volume, it seems fitting to reflect on the circumstances that led to its writing.

The original edition was planned and issued in the interval between the termination of World War I and the Great Depression of 1929. During this time I had a brief career on Wall Street, the outstanding event of which was witnessing a man depressed over investment losses take his life.

My fleeting contact with high finance resulted in serious doubts concerning business as it was being conducted at that time. It was apparent that materialism was in complete control of the economic structure, the final objective of which was for the individual to become part of a system providing an economic security at the expense of the human soul, mind, and body.

I felt strongly moved to explore the problems of humanity, its origin and destiny, and I spent a number of quiet hours in the New York Public Library tracing the confused course of civilization. With a very few exceptions modern authorities downgraded all systems of idealistic philosophy and the deeper aspects of comparative religion. Translations of classical authors could differ greatly, but in most cases the noblest thoughts were eliminated or denigrated. Those more sincere authors whose knowledge of ancient languages was profound were never included as required reading, and scholarship was based largely upon the acceptance of a sterile materialism.

Fortunately, since contemporary scholarship had little regard for the wisdom of the past, there was no premium on the earlier texts. As a result I assembled a fair collection of the works of those forgotten sages to whose labors the world owes a tremendous debt of gratitude. It seems that my efforts were timely, and the first two editions of the book were sold out before the volume came off the press. There was certainly a blessing upon the book. Written by a young man in his twenties, it has now passed through a number of editions with over thirty printings and is still a best seller in its field.

We are now coming to the end of the twentieth century, and the great materialistic progress which we have venerated for so long is on the verge of bankruptcy. We can no longer believe that we are born into this world to accumulate wealth and abandon ourselves to mortal pleasures. We see the dangers and realize that we have been exploited for centuries. We were told that the twentieth century was the most progressive that the world has ever known, but unfortunately the progression was in the direction of self-destruction.

To avoid a future of war, crime, and bankruptcy, the individual must begin to plan his own destiny, and the best source of the necessary information comes down to us through the writings of the ancients. We have tried to select the most useful and practical elements of classical idealism, combining them into a single volume. The greatest knowledge of all time should be available to the twentieth century not only in the one shilling editions of the Bohn Library in small type and shabby binding, but in a book that would be a monument, not merely a coffin. John Henry Nash, who designed this book, agreed with me.

It is our sincere hope that this book will endure into the twenty-first century and continue to make available the contents of countless books and manuscripts that have been destroyed by the ravages of war. This volume is not devoted to my own opinions but is a tribute to the memories and labors of the noblest of mankind. May the twenty-first century bring with it a restoration of those systems of inspired instruction so desperately needed.

> —MANLY P. HALL
> Los Angeles, California
> October 1, 1988

Foreword

I t is an honor to have been invited to write this Foreword. My aim shall be to set forth briefly what a careful study of this important volume, over a period of years, has meant to me.

Associations of men and women bound together by oaths and obligations into esoteric fraternities have descended from the earliest times and bear witness to a natural inclination to perpetuate doctrines which lead to the good of mankind.

With the growth of social consciousness, these secret societies became the custodians of the highest cultural concepts. Their initiation rites were symbolic pageantries suitable to inspire veneration for the Divine Mysteries, and admiration for the powers of nature and of God. Most of the mythologies of classical nations were originally rituals of secret societies, and it is a mistake to assume that earlier cultures accepted as literal the elaborate theology and legendry found in their traditions.

Historically the secret societies were closely identified with state religions. Basic knowledge was believed to have been bestowed by the gods in a remote age. The esoteric philosophies have always been taught by means of secret organizations, to which candidates were admitted only after appropriate preparation and initiatory rites. These spiritual brotherhoods of scholars, sages, and mystics have flourished among all peoples, ancient and modern, and in all parts of the world.

In the program of the Mysteries each individual must grow into the comprehension of truth. Before he could be entrusted with the divine powers of mind and will, he must accept knowledge as a responsibility to his Creator and his world, rather than as an opportunity for the advancement of personal ambitions. The masters of the Mysteries taught secret practices and disciplines by which the properly qualified disciples could develop the potent abilities latent within the soul, and so, come into conscious communication with spiritual realities.

Initiates of the philosophical societies came to be regarded as possessing extraordinary faculties and powers. They enjoyed the special favor of the divinities, performed miracles, and were worthy of the title "Twice-Born," for they had come to second birth from the womb of the Mysteries. These adepts-philosophers were the truly evolved human beings. Most of the arts and sciences which enriched the modern world were discovered, developed, and in many instances perfected by these initiate philosophers and priests.

Scholarship was recognized as the pursuit most suitable to the abilities of man. But scholarship was always the means, never the end. The end of the sacred sciences was the abstraction of the human soul from bondage to the senses and its preparation to receive within itself the light of vast truths. Some men are naturally suited to higher learning for they possess integrity of motive, the patience of effort, and the vision of ends—these labored toward the soul's improvement, and championed enlightened progress above other considerations. Those of different opinion opposed the Mystery Schools.

It was inevitable that the initiates of the Mysteries should unite themselves against the forces seeking their extinction. Thus, while the secret doctrine with its body of disciples functioned more or less openly in ancient society, it later passed almost completely from public view. This circumstance should not be interpreted as a decline of plan or purpose. The esoteric schools remained as a powerful force for the regeneration of human institutions.

Those who do not understand the spiritual sciences question their use of unusual symbols, myths, and figures employed to conceal the essential teaching. Let it be remembered that these "clouds" were no part of the original doctrine, but were made necessary by intolerance and bigotry. The use of indirect communication was based entirely upon practical considerations. To remain unknown was the best way to prevent a repetition of the disaster which occurred to the Knights Templars. The "veils" which concealed the arcana of the Mysteries were not employed to cover ignorance, but to protect wisdom, and in Europe it was protected for a thousand years.

The secrets of the Mysteries are obviously metaphysical, philosophical, and esoteric and relate to processes taking place within the fields of the human psyche during the practice of the spiritual disciplines. Discipleship ends in the attainment of an inner capacity suitable for the realization of the esoteric tradition. The disciplines, by expanding consciousness, give the initiate practical mastery over that which is learned and constant awareness as to the proper use of higher learning.

If these sacred academies imparted only scientific, intellectual, ethical or cultural doctrines somewhat in advance of their time, they could produce only scholars. The initiates of the esoteric tradition were never regarded merely as brilliant intellectuals. From white-walled Memphis to rock-hewn Ellora, they were honored as practicing a higher dimension of essential knowledge. History preserves the records of numerous persons, living in different times and in various places, who have exhibited a knowledge and skill which cannot be explained according to present standards of erudition. We cannot ignore the testimonies of such learned men as Pythagoras, Buddha, and Plotinus. Many of the noblest members of our race have expressed their profound admiration for the esoteric institutions flourishing in their own times. Not to recognize the esoteric sciences is to disregard most that has contributed to the advancement and improvement of the human state during the last five thousand years. There being a divine order of learning superior to mundane knowledge, and its being available—the time is most appropriate for the further restoration of this sacred tradition.

Adeptship is the state of complete spiritual maturity so far as this is possible to a member of the human family. Deficient in nothing necessary to a life of wisdom, the adept is sufficient to his own needs and capable of determining that course of personal action most likely to contribute to enlightenment. The adepts foreshadow the state of mankind when it will have attained the full release of its faculties and its powers. The adept is, therefore, the truly evolved of our species. Accordingly, the adepts, considered together as the citizens of an invisible empire of the philosophic elect, constitute the heroic elder brothers, the custodians and protectors of humanity. As the interpreters of the Mysteries, they are the true educators and illuminators. As the redeemed, the servants of Divine purpose, they comprise a powerful, creative and directive force in the world.

The science of life is, therefore, the supreme science, and the art of living, the finest of the arts. There have always been truth-seekers willing to acknowledge the sovereignty of the eternal over the temporal. These have dedicated themselves to the mastery of life, and have perpetuated from generation to generation the knowledge and skill they accumulated. This body of essential knowledge is the esoteric tradition. The institutions which perpetuated this tradition are the Mystery Schools, and the graduates of these schools are the adepts.

This volume reveals that the lore and legendry of the world, the scriptures and sacred books, and the great philosophical systems all tell the same story. Human ambition may produce the tyrant; divine aspiration will produce the adept. This then, seems to me to be the significant message of Manly P. Hall's encyclopedic tome. So, my sincere wish is that this contribution by our friend may mean as much in your life as it has in mine.

> —Henry L. Drake
> Vice President
> Philosophical Research Society
> 1975

Preface

umerous volumes have been written as commentaries upon the secret systems of philosophy existing in the ancient world, but the ageless truths of life, like many of the earth's greatest thinkers, have usually been clothed in shabby garments. The present work is an attempt to supply a tome worthy of those seers and sages whose thoughts are the substance of its pages. To bring about this coalescence of Beauty and Truth has proved most costly, but I believe that the result will produce an effect upon the mind of the reader which will more than justify the expenditure.

Work upon the text of this volume was begun the first day of January, 1926, and has continued almost uninterruptedly for over two years. The greater part of the research work, however, was carried on prior to the writing of the manuscript. The collection of reference material was begun in 1921, and three years later the plans for the book took definite form. For the sake of clarity, all footnotes were eliminated, the various quotations and references to other authors being embodied in the text in their logical order. The bibliography is appended primarily to assist those interested in selecting for future study the most authoritative and important items dealing with philosophy and symbolism. To make readily accessible the abstruse information contained in the book, an elaborate topical cross index is included.

I make no claim for either the infallibility or the originality of any statement herein contained. I have studied the fragmentary writings of the ancients sufficiently to realize that dogmatic utterances concerning their tenets are worse than foolhardy. Traditionalism is the curse of modern philosophy, particularly that of the European schools. While many of the statements contained in this treatise may appear at first wildly fantastic, I have sincerely endeavored to refrain from haphazard metaphysical speculation, presenting the material as far as possible in the spirit rather than the letter of the original authors. By assuming responsibility only for the mistakes which may appear herein, I hope to escape the accusation of plagiarism which has been directed against nearly every writer on the subject of mystical philosophy.

Having no particular *ism* of my own to promulgate, I have not attempted to twist the original writings to substantiate preconceived notions, nor have I distorted doctrines in any effort to reconcile the irreconcilable differences present in the various systems of religio-philosophic thought.

The entire theory of the book is diametrically opposed to the modern method of thinking, for it is concerned with subjects openly ridiculed by the sophists of the twentieth century. Its true purpose is to introduce the mind of the reader to a hypothesis of living wholly beyond the pale of materialistic theology, philosophy, or science. The mass of abstruse material between its covers is not susceptible to perfect organization, but so far as possible related topics have been grouped together.

Rich as the English language is in media of expression, it is curiously lacking in terms suitable to the conveyance of abstract philosophical premises. A certain intuitive grasp of the subtler meanings concealed within groups of inadequate words is necessary therefore to an understanding of the ancient Mystery Teachings.

Although the majority of the items in the bibliography are in my own library, I wish to acknowledge gratefully the assistance rendered by the Public Libraries of San Francisco and Los Angeles, the libraries of the Scottish Rite in San Francisco and Los Angeles, the libraries of the University of California in Berkeley and Los Angeles, the Mechanics' Library in San Francisco, and the Krotona Theosophical Library at Ojai, California. Special recognition for their help is also due to the following persons: Mrs. Max Heindel, Mrs. Alice Palmer Henderson, Mr. Ernest Dawson and staff, Mr. John Howell, Mr. Paul Elder, Mr. Phillip Watson Hackett, and Mr. John R. Ruckstell. Single books were lent by other persons and organizations, to whom thanks are also given.

The matter of translation was the greatest single task in the research work incident to the preparation of this volume. The necessary German translations, which required nearly three years, were generously undertaken by Mr. Alfred Beri, who declined all remuneration for his labor. The Latin, Italian, French, and Spanish translations were made by Prof. Homer P. Earle. The Hebrew text was edited by Rabbi Jacob M. Alkow. Miscellaneous short translations and checking also were done by various individuals.

The editorial work was under the supervision of Dr. C. B. Rowlingson, through whose able efforts literary order was often brought out of literary chaos. Special recognition is also due the services rendered by Mr. Robert B. Tum-monds, of the staff of H. S. Crocker Company, Inc., to whom were assigned the technical difficulties of fitting the text matter into its allotted space. For much of the literary charm of the work I am also indebted to Mr. M. M. Saxton, to whom the entire manuscript was first dictated and to whom was also entrusted the preparation of the index. The splendid efforts of Mr. J. Augustus Knapp, the illustrator, have resulted in a series of color plates which add materially to the beauty and completeness of the work.

The printing of the book was in the hands of Mr. Frederick E. Keast, of H. S. Crocker Company, Inc., whose great personal interest in the volume has been manifested by an untiring effort to improve the quality thereof. Through the gracious cooperation of Dr. John Henry Nash, the foremost designer of printing on the American Continent, the book appears in a unique and appropriate form, embodying the finest elements of the printer's craft. An increase in the number of plates and also a finer quality of workmanship than was first contemplated have been made possible by Mr. C. E. Benson, of the Los Angeles Engraving Company, who entered heart and soul into the production of this volume.

The pre-publication sale of this book has been without known precedent. The subscription list for the first edition of 550 copies was closed a year before the manuscript was given to the printer. The second, or King Solomon, edition, 550 copies; the third, or Theosophical, edition, 200 copies; and the fourth, or Rosicrucian, edition, 100 copies, were sold before the finished volume was received from the printer. For so ambitious a production, this constitutes a unique achievement. The credit for this extraordinary sales program belongs to Mrs. Maud F. Galigher, who had as her ideal not to sell the book in the commercial sense of the word but to place it in the hands of those particularly interested in the subject matter it contains. Valuable assistance in this respect was also rendered by numerous friends who had attended my lectures and who without compensation undertook and successfully accomplished the distribution of the book.

In conclusion, the author wishes to acknowledge gratefully his indebtedness to each one of the hundreds of subscribers through whose advance payments the publication of this folio was made possible. To undertake the enormous expense involved was entirely beyond his individual means and those who invested in the volume had no assurance of its production and no security other than their faith in the integrity of the writer.

I sincerely hope that each reader will profit from the perusal of this book, even as I have profited from the writing of it. The years of labor and thought expended upon it have meant much to me. The research work discovered to me many great truths; the writing of it discovered to me the laws of order and patience; the printing of it discovered to me new wonders of the arts and crafts; and the whole enterprise has discovered to me a multitude of friends whom otherwise I might never have known. And so, in the words of John Bunyan:

I penned
It down, until at last it came to be,
For length and breadth, the bigness which you see.

—MANLY P. HALL
Los Angeles, California
May 28, 1928

Introduction

hilosophy is the science of estimating values. The superiority of any state or substance over another is determined by philosophy. By assigning a position of primary importance to what remains when all that is secondary has been removed, philosophy thus becomes the true index of priority or emphasis in the realm of speculative thought. The mission of philosophy *a priori* is to establish the relation of manifested things to their invisible ultimate cause or nature.

"Philosophy," writes Sir William Hamilton, "has been defined [as]: The science of things divine and human, and of the causes in which they are contained [Cicero]; The science of effects by their causes [Hobbes]; The science of sufficient reasons [Leibnitz]; The science of things possible, inasmuch as they are possible [Wolf]; The science of things evidently deduced from first principles [Descartes]; The science of truths, sensible and abstract [de Condillac]; The application of reason to its legitimate objects [Tennemann]; The science of the relations of all knowledge to the necessary ends of human reason [Kant]; The science of the original form of the ego or mental self [Krug]; The science of sciences [Fichte]; The science of the absolute [von Schelling]; The science of the absolute indifference of the ideal and real [von Schelling]—or, The identity of identity and non-identity [Hegel]." (See *Lectures on Metaphysics and Logic.*)

The six headings under which the disciplines of philosophy are commonly classified are: *metaphysics,* which deals with such abstract subjects as cosmology, theology, and the nature of being; *logic,* which deals with the laws governing rational thinking, or, as it has been called, "the doctrine of fallacies"; *ethics,* which is the science of morality, individual responsibility, and character—concerned chiefly with an effort to determine the nature of good; *psychology,* which is devoted to investigation and classification of those forms of phenomena referable to a mental origin; *epistemology,* which is the science concerned primarily with the nature of knowledge itself and the question of whether it may exist in an absolute form; and *asthetics,* which is the science of the nature of and the reactions awakened by the beautiful, the harmonious, the elegant, and the noble.

FROM THOMASSIN'S *RECUEIL DES FIGURES, GROUPES, THERMES, FONTAINES, VASES ET AUTRES ORNEMENTS.*

PLATO.

Plato's real name was Aristocles. When his father brought him to study with Socrates, the great Skeptic declared that on the previous night he had dreamed of a white swan, which was an omen that his new disciple was to become one of the world's illumined. There is a tradition that the immortal Plato was sold as a slave by the King of Sicily.

Plato regarded philosophy as the greatest good ever imparted by Divinity to man. In the twentieth century, however, it has become a ponderous and complicated structure of arbitrary and irreconcilable notions—yet each substantiated by almost incontestible logic. The lofty theorems of the old Academy which Iamblichus likened to the nectar and ambrosia of the gods have been so adulterated by opinion—which Heraclitus declared to be a falling sickness of the mind—that the heavenly mead would now be quite unrecognizable to this great Neo-Platonist. Convincing evidence of the increasing superficiality of modern scientific and philosophic thought is its persistent drift towards materialism. When the great astronomer Laplace was asked by Napoleon why he had not mentioned God in his *Traité de la Mécanique Céleste,* the mathematician naïvely replied: "Sire, I had no need for that hypothesis!"

In his treatise on *Atheism,* Sir Francis Bacon tersely summarizes the situation thus: "A little philosophy inclineth man's mind to atheism; but depth in philosophy bringeth men's minds about to religion." *The Metaphysics* of Aristotle opens with these words: "All men naturally desire to know." To satisfy this common urge the unfolding human intellect has explored the extremities of imaginable space without and the extremities of imaginable self within, seeking to estimate the relationship between the one and the all; the effect and the cause; Nature and the groundwork of Nature; the mind and the source of the mind; the spirit and the substance of the spirit; the illusion and the reality.

An ancient philosopher once said: "He who has not even a knowledge of common things is a brute among men. He who has an accurate knowledge of human concerns alone is a man among brutes. But he who knows all that can be known by intellectual energy, is a God among men." Man's status in the natural world is determined, therefore, by the *quality* of his thinking. He whose mind is enslaved to his bestial instincts is philosophically not superior to the brute; he whose rational faculties ponder human affairs is a man; and he whose intellect is elevated to the consideration of divine realities is already a demigod, for his being partakes of the luminosity with which his reason has brought him into proximity. In his encomium of "the science of sciences" Cicero is led to exclaim: "O philosophy, life's guide! O searcher-out of virtue and expeller of vices! What could we and every age of men have been without thee? Thou hast produced cities; thou hast called men scattered about into the social enjoyment of life."

In this age the word *philosophy* has little meaning unless accompanied by some other qualifying term. The body of philosophy has been broken up into numerous *isms* more or less antagonistic, which have become so concerned with the effort to disprove each other's fallacies that the sublimer issues of divine order and human destiny have suffered deplorable neglect. The ideal function of philosophy is to serve as the stabilizing influence in human thought. By virtue of its intrinsic nature it should prevent man from ever establishing unreasonable codes of life. Philosophers themselves, however, have frustrated the ends of philosophy by exceeding in their woolgathering those untrained minds whom they are supposed to lead in the straight and narrow path of rational thinking. To list and classify any but the more important of the now recognized schools of the philosophy is beyond the space limitations of this volume. The vast area of speculation covered by philosophy will be appreciated best after a brief consideration of a few of the outstanding systems of philosophic discipline which have swayed the world of thought during the last twenty-six centuries.

The Greek school of philosophy had its inception with the seven immortalized thinkers upon whom was first conferred the appellation of *Sophos,* "the wise." According to Diogenes Laertius, these were Thales, Solon, Chilon, Pittacus, Bias, Cleobulus, and Periander. Water was conceived by Thales to be the primal principle or element, upon which the earth floated like a ship, and earthquakes were the result of disturbances in this universal sea. Since Thales was an Ionian, the school perpetuating his tenets became known as the Ionic. He died in 546 B.C., and was succeeded by Anaximander, who in turn was followed by Anaximenes, Anaxagoras, and Archelaus, with whom the Ionic school ended. Anaximander, differing from his master Thales, declared measureless and indefinable infinity to be the principle from which all things were generated.

Anaximenes asserted air to be the first element of the universe; that souls and even the Deity itself were composed of it.

Anaxagoras (whose doctrine savors of atomism) held God to be "an infinite self-moving mind; that this divine infinite Mind, not inclosed in any body, is the efficient cause of all things; out of the infinite matter consisting of similar parts, everything being made according to its species by the divine mind, who when all things were at first confusedly mingled together, came and reduced them to order." Archelaus declared the principle of all things to be twofold: mind (which was incorporeal) and air (which was corporeal), the rarefaction and condensation of the latter resulting in fire and water respectively. The stars were conceived by Archelaus to be burning iron plates. Heraclitus (who lived 536–470 B.C. and is sometimes included in the Ionic school) in his doctrine of change and eternal flux asserted fire to be the first element and also the state into which the world would ultimately be reabsorbed. The soul of the world he regarded as an exhalation from its humid parts, and he declared the ebb and flow of the sea to be caused by the sun.

After Pythagoras of Samos, its founder, the *Italic* or *Pythagorean* school numbers among its most distinguished representatives Empedocles, Epicharmus, Archytas, Alcmæon, Hippasus, Philolaus, and Eudoxus. Pythagoras (580–500? B.C.) conceived mathematics to be the most sacred and exact of all the sciences, and demanded of all who came to him for study a familiarity with arithmetic, music, astronomy, and geometry. He laid special emphasis upon the *philosophic life* as a prerequisite to wisdom. Pythagoras was one of the first teachers to establish a community wherein all the members were of mutual assistance to one another in the common attainment of the higher sciences. He also introduced the discipline of retrospection as essential to the development of the spiritual mind. Pythagoreanism may be summarized as a system of metaphysical speculation concerning the relationships between numbers and the causal agencies of existence. This school also first expounded the theory of celestial harmonics or "the music of the spheres." John Reuchlin said of Pythagoras that he taught nothing to his disciples before the discipline of silence, silence being the first rudiment of contemplation. In his *Sophist,* Aristotle credits Empedocles with the discovery of rhetoric. Both Pythagoras and Empedocles accepted the theory of transmigration, the latter saying: "A boy I was, then did a maid become; a plant, bird, fish, and in the vast sea swum." Archytas is credited with invention of the screw and the crane. Pleasure he declared to be a pestilence because it was opposed to the temperance of the mind; he considered a man without deceit to be as rare as a fish without bones.

The *Eleatic* sect was founded by Xenophanes (570–480 B.C.), who was conspicuous for his attacks upon the cosmologic and theogonic fables of Homer and Hesiod. Xenophanes declared that God was "one and incorporeal, in substance and figure round, in no way resembling man; that He is all sight and all hearing, but breathes not; that He is all things, the mind and wisdom, not generate but eternal, impassible, immutable, and rational." Xenophanes believed that all existing things were eternal, that the world was without beginning or end, and that everything which was generated was subject to corruption. He lived to great age and is said to have buried his sons with his own hands. Parmenides studied under Xenophanes, but never entirely subscribed to his doctrines. Parmenides declared the senses to be uncertain and reason the only criterion of truth. He first asserted the earth to be round and also divided its surface into zones of heat and cold.

Melissus, who is included in the Eleatic school, held many opinions in common with Parmenides. He declared the universe to be immovable because, occupying all space, there was no place to which it could be moved. He further rejected the theory of a vacuum in space. Zeno of Elea also maintained that a vacuum could not exist. Rejecting the theory of motion, he asserted that there was but one God, who was an eternal, ungenerated Being. Like Xenophanes, he conceived Deity to be spherical in shape. Leucippus held the Universe to consist of two parts: one full and the other a vacuum. From the Infinite a host of minute fragmentary bodies descended into the vacuum, where, through continual agitation, they organized themselves into spheres of substance.

The great Democritus to a certain degree enlarged upon the atomic theory of Leucippus. Democritus declared the principles of all things to be twofold: atoms and vacuum. Both, he asserted, are infinite—atoms in number, vacuum in magnitude. Thus all bodies must be composed of atoms or vacuum. Atoms possessed two properties, form and size, both characterized by infinite variety. The soul Democritus also conceived to be atomic in structure and subject to dissolution with the body. The mind he believed to be composed of spiritual atoms. Aristotle intimates that Democritus obtained his atomic theory from the Pythagorean doctrine of the *Monad.* Among the Eleatics are also included Protagoras and Anaxarchus.

Socrates (469–399 B.C.), the founder of the *Socratic* sect, being fundamentally a Skeptic, did not force his opinions upon others, but through the medium of questionings caused each man to give expression to his own philosophy. According to Plutarch, Socrates conceived every place as appropriate for teaching in that the whole world was a school of virtue. He held that the soul existed before the body and, prior to immersion therein, was endowed with all knowledge; that when the soul entered into the material form it became stupefied, but that by discourses upon sensible objects it was caused to reawaken and to recover its original knowledge. On these premises was based his attempt to stimulate the soul-power through irony and inductive reasoning. It has been said of Socrates that the sole subject of his philosophy was man. He himself declared philosophy to be the way of true happiness and its purpose twofold: (1) to contemplate God, and (2) to abstract the soul from corporeal sense.

The principles of all things he conceived to be three in number: *God, matter,* and *ideas.* Of God he said: "What He is I know not; what He is not I know." Matter he defined as the subject of generation and corruption; idea, as an incorruptible substance—the intellect of God. Wisdom he considered the sum of the virtues. Among the prominent members of the Socratic sect were Xenophon, Æschines, Crito, Simon, Glauco, Simmias, and Cebes. Professor Zeller, the great authority on ancient philosophies, has recently declared the writings of Xenophon relating to Socrates to be forgeries. When *The Clouds of Aristophanes,* a comedy written to ridicule the theories of Socrates, was first presented, the great Skeptic himself attended the play. During the performance, which caricatured him seated in a basket high in the air studying the sun, Socrates rose calmly in his seat, the better to enable the Athenian spectators to compare his own unprepossessing features with the grotesque mask worn by the actor impersonating him.

The *Elean* sect was founded by Phædo of Elis, a youth of noble family, who was bought from slavery at the instigation of Socrates and who became his devoted disciple. Plato so highly admired Phædo's mentality that he named one of the most famous of his discourses the *Phædo.* Phædo was succeeded in his school by Plisthenes, who in turn was followed by Menedemus. Of the doctrines of the Elean sect little is known. Menedemus is presumed to have been inclined toward the teachings of Stilpo and the Megarian sect. When Menedemus' opinions were demanded, he answered that he was free, thus intimating that most men were enslaved to their opinions. Menedemus was apparently of a somewhat belligerent temperament and often returned from his lectures in a badly bruised condition. The most famous of his propositions is stated thus: That which is not the same is different from that with which it is not the same. This point being admitted, Menedemus continued: To benefit is not the same as good, therefore good does not benefit. After the time of Menedemus the Elean sect became known as the Eretrian. Its exponents denounced all negative propositions and all complex and abstruse theories, declaring that only affirmative and simple doctrines could be true.

The *Megarian* sect was founded by Euclid of Megara (not the celebrated mathematician), a great admirer of Socrates. The Athenians passed a law decreeing death to any citizen of Megara found in the city of Athens. Nothing daunted, Euclid donned woman's clothing and went at night to study with Socrates. After the cruel death of their teacher, the disciples of Socrates, fearing a similar fate, fled to Megara, where they were entertained with great honor by Euclid. The Megarian school accepted the Socratic doctrine that virtue is wisdom, adding to it the Eleatic concept that goodness is absolute unity and all change an illusion of the senses. Euclid maintained that good has no opposite and therefore evil does not exist. Being asked about the nature of the gods, he declared himself ignorant of their disposition save that they hated curious persons.

The Megarians are occasionally included among the dialectic philosophers. Euclid (who died in 374? B.C.) was succeeded in his school by Eubulides, among whose disciples were Alexinus and Apollonius Cronus. Euphantus, who lived to great age and wrote many tragedies, was among the foremost followers of Eubulides. Diodorus is usually included in the Megarian school, having heard Eubulides lecture. According to legend, Diodorus died of grief because he could not answer instantly certain questions asked him by Stilpo, at one time master of the Megarian school. Diodorus held that nothing can be moved, since to be moved it must be taken out of the place in which it is and put into the place where it is not, which is impossible because all things must always be in the places where they are.

The *Cynics* were a sect founded by Antisthenes of Athens (444–365? B.C.), a disciple of Socrates. Their doctrine may be described as an extreme individualism which considers man as existing for himself alone and advocates surrounding him by inharmony, suffering, and direst need that he may thereby be driven to retire more completely into his own nature. The Cynics renounced all worldly possessions, living in the rudest shelters and subsisting upon the coarsest and simplest food. On the assumption that the gods wanted nothing, the Cynics affirmed that those whose needs were fewest consequently approached closest to the divinities. Being asked what he gained by a life of philosophy, Antisthenes replied that he had learned how to converse with himself.

Diogenes of Sinopis is remembered chiefly for the tub in the Metroum which for many years served him as a home. The people of Athens loved the beggar-philosopher, and when a youth in jest bored holes in the tub, the city presented Diogenes with a new one and punished the youth. Diogenes believed that nothing in life can be rightly accomplished without exercitation. He maintained that everything in the world belongs to the wise, a declaration which he proved by the following logic: "All things belong to the gods; the gods are friends to wise persons; all things are common amongst friends; therefore all things belong to the wise." Among the Cynics are Monimus, Onesicritus, Crates, Metrocles, Hipparchia (who married Crates), Menippus, and Menedemus.

The *Cyrenaic* sect, founded by Aristippus of Cyrene (435–356? B.C.), promulgated the doctrine of hedonism. Learning of the fame of Socrates, Aristippus journeyed to Athens and applied himself to the teachings of the great Skeptic. Socrates, pained by the voluptuous and mercenary tendencies of Aristippus, vainly labored to reform the young man. Aristippus has the distinction of being consistent in principle and practice, for he lived in perfect harmony with his philosophy that the quest of pleasure was the chief purpose of life. The doctrines of the Cyrenaics may be summarized thus: All that is actually known concerning any object or condition is the feeling which it awakens in man's own nature. In the sphere of ethics that which awakens the most pleasant feeling is consequently to be esteemed as the greatest good. Emotional reactions are classified as pleasant or gentle, harsh, and mean. The end of pleasant emotion is pleasure; the end of harsh emotion, grief; the end of mean emotion, nothing.

Through mental perversity some men do not desire pleasure. In reality, however, pleasure (especially of a physical nature) is the true end of existence and exceeds in every way mental and spiritual enjoyments. Pleasure, furthermore, is limited wholly to the moment; *now* is the only time. The past cannot be regarded without regret and the future cannot be faced without misgiving; therefore neither is conducive to pleasure. No man should grieve, for grief is the most serious of all diseases. Nature permits man to do anything he desires; he is limited only by his own laws and customs. A philosopher is one free from envy, love, and superstition, and whose days are one long round of pleasure. Indulgence was thus elevated by Aristippus to the chief position among the virtues. He further declared philosophers to differ markedly from other men in that they alone would not change the order of their lives if all the laws of men were abolished. Among prominent philosophers influenced by the Cyrenaic doctrines were Hegesias, Anniceris, Theodorus, and Bion.

The sect of the *Academic* philosophers instituted by Plato (427–347 B.C.) was divided into three major parts—the old, the middle, and the new Academy. Among the old Academics were Speusippus, Zenocrates, Poleman, Crates, and Crantor. Arcesilaus instituted the middle Academy and Carneades founded the new. Chief among the masters of Plato was Socrates. Plato traveled widely and was initiated by the Egyptians into the profundities of Hermetic philosophy. He also derived much from the doctrines of the Pythagoreans. Cicero describes the threefold constitution of Platonic philosophy as comprising ethics, physics, and dialectics. Plato defined *good* as threefold in character: good in the soul, expressed through the virtues; good in the body, expressed through the symmetry and endurance of the parts; and good in the external world, expressed through social position and companionship. In *The Book of Speusippus on Platonic Definitions,* that great Platonist thus defines God: "A being that lives immortally by means of Himself alone, sufficing for His own blessedness, the eternal Essence, cause of His own goodness." According to Plato, the *One* is the term most suitable for defining the Absolute, since the whole precedes the parts and diversity is dependent on unity, but unity not on diversity. The One, moreover, is before being, for *to be* is an attribute or condition of the One.

Platonic philosophy is based upon the postulation of three orders of being: that which moves unmoved, that which is self-moved, and that which is moved. That which is immovable but moves is anterior to that which is self-moved, which likewise is anterior to that which it moves. That in which motion is inherent cannot be separated from its motive power; it is therefore incapable of dissolution. Of such nature are the immortals. That which has motion imparted to it from another can be separated from the source of its animating principle; it is therefore subject to dissolution. Of such nature are mortal beings. Superior to both the mortals and the immortals is that condition which continually moves yet itself is unmoved. To this constitution the power of abidance is inherent; it is therefore the Divine Permanence upon which all things are established. Being nobler even than self-motion, the unmoved Mover is the first of all dignities. The Platonic discipline was founded upon the theory that learning is really reminiscence, or the bringing into objectivity of knowledge formerly acquired by the soul in a previous state of existence. At the entrance of the Platonic school in the Academy were written the words: "Let none ignorant of geometry enter here."

After the death of Plato, his disciples separated into two groups. One, the *Academics,* continued to meet in the Academy where once he had presided; the other, the *Peripatetics,* removed to the Lyceum under the leadership of Aristotle (384–322 B.C.). Plato recognized Aristotle as his greatest disciple and, according to Philoponus, referred to him as "the mind of the school." If Aristotle were absent from the lectures, Plato would say: "The intellect is not here." Of the prodigious genius of Aristotle, Thomas Taylor writes in his introduction to *The Metaphysics:*

"When we consider that he was not only well acquainted with every science, as his works abundantly evince, but that he wrote on almost every subject which is comprehended in the circle of human knowledge, and this with matchless accuracy and skill, we know not which to admire most, the penetration or extent of his mind." Of the philosophy of Aristotle, the same author says: "The end of Aristotle's moral philosophy is perfection through the virtues, and the end of his contemplative philosophy an union with the one principle of all things."

Aristotle conceived philosophy to be twofold: practical and theoretical. Practical philosophy embraced ethics and politics; theoretical philosophy, physics and logic. Metaphysics he considered to be the science concerning that substance which has the principle of motion and rest inherent to itself. To Aristotle the soul is that by which man first lives, feels, and understands. Hence to the soul he assigned three faculties: nutritive, sensitive, and intellective. He further considered the soul to be twofold—rational and irrational—and in some particulars elevated the sense perceptions above the mind. Aristotle defined wisdom as the science of first Causes. The four major divisions of his philosophy are dialectics, physics, ethics, and metaphysics. God is defined as the First Mover, the Best of beings, an immovable Substance, separate from sensible things, void of corporeal quantity, without parts and indivisible. Platonism is based upon *a priori* reasoning; Aristotelianism upon *a posteriori* reasoning. Aristotle taught his pupil, Alexander the Great, to feel that if he had not done a good deed he had not reigned that day. Among his followers were Theophrastus, Strato, Lyco, Aristo, Critolaus, and Diodorus.

Of *Skepticism* as propounded by Pyrrho of Elis (365–275 B.C.) and by Timon, Sextus Empiricus said that those who seek must find or deny they have found or can find, or persevere in the inquiry. Those who suppose they have found truth are called *Dogmatists;* those who think it incomprehensible are the *Academics;* those who still seek are the *Skeptics.* The attitude of Skepticism towards the knowable is summed up by Sextus Empiricus in the following words: "But the chief ground of Skepticism is that to every reason there is an opposite reason equivalent, which makes us forbear to dogmatize." The Skeptics were strongly opposed to the Dogmatists and were agnostic in that they held the accepted theories regarding Deity to be self-contradictory and undemonstrable. "How," asked the Skeptic, "can we have indubitate knowledge of God, knowing not His substance, form or place; for, while philosophers disagree irreconcilably on these points, their conclusions cannot be considered as undoubtably true?" Since absolute knowledge was considered unattainable, the Skeptics declared the end of their discipline to be: "In opinionatives, indisturbance; in impulsives, moderation; and in disquietives, suspension."

The sect of the *Stoics* was founded by Zeno (340–265 B.C.), the Cittiean, who studied under Crates the Cynic, from which sect the Stoics had their origin.

Zeno was succeeded by Cleanthes, Chrysippus, Zeno of Tanis, Diogenes, Antipater, Panætius, and Posidonius. Most famous of the Roman Stoics are Epictetus and Marcus Aurelius. The Stoics were essentially pantheists, since they maintained that as there is nothing better than the world, the world is God. Zeno declared that the reason of the world is diffused throughout it as seed. Stoicism is a materialistic philosophy, enjoining voluntary resignation to natural law. Chrysippus maintained that good and evil being contrary, both are necessary since each sustains the other. The soul was regarded as a body distributed throughout the physical form and subject to dissolution with it. Though some of the Stoics held that wisdom prolonged the existence of the soul, actual immortality is not included in their tenets. The soul was said to be composed of eight parts: the five senses, the generative power, the vocal power, and an eighth, or hegemonic, part. Nature was defined as God mixed throughout the substance of the world. All things were looked upon as bodies either corporeal or incorporeal.

Meekness marked the attitude of the Stoic philosopher. While Diogenes was delivering a discourse against anger, one of his listeners spat contemptuously in his face. Receiving the insult with humility, the great Stoic was moved to retort: "I am not angry, but am in doubt whether I ought to be so or not!"

Epicurus of Samos (341–270 B.C.) was the founder of the *Epicurean* sect, which in many respects resembles the Cyrenaic but is higher in ethical standards. The Epicureans also posited pleasure as the most desirable state, but conceived it to be a grave and dignified state achieved through renunciation of those mental and emotional inconstancies which are productive of pain and sorrow. Epicurus held that as the pains of the mind and soul are more grievous than those of the body, so the joys of the mind and soul exceed those of the body. The Cyrenaics asserted pleasure to be dependent upon action or motion; the Epicureans claimed rest or lack of action to be equally productive of pleasure. Epicurus accepted the philosophy of Democritus concerning the nature of atoms and based his physics upon this theory. The Epicurean philosophy may be summed up in four canons:

"(1) Sense is never deceived; and therefore every sensation and every perception of an appearance is true. (2) Opinion follows upon sense and is superadded to sensation, and capable of truth or falsehood. (3) All opinion arrested, or not contradicted by the evidence of sense, is true. (4) An opinion contradicted, or not arrested by the evidence of sense, is false." Among the Epicureans of note were Metrodorus of Lampsacus, Zeno of Sidon, and Phædrus.

Eclecticism may be defined as the practice of choosing apparently irreconcilable doctrines from antagonistic schools and constructing therefrom a composite philosophic system in harmony with the convictions of the eclectic himself. Eclecticism can scarcely be considered philosophically or logically sound, for as individual schools arrive at their conclusions by different methods of reasoning, so the philosophic product of fragments from these schools must necessarily be built upon the foundation of conflicting premises. Eclecticism, accordingly, has been designated the layman's cult. In the Roman Empire little thought was devoted to philosophic theory; consequently most of its thinkers were of the eclectic type. Cicero is the outstanding example of early Eclecticism, for his writings are a veritable potpourri of invaluable fragments from earlier schools of thought. Eclecticism appears to have had its inception at the moment when men first doubted the possibility of discovering ultimate truth. Observing all so-called knowledge to be mere opinion at best, the less studious furthermore concluded that the wiser course to pursue was to accept that which appeared to be the most reasonable of the teachings of any school or individual. From this practice, however, arose a pseudo-broadmindedness devoid of the element of preciseness found in true logic and philosophy.

The *Neo-Pythagorean* school flourished in Alexandria during the first century of the Christian Era. Only two names stand out in connection with it— Apollonius of Tyana and Moderatus of Gades. Neo-Pythagoreanism is a link between the older pagan philosophies and Neo-Platonism. Like the former, it contained many exact elements of thought derived from Pythagoras and Plato; like the latter, it emphasized metaphysical speculation and ascetic habits. A striking similarity has been observed by several authors between Neo-Pythagoreanism and the doctrines of the Essenes. Special emphasis was laid upon the mystery of numbers, and it is possible that the Neo-Pythagoreans had a far wider knowledge of the true teachings of Pythagoras than is available today. Even in the first century Pythagoras was regarded more as a god than a man, and the revival of his philosophy was resorted to apparently in the hope that his name would stimulate interest in the deeper systems of learning. But Greek philosophy had passed the zenith of its splendor; the mass of humanity was awakening to the importance of physical life and physical phenomena. The emphasis upon earthly affairs which began to assert itself later reached maturity of expression in twentieth century materialism and commercialism, even though Neo-Platonism was to intervene and many centuries pass before this emphasis took definite form.

Although Ammonius Saccus was long believed to be the founder of *Neo-Platonism,* the school had its true beginning in Plotinus (A.D. 204–269?). Prominent among the Neo-Platonists of Alexandria, Syria, Rome, and Athens were Porphyry, Iamblichus, Sallustius, the Emperor Julian, Plutarch, and Proclus. Neo-Platonism was the supreme effort of decadent pagandom to publish and thus preserve for posterity its secret (or unwritten) doctrine. In its teachings ancient idealism found its most perfect expression. Neo-Platonism was concerned

FROM AN OLD PRINT, COURTESY OF CARL OSCAR BORG.

THE PTOLEMAIC SCHEME OF THE UNIVERSE.

In ridiculing the geocentric system of astronomy expounded by Claudius Ptolemy, modern astronomers have overlooked the philosophic key to the Ptolemaic system. The universe of Ptolemy is a diagrammatic representation of the relationships existing between the various divine and elemental parts of every creature, and is not concerned with astronomy as that science is now comprehended. In the above figure, special attention is called to the three circles of zodiacs surrounding the orbits of the planets. These zodiacs represent the threefold spiritual constitution of the universe. The orbits of the planets are the Governors of the World and the four elemental spheres in the center represent the physical constitution of both man and the universe. Ptolemy's scheme of the universe is simply a cross section of the universal aura, the planets and elements to which he refers having no relation to those recognized by modern astronomers.

almost exclusively with the problems of higher metaphysics. It recognized the existence of a secret and all-important doctrine which from the time of the earliest civilizations had been concealed within the rituals, symbols, and allegories of religions and philosophies. To the mind unacquainted with its fundamental tenets, Neo-Platonism may appear to be a mass of speculations interspersed with extravagant flights of fancy. Such a viewpoint, however, ignores the institutions of the Mysteries—those secret schools into whose profundities of idealism nearly all of the first philosophers of antiquity were initiated.

When the physical body of pagan thought collapsed, an attempt was made to resurrect the form by instilling new life into it by the unveiling of its mystical truths. This effort apparently was barren of results. Despite the antagonism, however, between pristine Christianity and Neo-Platonism many basic tenets of the latter were accepted by the former and woven into the fabric of Patristic philosophy. Briefly described, Neo-Platonism is a philosophic code which conceives every physical or concrete body of doctrine to be merely the shell of a spiritual verity which may be discovered through meditation and certain exercises of a mystic nature. In comparison to the esoteric spiritual truths which they contain, the corporeal bodies of religion and philosophy were considered relatively of little value. Likewise, no emphasis was placed upon the material sciences.

The term *Patristic* is employed to designate the philosophy of the Fathers of the early Christian Church. Patristic philosophy is divided into two general epochs: ante-Nicene and post-Nicene. The ante-Nicene period in the main was devoted to attacks upon paganism and to apologies and defenses of Christianity. The entire structure of pagan philosophy was assailed and the dictates of faith elevated above those of reason. In some instances efforts were made to reconcile the evident truths of paganism with Christian revelation. Eminent among the ante-Nicene Fathers were St. Irenæus, Clement of Alexandria, and Justin Martyr. In the post-Nicene period more emphasis was placed upon the unfoldment of Christian philosophy along Platonic and Neo-Platonic lines, resulting in the appearance of many strange documents of a lengthy, rambling, and ambiguous nature, nearly all of which were philosophically unsound. The post-Nicene philosophers included Athanasius, Gregory of Nyssa, and Cyril of Alexandria. The Patristic school is notable for its emphasis upon the supremacy of man throughout the universe. Man was conceived to be a separate and divine creation—the crowning achievement of Deity and an exception to the suzerainty of natural law. To the Patristics it was inconceivable that there should ever exist another creature so noble, so fortunate, or so able as man, for whose sole benefit and edification all the kingdoms of Nature were primarily created.

Patristic philosophy cluminated in *Augustinianism,* which may best be defined as Christian Platonism. Opposing the *Pelasgian* doctrine that man is the author of his own salvation, Augustinianism elevated the church and its dogmas to a position of absolute infallibility—a position which it successfully maintained until the Reformation. *Gnosticism,* a system of emanationism, interpreting Christianity in terms of Greek, Egyptian, and Persian metaphysics, appeared in the latter part of the first century of the Christian Era. Practically all the information extant regarding the Gnostics and their doctrines, stigmatized as heresy by the ante-Nicene Church Fathers, is derived from the accusations made against them, particularly from the writings of St. Irenæus. In the third century appeared *Manichæism*, a dualistic system of Persian origin, which taught that Good and Evil were forever contending for universal supremacy. In Manichæism, Christ is conceived to be the Principle of redeeming Good in contradistinction to the man Jesus, who was viewed as an evil personality.

The death of Boethius in the sixth century marked the close of the ancient Greek school of philosophy. The ninth century saw the rise of the new school of *Scholasticism,* which sought to reconcile philosophy with theology. Representative of the main divisions of the Scholastic school were the *Eclecticism* of John of Salisbury, the *Mysticism* of Bernard of Clairvaux and St. Bonaventura, the *Rationalism* of Peter Abelard, and the pantheistic *Mysticism* of Meister Eckhart. Among the Arabian Aristotelians were Avicenna and Averroes. The zenith of Scholasticism was reached with the advent of Albertus Magnus and his illustrious disciple, St. Thomas Aquinas. *Thomism* (the philosophy of St. Thomas Aquinas, sometimes referred to as the Christian Aristotle) sought to reconcile the various factions of the Scholastic school. Thomism was basically Aristotelian with the added concept that faith is a projection of reason.

Scotism, or the doctrine of *Voluntarism* promulgated by Joannes Duns Scotus, a Franciscan Scholastic, emphasized the power and efficacy of the individual will, as opposed to Thomism. The outstanding characteristic of Scholasticism was its frantic effort to cast all European thought in an Aristotelian mold. Eventually the Schoolmen descended to the level of mere word-mongers who picked the words of Aristotle so clean that nothing but the bones remained. It was this decadent school of meaningless verbiage against which Sir Francis Bacon directed his bitter shafts of irony and which he relegated to the potter's field of discarded notions.

The Baconian, or inductive, system of reasoning (whereby facts are arrived at by a process of observation and verified by experimentation) cleared the way for the schools of modern science. Bacon was followed by Thomas Hobbes (for some time his secretary), who held mathematics to be the only exact science and thought to be essentially a mathematical process. Hobbes declared matter to be the only reality, and scientific investigation to be limited to the study of bodies, the phenomena relative to their probable causes, and the consequences which flow from them under every variety of circumstance. Hobbes laid special stress upon the significance of words, declaring understanding to be the faculty of perceiving the relationship between words and the objects for which they stand.

Having broken away from the scholastic and theological schools, *Post-Reformation,* or modern, philosophy experienced a most prolific growth along many diverse lines. According to *Humanism,* man is the measure of all things; *Rationalism* makes the reasoning faculties the basis of all knowledge; *Political Philosophy* holds that man must comprehend his natural, social, and national privileges; *Empiricism* declares that alone to be true which is demonstrable by experiment or experience; *Moralism* emphasizes the necessity of right conduct as a fundamental philosophic tenet; *Idealism* asserts the realities of the universe to be superphysical—either mental or psychical; *Realism,* the reverse; and *Phenomenalism* restricts knowledge to facts or events which can be scientifically described or explained. The most recent developments in the field of philosophic thought are *Behaviorism* and *Neo-Realism.* The former estimates the intrinsic characteristics through an analysis of behavior; the latter may be summed up as the total extinction of idealism.

Baruch de Spinoza, the eminent Dutch philosopher, conceived God to be a substance absolutely self-existent and needing no other conception besides itself to render it complete and intelligible. The nature of this Being was held by Spinoza to be comprehensible only through its attributes, which are *extension* and *thought:* these combine to form an endless variety of *aspects* or *modes.* The mind of man is one of the modes of infinite thought; the body of man one of the modes of infinite extension. Through reason man is enabled to elevate himself above the illusionary world of the senses and find eternal repose in perfect union with the Divine Essence. Spinoza, it has been said, deprived God of all personality, making Deity synonymous with the universe.

German philosophy had its inception with Gottfried Wilhelm von Leibnitz, whose theories are permeated with the qualities of optimism and idealism. Leibnitz's criteria of *sufficient reason* revealed to him the insufficiency of Descartes' theory of extension, and he therefore concluded that substance itself contained an inherent power in the form of an incalculable number of separate and all-sufficient units. Matter reduced to its ultimate particles ceases to exist as a substantial body, being resolved into a mass of immaterial ideas or metaphysical units of power, to which Leibnitz applied the term *monad.* Thus the universe is composed of an infinite number of separate monadic entities unfolding spontaneously through the objectification of innate active qualities. All things are conceived as consisting of single monads of varying magnitudes or of aggregations of these bodies, which may exist as physical, emotional, mental, or spiritual substances. God is the first and greatest Monad; the spirit of man is an awakened monad in contradistinction to the lower kingdoms whose governing monadic powers are in a semidormant state.

Though a product of the Leibnitzian-Wolfian school, Immanuel Kant, like Locke, dedicated himself to investigation of the powers and limits of human understanding. The result was his critical philosophy, embracing the critique of pure reason, the critique of practical reason, and the critique of judgment. Dr. W. J. Durant sums up Kant's philosophy in the concise statement that he rescued mind from matter. The mind Kant conceived to be the selector and coordinator of all perceptions, which in turn are the result of sensations grouping themselves about some external object. In the classification of sensations and ideas the mind employs certain categories: of sense, time and space; of understanding, quality, relation, modality, and causation; and the unity of apperception. Being subject to mathematical laws, time and space are considered absolute and sufficient bases for exact thinking. Kant's practical reason declared that while the nature of *noumenon* could never be comprehended by the reason, the fact of morality proves the existence of three necessary postulates: free will, immortality, and God. In the critique of judgment Kant demonstrates the union of the *noumenon* and the *phenomenon* in art and biological evolution. German *superintellectualism* is the outgrowth of an overemphasis of Kant's theory of the autocratic supremacy of the mind over sensation and thought. The philosophy of Johann Gottlieb Fichte was a projection of Kant's philosophy, wherein he attempted to unite Kant's practical reason with his pure reason. Fichte held that the known is merely the contents of the consciousness of the knower, and that nothing can exist to the knower until it becomes part of those contents. Nothing is actually real, therefore, except the facts of one's own mental experience.

Recognizing the necessity of certain objective realities, Friedrich Wilhelm Joseph von Schelling, who succeeded Fichte in the chair of philosophy at Jena, first employed the doctrine of identity as the groundwork for a complete system of philosophy. Whereas Fichte regarded self as the Absolute, von Schelling conceived infinite and eternal Mind to be the all-pervading Cause. Realization of the Absolute is made possible by intellectual intuition which, being a superior or spiritual sense, is able to dissociate itself from both subject and object. Kant's categories of space and time von Schelling conceived to be positive and negative respectively, and material existence the result of the reciprocal action of these two expressions. Von Schelling also held that the Absolute in its process of self-development proceeds according to a law or rhythm consisting of three movements. The first, a reflective movement, is the attempt of the Infinite to embody itself in the finite. The second, that of subsumption, is the attempt of the Absolute to return to the Infinite after involvement in the finite. The third, that of reason, is the neutral point wherein the two former movements are blended.

Georg Wilhelm Friedrich Hegel considered the intellectual intuition of von Schelling to be philosophically unsound and hence turned his attention to the establishment of a system of philosophy based upon pure logic. Of Hegel it has been said that he began with nothing and showed with logical precision how everything had proceeded from it in logical order. Hegel elevated logic to a position of supreme importance, in fact as a quality of the Absolute itself. God he conceived to be a process of unfolding which never attains to the condition of unfoldment. In like manner, thought is without either beginning or end. Hegel further believed that all things owe their existence to their opposites and that all opposites are actually identical. Thus the only existence is the relationship of opposites to each other, through whose combinations new elements are produced. As the Divine Mind is an eternal process of thought never accomplished, Hegel assails the very foundation of theism and his philosophy limits immortality to the everflowing Deity alone. Evolution is consequently the never-ending flow of Divine Consciousness out of itself; all creation, though continually moving, never arrives at any state other than that of ceaseless flow.

Johann Friedrich Herbart's philosophy was a realistic reaction from the idealism of Fichte and von Schelling. To Herbart the true basis of philosophy was the great mass of phenomena continually moving through the human mind. Examination of phenomena, however, demonstrates that a great part of it is unreal, at least incapable of supplying the mind with actual truth. To correct the false impressions caused by phenomena and discover reality, Herbart believed it necessary to resolve phenomena into separate elements, for reality exists in the elements and not in the whole. He stated that objects can be classified by three general terms: thing, matter, and mind; the first a unit of several properties, the second an existing object, the third a self-conscious being. All three notions give rise, however, to certain contradictions, with whose solution Herbart is primarily concerned. For example, consider matter. Though capable of filling space, if reduced to its ultimate state it consists of incomprehensibly minute units of divine energy occupying no physical space whatsoever.

The true subject of Arthur Schopenhauer's philosophy is the will; the object of his philosophy is the elevation of the mind to the point where it is capable of controlling the will. Schopenhauer likens the will to a strong blind man who carries on his shoulders the intellect, which is a weak lame man possessing the power of sight. The will is the tireless cause of manifestation and every part of

Nature the product of will. The brain is the product of the will to know; the hand the product of the will to grasp. The entire intellectual and emotional constitutions of man are subservient to the will and are largely concerned with the effort to justify the dictates of the will. Thus the mind creates elaborate systems of thought simply to prove the necessity of the thing willed. Genius, however, represents the state wherein the intellect has gained supremacy over the will and the life is ruled by reason and not by impulse. The strength of Christianity, said Schopenhauer, lay in its pessimism and conquest of individual will. His own religious viewpoints resembled closely the Buddhistic. To him Nirvana represented the subjugation of will. Life—the manifestation of the blind will to live—he viewed as a misfortune, claiming that the true philosopher was one who, recognizing the wisdom of death, resisted the inherent urge to reproduce his kind.

Of Friedrich Wilhelm Nietzsche it has been said that his peculiar contribution to the cause of human hope was the glad tidings that God had died of pity! The outstanding features of Nietzsche's philosophy are his doctrine of eternal recurrence and the extreme emphasis placed by him upon the *will to power*—a projection of Schopenhauer's *will to live*. Nietzsche believed the purpose of existence to be

FROM HONE'S *ANCIENT MYSTERIES DESCRIBED*.

A CHRISTIAN TRINITY.

In an effort to set forth in an appropriate figure the Christian doctrine of the Trinity, it was necessary to devise an image in which the three persons—Father, Son, and Holy Ghost—were separate and yet one. In different parts of Europe may be seen figures similar to the above, wherein three faces are united in one head. This is a legitimate method of symbolism, for to those able to realize the sacred significance of the threefold head a great mystery is revealed. However, in the presence of such applications of symbology in Christian art, it is scarcely proper to consider the philosophers of other faiths as benighted if, like the Hindus, they have a three-faced Brahma, or, like the Romans, a two-faced Janus.

the production of a type of all-powerful individual, designated by him the superman. This superman was the product of careful culturing, for if not separated forcibly from the mass and consecrated to the production of power, the individual would sink back to the level of the deadly mediocre. Love, Nietzsche said, should be sacrificed to the production of the superman and those only should marry who are best fitted to produce this outstanding type. Nietzsche also believed in the rule of the aristocracy, both blood and breeding being essential to the establishment of this superior type. Nietzsche's doctrine did not liberate the masses; it rather placed over them supermen for whom their inferior brothers and sisters should be perfectly reconciled to die. Ethically and politically, the superman was a law unto himself. To those who understand the true meaning of power to be virtue, self-control, and truth, the ideality behind Nietzsche's theory is apparent. To the superficial, however, it is a philosophy heartless and calculating, concerned solely with the survival of the fittest.

Of the other German schools of philosophic thought, limitations of space preclude detailed mention. The more recent developments of the German school are *Freudianism* and *Relativism* (often called the Einstein theory). The former is a system of psychoanalysis through psychopathic and neurological phenomena; the latter attacks the accuracy of mechanical principles dependent upon the present theory of velocity.

René Descartes stands at the head of the French school of philosophy and shares with Sir Francis Bacon the honor of founding the systems of modern science and philosophy. As Bacon based his conclusions upon observation of external things, so Descartes founded his metaphysical philosophy upon observation of internal things. *Cartesianism* (the philosophy of Descartes) first eliminates all things and then replaces as fundamental those premises without which existence is impossible. Descartes defined an idea as that which fills the mind when we conceive a thing. The truth of an idea must be determined by the criteria of clarity and distinctness. Hence Descartes held that a clear and distinct idea must be true. Descartes has the distinction also of evolving his own philosophy without recourse to authority. Consequently his conclusions are built up from the simplest of premises and grow in complexity as the structure of his philosophy takes form.

The *Positive* philosophy of Auguste Comte is based upon the theory that the human intellect develops through three stages of thought. The first and lowest stage is theological; the second, metaphysical; and the third and highest, positive. Thus theology and metaphysics are the feeble intellectual efforts of humanity's child-mind and positivism is the mental expression of the adult intellect. In his *Cours de Philosophie positive,* Comte writes:

"In the final, the positive state, the mind has given over the vain search after Absolute notions, the origin and destination of the universe, and the causes of phenomena, and applies itself to the study of their laws,—that is, their invariable relations of succession and resemblance. Reasoning and observation, duly combined, are the means of this knowledge." Comte's theory is described as an "enormous system of materialism." According to Comte, it was formerly said that the heavens declare the glory of God, but now they only recount the glory of Newton and Laplace.

Among the French schools of philosophy are *Traditionalism* (often applied to Christianity), which esteems tradition as the proper foundation for philosophy; the *Sociological* school, which regards humanity as one vast social organism; the *Encyclopedists,* whose efforts to classify knowledge according to the Baconian system revolutionized European thought; *Voltairism,* which assailed the divine origin of the Christian faith and adopted an attitude of extreme skepticism towards all matters pertaining to theology; and *Neo-Criticism,* a French revision of the doctrines of Immanuel Kant.

Henri Bergson, the intuitionalist, undoubtedly the greatest living French philosopher, presents a theory of mystic anti-intellectualism founded upon the premise of creative evolution. His rapid rise to popularity is due to his appeal to the finer sentiments in human nature, which rebel against the hopelessness and helplessness of materialistic science and realistic philosophy. Bergson sees God as life continually struggling against the limitations of matter. He even conceives the possible victory of life over matter, and in time the annihilation of death.

Applying the Baconian method to the mind, John Locke, the great English philosopher, declared that everything which passes through the mind is a legitimate object of mental philosophy, and that these mental phenomena are as real and valid as the objects of any other science. In his investigations of the origin of phenomena Locke departed from the Baconian requirement that it was first necessary to make a natural history of facts. The mind was regarded by Locke to be blank until experience is inscribed upon it. Thus the mind is built up of received impressions plus reflection. The soul Locke believed to be incapable of apprehension of Deity, and man's realization or cognition of God to be merely an inference of the reasoning faculty. David Hume was the most enthusiastic and also the most powerful of the disciples of Locke.

Attacking Locke's sensationalism, Bishop George Berkeley substituted for it a philosophy founded on Locke's fundamental premises but which he developed as a system of idealism. Berkeley held that ideas are the real objects of knowledge. He declared it impossible to adduce proof that sensations are occasioned by material objects; he also attempted to prove that matter has no existence. *Berkeleianism* holds that the universe is permeated and governed by mind. Thus the belief in the existence of material objects is merely a mental condition, and the objects themselves may well be fabrications of the mind. At the same time Berkeley considered it worse than insanity to question the accuracy of the perceptions; for if the power of the perceptive faculties be questioned man is reduced to a creature incapable of knowing, estimating, or realizing anything whatsoever.

In the *Associationalism* of Hartley and Hume was advanced the theory that the association of ideas is the fundamental principle of psychology and the explanation for all mental phenomena. Hartley held that if a sensation be repeated several times there is a tendency towards its spontaneous repetition, which may be awakened by association with some other idea even though the object causing the original reaction be absent. The *Utilitarianism* of Jeremy Bentham, Archdeacon Paley, and James and John Stuart Mill declares that to be the greatest good which is the most useful to the greatest number. John Stuart Mill believed that if it is possible through sensation to secure knowledge of the *properties* of things, it is also possible through a higher state of the mind—that is, intuition or reason—to gain a knowledge of the true *substance* of things.

Darwinism is the doctrine of natural selection and physical evolution. It has been said of Charles Robert Darwin that he determined to banish *spirit* altogether from the universe and make the infinite and omnipresent Mind itself synonymous with the all-pervading powers of an impersonal Nature. *Agnosticism* and *Neo-Hegelianism* are also noteworthy products of this period of philosophic thought. The former is the belief that the nature of ultimates is unknowable; the latter an English and American revival of Hegel's idealism.

Dr. W. J. Durant declares that Herbert Spencer's great work, *First Principles,* made him almost at once the most famous philosopher of his time. *Spencerianism* is a philosophic positivism which describes evolution as an ever-increasing complexity with equilibrium as its highest possible state. According to Spencer, life is a continuous process from homogeneity to heterogeneity and back from heterogeneity to homogeneity. Life also involves the continual adjustment of internal relations to external relations. Most famous of all Spencer's aphorisms is his definition of Deity: "God is infinite intelligence, infinitely diversified through infinite time and infinite space, manifesting through an infinitude of ever-evolving individualities." The universality of the law of evolution was emphasized by Spencer, who applied it not only to the form but also to the intelligence behind the form. In every manifestation of being he recognized the fundamental tendency of unfoldment from simplicity to complexity, observing that when the point of equilibrium is reached it is always followed by the process of dissolution. According to Spencer, however, disintegration took place only that reintegration might follow upon a higher level of being.

The chief position in the Italian school of philosophy should be awarded to Giordano Bruno, who, after enthusiastically accepting Copernicus' theory that the sun is the center of the solar system, declared the sun to be a star and all the stars to be suns. In Bruno's time the earth was regarded as the center of all creation. Consequently when he thus relegated the world and man to an obscure corner in space the effect was cataclysmic. For the heresy of affirming a multiplicity of universes and conceiving Cosmos to be so vast that no single creed could fill it, Bruno paid the forfeit of his life.

Vicoism is a philosophy based upon the conclusions of Giovanni Battista Vico, who held that God controls His world not miraculously but through natural law. The laws by which men rule themselves, Vico declared, issue from a spiritual source within mankind which is *en rapport* with the law of the Deity. Hence material law is of divine origin and reflects the dictates of the Spiritual Father. The philosophy of *Ontologism* developed by Vincenzo Gioberti (generally considered more as a theologian than a philosopher) posits God as the only being and the origin of all knowledge, knowledge being identical with Deity itself. God is consequently called Being; all other manifestations are existences. Truth is to be discovered through reflection upon this mystery.

The most important of modern Italian philosophers is Benedetto Croce, a Hegelian idealist. Croce conceives ideas to be the only reality. He is anti-theological in his viewpoints, does not believe in the immortality of the soul, and seeks to substitute ethics and æsthetics for religion. Among other branches of Italian philosophy should be mentioned *Sensism* (Sensationalism), which posits the sense perceptions as the sole channels for the reception of knowledge; *Criticism,* or the philosophy of accurate judgment; and *Neo-Scholasticism,* which is a revival of Thomism encouraged by the Roman Catholic Church.

The two outstanding schools of American philosophy are *Transcendentalism* and *Pragmatism*. Transcendentalism, exemplified in the writings of Ralph Waldo Emerson, emphasizes the power of the transcendental over the physical. Many of Emerson's writings show pronounced Oriental influence, particularly his essays on the Oversoul and the Law of Compensation. The theory of Pragmatism, while not original with Professor William James, owes its widespread popularity as a philosophic tenet to his efforts. Pragmatism may be defined as the doctrine that the meaning and nature of things are to be discovered from consideration of their consequences. The true, according to James, "is only an expedient in the way of our thinking, just as 'the right' is only an expedient in the way of our behaving." (See his *Pragmatism.*) John Dewey, the *Instrumentalist,* who applies the experimental attitude to all the aims of life, should be considered a commentator of James. To Dewey, growth and change are limitless and no ultimates are postulated. The long residence in America of George Santayana warrants the listing of this great Spaniard among the ranks of American philosophers. Defending himself with the shield of skepticism alike from the illusions of the senses and the cumulative errors of the ages, Santayana seeks to lead mankind into a more apprehending state denominated by him *the life of reason.*

(In addition to the authorities already quoted, in the preparation of the foregoing abstract of the main branches of philosophic thought the present writer has had recourse to Stanley's *History of Philosophy;* Morell's *An Historical and Critical View of the Speculative Philosophy of Europe in the Nineteenth Century;* Singer's *Modern Thinkers and Present Problems;* Rand's *Modern Classical Philosophers;* Windelband's *History of Philosophy;* Perry's *Present Philosophical Tendencies;* Hamilton's *Lectures on Metaphysics and Logic;* and Durant's *The Story of Philosophy.*)

Having thus traced the more or less sequential development of philosophic speculation from Thales to James and Bergson, it is now in order to direct the reader's attention to the elements leading to and the circumstances attendant upon the genesis of philosophic thinking. Although the Hellenes proved themselves peculiarly responsive to the disciplines of philosophy, this science of sciences should not be considered indigenous to them. "Although some of the Grecians," writes Thomas Stanley, "have challenged to their nation the original of philosophy, yet the more learned of them have acknowledged it [to be] derived from the East." The magnificent institutions of Hindu, Chaldean, and Egyptian learning must be recognized as the actual source of Greek wisdom. The last was patterned after the shadow cast by the sanctuaries of Ellora, Ur, and Memphis upon the thought substance of a primitive people. Thales, Pythagoras, and Plato in their philosophic wanderings contacted many distant cults and brought back the lore of Egypt and the inscrutable Orient.

From indisputable facts such as these it is evident that philosophy emerged from the religious Mysteries of antiquity, not being separated from religion until after the decay of the Mysteries. Hence he who would fathom the depths of philosophic thought must familiarize himself with the teachings of those initiated priests designated as the first custodians of divine revelation. The Mysteries claimed to be the guardians of a transcendental knowledge so profound as to be incomprehensible save to the most exalted intellect and so potent as to be revealed with safety only to those in whom personal ambition was dead and who had consecrated their lives to the unselfish service of humanity. Both the dignity of these sacred institutions and the validity of their claim to possession of Universal Wisdom are attested by the most illustrious philosophers of antiquity, who were themselves initiated into the profundities of the secret doctrine and who bore witness to its efficacy.

The question may legitimately be propounded: If these ancient mystical institutions were of such "great pith and moment," why is so little information now available concerning them and the arcana they claimed to possess? The answer is simple enough: The Mysteries were secret societies, binding their initiates to inviolable secrecy, and avenging with death the betrayal of their sacred trusts. Although these schools were the true inspiration of the various doctrines promulgated by the ancient philosophers, the fountainhead of those doctrines was never revealed to the profane. Furthermore, in the lapse of time the teachings became so inextricably linked with the names of their disseminators that the actual but recondite source—the Mysteries—came to be wholly ignored.

Symbolism is the language of the Mysteries; in fact it is the language not only of mysticism and philosophy but of all Nature, for every law and power active in universal procedure is manifested to the limited sense perceptions of man through the medium of symbol. Every form existing in the diversified sphere of being is symbolic of the divine activity by which it is produced. By symbols men have ever sought to communicate to each other those thoughts which transcend the limitations of language. Rejecting man-conceived dialects as inadequate and unworthy to perpetuate divine ideas, the Mysteries thus chose symbolism as a far more ingenious and ideal method of preserving their transcendental knowledge. In a single figure a symbol may both reveal and conceal, for to the wise the subject of the symbol is obvious, while to the ignorant the figure remains inscrutable. Hence, he who seeks to unveil the secret doctrine of antiquity must search for that doctrine not upon the open pages of books which might fall into the hands of the unworthy but in the place where it was originally concealed.

Far-sighted were the initiates of antiquity. They realized that nations come and go, that empires rise and fall, and that the golden ages of art, science, and idealism are succeeded by the dark ages of superstition. With the needs of posterity foremost in mind, the sages of old went to inconceivable extremes to make certain that their knowledge should be preserved. They engraved it upon the face of mountains and concealed it within the measurements of colossal images, each of which was a geometric marvel. Their knowledge of chemistry and mathematics they hid within mythologies which the ignorant would perpetuate, or in the spans and arches of their temples which time has not entirely obliterated. They wrote in characters that neither the vandalism of men nor the ruthlessness of the elements could completely efface. Today men gaze with awe and reverence upon the mighty Memnons standing alone on the sands of Egypt, or upon the strange terraced pyramids of Palanque. Mute testimonies these are of the lost arts and sciences of antiquity; and concealed this wisdom must remain until this race has learned to read the universal language—SYMBOLISM.

The book to which this is the introduction is dedicated to the proposition that concealed within the emblematic figures, allegories, and rituals of the ancients is a secret doctrine concerning the inner mysteries of life, which doctrine has been preserved *in toto* among a small band of initiated minds since the beginning of the world. Departing, these illumined philosophers left their formulæ that others, too, might attain to understanding. But, lest these secret processes fall into uncultured hands and be perverted, the Great Arcanum was always concealed in symbol or allegory; and those who can today discover its lost keys may open with them a treasure house of philosophic, scientific, and religious truths.

The Ancient Mysteries
and Secret Societies
Which Have Influenced
Modern Masonic Symbolism

PART I

hen confronted with a problem involving the use of the reasoning faculties, individuals of strong intellect keep their poise, and seek to reach a solution by obtaining facts bearing upon the question. Those of immature mentality, on the other hand, when similarly confronted, are overwhelmed. While the former may be qualified to solve the riddle of their own destiny, the latter must be led like a flock of sheep and taught in simple language. They depend almost entirely upon the ministrations of the shepherd. The Apostle Paul said that these little ones must be fed with milk, but that meat is the food of strong men. Thought*less*ness is almost synonymous with childishness, while thought*ful*ness is symbolic of maturity.

There are, however, but few mature minds in the world; and thus it was that the philosophic-religious doctrines of the pagans were divided to meet the needs of these two fundamental groups of human intellect—one philosophic, the other incapable of appreciating the deeper mysteries of life. To the discerning few were revealed the *esoteric*, or spiritual, teachings, while the unqualified many received only the literal, or *exoteric*, interpretations. In order to make simple the great truths of Nature and the abstract principles of natural law, the vital forces of the universe were personified, becoming the gods and goddesses of the ancient mythologies. While the ignorant multitudes brought their offerings to the altars of Priapus and Pan (deities representing the procreative energies), the wise recognized in these marble statues only symbolic concretions of great abstract truths.

In all cities of the ancient world were temples for public worship and offering. In every community also were philosophers and mystics, deeply versed in Nature's lore. These individuals were usually banded together, forming seclusive philosophic and religious schools. The more important of these groups were known as the *Mysteries.* Many of the great minds of antiquity were initiated into these secret fraternities by strange and mysterious rites, some of which were extremely cruel. Alexander Wilder defines the Mysteries as "Sacred dramas performed at stated periods. The most celebrated were those of Isis, Sabazius, Cybele, and Eleusis." After being admitted, the initiates were instructed in the secret wisdom which had been preserved for ages. Plato, an initiate of one of these sacred orders, was severely criticized because in his writings he revealed to the public many of the secret philosophic principles of the Mysteries.

Every pagan nation had (and has) not only its state religion, but another into which the philosophic elect alone have gained entrance. Many of these ancient cults vanished from the earth without revealing their secrets, but a few have survived the test of ages and their mysterious symbols are still preserved. Much of the ritualism of Freemasonry is based on the trials to which candidates were subjected by the ancient hierophants before the keys of wisdom were entrusted to them.

Few realize the extent to which the ancient secret schools influenced contemporary intellects and, through those minds, posterity. Robert Macoy, 33°, in his *General History of Freemasonry,* pays a magnificent tribute to the part played by the ancient Mysteries in the rearing of the edifice of human culture. He says, in part: "It appears that all the perfection of civilization, and all the advancement made in philosophy, science, and art among the ancients are due to those institutions which, under the veil of mystery, sought to illustrate the sublimest truths of religion, morality, and virtue, and impress them on the hearts of their disciples.* * * Their chief object was to teach the doctrine of one God, the resurrection of man to eternal life, the dignity of the human soul, and to lead the people to see the shadow of the deity, in the beauty, magnificence, and splendor of the universe."

With the decline of virtue, which has preceded the destruction of every nation of history, the Mysteries became perverted. Sorcery took the place of the divine magic. Indescribable practices (such as the Bacchanalia) were introduced, and perversion ruled supreme; for no institution can be any better than the members of which it is composed. In despair, the few who were true sought to preserve the secret doctrines from oblivion. In some cases they succeeded, but more often the arcanum was lost and only the empty shell of the Mysteries remained.

Thomas Taylor has written, "Man is naturally a religious animal." From the earliest dawning of his consciousness, man has worshiped and revered *things* as symbolic of the invisible, omnipresent, indescribable *Thing,* concerning which he could discover practically nothing. The pagan Mysteries opposed the Christians during the early centuries of their church, declaring that the new faith (Christianity) did not demand virtue and integrity as requisites for salvation. Celsus expressed himself on the subject in the following caustic terms:

"That I do not, however, accuse the Christians more bitterly than truth compels, may be conjectured from hence, that the cryers who call men to other mysteries proclaim as follows: 'Let him approach whose hands are pure, and whose words are wise.' And again, others proclaim: 'Let him approach who is pure from all wickedness, whose soul is not conscious of any evil, and who leads a just and upright life.' And these things are proclaimed by those who promise a purification from error. Let us now hear who those are that are called to the Christian mysteries: Whoever is a sinner, whoever is unwise, whoever is a fool, and whoever, in short, is miserable, him the kingdom of God will receive. Do you not, therefore, call a sinner, an unjust man, a thief, a housebreaker, a wizard, one who is sacrilegious, and a robber of sepulchres? What other persons would the cryer nominate, who should call robbers together?"

It was not the true faith of the early Christian mystics that Celsus attacked, but the false forms that were creeping in even during his day. The ideals of early Christianity were based upon the high moral standards of the pagan Mysteries, and the first Christians who met under the city of Rome used as their places of worship the subterranean temples of Mithras, from whose cult has been borrowed much of the sacerdotalism of the modern church.

The ancient philosophers believed that no man could live intelligently who did not have a fundamental knowledge of Nature and her laws. Before man can obey, he must understand, and the Mysteries were devoted to instructing man concerning the operation of divine law in the terrestrial sphere. Few of the early cults actually worshiped anthropomorphic deities, although their symbolism might lead one to believe they did. They were moralistic rather than religionistic; philosophic rather than theologic. They taught man to use his faculties more intelligently, to be patient in the face of adversity, to be courageous when confronted by danger, to be true in the midst of temptation, and, most of all, to view a worthy life as the most acceptable sacrifice to God, and his body as an altar sacred to the Deity.

Sun worship played an important part in nearly all the early pagan Mysteries. This indicates the probability of their Atlantean origin, for the people of

Atlantis were sun worshipers. The Solar Deity was usually personified as a beautiful youth, with long golden hair to symbolize the rays of the sun. This golden Sun God was slain by wicked ruffians, who personified the evil principle of the universe. By means of certain rituals and ceremonies, symbolic of purification and regeneration, this wonderful God of Good was brought back to life and became the Savior of His people. The secret processes whereby He was resurrected symbolized those cultures by means of which man is able to overcome his lower nature, master his appetites, and give expression to the higher side of himself. The Mysteries were organized for the purpose of assisting the struggling human creature to reawaken the spiritual powers which, surrounded by the flaming ring of lust and degeneracy, lay asleep within his soul. In other words, man was offered a way by which he could regain his lost estate. (See Wagner's *Siegfried.*)

In the ancient world, nearly all the secret societies were philosophic and religious. During the mediæval centuries, they were chiefly religious and political, although a few philosophic schools remained. In modern times, secret societies, in the Occidental countries, are largely political or fraternal, although in a few of them, as in Masonry, the ancient religious and philosophic principles still survive.

Space prohibits a detailed discussion of the secret schools. There were literally scores of these ancient cults, with branches in all parts of the Eastern and Western worlds. Some, such as those of Pythagoras and the Hermetists, show a decided Oriental influence, while the Rosicrucians, according to their own proclamations, gained much of their wisdom from Arabian mystics. Although the Mystery schools are usually associated with civilization, there is evidence that the most uncivilized peoples of prehistoric times had a knowledge of them. Natives of distant islands, many in the lowest forms of savagery, have mystic rituals and secret practices which, although primitive, are of a decided Masonic tinge.

The Druidic Mysteries of Britain and Gaul

"The original and primitive inhabitants of Britain, at some remote period, revived and reformed their national institutes. Their priest, or instructor, had hithero been simply named Gwydd, but it was considered to have become necessary to divide this office between the national, or superior, priest and another whose influence [would] be more limited. From henceforth the former became Der-Wydd (Druid), or superior instructor, and [the latter] Go-Wydd, or

O-Vydd (Ovate), subordinate instructor; and both went by the general name of Beirdd (Bards), or teachers of wisdom. As the system matured and augmented, the Bardic Order consisted of three classes, the Druids, Beirdd Braint, or privileged Bards, and Ovates." (See Samuel Meyrick and Charles Smith, *The Costume of The Original Inhabitants of The British Islands.*)

The origin of the word *Druid* is under dispute. Max Müller believes that, like the Irish word *Drui,* it means "the men of the oak trees." He further draws attention to the fact that the forest gods and tree deities of the Greeks were called *dryades.* Some believe the word to be of Teutonic origin; others ascribe it to the Welsh. A few trace it to the Gaelic *druidh,* which means "a wise man" or "a sorcerer." In Sanskrit the word *dru* means "timber."

At the time of the Roman conquest, the Druids were thoroughly ensconced in Britain and Gaul. Their power over the people was unquestioned, and there were instances in which armies, about to attack each other, sheathed their swords when ordered to do so by the white-robed Druids. No undertaking of great importance was started without the assistance of these patriarchs, who stood as mediators between the gods and men. The Druidic Order is deservedly credited with having had a deep understanding of Nature and her laws. The *Encyclopædia Britannica* states that geography, physical science, natural theology, and astrology were their favorite studies. The Druids had a fundamental knowledge of medicine, especially the use of herbs and *simples.* Crude surgical instruments also have been found in England and Ireland. An odd treatise on early British medicine states that every practitioner was expected to have a garden or back yard for the growing of certain herbs necessary to his profession. Eliphas Levi, the celebrated transcendentalist, makes the following significant statement:

"The Druids were priests and physicians, curing by magnetism and charging amylets with their fluidic influence. Their universal remedies were mistletoe and serpents' eggs, because these substances attract the astral light in a special manner. The solemnity with which mistletoe was cut down drew upon this plant the popular confidence and rendered it powerfully magnetic.* * * The progress of magnetism will some day reveal to us the absorbing properties of mistletoe. We shall then understand the secret of those spongy growths which drew the unused virtues of plants and become surcharged with tinctures and savors. Mushrooms, truffles, gall on trees, and the different kinds of mistletoe will be employed with understanding by a medical science, which will be new because it is old * * * but one must not move quicker than science, which recedes that it may advance the further." (See *The History of Magic.*)

Not only was the mistletoe sacred as symbolic of the universal medicine, or panacea, but also because of the fact that it grew upon the oak tree. Through the symbol of the oak, the Druids worshiped the Supreme Deity; therefore, anything growing upon that tree was sacred to Him. At certain seasons, according to the positions of the sun, moon, and stars, the Arch-Druid climbed the oak tree and cut the mistletoe with a golden sickle consecrated for that service. The parasitic growth was caught in white cloths provided for the purpose, lest it touch the earth and be polluted by terrestrial vibrations. Usually a sacrifice of a white bull was made under the tree.

The Druids were initiates of a secret school that existed in their midst. This school, which closely resembled the Bacchic and Eleusinian Mysteries of Greece or the Egyptian rites of Isis and Osiris, is justly designated the *Druidic Mysteries.* There has been much speculation concerning the secret wisdom that the Druids claimed to possess. Their secret teachings were never written, but were communicated orally to specially prepared candidates. Robert Brown, 32°, is of the opinion that the British priests secured their information from Tyrian and Phœnician navigators who, thousands of years before the Christian Era, established colonies in Britain and Gaul while searching for tin. Thomas Maurice, in his *Indian Antiquities,* discourses at length on Phœnician, Carthaginian, and Greek expeditions to the British Isles for the purpose of procuring tin. Others are of the opinion that the Mysteries as celebrated by the Druids were of Oriental origin, possibly Buddhistic.

The proximity of the British Isles to the lost Atlantis may account for the sun worship which plays an important part in the rituals of Druidism. According to Artemidorus, Ceres and Persephone were worshiped on an island close to Britain with rites and ceremonies similar to those of Samothrace. There is no doubt that the Druidic Pantheon includes a large number of Greek and Roman deities. This greatly amazed Cæsar during his conquest of Britain and Gaul, and caused him to affirm that these tribes adored Mercury, Apollo, Mars, and Jupiter, in a manner similar to that of the Latin countries. It is almost certain that the Druidic Mysteries were not indigenous to Britain or Gaul, but migrated from one of the more ancient civilizations.

The school of the Druids was divided into three distinct parts, and the secret teachings embodied therein are practically the same as the mysteries concealed under the allegories of Blue Lodge Masonry. The lowest of the three divisions was that of Ovate (Ovydd). This was an honorary degree, requiring no special purification or preparation. The Ovates dressed in green, the Druidic color of learning, and were expected to know something about medicine, astronomy, poetry if possible, and sometimes music. An Ovate was an individual admitted to the Druidic Order because of his general excellence and superior knowledge concerning the problems of life.

The second division was that of Bard (Beirdd). Its members were robed in sky-blue, to represent harmony and truth, and to them was assigned the labor of memorizing, at least in part, the twenty thousand verses of Druidic sacred poetry. They were often pictured with the primitive British or Irish harp—an instrument strung with human hair, and having as many strings as there were ribs on one side of the human body. These Bards were often chosen as teachers of candidates seeking entrance into the Druidic Mysteries. Neophytes wore striped robes of blue, green, and white, these being the three sacred colors of the Druidic Order.

The third division was that of Druid (Derwyddon). Its particular labor was to minister to the religious needs of the people. To reach this dignity, the candidate must first become a Bard Braint. The Druids always dressed in white—symbolic of their purity, and the color used by them to symbolize the sun.

In order to reach the exalted position of *Arch-Druid,* or spiritual head of the organization, it was necessary for a priest to pass through the six successive degrees of the Druidic Order. (The members of the different degrees were differentiated by the colors of their sashes, for all of them wore robes of white.) Some writers are of the opinion that the title of *Arch-Druid* was hereditary, descending from father to son, but it is more probable that the honor was conferred by ballot election. Its recipient was chosen for his virtues and integrity from the most learned members of the higher Druidic degrees.

According to James Gardner, there were usually two *Arch-Druids* in Britain, one residing on the Isle of Anglesea and the other on the Isle of Man. Presumably there were others in Gaul. These dignitaries generally carried golden scepters and were crowned with wreaths of oak leaves, symbolic of their authority. The younger members of the Druidic Order were clean-shaven and modestly dressed, but the more aged had long gray beards and wore magnificent golden ornaments. The educational system of the Druids in Britain was superior to that of their colleagues on the Continent, and consequently many of the Gallic youths were sent to the Druidic colleges in Britain for their philosophical instruction and training.

Eliphas Levi states that the Druids lived in strict abstinence, studied the natural sciences, preserved the deepest secrecy, and admitted new members only after long probationary periods. Many of the priests of the order lived in buildings not unlike the monasteries of the modern world. They were associated in groups like ascetics of the Far East. Although celibacy was not demanded of them, few married. Many of the Druids retired from the world and lived as recluses in caves, in rough-stone houses, or in little shacks built in the depths of a forest. Here they prayed and meditated, emerging only to perform their religious duties.

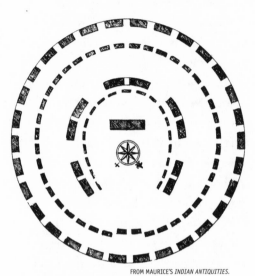

FROM MAURICE'S *INDIAN ANTIQUITIES.*

THE GROUND PLAN OF STONEHENGE.

The Druid temples or places of religious worship were not patterned after those of other nations. Most of their ceremonies were performed at night, either in thick groves of oak trees or around open-air altars built of great uncut stones. How these masses of rock were moved has not been satisfactorily explained. The most famous of their altars, a great ring of rocks, is Stonehenge, in Southwestern England. This structure, laid out on an astronomical basis, still stands, a wonder of antiquity.

James Freeman Clarke, in his *Ten Great Religions,* describes the beliefs of the Druids as follows: "The Druids believed in three worlds and in transmigration from one to the other: In a world above this, in which happiness predominated; a world below, of misery; and this present state. This transmigration was to punish and reward and also to purify the soul. In the present world, said they, Good and Evil are so exactly balanced that man has the utmost freedom and is able to choose or reject either. The Welsh Triads tell us there are three objects of metempsychosis: to collect into the soul the properties of all being, to acquire a knowledge of all things, and to get power to conquer evil. There are also, they say, three kinds of knowledge: knowledge of the name of each thing, of its cause, and its influence. There are three things which continually grow less: darkness, falsehood, and death. There are three which constantly increase: light, life, and truth."

Like nearly all schools of the Mysteries, the teachings of the Druids were divided into two distinct sections. The simpler, a moral code, was taught to all the people, while the deeper, esoteric doctrine was given only to initiated priests. To be admitted to the order, a candidate was required to be of good family and of high moral character. No important secrets were intrusted to him until he had been tempted in many ways and his strength of character severely tried. The Druids taught the people of Britain and Gaul concerning the immortality of the soul. They believed in transmigration and apparently in reincarnation. They borrowed in one life, promising to pay back in the next. They believed in a purgatorial type of hell where they would be purged of their sins, afterward passing on to the happiness of unity with the gods. The Druids taught that all men would be saved, but that some must return to earth many times to learn the lessons of human life and to overcome the inherent evil of their own natures.

Before a candidate was intrusted with the secret doctrines of the Druids, he was bound with a vow of secrecy. These doctrines were imparted only in the depths of forests and in the darkness of caves. In these places, far from the haunts of men, the neophyte was instructed concerning the creation of the universe, the personalities of the gods, the laws of Nature, the secrets of occult medicine, the mysteries of the celestial bodies, and the rudiments of magic and sorcery. The Druids had a great number of feast days. The new and full moon and the sixth day of the moon were sacred periods. It is believed that initiations took place only at the two solstices and the two equinoxes. At dawn of the 25th day of December, the birth of the Sun God was celebrated.

The secret teachings of the Druids are said by some to be tinctured with Pythagorean philosophy. The Druids had a Madonna, or Virgin Mother, with a Child in her arms, who was sacred to their Mysteries; and their Sun God was resurrected at the time of the year corresponding to that at which modern Christians celebrate Easter.

Both the cross and the serpent were sacred to the Druids, who made the former by cutting off all the branches of an oak tree and fastening one of them to the main trunk in the form of the letter **T**. This oaken cross became symbolic of their superior Deity. They also worshiped the sun, moon, and stars. The moon received their special veneration. Cæsar stated that Mercury was one of the chief deities of the Gauls. The Druids are believed to have worshiped Mercury under the similitude of a stone cube. They also had great veneration for the Nature spirits (fairies, gnomes, and undines), little creatures of the forests and rivers to whom many offerings were made. Describing the temples of the Druids, Charles Heckethorn, in *The Secret Societies of All Ages & Countries,* says:

"Their temples wherein the sacred fire was preserved were generally situate on eminences and in dense groves of oak, and assumed various forms—circular, because a circle was the emblem of the universe; oval, in allusion to the mundane egg, from which issued, according to the traditions of many nations, the universe, or, according to others, our first parents; serpentine, because a serpent was the symbol of Hu, the Druidic Osiris; cruciform, because a cross is an emblem of regeneration; or winged, to represent the motion of the Divine Spirit. * * * Their chief deities were reducible to two—a male and a female, the great father and mother—Hu and Ceridwen, distinguished by the same characteristics as belong to Osiris and Isis, Bacchus and Ceres, or any other supreme god and goddess representing the two principles of all Being."

Godfrey Higgins states that *Hu,* the Mighty, regarded as the first settler of Britain, came from a place which the Welsh *Triads* call the Summer Country, the present site of Constantinople. Albert Pike says that the Lost Word of Masonry is concealed in the name of the Druid god *Hu.* The meager information extant concerning the secret initiations of the Druids indicates a decided similarity between their Mystery school and the schools of Greece and Egypt. *Hu,* the Sun God, was murdered and, after a number of strange ordeals and mystic rituals, was restored to life.

There were three degrees of the Druidic Mysteries, but few successfully passed them all. The candidate was buried in a coffin, as symbolic of the death of the Sun God. The supreme test, however, was being sent out to sea in an open boat. While undergoing this ordeal, many lost their lives. Taliesin, an ancient scholar, who passed through the Mysteries, describes the initiation of the open boat in Faber's *Pagan Idolatry.* The few who passed this third degree were said to have been "born again," and were instructed in the secret and hidden truths which the Druid priests had preserved from antiquity. From these initiates were chosen many of the dignitaries of the British religious and political world. (For further details, see Faber's *Pagan Idolatry,* Albert Pike's *Morals and Dogma,* and Godfrey Higgins' *Celtic Druids.*)

The Rites of Mithras

When the Persian Mysteries immigrated into Southern Europe, they were quickly assimilated by the Latin mind. The cult grew rapidly, especially among the Roman soldiery, and during the Roman wars of conquest the teachings were carried by the legionaries to nearly all parts of Europe. So powerful did the cult of Mithras become that at least one Roman Emperor was initiated into the order, which met in caverns under the city of Rome. Concerning the spread of this Mystery school through different parts of Europe, C. W. King, in his *Gnostics and Their Remains,* says:

"Mithraic bas-reliefs cut on the faces of rocks or on stone tablets still abound in the countries formerly the western provinces of the Roman Empire; many exist in Germany, still more in France, and in this island (Britain) they have often been discovered on the line of the Picts' Wall and the noted one at Bath."

Alexander Wilder, in his *Philosophy and Ethics of the Zoroasters,* states that *Mithras* is the Zend title for the sun, and he is supposed to dwell within that shining orb. *Mithras* has a male and a female aspect, though not himself androgynous. As *Mithras,* he is the lord of the sun, powerful and radiant, and most magnificent of the *Yazatas* (Izads, or Genii, of the sun). As *Mithra,* this deity represents the feminine principle; the mundane universe is recognized as her symbol. She represents Nature as receptive and terrestrial, and as fruitful only when bathed in the glory of the solar orb. The Mithraic cult is a simplication of the more elaborate teachings of Zarathustra (Zoroaster), the Persian fire magician.

According to the Persians, there coexisted in eternity two principles. The first of these, *Ahura-Mazda,* or *Ormuzd,* was the Spirit of Good. From Ormuzd came forth a number of hierarchies of good and beautiful spirits (angels and archangels). The second of these eternally existing principles was called *Ahriman.* He was also a pure and beautiful spirit, but he later rebelled against Ormuzd, being jealous of his power. This did not occur, however, until after Ormuzd had created light, for previously Ahriman had not been conscious of the existence of Ormuzd. Because of his jealousy and rebellion, Ahriman became the Spirit of Evil. From himself he individualized a host of destructive creatures to injure Ormuzd.

FROM LUNDY'S *MONUMENTAL CHRISTIANITY.*

MITHRAS SLAYING THE BULL.

The most famous sculpturings and reliefs of this prototokos show Mithras kneeling upon the recumbent form of a great bull, into whose throat he is driving a sword. The slaying of the bull signifies that the rays of the sun, symbolized by the sword, release at the vernal equinox the vital essences of the earth—the blood of the bull—which, pouring from the wound made by the Sun God, fertilize the seeds of living things. Dogs were held sacred to the cult of Mithras, being symbolic of sincerity and trustworthiness. The Mithraics used the serpent as an emblem of Ahriman, the Spirit of Evil, and water rats were held sacred to him. The bull is esoterically the Constellation of Taurus; the serpent, its opposite in the zodiac, Scorpio; the sun, Mithras, entering into the side of the bull, slays the celestial creature and nourishes the universe with its blood.

When Ormuzd created the earth, Ahriman entered into its grosser elements. Whenever Ormuzd did a good deed, Ahriman placed the principle of evil within it. At last when Ormuzd created the human race, Ahriman became incarnate in the lower nature of man so that in each personality the Spirit of Good and the Spirit of Evil struggle for control. For 3,000 years Ormuzd ruled the celestial worlds with light and goodness. Then he created man. For another 3,000 years he ruled man with wisdom and integrity. Then the power of Ahriman began, and the struggle for the soul of man continues through the next period of 3,000 years. During the fourth period of 3,000 years, the power of Ahriman will be destroyed. Good will return to the world again, evil and death will be vanquished, and at last the Spirit of Evil will bow humbly before the throne of Ormuzd. While Ormuzd and Ahriman are struggling for control of the human soul and for supremacy in Nature, Mithras, God of Intelligence, stands as mediator between the two. Many authors have noted the similarity between mercury and Mithras. As the chemical mercury acts as a solvent (according to alchemists), so Mithras seeks to harmonize the two celestial opposites.

There are many points of resemblance between Christianity and the cult of Mithras. One of the reasons for this probably is that the Persian mystics invaded Italy during the first century after Christ and the early history of both cults was closely interwoven. The *Encyclopædia Britannica* makes the following statement concerning the Mithraic and Christian Mysteries:

"The fraternal and democratic spirit of the first communities, and their humble origin; the identification of the object of adoration with light and the sun; the legends of the shepherds with their gifts and adoration, the flood, and the ark; the representation in art of the fiery chariot, the drawing of water from the rock; the use of bell and candle, holy water and the communion; the sanctification of Sunday and of the 25th of December; the insistence on moral conduct, the emphasis placed on abstinence and self-control; the doctrine of heaven and hell, of primitive revelation, of the mediation of the Logos emanating from the divine, the atoning sacrifice, the constant warfare between good and evil and the final triumph of the former, the immortality of the soul, the last judgment, the resurrection of the flesh and the fiery destruction of the universe—[these] are some of the resemblances which, whether real or only apparent, enabled Mithraism to prolong its resistance to Christianity."

The rites of Mithras were performed in caves. Porphyry, in his *Cave of the Nymphs,* states that Zarathustra (Zoroaster) was the first to consecrate a cave to the worship of God, because a cavern was symbolic of the earth, or the lower world of darkness. John P. Lundy, in his *Monumental Christianity,* describes the cave of Mithras as follows:

"But this cave was adorned with the signs of the zodiac, Cancer and Capricorn. The summer and winter solstices were chiefly conspicuous, as the gates of souls descending into this life, or passing out of it in their ascent to the Gods; Cancer being the gate of descent, and Capricorn of ascent. These are the two avenues of the immortals passing up and down from earth to heaven, and from heaven to earth."

The so-called chair of St. Peter, in Rome, was believed to have been used in one of the pagan Mysteries, possibly that of Mithras, in whose subterranean grottoes the votaries of the Christian Mysteries met in the early days of their faith. In *Anacalypsis,* Godfrey Higgins writes that in 1662, while cleaning this sacred chair of Bar-Jonas, the Twelve Labors of Hercules were discovered upon it, and that later the French discovered upon the same chair the Mohammedan confession of faith, written in Arabic.

Initiation into the rites of Mithras, like initiation into many other ancient schools of philosophy, apparently consisted of three important degrees. Preparation for these degrees consisted of self-purification, the building up of the intellectual powers, and the control of the animal nature. In the first degree the candidate was given a crown upon the point of a sword and instructed in the mysteries of Mithras' hidden power. Probably he was taught that the golden crown represented his own spiritual nature, which must be objectified and unfolded before he could truly glorify Mithras; for Mithras was his own soul, standing as mediator between Ormuzd, his spirit, and Ahriman, his animal nature. In the second degree he was given the armor of intelligence and purity and sent into the darkness of subterranean pits to fight the beasts of lust, passion, and degeneracy. In the third degree he was given a cape, upon which were drawn or woven the signs of the zodiac and other astronomical symbols. After his initiations were over, he was hailed as one who had risen from the dead, was instructed in the secret teachings of the Persian mystics, and became a full-fledged member of the order. Candidates who successfully passed the Mithraic initiations were called *Lions* and were marked upon their foreheads with the Egyptian cross. Mithras himself is often pictured with the head of a lion and two pairs of wings. Throughout the entire ritual were repeated references to the birth of Mithras as the Sun God, his sacrifice for man, his death that men might have eternal life, and lastly, his resurrection and the saving of all humanity by his intercession before the throne of Ormuzd. (See Heckethorn.)

While the cult of Mithras did not reach the philosophic heights attained by Zarathustra, its effect upon the civilization of the Western world was far-reaching, for at one time nearly all Europe was converted to its doctrines. Rome, in her intercourse with other nations, inoculated them with her religious principles; and many later institutions have exhibited Mithraic culture. The reference to the "Lion" and the "Grip of the Lion's Paw" in the Master Mason's degree have a strong Mithraic tinge and may easily have originated from this cult. A ladder of seven rungs appears in the Mithraic initiation. Faber is of the opinion that this ladder was originally a pyramid of seven steps. It is possible that the Masonic ladder with seven rungs had its origin in this Mithraic symbol. Women were never permitted to enter the Mithraic Order, but children of the male sex were initiates long before they reached maturity. The refusal to permit women to join the Masonic Order may be based on the esoteric reason given in the secret instructions of the Mithraics. This cult is another excellent example of those secret societies whose legends are largely symbolic representations of the sun and his journey through the houses of the heavens. Mithras, rising from a stone, is merely the sun rising over the horizon, or, as the ancients supposed, out of the horizon, at the vernal equinox.

John O'Neill disputes the theory that Mithras was intended as a solar deity. In *The Night of the Gods* he writes: "The Avestan Mithra, the yazata of light, has '10,000 eyes, high, with full knowledge (perethuvaedayana), strong, sleepless and ever awake (jaghaurvaunghem).' The supreme god Ahura Mazda also has one Eye, or else it is said that 'with his eyes, the sun, moon and stars, he sees everything.' The theory that Mithra was *originally* a title of the supreme heavens-god—putting the sun out of court—is the only one that answers all requirements. It will be evident that here we have origins in abundance for the Freemason's Eye and 'its nunquam dormio.'" The reader must not confuse the Persian Mithra with the Vedic Mitra. According to Alexander Wilder, "The Mithraic rites superseded the Mysteries of Bacchus, and became the foundation of the Gnostic system, which for many centuries prevailed in Asia, Egypt, and even the remote West."

The Ancient Mysteries
and Secret Societies

The entire history of Christian and pagan Gnosticism is shrouded in the deepest mystery and obscurity; for, while the Gnostics were undoubtedly prolific writers, little of their literature has survived. They brought down upon themselves the animosity of the early Christian Church, and when this institution reached its position of world power it destroyed all available records of the Gnostic *cultus*. The name *Gnostic* means *wisdom,* or *knowledge,* and is derived from the Greek *Gnosis.* The members of the order claimed to be familiar with the secret doctrines of early Christianity. They interpreted the Christian Mysteries according to pagan symbolism. Their secret information and philosophic tenets they concealed from the profane and taught to a small group only of especially initiated persons.

Simon Magus, the magician of New Testament fame, is often supposed to have been the founder of Gnosticism. If this be true, the sect was formed during the century after Christ and is probably the first of the many branches which have sprung from the main trunk of Christianity. Everything with which the enthusiasts of the early Christian Church might not agree they declared to be inspired by the Devil. That Simon Magus had mysterious and supernatural powers is conceded even by his enemies, but they maintained that these powers were lent to him by the infernal spirits and furies which they asserted were his ever present companions. Undoubtedly the most interesting legend concerning Simon is that which tells of his theosophic contests with the Apostle Peter while the two were promulgating their differing doctrines in Rome. According to the

FROM THE *NUREMBERG CHRONICLE*.

THE DEATH OF SIMON THE MAGICIAN.

Simon Magus, having called upon the Spirits of the Air, is here shown being picked up by the demons. St. Peter demands that the evil genii release their hold upon the magician. The demons are forced to comply and Simon Magus is killed by the fall.

story that the Church Fathers have preserved, Simon was to prove his spiritual superiority by ascending to heaven in a chariot of fire. He was actually picked up and carried many feet into the air by invisible powers. When St. Peter saw this, he cried out in a loud voice, ordering the demons (spirits of the air) to release their hold upon the magician. The evil spirits, when so ordered by the great saint, were forced to obey. Simon fell a great distance and was killed, which decisively proved the superiority of the Christian powers. This story is undoubtedly manufactured out of whole cloth, as it is only one out of many accounts concerning his death, few of which agree. As more and more evidence is being amassed to the effect that St. Peter was never in Rome, its last possible vestige of authenticity is rapidly being dissipated.

That Simon was a philosopher there is no doubt, for wherever his exact words are preserved his synthetic and transcending thoughts are beautifully expressed. The principles of Gnosticism are well described in the following verbatim statement by him, supposed to have been preserved by Hippolytus: "To you, therefore, I say what I say, and write what I write. And the writing is this. Of the universal Æons [periods, planes, or cycles of creative and created life in substance and space, celestial creatures] there are two shoots, without beginning or end, springing from one Root, which is the power invisible, inapprehensible silence [Bythos]. Of these shoots one is manifested from above, which is the Great Power, the Universal Mind ordering all things, male, and the other, [is manifested] from below, the Great Thought, female, producing all things. Hence pairing with each other, they unite and manifest the Middle Distance, incomprehensible Air, without beginning or end. In this is the Father Who sustains all things, and nourishes those things which have a beginning and end." (See *Simon Magus,* by G.R.S. Mead.) By this we are to understand that manifestation is the result of a positive and a negative principle, one acting upon the other, and it takes place in the middle plane, or point of equilibrium, called the *pleroma.* This *pleroma* is a peculiar substance produced out of the blending of the spiritual and material æons. Out of the *pleroma* was individualized the *Demiurgus,* the immortal mortal, to whom we are responsible for our physical existence and the suffering we must go through in connection with it. In the Gnostic system, three pairs of opposites, called *Syzygies,* emanated from the Eternal One. These, with Himself, make the total of seven. The six (three pairs) Æons (living, divine principles) were described by Simon in the *Philosophumena* in the following manner: The first two were *Mind* (Nous) and *Thought* (Epinoia). Then came *Voice* (Phone) and its opposite, *Name* (Onoma), and lastly, *Reason* (Logismos) and *Reflection* (Enthumesis). From these primordial six, united with the *Eternal Flame,* came forth the Æons (Angels) who formed the lower worlds through the direction of the Demiurgus. (See the works of H. P. Blavatsky.) How this first Gnosticism of Simon Magus and Menander, his disciple, was amplified, and frequently distorted, by later adherents to the cult must now be considered.

The School of Gnosticism was divided into two major parts, commonly called the Syrian Cult and the Alexandrian Cult. These schools agreed in essentials, but the latter division was more inclined to be pantheistic, while the former was dualistic. While the Syrian cult was largely Simonian, the Alexandrian School was the outgrowth of the philosophical deductions of a clever Egyptian Christian, Basilides by name, who claimed to have received his instructions from the Apostle Matthew. Like Simon Magus, he was an emanationist, with Neo-Platonic inclinations. In fact, the entire Gnostic Mystery is based upon the hypothesis of emanations as being the logical connection between the irreconcilable opposites Absolute Spirit and Absolute Substance, which the Gnostics believed to have been coexistent in Eternity. Some assert that Basilides was the true founder of Gnosticism, but there is much evidence to the effect that Simon Magus laid down its fundamental principles in the preceding century.

The Alexandrian Basilides inculcated Egyptian Hermeticism, Oriental occultism, Chaldean astrology, and Persian philosophy in his followers, and in his doctrines sought to unite the schools of early Christianity with the ancient pagan Mysteries. To him is attributed the formulation of that peculiar concept of the Deity which carries the name of *Abraxas*. In discussing the original meaning of this word, Godfrey Higgins, in his *Celtic Druids,* has demonstrated that the numerological powers of the letters forming the word *Abraxas* when added together result in the sum of 365. The same author also notes that the name *Mithras* when treated in a similar manner has the same numerical value. Basilides taught that the powers of the universe were divided into 365 Æons, or spiritual cycles, and that the sum of all these together was the Supreme Father, and to Him he gave the Qabbalistical appellation *Abraxas,* as being symbolical, numerologically, of His divine powers, attributes, and emanations. *Abraxas* is usually symbolized as a composite creature, with the body of a human being and the head of a rooster, and with each of his legs ending in a serpent. C. W. King, in his *Gnostics and Their Remains,* gives the following concise description of the Gnostic philosophy of Basilides, quoting from the writings of the early Christian bishop and martyr, St. Irenæus: "He asserted that God, the uncreated, eternal Father, had first brought forth Nous, or Mind; this the Logos, Word; this again Phronesis, Intelligence; from Phronesis sprung Sophia, Wisdom, and Dynamis, Strength."

In describing Abraxas, C. W. King says: "Bellermann considers the composite image, inscribed with the actual name Abraxas, to be a Gnostic Pantheos, representing the Supreme Being, with the Five Emanations marked out by appropriate symbols. From the human body, the usual form assigned to the Deity, spring the two supporters, Nous and Logos, expressed in the serpents, symbols of the inner senses, and the quickening understanding; on which account the Greeks had made the serpent the attribute of Pallas. His head—that of a cock—represents Phronesis, that bird being the emblem of foresight and of vigilance. His two arms hold the symbols of Sophia and Dynamis: the shield of Wisdom and the whip of Power."

The Gnostics were divided in their opinions concerning the Dermiurgus, or creator of the lower worlds. He established the terrestrial universe with the aid of six sons, or emanations (possibly the planetary Angels) which He formed out of, and yet within, Himself. As stated before, the Demiurgus was individualized as the lowest creation out of the substance called *pleroma*. One group of the Gnostics was of the opinion that the Demiurgus was the cause of all misery and was an evil creature, who by building this lower world had separated the souls of men from truth by encasing them in mortal vehicles. The other sect viewed the Demiurgus as being divinely inspired and merely fulfilling the dictates of the invisible Lord. Some Gnostics were of the opinion that the Jewish God, *Jehovah,* was the Demiurgus. This concept, under a slightly different name, apparently influenced mediæval Rosicrucianism, which viewed Jehovah as the Lord of the material universe rather than as the Supreme Deity. Mythology abounds with the stories of gods who partook of both celestial and terrestrial natures. Odin, of Scandinavia, is a good example of a deity subject to mortality, bowing before the laws of Nature and yet being, in certain senses at least, a Supreme Deity.

The Gnostic viewpoint concerning the Christ is well worthy of consideration. This order claimed to be the only sect to have actual pictures of the Divine Syrian. While these were, in all probability, idealistic conceptions of the Savior based upon existing sculpturings and paintings of the pagan sun gods, they were all Christianity had. To the Gnostics, the Christ was the personification of *Nous,* the Divine Mind, and emanated from the higher spiritual Æons. He descended into the body of Jesus at the baptism and left it again before the crucifixion. The Gnostics declared that the Christ was not crucified, as this Divine *Nous* could not suffer death, but that Simon, the Cyrenian, offered his life instead and that the *Nous,* by means of its power, caused Simon to resemble Jesus. Irenæus makes the following statement concerning the cosmic sacrifice of the Christ:

"When the uncreated, unnamed Father saw the corruption of mankind, He sent His firstborn, Nous, into the world, in the form of Christ, for the redemption of all who believe in Him, out of the power of those that have fabricated the world (the Demiurgus, and his six sons, the planetary genii). He appeared amongst men as the Man Jesus, and wrought miracles." (See King's *Gnostics and Their Remains*.)

The Gnostics divided humanity into three parts: those who, as savages, worshiped only the visible Nature; those who, like the Jews, worshiped the Demiurgus; and lastly, themselves, or others of a similar cult, including certain sects of Christians, who worshiped *Nous* (Christ) and the true spiritual light of the higher Æons.

After the death of Basilides, Valentinus became the leading inspiration of the Gnostic movement. He still further complicated the system of Gnostic philosophy by adding infinitely to the details. He increased the number of emanations from the Great One (the Abyss) to fifteen pairs and also laid much emphasis on the *Virgin Sophia,* or Wisdom. In the *Books of the Savior,* parts of which are commonly known as the *Pistis Sophia,* may be found much material concerning this strange doctrine of Æons and their strange inhabitants. James Freeman Clarke, in speaking of the doctrines of the Gnostics, says: "These doctrines, strange as they seem to us, had a wide influence in the Christian Church." Many of the theories of the ancient Gnostics, especially those concerning scientific subjects, have been substantiated by modern research. Several sects branched off from the main stem of Gnosticism, such as the Valentinians, the Ophites (serpent worshipers), and the Adamites. After the third century their power waned, and the Gnostics practically vanished from the philosophic world. An effort was made during the Middle Ages to resurrect the principles of Gnosticism, but owing to the destruction of their records the material necessary was not available. Even today there are evidences of Gnostic philosophy in the modern world, but they bear other names and their true origin is not suspected. Many of the Gnostic concepts have actually been incorporated into the dogmas of the Christian Church, and our newer interpretations of Christianity are often along the lines of Gnostic emanationism.

The Mysteries of Asar-Hapi

The identity of the Greco-Egyptian Serapis (known to the Greeks as *Serapis* and the Egyptians as *Asar-Hapi*) is shrouded by an impenetrable veil of mystery. While this deity was a familiar figure among the symbols of the secret Egyptian initiatory rites, his arcane nature was revealed only to those who had fulfilled the requirements of the Serapic cultus. Therefore, in all probability, excepting the initiated priests, the Egyptians themselves were ignorant of his true character. So far as known, there exists no authentic account of the rites of Serapis, but an analysis of the deity and his accompanying symbols reveals their salient points. In an oracle delivered to the King of Cyprus, Serapis described himself thus:

"A god I am such as I show to thee,
  The Starry Heavens are my head, my trunk the sea,
  Earth forms my feet, mine ears the air supplies,
  The Sun's far-darting, brilliant rays, mine eyes."

Several unsatisfactory attempts have been made to etymologize the word *Serapis.* Godfrey Higgins notes that *Soros* was the name given by the Egyptians to a stone coffin, and *Apis* was Osiris incarnate in the sacred bull. These two words combined result in *Soros-Apis* or *Sor-Apis,* "the tomb of the bull." But it is improbable that the Egyptians would worship a coffin in the form of a man.

Several ancient authors, including Macrobius, have affirmed that Serapis was a name for the Sun, because his image so often had a halo of light about its head. In his *Oration Upon the Sovereign Sun,* Julian speaks of the deity in these words: "One Jove, one Pluto, one Sun is Serapis." In Hebrew, Serapis is *Saraph,* meaning "to blaze out" or "to blaze up." For this reason the Jews designated one of their hierarchies of spiritual beings, *Seraphim.*

The most common theory, however, regarding the origin of the name *Serapis* is that which traces its derivation from the compound *Osiris-Apis.* At one time the Egyptians believed that the dead were absorbed into the nature of Osiris, the god of the dead. While marked similarity exists between Osiris-Apis and Serapis, the theory advanced by Egyptologists that Serapis is merely a name given to the dead Apis, or sacred bull of Egypt, is untenable in view of the transcendent wisdom possessed by the Egyptian priestcraft, who, in all probability, used the god to symbolize the soul of the world (*anima mundi*). The material body of Nature was called *Apis;* the soul which escaped from the body at death but was enmeshed with the form during physical life was designated *Serapis.*

C. W. King believes Serapis to be a deity of Brahmanic extraction, his name being the Grecianized form of *Ser-adah* or *Sri-pa,* two titles ascribed to *Yama,* the Hindu god of death. This appears reasonable, especially since there is a legend to the effect that Serapis, in the form of a bull, was driven by Bacchus from India to Egypt. The priority of the Hindu Mysteries would further substantiate such a theory.

Among other meanings suggested for the word *Serapis* are: "The Sacred Bull," "The Sun in Taurus," "The Soul of Osiris," "The Sacred Serpent," and

"The Retiring of the Bull." The last appellation has reference to the ceremony of drowning the sacred Apis in the waters of the Nile every twenty-five years.

There is considerable evidence that the famous statue of Serapis in the Serapeum at Alexandria was originally worshiped under another name at Sinope, from which it was brought to Alexandria. There is also a legend which tells that Serapis was a very early king of the Egyptians, to whom they owed the foundation of their philosophical and scientific power. After his death this king was elevated to the estate of a god. Phylarchus declared that the word *Serapis* means "the power that disposed the universe into its present beautiful order."

In his *Isis* and *Osiris,* Plutarch gives the following account of the origin of the magnificent statue of Serapis which stood in the Serapeum at Alexandria:

While he was Pharaoh of Egypt, Ptolemy Soter had a strange dream in which he beheld a tremendous statue, which came to life and ordered the Pharaoh to bring it to Alexandria with all possible speed. Ptolemy Soter, not knowing the whereabouts of the statue, was sorely perplexed as to how he could discover it. While the Pharaoh was relating his dream, a great traveler by the name of Sosibius, coming forward,

THE ALEXANDRIAN SERAPIS.

Serapis is often shown standing on the back of the sacred crocodile, carrying in his left hand a rule with which to measure the inundations of the Nile, and balancing with his right hand a curious emblem consisting of an animal with three heads. The first head—that of a lion—signified the present; the second head—that of a wolf—the past; and the third head—that of a dog—the future. The body with its three heads was enveloped by the twisted coils of a serpent. Figures of Serapis are occasionally accompanied by Cerberus, the three-headed dog of Pluto, and—like Jupiter—carry baskets of grain upon their heads.

FROM MOSAIZE
HISTORIE DER HEBREEUWSE KERKE.

declared that he had seen such an image at Sinope. The Pharaoh immediately dispatched Soteles and Dionysius to negotiate for the removal of the figure to Alexandria. Three years elapsed before the image was finally obtained, the representatives of the Pharaoh finally stealing it and concealing the theft by spreading a story that the statue had come to life and, walking down the street leading from its temple, had boarded the ship prepared for its transportation to Alexandria. Upon its arrival in Egypt, the figure was brought into the presence of two Egyptian Initiates—the Eumolpid Timotheus and Manetho the Sebennite— who immediately pronounced it to be Serapis. The priests then declared that it was equipollent to Pluto. This was a masterly stroke, for in Serapis the Greeks and Egyptians found a deity in common and thus religious unity was consummated between the two nations.

Several figures of Serapis that stood in his various temples in Egypt and Rome have been described by early authors. Nearly all these showed Grecian rather than Egyptian influence. In some the body of the god was encircled by the coils of a great serpent. Others showed him as a composite of Osiris and Apis.

A description of the god that in all probability is reasonably accurate is that which represents him as a tall, powerful figure, conveying the twofold impression of manly strength and womanly grace. His face portrayed a deeply pensive mood, the expression inclining toward sadness. His hair was long and arranged in a somewhat feminine manner, resting in curls upon his breast and shoulders. The face, save for its heavy beard, was also decidedly feminine. The figure of Serapis was usually robed from head to foot in heavy draperies, believed by initiates to conceal the fact that his body was androgynous.

Various substances were used in making the statues of Serapis. Some undoubtedly were carved from stone or marble by skilled craftsmen; others may have been cast from base or precious metals. One colossus of Serapis was composed of plates of various metals fitted together. In a labyrinth sacred to Serapis stood a thirteen-foot statue of him reputed to have been made from a single emerald. Modern writers, discussing this image, state that it was made of green glass poured into a mold. According to the Egyptians, however, it withstood all the tests of an actual emerald.

Clement of Alexandria describes a figure of Serapis compounded from the following elements: First, filings of gold, silver, lead, and tin; second, all manner of Egyptian stones, including sapphires, hematites, emeralds, and topazes; all these being ground down and mixed together with the coloring matter left over from the funeral of Osiris and Apis. The result was a rare and curious figure, indigo in color. Some of the statues of Serapis must have been formed of extremely hard substances, for when a Christian soldier, carrying out the edict of Theodosius, struck the Alexandrian Serapis with his ax, that instrument was shattered into fragments and sparks flew from it. It is also quite probable that Serapis was worshiped in the form of a serpent, in common with many of the higher deities of the Egyptian and Greek pantheons.

Serapis was called *Theon Heptagrammaton,* or the god with the name of seven letters. The name *Serapis* (like Abraxas and Mithras) contains seven letters. In their hymns to Serapis the priests chanted the seven vowels. Occasionally Serapis is depicted with horns or a coronet of seven rays. That evidently represented the seven divine intelligences manifesting through the solar light. The *Encyclopædia Britannica* notes that the earliest authentic mention of Serapis is in connection with the death of Alexander. Such was the prestige of Serapis that he alone of the gods was consulted in behalf of the dying king.

The Egyptian secret school of philosophy was divided into the Lesser and the Greater Mysteries, the former being sacred to Isis and the latter to Serapis and Osiris. Wilkinson is of the opinion that only the priests were permitted to enter the Greater Mysteries. Even the heir to the throne was not eligible until he had been crowned Pharaoh, when, by virtue of his kingly office, he automatically became a priest and the temporal head of the state religion. (See Wilkinson's *Manners and Customs of the Egyptians.*) A limited number were admitted into the Greater Mysteries: these preserved their secrets inviolate.

Much of the information concerning the rituals of the higher degrees of the Egyptian Mysteries has been gleaned from an examination of the chambers and passageways in which the initiations were given. Under the temple of Serapis destroyed by Theodosius were found strange mechanical contrivances constructed by the priests in the subterranean crypts and caverns where the nocturnal initiatory rites were celebrated. These machines indicate the severe tests of moral and physical courage undergone by the candidates. After passing through these tortuous ways, the neophytes who survived the ordeals were ushered into the presence of Serapis, a noble and awe-inspiring figure illumined by unseen lights.

Labyrinths were also a striking feature in connection with the Rite of Serapis, and E. A. Wallis Budge, in his *Gods of the Egyptians,* depicts Serapis (Minotaur-like) with the body of a man and the head of a bull. Labyrinths were symbolic of the involvements and illusions of the lower world through which wanders the soul of man in its search for truth. In the labyrinth dwells the lower animal man with the head of the bull, who seeks to destroy the soul entangled in the maze of worldly ignorance. In this relation Serapis becomes the Tryer or Adversary who tests the souls of those seeking union with the Immortals. The maze was also doubtless used to represent the solar system, the Bull-Man representing the sun dwelling in the mystic maze of its planets, moons, and asteroids.

The Gnostic Mysteries were acquainted with the arcane meaning of Serapis, and through the medium of Gnosticism this god became inextricably associated with early Christianity. In fact, the Emperor Hadrian, while traveling in Egypt in A.D. 134, declared in a letter to Servianus that the worshipers of Serapis were Christians and that the Bishops of the church also worshiped at his shrine. He even declared that the Patriarch himself, when in Egypt, was forced to adore Serapis as well as Christ. (See Parsons' *New Light on the Great Pyramid.*)

The little-suspected importance of Serapis as a prototype of Christ can be best appreciated after a consideration of the following extract from C. W. King's *Gnostics and Their Remains:* "There can be no doubt that the head of Serapis, marked as the face is by a grave and pensive majesty, supplied the first idea for the conventional portraits of the Saviour. The Jewish prejudices of the first converts were so powerful that we may be sure no attempt was made to depict His countenance until some generations after all that had beheld it on earth had passed away."

Serapis gradually usurped the positions previously occupied by the other Egyptian and Greek gods, and became the supreme deity of both religions. His power continued until the fourth century of the Christian Era. In A.D. 385, Theodosius, that would-be exterminator of pagan philosophy, issued his memorable edict *De Idolo Serapidis Diruendo.* When the Christian soldiers, in obedience to this order, entered the Serapeum at Alexandria to destroy the image of Serapis which had stood there for centuries, so great was their veneration for the god that they dared not touch the image lest the ground should open at their feet and engulf them. At length, overcoming their fear, they demolished the statue, sacked the building, and finally as a fitting climax to their offense burned the magnificent library which was housed within the lofty apartments of the Serapeum. Several writers have recorded the remarkable fact that Christian symbols were found in the ruined foundations of this pagan temple. Socrates, a church historian of the fifth century, declared that after the pious Christians had razed the Serapeum at Alexandria and scattered the demons who dwelt there under the guise of gods, beneath the foundations was found the monogram of Christ!

Two quotations will further establish the relationship existing between the Mysteries of Serapis and those of other ancient peoples. The first is from

Richard Payne Knight's *Symbolical Language of Ancient Art and Mythology:* "Hence Varro [in *De Lingua Latina*] says that Cœlum and Terra, that is universal mind and productive body, were the Great Gods of the Samothracian Mysteries; and the same as the Serapis and Isis of the later Ægyptians: the Taautos and Astarte of the Phœnicians, and the Saturn and Ops of the Latins." The second quotation is from Albert Pike's *Morals and Dogma:* " 'Thee,' says Martianus Capella, in his hymn to the Sun, 'dwellers on the Nile adore as Serapis, and Memphis worships as Osiris: in the sacred rites of Persia thou art Mithras, in Phrygia, Atys, and Libya bows down to thee as Ammon, and Phœnician Byblos as Adonis; thus the whole world adores thee under different names.' "

The Odinic Mysteries

The date of the founding of the Odinic Mysteries is uncertain, some writers declaring that they were established in the first century before Christ; others, the first century after Christ. Robert Macoy, *33°*, gives the following description of their origin: "It appears from the northern chronicles that in the first century of the Christian Era, Sigge, the chief of the Aser, an Asiatic tribe, emigrated from the Caspian sea and the Caucasus into northern Europe. He directed his course northwesterly from the Black sea to Russia, over which, according to tradition, he placed one of his sons as a ruler, as he is said to have done over the Saxons and the Franks. He then advanced through Cimbria to Denmark, which acknowledged his fifth son Skiold as its sovereign, and passed over to Sweden, where Gylf, who did homage to the wonderful stranger, and was initiated into his mysteries, then ruled. He soon made himself master here, built Sigtuna as the capital of his empire, and promulgated a new code of laws, and established the sacred mysteries. He, himself, assumed the name of Odin, founded the priesthood of the twelve Drottars (Druids?) who conducted the secret worship, and the administration of justice, and, as prophets, revealed the future. The secret rites of these mysteries celebrated the death of Balder, the beautiful and lovely, and represented the grief of Gods and men at his death, and his restoration to life." (*General History of Freemasonry.*)

After his death, the historical Odin was apotheosized, his identity being merged into that of the mythological Odin, god of wisdom, whose cult he had promulgated. Odinism then supplanted the worship of Thor, the thunderer, the supreme deity of the ancient Scandinavian pantheon. The mound where, according to legend, King Odin was buried is still to be seen near the site of his great temple at Upsala.

The twelve *Drottars* who presided over the Odinic Mysteries evidently personified the twelve holy and ineffable names of Odin. The rituals of the Odinic Mysteries were very similar to those of the Greeks, Persians, and Brahmins, after which they were patterned. The Drottars, who symbolized the signs of the zodiac, were the custodians of the arts and sciences, which they revealed to those who passed successfully the ordeals of initiation. Like many other pagan cults, the Odinic Mysteries, as an institution, were destroyed by Christianity, but the underlying cause of their fall was the corruption of the priesthood.

Mythology is nearly always the ritual and the symbolism of a Mystery school. Briefly stated, the sacred drama which formed the basis of the Odinic Mysteries was as follows:

The Supreme, invisible Creator of all things was called All-Father. His regent in Nature was Odin, the one-eyed god. Like Quetzalcoatl, Odin was elevated to the dignity of the Supreme Deity. According to the Drottars, the universe was fashioned from the body of *Ymir,* the hoarfrost giant. Ymir was formed from the clouds of mist that rose from Ginnungagap, the great cleft in chaos into which the primordial frost giants and flame giants had hurled snow and fire. The three gods—Odin, Vili, and Ve—slew Ymir and from him formed the world. From Ymir's various members the different parts of Nature were fashioned.

After Odin had established order, he caused a wonderful palace, called Asgard, to be built on the top of a mountain, and here the twelve Æsir (gods) dwelt together, far above the limitations of mortal men. On this mountain also was Valhalla, the palace of the slain, where those who had heroically died fought and feasted day after day. Each night their wounds were healed and the boar whose flesh they ate renewed itself as rapidly as it was consumed.

Balder the Beautiful—the Scandinavian Christ—was the beloved son of Odin. Balder was not warlike; his kindly and beautiful spirit brought peace and joy to the hearts of the gods, and they all loved him save one. As Jesus had a Judas among His twelve disciples, so one of the twelve gods was false—Loki, the personification of evil. Loki caused Höthr, the blind god of fate, to shoot Balder with a mistletoe arrow. With the death of Balder, light and joy vanished from the lives of the other deities. Heartbroken, the gods gathered to find a method whereby they could resurrect this spirit of eternal life and youth. The result was the establishment of the Mysteries.

The Odinic Mysteries were given in underground crypts or caves, the chambers, nine in number, representing the Nine Worlds of the Mysteries. The candidate seeking admission was assigned the task of raising Balder from the dead. Although he did not realize it, he himself played the part of Balder. He called himself a wanderer; the caverns through which he passed were symbolic of the worlds and spheres of Nature. The priests who initiated him were emblematic of the sun, the moon, and the stars. The three supreme initiators—the Sublime, the Equal to the Sublime, and the Highest—were analogous to the Worshipful Master and the Junior and Senior Wardens of a Masonic lodge.

After wandering for hours through the intricate passageways, the candidate was ushered into the presence of a statue of Balder the Beautiful, the prototype of all initiates into the Mysteries. This figure stood in the center of a great apartment roofed with shields. In the midst of the chamber stood a plant with seven blossoms, emblematic of the planets. In this room, which symbolized the home of the Æsir, or Wisdom, the neophyte took his oath of secrecy and piety upon the naked blade of a sword. He drank the sanctified mead from a bowl made of a human skull and, having passed successfully through all the tortures and trials designed to divert him from the course of wisdom, he was finally permitted to unveil the mystery of Odin—the personification of wisdom. He was presented, in the name of Balder, with the sacred ring of the order; he was hailed as a man reborn; and it was said of him that he had died and had been raised again without passing through the gates of death.

Richard Wagner's immortal composition, *Der Ring des Nibelungen,* is based upon the Mystery rituals of the Odinic cult. While the great composer took many liberties with the original story, the Ring Operas, declared to be the grandest tetralogy of music dramas the world possesses, have caught and preserved in a remarkable manner the majesty and power of the original sagas. Beginning with *Das Rheingold,* the action proceeds through *Die Walküre* and *Siegfried* to an awe-inspiring climax in *Götterdämmerung,* "The Twilight of the Gods."

The Ancient Mysteries
and Secret Societies

he most famous of the ancient religious Mysteries were the Eleusinian, whose rites were celebrated every five years in the city of Eleusis to honor Ceres (Demeter, Rhea, or Isis) and her daughter, Persephone. The initiates of the Eleusinian School were famous throughout Greece for the beauty of their philosophic concepts and the high standards of morality which they demonstrated in their daily lives. Because of their excellence, these Mysteries spread to Rome and Britain, and later the initiations were given in both these countries. The Eleusinian Mysteries, named for the community in Attica where the sacred dramas were first presented, are generally believed to have been founded by Eumolpos about fourteen hundred years before the birth of Christ, and through the Platonic system of philosophy their principles have been preserved to modern times.

The rites of Eleusis, with their mystic interpretations of Nature's most precious secrets, overshadowed the civilizations of their time and gradually absorbed many smaller schools, incorporating into their own system whatever valuable information these lesser institutions possessed. Heckethorn sees in the Mysteries of Ceres and Bacchus a metamorphosis of the rites of Isis and Osiris, and there is every reason to believe that all so-called secret schools of the ancient world were branches from one philosophic tree which, with its root in heaven and its branches on the earth, is—like the spirit of man—an invisible but everpresent cause of the objectified vehicles that give it expression. The Mysteries were the channels through which this one philosophic light was disseminated;

and their initiates, resplendent with intellectual and spiritual understanding, were the perfect fruitage of the divine tree, bearing witness before the material world of the recondite source of all Light and Truth.

The rites of Eleusis were divided into what were called the Lesser and the Greater Mysteries. According to James Gardner, the Lesser Mysteries were celebrated in the spring (probably at the time of the vernal equinox) in the town of Agræ, and the Greater, in the fall (the time of the autumnal equinox) at Eleusis or Athens. It is supposed that the former were given annually and the latter every five years. The rituals of the Eleusinians were highly involved, and to understand them required a deep study of Greek mythology, which they interpreted in its esoteric light with the aid of their secret keys.

The Lesser Mysteries were dedicated to Persephone. In his *Eleusinian and Bacchic Mysteries,* Thomas Taylor sums up their purpose as follows: "The Lesser Mysteries were designed by the ancient theologists, their founders, to signify occultly the condition of the unpurified soul invested with an earthy body, and enveloped in a material and physical nature."

The legend used in the Lesser rites is that of the abduction of the goddess Persephone, the daughter of Ceres, by Pluto, the lord of the underworld, or Hades. While Persephone is picking flowers in a beautiful meadow, the earth suddenly opens and the gloomy lord of death, riding in a magnificent chariot, emerges from its somber depths and, grasping her in his arms, carries the screaming and struggling goddess to his subterranean palace, where he forces her to become his queen.

It is doubtful whether many of the initiates themselves understood the mystic meaning of this allegory, for most of them apparently believed that it referred solely to the succession of the seasons. It is difficult to obtain satisfactory information concerning the Mysteries, for the candidates were bound by inviolable oaths never to reveal their inner secrets to the profane. At the beginning of the ceremony of initiation, the candidate stood upon the skins of animals sacrificed for the purpose, and vowed that death should seal his lips before he would divulge the sacred truths which were about to be communicated to him. Through indirect channels, however, some of their secrets have been preserved. The teachings given to the neophytes were substantially as follows:

The soul of man—often called *Psyche*, and in the Eleusinian Mysteries symbolized by Persephone—is essentially a spiritual thing. Its true home is in the higher worlds, where, free from the bondage of material form and material concepts, it is said to be truly alive and self-expressive. The human, or physical, nature of man, according to this doctrine, is a tomb, a quagmire, a false and impermanent thing, the source of all sorrow and suffering. Plato describes the body as the sepulcher of the soul; and by this he means not only the human form but also the human nature.

The gloom and depression of the Lesser Mysteries represented the agony of the spiritual soul unable to express itself because it has accepted the limitations and illusions of the human environment. The crux of the Eleusinian argument was that man is neither better nor wiser after death than during life. If he does not rise above ignorance during his sojourn here, man goes at death into eternity to wander about forever, making the same mistakes which he made here. If he does not outgrow the desire for material possessions here, he will carry it with him into the invisible world, where, because he can never gratify the desire, he will continue in endless agony. Dante's *Inferno* is symbolically descriptive of the sufferings of those who never freed their spiritual natures from the cravings, habits, viewpoints, and limitations of their Plutonic personalities. Those who made no endeavor to improve themselves (whose souls have slept) during their physical lives, passed at death into Hades, where, lying in rows, they slept through all eternity as they had slept through life.

To the Eleusinian philosophers, birth into the physical world was death in the fullest sense of the word, and the only true birth was that of the spiritual soul of man rising out of the womb of his own fleshly nature. "The soul is dead that slumbers," says Longfellow, and in this he strikes the keynote of the Eleusinian Mysteries. Just as Narcissus, gazing at himself in the water (the ancients used this mobile element to symbolize the transitory, illusionary, material universe) lost his life trying to embrace a reflection, so man, gazing into the mirror of Nature and accepting as his real self the senseless clay that he sees reflected, loses the opportunity afforded by physical life to unfold his immortal, invisible Self.

An ancient initiate once said that the living are ruled by the dead. Only those conversant with the Eleusinian concept of life could understand that statement. It means that the majority of people are not ruled by their living spirits but by their senseless (hence dead) animal personalities. Transmigration and reincarnation were taught in these Mysteries, but in a somewhat unusual manner. It was believed that at midnight the invisible worlds were closest to the terrestrial sphere and that souls coming into material existence slipped in during the midnight hour. For this reason many of the Eleusinian ceremonies were performed at midnight. Some of those sleeping spirits who had failed to awaken their higher natures during the earth life and who now floated around in the invisible worlds, surrounded by a darkness of their own making, occasionally slipped through at this hour and assumed the forms of various creatures.

The mystics of Eleusis also laid stress upon the evil of suicide, explaining that there was a profound mystery concerning this crime of which they could not speak, but warning their disciples that a great sorrow comes to all who take their own lives. This, in substance, constitutes the esoteric doctrine given to the initiates of the Lesser Mysteries. As the degree dealt largely with the miseries of those who failed to make the best use of their philosophic opportunities, the chambers of initiation were subterranean and the horrors of Hades were vividly depicted in a complicated ritualistic drama. After passing successfully through the tortuous passageways, with their trials and dangers, the candidate received the honorary title of *Mystes*. This meant one who saw through a veil or had a clouded vision. It also signified that the candidate had been brought up to the veil, which would be torn away in the higher degree. The modern word *mystic,* as referring to a seeker after truth according to the dictates of the heart along the path of faith, is probably derived from this ancient word, for faith is belief in the reality of things unseen or veiled.

The Greater Mysteries (into which the candidate was admitted only after he had successfully passed through the ordeals of the Lesser, and not always then) were sacred to Ceres, the mother of Persephone, and represent her as wandering through the world in quest of her abducted daughter. Ceres carried two torches, intuition and reason, to aid her in the search for her lost child (the soul). At last she found Persephone not far from Eleusis, and out of gratitude taught the people there to cultivate corn, which is sacred to her. She also founded the Mysteries. Ceres appeared before Pluto, god of the souls of the dead, and pleaded with him to allow Persephone to return to her home. This the god at first refused to do, because Persephone had eaten of the pomegranate, the fruit of mortality. At last, however, he compromised and agreed to permit Persephone to live in the upper world half of the year if she would stay with him in the darkness of Hades for the remaining half.

The Greeks believed that Persephone was a manifestation of the solar energy, which in the winter months lived under the earth with Pluto, but in the summer returned again with the goddess of productiveness. There is a legend that the flowers loved Persephone and that every year when she left for the dark realms of Pluto, the plants and shrubs would die of grief. While the profane and uninitiated had their own opinions on these subjects, the truths of the Greek allegories remained safely concealed by the priests, who alone recognized the sublimity of these great philosophic and religious parables.

Thomas Taylor epitomizes the doctrines of the Greater Mysteries in the following statement: "The Greater (Mysteries) obscurely intimated, by mystic and splendid visions, the felicity of the soul both here and hereafter when purified from the defilement of a material nature, and constantly elevated to the realities of intellectual (spiritual) vision."

Just as the Lesser Mysteries discussed the prenatal epoch of man when the consciousness in its nine days (embryologically, months) was descending into the realm of illusion and assuming the veil of unreality, so the Greater Mysteries discussed the principles of spiritual regeneration and revealed to initiates not only the simplest but also the most direct and complete method of liberating their higher natures from the bondage of material ignorance. Like Prometheus chained to the top of Mount Caucasus, man's higher nature is chained to his inadequate personality. The nine days of initiation were also symbolic of the nine spheres through which the human soul descends during the process of assuming a terrestrial form. The secret exercises for spiritual unfoldment given to disciples of the higher degrees are unknown, but there is every reason to believe that they were similar to the Brahmanic Mysteries, since it is known that the Eleusinian ceremonies were closed with the Sanskrit words "Konx Om Pax."

FROM A MURAL PAINTING IN POMPEII.

CERES, THE PATRON OF THE MYSTERIES.

Ceres, or Demeter, was the daughter of Kronos and Rhea, and by Zeus the mother of Persephone. Some believe her to be the goddess of the earth, but more correctly she is the deity protecting agriculture in general and corn in particular. The poppy is sacred to Ceres and she is often shown carrying or ornamented by a garland of these flowers. In the Mysteries, Ceres is represented riding in a chariot drawn by winged serpents.

That part of the allegory referring to the two six-month periods during one of which Peresphone must remain with Pluto, while during the other she may revisit the upper world, offers material for deep consideration. It is probable that the Eleusinians realized that the soul left the body during sleep, or at least was made capable of leaving by the special training which undoubtedly they were in a position to give. Thus Persephone would remain as the queen of Pluto's realm during the waking hours, but would ascend to the spiritual worlds during the periods of sleep. The initiate was taught how to intercede with Pluto to permit Persephone (the initiate's soul) to ascend from the darkness of his material nature into the light of understanding. When thus freed from the shackles of clay and crystallized concepts, the initiate was liberated not only for the period of his life but for all eternity, for never thereafter was he divested of those soul qualities which after death were his vehicles for manifestation and expression in the so-called heaven world.

In contrast to the idea of Hades as a state of darkness below, the gods were said to inhabit the tops of mountains, a well-known example being Mount Olympus, where the twelve deities of the Greek pantheon were said to dwell together. In his initiatory wanderings the neophyte therefore entered chambers of ever-increasing brilliancy to portray the ascent of the spirit from the lower worlds into the realms of bliss. As the climax to such wanderings he entered a great vaulted room, in the center of which stood a brilliantly illumined statue of the goddess Ceres. Here, in the presence of the hierophant and surrounded by priests in magnificent robes, he was instructed in the highest of the secret mysteries of the Eleusis. At the conclusion of this ceremony he was hailed as an *Epoptes,* which means one who has beheld or seen directly. For this reason also initiation was termed *autopsy.* The Epoptes was then given certain sacred books, probably written in cipher, together with tablets of stone on which secret instructions were engraved.

In *The Obelisk in Freemasonry,* John A. Weisse describes the officiating personages of the Eleusinian Mysteries as consisting of a male and a female hierophant who directed the initiations; a male and a female torchbearer; a male herald; and a male and a female altar attendant. There were also numerous minor officials. He states that, according to Porphyry, the hierophant represents Plato's *Demiurgus,* or Creator of the world; the torch bearer, the Sun; the altar man, the Moon; the herald, Hermes, or Mercury; and the other officials, minor stars.

From the records available, a number of strange and apparently supernatural phenomena accompanied the rituals. Many initiates claim to have actually seen the living gods themselves. Whether this was the result of religious ecstasy or the actual cooperation of invisible powers with the visible priests must remain a mystery. In *The Metamorphosis, or Golden Ass,* Apuleius thus describes what in all probability is his initiation into the Eleusinian Mysteries:

"I approached to the confines of death, and having trod on the threshold of Proserpine I returned from it, being carried through all the elements. At midnight I saw the sun shining with a splendid light; and I manifestly drew near to the gods beneath, and the gods above, and proximately adored them."

Women and children were admitted to the Eleusinian Mysteries, and at one time there were literally thousands of initiates. Because this vast host was not prepared for the highest spiritual and mystical doctrines, a division necessarily took place within the society itself. The higher teachings were given to only a limited number of initiates who, because of superior mentality, showed a comprehensive grasp of their underlying philosophical concepts. Socrates refused to be initiated into the Eleusinian Mysteries, for knowing its principles without being a member of the order he realized that membership would seal his tongue. That the Mysteries of Eleusis were based upon great and eternal truths is attested by the veneration in which they were held by the great minds of the ancient world. M. Ouvaroff asks, "Would Pindar, Plato, Cicero, Epictetus, have spoken of them with such admiration, if the hierophant had satisfied himself with loudly proclaiming his own opinions, or those of his order?"

The garments in which candidates were initiated were preserved for many years and were believed to possess almost sacred properties. Just as the soul can have no covering save wisdom and virtue, so the candidates—being as yet without true knowledge—were presented to the Mysteries unclothed, being first given the skin of an animal and later a consecrated robe to symbolize the philosophical teachings received by the initiate. During the course of initiation the candidate passed through two gates. The first led downward into the lower worlds and symbolized his birth into ignorance. The second led upward into a room brilliantly lighted by unseen lamps, in which was the statue of Ceres and which symbolized the upper world, or the abode of Light and Truth. Strabo states that the great temple of Eleusis would hold between twenty and thirty thousand people. The caves dedicated by Zarathustra also had these two doors, symbolizing the avenues of birth and death.

The following paragraph from Porphyry gives a fairly adequate conception of Eleusinian symbolism: "God being a luminous principle, residing in the midst of the most subtile fire, he remains for ever invisible to the eyes of those who do not elevate themselves above material life: on this account, the sight of transparent bodies, such as crystal, Parian marble, and even ivory, recalls the idea of divine light; as the sight of gold excites an idea of its purity, for gold cannot be sullied. Some have thought by a black stone was signified the invisibility of the divine essence. To express supreme reason, the Divinity was represented under the human form—and beautiful, for God is the source of beauty; of different ages, and in various attitudes, sitting or upright; of one or the other sex, as a virgin or a young man, a husband or a bride, that all the shades and gradations might be marked. Every thing luminous was subsequently attributed to the gods; the sphere, and all that is spherical, to the universe, to the sun and the moon—sometimes to Fortune and to Hope. The circle, and all circular figures, to eternity—to the celestial movements, to the circles and zones of the heavens. The section of circles, to the phases of the moon; and pyramids and obelisks, to the igneous principle, and through that to the gods of Heaven. A cone expresses the sun; a cylinder the earth; the phallus and triangle (a symbol of the matrix) designate generation." (From *Essay on the Mysteries of Eleusis* by M. Ouvaroff.)

The Eleusinian Mysteries, according to Heckethorn, survived all others and did not cease to exist as an institution until nearly four hundred years after Christ, when they were finally suppressed by Theodosius (styled the *Great*), who cruelly destroyed all who did not accept the Christian faith. Of this greatest of all philosophical institutions Cicero said that it taught men not only how to live but also how to die.

The Orphic Mysteries

Orpheus, the Thracian bard, the great initiator of the Greeks, ceased to be known as a man and was celebrated as a divinity several centuries before the Christian Era. "As to Orpheus himself * * *," writes Thomas Taylor, "scarcely a vestige of his life is to be found amongst the immense ruins of time. For who has ever been able to affirm any thing with certainty of his origin, his age, his country, and condition? This alone may be depended on, from general assent, that there formerly lived a person named Orpheus, who was the founder of theology among the Greeks; the institutor of their lives and morals; the first of prophets, and the prince of poets; himself the offspring of a Muse; who taught the Greeks their sacred rites and mysteries, and from whose wisdom, as from a perennial and abundant fountain, the divine muse of Homer and the sublime theology of Pythagoras and Plato flowed." (See *The Mystical Hymns of Orpheus.*)

Orpheus was founder of the Grecian mythological system which he used as the medium for the promulgation of his philosophical doctrines. The origin of his philosophy is uncertain. He may have got it from the Brahmins, there being legends to the effect that he was a Hindu, his name possibly being derived from ὀρφναῖος, meaning "dark." Orpheus was initiated into the Egyptian Mysteries, from which he secured extensive knowledge of magic, astrology, sorcery, and medicine. The Mysteries of the Cabiri at Samothrace were also conferred upon him, and these undoubtedly contributed to his knowledge of medicine and music.

The romance of Orpheus and Eurydice is one of the tragic episodes of Greek mythology and apparently constitutes the outstanding feature of the

Orphic Rite. Eurydice, in her attempt to escape from a villain seeking to seduce her, died from the venom of a poisonous serpent which stung her in the heel. Orpheus, penetrating to the very heart of the underworld, so charmed Pluto and Persephone with the beauty of his music that they agreed to permit Eurydice to return to life if Orpheus could lead her back to the sphere of the living without once looking round to see if she were following. So great was his fear, however, that she would stray from him that he turned his head, and Eurydice with a heartbroken cry was swept back into the land of death.

Orpheus wandered the earth for a while disconsolate, and there are several conflicting accounts of the manner of his death. Some declare that he was slain by a bolt of lightning; others, that failing to save his beloved Eurydice, he committed suicide. The generally accepted version of his death, however, is that he was torn to pieces by Ciconian women whose advances he had spurned. In the tenth book of Plato's *Republic* it is declared that, because of his sad fate at the hands of women, the soul that had once been Orpheus, upon being destined to live again in the physical world, chose rather to return in the body of a swan than be born of woman. The head of Orpheus, after being torn from his body, was cast with his lyre into the river Hebrus, down which it floated to the sea, where, wedging in a cleft in a rock, it gave oracles for many years. The lyre, after being stolen from its shrine and working the destruction of the thief, was picked up by the gods and fashioned into a constellation.

Orpheus has long been sung as the patron of music. On his seven-stringed lyre he played such perfect harmonies that the gods themselves were moved to acclaim his power. When he touched the strings of his instrument the birds and beasts gathered about him, and as he wandered through the forests his enchanting melodies caused even the ancient trees with mighty effort to draw their gnarled roots from out the earth and follow him. Orpheus is one of the many Immortals who have sacrificed themselves that mankind might have the wisdom of the gods. By the symbolism of his music he communicated the divine secrets to humanity, and several authors have declared that the gods, though loving him, feared that he would overthrow their kingdom and therefore reluctantly encompassed his destruction.

As time passed on the historical Orpheus became hopelessly confounded with the doctrine he represented and eventually became the symbol of the Greek school of the ancient wisdom. Thus Orpheus was declared to be the son of Apollo, the divine and perfect truth, and Calliope, the Muse of harmony and rhythm. In other words, Orpheus is the secret doctrine (Apollo) revealed through music (Calliope). Eurydice is humanity dead from the sting of the serpent of false knowledge and imprisoned in the underworld of ignorance. In this allegory Orpheus signifies theology, which wins her from the king of the dead but fails to accomplish her resurrection because it falsely estimates and mistrusts the innate understanding within the human soul. The Ciconian women who tore Orpheus limb from limb symbolize the various contending theological factions which destroy the body of Truth. They cannot accomplish this, however, until their discordant cries drown out the harmony drawn by Orpheus from his magic lyre. The head of Orpheus signifies the esoteric doctrines of his cult. These doctrines continue to live and speak even after his body (the cult) has been destroyed. The lyre is the secret teaching of Orpheus; the seven strings are the seven divine truths which are the keys to universal knowledge. The differing accounts of his death represent the various means used to destroy the secret teachings: wisdom can die in many ways at the same time. The allegory of Orpheus incarnating in the white swan merely signifies that the spiritual truths he promulgated will continue and will be taught by the illumined initiates of all future ages. The swan is the symbol of the initiates of the Mysteries; it is a symbol also of the divine power which is the progenitor of the world.

The Bacchic and Dionysiac Rites

The Bacchic Rite centers around the allegory of the youthful Bacchus (Dionysos or Zagreus) being torn to pieces by the Titans. These giants accomplished the destruction of Bacchus by causing him to become fascinated by his own image in a mirror. After dismembering him, the Titans first boiled the pieces in water and afterwards roasted them. Pallas rescued the heart of the murdered god, and by this precaution Bacchus (Dionysos) was enabled to spring forth again in all his former glory. Jupiter, the Demiurgus, beholding the crime of the Titans, hurled his thunderbolts and slew them, burning their bodies to ashes with heavenly fire. Out of the ashes of the Titans—which also contained a portion of the flesh of Bacchus, whose body they had partly devoured—the human race was created. Thus the mundane life of every man was said to contain a portion of the Bacchic life.

For this reason the Greek Mysteries warned against suicide. He who attempts to destroy himself raises his hand against the nature of Bacchus within him, since man's body is indirectly the tomb of this god and consequently must be preserved with the greatest care.

Bacchus (Dionysos) represents the rational soul of the inferior world. He is the chief of the Titans—the artificers of the mundane spheres. The Pythagoreans called him the *Titanic monad.* Thus Bacchus is the all-inclusive *idea* of the Titanic sphere and the Titans—or *gods of the fragments*—the active agencies by means of which universal substance is fashioned into the pattern of this idea. The Bacchic state signifies the unity of the rational soul in a state of self-knowledge, and the Titanic state the diversity of the rational soul which, being scattered throughout creation, loses the consciousness of its own essential one-ness. The mirror into which Bacchus gazes and which is the cause of his fall is the great sea of illusion—the lower world fashioned by the Titans. Bacchus (the mundane rational soul), seeing his image before him, accepts the image as a likeness of himself and ensouls the likeness; that is, the rational idea ensouls its reflection— the irrational universe. By ensouling the irrational image it implants in it the urge to become like its source, the rational image. Therefore the ancients said that man does not know the gods by logic or by reason but rather by realizing the presence of the gods within himself.

After Bacchus gazed into the mirror and followed his own reflection into matter, the rational soul of the world was broken up and distributed by the Titans throughout the mundane sphere of which it is the essential nature, but the heart, or source, of it they could not scatter. The Titans took the dismembered body of Bacchus and boiled it in water—symbol of immersion in the material universe—which represents the incorporation of the Bacchic principle in form. The pieces were afterwards roasted to signify the subsequent ascension of the spiritual nature out of form.

When Jupiter, the father of Bacchus and the Demiurgus of the universe, saw that the Titans were hopelessly involving the rational or divine idea by scattering its members through the constituent parts of the lower world, he slew the Titans in order that the divine idea might not be entirely lost. From the ashes of the Titans he formed mankind, whose purpose of existence was to preserve and eventually to release the Bacchic idea, or rational soul, from the Titanic fabrication. Jupiter, being the Demiurgus and fabricator of the material universe, is the third person of the Creative Triad, consequently the Lord of Death, for death exists only in the lower sphere of being over which he presides. Disintegration takes place so that reintegration may follow upon a higher level of form or intelligence. The thunderbolts of Jupiter are emblematic of his disintegrative power; they reveal the purpose of death, which is to rescue the rational soul from the devouring power of the irrational nature.

Man is a composite creature, his lower nature consisting of the fragments of the Titans and his higher nature the sacred, immortal flesh (life) of Bacchus. Therefore man is capable of either a Titanic (irrational) or a Bacchic (rational) existence. The Titans of Hesiod, who were twelve in number, are probably analogous to the celestial zodiac, whereas the Titans who murdered and dismembered Bacchus represent the zodiacal powers distorted by their involvement in the material world. Thus Bacchus represents the sun who is dismembered by the signs of the zodiac and from whose body the universe is formed. When the terrestrial forms were created from the various parts of his body the sense of wholeness was lost and the sense of separateness established. The heart of Bacchus, which was saved by Pallas, or Minerva, was lifted out of the four elements symbolized by his dismembered body and placed in the ether. The heart of Bacchus is the immortal center of the rational soul.

After the rational soul had been distributed throughout creation and the nature of man, the Bacchic Mysteries were instituted for the purpose of disentangling it from the irrational Titanic nature. This disentanglement was the process of lifting the soul out of the state of separateness into that of unity. The various parts and members of Bacchus were collected from the different corners of the earth. When all the rational parts are gathered Bacchus is resurrected.

The Rites of Dionysos were very similar to those of Bacchus, and by many these two gods are considered as one. Statues of Dionysos were carried in the Eleusinian Mysteries, especially the lesser degrees. Bacchus, representing the soul of the mundane sphere, was capable of an infinite multiplicity of form and designations. Dionysos apparently was his solar aspect.

The Dionysiac Architects constituted an ancient secret society, in principles and doctrines much like the modern Freemasonic Order. They were an organization of builders bound together by their secret knowledge of the relationship between the earthly and the divine sciences of architectonics. They were supposedly employed by King Solomon in the building of his Temple, although they were not Jews, nor did they worship the God of the Jews, being followers of Bacchus and Dionysos. The Dionysiac Architects erected many of the great monuments of antiquity. They possessed a secret language and a system of marking their stones. They had annual convocations and sacred feasts. The exact nature of their doctrines is unknown. It is believed that CHiram Abiff was an initiate of this society.

Atlantis and the Gods of Antiquity

tlantis is the subject of a short but important article appearing in the *Annual Report of the Board of Regents of The Smithsonian Institution for the year ending June 30th, 1915*. The author, M. Pierre Termier, a member of the Academy of Sciences and Director of Service of the Geologic Chart of France, in 1912 delivered a lecture on the Atlantean hypothesis before the Institut Océanographique; it is the translated notes of this remarkable lecture that are published in the Smithsonian report.

"After a long period of disdainful indifference," writes M. Termier, "observe how in the last few years science is returning to the study of Atlantis. How many naturalists, geologists, zoologists, or botanists are asking one another today whether Plato has not transmitted to us, with slight amplification, a page from the actual history of mankind. No affirmation is yet permissible; but it seems more and more evident that a vast region, continental or made up of great islands, has collapsed west of the Pillars of Hercules, otherwise called the Strait of Gibraltar, and that its collapse occurred in the not far distant past. In any event, the question of Atlantis is placed anew before men of science; and since I do not believe that it can ever be solved without the aid of oceanography, I have thought it natural to discuss it here, in this temple of maritime science, and to call to such a problem, long scorned but now being revived, the attention of oceanographers, as well as the attention of those who, though immersed in the tumult of cities, lend an ear to the distant murmur of the sea."

In his lecture M. Termier presents geologic, geographic, and zoologic data in substantiation of the Atlantis theory. Figuratively draining the entire bed of the Atlantic Ocean, he considers the inequalities of its basin and cites locations on a line from the Azores to Iceland where dredging has brought lava to the surface from a depth of 3,000 meters. The volcanic nature of the islands now existing in the Atlantic Ocean corroborates Plato's statement that the Atlantean continent was destroyed by volcanic cataclysms. M. Termier also advances the conclusions of a young French zoologist, M. Louis Germain, who admitted the existence of an Atlantic continent connected with the Iberian Peninsula and with Mauritania and prolonged toward the south so as to include some regions of desert climate. M. Termier concludes his lecture with a graphic picture of the engulfment of that continent.

The description of the Atlantean civilization given by Plato in the *Critias* may be summarized as follows. In the first ages the gods divided the earth among themselves, proportioning it according to their respective dignities. Each became the peculiar deity of his own allotment and established therein temples to himself, ordained a priestcraft, and instituted a system of sacrifice. To Poseidon was given the sea and the island continent of Atlantis. In the midst of the island was a mountain which was the dwelling place of three earth-born primitive human beings—Evenor; his wife, Leucipe; and their only daughter, Cleito. The maiden was very beautiful, and after the sudden death of her parents she was wooed by Poseidon, who begat by her five pairs of male children. Poseidon apportioned his continent among these ten, and Atlas, the eldest, he made overlord of the other nine. Poseidon further called the country *Atlantis* and the surrounding sea the *Atlantic* in honor of Atlas. Before the birth of his ten sons, Poseidon divided the continent and the coastwise sea into concentric zones of land and water, which were as perfect as though turned upon a lathe. Two zones of land and three of water surrounded the central island, which Poseidon caused to be irrigated with two springs of water—one warm and the other cold.

The descendants of Atlas continued as rulers of Atlantis, and with wise government and industry elevated the country to a position of surpassing dignity. The natural resources of Atlantis were apparently limitless. Precious metals were mined, wild animals domesticated, and perfumes distilled from its fragrant flowers. While enjoying the abundance natural to their semitropic location, the Atlanteans employed themselves also in the erection of palaces, temples, and docks. They bridged the zones of sea and later dug a deep canal to connect the outer ocean with the central island, where stood the palaces and temple of Poseidon, which excelled all other structures in magnificence. A network of bridges and canals was created by the Atlanteans to unite the various parts of their kingdom.

Plato then describes the white, black, and red stones which they quarried from beneath their continent and used in the construction of public buildings and docks. They circumscribed each of the land zones with a wall, the outer wall being covered with brass, the middle with tin, and the inner, which encompassed the citadel, with orichalch. The citadel, on the central island, contained the palaces, temples, and other public buildings. In its center, surrounded by a wall of gold, was a sanctuary dedicated to Cleito and Poseidon. Here the first ten princes of the island were born and here each year their descendants brought offerings. Poseidon's own temple, its exterior entirely covered with silver and its pinnacles with gold, also stood within the citadel. The interior of the temple was of ivory, gold, silver, and orichalch, even to the pillars and floor. The temple contained a colossal statue of Poseidon standing in a chariot drawn by six winged horses, about him a hundred Nereids riding on dolphins. Arranged outside the building were golden statues of the first ten kings and their wives.

In the groves and gardens were hot and cold springs. There were numerous temples to various deities, places of exercise for men and for beasts, public baths, and a great race course for horses. At various vantage points on the zones were fortifications, and to the great harbor came vessels from every maritime nation. The zones were so thickly populated that the sound of human voices was ever in the air.

That part of Atlantis facing the sea was described as lofty and precipitous, but about the central city was a plain sheltered by mountains renowned for their size, number, and beauty. The plain yielded two crops each year, in the winter being watered by rains and in the summer by immense irrigation canals, which were also used for transportation. The plain was divided into sections, and in time of war each section supplied its quota of fighting men and chariots.

The ten governments differed from each other in details concerning military requirements. Each of the kings of Atlantis had complete control over his own kingdom, but their mutual relationships were governed by a code engraved by the first ten kings on a column of orichalch standing in the temple of Poseidon. At alternate intervals of five and six years a pilgrimage was made to this temple that equal honor might be conferred upon both the odd and the even numbers. Here, with appropriate sacrifice, each king renewed his oath of loyalty upon the sacred inscription. Here also the kings donned azure robes and sat in judgment. At daybreak they wrote their sentences upon a golden tablet and deposited them with their robes as memorials. The chief laws of the Atlantean kings were that they should not take up arms against each other and that they should come to the assistance of any of their number who was attacked. In matters of war and great moment the final decision was in the hands of the direct descendants of the family of Atlas. No king had the power of life and death over his kinsmen without the assent of a majority of the ten.

Plato concludes his description by declaring that it was this great empire which attacked the Hellenic states. This did not occur, however, until their power and glory had lured the Atlantean kings from the pathway of wisdom and virtue. Filled with false ambition, the rulers of Atlantis determined to conquer the entire world. Zeus, perceiving the wickedness of the Atlanteans, gathered the gods into his holy habitation and addressed them. Here Plato's narrative comes to an abrupt end, for the *Critias* was never finished. In the *Timæus* is a further description of Atlantis, supposedly given to Solon by an Egyptian priest and which concludes as follows:

"But afterwards there occurred violent earthquakes and floods; and in a single day and night of rain all your warlike men in a body sank into the earth, and the island of Atlantis in like manner disappeared, and was sunk beneath the sea. And that is the reason why the sea in those parts is impassable and impenetrable, because there is such a quantity of shallow mud in the way; and this was caused by the subsidence of the island."

In the introduction to his translation of the *Timæus*, Thomas Taylor quotes from a *History of Ethiopia* written by Marcellus, which contains the following reference to Atlantis: "For they relate that in their time there were seven islands in the Atlantic sea, sacred to Proserpine; and besides these, three others of an immense magnitude; one of which was sacred to Pluto, another to Ammon, and another, which is the middle of these, and is of a thousand stadia, to Neptune." Crantor, commenting upon Plato, asserted that the Egyptian priests declared the story of Atlantis to be written upon pillars which were still preserved *circa* 300 B.C. (See *Beginnings or Glimpses of Vanished Civilizations.*) Ignatius Donnelly, who gave the subject of Atlantis profound study, believed that horses were first domesticated by the Atlanteans, for which reason they have always been considered peculiarly sacred to Poseidon. (See *Atlantis.*)

From a careful consideration of Plato's description of Atlantis it is evident that the story should not be regarded as wholly historical but rather as both allegorical and historical. Origen, Porphyry, Proclus, Iamblichus, and Syrianus realized that the story concealed a profound philosophical mystery, but they disagreed as to the actual interpretation. Plato's Atlantis symbolizes the threefold nature of both the universe and the human body. The ten kings of Atlantis are the *tetractys*, or numbers, which are born as five pairs of opposites. (Consult Theon of Smyrna for the Pythagorean doctrine of opposites.) The numbers 1 to

10 rule every creature, and the numbers, in turn, are under the control of the Monad, or 1—the Eldest among them.

With the trident scepter of Poseidon these kings held sway over the inhabitants of the seven small and three great islands comprising Atlantis. Philosophically, the ten islands symbolize the triune powers of the Superior Deity and the seven regents who bow before His eternal throne. If Atlantis be considered as the archetypal sphere, then its immersion signifies the descent of rational, organized consciousness into the illusionary, impermanent realm of irrational, mortal ignorance. Both the sinking of Atlantis and the Biblical story of the "fall of man" signify spiritual involution—a prerequisite to conscious evolution.

Either the initiated Plato used the Atlantis allegory to achieve two widely different ends or else the accounts preserved by the Egyptian priests were tampered with to perpetuate the secret doctrine. This does not mean to imply that Atlantis is purely mythological, but it overcomes the most serious obstacle to acceptance of the Atlantis theory, namely, the fantastic accounts of its origin, size, appearance, and date of destruction—9600 B.C. In the midst of the central island of Atlantis was a lofty mountain which cast a shadow five thousand stadia in extent and whose summit touched the sphere of *æther*. This is the axle mountain of the world, sacred among many races and symbolic of the human head, which rises out of the four elements of the body. This sacred mountain, upon whose summit stood the temple of the gods, gave rise to the stories of Olympus, Meru, and Asgard. The City of the Golden Gates—the capital of Atlantis—is the one now preserved among numerous religions as the *City of the Gods* or the *Holy City*. Here is the archetype of the *New Jerusalem*, with its streets paved with gold and its twelve gates shining with precious stones.

"The history of Atlantis," writes Ignatius Donnelly, "is the key of the Greek mythology. There can be no question that these gods of Greece were human beings. The tendency to attach divine attributes to great earthly rulers is one deeply implanted in human nature." (See *Atlantis*.)

The same author sustains his views by noting that the deities of the Greek pantheon were not looked upon as creators of the universe but rather as regents set over it by its more ancient original fabricators. The Garden of Eden from which humanity was driven by a flaming sword is perhaps an allusion to the earthly paradise supposedly located west of the Pillars of Hercules and destroyed by volcanic cataclysms. The Deluge legend may be traced also to the Atlantean inundation, during which a "world" was destroyed by water.

Was the religious, philosophic, and scientific knowledge possessed by the priestcrafts of antiquity secured from Atlantis, whose submergence obliterated every vestige of its part in the drama of world progress? Atlantean sun worship has been perpetuated in the ritualism and ceremonialism of both Christianity and pagandom. Both the cross and the serpent were Atlantean emblems of divine wisdom. The divine (Atlantean) progenitors of the Mayas and Quichés of Central America coexisted within the green and azure radiance of Gucumatz, the "plumed" serpent. The six sky-born sages came into manifestation as centers of light bound together or synthesized by the seventh—and chief—of their order, the "feathered" snake. (See the *Popol Vuh*.) The title of "winged" or "plumed" snake was applied to Quetzalcoatl, or Kukulcan, the Central American initiate. The center of the Atlantean Wisdom-Religion was presumably a great pyramidal temple standing on the brow of a plateau rising in the midst of the City of the Golden Gates. From here the Initiate-Priests of the Sacred Feather went forth, carrying the keys of Universal Wisdom to the uttermost parts of the earth.

The mythologies of many nations contain accounts of gods who "came out of the sea." Certain *shamans* among the American Indians tell of holy men dressed in birds' feathers and wampum who rose out of the blue waters and instructed them in the arts and crafts. Among the legends of the Chaldeans is that of Oannes, a partly amphibious creature who came out of the sea and taught the savage peoples along the shore to read and write, till the soil, cultivate herbs for healing, study the stars, establish rational forms of government, and become conversant with the sacred Mysteries. Among the Mayas, Quetzalcoatl, the Savior-God (whom some Christian scholars believe to have been St. Thomas), issued from the waters and, after instructing the people in the essentials of civilization, rode out to sea on a magic raft of serpents to escape the wrath of the fierce god of the Fiery Mirror, Tezcatlipoca.

May it not have been that these demigods of a fabulous age who, Esdras-like, came out of the sea were Atlantean priests? All that primitive man remembered of the Atlanteans was the glory of their golden ornaments, the transcendency of their wisdom, and the sanctity of their symbols—the cross and the serpent. That they came in ships was soon forgotten, for untutored minds considered even boats as supernatural. Wherever the Atlanteans proselyted they erected pyramids and temples patterned after the great sanctuary in the City of the Golden Gates. Such is the origin of the pyramids of Egypt, Mexico, and Central America. The mounds in Normandy and Britain, as well as those of the American Indians, are remnants of a similar culture. In the midst of the Atlantean program of world colonization and conversion, the cataclysms which sank Atlantis began. The Initiate-Priests of the Sacred Feather who promised to come back to their missionary settlements never returned; and after the lapse of centuries tradition preserved only a fantastic account of gods who came from a place where the sea now is.

H. P. Blavatsky thus sums up the causes which precipitated the Atlantean disaster: "Under the evil insinuations of their demon, Thevetat, the Atlantis-race became a nation of wicked *magicians*. In consequence of this, war was declared, the story of which would be too long to narrate; its substance may be found in the disfigured allegories of the race of Cain, the giants, and that of Noah and his righteous family. The conflict came to an end by the submersion of the Atlantis; which finds its imitation in the stories of the Babylonian and Mosaic flood: The giants and magicians '* * * and all flesh died * * * and every man.' All except Xisuthrus and Noah, who are substantially identical with the great Father of the Thlinkithians in the *Popol Vuh,* or the sacred book of the Guatemaleans, which also tells of his escaping in a large boat, like the Hindu Noah—Vaiswasvata." (See *Isis Unveiled.*)

From the Atlanteans the world has received not only the heritage of arts and crafts, philosophies, and sciences, ethics and religions, but also the heritage of hate, strife, and perversion. The Atlanteans instigated the first war; and it has been said that all subsequent wars were fought in a fruitless effort to justify the first one and right the wrong which it caused. Before Atlantis sank, its spiritually illumined Initiates, who realized that their land was doomed because it had departed from the Path of Light, withdrew from the ill-fated continent. Carrying with them the sacred and secret doctrine, these Atlanteans established themselves in Egypt, where they became its first "divine" rulers. Nearly all the great cosmologic myths forming the foundation of the various sacred books of the world are based upon the Atlantean Mystery rituals.

The Myth of the Dying God

The myth of *Tammuz* and *Ishtar* is one of the earliest examples of the dying-god allegory, probably antedating 4000 B.C. (See *Babylonia and Assyria* by Lewis Spence.) The imperfect condition of the tablets upon which the legends are inscribed makes it impossible to secure more than a fragmentary account of the Tammuz rites. Being the esoteric god of the sun, Tammuz did not occupy a position among the first deities venerated by the Babylonians, who for lack of deeper knowledge looked upon him as a god of agriculture or a vegetation spirit. Originally he was described as being one of the guardians of the gates of the underworld. Like many other Savior-Gods, he is referred to as a "shepherd" or "the lord of the shepherd seat." Tammuz occupies the remarkable position of son and husband of Ishtar, the Babylonian and Assyrian Mother-goddess. Ishtar— to whom the planet Venus was sacred—was the most widely venerated deity of the Babylonian and Assyrian pantheon. She was probably identical with Ashteroth, Astarte, and Aphrodite. The story of her descent into the underworld in search presumably for the sacred elixir which alone could restore Tammuz to life is the key to the ritual of her Mysteries. Tammuz, whose annual festival took place just before the summer solstice, died in midsummer in the ancient month which bore his name, and was mourned with elaborate ceremonies. The manner of his death is unknown, but some of the accusations made against Ishtar by Izdubar (Nimrod) would indicate that she, indirectly at least, had contributed to his demise. The resurrection of Tammuz was the occasion of great rejoicing, at which time he was hailed as a "redeemer" of his people.

With outspread wings, Ishtar, the daughter of Sin (the Moon), sweeps downward to the gates of death. The house of darkness—the dwelling of the god Irkalla—is described as "the place of no return." It is without light; the nourishment of those who dwell therein is dust and their food is mud. Over the bolts on the door of the house of Irkalla is scattered dust, and the keepers of the house are covered with feathers like birds. Ishtar demands that the keepers open the gates, declaring that if they do not she will shatter the doorposts and strike the hinges and raise up dead devourers of the living. The guardians of the gates beg her to be patient while they go to the queen of Hades from whom they secure permission to admit Ishtar, but only in the same manner as all others came to this dreary house. Ishtar thereupon descends through the seven gates which lead downward into the depths of the underworld. At the first gate the great crown is removed from her head, at the second gate the earrings from her ears, at the third gate the necklace from her neck, at the fourth gate the ornaments from her breast, at the fifth gate the girdle from her waist, at the sixth gate the bracelets from her hands and feet, and at the seventh gate the covering cloak of her body. Ishtar remonstrates as each successive article of apparel is taken from her, but the guardian tells her that this is the experience of all who enter the somber domain of death. Enraged upon beholding Ishtar, the Mistress of Hades inflicts upon her all manner of disease and imprisons her in the underworld.

As Ishtar represents the spirit of fertility, her loss prevents the ripening of the crops and the maturing of all life upon the earth. In this respect the story parallels the legend of Persephone. The gods, realizing that the loss of Ishtar is disorganizing all Nature, send a messenger to the underworld and demand her release. The Mistress of Hades is forced to comply, and the water of life is poured over Ishtar. Thus cured of the infirmities inflicted on her, she retraces her way upward through the seven gates, at each of which she is reinvested with the article of apparel which the guardians had removed. (See *The Chaldean Account of Genesis*.) No record exists that Ishtar secured the water of life which would have wrought the resurrection of Tammuz.

The myth of Ishtar symbolizes the descent of the human spirit through the seven worlds, or spheres of the sacred planets, until finally, deprived of its spiritual adornments, it incarnates in the physical body—Hades—where the mistress of that body heaps every form of sorrow and misery upon the imprisoned consciousness. The waters of life—the secret doctrine—cure the diseases of ignorance; and the spirit, ascending again to its divine source, regains its God-given adornments as it passes upward through the rings of the planets.

Another Mystery ritual among the Babylonians and Assyrians was that of Merodach and the Dragon. Merodach, the creator of the inferior universe, slays a horrible monster and out of her body forms the universe. Here is the probable source of the so-called Christian allegory of St. George and the Dragon.

The Mysteries of *Adonis,* or *Adoni,* were celebrated annually in many parts of Egypt, Phœnicia, and Biblos. The name *Adonis,* or *Adoni,* means "Lord" and was a designation applied to the sun and later borrowed by the Jews as the exoteric name of their God. Smyrna, mother of Adonis, was turned into a tree by the gods and after a time the bark burst open and the infant Savior issued forth. According to one account, he was liberated by a wild boar which split the wood of the maternal tree with its tusks. Adonis was born at midnight of the 24th of December, and through his unhappy death a Mystery rite was established that wrought the salvation of his people. In the Jewish month of Tammuz (another name for this deity) he was gored to death by a wild boar sent by the god Ares (Mars). The *Adoniasmos* was the ceremony of lamenting the premature death of the murdered god.

In Ezekiel viii. 14, it is written that women were weeping for Tammuz (Adonis) at the north gate of the Lord's House in Jerusalem. Sir James George Frazer cites Jerome thus: "He tells us that Bethlehem, the traditional birthplace of the Lord, was shaded by a grove of that still older Syrian Lord, Adonis, and that where the infant Jesus had wept, the lover of Venus was bewailed." (See *The Golden Bough.*) The effigy of a wild boar is said to have been set over one of the gates of Jerusalem in honor of Adonis, and his rites celebrated in the grotto of the Nativity at Bethlehem. Adonis as the "gored" (or "god") man is one of the keys to Sir Francis Bacon's use of the "wild boar" in his cryptic symbolism.

Adonis was originally an androgynous deity who represented the solar power which in the winter was destroyed by the evil principle of cold—the boar. After three days (months) in the tomb, Adonis rose triumphant on the 25th day of March, amidst the acclamation of his priests and followers, "He is risen!" Adonis was born out of a myrrh tree. Myrrh, the symbol of death because of its connection with the process of embalming, was one of the gifts brought by the three Magi to the manger of Jesus.

In the Mysteries of Adonis the neophyte passed through the symbolic death of the god and, "raised" by the priests, entered into the blessed state of redemption made possible by the sufferings of Adonis. Nearly all authors believe Adonis to have been originally a vegetation god directly connected with the growth and maturing of flowers and fruits. In support of this viewpoint they describe the "gardens of Adonis," which were small baskets of earth in which seeds were planted and nurtured for a period of eight days. When those plants prematurely died for lack of sufficient earth, they were considered emblematic of the murdered Adonis and were usually cast into the sea with images of the god.

In Phrygia there existed a remarkable school of religious philosophy which centered around the life and untimely fate of another Savior-God known as *Atys*, or *Attis*, by many considered synonymous with Adonis. This deity was born at midnight on the 24th day of December. Of his death there are two accounts. In one he was gored to death like Adonis; in the other he emasculated himself under a pine tree and there died. His body was taken to a cave by the Great Mother (Cybele), where it remained through the ages without decaying. To the rites of Atys the modern world is indebted for the symbolism of the Christmas tree. Atys imparted his immortality to the tree beneath which he died, and Cybele took the tree with her when she removed the body. Atys remained three days in the tomb, rose upon a date corresponding with Easter morn, and by this resurrection overcame death for all who were initiated into his Mysteries.

"In the Mysteries of the Phrygians," says Julius Firmicus, "which are called those of the MOTHER OF THE GODS, every year a PINE TREE is cut down and in the inside of the tree the image of a YOUTH is tied in! In the Mysteries of Isis the trunk of a PINE TREE is cut: the middle of the trunk is nicely hollowed out; the idol of Osiris made from those hollowed pieces is BURIED. In the Mysteries of Proserpine a tree cut is put together into the effigy and form of the VIRGIN, and when it has been carried within the city it is MOURNED 40 nights, but the fortieth night it is BURNED!" (See *Sod, the Mysteries of Adoni.*)

The Mysteries of Atys included a sacramental meal during which the neophyte ate out of a drum and drank from a cymbal. After being baptized by the blood of a bull, the new initiate was fed entirely on milk to symbolize that he was still a philosophical infant, having but recently been born out of the sphere of materiality. (See Frazer's *The Golden Bough*.) Is there a possible connection between this lacteal diet prescribed by the Attic rite and St. Paul's allusion to the food for spiritual babes? Sallust gives a key to the esoteric interpretation of the Attic rituals. Cybele, the Great Mother, signifies the vivifying powers of the universe, and Atys that aspect of the spiritual intellect which is suspended between the divine and animal spheres. The Mother of the gods, loving Atys, gave him a starry hat, signifying celestial powers, but Atys (mankind), falling in love with a nymph (symbolic of the lower animal propensities), forfeited his divinity and lost his creative powers. It is thus evident that Atys represents the human consciousness and that his Mysteries are concerned with the reattainment of the starry hat. (See *Sallust on the Gods and the World*.)

The rites of *Sabazius* were very similar to those of Bacchus and it is generally believed that the two deities are identical. Bacchus was born at Sabazius, or Sabaoth, and these names are frequently assigned to him. The Sabazian Mysteries were performed at night, and the ritual included the drawing of a live snake across the breast of the candidate. Clement of Alexandria writes: "The token of the Sabazian Mysteries to the initiated is 'the deity gliding over the breast.'" A golden serpent was the symbol of Sabazius because this deity represented the annual renovation of the world by the solar power. The Jews borrowed the name *Sabaoth* from these Mysteries and adopted it as one of the appellations of their supreme God. During the time the Sabazian Mysteries were celebrated in Rome, the cult gained many votaries and later influenced the symbolism of Christianity.

The Cabiric Mysteries of Samothrace were renowned among the ancients, being next to the Eleusinian in public esteem. Herodotus declares that the Samothracians received their doctrines, especially those concerning Mercury, from the Pelasgians. Little is known concerning the Cabiric rituals, for they were enshrouded in the profoundest secrecy. Some regard the Cabiri as seven in number and refer to them as "the Seven Spirits of fire before the throne of Saturn." Others believe the Cabiri to be the seven sacred wanderers, later called the planets.

While a vast number of deities are associated with the Samothracian Mysteries, the ritualistic drama centers around four brothers. The first three—Aschieros, Achiochersus, and Achiochersa—attack and murder the fourth—Cashmala (or Cadmillus). Dionysidorus, however, identifies Aschieros with Demeter, Achiochersus with Pluto, Achiochersa with Persephone, and Cashmala with Hermes. Alexander Wilder notes that in the Samothracian ritual "Cadmillus is made to include the Theban Serpent-god, Cadmus, the Thoth of Egypt, the Hermes of the Greeks, and the Emeph or Æsculapius of the Alexandrians and Phœnicians." Here again is a repetition of the story of Osiris, Bacchus, Adonis, Balder, and Hiram Abiff. The worship of Atys and Cybele was also involved in the Samothracian Mysteries. In the rituals of the Cabiri is to be traced a form of pinetree worship, for this tree, sacred to Atys, was first trimmed into the form of a cross and then cut down in honor of the murdered god whose body was discovered at its foot.

"If you wish to inspect the orgies of the Corybantes," writes Clement, "then know that, having killed their third brother, they covered the head of the dead body with a purple cloth, crowned it, and carrying it on the point of a spear, buried it under the roots of Olympus. These mysteries are, in short, murders and funerals. [This ante-Nicene Father in his efforts to defame the pagan rites apparently ignores the fact that, like the Cabirian martyr, Jesus Christ was foully betrayed, tortured, and finally murdered!] And the priests of these rites, who are called kings of the sacred rites by those whose business it is to name them, give additional strangeness to the tragic occurrence, by forbidding parsley with the roots from being placed on the table, for they think that parsley grew from the Corybantic blood that flowed forth; just as the women, in celebrating the Thesmophoria, abstain from eating the seeds of the pomegranate, which have fallen on the ground, from the idea that pomegranates sprang from the drops of the blood of Dionysus. Those Corybantes also they call Cabiric; and the ceremony itself they announce as the Cabiric mystery."

The Mysteries of the Cabiri were divided into three degrees, the first of which celebrated the death of Cashmala at the hands of his three brothers; the second, the discovery of his mutilated body, the parts of which had been found and gathered after much labor; and the third—accompanied by great rejoicing and happiness—his resurrection and the consequent salvation of the world. The temple of the Cabiri at Samothrace contained a number of curious divinities, many of them misshapen creatures representing the elemental powers of Nature, possibly the Bacchic Titans. Children were initiated into the Cabirian cult with the same dignity as adults, and criminals who reached the sanctuary were safe from pursuit. The Samothracian rites were particularly concerned with navigation, the Dioscuri—Castor and Pollux, or the gods of navigation— being among those propitiated by members of that cult. The Argonautic expedition, listening to the advice of Orpheus, stopped at the island of Samothrace for the purpose of having its members initiated into the Cabiric rites.

Herodotus relates that when Cambyses entered the temple of the Cabiri he was unable to restrain his mirth at seeing before him the figure of a man standing upright and, facing the man, the figure of a woman standing on her head. Had Cambyses been acquainted with the principles of divine astronomy, he would have realized that he was then in the presence of the key to universal equilibrium. "'I ask,' says Voltaire, 'who were these Hierophants, these sacred Freemasons, who celebrated their Ancient Mysteries of Samothracia, and whence came they and their gods Cabiri?'" (See Mackey's *Encyclopædia of Freemasonry*.) Clement speaks of the Mysteries of the Cabiri as "the sacred mystery of a brother slain by his brethren," and the "Cabiric death" was one of the secret symbols of antiquity. Thus the allegory of the Self murdered by the not-self is perpetuated through the religious mysticism of all peoples. The *philosophic death* and the *philosophic resurrection* are the Lesser and the Greater Mysteries respectively.

A curious aspect of the *dying-god* myth is that of the Hanged Man. The most important example of this peculiar conception is found in the Odinic rituals where Odin hangs himself for nine nights from the branches of the World Tree and upon the same occasion also pierces his own side with the sacred spear. As the result of this great sacrifice, Odin, while suspended over the depths of Nifl-heim, discovered by meditation the runes or alphabets by which later the records of his people were preserved. Because of this remarkable experience, Odin is sometimes shown seated on a gallows tree and he became the patron deity of all who died by the noose. Esoterically, the Hanged Man is the human spirit which is suspended from heaven by a single thread. Wisdom, not death, is the reward for this voluntary sacrifice during which the human soul, suspended above the world of illusion, and meditating upon its unreality, is rewarded by the achievement of self-realization.

From a consideration of all these ancient and secret rituals it becomes evident that the mystery of the *dying god* was universal among the illumined and venerated colleges of the sacred teaching. This mystery has been perpetuated in Christianity in the crucifixion and death of the God-man—Jesus the Christ. The secret import of this world tragedy and the Universal Martyr must be rediscovered if Christianity is to reach the heights attained by the pagans in the days of their philosophic supremacy. The myth of the *dying god* is the key to both universal and individual redemption and regeneration, and those who do not comprehend the true nature of this supreme allegory are not privileged to consider themselves either wise or truly religious.

The Life and Writings of Thoth Hermes Trismegistus

hunder rolled, lightning flashed, the veil of the Temple was rent from top to bottom. The venerable initiator, in his robes of blue and gold, slowly raised his jeweled wand and pointed with it into the darkness revealed by the tearing of the silken curtain: "Behold the Light of Egypt!" The candidate, in his plain white robe, gazed into the utter blackness framed by the two great lotus-headed columns between which the veil had hung. As he watched, a luminous haze distributed itself throughout the atmosphere until the air was a mass of shining particles. The face of the neophyte was illumined by the soft glow as he scanned the shimmering cloud for some tangible object. The initiator spoke again: "This Light which ye behold is the secret luminance of the Mysteries. Whence it comes none knoweth, save the 'Master of the Light.' Behold Him!" Suddenly, through the gleaming mist a figure appeared, surrounded by a flickering greenish sheen. The initiator lowered his wand and, bowing his head, placed one hand edgewise against his breast in humble salutation. The neophyte stepped back in awe, partly blinded by the glory of the revealed figure. Gaining courage, the youth gazed again at the Divine One. The Form before him was considerably larger than that of a mortal man. The body seemed partly transparent so that the heart and brain could be seen pulsating and radiant. As the candidate watched, the heart changed into an ibis, and the brain into a flashing emerald. In Its hand this mysterious Being bore a winged rod, entwined with serpents. The aged initiator, raising his wand, cried out in a loud voice: "All hail Thee, Thoth Hermes, Thrice Greatest; all hail Thee, Prince of Men; all hail Thee who standeth upon the head of Typhon!" At the same instant a lurid writhing dragon appeared—a hideous monster, part *serpent, part crocodile, and part hog. From its mouth and nostrils poured sheets of flame and horrible sounds echoed through the vaulted chambers. Suddenly Hermes struck the advancing reptile with the serpent-wound staff and with snarling cry the dragon fell over upon its side, while the flames about it slowly died away. Hermes placed His foot upon the skull of the vanquished Typhon. The next instant, with a blaze of unbearable glory that sent the neophyte staggering backward against a pillar, the immortal Hermes, followed by streamers of greenish mist, passed through the chamber and faded into nothingness.*

Suppositions Concerning the Identity of Hermes

Iamblichus averred that Hermes was the author of twenty thousand books; Manetho increased the number to more than thirty-six thousand (see James Gardner)—figures which make it evident that a solitary individual, even though he be overshadowed by divine prerogative, could scarcely have accomplished such a monumental labor. Among the arts and sciences

FROM *HISTORIA DEORUM FATIDICORUM.*

HERMES MERCURIUS TRISMEGISTUS.

Master of all arts and sciences, perfect in all crafts, Ruler of the Three Worlds, Scribe of the Gods, and Keeper of the Books of Life, Thoth Hermes Trismegistus—the Three Times Greatest, the "First Intelligencer"—was regarded by the ancient Egyptians as the embodiment of the Universal Mind. While in all probability there actually existed a great sage and educator by the name of Hermes, it is impossible to extricate the historical man from the mass of legendary accounts which attempt to identify him with the Cosmic Principle of Thought.

which it is affirmed Hermes revealed to mankind were medicine, chemistry, law, art, astrology, music, rhetoric, magic, philosophy, geography, mathematics (especially geometry), anatomy, and oratory. Orpheus was similarly acclaimed by the Greeks.

In his *Biographia Antiqua,* Francis Barrett says of Hermes: "* * * if God ever appeared in man, he appeared in him, as is evident both from his books and his Pymander; in which works he has communicated the sum of the Abyss, and the divine knowledge to all posterity; by which he has demonstrated himself to have been not only an inspired divine, but also a deep philosopher, obtaining his wisdom from God and heavenly things, and not from man."

His transcendent learning caused Hermes to be identified with many of the early sages and prophets. In his *Ancient Mythology,* Bryant writes: "I have mentioned that Cadmus was the same as the Egyptian Thoth; and it is manifest from his being Hermes, and from the invention of letters being attributed to him." (In the chapter on the theory of *Pythagorean Mathematics* will be found the table of the original Cadmean letters.) Investigators believe that it was Hermes who was known to the Jews as "Enoch," called by Kenealy the "Second Messenger of God." Hermes was accepted into the mythology of the Greeks, later becoming the Mercury of the Latins. He was revered through the form of the planet Mercury because this body is nearest to the sun: Hermes of all creatures was nearest to God, and became known as the Messenger of the Gods.

In the Egyptian drawings of him, Thoth carries a waxen writing tablet and serves as the recorder during the weighing of the souls of the dead in the Judgment Hall of Osiris—a ritual of great significance. Hermes is of first importance to Masonic scholars, because he was the author of the Masonic initiatory rituals, which were borrowed from the Mysteries established by Hermes. Nearly all of the Masonic symbols are Hermetic in character. Pythagoras studied mathematics with the Egyptians and from them gained his knowledge of the symbolic geometric solids. Hermes is also revered for his reformation of the calendar system. He increased the year from 360 to 365 days, thus establishing a precedent which still prevails. The appellation "Thrice Greatest" was given to Hermes because he was considered the greatest of all philosophers, the greatest of all priests, and the greatest of all kings. It is worthy of note that the last poem of America's beloved poet, Henry Wadsworth Longfellow, was a lyric ode to Hermes. (See *Chambers' Encyclopædia.*)

The Mutilated Hermetic Fragments

On the subject of the Hermetic books, James Campbell Brown, in his *History of Chemistry,* has written: "Leaving the Chaldean and earliest Egyptian periods, of which we have remains but no record, and from which no names of either chemists or philosophers have come down to us, we now approach the Historic Period, when books were written, not at first upon parchment or paper, but upon papyrus. A series of early Egyptian books is attributed to Hermes Trismegistus, who may have been a real *savant,* or may be a personification of a long succession of writers. * * * He is identified by some with the Greek god Hermes, and the

Egyptian Thoth or Tuti, who was the moon-god, and is represented in ancient paintings as ibis-headed with the disc and crescent of the moon. The Egyptians regarded him as the god of wisdom, letters, and the recording of time. It is in consequence of the great respect entertained for Hermes by the old alchemists that chemical writings were called 'hermetic,' and that the phrase 'hermetically sealed' is still in use to designate the closing of a glass vessel by fusion, after the manner of chemical manipulators. We find the same root in the hermetic medicines of Paracelsus, and the hermetic freemasonry of the Middle Ages."

Among the fragmentary writings believed to have come from the stylus of Hermes are two famous works. The first is the *Emerald Table,* and the second is the *Divine Pymander,* or, as it is more commonly called, *The Shepherd of Men,* a discussion of which follows. One outstanding point in connection with Hermes is that he was one of the few philosopher-priests of pagandom upon whom the early Christians did not vent their spleen. Some Church Fathers went so far as to declare that Hermes exhibited many symptoms of intelligence, and that if he had only been born in a more enlightened age so that he might have benefited by *their* instructions he would have been a really great man!

In his *Stromata,* Clement of Alexandria, one of the few chroniclers of pagan lore whose writings have been preserved to this age, gives practically all the information that is known concerning the original forty-two books of Hermes and the importance with which these books were regarded by both the temporal and spiritual powers of Egypt. Clement describes one of their ceremonial processions as follows:

"For the Egyptians pursue a philosophy of their own. This is principally shown by their sacred ceremonial. For first advances the Singer, bearing some one of the symbols of music. For they say that he must learn two of the books of Hermes, the one of which contains the hymns of the gods, the second the regulations for the king's life. And after the Singer advances the Astrologer, with a horologe in his hand, and a palm, the symbols of astrology. He must have the astrological books of Hermes, which are four in number, always in his mouth. Of these, one is about the order of the fixed stars that are visible, and another about the conjunctions and luminous appearances of the sun and moon; and the rest respecting their risings. Next in order advances the sacred Scribe, with wings on his head, and in his hand a book and rule, in which were writing ink and the reed, with which they write. And he must be acquainted with what are called hieroglyphics, and know about cosmography and geography, the position of the sun and moon, and about the five planets; also the description of Egypt, and the chart of the Nile; and the description of the equipment of the priests and of the place consecrated to them, and about the measures and the things in use in the sacred rites. Then the Stole-keeper follows those previously mentioned, with the cubit of justice and the cup for libations. He is acquainted with all points called Pædeutic (relating to training) and Moschophaltic (sacrificial). There are also ten books which relate to the honour paid by them to their gods, and containing the Egyptian worship; as that relating to sacrifices, first-fruits, hymns, prayers, processions, festivals, and the like. And behind all walks the Prophet, with the water-vase carried openly in his arms; who is followed by those who carry the issue of loaves. He, as being the governor of the temple, learns the ten books called 'Hieratic'; and they contain all about the laws, and the gods, and the whole of the training of the priests. For the Prophet is, among the Egyptians, also over the distribution of the revenues. There are then forty-two books of Hermes indispensably necessary; of which the six-and-thirty containing the whole philosophy of the Egyptians are learned by the forementioned personages; and the other six, which are medical, by the Pastophoroi (image-bearers),—treating of the structure of the body, and of diseases, and instruments, and medicines, and about the eyes, and the last about women."

One of the greatest tragedies of the philosophic world was the loss of nearly all of the forty-two books of Hermes mentioned in the foregoing. These books disappeared during the burning of Alexandria, for the Romans—and later the Christians—realized that until these books were eliminated they could never bring the Egyptians into subjection. The volumes which escaped the fire were buried in the desert and their location is now known to only a few initiates of the secret schools.

The Book of Thoth

While Hermes still walked the earth with men, he entrusted to his chosen successors the sacred *Book of Thoth*. This work contained the secret processes by which the regeneration of humanity was to be accomplished and also served as the key to his other writings. Nothing definite is known concerning the contents of the *Book of Thoth* other than that its pages were covered with strange hieroglyphic figures and symbols, which gave to those acquainted with their use unlimited power over the spirits of the air and the subterranean divinities. When certain areas of the brain are stimulated by the secret processes of the Mysteries, the consciousness of man is extended and he is permitted to behold the Immortals and enter into the presence of the superior gods. The *Book of Thoth* described the method whereby this stimulation was accomplished. In truth, therefore, it was the "Key to Immortality."

According to legend, the *Book of Thoth* was kept in a golden box in the inner sanctuary of the temple. There was but one key and this was in the possession of the "Master of the Mysteries," the highest initiate of the Hermetic Arcanum. He alone knew what was written in the secret book. The *Book of Thoth* was lost to the ancient world with the decay of the Mysteries, but its faithful initiates carried it sealed in the sacred casket into another land. The book is still in existence and continues to lead the disciples of this age into the presence of the Immortals. No other information can be given to the world concerning it now, but the apostolic succession from the first hierophant initiated by Hermes himself remains unbroken to this day, and those who are peculiarly fitted to serve the Immortals may discover this priceless document if they will search sincerely and tirelessly for it.

It has been asserted that the *Book of Thoth* is, in reality, the mysterious *Tarot* of the Bohemians— a strange emblematic book of seventy-eight leaves which has been in possession of the gypsies since the time when they were driven from their ancient temple, the Serapeum. (According to the Secret Histories the gypsies were originally Egyptian priests.) There are now in the world several secret schools privileged to initiate candidates into the Mysteries, but in nearly every instance they lighted their altar fires from the flaming torch of *Herm.* Hermes in his *Book of Thoth* revealed to all mankind the "One Way," and for ages the wise of every nation and every faith have reached immortality by the "Way" established by Hermes in the midst of the darkness for the redemption of humankind.

FROM WILKINSON'S *MANNERS & CUSTOMS OF THE ANCIENT EGYPTIANS.*

THOTH, THE IBIS-HEADED.

It is doubtful that the deity called *Thoth* by the Egyptians was originally Hermes, but the two personalities were blended together and it is now impossible to separate them. Thoth was called "The Lord of the Divine Books" and "Scribe of the Company of the Gods." He is generally pictured with the body of a man and the head of an ibis. The exact symbolic meaning of this latter bird has never been discovered. A careful analysis of the peculiar shape of the ibis—especially its head and beak—should prove illuminating.

Poimandres, the Vision of Hermes

The Divine Pymander of Hermes Mercurius Trismegistus is one of the earliest of the Hermetic writings now extant. While probably not in its original form, having been remodeled during the first centuries of the Christian Era and incorrectly translated since, this work undoubtedly contains many of the original concepts of the Hermetic *cultus*. *The Divine Pymander* consists of seventeen fragmentary writings gathered together and put forth as one work. The second book of *The Divine Pymander,* called *Poimandres,* or *The Vision,* is believed to describe the method by which the divine wisdom was first revealed to Hermes. It was after Hermes had received this revelation that he began his ministry, teaching to all who would listen the secrets of the invisible universe as they had been unfolded to him.

The Vision is the most famous of all the Hermetic fragments, and contains an exposition of Hermetic cosmogony and the secret sciences of the Egyptians regarding the culture and unfoldment of the human soul. For some time it was erroneously called "The Genesis of Enoch," but that mistake has now been rectified. At hand while preparing the following interpretation of the symbolic philosophy concealed within *The Vision of Hermes* the present author has had these reference works: *The Divine Pymander of Hermes Mercurius Trismegistus* (London, 1650), translated out of the Arabic and Greek by Dr. Everard; *Hermetica* (Oxford, 1924), edited by Walter Scott; *Hermes, The Mysteries of Egypt* (Philadelphia, 1925), by Edouard Schure; and the *Thrice-Greatest Hermes* (London, 1906), by G.R.S. Mead. To the material contained in the above volumes he has added commentaries based upon the esoteric philosophy of the ancient Egyptians, together with amplifications derived partly from other Hermetic fragments and partly from the secret arcanum of the Hermetic sciences. For the sake of clarity, the narrative form has been chosen in preference to the original dialogic style, and obsolete words have given place to those in current use.

Hermes, while wandering in a rocky and desolate place, gave himself over to meditation and prayer. Following the secret instructions of the Temple, he gradually freed his higher consciousness from the bondage of his bodily senses; and, thus released, his divine nature revealed to him the mysteries of the transcendental spheres. He beheld a figure, terrible and awe-inspiring. It was the Great Dragon, with wings stretching across the sky and light streaming in all directions from its body. (The Mysteries taught that the Universal Life was personified as a dragon.) The Great Dragon called Hermes by name, and asked him why he thus meditated upon the World Mystery. Terrified by the spectacle, Hermes prostrated himself before the Dragon, beseeching it to reveal its identity. The great creature answered that it was *Poimandres,* the *Mind of the Universe,* the Creative Intelligence, and the Absolute Emperor of all. (Schure identifies

Poimandres as the god Osiris.) Hermes then besought Poimandres to disclose the nature of the universe and the constitution of the gods. The Dragon acquiesced, bidding Trismegistus hold its image in his mind.

Immediately the form of Poimandres changed. Where it had stood there was a glorious and pulsating Radiance. This Light was the spiritual nature of the Great Dragon itself. Hermes was "raised" into the midst of this divine Effulgence and the universe of material things faded from his consciousness. Presently a great darkness descended and, expanding, swallowed up the Light. Everything was troubled. About Hermes swirled a mysterious watery substance which gave forth a smokelike vapor. The air was filled with inarticulate moanings and sighings which seemed to come from the Light swallowed up in the darkness. His mind told Hermes that the Light was the form of the spiritual universe and that the swirling darkness which had engulfed it represented material substance.

Then out of the imprisoned Light a mysterious and Holy Word came forth and took its stand upon the smoking waters. This Word—the Voice of the Light—rose out of the darkness as a great pillar, and the fire and the air followed after it, but the earth and the water remained unmoved below. Thus the waters of Light were divided from the waters of darkness, and from the waters of Light were formed the worlds above and from the waters of darkness were formed the worlds below. The earth and the water next mingled, becoming inseparable, and the Spiritual Word which is called *Reason* moved upon their surface, causing endless turmoil.

Then again was heard the voice of Poimandres, but His form was not revealed: "I Thy God am the Light and the Mind which were before substance was divided from spirit and darkness from Light. And the Word which appeared as a pillar of flame out of the darkness is the Son of God, born of the mystery of the Mind. The name of that Word is *Reason*. Reason is the offspring of Thought and Reason shall divide the Light from the darkness and establish Truth in the midst of the waters. Understand, O Hermes, and meditate deeply upon the mystery. That which in you sees and hears is not of the earth, but is the Word of God incarnate. So it is said that Divine Light dwells in the midst of mortal darkness, and ignorance cannot divide them. The union of the Word and the Mind produces that mystery which is called *Life*. As the darkness without you is divided against itself, so the darkness within you is likewise divided. The Light and the fire which rise are the divine man, ascending in the path of the Word, and that which fails to ascend is the mortal man, which may not partake of immortality. Learn deeply of the Mind and its mystery, for therein lies the secret of immortality."

The Dragon again revealed its form to Hermes, and for a long time the two looked steadfastly one upon the other, eye to eye, so that Hermes trembled before the gaze of Poimandres. At the Word of the Dragon the heavens opened and the innumerable Light Powers were revealed, soaring through Cosmos on pinions of streaming fire. Hermes beheld the spirits of the stars, the celestials controlling the universe, and all those Powers which shine with the radiance of the One Fire—the glory of the Sovereign Mind. Hermes realized that the sight which he beheld was revealed to him only because Poimandres had spoken a Word. The Word was Reason, and by the Reason of the Word invisible things were made manifest. Divine Mind—the Dragon—continued its discourse:

"Before the visible universe was formed its mold was cast. This mold was called the *Archetype,* and this Archetype was in the Supreme Mind long before the process of creation began. Beholding the Archetypes, the Supreme Mind became enamored with Its own thought; so, taking the Word as a mighty hammer, It gouged out caverns in primordial space and cast the form of the spheres in the Archetypal mold, at the same time sowing in the newly fashioned bodies the seeds of living things. The darkness below, receiving the hammer of the Word, was fashioned into an orderly universe. The elements separated into strata and each brought forth living creatures. The Supreme Being—the Mind—male and female, brought forth the Word; and the Word, suspended between Light and darkness, was delivered of another Mind called the *Workman,* the *Master-Builder,* or the *Maker of Things.*

"In this manner it was accomplished, O Hermes: The Word moving like a breath through space called forth the *Fire* by the friction of its motion. Therefore, the Fire is called the *Son of Striving.* The Workman passed as a whirlwind through the universe, causing the substances to vibrate and glow with its friction. The Son of Striving thus formed *Seven Governors,* the Spirits of the Planets, whose orbits bounded the world; and the Seven Governors controlled the world by the mysterious power called *Destiny* given them by the Fiery Workman. When the *Second Mind* (The Workman) had organized Chaos, the Word of God rose straightway out of its prison of substance, leaving the elements without Reason, and joined Itself to the nature of the Fiery Workman. Then the Second Mind, together with the risen Word, established Itself in the midst of the universe and whirled the wheels of the Celestial Powers. This shall continue from an infinite beginning to an infinite end, for the beginning and the ending are in the same place and state.

"Then the downward-turned and unreasoning elements brought forth creatures without Reason. Substance could not bestow Reason, for Reason had ascended out of it. The air produced flying things and the waters such as swim. The earth conceived strange four-footed and creeping beasts, dragons, composite demons, and grotesque monsters. Then the Father—the Supreme Mind— being Light and Life, fashioned a glorious Universal Man in Its own image, not an earthy man but a heavenly Man dwelling in the Light of God. The *Supreme Mind* loved the Man It had fashioned and delivered to Him the control of the creations and workmanships.

"The Man, desiring to labor, took up His abode in the sphere of generation and observed the works of His brother—the Second Mind—which sat upon the Ring of the Fire. And having beheld the achievements of the Fiery Workman, He willed also to make things, and His Father gave permission. The Seven Governors, of whose powers He partook, rejoiced and each gave the Man a share of Its own nature.

"The Man longed to pierce the circumference of the circles and understand the mystery of Him who sat upon the Eternal Fire. Having already all power, He stooped down and peeped through the seven Harmonies and, breaking through the strength of the circles, made Himself manifest to Nature stretched out below. The Man, looking into the depths, smiled, for He beheld a shadow upon the earth and a likeness mirrored in the waters, which shadow and likeness were a reflection of Himself. The Man fell in love with His own shadow and desired to descend into it. Coincident with the desire, the Intelligent Thing united Itself with the unreasoning image or shape.

"Nature, beholding the descent, wrapped herself about the Man whom she loved, and the two were mingled. For this reason, earthy man is composite. Within him is the Sky Man, immortal and beautiful; without is Nature, mortal and destructible. Thus, suffering is the result of the Immortal Man's falling in love with His shadow and giving up Reality to dwell in the darkness of illusion; for, being immortal, man has the power of the Seven Governors—also the Life, the Light, and the Word—but being mortal, he is controlled by the Rings of the Governors—Fate or Destiny.

"Of the Immortal Man it should be said that He is hermaphrodite, or male and female, and eternally watchful. He neither slumbers nor sleeps, and is governed by a Father also both male and female, and ever watchful. Such is the mystery kept hidden to this day, for Nature, being mingled in marriage with the Sky Man, brought forth a wonder most wonderful—seven men, all bisexual, male and female, and upright of stature, each one exemplifying the natures of the Seven Governors. These, O Hermes, are the seven races, species, and wheels.

"After this manner were the seven men generated. Earth was the female element and water the male element, and from the fire and the æther they received their spirits, and Nature produced bodies after the species and shapes of men. And man received the Life and Light of the Great Dragon, and of the Life was made his Soul and of the Light his Mind. And so, all these composite creatures containing immortality, but partaking of mortality, continued in this state for the duration of a period. They reproduced themselves out of themselves, for each was male and female. But at the end of the period the knot of Destiny was untied by the will of God and the bond of all things was loosened.

"Then all living creatures, including man, which had been hermaphroditical, were separated, the males being set apart by themselves and the females likewise, according to the dictates of Reason.

"Then God spoke to the Holy Word within the soul of all things, saying: 'Increase in increasing and multiply in multitudes, all you, my creatures and workmanships. Let him that is endued with Mind know himself to be immortal and that the cause of death is the love of the body; and let him learn all things that are, for he who has recognized himself enters into the state of Good.'

"And when God had said this, Providence, with the aid of the Seven Governors and Harmony, brought the sexes together, making the mixtures and establishing the generations, and all things were multiplied according to their kind. He who through the error of attachment loves his body, abides wandering in darkness, sensible and suffering the things of death, but he who realizes that the body is but the tomb of his soul, rises to immortality."

Then Hermes desired to know why men should be deprived of immortality for the sin of ignorance alone. The Great Dragon answered: "To the ignorant the body is supreme and they are incapable of realizing the immortality that is within them. Knowing only the body which is subject to death, they believe in death because they worship that substance which is the cause and reality of death."

Then Hermes asked how the righteous and wise pass to God, to which Poimandres replied: "That which the Word of God said, say I: 'Because the Father of all things consists of Life and Light, whereof man is made.' If, therefore, a man shall learn and understand the nature of Life and Light, then he shall pass into the eternity of Life and Light."

Hermes next inquired about the road by which the wise attained to Life eternal, and Poimandres continued: "Let the man endued with a Mind mark, consider, and learn of himself, and with the power of his Mind divide himself from his not-self and become a servant of Reality."

Hermes asked if all men did not have Minds, and the Great Dragon replied: "Take heed what you say, for I am the Mind—the Eternal Teacher. I am the Father of the *Word*—the Redeemer of all men—and in the nature of the wise the Word takes flesh. By means of the Word, the world is saved. I, *Thought* (Thoth)—the Father of the Word, the Mind—come only unto men that are holy and good, pure and merciful, and that live piously and religiously, and my presence is an inspiration and a help to them, for when I come they immediately know all things and adore the Universal Father. Before such wise and philosophic ones die, they learn to renounce their senses, knowing that these are the enemies of their immortal souls.

"I will not permit the evil senses to control the bodies of those who love me, nor will I allow evil emotions and evil thoughts to enter them. I become as a porter or doorkeeper, and shut out evil, protecting the wise from their own lower nature. But to the wicked, the envious and the covetous, I come not, for such cannot understand the mysteries of *Mind;* therefore, I am unwelcome. I leave them to the avenging demon that they are making in their own souls, for evil each day increases itself and torments man more sharply, and each evil deed adds to the evil deeds that are gone before until finally evil destroys itself. The punishment of desire is the agony of unfulfillment."

Hermes bowed his head in thankfulness to the Great Dragon who had taught him so much, and begged to hear more concerning the ultimate of the human soul. So Poimandres resumed: "At death the material body of man is returned to the elements from which it came, and the invisible divine man ascends to the source from whence he came, namely the *Eighth Sphere.* The evil passes to the dwelling place of the demon, and the senses, feelings, desires, and body passions return to their source, namely the Seven Governors, whose natures in the lower man destroy but in the invisible spiritual man give life.

"After the lower nature has returned to the brutishness, the higher struggles again to regain its spiritual estate. It ascends the seven Rings upon which sit the Seven Governors and returns to each their lower powers in this manner: Upon the first ring sits the Moon, and to it is returned the ability to increase and diminish. Upon the second ring sits Mercury, and to it are returned machinations, deceit, and craftiness. Upon the third ring sits Venus, and to it are returned the lusts and passions. Upon the fourth ring sits the Sun, and to this Lord are returned ambitions. Upon the fifth ring sits Mars, and to it are returned rashness and profane boldness. Upon the sixth ring sits Jupiter, and to it are returned the sense of accumulation and riches. And upon the seventh ring sits Saturn, at the Gate of Chaos, and to it are returned falsehood and evil plotting.

"Then, being naked of all the accumulations of the seven Rings, the soul comes to the Eighth Sphere, namely, the ring of the fixed stars. Here, freed of all illusion, it dwells in the Light and sings praises to the Father in a voice which only the pure of spirit may understand. Behold, O Hermes, there is a great mystery in the Eighth Sphere, for the Milky Way is the seed-ground of souls, and from it they drop into the Rings, and to the Milky Way they return again from the wheels of Saturn. But some cannot climb the seven-runged ladder of the Rings. So they wander in darkness below and are swept into eternity with the illusion of sense and earthiness.

"The path to immortality is hard, and only a few find it. The rest await the Great Day when the wheels of the universe shall be stopped and the immortal sparks shall escape from the sheaths of substance. Woe unto those who wait, for they must return again, unconscious and unknowing, to the seed-ground of stars, and await a new beginning. Those who are saved by the light of the mystery which I have revealed unto you, O Hermes, and which I now bid you to establish among men, shall return again to the Father who dwelleth in the White Light, and shall deliver themselves up to the Light and shall be absorbed into the Light, and in the Light they shall become Powers in God. This is the Way of *Good* and is revealed only to them that have wisdom.

"Blessed art thou, O Son of Light, to whom of all men, I, Poimandres, the Light of the World, have revealed myself. I order you to go forth, to become as a guide to those who wander in darkness, that all men within whom dwells the spirit of *My Mind* (The Universal Mind) may be saved by My Mind in you, which shall call forth My Mind in them. Establish My Mysteries and they shall not fail from the earth, for I am the Mind of the Mysteries and until Mind fails (which is never) my Mysteries cannot fail." With these parting words, Poimandres, radiant with celestial light, vanished, mingling with the powers of the heavens. Raising his eyes unto the heavens, Hermes blessed the Father of All Things and consecrated his life to the service of the Great Light.

Thus preached Hermes: "O people of the earth, men born and made of the elements, but with the spirit of the Divine Man within you, rise from your sleep of ignorance! Be sober and thoughtful. Realize that your home is not in the earth but in the Light. Why have you delivered yourselves over unto death, having power to partake of immortality? Repent, and *change your minds*. Depart from the dark light and forsake corruption forever. Prepare yourselves to climb through the Seven Rings and to blend your souls with the eternal Light."

Some who heard mocked and scoffed and went their way, delivering themselves to the Second Death from which there is no salvation. But others, casting themselves before the feet of Hermes, besought him to teach them the Way of Life. He lifted them gently, receiving no approbation for himself, and staff in hand, went forth teaching and guiding mankind, and showing them how they might be saved. In the worlds of men, Hermes sowed the seeds of wisdom and nourished the seeds with the Immortal Waters. And at last came the evening of his life, and as the brightness of the light of earth was beginning to go down, Hermes commanded his disciples to preserve his doctrines inviolate throughout all ages. The *Vision of Poimandres* he committed to writing that all men desiring immortality might therein find the way.

In concluding his exposition of the *Vision*, Hermes wrote: "The sleep of the body is the sober watchfulness of the Mind and the shutting of my eyes reveals the true Light. My silence is filled with budding life and hope, and is full of good. My words are the blossoms of fruit of the tree of my soul. For this is the faithful account of what I received from my true Mind, that is Poimandres, the Great Dragon, the Lord of the Word, through whom I became inspired by God with the Truth. Since that day my Mind has been ever with me and in my own soul it hath given birth to the Word: the Word is Reason, and Reason hath redeemed me. For which cause, with all my soul and all my strength, I give praise and blessing unto God the Father, the Life and the Light, and the Eternal Good.

> "Holy is God, the Father of all things, the One who is before the First Beginning.
>
> "Holy is God, whose will is performed and accomplished by His own Powers which He hath given birth to out of Himself.
>
> "Holy is God, who has determined that He shall be known, and who is known by His own to whom He reveals Himself.
>
> "Holy art Thou, who by Thy Word (Reason) hast established all things.
>
> "Holy art Thou, of whom all Nature is the image.
>
> "Holy art Thou, whom the inferior nature has not formed.
>
> "Holy art Thou, who art stronger than all powers.
>
> "Holy art Thou, who art greater than all excellency.
>
> "Holy art Thou, who art better than all praise.
>
> "Accept these reasonable sacrifices from a pure soul and a heart stretched out unto Thee.

"O Thou Unspeakable, Unutterable, to be praised with silence!

"I beseech Thee to look mercifully upon me, that I may not err from the knowledge of Thee and that I may enlighten those that are in ignorance, my brothers and Thy sons.

"Therefore I believe Thee and bear witness unto Thee, and depart in peace and in trustfuless into Thy Light and Life.

"Blessed art Thou, O Father! The man Thou hast fashioned would be sanctified with Thee as Thou hast given him power to sanctify others with Thy Word and Thy Truth."

The *Vision of Hermes,* like nearly all of the Hermetic writings, is an allegorical exposition of great philosophic and mystic truths, and its hidden meaning may be comprehended only by those who have been "raised" into the presence of the True Mind.

VII

The Initiation of the Pyramid

 upreme among the wonders of antiquity, unrivaled by the achievements of later architects and builders, the Great Pyramid of Gizeh bears mute witness to an unknown civilization which, having completed its predestined span, passed into oblivion. Eloquent in its silence, inspiring in its majesty, divine in its simplicity, the Great Pyramid is indeed a sermon in stone. Its magnitude overwhelms the puny sensibilities of man. Among the shifting sands of time it stands as a fitting emblem of eternity itself. Who were the illumined mathematicians who planned its parts and dimensions, the master craftsmen who supervised its construction, the skilled artisans who trued its blocks of stone?

The earliest and best-known account of the building of the Great Pyramid is that given by that highly revered but somewhat imaginative historian, Herodotus. "The pyramid was built in steps, battlement-wise, as it is called, or, according to others, altar-wise. After laying the stones for the base, they raised the remaining stones to their places by means of machines formed to short wooden planks. The first machine raised them from the ground to the top of the first step. On this there was another machine, which received the stone upon its arrival, and conveyed it to the second step, whence a third machine advanced it still higher. Either they had as many machines as there were steps in the pyramid, or possibly they had but a single machine, which, being easily moved, was transferred from tier to tier as the stone rose. Both accounts are given, and therefore I mention both. The upper portion of the pyramid was finished first, then the middle, and finally the part which was lowest and nearest the ground. There is an inscription in Egyptian characters on the pyramid which records the quantity of radishes, onions, and garlick consumed by the labourers who constructed it; and I perfectly well remember that the interpreter who read the writing to me said that the

ŒDIPUS AND THE SPHINX.

The Egyptian Sphinx is closely related to the Greek legend of Œdipus, who first solved the famous riddle propounded by the mysterious creature with the body of a winged lion and the head of a woman which frequented the highway leading to Thebes. To each who passed her lair the sphinx addressed the question, "What aminal is it that in the morning goes on four feet, at noon on two feet, and in the evening on three feet?" Those who failed to answer her riddle she destroyed. Œdipus declared the answer to be man himself, who in childhood crawled upon his hands and knees, in manhood stood erect, and in old age shuffled along supporting himself by a staff. Discovering one who knew the answer to her riddle, the sphinx cast herself from the cliff which bordered the road and perished.

There is still another answer to the riddle of the sphinx, an answer best revealed by a consideration of the Pythagorean values of numbers. The 4, the 2, and the 3 produce the sum of 9, which is that natural number of man and also of the lower worlds. The 4 represents the ignorant man, the 2 the intellectual man, and the 3 the spiritual man. Infant humanity walks on four legs, evolving humanity on two legs, and to the power of his own mind the redeemed and illuminated *magus* adds the staff of wisdom. The sphinx is therefore the mystery of Nature, the embodiment of the secret doctrine, and all who cannot solve her riddle perish. To pass the sphinx is to attain personal immortality.

money expended in this way was 1600 talents of silver. If this then is a true record, what a vast sum must have been spent on the iron tools used in the work, and on the feeding and clothing of the labourers, considering the length of time the work lasted, which has already been stated [ten years], and the additional time—no small space, I imagine—which must have been occupied by the quarrying of the stones, their conveyance, and the formation of the underground apartments."

While his account is extremely colorful, it is apparent that the Father of History, for reasons which he doubtless considered sufficient, concocted a fraudulent story to conceal the true origin and the purpose of the Great Pyramid. This is but one of several instances in his writings which would lead the thoughtful reader to suspect that Herodotus himself was an initiate of the Sacred Schools and consequently obligated to preserve inviolate the secrets of the ancient orders. The theory advanced by Herodotus and now generally accepted that the Pyramid was the tomb of the Pharaoh Cheops cannot be substantiated. In fact, Manetho, Eratosthenes, and Diodorus Siculus all differ from Herodotus—as well as from each other—regarding the name of the builder of this supreme edifice. The sepulchral vault, which, according to the Lepsius Law of pyramid construction, should have been finished at the same time as the monument or sooner, was never completed. There is no proof that the building was erected by the Egyptians, for the elaborate carvings with which the burial chambers of Egyptian royalty are almost invariably ornamented are entirely lacking and it embodies none of the elements of their architecture or decoration, such as inscriptions, images, cartouches, paintings, and other distinctive features associated with dynastic mortuary art. The only hieroglyphics to be found within the Pyramid are a few builders' marks sealed up in the *chambers of construction,* first opened by Howard Vyse. These apparently were painted upon the stones before they were set in position, for in a number of instances the marks were either inverted or disfigured by the operation of fitting the blocks together. While Egyptologists have attempted to identify the crude dabs of paint as cartouches of Cheops, it is almost inconceivable that this ambitious ruler would have permitted his royal name to suffer such indignities. As the most eminent authorities on the subject are still uncertain as to the true meaning of these crude markings, whatever proof they might be that the building was erected during the fourth dynasty is certainly offset by the sea shells at the base of the Pyramid which Mr. Gab advances as evidence that it was erected before the Deluge—a theory substantiated by the much-abused Arabian traditions. One Arabian historian declared that the Pyramid was built by the Egyptian sages as a refuge against the Flood, while another proclaimed it to have been the treasure house of the powerful antediluvian king Sheddad Ben Ad. A panel of hieroglyphs over the entrance, which the casual observer might consider to afford a solution of the mystery, unfortunately dates back no further than A.D. 1843, having been cut at that time by Dr. Lepsius as a tribute to the King of Prussia.

Caliph al Mamoun, an illustrious descendant of the Prophet, inspired by stories of the immense treasures sealed within its depths, journeyed from Bagdad to Cairo, A.D. 820, with a great force of workmen to open the mighty Pyramid. When Caliph al Mamoun first reached the foot of the "Rock of Ages" and gazed up at its smooth glistening surface, a tumult of emotions undoubtedly racked his soul. The casing stones must have been in place at the time of his visit, for the Caliph could find no indication of an entrance—four perfectly smooth surfaces confronted him. Following vague rumors, he set his followers to work on the north side of the Pyramid, with instructions to keep on cutting and chiseling until they discovered something. To the Moslems with their crude instruments and vinegar it was a herculean effort to tunnel a full hundred feet through the limestone. Many times they were on the point of rebellion, but the word of the Caliph was law and the hope of a vast fortune buoyed them up.

At last on the eve of total discouragement fate came to their rescue. A great stone was heard to fall somewhere in the wall near the toiling and disgruntled

Arabs. Pushing on toward the sound with renewed enthusiasm, they finally broke into the descending passage which leads into the subterranean chamber. They then chiseled their way around the great stone portcullis which had fallen into a position barring their progress, and attacked and removed one after another the granite plugs which for a while continued to slide down the passage leading from the Queen's Chamber above.

Finally no more blocks descended and the way was clear for the followers of the Prophet. But where were the treasures? From room to room the frantic workmen rushed, looking in vain for loot. The discontent of the Moslems reached such a height that Caliph al Mamoun—who had inherited much of the wisdom of his illustrious father, the Caliph al Raschid—sent to Bagdad for funds, which he caused to be secretly buried near the entrance of the Pyramid. He then ordered his men to dig at that spot and great was their rejoicing when the treasure was discovered, the workmen being deeply impressed by the wisdom of the antediluvian monarch who had carefully estimated their wages and thoughtfully caused the exact amount to be buried for their benefit!

The Caliph then returned to the city of his fathers and the Great Pyramid was left to the mercy of succeeding generations. In the ninth century the sun's rays striking the highly polished surfaces of the original casing stones caused each side of the Pyramid to appear as a dazzling triangle of light. Since that time, all but two of these casing stones have disappeared. Investigation has resulted in their discovery, recut and resurfaced, in the walls of Mohammedan mosques and palaces in various parts of Cairo and its environs.

Pyramid Problems

C. Piazzi Smyth asks: "Was the Great Pyramid, then, erected before the invention of hieroglyphics, and previous to the birth of the Egyptian religion?" Time may yet prove that the upper chambers of the Pyramid were a sealed mystery before the establishment of the Egyptian empire. In the subterranean chamber, however, are markings which indicate that the Romans gained admission there. In the light of the secret philosophy of the Egyptian initiates, W. W. Harmon, by a series of extremely complicated yet exact mathematical calculations, determines that the first ceremonial of the Pyramid was performed 68,890 years ago on the occasion when the star Vega for the first time sent its ray down the descending passage into the pit. The actual building of the Pyramid was accomplished in the period of from ten to fifteen years immediately preceding this date.

While such figures doubtless will evoke the ridicule of modern Egyptologists, they are based upon an exhaustive study of the principles of sidereal mechanics as incorporated into the structure of the Pyramid by its initiated builders. If the casing stones were in position at the beginning of the ninth century, the so-called erosion marks upon the outside were not due to water. The theory also that the salt upon the interior stones of the Pyramid is evidence that the building was once submerged is weakened by the scientific fact that this kind of stone is subject to exudations of salt. While the building may have been submerged, at least in part, during the many thousands of years since its erection, the evidence adduced to prove this point is not conclusive.

The Great Pyramid was built of limestone and granite throughout, the two kinds of rock being combined in a peculiar and significant manner. The stones were trued with the utmost precision, and the cement used was of such remarkable quality that it is now practically as hard as the stone itself. The limestone blocks were sawed with bronze saws, the teeth of which were diamonds or other jewels. The chips from the stones were piled against the north side of the plateau on which the structure stands, where they form an additional buttress to aid in supporting the weight of the structure. The entire Pyramid is an example of perfect orientation and actually squares the circle. This last is accomplished by dropping a vertical line from the apex of the Pyramid to its base line. If this vertical line be considered as the radius of an imaginary circle, the length of the circumference of such a circle will be found to equal the sum of the base lines of the four sides of the Pyramid.

If the passage leading to the King's Chamber and the Queen's Chamber was sealed up thousands of years before the Christian Era, those later admitted into the Pyramid Mysteries must have received their initiations in subterranean galleries now unknown. Without such galleries there could have been no possible means of ingress or egress, since the single surface entrance was completely closed with casing stones. If not blocked by the mass of the Sphinx or concealed in some part of that image, the secret entrance may be either in one of the adjacent temples or upon the sides of the limestone plateau.

Attention is called to the granite plugs filling the ascending passageway to the Queen's Chamber which Caliph al Mamoun was forced practically to pulverize before he could clear a way into the upper chambers. C. Piazzi Smyth notes that the position of the stones demonstrate that they were set in place from above—which made it necessary for a considerable number of workmen to depart from the upper chambers. How did they do it? Smyth believes they descended through the wall (see diagram), dropping the ramp stone into place behind them. He further contends that robbers probably used the well as a means of getting into the upper chambers. The ramp stone having been set in a bed of plaster, the robbers were forced to break through it, leaving a jagged opening. Mr. Dupré, an architect who has spent years investigating the pyramids, differs from Smyth, however, in that he believes the well itself to be a robbers' hole, being the first successful attempt made to enter the upper chambers from the subterranean chamber, then the only open section of the Pyramid.

Mr. Dupré bases his conclusion upon the fact that the well is merely a rough hole and the grotto an irregular chamber, without any evidence of the architectural precision with which the remainder of the structure was erected. The diameter of the well also precludes the possibility of its having been dug downward; it must have been gouged out from below, and the grotto was necessary to supply air to the thieves. It is inconceivable that the Pyramid builders would break one of their own ramp stones and leave its broken surface and a gaping hole in the side wall of their otherwise perfect gallery. If the well is a robbers' hole, it may explain why the Pyramid was empty when Caliph al Mamoun entered it and what happened to the missing coffer lid. A careful examination of the so-called unfinished subterranean chamber, which must have been the base of operations for the robbers, might disclose traces of their presence or show where they piled the rubble which must have accumulated as a result of their operations. While it is not entirely clear by what entrance the robbers reached the subterranean chamber, it is improbable that they used the descending passageway.

There is a remarkable niche in the north wall of the Queen's Chamber which the Mohammedan guides glibly pronounce to be a shrine. The general shape of this niche, however, with its walls converging by a series of overlaps like those of the Grand Gallery, would indicate that originally it had been intended as a passageway. Efforts made to explore this niche have been nonproductive, but Mr. Dupré believes an entrance to exist here through which—if the well did not exist at the time—the workmen made their exit through the Pyramid after dropping the stone plugs into the ascending gallery.

Biblical scholars have contributed a number of most extraordinary conceptions regarding the Great Pyramid. This ancient edifice has been identified by them as Joseph's granary (despite its hopelessly inadequate capacity); as the tomb prepared for the unfortunate Pharaoh of the Exodus who could not be buried there because his body was never recovered from the Red Sea; and finally as a perpetual confirmation of the infallibility of the numerous prophecies contained in the Authorized Version!

The Sphinx

Although the Great Pyramid, as Ignatius Donnelly has demonstrated, is patterned after an antediluvian type of architecture, examples of which are to be found in nearly every part of the world, the Sphinx (*Hu*) is typically Egyptian. The stele between its paws states the Sphinx is an image of the Sun God, Harmackis, which was evidently made in the similitude of the Pharaoh during whose reign it was chiseled. The statue was restored and completely excavated by Tahutmes IV as the result of a vision in which the god had appeared and declared himself oppressed by the weight of the sand about his body. The broken beard of the Sphinx was discovered during excavations between the front paws. The steps leading up to the Sphinx and also the temple and altar between the paws are much later additions, probably Roman, for it is known that the Romans reconstructed many Egyptian antiquities. The shallow depression in the crown of the head, once thought to be the terminus of a closed-up passageway leading from the Sphinx to the Great Pyramid, was merely intended to help support a headdress now missing.

Metal rods have been driven into the Sphinx in a vain effort to discover chambers or passages within its body. The major part of the Sphinx is a single stone, but the front paws have been built up of smaller stones. The Sphinx is about 200 feet long, 70 feet high, and 38 feet wide across the shoulders. The main stone from which it was carved is believed by some to have been transported from distant quarries by methods unknown, while others assert it to be native rock, possibly an outcropping somewhat resembling the form into which it was later carved. The theory once advanced that both the Pyramid and the Sphinx were built from artificial stones made on the spot has been abandoned. A careful analysis of the limestone shows it to be composed of small sea creatures called *mummulites.*

The popular supposition that the Sphinx was the true portal of the Great Pyramid, while it survives with surprising tenacity, has never been substantiated. P. Christian presents this theory as follows, basing it in part upon the authority of Iamblichus:

"The Sphinx of Gizeh, says the author of the *Traité des Mystères,* served as the entrance to the sacred subterranean chambers in which the trials of the initiate were undergone. This entrance, obstructed in our day by sands and rubbish, may still be traced between the forelegs of the crouched colossus. It was formerly closed by a bronze gate whose secret spring could be operated only by the Magi. It was guarded by public respect and a sort of religious fear maintained its inviolability better than armed protection would have done. In the belly of the Sphinx were cut out galleries leading to the subterranean part of the Great Pyramid. These galleries were so artfully crisscrossed along their course to the Pyramid that in setting forth into the passage without a guide through this network, one ceaselessly and inevitably returned to the starting point." (See *Histoire de la Magie.*)

Unfortunately, the bronze door referred to cannot be found, nor is there any evidence that it ever existed. The passing centuries have wrought many changes in the colossus, however, and the original opening may have been closed.

Nearly all students of the subject believe that subterranean chambers exist beneath the Great Pyramid. Robert Ballard writes: "The priests of the Pyramids of Lake Moeris had their vast subterranean residences. It appears to me more than probable that those of Gizeh were similarly provided. And I may go further:—Out of these very caverns may have been excavated the limestone of which the Pyramids were built. * * * In the bowels of the limestone ridge on which the Pyramids are built will yet be found, I feel convinced, ample information as to their uses. A good diamond drill with two or three hundred feet of rods is what is wanted to test this, and the solidarity of the Pyramids at the same time." (See *The Solution of the Pyramid Problem.*)

Mr. Ballard's theory of extensive underground apartments and quarries brings up an important problem in architectonics. The Pyramid builders were too farsighted to endanger the permanence of the Great Pyramid by placing over five million tons of limestone and granite on any but a solid foundation. It is therefore reasonably certain that such chambers or passageways as may exist beneath the building are relatively insignificant, like those within the body of the structure, which occupy less than one sixteen-hundredth of the cubic contents of the Pyramid.

The Sphinx was undoubtedly erected for symbolical purposes at the instigation of the priestcraft. The theories that the uræus upon its forehead was originally the finger of an immense sundial and that both the Pyramid and the Sphinx were used to measure time, the seasons, and the precession of the equinoxes are ingenious but not wholly convincing. If this great creature was erected to obliterate the ancient passageway leading into the subterranean temple of the Pyramid, its symbolism would be most appropriate. In comparison with the overwhelming size and dignity of the Great Pyramid, the Sphinx is almost insignificant. Its battered face, upon which may still be seen vestiges of the red paint with which the figure was originally covered, is disfigured beyond recognition. Its nose was broken off by a fanatical Mohammedan, lest the follow-

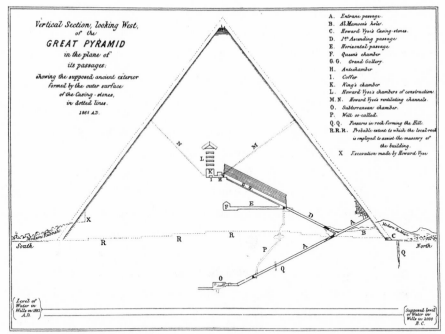

Vertical Section, looking West,
of the
GREAT PYRAMID
in the plane of
its passages:

showing the supposed ancient exterior
formed by the outer surface
of the Casing-stones,
in dotted lines.
1865 AD.

A. Entrance passage.
B. Al Mamoun's hole.
C. Howard Vyse's Casing-stones.
D. 1st Ascending passage.
E. Horizontal passage.
F. Queen's chamber.
G. G. Grand Gallery.
H. Antechamber.
I. Coffer.
K. King's chamber.
L. Howard Vyse's chambers of construction.
M. N. Howard Vyse's ventilating channels.
O. Subterranean chamber.
P. Well so-called.
Q. Q. Fissures in rock forming the Hill.
R.R.R. Probable extent to which the local rock is employed to assist the masonry of the building.
X Excavation made by Howard Vyse.

FROM SMYTH'S LIFE AND WORK AT THE GREAT PYRAMID.

A VERTICAL SECTION OF THE GREAT PYRAMID.

The Great Pyramid stands upon a limestone plateau at the base of which, according to ancient history, the Nile once flowed, thus supplying a method of transportation for the huge blocks used in its construction. Presuming that the capstone was originally in place, the Pyramid is, according to John Taylor, in round figures 486 feet high; the base of each side is 764 feet long, and the entire structure covers a ground area of more than 13 acres.

The Great Pyramid is the only one in the group at Gizeh—in fact, as far as known, the only one in Egypt—that has chambers within the actual body of the Pyramid itself. For this reason it is said to refute the Lepsius Law, which asserts that each of these structures is a monument raised over a subterranean chamber in which a ruler is entombed. The Pyramid contains four chambers, which in the diagram are lettered K, H, F, and O.

The King's Chamber (K) is an oblong apartment 39 feet long, 17 feet wide, and 19 feet high (disregarding fractional parts of a foot in each case), with a flat roof consisting of nine great stones, the largest in the Pyramid. Above the King's Chamber are five low compartments (L), generally termed construction chambers. In the lowest of these the so-called hieroglyphs of the Pharaoh Cheops are located. The roof of the fifth construction chamber is peaked. At the end of the King's Chamber opposite the entrance stands the famous sarcophagus, or coffer (I), and behind it is a shallow opening that was dug in the hope of discovering valuables. Two air vents (M, N) passing through the entire body of the Pyramid ventilate the King's Chamber. In itself this is sufficient to establish that the building was not intended for a tomb.

Between the upper end of the Grand Gallery (G. G.) and the King's Chamber is a small antechamber (H), its extreme length 9 feet, its extreme width 5 feet, and its extreme height 12 feet, with its walls grooved for purposes now unknown. In the groove nearest the Grand Gallery is a slab of stone in two sections, with a peculiar boss or knob protruding about an inch from the surface of the upper part facing the Grand Gallery. This stone does not reach to the floor of the antechamber and those entering the King's Chamber must pass under the slab. From the King's Chamber the Grand Gallery—157 feet in length, 28 feet in height, 7 feet in width at its widest point and decreasing to 3½ feet as the result of seven converging overlaps of the stones forming the walls—descends to a little above the Queen's Chamber. Here a gallery (E) branches off, passing more than 100 feet back towards the center of the Pyramid and opening into the Queen's Chamber (F). The Queen's Chamber is 19 feet long, 17 feet wide, and 20 feet high. Its roof is peaked and composed of great slabs of stone. Air passages not shown lead from the Queen's Chamber, but these were not open originally. In the east wall of the Queen's Chamber is a peculiar niche of gradually converging stone, which, in all likelihood, may prove to be a now lost entrance way.

At the point where the Grand Gallery ends and the horizontal passage towards the Queen's Chamber begins is the entrance to the well and also the opening leading down the first ascending passage (D) to the point where this passage meets the descending passage (A) leading from the outer wall of the Pyramid down to the subterranean chamber. After descending 59 feet down the well (P), the grotto is reached. Continuing through the floor of the grotto the well leads downward 133 feet to the descending entrance passage (A), which it meets a short distance before this passage becomes horizontal and leads into the subterranean chamber.

The subterranean chamber (O) is about 46 feet long and 27 feet wide, but is extremely low, the ceiling varying in height from a little over 3 feet to about 13 feet from the rough and apparently unfinished floor. From the south side of the subterranean chamber a low tunnel runs about 50 feet and then meets a blank wall. These constitute the only known openings in the Pyramid, with the exception of a few niches, exploration holes, blind passages, and the rambling cavernous tunnel (B) hewn out by the Moslems under the leadership of the Prophet's descendant, Caliph al Mamoun.

ers of the Prophet be led into idolatry. The very nature of its construction and the present repairs necessary to prevent the head from falling off indicate that it could not have survived the great periods of time which have elapsed since the erection of the Pyramid.

To the Egyptians, the Sphinx was the symbol of strength and intelligence. It was portrayed as androgynous to signify that they recognized the initiates and gods as partaking of both the positive and negative creative powers. Gerald Massey writes: "This is the secret of the Sphinx. The orthodox sphinx of Egypt is masculine in front and feminine behind. So is the image of Sut-Typhon, a type of horn and tail, male in front and female behind. The Pharaohs, who wore the tail of the Lioness or Cow behind them, were male in front and female behind. Like the Gods they included the dual totality of Being in one person, born of the Mother, but of *both sexes as the Child.*" (See *The Natural Genesis.*)

Most investigators have ridiculed the Sphinx and, without even deigning to investigate the great colossus, have turned their attention to the most over-whelming mystery of the Pyramid.

The Pyramid Mysteries

The word *pyramid* is popularly supposed to be derived from πῦρ, *fire,* thus signifying that it is the symbolic representation of the One Divine Flame, the life of every creature. John Taylor believes the word *pyramid* to mean a "measure of wheat," while C. Piazzi Smyth favors the Coptic meaning, "a division into ten." The initiates of old accepted the pyramid form as the ideal symbol of both the secret doctrine and chose institutions established for its dissemination. Both pyramids and mounds are antitypes of the Holy Mountain, or High Place of God, which was believed to stand in the "midst" of the earth. John P. Lundy relates the Great Pyramid to the fabled Olympus, further assuming that its subterranean passages correspond to the tortuous byways of Hades.

The square base of the Pyramid is a constant reminder that the House of Wisdom is firmly founded upon Nature and her immutable laws. "The Gnostics," writes Albert Pike, "claimed that the whole edifice of their science rested on a square whose angles were: Σιγη, Silence; Βυθος, Profundity; Νους, Intelligence; Αληθεια, Truth." (See *Morals and Dogma.*) The sides of the Great Pyramid face the four cardinal angles, the latter signifying according to Eliphas Levi the extremities of heat and cold (south and north) and the extremities of light and darkness (east and west). The base of the Pyramid further represents the four material elements or substances from the combinations of which the quaternary body of man is formed. From each side of the square there rises a triangle, typifying the threefold divine being enthroned within every quaternary material nature. If each base line be considered a square from which ascends a threefold spiritual power, then the sum of the lines of the four faces (12) and the four hypothetical squares (16) constituting the base is 28, the sacred number of the lower world. If this be added to the three septenaries composing the sun (21), it equals 49, the square of 7 and the number of the universe.

The twelve signs of the zodiac, like the Governors of the lower worlds, are symbolized by the twelve lines of the four triangles—of the faces of the Pyramid. In the midst of each face is one of the beasts of Ezekiel, and the structure as a whole becomes the Cherubim. The three main chambers of the Pyramid are related to the heart, the brain, and the generative system—the spiritual centers of the human constitution. The triangular form of the Pyramid also is similar to the posture assumed by the body during the ancient meditative exercises. The Mysteries taught that the divine energies from the gods descended upon the top of the Pyramid, which was likened to an inverted tree with its branches below and its roots at the apex. From this inverted tree the divine wisdom is disseminated by streaming down the diverging sides and radiating throughout the world.

The size of the capstone of the Great Pyramid cannot be accurately determined, for, while most investigators have assumed that it was once in place, no vestige of it now remains. There is a curious tendency among the builders of great religious edifices to leave their creations unfinished, thereby signifying that God alone is complete. The capstone—if it existed—was itself a miniature pyramid, the apex of which again would be capped by a smaller block of similar shape, and so on *ad infinitum*. The capstone therefore is the epitome of the entire structure. Thus, the Pyramid may be likened to the universe and the capstone to man. Following the chain of analogy, the mind is the capstone of man, the spirit the capstone of the mind, and God—the epitome of the whole—the capstone of the spirit. As a rough and unfinished block, man is taken from the quarry and by the secret culture of the Mysteries gradually transformed into a trued and perfect pyramidal capstone. The temple is complete only when the initiate himself becomes the living apex through which the divine power is focused into the diverging structure below.

W. Marsham Adams calls the Great Pyramid "the House of the Hidden Places"; such indeed it was, for it represented the inner sanctuary of pre-Egyptian wisdom. By the Egyptians the Great Pyramid was associated with Hermes, the god of wisdom and letters and the Divine Illuminator worshiped through the planet Mercury. Relating Hermes to the Pyramid emphasizes anew the fact that it was in reality the supreme temple of the Invisible and Supreme Deity. The Great Pyramid was not a lighthouse, an observatory, or a tomb, but the first temple of the Mysteries, the first structure erected as a repository for those secret truths which are the certain foundation of all arts and sciences. It was the perfect emblem of the *microcosm* and the *macrocosm* and, according to the secret teachings, the tomb of Osiris, the black god of the Nile. Osiris represents a certain manifestation of solar energy, and therefore his house or tomb is emblematic of the universe within which he is entombed and upon the cross of which he is crucified.

Through the mystic passageways and chambers of the Great Pyramid passed the illumined of antiquity. They entered its portals as *men;* they came forth as *gods.* It was the place of the "second birth," the "womb of the Mysteries," and wisdom dwelt in it as God dwells in the hearts of men. Somewhere in the depths of its recesses there resided an unknown being who was called "The Initiator," or "The Illustrious One," robed in blue and gold and bearing in his hand the sevenfold key of Eternity. This was the lion-faced hierophant, the Holy One, the Master of Masters, who never left the House of Wisdom and whom no man ever saw save he who had passed through the gates of preparation and purification. It was in these chambers that Plato—he of the broad brow—came face to face with the wisdom of the ages personified in the Master of the Hidden House.

Who was the Master dwelling in the mighty Pyramid, the many rooms of which signified the worlds in space; the Master whom none might behold save those who had been "born again"? He alone fully knew the secret of the Pyramid, but he has departed the way of the wise and the house is empty. The hymns of praise no longer echo in muffled tones through the chambers; the neophyte no longer passes through the elements and wanders among the seven stars; the candidate no longer receives the "Word of Life" from the lips of the Eternal One. Nothing now remains that the eye of man can see but an empty shell—the outer symbol of an inner truth—and men call the House of God a tomb!

The technique of the Mysteries was unfolded by the Sage Illuminator, the Master of the Secret House. The power to know his guardian spirit was revealed to the new initiate; the method of disentangling his material body from his divine vehicle was explained; and to consummate the *magnum opus,* there was revealed the Divine Name—the secret and unutterable designation of the Supreme Deity, by the very knowledge of which man and his God are made consciously one. With the giving of the Name, the new initiate became himself a *pyramid,* within the chambers of whose soul numberless other human beings might also receive spiritual enlightenment.

In the King's Chamber was enacted the drama of the "second death." Here the candidate, after being crucified upon the cross of the solstices and the equinoxes, was buried in the great coffer. There is a profound mystery to the atmosphere and temperature of the King's Chamber: it is of a peculiar deathlike cold which cuts to the marrow of the bone. This room was a doorway between the material world and the transcendental spheres of Nature. While his body lay in the coffer, the soul of the neophyte soared as a human-headed hawk through the celestial realms, there to discover first hand the eternity of Life, Light, and Truth, as well as the illusion of Death, Darkness, and Sin. Thus in one sense the Great Pyramid may be likened to a gate through which the ancient priests permitted a few to pass toward the attainment of individual completion. It is also to be noted incidentally that if the coffer in the King's Chamber be struck, the sound emitted has no counterpart in any known musical scale. This tonal value may have formed part of that combination of circumstances which rendered the King's Chamber an ideal setting for the conferment of the highest degree of the Mysteries.

The modern world knows little of these ancient rites. The scientist and the theologian alike gaze upon the sacred structure, wondering what fundamental urge inspired the herculean labor. If they would but think for a moment, they would realize that there is only *one* urge in the soul of man capable of supplying the required incentive—namely, the desire to know, to understand, and to exchange the narrowness of human mortality for the greater breadth and scope of divine enlightenment. So men say of the Great Pyramid that it is the most perfect building in the world, the source of weights and measures, the original Noah's Ark, the origin of languages, alphabets, and scales of temperature and humidity. Few realize, however, that it is the gateway to the Eternal.

Though the modern world may know a million secrets, the ancient world knew one—and that one was greater than the million; for the *million* secrets breed death, disaster, sorrow, selfishness, lust, and avarice, but the *one* secret confers life, light, and truth. The time will come when the secret wisdom shall again be the dominating religious and philosophical urge of the world. The day is at hand when the doom of dogma shall be sounded. The great theological Tower of Babel, with its confusion of tongues, was built of bricks of mud and the mortar of slime. Out of the cold ashes of lifeless creeds, however, shall rise *phoenixlike* the ancient Mysteries. No other institution has so completely satisfied the religious aspirations of humanity, for since the destruction of the Mysteries there never has been a religious code to which Plato could have subscribed. The unfolding of man's spiritual nature is as much an exact science as astronomy, medicine or jurisprudence. To accomplish this end religions were primarily established; and out of religion have come science, philosophy, and logic as methods whereby this divine purpose might be realized.

The Dying God shall rise again! The secret room in the House of the Hidden Places shall be rediscovered. The Pyramid again shall stand as the ideal emblem of solidarity, inspiration, aspiration, resurrection, and regeneration. As the passing sands of time bury civilization upon civilization beneath their weight, the Pyramid shall remain as the visible covenant between Eternal Wisdom and the world. The time may yet come when the chants of the illumined shall be heard once more in its ancient passageways and the Master of the Hidden House shall await in the Silent Place for the coming of that man who, casting aside the fallacies of dogma and tenet, seeks simply Truth and will be satisfied with neither substitute nor counterfeit.

VIII

Isis, the Virgin of the World

t is especially fitting that a study of Hermetic symbolism should begin with a discussion of the symbols and attributes of the *Saitic Isis*. This is the Isis of Sais, famous for the inscription concerning her which appeared on the front of her temple in that city: *"I, Isis, am all that has been, that is or shall be; no mortal Man hath ever me unveiled."*

Plutarch affirms that many ancient authors believed this goddess to be the daughter of Hermes; others held the opinion that she was the child of Prometheus. Both of these demigods were noted for their divine wisdom. It is not improbable that her kinship to them is merely allegorical. Plutarch translates the name Isis to mean *wisdom*. Godfrey Higgins, in his *Anacalypsis,* derives the name of *Isis* from the Hebrew יש׳ , *Iso,* and the Greek ζωω, *to save.* Some authorities, however, for example, Richard Payne Knight (as stated in his *Symbolical Language of Ancient Art and Mythology*), believe the word to be of Northern extraction, possibly Scandinavian or Gothic. In these languages the name is pronounced *Isa,* meaning *ice,* or water in its most passive, crystallized, negative state.

This Egyptian deity under many names appears as the principle of natural fecundity among nearly all the religions of the ancient world. She was known as the goddess with ten thousand appellations and was metamorphosed by Christianity into the Virgin Mary, for Isis, although she gave birth to all living things—chief among them the Sun—still remained a virgin, according to the legendary accounts.

Apuleius in the eleventh book of *The Golden Ass* ascribes to the goddess the following statement concerning her powers and attributes: "Behold, * *, I, moved by thy prayers, am present with thee; I, who am Nature, the parent of things, the queen of all the elements, the primordial progeny of ages, the supreme of Divinities, the sovereign of the spirits of the dead, the first of the celestials, and the uni-form resemblance of Gods and Goddesses. I, who rule by my nod the luminous summits of the heavens, the salubrious breezes of the sea, and the deplorable silences of the realms beneath and whose one divinity the whole orb of the earth venerates under a mani-fold form, by different rites and a variety of appellations. Hence the primogenial Phrygians call me Pessinuntica, the mother of the Gods; the Attic Aborigines, Cecropian Minerva; the floating Cyprians, Paphian Venus; arrow-bearing Cretans, Diana Dictynna; the three-tongued Sicilians, Sty-gian Proserpine; and the Eleusini-ans, the ancient Goddess Ceres. Some also call me Juno, others Bellona, others Hecate, and others Rhamnusia. And those who are illuminated by the incipient rays of that divinity the Sun, when he rises, viz. the Ethiopians, the Arii, and the Egyptians skilled in ancient learning, worshipping me by ceremonies perfectly appropri-ate, call me by my true name, Queen Isis."

FROM *MOSAIZE HISTORIE DER HEBREEUWSE KERKE.*

ISIS, QUEEN OF HEAVEN.

Diodorus writes of a famous inscription carved on a column at Nysa, in Ara-bia, wherein Isis described herself as follows: "I am Isis, Queen of this coun-try. I was instructed by Mercury. No one can destroy the laws which I have es-tablished. I am the eldest daughter of Saturn, most ancient of the gods. I am the wife and sister of Osiris the King. I first made known to mortals the use of wheat. I am the mother of Orus the King. In my honor was the city of Bubaste built. Rejoice, O Egypt, rejoice, land that gave me birth!" (See "Morals and Dogma," by Albert Pike.)

Le Plongeon believes that the Egyptian myth of Isis had a histor-ical basis among the Mayas of Central America, where this god-dess was known as Queen Moo. In Prince Coh the same author finds a correspondence to Osiris, the brother-husband of Isis. Le Plongeon's theory is that Mayan civilization was far more ancient than that of Egypt. After the death of Prince Coh, his widow, Queen Moo, fleeing to escape the wrath of his murderers, sought refuge among the Mayan colonies in Egypt, where she was accepted as their queen and was given the name of *Isis*. While Le Plongeon may be right, the possible historical queen sinks into insignificance when compared with the allegorical, symbolic World Virgin; and the fact that she appears among so many different races and peoples discredits the theory that she was a historical individual.

According to Sextus Empyricus, the Trojan war was fought over a statue of the moon goddess. For this lunar Helena, and not for a woman, the Greeks and Trojans struggled at the gates of Troy.

Several authors have attempted to prove that Isis, Osiris, Typhon, Nephthys, and Aroueris (Thoth, or Mercury) were grandchildren of the great Jewish patriarch Noah by his son Ham. But as the story of Noah and his ark is a cosmic allegory concerning the repopulation of planets at the beginning of each world period, this only makes it less likely that they were historical personages. According to Robert Fludd, the sun has three properties—*life, light,* and *heat.* These three vivify and vitalize the three worlds—spiritual, intellectual, and material. Therefore, it is said *"from one light, three lights,"* i. e., the first three Master Masons. In all probability, Osiris represents the third, or material, aspect of solar activity, which by its beneficent influences vitalizes and enlivens the flora and fauna of the earth. Osiris is not the sun, but the sun is symbolic of the vital principle of Nature, which the ancients knew as Osiris. His symbol, therefore, was an opened eye, in honor of the Great Eye of the universe, the sun. Opposed to the active, radiant principle of impregnating fire, heat, and motion was the passive, receptive principle of Nature.

Modern science has proved that forms ranging in magnitude from solar systems to atoms are composed of positive, radiant nuclei surrounded by negative bodies that exist upon the emanations of the central life. From this allegory we have the story of Solomon and his wives, for Solomon is the sun and his wives and concubines are the planets, moons, asteroids, and other receptive bodies within his house—the solar mansion. Isis, represented in the Song of Solomon by the dark maid of Jerusalem, is symbolic of receptive Nature—the watery, maternal principle which creates all things out of herself after impregnation has been achieved by the virility of the sun.

In the ancient world the year had 360 days. The five extra days were gathered together by the God of Cosmic Intelligence to serve as the birthdays of the five gods and goddesses who are called the sons and daughters of Ham. Upon the first of these special days Osiris was born and upon the fourth of them Isis. (The number *four* shows the relation that this goddess bears to the earth and its elements.) Typhon, the Egyptian Demon or Spirit of the Adversary, was born upon the third day. Typhon is often symbolized by a crocodile; sometimes his body is a combination of crocodile and hog. Isis stands for knowledge and wisdom, and according to Plutarch the word *Typhon* means *insolence* and *pride*. Egotism, self-centeredness, and pride are the deadly enemies of understanding and truth. This part of the allegory is revealed.

After Osiris, here symbolized as the sun, had become King of Egypt and had given to his people the full advantage of his intellectual light, he continued his path through the heavens, visiting the peoples of other nations and converting all with whom he came in contact. Plutarch further asserts that the Greeks recognized in Osiris the same person whom they revered under the names of *Dionysos* and *Bacchus*. While he was away from his country, his brother, Typhon, the Evil One, like the Loki of Scandinavia, plotted against the Sun God to destroy him. Gathering seventy-two persons as fellow conspirators, he attained his nefarious end in a most subtle manner. He had a wonderful ornamented box made just the size of the body of Osiris. This he brought into a banquet hall where the gods and goddesses were feasting together. All admired the beautiful chest, and Typhon promised to give it to the one whose body fitted it most perfectly. One after another lay down in the box, but in disappointment rose again, until at last Osiris also tried. The moment he was in the chest Typhon and his accomplices nailed the cover down and sealed the cracks with molten lead. They then cast the box into the Nile, down which it floated to the sea. Plutarch states that the date upon which this occurred was the seventeenth day of the month Athyr, when the sun was in the constellation of Scorpio. This is most significant, for the Scorpion is the symbol of treachery. The time when Osiris entered the chest was also the same season that Noah entered the ark to escape from the Deluge.

Plutarch further declares that the Pans and Satyrs (the Nature spirits and elementals) first discovered that Osiris had been murdered. These immediately raised an alarm, and from this incident the word *panic*, meaning *fright* or *amazement* of the multitudes, originated. Isis, upon receiving the news of her husband's murder, which she learned from some children who had seen the murderers making off with the box, at once robed herself in mourning and started forth in quest of him.

At length Isis discovered that the chest had floated to the coast of Byblos. There it had lodged in the branches of a tree, which in a short time miraculously grew up around the box. This so amazed the king of that country that he ordered the tree to be cut down and a pillar made from its trunk to support the roof of his palace. Isis, visiting Byblos, recovered the body of her husband, but it was again stolen by Typhon, who cut it into fourteen parts, which he scattered all over the earth. Isis, in despair, began gathering up the severed remains of her husband, but found only thirteen pieces. The fourteenth part (the phallus) she reproduced in gold, for the original had fallen into the river Nile and had been swallowed by a fish.

Typhon was later slain in battle by the son of Osiris. Some of the Egyptians believed that the souls of the gods were taken to heaven, where they shone forth as stars. It was supposed that the soul of Isis gleamed from the Dog Star, while Typhon became the constellation of the Bear. It is doubtful, however, whether this idea was ever generally accepted.

Among the Egyptians, Isis is often represented with a headdress consisting of the empty throne chair of her murdered husband, and this peculiar structure was accepted during certain dynasties as her hieroglyphic. The headdresses of the Egyptians have great symbolic and emblematic importance, for they represent the auric bodies of the superhuman intelligences, and are used in the same way that the nimbus, halo, and aureole are used in Christian religious art. Frank C. Higgins, a well-known Masonic symbolist, has astutely noted that the ornate headgears of certain gods and Pharaohs are inclined backward at the same angle as the earth's axis. The robes, insignia, jewels, and ornamentations of the ancient hierophants symbolized the spiritual energies radiating from the human body. Modern science is rediscovering many of the lost secrets of Hermetic philosophy. One of these is the ability to gauge the mental development, the soul qualities, and the physical health of an individual from the streamers of semi-visible electric force which pour through the surface of the skin of every human being at all times during his life. (For details concerning a scientific process for making the auric emanations visible, see *The Human Atmosphere* by Dr. Walter J. Kilner.)

Isis is sometimes symbolized by the head of a cow; occasionally the entire animal is her symbol. The first gods of the Scandinavians were licked out of blocks of ice by the Mother Cow (Audhumla), who symbolized the principle of natural nutriment and fecundity because of her milk. Occasionally Isis is represented as a bird. She often carries in one hand the *crux ansata,* the symbol of eternal life, and in the other the flowered scepter, symbolic of her authority.

Thoth Hermes Trismegistus, the founder of Egyptian learning, the Wise Man of the ancient world, gave to the priests and philosophers of antiquity the secrets which have been preserved to this day in myth and legend. These allegories and emblematic figures conceal the secret formulæ for spiritual, mental, moral, and physical regeneration commonly known as the Mystic Chemistry of the Soul (alchemy). These sublime truths were communicated to the initiates of the Mystery Schools, but were concealed from the profane. The latter, unable to understand the abstract philosophical tenets, worshiped the concrete sculptured idols which were emblematic of these secret truths. The wisdom and secrecy of Egypt are epitomized in the Sphinx, which has preserved its secret from the seekers of a hundred generations. The mysteries of Hermeticism, the great spiritual truths hidden from the world by the ignorance of the world, and the keys of the secret doctrines of the ancient philosophers, are all symbolized by the Virgin Isis. Veiled from head to foot, she reveals her wisdom only to the tried and initiated few who have earned the right to enter her sacred presence, tear from the veiled figure of Nature its shroud of obscurity, and stand face to face with the Divine Reality.

The explanations in these pages of the symbols peculiar to the Virgin Isis are based (unless otherwise noted) on selections from a free translation of the fourth book of *Bibliothèque des Philosophes Hermétiques,* entitled "The Hermetical Signification of the Symbols and Attributes of Isis," with interpolations by the compiler to amplify and clarify the text.

The statues of Isis were decorated with the sun, moon, and stars, and many emblems pertaining to the earth, over which Isis was believed to rule (as the guardian spirit of Nature personified). Several images of the goddess have been found upon which the marks of her dignity and position were still intact. According to the ancient philosophers, she personified Universal Nature, the mother of all productions. The deity was generally represented as a partly nude woman, often pregnant, sometimes loosely covered with a garment either of green or black color, or of four different shades intermingled—black, white, yellow, and red.

Apuleius describes her as follows: "In the first place, then, her most copious and long hairs, being gradually intorted, and promiscuously scattered on her divine neck, were softly defluous. A multiform crown, consisting of various flowers, bound the sublime summit of her head. And in the middle of the crown, just on her forehead, there was a smooth orb resembling a mirror, or rather a white refulgent light, which indicated that she was the moon. Vipers rising up after the manner of furrows, environed the crown on the right hand and on the left, and Cerealian ears of corn were also extended from above. Her garment was of many colours, and woven from the finest flax, and was at one time lucid with a white splendour, at another yellow from the flower of crocus, and at another flaming with a rosy redness. But that which most excessively dazzled my sight, was a very black robe, fulgid with a dark splendour, and which, spreading round and passing under her right side, and ascending to her left shoulder, there rose protuberant like the center of a shield, the dependent part of the robe falling in many folds, and having small knots of fringe, gracefully flowing in its extremities. Glittering stars were dispersed through the embroidered border of the robe, and through the whole of its surface: and the full moon, shining in the middle of the stars, breathed forth flaming fires. Nevertheless, a crown, wholly consisting of flowers and fruits of every kind, adhered with indivisible connexion to the border of that conspicuous robe, in all its undulating motions. What she carried in her hands also consisted of things of a very different nature. For her right hand, indeed, bore a brazen rattle [sistrum] through the narrow lamina of which bent like a belt, certain rods passing, produced a sharp triple sound, through the vibrating motion of her arm. An oblong vessel, in the shape of a boat, depended from her left hand, on the handle of which, in that part in which it was conspicuous, an asp raised its erect head and largely swelling neck. And shoes woven from the leaves of the victorious palm tree covered her immortal feet."

The green color alludes to the vegetation which covers the face of the earth, and therefore represents the robe of Nature. The black represents death and corruption as being the way to a new life and generation. "Except a man be born again, he cannot see the kingdom of God." (John iii. 3.) White, yellow, and red signify the three principal colors of the alchemical, Hermetical, universal medicine after the blackness of its putrefaction is over.

The ancients gave the name *Isis* to one of their occult medicines; therefore the description here given relates somewhat to chemistry. Her black drape also signifies that the moon, or the lunar humidity—the sophic universal mercury and the operating substance of Nature in alchemical terminology—has no light of its own, but receives its light, its fire, and its vitalizing force from the sun. Isis was the image or representative of the great works of the wise men: the Philosopher's Stone, the Elixir of Life, and the Universal Medicine.

Other hieroglyphics seen in connection with Isis are no less curious than those already described, but it is impossible to enumerate all, for many symbols were used interchangeably by the Egyptian Hermetists. The goddess often wore upon her head a hat made of cypress branches, to signify mourning for her dead husband and also for the physical death which she caused every creature to undergo in order to receive a new life in posterity or a periodic resurrection. The head of Isis is sometimes ornamented with a crown of gold or a garland of olive leaves, as conspicuous marks of her sovereignty as queen of the world and mistress of the entire universe. The crown of gold signifies also the aurific unctuosity or sulphurous fatness of the solar and vital fires which she dispenses to every individual by a continual circulation of the elements, this circulation being symbolized by the musical rattle which she carries in her hand. This sistrum is also the yonic symbol of purity.

A serpent interwoven among the olive leaves on her head, devouring its own tail, denotes that the aurific unctuosity was soiled with the venom of terrestrial corruption which surrounded it and must be mortified and purified by seven planetary circulations or purifications called *flying eagles* (alchemical terminology) in order to make it medicinal for the restoration of health. (Here the emanations from the sun are recognized as a medicine for the healing of human ills.) The seven planetary circulations are represented by the circumambulations of the Masonic lodge; by the marching of the Jewish priests seven times around the walls of Jericho, and of the Mohammedan priests seven times around the Kabba at Mecca. From the crown of gold project three horns of plenty, signifying the abundance of the gifts of Nature proceeding from one root having its origin in the heavens (head of Isis).

In this figure the pagan naturalists represent all the vital powers of the three kingdoms and families of sublunary nature—mineral, plant, and animal (man considered as an animal). At one of her ears was the moon and at the other the sun, to indicate that these two were the agent and patient, or father and mother principles of all natural objects; and that Isis, or Nature, makes use of these two luminaries to communicate her powers to the whole empire of animals, vegetables, and minerals. On the back of her neck were the characters of the planets and the signs of the zodiac which assisted the planets in their functions. This signified that the heavenly influences directed the destinies of the principles and sperms of all things, because they were the governors of all sublunary bodies, which they transformed into little worlds made in the image of the greater universe.

Isis holds in her right hand a small sailing ship with the spindle of a spinning wheel for its mast. From the top of the mast projects a water jug, its handle shaped like a serpent swelled with venom. This indicates that Isis steers the bark of life, full of troubles and miseries, on the stormy ocean of Time. The spindle symbolizes the fact that she spins and cuts the thread of Life. These emblems further signify that Isis abounds in humidity, by means of which she nourishes all natural bodies, preserving them from the heat of the sun by humidifying them with nutritious moisture from the atmosphere. Moisture supports vegetation, but this subtle humidity (life ether) is always more or less infected by some venom proceeding from corruption or decay. It must be purified by being brought into contact with the invisible cleansing fire of Nature. This fire digests, perfects, and revitalizes this substance, in order that the humidity may become a universal medicine to heal and renew all the bodies in Nature.

The serpent throws off its skin annually and is thereby renewed (symbolic of the resurrection of the spiritual life from the material nature). This renewal of the earth takes place every spring, when the vivifying spirit of the sun returns to the countries of the Northern Hemisphere.

The symbolic Virgin carries in her left hand a sistrum and a cymbal, or square frame of metal, which when struck gives the keynote of Nature (Fa); sometimes also an olive branch, to indicate the harmony she preserves among natural things with her regenerating power. By the processes of death and corruption she gives life to a number of creatures of diverse forms through periods of perpetual change. The cymbal is made square instead of the usual triangular shape in order to symbolize that all things are transmuted and regenerated according to the harmony of the four elements.

Dr. Sigismund Bacstrom believed that if a physician could establish harmony among the elements of earth, fire, air, and water, and unite them into a stone (the Philosopher's Stone) symbolized by the six-pointed star or two interlaced triangles, he would possess the means of healing all disease. Dr. Bacstrom further stated that there was no doubt in his mind that the universal, omnipresent fire (spirit) of Nature "does all and is all in all." By attraction, repulsion, motion, heat, sublimation, evaporation, exsiccation, inspissation, coagulation, and fixation, the Universal Fire (Spirit) manipulates matter, and manifests throughout creation. Any individual who can understand these principles and adapt them to the three departments of Nature becomes a true philosopher.

From the right breast of Isis protruded a bunch of grapes and from the left an ear of corn or a sheaf of wheat, golden in color. These indicate that Nature is the source of nutrition for plant, animal, and human life, nourishing all things from herself. The golden color in the wheat (corn) indicates that in the sunlight or spiritual gold is concealed the first sperm of all life.

On the girdle surrounding the upper part of the body of the statue appear a number of mysterious emblems. The girdle is joined together in front by four golden plates (the elements), placed in the form of a square. This signified that Isis, or Nature, the first matter (alchemical terminology), was the essence of the four elements (life, light, heat, and force), which quintessence generated all things. Numerous stars are represented on this girdle, thereby indicating their influence in darkness as well as the influence of the sun in light. Isis is the Virgin immortalized in the constellation of Virgo, where the World Mother is placed with the serpent under her feet and a crown of stars on her head. In her arms she carries a sheaf of grain and sometimes the young Sun God.

The statue of Isis was placed on a pedestal of dark stone ornamented with rams' heads. Her feet trod upon a number of venomous reptiles. This indicates that Nature has power to free from acidity or saltness all corrosives and to overcome all impurities from terrestrial corruption adhering to bodies. The rams' heads indicate that the most auspicious time for the generation of life is during the period when the sun passes through the sign of Aries. The serpents under her feet indicate that Nature is inclined to preserve life and to heal disease by expelling impurities and corruption.

In this sense the axioms known to the ancient philosophers are verified; namely:

> *Nature contains Nature;*
> *Nature rejoices in her own nature;*
> *Nature surmounts Nature;*
> *Nature cannot be amended but in her own nature.*

Therefore, in contemplating the statue of Isis, we must not lose sight of the occult sense of its allegories; otherwise, the Virgin remains an inexplicable enigma.

From a golden ring on her left arm a line descends, to the end of which is suspended a deep box filled with flaming coals and incense. Isis, or Nature personified, carries with her the sacred fire, religiously preserved and kept burning in a special temple by the vestal virgins. This fire is the genuine, immortal flame of Nature—ethereal, essential, the author of life. The inconsumable oil, the balsam of life, so much praised by the wise and so often referred to in the Scriptures, is frequently symbolized as the fuel of this immortal flame.

From the right arm of the figure also descends a thread, to the end of which is fastened a pair of scales, to denote the exactitude of Nature in her weights and measures. Isis is often represented as the symbol of Justice, because Nature is eternally consistent.

The World Virgin is sometimes shown standing between two great pillars—the Jachin and Boaz of Freemasonry—symbolizing the fact that Nature attains productivity by means of polarity. As wisdom personified, Isis stands between the pillars of opposites, demonstrating that understanding is always found at the point of equilibrium and that truth is often crucified between the two thieves of apparent contradiction.

The sheen of gold in her dark hair indicates that while she is lunar, her power is due to the sun's rays, from which she secures her ruddy complexion.

As the moon is robed in the reflected light of the sun, so Isis, like the virgin of Revelation, is clothed in the glory of solar luminosity. Apuleius states that while he was sleeping he beheld the venerable goddess Isis rising out of the ocean. The ancients realized that the primary forms of life first came out of water, and modern science concurs in this view. H. G. Wells, in his *Outline of History,* describing primitive life on the earth, states: "But though the ocean and inter-tidal water already swarmed with life, the land above the high-tide line was still, so far as we can guess, a stony wilderness without a trace of life." In the next chapter he adds: "Wherever the shore-line ran there was life, and that life went on in and by and with water as its home, its medium, and its fundamental neces-sity." The ancients believed that the universal sperm proceeded with warm vapor, humid but fiery. The veiled Isis, whose very coverings represent vapor, is symbolic of this humidity, which is the carrier or vehicle for the sperm life of the sun, represented by a child in her arms. Because the sun, moon, and stars in set-ting appear to sink into the sea and also because the water receives their rays into itself, the sea was believed to be the breeding ground for the sperm of living things. The sperm is generated from the combination of the influences of the celestial bodies; hence Isis is sometimes represented as pregnant.

Frequently the statue of Isis was accompanied by the figure of a large black and white ox. The ox represents either Osiris as Taurus, the bull of the zodiac, or Apis, an animal sacred to Osiris because of its peculiar markings and color-ings. Among the Egyptians, the bull was a beast of burden. Hence the presence of the animal was a reminder of the labors patiently performed by Nature that all creatures may have life and health. Harpocrates, the God of Silence, holding his fingers to his mouth, often accompanies the statue of Isis. He warns all to keep the secrets of the wise from those unfit to know them.

The Druids of Britain and Gaul had a deep knowledge concerning the mys-teries of Isis and worshiped her under the symbol of the moon. Godfrey Higgins considers it a mistake to regard Isis as synonymous with the moon. The moon was chosen for Isis because of its dominion over water. The Druids considered the sun to be the father and the moon the mother of all things. By means of these symbols they worshiped Universal Nature.

The figure of Isis is sometimes used to represent the occult and magical arts, such as necromancy, invocation, sorcery, and thaumaturgy. In one of the myths concerning her, Isis is said to have conjured the invincible God of Eterni-ties, *Ra,* to tell her his secret and sacred name, which he did. This name is equivalent to the Lost Word of Masonry. By means of this Word, a magician can demand obedience from the invisible and superior deities. The priests of Isis became adepts in the use of the unseen forces of Nature. They understood hypnotism, mesmerism, and similar practices long before the modern world dreamed of their existence.

Plutarch describes the requisites of a follower of Isis in this manner: "For as 'tis not the length of the beard, or the coarseness of the habit which makes a philosopher, so neither will those frequent shavings, or the mere wearing [of] a linen vestment constitute a votary of Isis; but he alone is a true servant or follower of this Goddess, who after he has heard, and been made acquainted in a proper manner with the history of the actions of these Gods, searches into the hidden truths which lie concealed under them, and examines the whole by the dictates of reason and philosophy."

During the Middle Ages the troubadours of Central Europe preserved in song the legends of this Egyptian goddess. They composed sonnets to the most beautiful woman in the world. Though few ever discovered her identity, she was *Sophia,* the Virgin of Wisdom, whom all the philosophers of the world have wooed. Isis represents the mystery of motherhood, which the ancients recognized as the most apparent proof of Nature's omniscient wisdom and God's overshadowing power. To the modern seeker she is the epitome of the Great Unknown, and only those who unveil her will be able to solve the mysteries of life, death, generation, and regeneration.

Mummification of the Egyptian Dead

Servius, commenting on Virgil's *Æneid,* observes that "the wise Egyptians took care to embalm their bodies, and deposit them in catacombs, in order that the soul might be preserved for a long time in connection with the body, and might not soon be alienated; while the Romans, with an opposite design, committed the remains of their dead to the funeral pyre, intending that the vital spark might immediately be restored to the general element, or return to its pristine nature." (From Prichard's *An Analysis of the Egyptian Mythology.*)

No complete records are available which give the secret doctrine of the Egyptians concerning the relationship existing between the spirit, or consciousness, and the body which it inhabited. It is reasonably certain, however, that Pythagoras, who had been initiated in the Egyptian temples, when he promulgated the doctrine of metempsychosis, restated, in part at least, the teachings of the Egyptian initiates. The popular supposition that the Egyptians mummified their dead in order to preserve the form for a physical resurrection is untenable in the light of modern knowledge regarding their philosophy of death. In the fourth book of *On Abstinence from Animal Food,* Porphyry describes an Egyptian custom of purifying the dead by removing the contents of the abdominal cavity, which they placed in a separate chest. He then reproduces the following oration which had been translated out of the Egyptian tongue by Euphantus: "O sovereign Sun, and all ye Gods who impart life to men, receive me, and deliver me to the eternal Gods as a cohabitant. For I have always piously worshipped those divinities which were pointed out to me by my parents as long as I lived in this age, and have likewise always honored those who procreated my body. And, with respect to other men, I have never slain any one, nor defrauded any one of what he deposited with me, nor have I committed any other atrocious deed. If, therefore, during my life I have acted erroneously, by eating or drinking things which it is unlawful to eat or drink, I have not erred through myself, but through these" (pointing to the chest which contained the viscera). The removal of the organs identified as the seat of the appetites was considered equivalent to the purification of the body from their evil influences.

So literally did the early Christians interpret their Scriptures that they preserved the bodies of their dead by pickling them in salt water, so that on the day of resurrection the spirit of the dead might reenter a complete and perfectly preserved body. Believing that the incisions necessary to the embalming process and the removal of the internal organs would prevent the return of the spirit to its body, the Christians buried their dead without resorting to the more elaborate mummification methods employed by the Egyptian morticians.

In his work on *Egyptian Magic,* S.S.D.D. hazards the following speculation concerning the esoteric purposes behind the practice of mummification. "There is every reason to suppose," he says, "that only those who had received some grade of initiation were mummified; for it is certain that, in the eyes of the Egyptians, mummification effectually prevented reincarnation. Reincarnation was necessary to imperfect souls, to those who had failed to pass the tests of initiation; but for those who had the Will and the capacity to enter the Secret Adytum, there was seldom necessity for that liberation of the soul which is said to be effected by the destruction of the body. The body of the Initiate was therefore preserved after death as a species of Talisman or material basis for the manifestation of the Soul upon earth."

During the period of its inception mummification was limited to the Pharaoh and such other persons of royal rank as presumably partook of the attributes of the great Osiris, the divine, mummified King of the Egyptian Underworld.

IX

The Sun,
a Universal Deity

The adoration of the sun was one of the earliest and most natural forms of religious expression. Complex modern theologies are merely involvements and amplifications of this simple aboriginal belief. The primitive mind, recognizing the beneficent power of the solar orb, adored it as the proxy of the Supreme Deity. Concerning the origin of sun worship, Albert Pike makes the following concise statement in his *Morals and Dogma:* "To them [aboriginal peoples] he [the sun] was the innate fire of bodies, the fire of Nature. Author of Life, heat, and ignition, he was to them the efficient cause of all generation, for without him there was no movement, no existence, no form. He was to them immense, indivisible, imperishable, and everywhere present. It was their need of light, and of his creative energy, that was felt by all men; and nothing was more fearful to them than his absence. His beneficent influences caused his identification with the Principle of Good; and the BRAHMA of the Hindus, and MITHRAS of the Persians, and ATHOM, AMUN, PHTHA, and OSIRIS, of the Egyptians, the BEL of the Chaldeans, the ADONAI of the Phoenicians, the ADONIS and APOLLO of the Greeks, became but personifications of the Sun, the regenerating Principle, image of that fecundity which perpetuates and rejuvenates the world's existence."

Among all the nations of antiquity, altars, mounds, and temples were dedicated to the worship of the orb of day. The ruins of these sacred places yet remain, notable among them being the pyramids of Yucatan and Egypt, the snake mounds of the American Indians, the Zikkurats of Babylon and Chaldea, the round towers of Ireland, and the massive rings of uncut stone in Britain and Normandy. The Tower of Babel, which, according to the Scriptures, was built so that man might reach up to God, was probably an astronomical observatory.

THE WINGED GLOBE OF EGYPT.

This symbol, which appears over the pylons or gates of many Egyptian palaces and temples, is emblematic of the three persons of the Egyptian Trinity. The wings, the serpents, and the solar orb are the insignia of Ammon, Ra, and Osiris.

Many early priests and prophets, both pagan and Christian, were versed in astronomy and astrology; their writings are best understood when read in the light of these ancient sciences. With the growth of man's knowledge of the constitution and periodicity of the heavenly bodies, astronomical principles and terminology were introduced into his religious systems. The tutelary gods were given planetary thrones, the celestial bodies being named after the deities assigned to them. The fixed stars were divided into constellations, and through these constellations wandered the sun and its planets, the latter with their accompanying satellites.

The Solar Trinity

The sun, as supreme among the celestial bodies visible to the astronomers of antiquity, was assigned to the highest of the gods and became symbolic of the supreme authority of the Creator Himself. From a deep philosophic consideration of the powers and principles of the sun has come the concept of the Trinity as it is understood in the world today. The tenet of a Triune Divinity is not peculiar to Christian or Mosaic theology, but forms a conspicuous part of the dogma of the greatest religions of both ancient and modern times. The Persians, Hindus, Babylonians, and Egyptians had their Trinities. In every instance these represented the threefold form of one Supreme Intelligence. In modern Masonry, the Deity is symbolized by an equilateral triangle, its three sides representing the primary manifestations of the Eternal One who is Himself represented as a tiny flame, called by the Hebrews *Yod* (ᐟ). Jakob Böhme, the Teutonic mystic, calls the Trinity *The Three Witnesses,* by means of which the Invisible is made known to the visible, tangible universe.

The origin of the Trinity is obvious to anyone who will observe the daily manifestations of the sun. This orb, being the symbol of all Light, has three distinct phases: rising, midday, and setting. The philosophers therefore divided the life of all things into three distinct parts: growth, maturity, and decay. Between the twilight of dawn and the twilight of evening is the high noon of resplendent glory. God the Father, the Creator of the world, is symbolized by the dawn. His color is blue, because the sun rising in the morning is veiled in blue mist. God the Son, the Illuminating One sent to bear witness of His Father before all worlds, is the celestial globe at noonday, radiant and magnificent, the maned Lion of Judah, the Golden-haired Savior of the World. Yellow is His color and His power is without end. God the Holy Ghost is the sunset phase, when the orb of day, robed in flaming red, rests for a moment upon the horizon line and then vanishes into the darkness of the night to wander in the lower worlds and later rise again triumphant from the embrace of darkness.

To the Egyptians the sun was the symbol of immortality, for, while it died each night, it rose again with each ensuing dawn. Not only has the sun this diurnal activity, but it also has its annual pilgrimage, during which time it passes successively through the twelve celestial houses of the heavens, remaining in each for thirty days. Added to these it has a third path of travel, which is called the *precession of the equinoxes,* in which it retrogrades around the zodiac through the twelve signs at the rate of one degree every seventy-two years.

Concerning the annual passage of the sun through the twelve houses of the heavens, Robert Hewitt Brown, 32°, makes the following statement: "The Sun, as he pursued his way among these 'living creatures' of the zodiac, was said, in allegorical language, either to assume the nature of or to triumph over the sign he entered. The sun thus became a Bull in Taurus, and was worshipped as such by the Egyptians under the name of Apis, and by the Assyrians as Bel, Baal, or Bul. In Leo the sun became a Lion-slayer, Hercules, and an Archer in Sagittarius. In Pisces, the Fishes, he was a fish—Dagon, or Vishnu, the fish-god of the Philistines and Hindoos."

A careful analysis of the religious systems of pagandom uncovers much evidence of the fact that its priests served the solar energy and that their Supreme Deity was in every case this Divine Light personified. Godfrey Higgins, after thirty years of inquiry into the origin of religious beliefs, is of the opinion that "All the Gods of antiquity resolved themselves into the solar fire, sometimes itself as God, or sometimes an emblem or shekinah of that higher principle, known by the name of the creative Being or God."

The Egyptian priests in many of their ceremonies wore the skins of lions, which were symbols of the solar orb, owing to the fact that the sun is exalted, dignified, and most fortunately placed in the constellation of Leo, which he rules and which was at one time the keystone of the celestial arch. Again, Hercules is the Solar Deity, for as this mighty hunter performed his twelve labors, so the sun, in traversing the twelve houses of the zodiacal band, performs during his pilgrimage twelve essential and benevolent labors for the human race and for Nature in general. Hercules, like the Egyptian priests, wore the skin of a lion for a girdle. Samson, the Hebrew hero, as his name implies, is also a solar deity. His fight with the Nubian lion, his battles with the Philistines, who represent the Powers of Darkness, and his memorable feat of carrying off the gates of Gaza, all refer to aspects of solar activity. Many of the ancient peoples had more than one solar deity; in fact, all of the gods and goddesses were supposed to partake, in part at least, of the sun's effulgence.

The golden ornaments used by the priestcraft of the various world religions are again a subtle reference to the solar energy, as are also the crowns of kings. In ancient times, crowns had a number of points extending outward like the rays of the sun, but modern conventionalism has, in many cases, either removed the points or else bent them inward, gathered them together, and placed an orb or cross upon the point where they meet. Many of the ancient prophets, philosophers, and dignitaries carried a scepter, the upper end of which bore a representation of the solar globe surrounded by emanating rays. All the kingdoms of earth were but copies of the kingdoms of Heaven, and the kingdoms of Heaven were best symbolized by the solar kingdom, in which the sun was the supreme ruler, the planets his privy council, and all Nature the subjects of his empire.

Many deities have been associated with the sun. The Greeks believed that Apollo, Bacchus, Dionysos, Sabazius, Hercules, Jason, Ulysses, Zeus, Uranus, and Vulcan partook of either the visible or invisible attributes of the sun. The Norwegians regarded Balder the Beautiful as a solar deity, and Odin is often connected with the celestial orb, especially because of his one eye. Among the Egyptians, Osiris, Ra, Anubis, Hermes, and even the mysterious Ammon himself had points of resemblance with the solar disc. Isis was the mother of the sun, and even Typhon, the Destroyer, was supposed to be a form of solar energy. The Egyptian sun myth finally centered around the person of a mysterious deity called *Serapis*. The two Central American deities, *Tezcatlipoca* and *Quetzalcoatl*, while often associated with the winds, were also undoubtedly solar gods.

In Masonry the sun has many symbols. One expression of the solar energy is Solomon, whose name SOL-OM-ON is the name for the Supreme Light in three different languages. Hiram Abiff, the CHiram (Hiram) of the Chaldees, is also a solar deity, and the story of his attack and murder by the Ruffians, with its solar interpretation, will be found in the chapter *The Hiramic Legend*. A striking example of the important part which the sun plays in the symbols and rituals of Freemasonry is given by George Oliver, D.D., in his *Dictionary of Symbolical Masonry,* as follows:

"The sun rises in the east, and in the east is the place for the Worshipful Master. As the sun is the source of all light and warmth, so should the Worshipful Master enliven and warm the brethren to their work. Among the ancient Egyptians the sun was the symbol of divine providence." The hierophants of the Mysteries were adorned with many insignia emblematic of solar power. The sunbursts of gilt embroidery on the back of the vestments of the Catholic priesthood signify that the priest is also an emissary and representative of *Sol Invictus.*

Christianity and the Sun

For reasons which they doubtless considered sufficient, those who chronicled the life and acts of Jesus found it advisable to metamorphose him into a solar deity. The historical Jesus was forgotten; nearly all the salient incidents recorded in the four Gospels have their correlations in the movements, phases, or functions of the heavenly bodies.

Among other allegories borrowed by Christianity from pagan antiquity is the story of the beautiful, blue-eyed Sun God, with His golden hair falling upon His shoulders, robed from head to foot in spotless white and carrying in His arms the Lamb of God, symbolic of the vernal equinox. This handsome youth is a composite of Apollo, Osiris, Orpheus, Mithras, and Bacchus, for He has certain characteristics in common with each of these pagan deities.

The philosophers of Greece and Egypt divided the life of the sun during the year into four parts; therefore they symbolized the Solar Man by four different figures. When He was born in the winter solstice, the Sun God was symbolized as a dependent infant who in some mysterious manner had managed to escape the Powers of Darkness seeking to destroy Him while He was still in the cradle of winter. The sun, being weak at this season of the year, had no golden rays (or locks of hair), but the survival of the light through the darkness of winter was symbolized by one tiny hair which alone adorned the head of the Celestial Child. (As the birth of the sun took place in Capricorn, it was often represented as being suckled by a goat.)

At the vernal equinox, the sun had grown to be a beautiful youth. His golden hair hung in ringlets on his shoulders and his light, as Schiller said, extended to all parts of infinity. At the summer solstice, the sun became a strong man, heavily bearded, who, in the prime of maturity, symbolized the fact that Nature at this period of the year is strongest and most fecund. At the autumnal equinox, the sun was pictured as an aged man, shuffling along with bended back and whitened locks into the oblivion of winter darkness. Thus, twelve months were assigned to the sun as the length of its life. During this period it circled the twelve signs of the zodiac in a magnificent triumphal march. When fall came, it entered, like Samson, into the house of Delilah (Virgo), where its rays were cut off and it lost its strength. In Masonry, the cruel winter months are symbolized by three murderers who sought to destroy the God of Light and Truth.

The coming of the sun was hailed with joy; the time of its departure was viewed as a period to be set aside for sorrow and unhappiness. This glorious, radiant orb of day, the true light "which lighteth every man who cometh into the world," the supreme benefactor, who raised all things from the dead, who fed the hungry multitudes, who stilled the tempest, who after dying rose again and restored all things to life—this Supreme Spirit of humanitarianism and philanthropy is known to Christendom as Christ, the Redeemer of worlds, the Only Begotten of The Father, the Word made Flesh, and the Hope of Glory.

The Birthday of the Sun

The pagans set aside the 25th of December as the birthday of the Solar Man. They rejoiced, feasted, gathered in processions, and made offerings in the temples. The darkness of winter was over and the glorious son of light was returning to the Northern Hemisphere. With his last effort the old Sun God had torn down the house of the Philistines (the Spirits of Darkness) and had cleared the way for the new sun who was born that day from the depths of the earth amidst the symbolic beasts of the lower world.

Concerning this season of celebration, an anonymous Master of Arts of Balliol College, Oxford, in his scholarly treatise, *Mankind—Their Origin and Destiny,* says: "The Romans also had their solar festival, and their games of the circus in honor of the birth of the god of day. It took place the eighth day before the kalends of January—that is, on December 25. Servius, in his commentary on verse 720 of the seventh book of the Æneid, in which Virgil speaks of the new sun, says that, properly speaking, the sun is new on the 8th of the Kalends of January—that is, December 25. In the time of Leo I. (Leo, Serm. xxi., De Nativ. Dom. p. 148), some of the Fathers of the Church said that 'what rendered the festival (of Christmas) venerable was less the birth of Jesus Christ than the return, and, as they expressed it, the new birth of the sun.' It was on the same day that the birth of the Invincible Sun (Natalis solis invicti), was celebrated at Rome, as can be seen in the Roman calendars, published in the reign of Constantine and of Julian (Hymn to the Sun, p. 155). This epithet 'Invictus' is the same as the Persians gave to this same god, whom they worshipped by the name of Mithra, and whom they caused to be born in a grotto (Justin. Dial. cum Tryph. p. 305), just as he is represented as being born in a stable, under the name of Christ, by the Christians."

Concerning the Catholic Feast of the Assumption and its parallel in astronomy, the same author adds: "At the end of eight months, when the sun-god, having increased, traverses the eighth sign, he absorbs the celestial Virgin in his fiery course, and she disappears in the midst of the luminous rays and the glory of her son. This phenomenon, which takes place every year about the middle of August, gave rise to a festival which still exists, and in which it is supposed that the mother of Christ, laying aside her earthly life, is associated with the glory of her son, and is placed at his side in the heavens. The Roman calendar of Columella (Col. 1. II. cap. ii. p. 429) marks the death or disappearance of Virgo at this period. The sun, he says, passes into Virgo on the thirteenth day before the kalends of September. This is where the Catholics place the Feast of the Assumption, or the reunion of the Virgin to her Son. This feast was formerly called the feast of the Passage of the Virgin (Beausobre, tome i. p. 350); and in the Library of the Fathers (Bibl. Patr. vol. II. part ii. p. 212) we have an account of the Passage of the Blessed Virgin. The ancient Greeks and Romans fix the assumption of Astraea, who is also this same Virgin, on that day."

This Virgin mother, giving birth to the Sun God which Christianity has so faithfully preserved, is a reminder of the inscription concerning her Egyptian prototype, Isis, which appeared on the Temple of Sais: *"The fruit which l have brought forth is the Sun."* While the Virgin was associated with the moon by the early pagans, there is no doubt that they also understood her position as a constellation in the heavens, for nearly all the peoples of antiquity credit her as being the mother of the sun, and they realized that although the moon could not occupy that position, the sign of Virgo could, and did, give birth to the sun out of her side on the 25th day of December. Albertus Magnus states, "We know that the sign of the Celestial Virgin rose over the Horizon at the moment at which we fix the birth of our Lord Jesus Christ."

Among certain of the Arabian and Persian astronomers the three stars forming the sword belt of Orion were called the Magi who came to pay homage to the young Sun God. The author of *Mankind—Their Origin and Destiny* contributes the following additional information: "In Cancer, which had risen to the meridian at midnight, is the constellation of the Stable and of the Ass. The ancients called it Præsepe Jovis. In the north the stars of the Bear are seen, called by the Arabians Martha and Mary, and also the coffin of Lazarus." Thus the esotericism of pagandom was embodied in Christianity, although its keys are lost. The Christian church blindly follows ancient customs, and when asked for a reason gives superficial and unsatisfactory explanations, either forgetting or ignoring the indisputable fact that each religion is based upon the secret doctrines of its predecessor.

The Three Suns

The solar orb, like the nature of man, was divided by the ancient sages into three separate bodies. According to the mystics, there are three suns in each solar system, analogous to the three centers of life in each individual constitution. These are called three lights: the *spiritual* sun, the *intellectual* or *soular* sun, and the *material* sun (now symbolized in Freemasonry by three candles). The spiritual sun manifests the power of God the Father; the soular sun radiates the life of God the Son; and the material sun is the vehicle of manifestation for God the Holy Spirit. Man's

FROM MOOR'S *HINDU PANTHEON.*

SURYA, THE REGENT OF THE SUN.

Moor describes this figure as follows: "The cast is nine inches in height, representing the glorious god of day holding the attributes of VISHNU, seated on a seven-headed serpent; his car drawn by a seven-headed horse, driven by the legless ARUN, a personification of the dawn, or AURORA." (See Moor's *Hindu Pantheon.*)

nature was divided by the mystics into three distinct parts: spirit, soul, and body. His physical body was unfolded and vitalized by the material sun; his spiritual nature was illuminated by the spiritual sun; and his intellectual nature was redeemed by the true *light of grace*—the soular sun. The alignment of these three globes in the heavens was one explanation offered for the peculiar fact that the orbits of the planets are not circular but elliptical.

The pagan priests always considered the solar system as a *Grand Man,* and drew their analogy of these three centers of activity from the three main centers of life in the human body: the brain, the heart, and the generative system. The Transfiguration of Jesus describes three tabernacles, the largest being in the center (the heart), and a smaller one on either side (the brain and the generative system). It is possible that the philosophical hypothesis of the existence of the three suns is based upon a peculiar natural phenomenon which has occurred many times in history. In the fifty-first year after Christ three suns were seen at once in the sky and also in the sixty-sixth year. In the sixty-ninth year, two suns were seen together. According to William Lilly, between the years 1156 and 1648 twenty similar occurrences were recorded.

Recognizing the sun as the supreme benefactor of the material world, Hermetists believed that there was a spiritual sun which ministered to the needs of the invisible and divine part of Nature—human and universal. Anent this subject, the great Paracelsus wrote: "There is an earthly sun, which is the cause of all heat, and all who are able to see may see the sun; and those who are blind and cannot see him may feel his heat. There is an Eternal Sun, which is the source of all wisdom, and those whose spiritual senses have awakened to life will see that sun and be conscious of His existence; but those who have not attained spiritual consciousness may yet feel His power by an inner faculty which is called Intuition."

Certain Rosicrucian scholars have given special appellations to these three phases of the sun: the spiritual sun they called *Vulcan;* the soular and intellectual sun, *Christ* and *Lucifer* respectively; and the material sun, the Jewish Demiurgus *Jehovah.* Lucifer here represents the intellectual mind without the illumination of the spiritual mind; therefore it is "the false light." The false light is finally overcome and redeemed by the true light of the soul, called the *Second Logos* or *Christ.* The secret processes by which the Luciferian intellect is transmuted into the Christly intellect constitute one of the great secrets of alchemy, and are symbolized by the process of transmuting base metals into gold.

In the rare treatise, *The Secret Symbols of The Rosicrucians,* Franz Hartmann defines the sun alchemically as: "The symbol of Wisdom. The Centre of Power or Heart of things. The Sun is a centre of energy and a storehouse of power. Each living being contains within itself a centre of life, which may grow to be a Sun. In the heart of the regenerated, the divine power, stimulated by the Light of the Logos, grows into a Sun which illuminates his mind." In a note, the same author amplifies his description by adding: "The terrestrial sun is the image or reflection of the invisible celestial sun; the former is in the realm of Spirit what the latter is in the realm of Matter; but the latter receives its power from the former."

In the majority of cases, the religions of antiquity agree that the material visible sun was a reflector rather than a source of power. The sun was sometimes represented as a shield carried on the arm of the Sun God, as for example, Frey, the Scandinavian Solar Deity. This sun reflected the light of the invisible *spiritual* sun, which was the true source of life, light, and truth. The physical nature of the universe is receptive; it is a realm of effects. The invisible causes of these effects belong to the spiritual world. Hence, the spiritual world is the sphere of *causation;* the material world is the sphere of *effects;* while the intellectual—or soul—world is the sphere of *mediation.* Thus Christ, the personified higher intellect and soul nature, is called "the Mediator" who, by virtue of His position and power, says: "No man cometh to the Father, but by me."

What the sun is to the solar system, the spirit is to the bodies of man; for his natures, organs, and functions are as planets surrounding the central life (or sun) and living upon its emanations. The solar power in man is divided into three parts, which are termed the threefold human spirit of man. All three of these spiritual natures are said to be radiant and transcendent; united, they form the Divinity in man. Man's threefold lower nature—consisting of his physical organism, his emotional nature, and his mental faculties—reflects the light of his threefold Divinity and bears witness of It in the physical world. Man's three bodies are symbolized by an upright triangle; his threefold spiritual nature by an inverted triangle. These two triangles, when united in the form of a six-pointed star, were called by the Jews "the Star of David," "the Signet of Solomon," and are more commonly known today as "the Star of Zion." These triangles symbolize the spiritual and material universes linked together in the constitution of the human creature, who partakes of both Nature and Divinity. Man's animal nature partakes of the earth; his divine nature of the heavens; his human nature of the mediator.

The Celestial Inhabitants of the Sun

The Rosicrucians and the Illuminati, describing the angels, archangels, and other celestial creatures, declared that they resembled small suns, being centers of radiant energy surrounded by streamers of Vrilic force. From these outpouring streamers of force is derived the popular belief that angels have wings. These wings are corona-like fans of light, by means of which the celestial creatures propel themselves through the subtle essences of the superphysical worlds.

True mystics are unanimous in their denial of the theory that the angels and archangels are human in form, as so often pictured. A human figure would be utterly useless in the ethereal substances through which they manifest. Science has long debated the probability of the other planets being inhabited. Objections to the idea are based upon the argument that creatures with human organisms could not possibly exist in the environments of Mars, Jupiter, Uranus, and Neptune. This argument fails to take into account Nature's universal law of adjustment to environment. The ancients asserted that life originated from the sun, and that everything when bathed in the light of the solar orb was capable of absorbing the solar life elements and later radiating them as flora and fauna. One philosophical concept regarded the sun as a parent and the planets as embryos still connected to the solar body by means of ethereal umbilical cords which served as channels to convey life and nourishment to the planets.

Some secret orders have taught that the sun was inhabited by a race of creatures with bodies composed of a radiant, spiritual ether not unlike in its constituency the actual glowing ball of the sun itself. The solar heat had no harmful effect upon them, because their organisms were sufficiently refined and sensitized to harmonize with the sun's tremendous vibratory rate. These creatures resemble miniature suns, being a little larger than a dinner plate in size, although some of the more powerful are considerably larger. Their color is the golden white light of the sun, and from them emanate four streamers of Vril. These streamers are often of great length and are in constant motion. A peculiar palpitation is to be noted throughout the structure of the globe and is communicated in the form of ripples to the emanating streamers. The greatest and most luminous of these spheres is the Archangel Michael; and the entire order of solar life, which resemble him and dwell upon the sun, are called by modern Christians "the archangels" or "the spirits of the light."

The Sun in Alchemical Symbology

Gold is the metal of the sun and has been considered by many as crystallized sunlight. When gold is mentioned in alchemical tracts, it may be either the metal itself or the celestial orb which is the source, or spirit, of gold. Sulphur because of in fiery nature was also associated with the sun.

As gold was the symbol of spirit and the base metals represented man's lower nature, certain alchemists were called "miners" and were pictured with picks and shovels digging into the earth in search of the precious metal—those finer traits of character buried in the earthiness of materiality and ignorance. The diamond concealed in the heart of the black carbon illustrated the same principle. The Illuminati used a pearl hidden in the shell of an oyster at the bottom of the sea to signify spiritual powers. Thus the seeker after truth became a pearl-fisher: he descended into the sea of material illusion in search of understanding, termed by the initiates "the Pearl of Great Price."

When the alchemists stated that every animate and inanimate thing in the universe contained the seeds of gold, they meant that even the grains of sand possessed a spiritual nature, for gold was the spirit of all things. Concerning these seeds of spiritual gold the following Rosicrucian axiom is significant: "A seed is useless and impotent unless it is put in its appropriate matrix." Franz Hartmann comments on this axiom with these illuminating words: "A soul cannot develop and progress without an appropriate body, because it is the physical body that furnishes the material for its development." (See *In the Pronaos of the Temple of Wisdom*.)

The purpose of alchemy was not to make something out of nothing but rather to fertilize and nurture the seed which was already present. Its processes did not actually create gold but rather made the ever-present seed of gold grow and flourish. Everything which exists has a spirit—the seed of Divinity within itself—and regeneration is not the process of attempting to place something where it previously had not existed. Regeneration actually means the unfoldment of the omnipresent Divinity in man, that this Divinity may shine forth as a sun and illumine all with whom it comes in contact.

The Midnight Sun

Apuleius said when describing his initiation (*vide ante*): "At midnight I saw the sun shining with a splendid light." The midnight sun was also part of the mystery of alchemy. It symbolized the spirit in man shining through the darkness of his human organisms. It also referred to the *spiritual* sun in the solar system, which the mystic could see as well at midnight as at high noon, the material earth being powerless to obstruct the rays of this Divine orb. The mysterious lights which illuminated the temples of the Egyptian Mysteries during the nocturnal hours were said by some to be reflections of the *spiritual* sun gathered by the magical powers of the priests. The weird light seen ten miles below the surface of the earth by I-AM-THE-MAN in that remarkable Masonic allegory *Etidorhpa* (Aphrodite spelt backward) may well refer to the mysterious midnight sun of the ancient rites.

Primitive conceptions concerning the warfare between the principles of Good and Evil were often based upon the alternations of day and night. During the Middle Ages, the practices of black magic were confined to the nocturnal hours; and those who served the Spirit of Evil were called black magicians, while those who served the Spirit of Good were called white magicians. Black and white were associated respectively with night and day, and the endless conflict of light and shadow is alluded to many times in the mythologies of various peoples.

The Egyptian Demon, Typhon, was symbolized as part crocodile and part hog because these animals are gross and earthy in both appearance and temperament. Since the world began, living things have feared the darkness; those few creatures who use it as a shield for their maneuvers were usually connected with the Spirit of Evil. Consequently cats, bats, toads, and owls are associated with witchcraft. In certain parts of Europe it is still believed that at night black magicians assume the bodies of wolves and roam around destroying. From this notion originated the stories of the werewolves. Serpents, because they lived in the earth, were associated with the Spirit of Darkness. As the battle between Good and Evil centers around the use of the generative forces of Nature, winged serpents represent the regeneration of the animal nature of man or those Great Ones in whom this regeneration is complete. Among the Egyptians the sun's rays are often shown ending in human hands. Masons will find a connection between these hands and the well-known *Paw of the Lion* which raises all things to life with its grip.

Solar Colors

The theory so long held of three primary and four secondary colors is purely exoteric, for since the earliest periods it has been known that there are seven, and not three, primary colors, the human eye being capable of estimating only three of them. Thus, although green can be made by combining blue and yellow, there is also a true or primary green which is not a compound. This can be proved by breaking up the spectrum with a prism. Helmholtz found that the so-called secondary colors of the spectrum could not be broken up into their supposed primary colors. Thus the orange of the spectrum, if passed through a second prism, does not break up into red and yellow but remains orange.

Consciousness, intelligence, and force are fittingly symbolized by the colors blue, yellow, and red. The therapeutic effects of the colors, moreover, are in harmony with this concept, for blue is a fine, soothing, electrical color; yellow, a vitalizing and refining color; and red, an agitating and heat-giving color. It has also been demonstrated that minerals and plants affect the human constitution according to their colors. Thus a yellow flower generally yields a medicine that affects the constitution in a manner similar to yellow light or the musical tone *mi*. An orange flower will influence in a manner similar to orange light and, being one of the so-called secondary colors, corresponds either to the tone *re* or to the chord of *do* and *mi*.

The ancients conceived the spirit of man to correspond with the color blue, the mind with yellow, and the body with red. Heaven is therefore blue, earth yellow, and hell—or the underworld—red. The fiery condition of the inferno merely symbolizes the nature of the sphere or plane of force of which it is composed. In the Greek Mysteries the irrational sphere was always considered as red, for it represented that condition in which the consciousness is enslaved by the lusts and passions of the lower nature. In India certain of the gods—usually attributes of Vishnu—are depicted with blue skin to signify their divine and supermundane constitution. According to esoteric philosophy, blue is the true and sacred color of the sun. The apparent orange-yellow shade of this orb is the result of its rays being immersed in the substances of the illusionary world.

In the original symbolism of the Christian Church, colors were of first importance and their use was regulated according to carefully prepared rules. Since the Middle Ages, however, the carelessness with which colors have been employed has resulted in the loss of their deeper emblematic meanings. In its primary aspect, white or silver signified life, purity, innocence, joy, and light; red, the suffering and death of Christ and His saints, and also divine love, blood, and warfare or suffering; blue, the heavenly sphere and the states of godliness and contemplation; yellow or gold, glory, fruitfulness, and goodness; green, fecundity, youthfulness, and prosperity; violet, humility, deep affection, and sorrow; black, death, destruction, and humiliation. In early church art the colors of robes and ornaments also revealed whether a saint had been martyred, as well as the character of the work that he had done to deserve canonization.

In addition to the colors of the spectrum there are a vast number of vibratory color waves, some too low and others too high to be registered by the human optical apparatus. It is appalling to contemplate man's colossal ignorance concerning these vistas of abstract space. As in the past man explored unknown continents, so in the future, armed with curious implements fashioned for the purpose, he will explore these little known fastnesses of light, color, sound, and consciousness.

X

The Zodiac and Its Signs

t is difficult for this age to estimate correctly the profound effect produced upon the religions, philosophies, and sciences of antiquity by the study of the planets, luminaries, and constellations. Not without adequate reason were the Magi of Persia called the Star Gazers. The Egyptians were honored with a special appellation because of their proficiency in computing the power and motion of the heavenly bodies and their effect upon the destinies of nations and individuals.

Ruins of primitive astronomical observatories have been discovered in all parts of the world, although in many cases modern archæologists are unaware of the true purpose for which these structures were erected. While the telescope was unknown to ancient astronomers, they made many remarkable calculations with instruments cut from blocks of granite or pounded from sheets of brass and copper. In India such instruments are still in use, and they possess a high degree of accuracy. In Jaipur, Rajputana, India, an observatory consisting largely of immense stone sundials is still in operation. The famous Chinese observatory on the wall of Peking consists of immense bronze instruments, including a telescope in the form of a hollow tube without lenses.

The pagans looked upon the stars as living things, capable of influencing the destinies of individuals, nations, and races. That the early Jewish patriarchs believed that the celestial bodies participated in the affairs of men is evident to any student of Biblical literature, as, for example, in the Book of Judges: "They fought from heaven, even the stars in their courses fought against Sisera." The Chaldeans, Phœnicians, Egyptians, Persians, Hindus, and Chinese all had zodiacs that were much alike in general character, and different authorities have credited each of these nations with being the cradle of astrology and astronomy. The Central and North American Indians also had an understanding of the zodiac, but the patterns and numbers of the signs differed in many details from those of the Eastern Hemisphere.

The word *zodiac* is derived from the Greek ζωδιακός (*zodiakos*), which means "a circle of animals," or, as some believe, "little animals." It is the name given by the old pagan astronomers to a band of fixed stars about sixteen degrees wide, apparently encircling the earth. Robert Hewitt Brown, 32°, states that the Greek word *zodiakos* comes from *zo-on*, meaning "an animal." He adds: "This latter word is compounded directly from the primitive Egyptian radicals, *zo*, life, and *on*, a being."

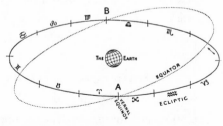

THE EQUINOXES AND SOLSTICES.

The plane of the zodiac intersects the celestial equator at an angle of approximately 23° 28'. The two points of intersection (*A* and *B*) are called the equinoxes.

The Greeks, and later other peoples influenced by their culture, divided the band of the zodiac into twelve sections, each being sixteen degrees in width and thirty degrees in length. These divisions were called the Houses of the Zodiac. The sun during its annual pilgrimage passed through each of these in turn. Imaginary creatures were traced in the star groups bounded by these rectangles; and because most of them were animal—or part animal—in form, they later became known as the Constellations, or Signs, of the Zodiac.

There is a popular theory concerning the origin of the zodiacal creatures to the effect that they were products of the imagination of shepherds, who, watching their flocks at night, occupied their minds by tracing the forms of animals and birds in the heavens. This theory is untenable, unless the "shepherds" be regarded as the shepherd priests of antiquity. It is unlikely that the zodiacal signs were derived from the star groups which they now represent. It is far more probable that the creatures assigned to the twelve houses are symbolic of the qualities and intensity of the sun's power while it occupies different parts of the zodiacal belt.

On this subject Richard Payne Knight writes: "The emblematical meaning, which certain animals were employed to signify, was only some particular property generalized; and, therefore, might easily be invented or discovered by the natural operation of the mind: but the collections of stars, named after certain animals, have no resemblance whatever to those animals; which are therefore merely signs of convention adopted to distinguish certain portions of the heavens, which were probably consecrated to those particular personified attributes, which they respectively represented." (*The Symbolical Language of Ancient Art and Mythology.*)

Some authorities are of the opinion that the zodiac was originally divided into ten (instead of twelve) houses, or "solar mansions." In early times there were two separate standards—one solar and the other lunar—used for the measurement of the months, years, and seasons. The solar year was composed of ten months of thirty-six days each, and five days sacred to the gods. The lunar year consisted of thirteen months of twenty-eight days each, with one day left over. The solar zodiac at that time consisted of ten houses of thirty-six degrees each.

The first six signs of the zodiac of twelve signs were regarded as benevolent, because the sun occupied them while traversing the Northern Hemisphere. The 6,000 years during which, according to the Persians, Ahura-Mazda ruled His universe in harmony and peace, were symbolic of these six signs. The second six were considered malevolent, because while the sun was traveling the Southern Hemisphere it was winter with the Greeks, Egyptians, and Persians. Therefore these six months were symbolic of the 6,000 years of misery and suffering caused by the evil genius of the Persians, Ahriman, who sought to overthrow the power of Ahura-Mazda.

Those who hold the opinion that before its revision by the Greeks the zodiac consisted of only ten signs adduce evidence to show that Libra (the Scales) was inserted into the zodiac by dividing the constellation of Virgo-Scorpio (at that time one sign) into two parts, thus establishing "the balance" at the point of equilibrium between the ascending northern and the descending southern signs. (See *The Rosicrucians, Their Rites and Mysteries*, by Hargrave Jennings.) On this subject Isaac Myer states: "We think that the Zodiacal constellations were first ten and represented an immense androgenic man or deity; subsequently this was changed, resulting in Scorpio and Virgo and making eleven; after this from Scorpio, Libra, the Balance, was taken, making the present twelve." (*The Qabbalah.*)

Each year the sun passes entirely around the zodiac and returns to the point from which it started—the vernal equinox—and each year it falls just a little short of making the complete circle of the heavens in the allotted period of time. As a result, it crosses the equator just a little behind the spot in the zodiacal sign where it crossed the previous year. Each sign of the zodiac consists of thirty degrees, and as the sun loses about one degree every seventy-two years, it regresses through one entire constellation (or sign) in approximately 2,160 years, and through the entire zodiac in about 25,920 years. (Authorities disagree concerning these figures.) This retrograde motion is called the *precession of the equinoxes.* This means that in the course of about 25,920 years, which constitute one Great Solar or Platonic Year, each one of the twelve constellations occupies a position at the vernal equinox for nearly 2,160 years, then gives place to the *previous* sign.

Among the ancients the sun was always symbolized by the figure and nature of the constellation through which it passed at the vernal equinox. For nearly the past 2,000 years the sun has crossed the equator at the vernal equinox in the constellation of Pisces (the Two Fishes). For the 2,160 years before that it crossed through the constellation of Aries (the Ram). Prior to that the vernal equinox was in the sign of Taurus (the Bull). It is probable that the form of the bull and the bull's proclivities were assigned to this constellation because the bull was used by the ancients to plow the fields, and the season set aside for plowing and furrowing corresponded to the time at which the sun reached the segment of the heavens named Taurus.

Albert Pike describes the reverence which the Persians felt for this sign and the method of astrological symbolism in vogue among them, thus: "In Zoroaster's cave of initiation, the Sun and Planets were represented, overhead, in gems and gold, as was also the Zodiac. The Sun appeared, emerging from the back of Taurus." In the constellation of the Bull are also to be found the "Seven Sisters"—the sacred Pleiades—famous to Freemasonry as the Seven Stars at the upper end of the Sacred Ladder.

In ancient Egypt it was during this period—when the vernal equinox was in the sign of Taurus—that the Bull, Apis, was sacred to the Sun God, who was worshiped through the animal equivalent of the celestial sign which he had impregnated with his presence at the time of its crossing into the Northern Hemisphere. This is the meaning of an ancient saying that the celestial Bull "broke the egg of the year with his horns."

Sampson Arnold Mackey, in his *Mythological Astronomy of the Ancients Demonstrated,* makes note of two very interesting points concerning the bull in Egyptian symbolism. Mr. Mackey is of the opinion that the motion of the earth that we know as the alternation of the poles has resulted in a great change of relative position of the equator and the zodiacal band. He believes that originally the band of the zodiac was at right angles to the equator, with the sign of Cancer opposite the north pole and the sign of Capricorn opposite the south pole. It is possible that the Orphic symbol of the serpent twisted around the egg attempts to show the motion of the sun in relation to the earth under such conditions. Mr. Mackey advances the *Labyrinth of Crete,* the name *Abraxas,* and the magic formula, *abracadabra,* among other things, to substantiate his theory. Concerning *abracadabra* he states:

"But the slow progressive disappearance of the Bull is most happily commemorated in the vanishing series of letters so emphatically expressive of the great astronomical fact. For ABRACADABRA is The Bull, the only Bull. The ancient sentence split into its component parts stands thus: Ab'r-achad-ab'ra, *i. e.,* Ab'r, the Bull; achad, the only, &c.—Achad is one of the names of the Sun, given him in consequence of his Shining ALONE,—he is the ONLY Star to be seen when he is seen—the remaining ab'ra, makes the whole to be, The Bull, the only Bull; while the repetition of the name omitting a letter, till all is gone, is the most simple, yet most satisfactory method that could have been devised to preserve the memory of the fact; and the name of Sorapis, or Serapis, given to the Bull at the above ceremony puts it beyond all doubt.* * * This word (Abracadabra) disappears in eleven decreasing stages; as in the figure. And what is very remarkable, a body with three heads is folded up by a Serpent with eleven Coils, and placed by Sorapis: and the eleven Volves of the Serpent form a triangle similar to that formed by the ELEVEN diminishing lines of the abracadabra."

Nearly every religion of the world shows traces of astrological influence. The Old Testament of the Jews, its writings overshadowed by Egyptian culture, is a mass of astrological and astronomical allegories. Nearly all the mythology of Greece and Rome may be traced in star groups. Some writers are of the opinion that the original twenty-two letters of the Hebrew alphabet were derived from groups of stars, and that the starry handwriting on the wall of the heavens referred to words spelt out, with fixed stars for consonants, and the planets, or luminaries, for vowels. These, coming into ever-different combinations, spelt words which, when properly read, foretold future events.

As the zodiacal band marks the pathway of the sun through the constellations, it results in the phenomena of the seasons. The ancient systems of measuring the year were based upon the equinoxes and the solstices. The year always began with the vernal equinox, celebrated March 21 with rejoicing to mark the moment when the sun crossed the equator northward up the zodiacal arc. The summer solstice was celebrated when the sun reached its most northerly position, and the day appointed was June 21. After that time the sun began to descend toward the equator, which it recrossed southbound at the autumnal equinox, September 21. The sun reached its most southerly position at the winter solstice, December 21.

Four of the signs of the zodiac have been permanently dedicated to the equinoxes and the solstices; and, while the signs no longer correspond with the ancient constellations to which they were assigned, and from which they secured their names, they are accepted by modern astronomers as a basis of cal-

culation. The vernal equinox is therefore said to occur in the constellation of
Aries (the Ram). It is fitting that of all beasts a Ram should be placed at the head
of the heavenly flock forming the zodiacal band. Centuries before the Christian
Era, the pagans revered this constellation. Godfrey Higgins states: "This constellation was called the 'Lamb of God.' He was also called the 'Savior,' and was
said to save mankind from their sins. He was always honored with the appellation of 'Dominus' or 'Lord.' He was called the 'Lamb of God which taketh away
the sins of the world.' The devotees addressing him in their litany, constantly
repeated the words, 'O Lamb of God, that taketh away the sin of the world, have
mercy upon us. Grant us Thy peace.'" Therefore, the *Lamb of God* is a title
given to the sun, who is said to be reborn every year in the Northern Hemisphere in the sign of the Ram, although, due to the existing discrepancy
between the signs of the zodiac and the actual star groups, it actually rises in the
sign of Pisces.

The summer solstice is regarded as occurring in Cancer (the Crab), which
the Egyptians called the *scarab*—a beetle of the family Lamellicornes, the head
of the insect kingdom, and sacred to the Egyptians as the symbol of Eternal Life.
It is evident that the constellation of the Crab is represented by this peculiar
creature because the sun, after passing through this house, proceeds to walk
backwards, or descend the zodiacal arc. Cancer is the symbol of generation, for
it is the house of the Moon, the great Mother of all things and the patroness of
the life forces of Nature. Diana, the moon goddess of the Greeks, is called the
Mother of the World. Concerning the worship of the feminine or maternal principle, Richard Payne Knight writes:

"By attracting or heaving the waters of the ocean, she naturally appeared to
be the sovereign of humidity; and by seeming to operate so powerfully upon the
constitutions of women, she equally appeared to be the patroness and regula-
tress of nutrition and passive generation: whence she is said to have received her
nymphs, or subordinate personifications, from the ocean; and is often represented by the symbol of the sea crab, an animal that has the property of spontaneously detaching from its own body any limb that has been hurt or mutilated,
and reproducing another in its place." (*The Symbolical Language of Ancient Art
and Mythology.*) This water sign, being symbolic of the maternal principle of
Nature, and recognized by the pagans as the origin of all life, was a natural and
consistent domicile of the moon.

The autumnal equinox apparently occurs in the constellation of Libra (the
Balances). The scales tipped and the solar globe began in pilgrimage toward the
home of winter. The constellation of the Scales was placed in the zodiac to sym-

bolize the power of choice, by means of which man may weigh one problem against another. Millions of years ago, when the human race was in the making, man was like the angels, who knew neither good nor evil. He *fell* into the state of the knowledge of good and evil when the gods gave him the seed for the mental nature. From man's mental reactions to his environments he distills the product of experience, which then aids him to regain his lost position plus an individualized intelligence. Paracelsus said: "The body comes from the elements, the soul from the stars, and the spirit from God. All that the intellect can conceive of comes from the stars [the spirits of the stars, rather than the material constellations]."

The constellation of Capricorn, in which the winter solstice theoretically takes place, was called *The House of Death,* for in winter all life in the Northern Hemisphere is at its lowest ebb. Capricorn is a composite creature, with the head and upper body of a goat and the tail of a fish. In this constellation the sun is least powerful in the Northern Hemisphere, and after passing through this constellation it immediately begins to increase. Hence the Greeks said that Jupiter (a name of the Sun God) was suckled by a goat. A new and different sidelight on zodiacal symbolism is supplied by John Cole, in *A Treatise on the Circular Zodiac of Tentyra, in Egypt:* "The symbol therefore of the Goat rising from the body of a fish [Capricorn], represents with the greatest propriety the mountainous buildings of Babylon rising out of its low and marshy situation; the two horns of the Goat being emblematical of the two towns, Nineveh and Babylon, the former built on the Tigris, the latter on the Euphrates; but both subjected to one sovereignty."

The period of 2,160 years required for the regression of the sun through one of the zodiacal constellations is often termed an *age.* According to this system, the *age* secured its name from the sign through which the sun passes year after year as it crosses the equator at the vernal equinox. From this arrangement are derived the terms *The Taurian Age, The Aryan Age, The Piscean Age,* and *The Aquarian Age.* During these periods, or *ages,* religious worship takes the form of the appropriate celestial sign—that which the sun is said to assume as a personality in the same manner that a spirit assumes a body. These twelve signs are the jewels of his breastplate and his light shines forth from them, one after the other.

From a consideration of this system, it is readily understood why certain religious symbols were adopted during different ages of the earth's history; for during the 2,160 years the sun was in the constellation of Taurus, it is said that the Solar Deity assumed the body of Apis, and the Bull became sacred to Osiris.

(For details concerning the astrological ages as related to Biblical symbolism, see *The Message of the Stars* by Max and Augusta Foss Heindel.) During the Aryan Age the Lamb was held sacred and the priests were called *shepherds*. Sheep and goats were sacrificed upon the altars, and a scapegoat was appointed to bear the sins of Israel.

During the Age of Pisces, the Fish was the symbol of divinity and the Sun God fed the multitude with two small fishes. The frontispiece of Inman's *Ancient Faiths* shows the goddess Isis with a fish on her head; and the Indian Savior God, Christna, in one of his incarnations was cast from the mouth of a fish.

Not only is Jesus often referred to as the *Fisher of Men*, but as John P. Lundy writes: "The word Fish is an abbreviation of this whole title, Jesus Christ, Son of God, Savior, and Cross; or as St. Augustine expresses it, 'If you join together the initial letters of the five Greek words, Ἰησοῦς Χριστος Θεου Υἱὸς Σωτήρ, which mean Jesus Christ, Son of God, Saviour, they will make ΙΧΘΥΣ, Fish, in which word Christ is mystically understood, because He was able to live in the abyss of this mortality as in the depth of waters, that is, without sin.'" (*Monumental Christianity*.) Many Christians observe Friday, which is sacred to the Virgin (Venus), upon which day they shall eat fish and not meat. The sign of the fish was one of the earliest symbols of Christianity; and when drawn upon the sand, it informed one Christian that another of the same faith was near.

Aquarius is called the *Sign of the Water Bearer*, or the man with a jug of water on his shoulder mentioned in the New Testament. This is sometimes shown as an angelic figure, supposedly androgynous, either pouring water from an urn or carrying the vessel upon its shoulder. Among Oriental peoples, a water vessel alone is often used. Edward Upham, in his *History and Doctrine of Budhism,* describes Aquarius as being "in the shape of a pot and of a color between blue and yellow; this Sign is the single house of Saturn." When Herschel discovered the planet Uranus (sometimes called by the name of its discoverer), the second half of the sign of Aquarius was allotted to this added member of the planetary family. The water pouring from the urn of Aquarius under the name of "the waters of eternal life" appears many times in symbolism. So it is with all the signs. Thus the sun in its path controls whatever form of worship man offers to the Supreme Deity.

There are two distinct systems of astrological philosophy. One of them, the Ptolemaic, is geocentric: the earth is considered the center of the solar system, around which the sun, moon, and planets revolve. Astronomically, the geocentric system is incorrect; but for thousands of years it had proved its accuracy when applied to the material nature of earthly things. A careful consideration of the writings of the great occultists and a study of their diagrams reveal the fact that many of them were acquainted with another method of arranging the heavenly bodies.

The other system of astrological philosophy is called the heliocentric. This posits the sun in the center of the solar system, where it naturally belongs, with the planets and their moons revolving about it. The great difficulty, however, with the heliocentric system is that, being comparatively new, there has not been sufficient time to experiment successfully and catalogue the effects of its various aspects and relationships. Geocentric astrology, as its name implies, is confined to the earthy side of nature, while heliocentric astrology may be used to analyze the higher intellectual and spiritual faculties of man.

The important point to be remembered is that when the sun was said to be in a certain sign of the zodiac, the ancients really meant that the sun occupied the opposite sign and cast its long ray into the house in which they enthroned it. Therefore, when it is said that the sun is in Taurus, it means (astronomically) that the sun is in the sign opposite to Taurus, which is Scorpio. This resulted in two distinct schools of philosophy: one geocentric and exoteric, the other heliocentric and esoteric. While the ignorant multitudes worshiped the house of the sun's reflection, which in the case described would be the Bull, the wise revered the house of the sun's actual dwelling, which would be the Scorpion, or the Serpent, the symbol of the concealed spiritual mystery. This sign has three different symbols. The most common is that of a Scorpion, who was called by the ancients the *backbiter,* being the symbol of deceit and perversion; the second (and less common) form of the sign is a Serpent, often used by the ancients to symbolize wisdom.

Probably the rarest form of Scorpio is that of an Eagle. The arrangement of the stars of the constellation bears as much resemblance to a flying bird as to a scorpion. Scorpio, being the sign of occult initiation, the flying eagle—the king of birds—represents the highest and most spiritual type of Scorpio, in which it transcends the venomous insect of the earth. As Scorpio and Taurus are opposite each other in the zodiac, their symbolism is often closely intermingled. The Hon. E. M. Plunket, in *Ancient Calendars and Constellations,* says: "The Scorpion (the constellation Scorpio of the Zodiac opposed to Taurus) joins with Mithras in his attack upon the Bull, and always the genii of the spring and autumn equinoxes are present in joyous and mournful attitudes."

The Egyptians, the Assyrians, and the Babylonians, who knew the sun as a

Bull, called the zodiac a series of furrows, through which the great celestial Ox dragged the plow of the sun. Hence the populace offered up sacrifice and led through the streets magnificent steers, bedecked with flowers and surrounded with priests, dancing girls of the temple, and musicians. The philosophic elect did not participate in these idolatrous ceremonials, but advocated them as most suitable for the types of mind composing the mass of the population. These few possessed a far deeper understanding, as the Serpent of Scorpio upon their foreheads—the *Uræus*—bore witness.

The sun is often symbolized with its rays in the form of a shaggy mane. Concerning the Masonic significance of Leo, Robert Hewitt Brown, 32°, has written: "On the 21st of June, when the sun arrives at the summer solstice, the constellation Leo—being but 30° in advance of the sun—appears to be leading the way, and to aid by his powerful paw in lifting the sun up to the summit of the zodiacal arch. * * * This visible connection between the constellation Leo and the return of the sun to his place of power and glory, at the summit of the Royal Arch of heaven, was the principal reason why that constellation was held in such high esteem and reverence by the ancients. The astrologers distinguished Leo as the 'sole house of the sun,' and taught that the world was created when the sun was in that sign. 'The lion was adored in the East and the West by the Egyptians and the Mexicans. The chief Druid of Britain was styled a lion.'" (*Stellar Theology and Masonic Astronomy.*) When the Aquarian Age is thoroughly established, the sun will be in Leo, as will be noted from the explanation previously given in this chapter regarding the distinction between geocentric and heliocentic astrology. Then, indeed, will the secret religions of the world include once more the raising to initiation by the Grip of the Lion's Paw. (Lazarus will come forth.)

The antiquity of the zodiac is much in dispute. To contend that it originated but a mere few thousand years before the Christian Era is a colossal mistake on the part of those who have sought to compile data concerning its origin. The zodiac necessarily must be ancient enough to go backward to that period when its signs and symbols coincided exactly with the positions of the constellations whose various creatures in their natural functions exemplified the outstanding features of the sun's activity during each of the twelve months. One author, after many years of deep study on the subject, believed man's concept of the zodiac to be at least five million years old. In all probability it is one of the many things for which the modern world is indebted to the Atlantean or the Lemurian civilizations. About ten thousand years before the Christian Era there was a period of many ages when knowledge of every kind was suppressed, tablets destroyed, monuments torn down, and every vestige of available material concerning previous civilizations completely obliterated. Only a few copper knives, some arrowheads, and crude carvings on the walls of caves bear mute witness of those civilizations which preceded this age of destruction. Here and

FROM KIRCHER'S *ŒDIPUS ÆGYPTIACUS*.

HIEROGLYPHIC PLAN, BY HERMES, OF THE ANCIENT ZODIAC.

The inner circle contains the hieroglyph of Hemphta, the triform and pantamorphic deity. In the six concentric bands surrounding the inner circle are (from within outward): (1) the numbers of the zodiacal houses in figures and also in words; (2) the modern names of the houses; (3) the Greek or the Egyptian names of the Egyptian deities assigned to the houses; (4) the complete figures of these deities; (5) the ancient or the modern zodiacal signs, sometimes both; (6) the number of decans or subdivisions of the houses.

there a few gigantic structures have remained which, like the strange monoliths on Easter Island, are evidence of lost arts and sciences and lost races. The human race is exceedingly old. Modern science counts its age in tens of thousands of years; occultism, in tens of millions. There is an old saying that "Mother Earth has shaken many civilizations from her back," and it is not beyond reason that the principles of astrology and astronomy were evolved millions of years before the first white man appeared.

The occultists of the ancient world had a most remarkable understanding of the principle of evolution. They recognized all life as being in various stages of *becoming*. They believed that grains of sand were in the process of *becoming* human in consciousness but not necessarily in form; that human creatures were in the process of *becoming* planets; that planets were in the process of *becoming* solar systems; and that solar systems were in the process of *becoming* cosmic chains; and so on *ad infinitum*. One of the stages between the solar system and the cosmic chain was called the *zodiac;* therefore they taught that at a certain time a solar system breaks up into a zodiac. The houses of the zodiac become the thrones for twelve Celestial Hierarchies, or as certain of the ancients state, ten Divine Orders. Pythagoras taught that 10, or the unit of the decimal system, was the most perfect of all numbers, and he symbolized the number ten by the *lesser tetractys,* an arrangement of ten dots in the form of an upright triangle.

The early star gazers, after dividing the zodiac into its houses, appointed the three brightest stars in each constellation to be the joint rulers of that house. Then they divided the house into three sections of ten degrees each, which they called *decans.* These, in turn, were divided in half, resulting in the breaking up of the zodiac into seventy-two duodecans of five degrees each. Over each of these duodecans the Hebrews placed a celestial intelligence, or angel, and from this sytem has resulted the Qabbalistic arrangement of the seventy-two sacred names, which correspond to the seventy-two flowers, knops, and almonds upon the seven-branched Candlestick of the Tabernacle, and the seventy-two men who were chosen from the Twelve Tribes to represent Israel.

The only two signs not already mentioned are Gemini and Sagittarius. The constellation of Gemini is generally represented as two small children, who, according to the ancients, were born out of eggs, possibly the ones that the Bull broke with his horns. The stories concerning Castor and Pollux, and Romulus and Remus, may be the result of amplifying the myths of these celestial Twins. The symbols of Gemini have passed through many modifications. The one used by the Arabians was the peacock. Two of the important stars in the constellation of Gemini still bear the names of Castor and Pollux. The sign of Gemini is supposed to have been the patron of phallic worship, and the two obelisks, or pillars, in front of temples and churches convey the same symbolism as the Twins.

The sign of Sagittarius consists of what the ancient Greeks called a centaur—a composite creature, the lower half of whose body was in the form of a horse, while the upper half was human. The centaur is generally shown with a bow and arrow in his hands, aiming a shaft far off into the stars. Hence Sagittarius stands for two distinct principles: first, it represents the spiritual evolution of man, for the human form is rising from the body of the beast; secondly, it is the symbol of aspiration and ambition, for as the centaur aims his arrow at the stars, so every human creature aims at a higher mark than he can reach.

Albert Churchward, in *The Signs and Symbols of Primordial Man,* sums up the influence of the zodiac upon religious symbolism in the following words: "The division here [is] in twelve parts, the twelve signs of the Zodiac, twelve tribes of Israel, twelve gates of heaven mentioned in Revelation, and twelve entrances or portals to be passed through in the Great Pyramid, before finally reaching the highest degree, and twelve Apostles in the Christian doctrines, and the twelve original and perfect points in Masonry."

The ancients believed that the theory of man's being made in the image of God was to be understood literally. They maintained that the universe was a great organism not unlike the human body, and that every phase and function of the Universal Body had a correspondence in man. The most precious Key to Wisdom that the priests communicated to the new initiates was what they termed *the law of analogy.* Therefore, to the ancients, the study of the stars was a sacred science, for they saw in the movements of the celestial bodies the ever-present activity of the Infinite Father.

The Pythagoreans were often undeservedly criticized for promulgating the so-called doctrine of metempsychosis, or the transmigration of souls. This concept as circulated among the uninitiated was merely a blind, however, to conceal a sacred truth. Greek mystics believed that the spiritual nature of man descended into material existence from the Milky Way—the seed ground of souls—through one of the twelve gates of the great zodiacal band. The spiritual nature was therefore said to incarnate in the form of the symbolic creature created by Magian star gazers to represent the various zodiacal constellations. If the spirit incarnated through the sign of Aries, it was said to be born in the body of a ram; if in Taurus, in the body of the celestial bull. All human beings were thus symbolized by twelve mysterious creatures through the natures of which they were able to incarnate into the material world. The theory of transmigration was not applicable to the visible material body of man, but rather to the invisible immaterial spirit wandering along the pathway of the stars and sequentially assuming in the course of evolution the forms of the sacred zodiacal animals.

In the Third Book of the *Mathesis* of Julius Firmicus Maternus appears the following extract concerning the positions of the heavenly bodies at the time of the establishment of the inferior universe: "According to Æsculapius, therefore, and Anubius, to whom especially the divinity Mercury committed the secrets of the astrological science, the geniture of the world is as follows: They constituted the Sun in the 15th part of Leo, the Moon in the 15th part of Cancer, Saturn in the 15th part of Capricorn, Jupiter in the 15th part of Sagittary, Man in the 15th part of Scorpio, Venus in the 15th part of Libra, Mercury in the 15th part of Virgo, and the Horoscope in the 15th part of Cancer. Conformably to this geniture, therefore, to these conditions of the stars, and the testimonies which they adduce in confirmation of this geniture, they are of opinion that the destinies of men, also, are disposed in accordance with the above arrangement as may be learnt from that book of Æsculapius which is called Μυριογενεσις (i.e., Ten Thousand, or an innumerable multitude of Genitures), in order that nothing in the several genitures of men may be found to be discordant with the above-mentioned geniture of the world." The seven ages of man are under the control of the planets in the following order: infancy, the moon; childhood, Mercury; adolescence, Venus; maturity, the sun; middle age, Mars; advanced age, Jupiter; and decrepitude and dissolution, Saturn.

XI

The Bembine Table of Isis

manuscript by Thomas Taylor contains the following remarkable paragraph:

"Plato was initiated into the 'Greater Mysteries' at the age of 49. The initiation took place in one of the subterranean halls of the Great Pyramid in Egypt. The ISIAC TABLE formed the altar, before which the Divine Plato stood and received that which was always his, but which the ceremony of the Mysteries enkindled and brought from its dormant state. With this ascent, after three days in the Great Hall, he was received by the Hierophant of the Pyramid (the hierophant was seen only by those who had passed the three days, the three degrees, the three dimensions) and given verbally the Highest Esoteric Teachings, each accompanied with Its appropriate Symbol. After a further three months' sojourn in the halls of the Pyramid, the Initiate Plato was sent out into the world to do the work of the Great Order, as Pythagoras and Orpheus had been before him."

Before the sacking of Rome in 1527 there is no historical mention of the *Mensa Isiaca* (Tablet of Isis). At that time the Tablet came into the possession of a certain locksmith or ironworker, who sold it at an exorbitant price to Cardinal Bembo, a celebrated antiquary, historiographer of the Republic of Venice, and afterwards librarian of St. Mark's. After his death in 1547 the Isiac Tablet was acquired by the House of Mantua, in whose museum it remained until 1630, when troops of Ferdinand II captured the city of Mantua. Several early writers on the subject have assumed that the Tablet was demolished by the ignorant soldiery for the silver it contained. The assumption, however, was erroneous. The Tablet fell into the hands of Cardinal Pava, who presented it to the Duke of Savoy, who in turn presented it to the King of Sardinia. When the French conquered Italy in 1797 the Tablet was carried to Paris. In 1809, Alexandre Lenoir, writing of the *Mensa Isiaca,* said it was on exhibition at the Bibliothèque

Nationale. Upon the establishment of peace between the two countries it was returned to Italy. In his Guide to Northern Italy, Karl Baedeker describes the *Mensa Isiaca* as being in the center of Gallery 2 in the Museum of Antiquities at Turin.

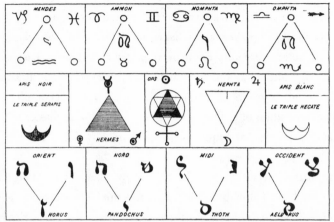

FROM LEVI'S *HISTORY OF MAGIC*.

LEVI'S KEY TO THE BEMBINE TABLE.

"The Isiac Tablet, writes Levi, is a Key to the Ancient Book of Thoth, which has survived to some extent the lapse of centuries and is pictured to us in the still comparatively ancient set of Tarocchi Cards. To him the Book of Thoth was a résumé of the esoteric learning of the Egyptians, after the decadence of their civilization, this lore became crystallized in an hieroglyphic form as the Tarot; this Tarot having become partially or entirely forgotten or misunderstood, its pictured symbols fell into the hands of the sham diviners, and of the providers of the public amusement by games of Cards. The modern Tarot, or Tarocchi pack of cards consists of 78 cards, of which 22 form a special group of trumps, or pictorial design: the remaining 56 are composed of four suits of 10 numerals and four court cards, King, Queen, Knight, and Knave or Valet; the suits are Swords (Militaryism), Cups (Sacerdocy), Clubs or Wands (Agriculture), and Shekels or Coins (Commerce), answering respectively to our Spades, Hearts, Clubs, and Diamonds. Our purpose is with the 22 trumps, these form the special characteristic of the pack and are the lineal descendants of the Hieroglyphics of the Tarot. These 22 correspond to the letters of the Hebrew and other sacred alphabets, which fall naturally into three classes of a Trio of Mothers, a Heptad of doubles, and a duodecad of simple letters. They are also considered as a triad of Heptads and one apart, a system of Initiation and an Uninitiate." (See Westcott's *The Isiac Tablet*.)

A faithful reproduction of the original Tablet was made in 1559 by the celebrated Æneas Vicus of Parma, and a copy of the engraving was given by the Chancellor of the Duke of Bavaria to the Museum of Hieroglyphics. Athanasius Kircher describes the Tablet as "five palms long and four wide." W. Wynn Westcott says it measures 50 by 30 inches. It was made of bronze and decorated with encaustic or smalt enamel and silver inlay. Fosbroke adds: "The figures are cut very shallow, and the contour of most of them is encircled by threads of silver. The bases upon which the figures were seated or reclined, and left blank in the prints, were of silver and are torn away." (See *Encyclopædia of Antiquities*.)

Those familiar with the fundamental principles of Hermetic philosophy will recognize in the *Mensa Isiaca* the key to Chaldean, Egyptian, and Greek theology. In his *Antiquities*, the learned Benedictine, Father Montfaucon, admits his inability to cope with the intricacies of its symbolism. He therefore doubts that the emblems upon the Tablet possess any significance worthy of consideration and ridicules Kircher, declaring him to be more obscure than the Tablet itself. Laurentius Pignorius reproduced the Tablet in connection with a descriptive essay in 1605, but his timidly advanced explanations demonstrated his ignorance concerning the actual interpretation of the figures.

In his *Œdipus Ægyptiacus,* published in 1654, Kircher attacked the problem with characteristic avidity. Being peculiarly qualified for such a task by years of research in matters pertaining to the secret doctrines of antiquity, and with the assistance of a group of eminent scholars, Kircher accomplished much towards an exposition of the mysteries of the Tablet. The master secret, however, eluded even him, as Eliphas Levi has shrewdly noted in his *History of Magic.*

"The learned Jesuit," writes Levi, "divined that it contained the hieroglyphic key to sacred alphabets, though he was unable to develop the explanation. It is divided into three equal compartments; above are the twelve houses of heaven and below are the corresponding distributions of labor [work periods] throughout the year, while in the middle place are twenty-one sacred signs answering to the letters of the alphabet. In the midst of all is a seated figure of the pantomorphic IYNX, emblem of universal being and corresponding as such to the Hebrew *Yod,* or to that unique letter from which all the other letters were formed. The IYNX is encircled by the Ophite triad, answering to the Three Mother Letters of the Egyptian and Hebrew alphabets. On the right are the Ibimorphic and Serapian triads; on the left are those of Nepthys and Hecate, representing active and passive, fixed and volatile, fructifying fire and generating water. Each pair of triads in conjunction with the center produces a septenary, and a septenary is contained in the center. The three septenaries furnish the absolute number of the three worlds, as well as the complete number of primitive letters, to which a complementary sign is added, like zero to the nine numerals."

Levi's hint may be construed to mean that the twenty-one figures in the center section of the Table represent the twenty-one major trumps of the Tarot cards. If this be so, is not the zero card, cause of so much controversy, the nameless crown of the Supreme Mind, the crown being symbolized by the hidden triad in the upper part of the throne in the center of the Table? Might not the first emanation of this Supreme Mind be well symbolized by a juggler or magician with the symbols of the four lower worlds spread out on a table before him: the rod, the sword, the cup, and the coin? Thus considered, the zero card belongs nowhere among the others but is in fact the fourth dimensional point from which they all emanated and consequently is broken up into the twenty-one cards (letters) which, when gathered together, produce the zero. The cipher appearing upon this card would substantiate this interpretation, for the cipher, or circle, is emblematic of the superior sphere from which issue the lower worlds, powers, and letters.

Westcott carefully collected the all too meager theories advanced by various authorities and in 1887 published his now extremely rare volume, which contains the only detailed description of the Isiac Tablet published in English since Humphreys translated Montfaucon's worthless description in 1721. After explaining his reticence to reveal that which Levi evidently felt was better left concealed, Westcott sums up his interpretation of the Tablet as follows:

"The diagram of Levi, by which he explains the mystery of the Tablet, shows the Upper Region divided into the four seasons of the year, each with three signs of the Zodiac, and he has added the four-lettered sacred name, the Tetragrammaton, assigning Jod to Aquarius, that is Canopus, He to Taurus, that is Apis, Vau to Leo, that is Momphta, and He final to Typhon. Note the Cherubic parallel—Man, Bull, Lion and Eagle. The fourth form is found either as Scorpion or Eagle depending upon the Occult good or evil intention: in the Demotic Zodiac, the Snake replaces the Scorpion.

"The Lower Region he ascribes to the twelve *simple* Hebrew letters, associating them with the four quarters of the horizon. Compare the Sepher Yetzirah, Cap. v., sec. 1.

"The Central Region he ascribes to the Solar powers and the Planetary. In the middle we see above, the Sun, marked Ops, and below it is a Solomon's Seal, above a cross; a double triangle Hexapla, one light and one dark triangle superposed, the whole forming a sort of complex symbol of Venus. To the Ibimorphos he gives the three dark planets, Venus, Mercury, and Mars placed around a dark triangle erect, denoting Fire. To the Nephthæan triad he gives three light planets, Saturn, Luna, and Jupiter, around a light inverted triangle which denotes Water. There is a necessary connection between water, female power, passive principle, Binah, and Sephirotic Mother, and Bride. (See the *Kabbalah* by Mathers.) Note the ancient signs for the planets were all composed of a Cross, Solar Disc and Crescent: Venus is a cross below a Sun disc, Mercury, a disc with a crescent above and cross below, Saturn is a Cross whose lowest point touches the apex of the crescent; Jupiter is a Crescent whose lowest point touches the left hand end of a cross: all these are deep mysteries. Note that Levi in his original plate transposed Serapis and Hecate, but not the Apis noir and

Apis blanc, perhaps because of the head of Bes being associated by him with Hecate. Note that having referred the 12 simple letters to the lower, the 7 double must correspond to the central region of the planets, and then the great triad A.M.S. the mother letters representing Air, Water, and Fire remain to be pictured, around S the Central lynx, or Yod, by the Ophionian Triad the two Serpents and the Leonine Sphynx. Levi's word OPS in the centre is the Latin Ops, Terra, genius of the Earth; and the Greek Ops, Rhea, or Kubele (Cybele) often drawn as a goddess seated in a chariot drawn by lions; she is crowned with turrets, and holds a Key." (See *The Isiac Tablet.*)

The essay published in French by Alexandre Lenoir in 1809, while curious and original, contains little real information on the Tablet, which the author seeks to prove was an Egyptian calendar or astrological chart. As both Montfaucon and Lenoir—in fact all writers on the subject since 1651—either have based their work upon that of Kircher or have been influenced considerably by him, a careful translation has been made of the latter's original article (eighty pages of seventeenth-century Latin). The double-page plate in the color insert is a faithful reproduction made by Kircher from the engraving in the Museum of Hieroglyphics. The small letters and numbers used to designate the figures were added by him to clarify his commentary and will be used for the same purpose in this work.

Like nearly all religious and philosophical antiquities, the Bembine Table of Isis has been the subject of much controversy. In a footnote, A. E. Waite—unable to differentiate between the true and the purported nature or origin of the Tablet—echoes the sentiments of J. G. Wilkinson, another eminent *exotericus:* "The original [Table] is exceedingly late and is roughly termed a forgery." On the other hand, Eduard Winkelmann, a man of profound learning, defends the genuineness and antiquity of the Tablet. A sincere consideration of the *Mensa Isiaca* discloses one fact of paramount importance: that although whoever fashioned the Table was not necessarily an Egyptian, he was an initiate of the highest order, conversant with the most arcane tenets of Hermetic esotericism.

Symbolism of the Bembine Table

The following necessarily brief elucidation of the Bembine Table is based upon a digest of the writings of Kircher supplemented by other information gleaned by the present author from the mystical writings of the Chaldeans, Hebrews, Egyptians, and Greeks. The temples of the Egyptians were so designed that the arrangement of chambers, decorations, and utensils was all of symbolic significance, as shown by the hieroglyphics that covered them. Beside the altar, which usually was in the center of each room, was the cistern of Nile water which flowed in and out through unseen pipes. Here also were images of the gods in concatenated series, accompanied by magical inscriptions. In these temples, by use of symbols and hieroglyphics, neophytes were instructed in the secrets of the sacerdotal caste.

The Tablet of Isis was originally a table or altar, and its emblems were part of the mysteries explained by priests. Tables were dedicated to the various gods and goddesses; in this case Isis was so honored. The substances from which the tables were made differed according to the relative dignities of the deities. The tables consecrated to Jupiter and Apollo were of gold; those to Diana, Venus, and Juno were of silver; those to the other superior gods, of marble; those to the lesser divinities, of wood. Tables were also made of metals corresponding to the planets governed by the various celestials. As food for the body is spread on a banquet table, so on these sacred altars were spread the symbols which, when understood, feed the invisible nature of man.

In his introduction to the Table, Kircher summarizes its symbolism thus: "It teaches, in the first place, the whole constitution of the threefold world—archetypal, intellectual, and sensible. The Supreme Divinity is shown moving from the center to the circumference of a universe made up of both sensible and inanimate things, all of which are animated and agitated by the one supreme power which they call the *Father Mind* and represented by a threefold symbol. Here also are shown three triads from the Supreme One, each manifesting one attribute of the first Trimurti. These triads are called the *Foundation,* or the base of all things. In the Table is also set forth the arrangement and distribution of those divine creatures that aid the *Father Mind* in the control of the universe. Here [in the upper panel] are to be seen the Governors of the worlds, each with its fiery, ethereal, and material insignia. Here also [in the lower panel] are the *Fathers of Fountains,* whose duty it is to care for and preserve the principles of all things and sustain the inviolable laws of Nature. Here are the gods of the spheres and also those who wander from place to place, laboring with all substances and forms (Zonia and Azonia), grouped together as figures of both sexes, with their faces turned to their superior deity."

The *Mensa Isiaca,* which is divided horizontally into three chambers or panels, may represent the ground plan of the chambers in which the Isiac Mysteries were given. The center panel is divided into seven parts or lesser rooms, and the lower has two gates, one at each end. The entire Table contains forty-five figures of first importance and a number of lesser symbols. The forty-five main figures are grouped into fifteen triads, of which four are in the upper panel, seven in the central, and four in the lower. According to both Kircher and Levi, the triads are divided in the following manner:

IN THE UPPER SECTION

1. P, S, V—Mendesian Triad.

2. X, Z, A—Ammonian Triad.

3. B, C, D—Momphtæan Triad.

4. F, G, H—Omphtæan Triad.

IN THE CENTER SECTION

1. G, I, K—Isiac Triad.

2. L, M, N—Hecatine Triad.

3. O, Q, R—lbimorphous Triad.

4. V, S, W—Ophionic Triad.

5. X, Y, Z—Nephtæan Triad.

6. ζ, η, θ—Serapæan Triad.

7. γ, δ (not shown), ε—Osirian Triad.

IN THE LOWER SECTION

1. λ, M, N—Horæan Triad.

2. ξ, O, Σ—Pandochæan Triad.

3. T, Φ, X—Thaustic Triad.

4. Ψ, F, H—Æluristic Triad.

Of these fifteen triads Kircher writes: "The figures differ from each other in eight highly important respects, i.e., according to form, position, gesture, act, raiment, headdress, staff, and, lastly, according to the hieroglyphics placed around them, whether these be flowers, shrubs, small letters or animals." These eight symbolic methods of portraying the secret powers of the figures are subtle reminders of the eight spiritual senses of cognition by means of which the Real Self in man may be comprehended. To express this spiritual truth the Buddhists used the wheel with eight spokes and raised their consciousness by means of the noble eightfold path. The ornamented border enclosing the three main panels of the Table contains many symbols consisting of birds, animals, reptiles, human beings, and composite forms. According to one reading of the Table, this border represents the four elements; the creatures are elemental beings. According to another interpretation, the border represents the archetypal spheres, and in its frieze of composite figures are the patterns of those forms which in various combinations will subsequently manifest themselves in the material world. The four flowers at the corners of the Table are those which, because their blossoms always face the sun and follow its course across the sky, are sacred emblems of that finer part of man's nature which delights in facing its Creator.

According to the secret doctrine of the Chaldeans, the universe is divided into four states of being (planes or spheres): archetypal, intellectual, sidereal, and elemental. Each of these reveals the others; the superior controlling the inferior, and the inferior receiving influence from the superior. The archetypal plane was considered synonymous with the intellect of the Triune Divinity. Within this divine, incorporeal, and eternal sphere are included all the lower manifestations of life—all that is, has been, or ever shall be. Within the Kosmic Intellect all things spiritual or material exist as archetypes, or divine thought-forms, which is shown in the Table by a chain of secret similes.

In the middle region of the Table appears the all-form-containing personified Spiritual Essence—the source and substance of all things. From this proceed the lower worlds as nine emanations in groups of three (the Ophionic, Ibimorphous, and Nephtæan Triads). Consider in this connection the analogy of the Qabbalistic Sephiroth, or the nine spheres issuing from Kether, the Crown. The twelve Governors of the Universe (the Mendesian, Ammonian, Momphtæan, and Omphtæan Triads)—vehicles for the distribution of the creative influences, and shown in the upper region of the Table—are directed in their activities by the Divine Mind patterns existing in the archetypal sphere. The archetypes are abstract patterns formulated in the Divine Mind and by them all the inferior activities are controlled. In the lower region of the Table are the Father Fountains (the Horæan, Pandochæan, Thaustic, and Æluristic Triads), keepers of the great gates of the universe. These distribute to the lower worlds the influences descending from the Governors shown above.

In the theology of the Egyptians, goodness takes precedence and all things partake of its nature to a higher or lower degree. Goodness is sought by all. It is the Prime Cause of causes. Goodness is self-diffused and hence exists in all things, for nothing can produce that which it does not have in itself. The Table demonstrates that all is in God and God is in all; that all is in all and each is in each. In the intellectual world are invisible spiritual counterparts of the crea-

MENDES	WINTER			AMMON	SPRING			MOMPHTA	SUMMER			OMPHTA	AUTUMN		
MENDES	MECHIR	CANOPUS	PHAMENOTH / ICHTON / PHARMUTHI	AMMON	PACHONS	APIS	PAONI / GEMINI / EPIPHI	HERMANUBIS	MESORI	MOMPHTA	THOTH / ISIS / PAOPHI	OMPHTA	ATHYR	TYPHON	CHOIAK / NEPHTHA / TYBI
P	S		V		X	Z	A	B		C	E	F		G	H

APIS ISIS			TRIAD		TRIAD		MNEVIS OSIRIS	
G I K		OF		OF		P V E	
		IBIMORPHOS	OPHIONIAN	NEPHTHA			
TRIAD		MASCULINE	TRIAD	FEMININE		TRIAD	
OF		ACTIVE	CENTRAL *IYNX*	PASSIVE		OF	
HECATE		O Q F	V S W	X Y Z		SERAPIS	
L M N						Z H Θ	

EAST GATE	NORTH GATE	SOUTH GATE	WEST GATE
HORUS	PANDOCHUS	THOTH	ÆLURUS
λ m N	ξ o Σ	T φ X	ψ F H

FROM WESTCOTT'S *THE ISIAC TABLET.*

WESTCOTT'S KEY TO THE BEMBINE TABLE.

Zoroaster declared that the number three shines throughout the world. This is revealed in the Bembine Table by a series of triads representing the creative impulses. Of the Isiac Table, Alexandre Lenoir writes: "The Isiac Table, as a work of art, is not of great interest. It is but a composition, rather cold and insignificant, whose figures, summarily sketched and methodically placed near each other, give but little impression of life. But, if on the contrary, after examining it, we understand the purpose of the author, we become soon convinced that the Isiac Table is an image of the heavenly sphere divided in small parts to be used very likely for general teaching. According to that idea, we can conclude that the Isiac Table was originally the introduction to a collection followed by the Mysteries of Isis. It was engraved on copper in order to be used in the ceremonial of initiation." (See *New Essay on the Isiac Table.*)

tures which inhabit the elemental world. Therefore, the lowest exhibits the highest, the corporeal declares the intellectual, and the invisible is made manifest by its works. For this reason the Egyptians made images of substances existing in the inferior sensible world to serve as visible exemplars of superior and invisible powers. To the corruptible images they assigned the virtues of the incorruptible divinities, thus demonstrating arcanely that this world is but the shadow of God, the outward picture of the paradise within. All that is in the invisible archetypal sphere is revealed in the sensible corporeal world by the light of Nature.

The Archetypal and Creative Mind—first through its Paternal Foundation and afterwards through secondary Gods called Intelligences—poured out the whole infinity of its powers by continuous exchange from highest to lowest. In their phallic symbolism the Egyptians used the sperm to represent the spiritual spheres, because each contains all that comes forth from it. The Chaldeans and Egyptians also held that everything which is a result dwells in the cause of itself and turns to that cause as the lotus to the sun. Accordingly, the Supreme Intellect, through its Paternal Foundation, first created light—the angelic world. Out of that light were then created the invisible hierarchies of beings which some call the stars; and out of the stars the four elements and the sensible world were formed. Thus all are in all, after their respective kinds. All visible bodies or elements are in the invisible stars or spiritual elements, and the stars are likewise in those bodies; the stars are in the angels and the angels in the stars; the angels are in God and God is in all. Therefore, all are divinely in the Divine, angelically in the angels, and corporeally in the corporeal world, and vice versa. Just as the seed is the tree folded up, so the world is God unfolded.

Proclus says: "Every property of divinity permeates all creation and gives itself to all inferior creatures." One of the manifestations of the Supreme Mind is the power of reproduction according to species which it confers upon every creature of which it is the divine part. Thus souls, heavens, elements, animals, plants, and stones generate themselves each according to its pattern, but all are dependent upon the one fertilizing principle existing in the Supreme Mind. The fecundative power, though of itself a unit, manifests differently through the various substances, for in the mineral it contributes to material existence, in the plant it manifests as vitality, and in the animal as sensibility. It imparts motion to the heavenly bodies, thought to the souls of men, intellectuality to the angels, and superessentiality to God. Thus it is seen that all forms are of one substance and all life of one force, and these are co-existent in the nature of the Supreme One.

This doctrine was first expounded by Plato. His disciple, Aristotle, set it forth in these words: "We say that this Sensible World is an image of another; therefore since this world is vivid or alive, how much more, then, that other must live. * * * Yonder, therefore, above the stellar virtues, stand other heavens to be attained, like the heavens of this world; beyond them, because they are of a higher kind, brighter and vaster; nor are they distant from each other like this one, for they are incorporeal. Yonder, too, exists an earth, not of inanimate matter, but vivid with animal life and all natural terrestrial phenomena like this one, but of other kinds and perfections. There are plants, also, and gardens, and flowing water; there are aquatic animals but of nobler species. Yonder is air and life appropriate to it, all immortal. And although the life there is analogous to ours, yet it is nobler, seeing that it is intellectual, perpetual and unalterable. For if anyone should object and ask, How in the world above do the plants, etc. above mentioned find footing, we should answer that they do not have objective existence, for they were produced by the primal Author in an absolute condition and without exteriorization. They are, therefore, in the same case as intellect and soul; they suffer no defect such as waste and corruption, since the beings yonder are full of energy, strength and joy, as living in a life sublime and being the issue of one fount and of one quality, compounded of all like sweet savors, delicate perfumes, harmonious color and sound, and other perfections. Nor do they move violently about nor intermix nor corrupt each other, but each perfectly preserves its own essential character; and they are simple and do not multiply as corporeal beings do."

In the midst of the Table is a great covered throne with a seated female figure representing Isis, but here called the Pantomorphic IYNX. G.R.S. Mead defines the IYNX as "a transmitting intelligence." Others have declared it to be a symbol of Universal Being. Over the head of the goddess the throne is surmounted by a triple crown, and beneath her feet is the house of material substance. The threefold crown is here symbolic of the Triune Divinity, called by the Egyptians the Supreme Mind, and described in the *Sepher ha Zohar* as being "hidden and unrevealed." According to the Hebrew system of Qabbalism, the Tree of the Sephiroth was divided into two parts, the upper invisible and the lower visible. The upper consisted of three parts and the lower of seven. The three uncognizable Sephiroth were called *Kether,* the Crown; *Chochmah,* Wisdom; and *Binah,* Understanding. These are too abstract to permit of comprehension, whereas the lower seven spheres that came forth from them were within the grasp of human consciousness. The central panel contains seven triads of figures. These represent the lower Sephiroth, all emanating from the concealed threefold crown over the throne.

Kircher writes: "The throne denotes the diffusion of the triform Supreme Mind along the universal paths of the three worlds. Out of these three intangible spheres emerges the sensible universe, which Plutarch calls the 'House of Horus' and the Egyptians, the 'Great Gate of the Gods.' The top of the throne is in the midst of diffused serpent-shaped flames, indicating that the Supreme Mind is filled with light and life, eternal and incorruptible, removed from all material contact. How the Supreme Mind communicated His fire to all creatures is clearly set forth in the symbolism of the Table. The Divine Fire is communicated to lower spheres through the universal power of Nature personified by the World Virgin, Isis, here denominated the IYNX, or the polymorphous all-containing Universal Idea." The word *Idea* is here used in its Platonic sense. "Plato believed that there are eternal forms of all possible things which exist without matter; and to these eternal and immaterial forms he gave the name of *ideas.* In the Platonic sense, *ideas* were the patterns according to which the Deity fashioned the phenomenal or ectypal world." (Sir W. Hamilton.)

Kircher describes the 21 figures in the central panel thus: "Seven principal triads, corresponding to seven superior worlds, are shown in the central section of the Table. They all originate from the fiery, invisible archetype [the triple crown of the throne]. The first, the Ophionic or IYNX Triad, V S W, corresponds to the vital and fiery world and is the first intellectual world, called by the ancients the *Aetherium.* Zoroaster says of it: 'Oh, what rigorous rulers this world has!' The second, or Ibimorphous Triad, O Q R, corresponds to the second intellectual, or ethereal, world, and is concerned with the principle of humidity. The third, or Nephtæan Triad, X Y Z, corresponds to the third intellectual and ethereal [world] and is concerned with fecundity. These are the three triads of the ethereal worlds, which correspond to the Father Foundation. Then follow the four triads of the sensible, or material, worlds, of which the first two correspond to the sidereal worlds, G I K and γ δ ε, namely, Osiris and Isis, Sun and Moon, indicated by two bulls. They are followed by two triads—the Hecatine, L M N, and the Serapæan, ζ η Θ, corresponding to the sublunary and subterranean worlds. These complete the seven worlds of primary Genii ruling the natural universe. Psellus quotes Zoroaster: 'The Egyptians and the Chaldeans taught that there were seven corporeal worlds (i.e., worlds ruled by the intellectual powers); the first is of pure fire; the second, third, and fourth, ethereal; the fifth, six, and seventh, material; the seventh being the one called terrestrial and hater of light, and is located under the Moon, comprising within itself the matter called *fundus,* or foundation.' These seven, plus the one invisible crown, constitute the eight worlds. * * *

"Plato writes that it is needful for the philosopher to know how the seven circles beneath the first one are arranged according to the Egyptians. The first triad of fire denotes life; the second, water, over which rule the Ibimorphous divinities; and the third, air, ruled by Nephta. From the fire the heavens were created, from the water the earth, and air was the mediator between them. In the Sephira Yetzirah it is said that from the three originate the seven, i. e., the height, the depth, the East, the West, the North, and the South, and the Holy Temple in the center sustaining them all. Is not the Holy Temple in the center the great throne of the many-formed Spirit of Nature which is shown in the middle of the Tablet? What are the seven triads but the seven Powers that rule over the world? Psellus writes: 'The Egyptians worshipped the triad of faith, truth, and love; and the seven fountains: the Sun as ruler—the fountain of matter; then the fountain of the archangels; the fountain of the senses; of judgment; of lightning; of reflections; and of characters of unknown composition. They say that the highest material fountains are those of Apollo, Osiris, and Mercury—the fountains of the centers of the elements.' Thus, they understood by the Sun as ruler the solar world; by the material archangelic, the lunar world; by the fountain of the senses, the world of Saturn; by judgment, Jupiter; by lightning, Mars; by that of the reflections, or mirrors, the world of Venus; by the fountain of characters, the world of Mercury. All these are shown by the figures in the center pane of the Tablet."

The upper panel contains the twelve figures of the zodiac arranged in four triads. The center figure in each group represents one of the four fixed signs of the zodiac. *S* is the sign of Aquarius; *Z*, Taurus; *C*, Leo; and *G*, Scorpio. These are called the *Fathers*. In the secret teachings of the Far East these four figures— the man, the bull, the lion, and the eagle—are called the winged globes or the four Maharajahs who stand upon the corners of creation. The four cardinal signs—*P*, Capricorn; *X*, Aries; *B*, Cancer; *F*, Libra—are called the Powers. The four common signs—*V*, Pisces; *A*, Gemini; *E*, Virgo; *H*, Sagittarius—are called the *Minds* of the Four Lords. This explains the meaning of the winged globes of Egypt, for the four central figures—Aquarius, Taurus, Leo, and Scorpio (called by Ezekiel the *Cherubim*)—are the globes; the cardinal and common signs on either side are the wings. Therefore the twelve signs of the zodiac may be symbolized by four globes, each with two wings.

The celestial triads are further shown by the Egyptians as a globe (the *Father*) from which issue a serpent (the *Mind*) and wings (the *Power*). These twelve forces are the fabricators of the world, and from them emanate the microcosm, or the mystery of the twelve sacred animals—representing in the universe the twelve parts of the world and in man the twelve parts of the human body. Anatomically, the twelve figures in the upper panel may well symbolize the twelve convolutions of the brain and the twelve figures in the lower panel the twelve zodiacal members and organs of the human body, for man is a creature formed of the twelve sacred animals with his members and organs under the direct control of the twelve governors or powers resident in the brain.

A more profound interpretation is found in the correspondences between the twelve figures in the upper panel and the twelve in the lower. This furnishes a key to one of the most arcane of ancient secrets—the relationship existing between the two great zodiacs—the *fixed* and the *movable*. The *fixed* zodiac is described as an immense dodecahedron, its twelve surfaces representing the outermost walls of abstract space. From each surface of this dodecahedron a great spiritual power, radiating inward, becomes embodied as one of the hierarchies of the *movable* zodiac, which is a band of circumambulating so-called fixed stars. Within this *movable* zodiac are posited the various planetary and elemental bodies. The relation of these two zodiacs to the subzodiacal spheres has a correlation in the respiratory system of the human body. The great *fixed* zodiac may be said to represent the atmosphere, the *movable* zodiac the lungs, and the subzodiacal worlds the body. The spiritual atmosphere containing the vivifying energies of the twelve divine powers of the great *fixed* zodiac is inhaled by the cosmic lungs—the *movable* zodiac—and distributed by them through the constitution of the twelve holy animals which are the parts and members of the material universe. The functional cycle is completed when the poisonous effluvia of the lower worlds collected by the *movable* zodiac are exhaled into the great *fixed* zodiac, there to be purified by being passed through the divine natures of its twelve eternal hierarchies.

The Table as a whole is susceptible of many interpretations. If the border of the Table with its hieroglyphic figures be accepted as the spiritual source, then the throne in the center represents the physical body within which human nature is enthroned. From this point of view the entire Table becomes emblematic of the auric bodies of man, with the border as the outer extremity or shell of the *auric egg*. If the throne be accepted as the symbol of the spiritual sphere, the border typifies the elements, and the various panels surrounding the central one become emblematic of the worlds or planes emanating from the one divine source. If the Table be considered from a purely physical basis, the throne becomes symbolic of the generative system and the Table reveals the secret processes of embryology as applied to the formation of the material worlds. If a purely physiological and anatomical interpretation be desired, the central throne becomes the heart, the Ibimorphous Triad the mind, the Nephtæan Triad the generative system, and the surrounding hieroglyphics the various parts and members of the human body. From the evolutionary viewpoint the central gate becomes the point of both entrance and exit. Here also is set forth the process of initiation, in which the candidate after passing successfully through the various ordeals is finally brought into the presence of his own soul, which he alone is capable of unveiling.

If cosmogony be the subject of consideration, the central panel represents the spiritual worlds, the upper panel the intellectual worlds, and the lower panel the material worlds. The central panel may also symbolize the nine invisible worlds, and the creature marked *T* the physical nature—the footstool of Isis, the Spirit of Universal Life. Considered in the light of alchemy, the central panel contains the metals and the borders the alchemical processes. The figure seated on the throne is the Universal Mercury—the "stone of the wise"; the flaming canopy of the throne above is the Divine Sulphur; and the cube of earth beneath is the elemental salt.

The three triads—or the *Paternal Foundation*—in the central panel represent the Silent Watchers, the three invisible parts of the nature of man; the two panels on either side are the quaternary lower nature of man. In the central panel are 21 figures. This number is sacred to the sun—which consists of three great powers, each with seven attributes—and by Qabbalistic reduction 21 becomes 3, or the Great Triad.

It will yet be proved that the Table of Isis is directly connected with Egyptian Gnosticism, for in a Gnostic papyrus preserved in the Bodleian Library there is a direct reference to the twelve *Fathers* or *Paternities* beneath whom are twelve Fountains. (See *Egyptian Magic* by S.S.D.D.) That the lower panel represents the underworld is further emphasized by the two gates—the great gate of the East and the great gate of the West—for in the Chaldean theology the sun rises and sets through gates in the underworld, where it wanders during the hours of darkness. As Plato was for thirteen years under the instruction of the Magi Patheneith, Ochoaps, Sechtnouphis, and Etymon of Sebbennithis, his philosophy consequently is permeated with the Chaldean and Egyptian system of triads. The Bembine Table is a diagrammatic exposition of the so-called Platonic philosophy, for in its design is epitomized the entire theory of mystic cosmogony and generation. The most valuable guide to the interpretation of this Table is the *Commentaries of Proclus on the Theology of Plato*. The *Chaldean Oracles of Zaroaster* also contains many allusions to the theogonic principles which are demonstrated by the Table.

The *Theogony* of Hesiod contains the most complete account of the Greek cosmogony myth. Orphic cosmogony has left its impress upon the various forms of philosophy and religion—Greek, Egyptian, and Syrian—which it contacted. Chief of the Orphic symbols was the *mundane egg* from which Phanes sprang into light. Thomas Taylor considers the Orphic egg to be synonymous with the *mixture* from *bound* and *infinity* mentioned by Plato in the *Philebus*. The egg is furthermore the third Intelligible Triad and the proper symbol of the Demiurgus, whose auric body is the egg of the inferior universe.

Eusebius, on the authority of Porphyry, declared that the Egyptians acknowledged one intellectual Author or Creator of the world under the name of *Cneph* and that they worshiped him in a statue of human form and dark blue complexion, holding in his hand a girdle and a scepter, wearing on his head a royal plume, and thrusting forth an egg out of his mouth. (See *An Analysis of the Egyptian Mythology.*) While the Bembine Table is rectangular-shaped, it signifies philosophically the Orphic egg of the universe with its contents. In the esoteric doctrines the supreme individual achievement is the breaking of the Orphic egg, which is equivalent to the return of the spirit to the Nirvana—the *absolute* condition—of the Oriental mystics.

The New Pantheon by Samuel Boyse contains three plates showing various sections of the Bembine Table. The author, however, makes no important contribution to the knowledge of the subject. In *The Mythology and Fables of the Ancients Explained from History,* the Abbé Banier devotes a chapter to a consideration of the *Mensa Isiaca.* After reviewing the conclusions of Montfaucon, Kircher, and Pignorius, he adds: "I am of the opinion that it was a votive table, which some prince or private person had consecrated to Isis, as an acknowledgment for some benefit which he believed she had conferred upon him."

Wonders of Antiquity

t was a common practice among the early Egyptians, Greeks, and Romans to seal lighted lamps in the sepulchers of their dead as offerings to the God of Death. Possibly it was also believed that the deceased could use these lights in finding his way through the Valley of the Shadow. Later as the custom became generally established, not only actual lamps but miniatures of them in terra cotta were buried with the dead. Some of the lamps were enclosed in circular vessels for protection; and instances have been recorded in which the original oil was found in them, in a perfect state of preservation, after more than 2,000 years. There is ample proof that many of these lamps were burning when the sepulchers were sealed, and it has been declared that they were still burning when the vaults were opened hundreds of years later. The possibility of preparing a fuel which would renew itself as rapidly as it was consumed has been a source of considerable controversy among mediæval authors. After due consideration of the evidence at hand, it seems well within the range of possibility that the ancient priest-chemists did manufacture lamps that burned, if not indefinitely, at least for considerable periods of time.

Numerous authorities have written on the subject of ever-burning lamps. W. Wynn Westcott estimates the number of writers who have given the subject consideration as more than 150, and H. P. Blavatsky as 173. While conclusions reached by different authors are at variance, a majority admit the existence of these phenomenal lamps. Only a few maintained that the lamps would burn forever, but many were willing to concede that they might remain alight for several centuries without replenishment of the fuel. Some considered the so-called perpetual lights as mere artifices of the crafty pagan priests, while a great many, admitting that the lamps actually burned, made the sweeping assertion that the Devil was using this apparent miracle to ensnare the credulous and thereby lead their souls to perdition.

On this subject the learned Jesuit, Athanasius Kircher, usually dependable, exhibits a striking inconsistency. In his *Œdipus Ægyptiacus* he writes: "Not a few of these everburning lamps have been found to be the devices of devils, * * * And I take it that all the lamps found in the tombs of the Gentiles dedicated to the worship of certain gods, were of this kind, not because they burned, or have been reported to burn, with a perpetual flame, but because probably the devil set them there, maliciously intending thereby to obtain fresh credence for a false worship."

Having admitted that dependable authorities defend the existence of the ever-burning lamps, and that even the Devil lends himself to their manufacture, Kircher next declared the entire theory to be desperate and impossible, and to be classed with perpetual motion and the Philosopher's Stone. Having already solved the problem to his satisfaction once, Kircher solves it again—but differently—in the following words: "In Egypt there are rich deposits of asphalt and petroleum. What did those clever fellows [the priests] do, then, but connect an oil deposit by a secret duct with one or more lamps, provided with wicks of abestos! How could such lamps help burning perpetually? * * * In my opinion this is the solution of the riddle of the supernatural everlastingness of these ancient lamps."

FROM MONTFAUCON'S *ANTIQUITIES*.

BASE OF A DELPHIAN TRIPOD.

The windings of these serpents formed the base, and the three heads sustained the three feet of the tripod. It is impossible to secure satisfactory information concerning the shape and size of the celebrated Delphian tripod. Theories concerning it are based (in most part) upon small ornamental tripods discovered in various temples.

Montfaucon, in his *Antiquities,* agrees in the main with the later deductions of Kircher, believing the fabled perpetual lamps of the temples to be cunning mechanical contrivances. He further adds that the belief that lamps burned indefinitely in tombs was the result of the noteworthy fact that in some cases fumes resembling smoke poured forth from the entrances of newly opened vaults. Parties going in later and discovering lamps scattered about the floor assumed that they were the source of the fumes.

There are several interesting stories concerning the discoveries of ever-burning lamps in various parts of the world. In a tomb on the Appian Way which was opened during the papacy of Paul III was found a burning lamp which had remained alight in a hermetically sealed vault for nearly 1,600 years. According to an account written by a contemporary, a body—that of a young and beautiful girl with long golden hair—was found floating in an unknown transparent liquid and as well preserved as though death had occurred but a few hours before. About the interior of the vault were a number of significant objects, which included several lamps, one of them alight. Those entering the sepulcher declared that the draft caused by the opening of the door blew out the light and the lamp could not be relighted. Kircher reproduces an epitaph, "TULLI-OLAE FILIAE MEAE," supposedly found in the tomb, but which Montfaucon declares never existed, the latter adding that although conclusive evidence was not found, the body was generally believed to be that of Tulliola, the daughter of Cicero.

Ever-burning lamps have been discovered in all parts of the world. Not only the Mediterranean countries but also India, Tibet, China, and South America have contributed records of lights which burned continuously without fuel. The examples which follow were selected at random from the imposing list of perpetual lamps found in different ages.

Plutarch wrote of a lamp that burned over the door of a temple to Jupiter Ammon; the priests declared that it had remained alight for centuries without fuel.

St. Augustine described a perpetual lamp, guarded in a temple in Egypt sacred to Venus, which neither wind nor water could extinguish. He believed it to be the work of the Devil.

An ever-burning lamp was found at Edessa, or Antioch, during the reign of the Emperor Justinian. It was in a niche over the city gate, elaborately enclosed to protect it from the elements. The date upon it proved that the lamp had been burning for more than 500 years. It was destroyed by soldiers.

During the early Middle Ages a lamp was found in England which had burned since the third century after Christ. The monument containing it was believed to be the tomb of the father of Constantine the Great.

The Lantern of Pallas was discovered near Rome in A.D. 1401. It was found in the sepulcher of Pallas, Son of Evander, immortalized by Virgil in his *Æneid*. The lamp was placed at the head of the body and had burned with a steady glow for more than 2,000 years.

In A.D. 1550 on the island of Nesis, in the Bay of Naples, a magnificent marble vault was opened in which was found a lamp still alight which had been placed there before the beginning of the Christian Era.

Pausanias described a beautiful golden lamp in the temple of Minerva which burned steadily for a year without refueling or having the wick trimmed. The ceremony of filling the lamp took place annually, and time was measured by the ceremony.

According to the *Fama Fraternitatis,* the crypt of Christian Rosencreutz when opened 120 years after his death was found to be brilliantly illuminated by a perpetual lamp suspended from the ceiling.

Numa Pompilius, King of Rome and magician of considerable power, caused a perpetual light to burn in the dome of a temple he had created in honor of an elemental being.

In England a curious tomb was found containing an automaton which moved when certain stones in the floor of the vault were stepped upon by an intruder. At that time the Rosicrucian controversy was at its height, so it was decided that the tomb was that of a Rosicrucian initiate. A countryman, discovering the tomb and entering, found the interior brilliantly lighted by a lamp hanging from the ceiling. As he walked, his weight depressed some of the floor stones. At once a seated figure in heavy armor began to move. Mechanically it rose to its feet and struck the lamp with an iron baton, completely destroying it, and thus effectually preventing the discovery of the secret substance which maintained the flame. How long the lamp had burned is unknown, but certainly it had been for a considerable number of years.

It is related that among the tombs near Memphis and in the Brahmin temples of India lights have been found in sealed chambers and vessels, but sudden exposure to the air has extinguished them and caused their fuel to evaporate.

It is now believed that the wicks of these perpetual lamps were made of braided or woven asbestos, called by the alchemists *salamander's wool,* and that the fuel was one of the products of alchemical research. Kircher attempted to extract oil from asbestos, being convinced that as the substance itself was indestructible by fire an oil extracted from it would supply the lamp with a fuel likewise indestructible. After spending two years in fruitless experimental work, he concluded that the task was impossible of accomplishment.

Several formulæ for the making of the fuel for the lamps have been preserved. In *Isis Unveiled,* H. P. Blavatsky reprints two of these formulæ from early authors—Tritenheim and Bartolomeo Korndorf. One will suffice to give a general understanding of the process:

"*Sulphur. Alum* ust. a 3 iv.; sublime them into flowers to 3 ij., of which add of crystalline Venetian borax (powdered) 3 j.; upon these affuse high rectified spirit of wine and digest it, then abstract it and pour on fresh; repeat this so often till the sulphur melts like wax without any smoke, upon a hot plate of brass: this is for the *pabulum,* but the wick is to be prepared after this manner: gather the threads or thrums of the *Lapis asbestos,* to the thickness of your middle and the length of your little finger, then put them into a Venetian glass, and covering them over with the aforesaid depurated sulphur or aliment set the glass in sand for the space of twenty-four hours, so hot that the sulphur may bubble all the while. The wick being thus besmeared and anointed, is to be put into a glass like a scallop-shell, in such manner that some part of it may lie above the mass of prepared sulphur; then setting this glass upon hot sand, you must melt the sulphur, so that it may lay hold of the wick, and when it is lighted, it will burn with a perpetual flame and you may set this lamp in any place where you please."

The Greek Oracles

The worship of Apollo included the establishment and maintenance of places of prophecy by means of which the gods could communicate with mankind and reveal futurity to such as deserved the boon. The early history of Greece abounds with accounts of talking trees, rivers, statues, and caves in which nymphs, dryads, or dæmons had taken up their abodes and from which they delivered oracles. While Christian authors have tried to prove that oracular revelations were delivered by the Devil for the purpose of misleading humanity, they have not dared to attack the theory of oracles, because of the repeated reference to it in their own sacred writings. If the onyx stones on the shoulders of Israel's high priest made known by their flashings the will of Jehovah, then a black dove, temporarily endowed with the faculty of speech, could indeed pronounce oracles in the temple of Jupiter Ammon. If the witch of Endor could invoke the shade of Samuel, who in turn gave prophecies to Saul, could not a priestess of Apollo call up the specter of her leige to foretell the destiny of Greece?

The most famous oracles of antiquity were those of Delphi, Dodona, Trophonius, and Latona, of which the talking oak trees of Dodona were the oldest. Though it is impossible to trace back to the genesis of the theory of oracular prophecy, it is known that many of the caves and fissures set aside by the Greeks as oracles were sacred long before the rise of Greek culture.

The oracle of Apollo at Delphi remains one of the unsolved mysteries of the ancients. Alexander Wilder derives the name *Delphi* from *delphos,* the womb. This name was chosen by the Greeks because of the shape of the cavern and the vent leading into the depths of the earth. The original name of the oracle was *Pytho,* so called because its chambers had been the abode of the great serpent *Python,* a fearsome creature that had crept out of the slime left by the receding flood that had destroyed all human beings except Deucalion and Pyrrha. Apollo, climbing the side of Mount Parnassus, slew the serpent after a prolonged combat, and threw the body down the fissure of the oracle. From that time the Sun God, surnamed the Pythian Apollo, gave oracles from the vent. With Dionysos he shared the honor of being the patron god of Delphi.

After being vanquished by Apollo, the spirit of Python remained at Delphi as the representative of his conqueror, and it was with the aid of his effluvium that the priestess was able to become *en rapport* with the god. The fumes rising from the fissure of the oracle were supposed to come from the decaying body of Python. The name *Pythoness,* or *Pythia,* given to the female hierophant of the oracle, means literally one who has been thrown into a religious frenzy by inhaling fumes rising from decomposing matter. It is of further interest to note that the Greeks believed the oracle of Delphi to be the umbilicus of the earth, thus proving that they considered the planet an immense human being. The connection between the principle of oracular revelation and the occult significance of the navel is an important secret belonging to the ancient Mysteries.

The oracle, however, is much older than the foregoing account indicates. A story of this kind was probably invented by the priests to explain the phenomena to those inquisitive persons whom they did not consider worthy of enlightenment regarding the true esoteric nature of the oracle. Some believe that the Delphic fissure was discovered by a Hypoborean priest, but as far back as recorded history goes the cave was sacred, and persons came from all parts of Greece and the surrounding countries to question the dæmon who dwelt in its chimney-like vent. Priests and priestesses guarded it closely and served the spirit who dwelt therein and who enlightened humanity through the gift of prophecy.

The story of the original discovery of the oracle is somewhat as follows: Shepherds tending their flocks on the side of Mount Parnassus were amazed at the peculiar antics of goats that wandered close to a great chasm on its southwestern spur. The animals jumped about as though trying to dance, and emitted strange cries unlike anything before heard. At last one of the shepherds, curious to learn the cause of the phenomenon, approached the vent, from which were rising noxious fumes. Immediately he was seized with a prophetic ecstasy; he danced with wild abandon, sang, jabbered inarticulate sounds, and foretold future events. Others went close to the fissure, with the same result. The fame of the place spread, and many came to learn of the future by inhaling the mephitic fumes, which exhilarated to the verge of delirium.

Some of those who came, being unable to control themselves, and having temporarily the strength of madmen, tore themselves from those seeking to restrain them, and, jumping into the vent, perished. In order to prevent others from doing likewise, a wall was erected around the fissure and a prophetess was appointed to act as mediator between the oracle and those who came to question it. According to later authorities, a tripod of gold, ornamented with carvings of Apollo in the form of Python, the great serpent, was placed over the cleft, and on this was arranged a specially prepared seat, so constructed that a person would have difficulty in falling off while under the influence of the oracular fumes. Just before this time, a story had been circulated that the fumes of the oracle arose from the decaying body of Python. It is possible that the oracle revealed its own origin.

For many centuries during its early history, virgin maidens were consecrated to the service of the oracle. They were called the *Phœbades,* or *Pythiœ,* and constituted that famous order now known as the Pythian priesthood. It is probable that women were chosen to receive the oracles because their sensitive and emotional nature responded more quickly and completely to "the fumes of enthusiasm." Three days before the time set to receive the communications from Apollo, the virgin priestess began the ceremony of purification. She bathed in the Castalian well, abstained from all food, drank only from the fountain of Cassotis, which was brought into the temple through concealed pipes, and just before mounting the tripod, she chewed a few leaves of the sacred bay tree. It has been said that the water was drugged to bring on distorted visions, or the priests of Delphi were able to manufacture an exhilarating and intoxicating gas, which they conducted by subterranean ducts and released into the shaft of the oracle several feet below the surface. Neither of these theories has been proved, however, nor does either in any way explain the accuracy of the predictions.

When the young prophetess had completed the process of purification, she was clothed in sanctified raiment and led to the tripod, upon which she seated herself, surrounded by the noxious vapors rising from the yawning fissure. Gradually, as she inhaled the fumes, a change came over her. It was as if a different spirit had entered her body. She struggled, tore her clothing, and uttered inarticulate cries. After a time her struggles ceased. Upon becoming calm a great majesty seemed to possess her, and with eyes fixed on space and body rigid, she uttered the prophetic words. The predictions were usually in the form of hexameter verse, but the words were often ambiguous and sometimes unintelligible. Every sound that she made, every motion of her body, was carefully recorded by the five Hosii, or holy men, who were appointed as scribes to preserve the minutest details of each divination. The Hosii were appointed for life, and were chosen from the direct descendants of Deucalion.

After the oracle was delivered, the Pythia began to struggle again, and the spirit released her. She was then carried or supported to a chamber of rest, where she remained till the nervous ecstasy had passed away.

Iamblichus, in his dissertation on *The Mysteries,* describes how the spirit of the oracle—a fiery dæmon, even Apollo himself—took control of the Pythoness and manifested through her: "But the prophetess in Delphi, whether she gives oracles to mankind through an attenuated and fiery spirit, bursting from the mouth of the cavern; or whether being seated in the adytum on a brazen tripod, or on a stool with four feet, she becomes sacred to the God; whichsoever of these is the case, she entirely gives herself up to a divine spirit, and is illuminated with a ray of divine fire. And when, indeed, fire ascending from the mouth of the cavern circularly invests her in collected abundance, she becomes filled from it with a divine splendour. But when she places herself on the seat of the God, she becomes coadapted to his stable prophetic power: and from both of these preparatory operations she becomes wholly possessed by the God. And then, indeed, he is present with and illuminates her in a separate manner, and is different from the fire, the spirit, the proper seat, and, in short, from all the visible apparatus of the place, whether physical or sacred."

Among the celebrities who visited the oracle of Delphi were the immortal Apollonius of Tyana and his disciple Damis. He made his offerings and, after being crowned with a laurel wreath and given a branch of the same plant to carry in his hand, he passed behind the statue of Apollo which stood before the entrance to the cave, and descended into the sacred place of the oracle. The priestess was also crowned with laurel and her head bound with a band of white wool. Apollonius asked the oracle if his name would be remembered by future generations. The Pythoness answered in the affirmative, but declared that it would always be calumniated. Apollonius left the cavern in anger, but time has proved the accuracy of the prediction, for the early church fathers perpetuated the name of Apollonius as the Antichrist. (For details of the story see *Histoire de la Magie.*)

The messages given by the virgin prophetess were turned over to the philosophers of the oracle, whose duty it was to interpret and apply them. The communications were then delivered to the poets, who immediately translated them into odes and lyrics, setting forth in exquisite form the statements supposedly made by Apollo and making them available for the populace.

Serpents were much in evidence at the oracle of Delphi. The base of the tripod upon which the Pythia sat was formed of the twisted bodies of three gigantic snakes. According to some authorities, one of the processes used to produce the prophetic ecstasy was to force the young priestess to gaze into the eyes of a serpent. Fascinated and hypnotized, she then spoke with the voice of the god.

Although the early Pythian priestesses were always maidens—some still in their teens—a law was later enacted that only women past fifty years of age should be the mouthpiece of the oracle. These older women dressed as young girls and went through the same ceremonial as the first Pythiæ. The change was probably the indirect result of a series of assaults made upon the persons of the priestesses by the profane.

During the early history of the Delphian oracle the god spoke only at each seventh birthday of Apollo. As time went on, however, the demand became so great that the Pythia was forced to seat herself upon the tripod every month. The times selected for the consultation and the questions to be asked were determined by lot or by vote of the inhabitants of Delphi.

It is generally admitted that the effect of the Delphian oracle upon Greek culture was profoundly constructive. James Gardner sums up its influence in the following words: "Its responses revealed many a tyrant and foretold his fate. Through its means many an unhappy being was saved from destruction and many a perplexed mortal guided in the right way. It encouraged useful institutions, and promoted the progress of useful discoveries. Its moral influence was on the side of virtue, and its political influence in favor of the advancement of civil liberty." (See *The Faiths of The World*.)

The oracle of Dodona was presided over by Jupiter, who uttered prophecies through oak trees, birds, and vases of brass. Many writers have noted the similarities between the rituals of Dodona and those of the Druid priests of Britain and Gaul. The famous oracular dove of Dodona, alighting upon the branches of the sacred oaks, not only discoursed at length in the Greek tongue upon philosophy and religion, but also answered the queries of those who came from distant places to consult it.

The "talking" trees stood together, forming a sacred grove. When the priests desired answers to important questions, after careful and solemn purifications they retired to the grove. They then accosted the trees, beseeching a reply from the god who dwelt therein. When they had stated their questions, the trees spoke with the voices of human beings, revealing to the priests the desired information. Some assert that there was but one tree which spoke—an oak or a beech standing in the very heart of the ancient grove. Because Jupiter was believed to inhabit this tree he was sometimes called *Phegonæus,* or one who lives in a beech tree.

Most curious of the oracles of Dodona were the "talking" vases, or kettles. These were made of brass and so carefully fashioned that when struck they gave off sound for hours. Some writers have described a row of these vases and have declared that if one of them was struck its vibrations would be communicated to all the others and a terrifying din ensue. Other authors describe a large single vase, standing upon a pillar, near which stood another column, supporting the statue of a child holding a whip. At the end of the whip were a number of swinging cords tipped with small metal balls, and the wind, which blew incessantly through the open building, caused the balls to strike against the vase. The number and intensity of the impacts and the reverberations of the vase were all carefully noted, and the priests delivered their oracles accordingly.

When the original priests of Dodona—the *Selloi*—mysteriously vanished, the oracle was served for many centuries by three priestesses who interpreted the vases and at midnight interrogated the sacred trees. The patrons of the oracles were expected to bring offerings and to make contributions.

Another remarkable oracle was the Cave of Trophonius, which stood upon the side of a hill with an entrance so small that it seemed impossible for a human being to enter. After the consultant had made his offering at the statue of Trophonius and had donned the sanctified garments, he climbed the hill to the cave, carrying in one hand a cake of honey. Sitting down at the edge of the opening, he lowered his feet into the cavern. Thereupon his entire body was precipitately drawn into the cave, which was described by those who had entered it as having only the dimensions of a fair-sized oven. When the oracle had completed its revelation, the consultant, usually delirious, was forcibly ejected from the cave, feet foremost.

Near the cave of the oracle two fountains bubbled out of the earth within a few feet of each other. Those about to enter the cave drank first from these fountains, the waters of which seemed to possess peculiar occult properties. The first contained the water of forgetfulness, and all who drank thereof forgot their earthly sorrows. From the second fountain flowed the sacred water of Mnemosyne, or remembrance, for later it enabled those who partook of it to recall their experiences while in the cave.

Though its entrance was marked by two brass obelisks, the cave, surrounded by a wall of white stones and concealed in the heart of a grove of sacred trees, did not present an imposing appearance. There is no doubt that those entering it passed through strange experiences, for they were obliged to leave at the adjacent temple a complete account of what they saw and heard while in the oracle. The prophecies were given in the form of dreams and visions, and were accompanied by severe pains in the head; some never completely recovered from the after effects of their delirium. The confused recital of their experiences was interpreted by the priests according to the question to be answered. While the priests probably used some unknown herb to produce the dreams or visions of the cavern, their skill in interpreting them bordered on the supernatural. Before consulting the oracle, it was necessary to offer a ram to the dæmon of the cave, and the priest decided by hieromancy whether the time chosen was propitious and the sacrifice was satisfactory.

The Seven Wonders of the World

Many of the sculptors and architects of the ancient world were initiates of the Mysteries, particularly the Eleusinian rites. Since the dawn of time, the truers of stone and the hewers of wood have constituted a divinely overshadowed caste. As civilization spread slowly over the earth, cities were built and deserted; monuments were erected to heroes at present unknown; temples were built to gods who lie broken in the dust of the nations they inspired. Research has proved not only that the builders of these cities and monuments and the sculptors who chiseled out the inscrutable faces of the gods were masters of their crafts, but that in the world today there are none to equal them. The profound knowledge of mathematics and astronomy embodied in ancient architecture, and the equally profound knowledge of anatomy revealed in Greek statuary, prove that the fashioners of both were master minds, deeply cultured in the wisdom which constituted the arcana of the Mysteries. Thus was established the Guild of the Builders, progenitors of modern Freemasons. When employed to build palaces, temples or tombs, or to carve statues for the wealthy, those initiated architects and artists concealed in their works the secret doctrine, so that now, long after their bones have returned to dust, the world realizes that those first artisans were indeed duly initiated and worthy to receive the wages of Master Masons.

The Seven Wonders of the World, while apparently designed for diverse reasons, were really monuments erected to perpetuate the arcana of the Mysteries. They were symbolic structures, placed in peculiar spots, and the real purpose of their erection can be sensed only by the initiated. Eliphas Levi has noted the marked correspondence between these Seven Wonders and the seven planets. The Seven Wonders of the World were built by Widow's sons in honor of the seven planetary genii. Their secret symbolism is identical with that of the seven seals of Revelation and the seven churches of Asia.

1. The Colossus of Rhodes, a gigantic brass statue about 109 feet in height and requiring over twelve years to build, was the work of an initiated artist, Charles of Lindus. The popular theory—accepted for several hundred years—that the figure stood with one foot on each side of the entrance to the harbor of Rhodes and that full-rigged ships passed between its feet, has never been substantiated. Unfortunately, the figure remained standing but fifty-six years, being thrown down by an earthquake in 224 B.C. The shattered parts of the Colossus lay scattered about the ground for more than 900 years, when they were finally sold to a Jewish merchant, who carried the metal away on the backs of 700 camels. Some believed that the brass was converted into munitions and others that it was made into drainage pipes. This gigantic gilded figure, with its crown of solar rays and its upraised torch, signified occultly the glorious Sun Man of the Mysteries, the Universal Savior.

2. The architect Ctesiphon, in the fifth century B.C., submitted to the Ionian cities a plan for erecting a joint monument to their patron goddess, Diana. The place chosen was Ephesus, a city south of Smyrna. The building was constructed of marble. The roof was supported by 127 columns, each 60 feet high and weighing over 150 tons. The temple was destroyed by black magic about 356 B.C., but the world fixes the odious crime upon the tool by means of which the destruction was accomplished—a mentally deranged man named Herostratus. It was later rebuilt, but the symbolism was lost. The original temple, designed as a miniature of the universe, was dedicated to the moon, the occult symbol of generation.

3. Upon his exile from Athens, Phidias—the greatest of all the Greek sculptors—went to Olympia in the province of Elis and there designed his colossal statue of Zeus, chief of the gods of Greece. There is not even an accurate description of this masterpiece now in existence; only a few old coins give an inadequate idea of its general appearance. The body of the god was overlaid with ivory and the robes were of beaten gold. In one hand he is supposed to have held a globe supporting a figure of the Goddess of Victory, in the other a scepter surmounted by an eagle. The head of Zeus was archaic, heavily bearded, and crowned with an olive wreath. The statue was seated upon an elaborately decorated throne. As its name implies, the monument was dedicated to the spirit of the planet Jupiter, one of the seven Logi who bow before the Lord of the Sun.

4. Eliphas Levi includes the Temple of Solomon among the Seven Wonders of the World, giving it the place occupied by the Pharos, or Lighthouse, of

Alexandria. The Pharos, named for the island upon which it stood, was designed and constructed by Sostratus of Cnidus during the reign of Ptolemy (283–247 B.C.). It is described as being of white marble and over 600 feet high. Even in that ancient day it cost nearly a million dollars. Fires were lighted in the top of it and could be seen for miles out at sea. It was destroyed by an earthquake in the thirteenth century, but remains of it were visible until A.D. 1350. Being the tallest of all the Wonders, it was naturally assigned to Saturn, the Father of the gods and the true illuminator of all humanity.

5. The Mausoleum at Halicarnassus was a magnificent monument erected by Queen Artemisia in memory of her dead husband, King Mausolus, from whose name the word *mausoleum* is derived. The designers of the building were Satyrus and Pythis, and four great sculptors were employed to orna- ment the edifice. The building, which was 114 feet long and 92 feet wide, was divided into five major sections (the senses) and surmounted by a pyra- mid (the spiritual nature of man). The pyramid rose in 24 steps (a sacred number), and upon the apex was a statue of King Mausolus in a chariot. His figure was 9 feet 9½ inches tall. Many attempts have been made to recon- struct the monument, which was destroyed by an earthquake, but none has been altogether successful. This monument was sacred to the planet Mars and was built by an initiate for the enlightenment of the world.

6. The Gardens of Semiramis at Babylon—more commonly known as the Hanging Gardens—stood within the palace grounds of Nebuchadnezzar, near the Euphrates River. They rose in a terrace-like pyramid and on the top was a reservoir for the watering of the gardens. They were built about 600 B.C., but the name of the landscape artist has not been preserved. They symbolized the planes of the invisible world, and were consecrated to Venus as the goddess of love and beauty.

7. The Great Pyramid was supreme among the temples of the Mysteries. In order to be true to its astronomical symbolism, it must have been con- structed about 70,000 years ago. It was the tomb of Osiris, and was believed to have been built by the gods themselves, and the architect may have been the immortal Hermes. It is the monument of Mercury, the messenger of the gods, and the universal symbol of wisdom and letters.

The Life and Philosophy of Pythagoras

hile Mnesarchus, the father of Pythagoras, was in the city of Delphi on matters pertaining to his business as a merchant, he and his wife, Parthenis, decided to consult the oracle of Delphi as to whether the Fates were favorable for their return voyage to Syria. When the Pythoness (prophetess of Apollo) seated herself on the golden tripod over the yawning vent of the oracle, she did not answer the question they had asked, but told Mnesarchus that his wife was then with child and would give birth to a son who was destined to surpass all men in beauty and wisdom, and who throughout the course of his life would contribute much to the benefit of mankind. Mnesarchus was so deeply impressed by the prophecy that he changed his wife's name to Pythasis, in honor of the Pythian priestess. When the child was born at Sidon in Phœnicia, it was—as the oracle had said—a son. Mnesarchus and Pythasis named the child Pythagoras, for they believed that he had been predestined by the oracle.

Many strange legends have been preserved concerning the birth of Pythagoras. Some maintained that he was no mortal man: that he was one of the gods who had taken a human body to enable him to come into the world and instruct the human race. Pythagoras was one of the many sages and saviors of antiquity for whom an immaculate conception is asserted. In his *Anacalypsis,* Godfrey Higgins writes: "The first striking circumstance in which the history of Pythagoras agrees with the history of Jesus is, that they were natives of nearly the same country; the former being born at Sidon, the latter at Bethlehem, both in Syria. The father of Pythagoras, as well as the father of Jesus, was prophetically informed that his wife should bring forth a son, who should be a benefactor to mankind. They were both born when their mothers were from home on journeys, Joseph and his wife having gone up to Bethlehem to be taxed, and the father of Pythagoras having travelled from Samos, his residence, to Sidon, about his mercantile concerns. Pythais [Pythasis], the mother of Pythagoras, had a connexion with an Apolloniacal spectre, or ghost, of the God Apollo, or God Sol, (of course this must have been a *holy* ghost, and here we have the Holy Ghost) which afterward appeared to her husband, and told him that he must have no connexion with his wife during her pregnancy—a story evidently the same as that relating to Joseph and Mary. From these peculiar circumstances, Pythagoras was known by the same title as Jesus, namely, the *son of God;* and was supposed by the multitude to be under the influence of Divine inspiration."

This most famous philosopher was born sometime between 600 and 590 B.C., and the length of his life has been estimated at nearly one hundred years.

The teachings of Pythagoras indicate that he was thoroughly conversant with the precepts of Oriental and Occidental esotericism. He traveled among the Jews and was instructed by the Rabbins concerning the secret traditions of Moses, the lawgiver of Israel. Later the School of the Essenes was conducted chiefly for the purpose of interpreting the Pythagorean symbols. Pythagoras was initiated into Egyptian, Babylonian, and Chaldean Mysteries. Although it is believed by some that he was a disciple of Zoroaster, it is doubtful whether his instructor of that name was the God-man now revered by the Parsees. While accounts of his travels differ, historians agree that he visited many countries and studied at the feet of many masters.

"After having acquired all which it was possible for him to learn of the Greek philosophers and, presumably, become an initiate in the Eleusinian mysteries, he went to Egypt, and after many rebuffs and refusals, finally succeeded in securing initiation in the Mysteries of Isis, at the hands of the priests of Thebes. Then this intrepid 'joiner' wended his way into Phœnicia and Syria where the Mysteries of Adonis were conferred upon him, and crossing to the valley of the Euphrates he tarried long enough to become versed in the secret lore of the Chaldeans, who still dwelt in the vicinity of Babylon. Finally, he made his greatest and most historic venture through Media and Persia into Hindustan where he remained several years as a pupil and initiate of the learned Brahmins of Elephanta and Ellora." (See *Ancient Freemasonry,* by Frank C. Higgins, 32°.) The same author adds that the name of Pythagoras is still preserved in the records of the Brahmins as *Yavancharya,* the Ionian Teacher.

Pythagoras was said to have been the first man to call himself a *philosopher;* in fact, the world is indebted to him for the word *philosopher.* Before that time the wise men had called themselves *sages,* which was interpreted to mean *those who know.* Pythagoras was more modest. He coined the word *philosopher*, which he defined as *one who is attempting to find out.*

After returning from his wanderings, Pythagoras established a school, or as it has been sometimes called, a university, at Crotona, a Dorian colony in Southern Italy. Upon his arrival at Crotona he was regarded askance, but after a short time those holding important positions in the surrounding colonies sought his counsel in matters of great moment. He gathered around him a small group of sincere disciples whom he instructed in the secret wisdom which had been revealed to him, and also in the fundamentals of occult mathematics, music, and astronomy, which he considered to be the triangular foundation of all the arts and sciences.

When he was about sixty years old, Pythagoras married one of his disciples, and seven children resulted from the union. His wife was a remarkably able woman, who not only inspired him during the years of his life but after his assassination continued to promulgate his doctrines.

As is so often the case with genius, Pythagoras by his outspokenness incurred both political and personal enmity. Among those who came for initiation was one who, because Pythagoras refused to admit him, determined to destroy both the man and his philosophy. By means of false propaganda, this disgruntled one turned the minds of the common people against the philosopher. Without warning, a band of murderers descended upon the little group of buildings where the great teacher and his disciples dwelt, burned the structures and killed Pythagoras.

Accounts of the philosopher's death do not agree. Some say that he was murdered with his disciples; others that, on escaping from Crotona with a small band of followers, he was trapped and burned alive by his enemies in a little house where the band had decided to rest for the night. Another account states that, finding themselves trapped in the burning structure, the disciples threw themselves into the flames, making of their own bodies a bridge over which Pythagoras escaped, only to die of a broken heart a short time afterwards as the result of grieving over the apparent fruitlessness of his efforts to serve and illuminate mankind.

His surviving disciples attempted to perpetuate his doctrines, but they were persecuted on every hand and very little remains today as a testimonial to the greatness of this philosopher. It is said that the disciples of Pythagoras never addressed him or referred to him by his own name, but always as *The Master* or *That Man*. This may have been because of the fact that the name Pythagoras was believed to consist of a certain number of specially arranged letters with great sacred significance. *The Word* magazine has printed an article by T. R. Prater, showing that Pythagoras initiated his candidates by means of a certain formula concealed within the letters of his own name. This may explain why the word Pythagoras was so highly revered.

After the death of Pythagoras his school gradually disintegrated, but those who had benefited by its teachings revered the memory of the great philosopher, as during his life they had reverenced the man himself. As time went on, Pythagoras came to be regarded as a god rather than a man, and his scattered disciples were bound together by their common admiration for the transcendent genius of their teacher. Edouard Schure, in his *Pythagoras and the Delphic Mysteries,* relates the following incident as illustrative of the bond of fellowship uniting the members of the Pythagorean School:

"One of them who had fallen upon sickness and poverty was kindly taken in by an innkeeper. Before dying he traced a few mysterious signs (the pentagram, no doubt) on the door of the inn and said to the host, 'Do not be uneasy, one of my brothers will pay my debts.' A year afterwards, as a stranger was passing by this inn he saw the signs and said to the host, 'I am a Pythagorean; one of my brothers died here; tell me what I owe you on his account.'"

Frank C. Higgins, 32°, gives an excellent compendium of the Pythagorean tenets in the following outline:

"Pythagoras' teachings are of the most transcendental importance to Masons, inasmuch as they are the necessary fruit of his contact with the leading philosophers of the whole civilized world of his own day, and must represent that in which all were agreed, shorn of all weeds of controversy. Thus, the determined stand made by Pythagoras, in defense of pure monotheism, is sufficient evidence that the tradition to the effect that the unity of God was the supreme secret of all the ancient initiations is substantially correct. The philosophical school of Pythagoras was, in a measure, also a series of initiations, for he caused his pupils to pass through a series of degrees and never permitted them personal contact with himself until they had reached the higher grades. According to his biographers, his degrees were three in number. The first, that of 'Mathematicus,' assuring his pupils proficiency in mathematics and geometry, which was then, as it would be now if Masonry were properly inculcated, the basis upon which all other knowledge was erected. Secondly, the degree of 'Theoreticus,' which dealt with superficial applications of the exact sciences, and, lastly, the degree of 'Electus,' which entitled the candidate to pass forward into the light of the fullest illumination which he was capable of absorbing. The pupils of the Pythagorean school were divided into 'exoterici,' or pupils in the outer grades, and 'esoterici,' after they had passed the third degree of initiation and were entitled to the secret wisdom. Silence, secrecy and unconditional obedience were cardinal principles of this great order." (See *Ancient Freemasonry.*)

Pythagoric Fundamentals

The study of geometry, music, and astronomy was considered essential to a rational understanding of God, man, or Nature, and no one could accompany Pythagoras as a disciple who was not thoroughly familiar with these sciences. Many came seeking admission to his school. Each applicant was tested on these three subjects, and if found ignorant, was summarily dismissed.

Pythagoras was not an extremist. He taught moderation in all things rather than excess in anything, for he believed that an excess of virtue was in itself a vice. One of his favorite statements was: "We must avoid with our utmost endeavor, and amputate with fire and sword, and by all other means, from the body, sickness; from the soul, ignorance; from the belly, luxury; from a city, sedition; from a family, discord; and from all things, excess." Pythagoras also believed that there was no crime equal to that of anarchy.

All men know what they *want*, but few know what they *need.* Pythagoras warned his disciples that when they prayed they should not pray for themselves; that when they asked things of the gods they should not ask things for themselves, because no man knows what is good for him and it is for this reason undesirable to ask for things which, if obtained, would only prove to be injurious.

The God of Pythagoras was the *Monad,* or the One that is Everything. He described God as the Supreme Mind distributed throughout all parts of the universe—the Cause of all things, the Intelligence

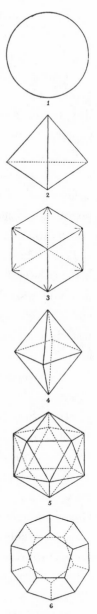

THE SYMMETRICAL GEOMETRIC SOLIDS.

To the five symmetrical solids of the ancients is added the sphere (1), the most perfect of all created forms. The five Pythagorean solids are: the tetrahedron (2) with four equilateral triangles as faces; the cube (3) with six squares as faces; the octahedron (4) with eight equilateral triangles as faces; the icosahedron (5) with twenty equilateral triangles as faces; and the dodecahedron (6) with twelve regular pentagons as faces.

of all things, and the Power within all things. He further declared the motion of God to be circular, the body of God to be composed of the substance of light, and the nature of God to be composed of the substance of truth.

Pythagoras declared that the eating of meat clouded the reasoning faculties. While he did not condemn its use or totally abstain therefrom himself, he declared that judges should refrain from eating meat before a trial, in order that those who appeared before them might receive the most honest and astute decisions. When Pythagoras decided (as he often did) to retire into the temple of God for an extended period of time to meditate and pray, he took with him a supply of specially prepared food and drink. The food consisted of equal parts of the seeds of poppy and sesame, the skin of the sea onion from which the juice had been thoroughly extracted, the flower of daffodil, the leaves of mallows, and a paste of barley and peas. These he compounded together with the addition of wild honey. For a beverage he took the seeds of cucumbers, dried raisins (with seeds removed), the flowers of coriander, the seeds of mallows and purslane, scraped cheese, meal, and cream, mixed together and sweetened with wild honey. Pythagoras claimed that this was the diet of Hercules while wandering in the Libyan desert and was according to the formula given to that hero by the goddess Ceres herself.

The favorite method of healing among the Pythagoreans was by the aid of poultices. These people also knew the magic properties of vast numbers of plants. Pythagoras highly esteemed the medicinal properties of the sea onion, and he is said to have written an entire volume on the subject. Such a work, however, is not known at the present time. Pythagoras discovered that music had great therapeutic power and he prepared special harmonies for various diseases. He apparently experimented also with color, attaining considerable success. One of his unique curative processes resulted from his discovery of the healing value of certain verses from the *Odyssey* and the *Iliad* of Homer. These he caused to be read to persons suffering from certain ailments. He was opposed to surgery in all its forms and also objected to cauterizing. He would not permit the disfigurement of the human body, for such, in his estimation, was a sacrilege against the dwelling place of the gods.

Pythagoras taught that friendship was the truest and nearest perfect of all relationships. He declared that in Nature there was a friendship of all for all; of gods for men; of doctrines one for another; of the soul for the body; of the rational part for the irrational part; of philosophy for its theory; of men for one another; of countrymen for one another; that friendship also existed between strangers, between a man and his wife, his children, and his servants. All bonds without friendship were shackles, and there was no virtue in their maintenance.

Pythagoras believed that relationships were essentially mental rather than phys-ical, and that a stranger of sympathetic intellect was closer to him than a blood relation whose viewpoint was at variance with his own. Pythagoras defined knowledge as the fruitage of mental accumulation. He believed that it would be obtained in many ways, but principally through observation. Wisdom was the understanding of the source or cause of all things, and this could be secured only by raising the intellect to a point where it intuitively cognized the invisible manifesting outwardly through the visible, and thus became capable of bringing itself *en rapport* with the spirit of things rather than with their forms. The ulti-mate source that wisdom could cognize was the *Monad,* the mysterious perma-nent atom of the Pythagoreans.

Pythagoras taught that both man and the universe were made in the image of God; that both being made in the same image, the understanding of one pred-icated the knowledge of the other. He further taught that there was a constant interplay between the Grand Man (the universe) and man (the little universe).

Pythagoras believed that all the sidereal bodies were alive and that the forms of the planets and stars were merely bodies encasing souls, minds, and spirits in the same manner that the visible human form is but the encasing vehicle for an invisible spiritual organism which is, in reality, the conscious individual. Pythagoras regarded the planets as magnificent deities, worthy of the adoration and respect of man. All these deities, however, he considered subservient to the One First Cause within whom they all existed temporarily, as mortality exists in the midst of immortality.

The famous Pythagorean Y signified the power of choice and was used in the Mysteries as emblematic of the Forking of the Ways. The central stem sepa-rated into two parts, one branching to the right and the other to the left. The branch to the right was called *Divine Wisdom* and the one to the left *Earthly Wisdom.* Youth, personified by the candidate, walking the Path of Life, symbol-ized by the central stem of the Y, reaches the point where the Path divides. The neophyte must then choose whether he will take the left-hand path and, follow-ing the dictates of his lower nature, enter upon a span of folly and thoughtless-ness which will inevitably result in his undoing, or whether he will take the right-hand road and through integrity, industry, and sincerity ultimately regain union with the immortals in the superior spheres.

It is probable that Pythagoras obtained his concept of the Y from the Egyp-tians, who included in certain of their initiatory rituals a scene in which the candidate was confronted by two female figures. One of them, veiled with the white robes of the temple, urged the neophyte to enter into the halls of learning;

the other, bedecked with jewels, symbolizing earthly treasures, and bearing in her hands a tray loaded with grapes (emblematic of false light), sought to lure him into the chambers of dissipation. This symbol is still preserved among the Tarot cards, where it is called The Forking of the Ways. The forked stick has been the symbol of life among many nations, and it was placed in the desert to indicate the presence of water.

Concerning the theory of transmigration as disseminated by Pythagoras, there are differences of opinion. According to one view, he taught that mortals who during their earthly existence had by their actions become like certain animals, returned to earth again in the form of the beasts which they had grown to resemble. Thus, a timid person would return in the form of a rabbit or a deer; a cruel person in the form of a wolf or other ferocious animal; and a cunning person in the guise of a fox. This concept, however, does not fit into the general Pythagorean scheme, and it is far more likely that it was given in an allegorical rather than a literal sense. It was intended to convey the idea that human beings become bestial when they allow themselves to be dominated by their own lower desires and destructive tendencies. It is probable that the term *transmigration* is to be understood as what is more commonly called *reincarnation,* a doctrine which Pythagoras must have contacted directly or indirectly in India and Egypt.

The fact that Pythagoras accepted the theory of successive reappearances of the spiritual nature in human form is found in a footnote to Levi's *History of Magic:* "He was an important champion of what used to be called the doctrine of metempsychosis, understood as the soul's transmigration into successive bodies. He himself had been (a) Aethalides, a son of Mercury; (b) Euphorbus, son of Panthus, who perished at the hands of Menelaus in the Trojan war; (c) Hermotimus, a prophet of Clazomenae, a city of Ionia; (d) a humble fisherman; and finally (e) the philosopher of Samos."

Pythagoras also taught that each species of creatures had what he termed a seal, given to it by God, and that the physical form of each was the impression of this seal upon the wax of physical substance. Thus each body was stamped with the dignity of its divinely given pattern. Pythagoras believed that ultimately man would reach a state where he would cast off his gross nature and function in a body of spiritualized ether which would be in juxtaposition to his physical form at all times and which might be the eighth sphere, or Antichthon. From this he would ascend into the realm of the immortals, where by divine birthright he belonged.

Pythagoras taught that everything in nature was divisible into three parts and that no one could become truly wise who did not view every problem as being diagrammatically triangular. He said, "Establish the triangle and the problem is two-thirds solved"; further, "All things consist of three." In conformity with this viewpoint, Pythagoras divided the universe into three parts, which he called the *Supreme World,* the *Superior World,* and the *Inferior World.* The highest, or Supreme World, was a subtle, interpenetrative spiritual essence pervading all things and therefore the true plane of the Supreme Deity itself, the Deity being in every sense omnipresent, omniactive, omnipotent, and omniscient. Both of the lower worlds existed within the nature of this supreme sphere.

The Superior World was the home of the immortals. It was also the dwelling place of the archetypes, or the seals; their natures in no manner partook of the material of earthiness, but they, casting their shadows upon the deep (the Inferior World), were cognizable only through their shadows. The third, or Inferior World, was the home of those creatures who partook of material substance or were engaged in labor with or upon material substance. Hence, this sphere was the home of the mortal gods, the Demiurgi, the angels who labor with men; also the dæmons who partake of the nature of the earth; and finally mankind and the lower kingdoms, those temporarily of the earth but capable of rising above that sphere by reason and philosophy.

The digits 1 and 2 are not considered numbers by the Pythagoreans, because they typify the two supermundane spheres. The Pythagorean numbers, therefore, begin with 3, the triangle, and 4, the square. These added to the 1 and the 2, produce the 10, the great number of all things, the archetype of the universe. The three worlds were called *receptacles.* The first was the receptacle of principles, the second was the receptacle of intelligences, and the third, or lowest, was the receptacle of quantities.

"The symmetrical solids were regarded by Pythagoras, and by the Greek thinkers after him, as of the greatest importance. To be perfectly symmetrical or regular, a solid must have an equal number of faces meeting at each of its angles, and these faces must be equal regular polygons, i. e., figures whose sides and angles are all equal. Pythagoras, perhaps, may be credited with the great discovery that there are only five such solids. * * *

"Now, the Greeks believed the world [material universe] to be composed of four elements—earth, air, fire, water—and to the Greek mind the conclusion was inevitable that the shapes of the particles of the elements were those of the regular solids. Earth-particles were cubical, the cube being the regular solid possessed of greatest stability; fire-particles were tetrahedral, the tetrahedron being the simplest and, hence, lightest solid. Water-particles were icosahedral for exactly the reverse reason, wilst air-particles, as intermediate between the two latter, were octahedral. The dodecahedron was, to these ancient mathematicians, the most mysterious of the solids; it was by far the most difficult to construct, the accurate drawing of the regular pentagon necessitating a rather elaborate application of Pythagoras' great theorem. Hence the conclusion, as Plato put it, that 'this (the regular dodecahedron) the Deity employed in tracing the plan of the Universe.'" (H. Stanley Redgrove, in *Bygone Beliefs.*)

Mr. Redgrove has not mentioned the fifth element of the ancient Mysteries, that which would make the analogy between the symmetrical solids and the elements complete. This fifth element, or ether, was called by the Hindus *akasa*. It was closely correlated with the hypothetical ether of modern science, and was the interpenetrative substance permeating all of the other elements and acting as a common solvent and common denominator of them. The twelve-faced solid also subtly referred to the Twelve Immortals who surfaced the universe, and also to the twelve convolutions of the human brain—the vehicles of those Immortals in the nature of man.

While Pythagoras, in accordance with others of his day, practiced divination (possibly arithmomancy), there is no accurate information concerning the methods which he used. He is believed to have had a remarkable wheel by means of which he could predict future events, and to have learned hydromancy from the Egyptians. He believed that brass had oracular powers, because even when everything was perfectly still there was always a rumbling sound in brass bowls. He once addressed a prayer to the spirit of a river and out of the water arose a voice, "Pythagoras, I greet thee." It is claimed for him that he was able to cause dæmons to enter into water and disturb its surface, and by means of the agitations certain things were predicted.

After having drunk from a certain spring one day, one of the Masters of Pythagoras announced that the spirit of the water had just predicted that a great earthquake would occur the next day—a prophecy which was fulfilled. It is highly probable that Pythagoras possessed hypnotic power, not only over man but also over animals. He caused a bird to change the course of its flight, a bear to cease its ravages upon a community, and a bull to change its diet, by the exercise of mental influence. He was also gifted with second sight, being able to see things at a distance and accurately describe incidents that had not yet come to pass.

The Symbolic Aphorisms of Pythagoras

Iamblichus gathered thirty-nine of the symbolic sayings of Pythagoras and interpreted them. These have been translated from the Greek by Thomas Taylor. Aphorismic statement was one of the favorite methods of instruction used in the Pythagorean university of Crotona. Ten of the most representative of these aphorisms are reproduced below with a brief elucidation of their concealed meanings.

I. *Declining from the public ways, walk in unfrequented paths.* By this it is to be understood that those who desire wisdom must seek it in solitude.

II. *Govern your tongue before all other things, following the gods.* This aphorism warns man that his words, instead of representing him, misrepresent him, and that when in doubt as to what he should say, he should always be silent.

III. *The wind blowing, adore the sound.* Pythagoras here reminds his disciples that the fiat of God is heard in the voice of the elements, and that all things in Nature manifest through harmony, rhythm, order, or procedure the attributes of the Deity.

IV. *Assist a man in raising a burden; but do not assist him in laying it down.* The student is instructed to aid the diligent but never to assist those who seek to evade their responsibilities, for it is a great sin to encourage indolence.

V. *Speak not about Pythagoric concerns without light.* The world is herein warned that it should not attempt to interpret the mysteries of God and the states of the sciences without spiritual and intellectual illumination.

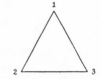

VI. *Having departed from your house, turn not back; for the furies will be your attendants.* Pythagoras here warns his followers that any who begin the search for truth and, after having learned part of the mystery, become discouraged and attempt to return again to their former ways of vice and ignorance, will suffer exceedingly; for it is better to know nothing about Divinity than to learn a little and then stop without learning all.

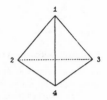

NUMBER RELATED TO FORM.

Pythagoras taught that the dot symbolized the power of the number 1, the line the power of the number 2, the surface the power of the number 3, and the solid the power of the number 4.

VII. *Nourish a cock, but sacrifice it not; for it is sacred to the sun and moon.* Two great lessons are concealed in this aphorism. The first is a warning against the sacrifice of

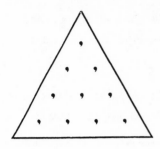

THE TETRACTYS.

Theon of Smyrna declares that the ten dots, or tetractys of Pythagoras, was a symbol of the greatest importance, for to the discerning mind it revealed the mystery of universal nature. The Pythagoreans bound themselves by the following oath: "By Him who gave to our soul the tetractys, which hath the fountain and root of ever-springing nature."

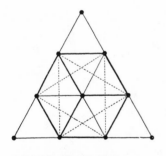

THE CUBE AND THE STAR.

By connecting the ten dots of the tetractys, nine triangles are formed. Six of these are involved in the forming of the cube. The same triangles, when lines are properly drawn between them, also reveal the six-pointed star with a dot in the center. Only seven dots are used in forming the cube and the star. Qabbalistically, the three unused corner dots represent the threefold, invisible causal universe, while the seven dots involved in the cube and the star are the Elohim—the Spirits of the seven creative periods. The Sabbath, or seventh day, is the central dot.

living things to the gods, because life is sacred and man should not destroy it even as an offering to the Deity. The second warns man that the human body here referred to as a cock is sacred to the sun (God) and the moon (Nature), and should be guarded and preserved as man's most precious medium of expression. Pythagoras also warned his disciples against suicide.

VIII.   *Receive not a swallow into your house.* This warns the seeker after truth not to allow drifting thoughts to come into his mind nor shiftless persons to enter into his life. He must ever surround himself with rationally inspired thinkers and with conscientious workers.

IX.   *Offer not your right hand easily to anyone.* This warns the disciple to keep his own counsel and not offer wisdom and knowledge (his right hand) to such as are incapable of appreciating them. The hand here represents Truth, which *raises* those who have fallen because of ignorance; but as many of the unregenerate do not desire wisdom they will cut off the hand that is extended in kindness to them. Time alone can effect the redemption of the ignorant masses.

X.   *When rising from the bedclothes, roll them together, and obliterate the impression of the body.* Pythagoras directed his disciples who had awakened from the sleep of ignorance into the waking state of intelligence to eliminate from their recollection all memory of their former spiritual darkness; for a wise man in passing leaves no form behind him which others less intelligent, seeing, shall use as a mold for the casting of idols.

The most famous of the Pythagorean fragments are the *Golden Verses,* ascribed to Pythagoras himself, but concerning whose authorship there is an element of doubt. The *Golden Verses* contain a brief summary of the entire system of philosophy forming the basis of the educational doctrines of Crotona, or, as it is more commonly known, the Italic School. These verses open by counseling the reader to love God, venerate the great heroes, and respect the dæmons and elemental inhabitants. They then urge man to think carefully and industriously concerning his daily life, and to prefer the treasures of the mind and soul to accumulations of earthly goods. The verses also promise man that if he will rise above his lower material nature and cultivate self-control, he will ultimately be acceptable in the sight of the gods, be reunited with them, and partake of their immortality. (It is rather significant to note that Plato paid a great price for some of the manuscripts of Pythagoras which had been saved from the destruction of Crotona. *See Historia Deorum Fatidicorum,* Geneva, 1675.)

Pythagorean Astronomy

According to Pythagoras, the position of each body in the universe was determined by the essential dignity of that body. The popular concept of his day was that the earth occupied the center of the solar system; that the planets, including the sun and moon, moved about the earth; and that the earth itself was flat and square. Contrary to this concept, and regardless of criticism, Pythagoras declared that fire was the most important of all the elements; that the center was the most important part of every body; and that, just as Vesta's fire was in the midst of every home, so in the midst of the universe was a flaming sphere of celestial radiance. This central globe he called the *Tower of Jupiter,* the *Globe of Unity,* the *Grand Monad,* and the *Altar of Vesta.* As the sacred number 10 symbolized the sum of all parts and the completeness of all things, it was only natural for Pythagoras to divide the universe into ten spheres, symbolized by ten concentric circles. These circles began at the center with the globe of Divine Fire; then came the seven planets, the earth, and another mysterious planet, called *Antichthon,* which was never visible.

Opinions differ as to the nature of *Antichthon.* Clement of Alexandria believed that it represented the mass of the heavens; others held the opinion that it was the moon. More probably it was the mysterious *eighth sphere* of the ancients, the dark planet which moved in the same orbit as the earth but which was always concealed from the earth by the body of the sun, being in exact opposition to the earth at all times. Is this the mysterious Lilith concerning which astrologers have speculated so long?

Isaac Myer has stated: "The Pythagoreans held that each star was a world having its own atmosphere, with an immense extent surrounding it, of aether." (See *The Qabbalah.*) The disciples of Pythagoras also highly revered the planet Venus, because it was the only planet bright enough to cast a shadow. As the morning star, Venus is visible before sunrise, and as the evening star it shines forth immediately after sunset. Because of these qualities, a number of names have been given to it by the ancients. Being visible in the sky at sunset, it was called *vesper,* and as it arose before the sun, it was called *the false light, the star of the morning,* or *Lucifer,* which means *the light-bearer.* Because of this relation to the sun, the planet was also referred to as Venus, Astarte, Aphrodite, Isis, and The Mother of the Gods. It is possible that at some seasons of the year in certain latitudes the fact that Venus was a crescent could be detected without the aid of a telescope. This would account for the crescent which is often seen in connection with the goddesses of antiquity, the stories of which do not agree with the phases of the moon. The accurate knowledge which Pythagoras possessed concerning astronomy he undoubtedly secured in the Egyptian temples, for their priests understood the true relationship of the heavenly bodies many thousands of years before that knowledge was revealed to the uninitiated world. The fact that the knowledge he acquired in the temples enabled him to make assertions requiring two thousand years to check proves why Plato and Aristotle so highly esteemed the profundity of the ancient Mysteries. In the midst of comparative scientific ignorance, and without the aid of any modern instruments, the priest-philosophers had discovered the true fundamentals of universal dynamics.

An interesting application of the Pythagorean doctrine of geometric solids as expounded by Plato is found in *The Canon.* "Nearly all the old philosophers," says its anonymous author, "devised an harmonic theory with respect to the universe, and the practice continued till the old mode of philosophizing died out. Kepler (1596), in order to demonstrate the Platonic doctrine, that the universe was formed of the five regular solids, proposed the following rule. 'The earth is a circle, the measurer of all. Round it describe a dodecahedron; the circle inclosing this will be Mars. Round Mars describe a tetrahedron; the sphere inclosing this will be Jupiter. Describe a cube round Jupiter; the sphere containing this will be Saturn. Now inscribe in the earth an icosahedron; the circle inscribed in it will be Venus. Inscribe an octahedron in Venus; the circle inscribed in it will be Mercury' (*Mysterium Cosmographicum,* 1596). This rule cannot be taken seriously as a real statement of the proportions of the cosmos, for it bears no real resemblance to the ratios published by Copernicus in the beginning of the sixteenth century. Yet Kepler was very proud of his formula, and said he valued it more than the Electorate of Saxony. It was also approved by those two eminent authorities, Tycho and Galileo, who evidently understood it. Kepler himself never gives the least hint of how his precious rule is to be interpreted." Platonic astronomy was not concerned with the material constitution or arrangement of the heavenly bodies, but considered the stars and planets primarily as focal points of Divine intelligence. Physical astronomy was regarded as the science of "shadows," philosophical astronomy the science of "realities."

Pythagorean Mathematics

oncerning the secret significance of numbers there has been much speculation. Though many interesting discoveries have been made, it may be safely said that with the death of Pythagoras the great key to this science was lost. For nearly 2500 years philosophers of all nations have attempted to unravel the Pythagorean skein, but apparently none has been successful. Notwithstanding attempts made to obliterate all records of the teachings of Pythagoras, fragments have survived which give clues to some of the simpler parts of his philosophy. The major secrets were never committed to writing, but were communicated orally to a few chosen disciples. These apparently dared not divulge their secrets to the profane, the result being that when death sealed their lips the arcana died with them.

Certain of the secret schools in the world today are perpetuations of the ancient Mysteries, and although it is quite possible that they may possess some of the original numerical formulæ, there is no evidence of it in the voluminous writings which have issued from these groups during the last five hundred years. These writings, while frequently discussing Pythagoras, show no indication of a more complete knowledge of his intricate doctrines than the post-Pythagorean Greek speculators had, who talked much, wrote little, knew less, and concealed their ignorance under a series of mysterious hints and promises. Here and there among the literary products of early writers are found enigmatic statements which they made no effort to interpret. The following example is quoted from Plutarch:

"The Pythagoreans indeed go farther than this, and honour even numbers and geometrical diagrams with the names and titles of the gods. Thus they call the equilateral triangle head-born Minerva and Tritogenia, because it may be equally divided by three perpendiculars drawn from each of the angles. So the unit they term Apollo, as to the number two they have affixed the name of strife and audaciousness, and to that of three, justice. For, as doing an injury is an extreme on the one side, and suffering one is an extreme on the other, justice properly takes place in the middle between them. In like manner the number thirty-six, their Tetraktys, or sacred Quaternion, being composed of the first four odd numbers added to the first four even ones, as is commonly reported, is looked upon by them as the most solemn oath they can take, and called Kosmos." (*Isis and Osiris*.)

Earlier in the same work, Plutarch also notes: "For as the power of the triangle is expressive of the nature of Pluto, Bacchus, and Mars; and the properties of the square of Rhea, Venus, Ceres, Vesta, and Juno; of the Dodecahedron of Jupiter; so, as we are informed by Eudoxus, is the figure of fifty-six angles expressive of the nature of Typhon." Plutarch did not pretend to explain the inner significance of the symbols, but believed that the relationship which Pythagoras established between the geometrical solids and the gods was the result of images the great sage had seen in the Egyptian temples.

Albert Pike, the great Masonic symbolist, admitted that there were many points concerning which he could secure no reliable information. In his *Symbolism*, for the 32° and 33°, he wrote: "I do not understand why the 7 should be called Minerva, or the cube, Neptune." Further on he added: "Undoubtedly the names given by the Pythagoreans to the different numbers were themselves enigmatical and symbolic—and there is little doubt that in the time of Plutarch the meanings these names concealed were lost. Pythagoras had succeeded too well in concealing his symbols with a veil that was from the first impenetrable, without his oral explanation * * *."

1	2	3	4	5	6	7	8
Aleph	א	א	1	A α	•	Alpha	A
Beth			2	B β	•	Beta	B
Gimel			3	Γ γ	•	Gamma	G
Daleth			4	Δ δ	•	Delta	D
He			5	E ε	•	Epsilon	E
Vau			6	F	•	Digamma	Fv
Zain			7	Z ζ		Zeta	
Heth			8	H η	•	Eta	
Teth			9	Θ θ		Theta	
Jod			10	I ι	•	Iota	I
Caph			20	K κ	•	Kappa	C
Lamed			30	Λ λ	•	Lambda	L
Mem			40	M μ	•	Mu	M
Nun			50	N ν	•	'Nu	N
Samech			60	Ξ ξ		Xi	
Oin			70	O o	•	Omicron	O
Pe			80	Π π	•	Pi	P
Tzadi			90	ϟ		Episemon bau	
Koph			100			επισημον ϧαυ	
			100	P ρ	•	Rho	R
Resh			200				
			200	Σ σ		Sigma	S
Shin			300				
			300	T τ	•	Tau	T
Tau			400				
			400	Υ υ	•	Upsilon	U
			500	Φ φ		Phi	
			600	X χ		Chi	
			700	Ψ ψ		Psi	
			800	Ω ω		Omega	
			900	ϡ		Sanpi	

FROM HIGGIN'S *CELTIC DRUIDS*.

THE NUMERICAL VALUES OF THE HEBREW, GREEK, AND SAMARITAN ALPHABETS.

Column

1. Names of the Hebrew letters.

2. Samaritan letters.

3. Hebrew and Chaldean letters.

4. Numerical equivalents of the letters.

5. Capital and small Greek letters.

6. The letters marked with asterisks are those brought to Greece from Phœnicia by Cadmus.

7. Names of the Greek letters.

8. Nearest English equivalents to the Hebrew, Greek, and Samaritan letters.

NOTE: When used at the end of a word, the Hebrew *Tau* has the numerical value of 400, *Caph* 500, *Mem* 600, *Nun* 700, *Pe* 800, *Tzadi* 900. A dotted *Alpha* and a dashed *Aleph* have a value of 1,000.

This uncertainty shared by all true students of the subject proves conclusively that it is unwise to make definite statements founded on the indefinite and fragmentary information available concerning the Pythagorean system of mathematical philosophy. The material which follows represents an effort to collect a few salient points from the scattered records preserved by disciples of Pythagoras and others who have since contacted his philosophy.

Method of Securing the Numerical Power of Words

The first step in obtaining the numerical value of a word is to resolve it back into its original tongue. Only words of Greek or Hebrew derivation can be successfully analyzed by this method, and *all words must be spelled in their most ancient and complete forms.* Old Testament words and names, therefore, must be translated back into the early Hebrew characters and New Testament words into the Greek. Two examples will help to clarify this principle.

The *Demiurgus* of the Jews is called in English *Jehovah,* but when seeking the numerical value of the name *Jehovah* it is necessary to resolve the name into its Hebrew letters. It becomes יהוה and is read from right to left. The Hebrew letters are: ה *He;* ו, *Vau;* ה, *He;* י, *Yod;* and when reversed into the English order from left to right read: *Yod-He-Vau-He.* By consulting the foregoing table of letter values, it is found that the four characters of this sacred name have the following numerical significance: *Yod* equals 10. *He* equals 5, *Vau* equals 6, and the second *He* equals 5. Therefore, 10 + 5 + 6 + 5=26, a synonym of *Jehovah.* If the English letters were used, the answer obviously would not be correct.

The second example is the mysterious Gnostic pantheos *Abraxas.* For this name the Greek table is used. *Abraxas* in Greek is Ἀβραξας. A = 1, β = 2, ρ = 100, α = 1, ξ = 60, α = 1, ς = 200, the sum being 365, the number of days in the year. This number furnishes the key to the mystery of Abraxas, who is symbolic of the 365 Æons, or Spirits of the Days, gathered together in one composite personality. *Abraxas* is symbolic of five creatures, and as the circle of the year actually consists of 360 degrees, each of the emanating deities is one-fifth of this power, or 72, one of the most sacred numbers in the Old Testament of the Jews and in their Qabbalistic system. This same method is used in finding the numerical value of the names of the gods and goddesses of the Greeks and Jews.

All higher numbers can be reduced to one of the original ten numerals, and the 10 itself to 1. Therefore, all groups of numbers resulting from the translation of names of deities into their numerical equivalents have a basis in one of the first ten numbers. By this system, in which the digits are added together, 666 becomes 6 + 6 + 6 or 18, and this, in turn, becomes 1 + 8 or 9. According to Revelation, 144,000 are to be saved. This number becomes 1 + 4 + 4 + 0 + 0 + 0, which equals 9, thus proving that both the Beast of Babylon and the number of the saved refer to man himself, whose symbol is the number 9. This system can be used successfully with both Greek and Hebrew letter values.

The original Pythagorean system of numerical philosophy contains nothing to justify the practice now in vogue of changing the given name or surname in the hope of improving the temperament or financial condition by altering the name vibrations.

There is also a system of calculation in vogue for the English language, but its accuracy is a matter of legitimate dispute. It is comparatively modern and has no relationship either to the Hebrew Qabbalistic system or to the Greek procedure. The claim made by some that it is Pythagorean is not supported by any tangible evidence, and there are many reasons why such a contention is untenable. The fact that Pythagoras used 10 as the basis of calculation, while this system uses 9—an imperfect number—is in itself almost conclusive. Furthermore, the arrangement of the Greek and Hebrew letters does not agree closely enough with the English to permit the application of the number sequences of one language to the number sequences of the others. Further experimentation with the system may prove profitable, but it is without basis in antiquity. The arrangement of the letters and numbers is as follows:

1	2	3	4	5	6	7	8	9
A	B	C	D	E	F	G	H	I
J	K	L	M	N	O	P	Q	R
S	T	U	V	W	X	Y	Z	

The letters under each of the numbers have the value of the figure at the top of the column. Thus, in the word *man*, $M = 4$, $A = 1$, $N = 5$: a total of 10. The values of the numbers are practically the same as those given by the Pythagorean system.

An Introduction to the Pythagorean Theory of Numbers

(The following outline of Pythagorean mathematics is a paraphrase of the opening chapters of Thomas Taylor's *Theoretic Arithmetic,* the rarest and most important compilation of Pythagorean mathematical fragments extant.)

The Pythagoreans declared arithmetic to be the mother of the mathematical sciences. This is proved by the fact that geometry, music, and astronomy are dependent upon it but it is not dependent upon them. Thus, geometry may be removed but arithmetic will remain; but if arithmetic be removed, geometry is eliminated. In the same manner music depends upon arithmetic, but the elimination of music affects arithmetic only by limiting one of its expressions. The Pythagoreans also demonstrated arithmetic to be prior to astronomy, for the latter is dependent upon both geometry and music. The size, form, and motion of the celestial bodies is determined by the use of geometry; their harmony and rhythm by the use of music. If astronomy be removed, neither geometry nor music is injured; but if geometry and music be eliminated, astronomy is destroyed. The priority of both geometry and music to astronomy is therefore established. Arithmetic, however, is prior to all; it is primary and fundamental.

Pythagoras instructed his disciples that the science of mathematics is divided into two major parts. The first is concerned with the *multitude,* or the constituent parts of a thing, and the second with the *magnitude,* or the relative size or density of a thing.

Magnitude is divided into two parts—magnitude which is stationary and magnitude which is movable, the stationary part having priority. *Multitude* is also divided into two parts, for it is related both to itself and to other things, the first relationship having priority. Pythagoras assigned the science of arithmetic to multitude related to itself, and the art of music to multitude related to other things. Geometry likewise was assigned to stationary magnitude, and spherics (used partly in the sense of astronomy) to movable magnitude. Both multitude and magnitude were circumscribed by the circumference of mind. The atomic theory has proved size to be the result of number, for a mass is made up of minute units though mistaken by the uninformed for a single simple substance.

Owing to the fragmentary condition of existing Pythagorean records, it is difficult to arrive at exact definitions of terms. Before it is possible, however, to unfold the subject further some light must be cast upon the meanings of the words *number, monad,* and *one.*

The *monad* signifies (a) the all-including ONE. The Pythagoreans called the monad the "noble number, Sire of Gods and men." The monad also signifies (b) the sum of any combination of numbers considered as a whole. Thus, the universe is considered as a monad, but the individual parts of the universe (such as the planets and elements) are monads in relation to the parts of which they themselves are composed, though they, in turn, are parts of the greater monad formed of their sum. The monad may also be likened (c) to the seed of a tree which, when it has grown, has many branches (the numbers). In other words, the numbers are to the monad what the branches of the tree are to the seed of the tree. From the study of the mysterious Pythagorean monad, Leibnitz evolved his magnificent theory of the world atoms—a theory in perfect accord with the ancient teachings of the Mysteries, for Leibnitz himself was an initiate of a secret school. By some Pythagoreans the monad is also considered (d) synonymous with the *one*.

Number is the term applied to all numerals and their combinations. (A strict interpretation of the term *number* by certain of the Pythagorean excludes 1 and 2.) Pythagoras defines number to be the extension and energy of the spermatic reasons contained in the monad. The followers of Hippasus declared number to be the first pattern used by the Demiurgus in the formation of the universe.

The *one* was defined by the Platonists as "the summit of the many." The one differs from the monad in that the term *monad* is used to designate the sum of the parts considered as a unit, whereas the *one* is the term applied to each of its integral parts.

There are two orders of number: *odd* and *even*. Because unity, or 1, always remains indivisible, the odd number cannot be divided equally. Thus, 9 is 4 + 1 + 4, the unity in the center being indivisible. Furthermore, if any odd number be divided into two parts, one part will always be odd and the other even. Thus, 9 may be 5 + 4, 3 + 6, 7 + 2, or 8 + 1. The Pythagoreans considered the odd number—of which the monad was the prototype—to be definite and masculine. They were not all agreed, however, as to the nature of unity, or 1. Some declared it to be positive, because if added to an even (negative) number, it produces an odd (positive) number. Others demonstrated that if unity be added to an odd number, the latter becomes even, thereby making the masculine to be feminine. Unity, or 1, therefore, was considered an androgynous number, partaking of both the masculine and the feminine attributes; consequently both odd and even. For this reason the Pythagoreans called it *evenly-odd*. It was customary for the Pythagoreans to offer sacrifices of an uneven number of objects to the superior gods, while to the goddesses and subterranean spirits an even number was offered.

Any even number may be divided into two equal parts, which are always either both odd or both even. Thus, 10 by equal division gives 5 + 5, both odd numbers. The same principle holds true if the 10 be unequally divided. For example, in 6 + 4, both parts are even; in 7 + 3, both parts are odd; in 8 + 2, both parts are again even; and in 9 + 1, both parts are again odd. Thus, in the even number, however it may be divided, the parts will always be both odd or both even. The Pythagoreans considered the even number—of which the *duad* was the prototype—to be indefinite and feminine.

The odd numbers are divided by a mathematical contrivance—called "the Sieve of Eratosthenes"—into three general classes: *incomposite, composite,* and *incomposite-composite.*

The *incomposite* numbers are those which have no divisor other than themselves and unity, such as 3, 5, 7, 11, 13, 17, 19, 23, 29, 31, 37, 41, 43, 47, and so forth. For example, 7 is divisible only by 7, which goes into itself once, and unity, which goes into 7 seven times.

The *composite* numbers are those which are divisible not only by themselves and unity but also by some other number, such as 9, 15, 21, 25, 27, 33, 39, 45, 51, 57, and so forth. For example, 21 is divisible not only by itself and by unity, but also by 3 and by 7.

The *incomposite-composite* numbers are those which have no common divisor, although each of itself is capable of division, such as 9 and 25. For example, 9 is divisible by 3 and 25 by 5, but neither is divisible by the divisor of the other; thus they have no common divisor. Because they have individual divisors, they are called *composite;* and because they have no common divisor, they are called *incomposite.* Accordingly, the term *incomposite-composite* was created to describe their properties.

Even numbers are divided into three classes: *evenly-even, evenly-odd,* and *oddly-odd.*

The *evenly-even* numbers are all in duple ratio from unity; thus: 1, 2, 4, 8, 16, 32, 64, 128, 256, 512, and 1,024. The proof of the perfect *evenly-even* number is that it can be halved and the halves again halved back to unity, as ½ of 64 = 32; ½ of 32 = 16; ½ of 16 = 8; ½ of 8 = 4; ½ of 4 = 2; ½ of 2 = 1; beyond unity it is impossible to go.

The *evenly-even* numbers possess certain unique properties. The sum of any number of terms but the last term is always equal to the last term minus one. For example: the sum of the first and second terms (1 + 2) equals the third term (4) minus one; or, the sum of the first, second, third, and fourth terms (1 + 2 + 4 + 8) equals the fifth term (16) minus one.

In a series of *evenly-even* numbers, the first multiplied by the last equals the last; the second multiplied by the second from the last equals the last, and so on until in an odd series one number remains, which multiplied by itself equals the last number of the series; or, in an even series two numbers remain, which multiplied by each other give the last number of the series. For example:

1, 2, 4, 8, 16 is an odd series. The first number (1) multiplied by the last number (16) equals the last number (16). The second number (2) multiplied by the second from the last number (8) equals the last number (16). Being an odd series, the 4 is left in the center, and this multiplied by itself also equals the last number (16).

The *evenly-odd* numbers are those which, when halved, are incapable of further division by halving. They are formed by taking the odd numbers in sequential order and multiplying them by 2. By this process the odd numbers 1, 3, 5, 7, 9, 11 produce the evenly-odd numbers 2, 6, 10, 14, 18, 22. Thus, every fourth number is evenly-odd. Each of the even-odd numbers may be divided once, as 2, which becomes two 1's and cannot be divided further; or 6, which becomes two 3's and cannot be divided further.

Another peculiarity of the evenly-odd numbers is that if the divisor be odd the quotient is always even, and if the divisor be even the quotient is always odd. For example: if 18 be divided by 2 (an even divisor) the quotient is 9 (an odd number); if 18 be divided by 3 (an odd divisor) the quotient is 6 (an even number).

The evenly-odd numbers are also remarkable in that each term is one-half of the sum of the terms on either side of it. For example: 10 is one-half of the sum of 6 and 14; 18 is one-half the sum of 14 and 22; and 6 is one-half the sum of 2 and 10.

The oddly-odd, or unevenly-even, numbers are a compromise between the evenly-even and the evenly-odd numbers. Unlike the evenly-even, they cannot be halved back to unity; and unlike the evenly-odd, they are capable of more than one division by halving. The oddly-odd numbers are formed by multiplying the evenly-even numbers above 2 by the odd numbers above one. The odd numbers above one are 3, 5, 7, 9, 11, and so forth. The evenly-even numbers above 2 are 4, 8, 16, 32, 64 and so on. The first odd number of the series (3) multiplied by 4 (the first evenly-even number of the series) gives 12, the first oddly-odd number. By multiplying 5, 7, 9, 11, and so forth, by 4, oddly-odd numbers are found. The other oddly-odd numbers are produced by multiplying 3, 5, 7, 9, 11, and so forth, in turn, by the other evenly-even numbers (8, 16, 32, 64, and so forth). An example of the halving of the oddly-odd number is as follows: ½ of 12 = 6; ½ of 6 = 3, which cannot be halved further because the Pythagoreans did not divide unity.

Even numbers are also divided into three other classes: *superperfect, deficient,* and *perfect.*

Superperfect or *superabundant* numbers are such as have the sum of their fractional parts greater than themselves. For example: ½ of 24 = 12; ¼ = 6; ⅓ = 8; ⅙ = 4; ¹⁄₁₂ = 2; and ¹⁄₂₄ = 1. The sum of these parts (12 + 6 + 8 + 4 + 2 + 1) is 33, which is in excess of 24, the original number.

Deficient numbers are such as have the sum of their fractional parts less than themselves. For example: ½ of 14 = 7; ⅐ = 2; and ¹⁄₁₄ = 1. The sum of these parts (7 + 2 + 1) is 10, which is less than 14, the original number.

Perfect numbers are such as have the sum of their fractional parts equal to themselves. For example: ½ of 28 = 14; ¼ = 7; ⅐ = 4; ¹⁄₁₄ = 2; and ¹⁄₂₈ = 1. The sum of these parts (14 + 7 + 4 + 2 + 1) is equal to 28.

The perfect numbers are extremely rare. There is only one between 1 and 10, namely, 6; one between 10 and 100, namely, 28; one between 100 and 1,000, namely, 496; and one between 1,000 and 10,000, namely, 8,128. The perfect numbers are found by the following rule: The first number of the evenly-even series of numbers (1, 2, 4, 8, 16, 32, and so forth) is added to the second number of the series, and if an incomposite number results it is multiplied by the last number of the series of evenly-even numbers whose sum produced it. The product is the first perfect number. For example: the first and second evenly-even numbers are 1 and 2. Their sum is 3, an incomposite number. If 3 be multiplied by 2, the last number of the series of evenly-even numbers used to produce it, the product is 6, the first perfect number. If the addition of the evenly-even numbers does not result in an incomposite number, the next evenly-even number of the series must be added until an incomposite number results. The second perfect number is found in the following manner: The sum of the evenly-even numbers 1, 2, and 4 is 7, an incomposite number. If 7 be multiplied by 4 (the last of the series of evenly-even numbers used to produce it) the product is 28, the second perfect number. This method of calculation may be continued to infinity.

Perfect numbers when multiplied by 2 produce superabundant numbers, and when divided by 2 produce deficient numbers.

The Pythagoreans evolved their philosophy from the science of numbers. The following quotation from *Theoretic Arithmetic* is an excellent example of this practice:

"Perfect numbers, therefore, are beautiful images of the virtues which are certain media between excess and defect, and are not summits, as by some of the ancients they were supposed to be. And evil indeed is opposed to evil, but both are opposed to one good. Good, however, is never opposed to good, but to two evils at one and the same time. Thus timidity is opposed to audacity, to both [of] which the want of true courage is common; but both timidity and audacity are opposed to fortitude. Craft also is opposed to fatuity, to both [of] which the want of intellect is common; and both these are opposed to prudence. Thus, too, profusion is opposed to avarice, to both [of] which illiberality is common; and both these are opposed to liberality. And in a similar manner in the other virtues; by all [of] which it is evident that perfect numbers have a great similitude to the virtues. But they also resemble the virtues on another account; for they are rarely found, as being few, and they are generated in a very constant order. On the contrary, an infinite multitude of superabundant and diminished numbers may be found, nor are they disposed in any orderly series, nor generated from any certain end; and hence they have a great similitude to the vices, which are numerous, inordinate, and indefinite."

The Table of the Ten Numbers

(The following outline of the Pythagorean numbers is a paraphrase of the writings of Nicomachus, Theon of Smyrna, Proclus, Porphyry, Plutarch, Clement of Alexandria, Aristotle, and other early authorities.)

Monad—1—is so called because it remains always in the same condition—that is, separate from multitude. Its attributes are as follows: It is called mind, because the mind is stable and has preeminence; hermaphrodism, because it is both male and female; odd and even, for being added to the even it makes odd, and to the odd, even; God, because it is the beginning and end of all, but itself has neither beginning nor end; good, for such is the nature of God; the receptacle of matter, because it produces the duad, which is essentially material.

By the Pythagoreans monad was called chaos, obscurity, chasm, Tartarus, Styx, abyss, Lethe, Atlas, Axis, Morpho (a name for Venus), and Tower or Throne of Jupiter, because of the great power which abides in the center of the universe and controls the circular motion of the planets about itself. Monad is also called germinal reason, because it is the origin of all the thoughts in the universe. Other names given to it were: Apollo, because of its relation to the sun; Prometheus, because he brought man light; Pyralios, one who exists in fire; geniture, because without it no number can exist; substance, because substance is primary; cause of truth; and constitution of symphony: all these because it is the primordial one.

Between greater and lesser the monad is equal; between intention and remission it is middle; in multitude it is mean; and in time it is now, because eternity knows neither past nor future. It is called Jupiter, because he is Father and head of the gods; Vesta, the fire of the home, because it is located in the midst of the universe and remains there inclining to no side as a dot in a circle; form, because it circumscribes, comprehends, and terminates; love, concord, and piety, because it is indivisible. Other symbolic names for the monad are ship, chariot, Proteus (a god capable of changing his form), Mnemosyne, and Polyonymous (having many names).

The following symbolic names were given to the duad—2—because it has been divided, and is two rather than one; and when there are two, each is opposed to the other: genius, evil, darkness, inequality, instability, movability, boldness, fortitude, contention, matter, dissimilarity, partition between multitude and monad, defect, shapelessness, indefiniteness, indeterminateness, harmony, tolerance, root, feet of fountain-abounding idea, top, Phanes, opinion, fallacy, alterity, diffidence, impulse, death, motion, generation, mutation, division, longitude, augmentation, composition, communion, misfortune, sustentation, imposition, marriage, soul, and science.

In his book, *Numbers,* W. Wynn Westcott says of the duad: "It was called 'Audacity,' from its being the earliest number to separate itself from the Divine One; from the 'Adytum of God-nourished Silence,' as the Chaldean oracles say."

As the monad is the father, so the duad is the mother; therefore, the duad has certain points in common with the goddesses Isis, Rhea (Jove's mother), Phrygia, Lydia, Dindymene (Cybele), and Ceres; Erato (one of the Muses); Diana, because the moon is forked; Dictynna, Venus, Dione, Cytherea; Juno, because she is both wife and sister of Jupiter; and Maia, the mother of Mercury.

While the monad is the symbol of wisdom, the duad is the symbol of ignorance, for in it exists the sense of separateness—which sense is the beginning of ignorance. The duad, however, is also the mother of wisdom, for ignorance—out of the nature of itself—invariably gives birth to wisdom.

The Pythagoreans revered the monad but despised the duad, because it was the symbol of polarity. By the power of the duad the deep was created in contradistinction to the heavens. The deep mirrored the heavens and became the symbol of illusion, for the below was merely a reflection of the above. The below was called *maya,* the illusion, the sea, the Great Void, and to symbolize it the Magi of Persia carried mirrors. From the duad arose disputes and contentions, until by bringing the monad between the duad, equilibrium was reestablished by the Savior-God, who took upon Himself the form of a number and was crucified between two thieves for the sins of men.

The triad—3—is the first number actually odd (monad not always being considered a number). It is the first equilibrium of unities; therefore, Pythagoras said that Apollo gave oracles from a tripod, and advised offer of libation three times. The keywords to the qualities of the triad are friendship, peace, justice, prudence, piety, temperance, and virtue. The following deities partake of the principles of the triad: Saturn (ruler of time), Latona, Cornucopiæ, Ophion (the great serpent), Thetis, Hecate, Polyhymnia (a Muse), Pluto, Triton, President of the Sea, Tritogenia, Achelous, and the Fates, Furies, and Graces. This number is called wisdom, because men organize the present, foresee the future, and benefit by the experiences of the past. It is cause of wisdom and understanding. The triad is the number of knowledge—music, geometry, and astronomy, and the science of the celestials and terrestrials. Pythagoras taught that the cube of this number had the power of the lunar circle.

The sacredness of the triad and its symbol—the triangle—is derived from the fact that it is made up of the monad and the duad. The monad is the symbol of the Divine Father and the duad of the Great Mother. The triad being made of these two is therefore androgynous and is symbolic of the fact that God gave birth to His worlds out of Himself, who in His creative aspect is always symbolized by the triangle. The monad passing into the duad was thus capable of becoming the parent of progeny, for the duad was the womb of Meru, within which the world was incubated and within which it still exists in embryo.

The tetrad—4—was esteemed by the Pythagoreans as the primogenial number, the root of all things, the fountain of Nature and the most perfect number. All tetrads are intellectual; they have an emergent order and encircle the world as the Empyreum passes through it. Why the Pythagoreans expressed God as a tetrad is explained in a sacred discourse ascribed to Pythagoras, wherein God is called the Number of Numbers. This is because the decad, or 10, is composed of 1, 2, 3, and 4. The number 4 is symbolic of God because it is symbolic of the first four numbers. Moreover, the tetrad is the center of the week, being halfway between 1 and 7. The tetrad is also the first geometric solid.

Pythagoras maintained that the soul of man consists of a tetrad, the four powers of the soul being mind, science, opinion, and sense. The tetrad connects all beings, elements, numbers, and seasons; nor can anything be named which does not depend upon the tetractys. It is the Cause and Maker of all things, the intelligible God, Author of celestial and sensible good. Plutarch interprets this tetractys, which he said was also called the world, to be 36, consisting of the first four odd numbers added to the first four even numbers, thus:

$$1 + 3 + 5 + 7 = 16$$
$$2 + 4 + 6 + 8 = \underline{20}$$
$$36$$

Keywords given to the tetrad are impetuosity, strength, virility, two-mothered, and the key keeper of Nature, because the universal constitution cannot be without it. It is also called harmony and the first profundity. The following deities partook of the nature of the tetrad: Hercules, Mercury, Vulcan, Bacchus, and Urania (one of the Muses).

The triad represents the primary colors and the major planets, while the tetrad represents the secondary colors and the minor planets. From the first triangle come forth the seven spirits, symbolized by a triangle and a square. These together form the Masonic apron.

The pentad—5—is the union of an odd and an even number (3 and 2). Among the Greeks, the pentagram was a sacred symbol of light, health, and vitality. It also symbolized the fifth element—ether—because it is free from the disturbances of the four lower elements. It is called equilibrium, because it divides the perfect number 10 into two equal parts.

The pentad is symbolic of Nature, for, when multiplied by itself it returns into itself, just as grains of wheat, starting in the form of seed, pass through Nature's processes and reproduce the seed of the wheat as the ultimate form of their own growth. Other numbers multiplied by themselves produce other numbers, but only 5 and 6 multiplied by themselves represent and retain their original number as the last figure in their products.

The pentad represents all the superior and inferior beings. It is sometimes referred to as the hierophant, or the priest of the Mysteries, because of its connection with the spiritual ethers, by means of which mystic development is attained. Keywords of the pentad are reconciliation, alternation, marriage, immortality, cordiality, providence, and sound. Among the deities who partook of the nature of the pentad were Pallas, Nemesis, Bubastia (Bast), Venus, Androgynia, Cytherea, and the messengers of Jupiter.

The tetrad (the elements) plus the monad equals the pentad. The Pythagoreans taught that the elements of earth, fire, air, and water were permeated by a substance called ether—the basis of vitality and life. Therefore, they chose the five-pointed star, or pentagram, as the symbol of vitality, health, and interpenetration.

It was customary for the philosophers to conceal the element of earth under the symbol of a dragon, and many of the heroes of antiquity were told to go forth and slay the dragon. Hence, they drove their sword (the monad) into the body of the dragon (the tetrad). This resulted in the formation of the pentad, a symbol of the victory of the spiritual nature over the material nature. The four elements are symbolized in the early Biblical writings as the four rivers that poured out of the

Garden of Eden. The elements themselves are under the control of the composite Cherubim of Ezekiel.

The Pythagoreans held the hexad—6—to represent, as Clement of Alexandria conceived, the creation of the world according to both the prophets and the ancient Mysteries. It was called by the Pythagoreans the perfection of all the parts. This number was particularly sacred to Orpheus, and also to the Fate, Lachesis, and the Muse Thalia. It was called the form of forms, the articulation of the universe, and the maker of the soul.

Among the Greeks, harmony and the soul were considered to be similar in nature, because all souls are harmonic. The hexad is also the symbol of marriage, because it is formed by the union of two triangles, one masculine and the other feminine. Among the keywords given to the hexad are: time, for it is the measure of duration; panacea, because health is equilibrium, and the hexad is a balance number; the world, because the world, like the hexad, is often seen to consist of contraries by harmony; omnisufficient, because its parts are sufficient for totality ($3 + 2 + 1 = 6$); unwearied, because it contains the elements of immortality.

By the Pythagoreans the heptad—7—was called "worthy of veneration." It was held to be the number of religion, because man is controlled by seven celestial spirits to whom it is proper for him to make offerings. It was called the number of life, because it was believed that human creatures born in the seventh month of embryonic life usually lived, but those born in the eighth month often died. One author called it the Motherless Virgin, Minerva, because it was not born of a mother but out of the crown, or the head of the Father, the monad. Keywords of the heptad are fortune, occasion, custody, control, government, judgment, dreams, voices, sounds, and that which leads all things to their end. Deities whose attributes were expressed by the heptad were Ægis, Osiris, Mars, and Cleo (one of the Muses).

Among many ancient nations the heptad is a sacred number. The Elohim of the Jews were supposedly seven in number. They were the Spirits of the Dawn, more commonly known as the Archangels controlling the planets. The seven Archangels, with the three spirits controlling the sun in its threefold aspect, constitute the 10, the sacred Pythagorean decad. The mysterious Pythagorean tetractys, or four rows of dots, increasing from 1 to 4, was symbolic of the stages of creation. The great Pythagorean truth that all things in Nature are regenerated through the decad, or 10, is subtly preserved in Freemasonry through the grips; these grips being effected by the uniting of 10 fingers, five on the hand of each person.

The 3 (spirit, mind, and soul) descend into the 4 (the world), the sum being the 7, or the mystic nature of man, consisting of a threefold spiritual body and a fourfold material form. These are symbolized by the cube, which has six surfaces and a mysterious seventh point within. The six surfaces are the directions: north, east, south, west, up, and down; or, front, back, right, left, above, and below; or again, earth, fire, air, water, spirit, and matter. In the midst of these stands the 1, which is the upright figure of man, from whose center in the cube radiate six pyramids. From this comes the great occult axiom: "The center is the father of the directions, the dimensions, and the distances."

The heptad is the number of the law, because it is the number of the Makers of Cosmic law, the Seven Spirits before the Throne.

The ogdoad—8—was sacred because it was the number of the first cube, which form had eight corners, and was the only evenly-even number under 10 (1-2-4-8-4-2-1). Thus, the 8 is divided into two 4's, each 4 is divided into two 2's, and each 2 is divided into two 1's, thereby reestablishing the monad. Among the keywords of the ogdoad are love, counsel, prudence, law, and convenience. Among the divinities partaking of its nature were Panarmonia, Rhea, Cibele, Cadmæa, Dindymene, Orcia, Neptune, Themis, and Euterpe (a Muse).

The ogdoad was a mysterious number associated with the Eleusinian Mysteries of Greece and the Cabiri. It was called the little holy number. It derived its form partly from the twisted snakes on the Caduceus of Hermes and partly from the serpentine motion of the celestial bodies; possibly also from the moon's nodes.

The ennead—9—was the first square of an odd number (3 × 3). It was associated with failure and shortcoming, because it fell short of the perfect number 10 by one. It was called the number of man, because of the nine months of his embryonic life. Among its keywords are ocean and horizon, because to the ancients these were boundless. The ennead is the limitless number because there is nothing beyond it but the infinite 10. It was called boundary and limitation, because it gathered all numbers within itself. It was called the sphere of the air, because it surrounded the numbers as air surrounds the earth. Among the gods and goddesses who partook in greater or less degree of its nature were Prometheus, Vulcan, Juno, the sister and wife of Jupiter, Pæan, and Aglaia, Tritogenia, Curetes, Proserpine, Hyperion, and Terpsichore (a Muse).

The 9 was looked upon as evil, because it was an inverted 6. According to the Eleusinian Mysteries, it was the number of the spheres through which the consciousness passed on its way to birth. Because of its close resemblance to the spermatozoon, the 9 has been associated with germinal life.

The decad—10—according to the Pythagoreans, is the greatest of numbers, not only because it is the tetractys (the 10 dots) but because it comprehends all arithmetic and harmonic proportions. Pythagoras said that 10 is the nature of number, because all nations reckon to it and when they arrive at it they return to the monad. The decad was called both heaven and the world, because the former includes the latter. Being a perfect number, the decad was applied by the Pythagoreans to those things relating to age, power, faith, necessity, and the power of memory. It was also called unwearied, because, like God, it was tireless. The Pythagoreans divided the heavenly bodies into ten orders. They also stated that the decad perfected all numbers and comprehended within itself the nature of odd and even, moved and unmoved, good and ill. They associated its power with the following deities: Atlas (for it carried the numbers on its shoulders), Urania, Mnemosyne, the Sun, Phanes, and the One God.

The decimal system can probably be traced back to the time when it was customary to reckon on the fingers, these being among the most primitive of calculating devices and still in use among many aboriginal peoples.

The Human Body in Symbolism

he oldest, the most profound, the most universal of all symbols is the human body. The Greeks, Persians, Egyptians, and Hindus considered a philosophical analysis of man's triune nature to be an indispensable part of ethical and religious training. The Mysteries of every nation taught that the laws, elements, and powers of the universe were epitomized in the human constitution; that everything which existed outside of man had its analogue within man. The universe, being immeasurable in its immensity and inconceivable in its profundity, was beyond mortal estimation. Even the gods themselves could comprehend but a part of the inaccessible glory which was their source. When temporarily permeated with divine enthusiasm, man may transcend for a brief moment the limitations of his own personality and behold in part that celestial effulgence in which all creation is bathed. But even in his periods of greatest illumination man is incapable of imprinting upon the substance of his rational soul a perfect image of the multiform expression of celestial activity.

Recognizing the futility of attempting to cope intellectually with that which transcends the comprehension of the rational faculties, the early philosophers turned their attention from the inconceivable Divinity to man himself, within the narrow confines of whose nature they found manifested all the mysteries of the external spheres. As the natural outgrowth of this practice there was fabricated a secret theological system in which God was considered as the Grand Man and, conversely, man as the little god. Continuing this analogy, the universe was regarded as a man and, conversely, man as a miniature universe. The greater universe was termed the *Macrocosm*—the Great World or Body—and the Divine Life or spiritual entity controlling its functions was called the *Macroprosophus.* Man's

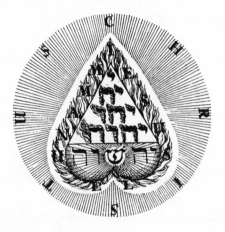

FROM BÖHME'S *LIBRI APOLOGETICI*.

THE TETRAGRAMMATON IN THE HUMAN HEART.

The Tetragrammaton, or four-lettered Name of God, is here arranged as a tetractys within the inverted human heart. Beneath, the name *Jehovah* is shown transformed into *Jehoshua* by the interpolation of the radiant Hebrew letter ש, *Shin*. The drawing as a whole represents the throne of God and His hierarchies within the heart of man. In the first book of his *Libri Apologetici*, Jakob Böhme thus describes the meaning of the symbol: "For we men have one book in common which points to God. Each has it within himself, which is the priceless Name of God. Its letters are the flames of His love, which He out of His heart in the priceless Name of Jesus has revealed in us. Read these letters in your hearts and spirits and you have books enough. All the writings of the children of God direct you unto that one book, for therein lie all the treasures of wisdom. * * * This book is Christ in you."

body, or the individual human universe, was termed the *Microcosm,* and the Divine Life or spiritual entity controlling its functions was called the *Microprosophus.* The pagan Mysteries were primarily concerned with instructing neophytes in the true relationship existing between the *Macrocosm* and the *Microcosm*—in other words, between God and man. Accordingly, the key to these analogies between the organs and functions of the *Microcosmic* man and those of the *Macrocosmic* Man constituted the most prized possession of the early initiates.

In *Isis Unveiled,* H. P. Blavatsky summarizes the pagan concept of man as follows: "Man is a little world—a microcosm inside the great universe. Like a fetus, he is suspended, by all his *three* spirits, in the matrix of the macrocosmos; and while his terrestrial body is in constant sympathy with its parent earth, his astral soul lives in unison with the sidereal *anima mundi.* He is in it, as it is in him, for the world-pervading element fills all space, and is space itself, only shoreless and infinite. As to his third spirit, the divine, what is it but an infinitesimal ray, one of the countless radiations proceeding directly from the Highest Cause—the Spiritual Light of the World? This is the trinity of organic and inorganic nature—the spiritual and the physical, which are three in one, and of which Proclus says that 'The first monad is the Eternal God; the second, eternity; the third, the paradigm, or pattern of the universe;' the three constituting the Intelligible Triad."

Long before the introduction of idolatry into religion, the early priests caused the statue of a man to be placed in the sanctuary of the temple. This human figure symbolized the Divine Power in all its intricate manifestations. Thus the priests of antiquity accepted man as their textbook, and through the study of him learned to understand the greater and more abstruse mysteries of the celestial scheme of which they were a part. It is not improbable that this mysterious figure standing over the primitive altars was made in the nature of a manikin and, like certain emblematic hands in the Mystery schools, was covered with either carved or painted hieroglyphs. The statue may have opened, thus showing the relative positions of the organs, bones, muscles, nerves, and other parts. After ages of research, the manikin became a mass of intricate hieroglyphs and symbolic figures. Every part had its secret meaning. The measurements formed a basic standard by means of which it was possible to measure all parts of cosmos. It was a glorious composite emblem of all the knowledge possessed by the sages and hierophants.

Then came the age of idolatry. The Mysteries decayed from within. The secrets were lost and none knew the identity of the mysterious man who stood over the altar. It was remembered only that the figure was a sacred and glorious symbol of the Universal Power, and it finally came to be looked upon as a god— the One in whose image man was made. Having lost the knowledge of the purpose for which the manikin was originally constructed, the priests worshiped this effigy until at last their lack of spiritual understanding brought the temple down in ruins about their heads and the statue crumbled with the civilization that had forgotten its meaning.

Proceeding from this assumption of the first theologians that man is actually fashioned in the image of God, the initiated minds of past ages erected the stupendous structure of theology upon the foundation of the human body. The religious world of today is almost totally ignorant of the fact that the science of biology is the fountainhead of its doctrines and tenets. Many of the codes and laws believed by modern divines to have been direct revelations from Divinity are in reality the fruitage of ages of patient delving into the intricacies of the human constitution and the infinite wonders revealed by such a study.

In nearly all the sacred books of the world can be traced an anatomical analogy. This is most evident in their creation myths. Anyone familiar with embryology and obstetrics will have no difficulty in recognizing the basis of the allegory concerning Adam and Eve and the Garden of Eden, the nine degrees of the Eleusinian Mysteries, and the Brahmanic legend of Vishnu's incarnations. The story of the Universal Egg, the Scandinavian myth of Ginnungagap (the dark cleft in space in which the seed of the world is sown), and the use of the fish as the emblem of the paternal generative power—all show the true origin of theological speculation. The philosophers of antiquity realized that man himself was the key to the riddle of life, for he was the living image of the Divine Plan, and in future ages humanity also will come to realize more fully the solemn import of those ancient words: "The proper study of mankind is man."

Both God and man have a twofold constitution, of which the superior part is invisible and the inferior visible. In both there is also an intermediary sphere, marking the point where these visible and invisible natures meet. As the spiritual nature of God controls His objective universal form—which is actually a crystallized idea—so the spiritual nature of man is the invisible cause and controlling power of his visible material personality. Thus it is evident that the spirit of man bears the same relationship to his material body that God bears to the objective universe. The Mysteries taught that spirit, or life, was anterior to form and that what is anterior includes all that is posterior to itself. Spirit being anterior to form, form is therefore included within the realm of spirit. It is also a popular statement or belief that man's spirit is within his body. According to the conclusions of philosophy and theology, however, this belief is erroneous, for spirit first circumscribes an area and then manifests within it. Philosophically speaking, form, being a part of spirit, is within spirit; but spirit is more than the sum of form. As the material nature of man is therefore within the sum of spirit, so the Universal Nature, including the entire system, is within the all-pervading essence of God—the Universal Spirit.

According to another concept of the ancient wisdom, all bodies—whether spiritual or material—have three centers, called by the Greeks the *upper* center, the *middle* center, and the *lower* center. An apparent ambiguity will here be noted. To diagram or symbolize adequately abstract mental verities is impossible, for the diagrammatic representation of one aspect of metaphysical relationships may be an actual contradiction of some other aspect. While that which is above is generally considered superior in dignity and power, in reality that which is in the center is superior and anterior to both that which is said to be above and that which is said to be below. Therefore, it must be said that the first—which is considered as being above—is actually in the center, while both of the others (which are said to be either above or below) are actually beneath. This point can be further simplified if the reader will consider *above* as indicating degree of proximity to source and *below* as indicating degree of distance from source, source being posited in the actual center and relative distance being the various points along the radii from the center toward the circumference. In matters pertaining to philosophy and theology, *up* may be considered as toward the center and *down* as toward the circumference. Center is spirit; circumference is matter. Therefore, *up* is toward spirit along an ascending scale of spirituality; *down* is toward matter along an ascending scale of materiality. The latter concept is partly expressed by the apex of a cone which, when viewed from above, is seen as a point in the exact center of the circumference formed by the base of the cone.

These three universal centers—the one above, the one below, and the link uniting them—represent three suns or three aspects of one sun—centers of effulgence. These also have their analogues in the three grand centers of the human body, which, like the physical universe, is a Demiurgic fabrication. "The first of these [suns]," says Thomas Taylor, "is analogous to light when viewed subsisting in its fountain the sun; the second to the light immediately proceeding from the sun; and the third to the splendour communicated to other natures by this light."

Since the superior (or spiritual) center is in the midst of the other two, its analogue in the physical body is the heart—the most spiritual and mysterious organ in the human body. The second center (or the link between the superior and inferior worlds) is elevated to the position of greatest physical dignity—the brain. The third (or lower) center is relegated to the position of least physical dignity but greatest physical importance—the generative system. Thus the heart is symbolically the source of life; the brain the link by which, through rational intelligence, life and form are united; and the generative system—or infernal creator—the source of that power by which physical organisms are produced. The ideals and aspirations of the individual depend largely upon which of these three centers of power predominates in scope and activity of expression. In the materialist the lower center is the strongest, in the intellectualist the higher center; but in the initiate the middle center—by bathing the two extremes in a flood of spiritual effulgence—controls wholesomely both the mind and the body.

As light bears witness of life—which is its source—so the mind bears witness of the spirit, and activity in a still lower plane bears witness of intelligence. Thus the mind bears witness of the heart, while the generative system, in turn, bears witness of the mind. Accordingly, the spiritual nature is most commonly symbolized by a heart; the intellectual power by an opened eye, symbolizing the pineal gland or Cyclopean eye, which is the two-faced Janus of the pagan Mysteries; and the generative system by a flower, a staff, a cup, or a hand.

While all the Mysteries recognized the heart as the center of spiritual consciousness, they often purposely ignored this concept and used the heart in its exoteric sense as the symbol of the emotional nature. In this arrangement the generative center represented the physical body, the heart the emotional body, and the brain the mental body. The brain represented the superior sphere, but after the initiates had passed through the lower degrees they were instructed that the brain was the proxy of the spiritual flame dwelling in the innermost recesses of the heart. The student of esotericism discovers ere long that the ancients often resorted to various blinds to conceal the true interpretations of their Mysteries. The substitution of the brain for the heart was one of these blinds.

The three degrees of the ancient Mysteries were, with few exceptions, given in chambers which represented the three great centers of the human and Universal bodies. If possible, the temple itself was constructed in the form of the human body. The candidate entered between the feet and received the highest degree in the point corresponding to the brain. Thus the first degree was the material mystery and its symbol was the generative system; it raised the candidate through the various degrees of concrete thought. The second degree was given in the chamber corresponding to the heart, but represented the middle power which was the mental link. Here the candidate was initiated into the mysteries of abstract thought and lifted as high as the mind was capable of penetrating. He then passed into the third chamber, which, analogous to the brain, occupied the highest position in the temple but, analogous to the heart, was of the greatest dignity. In the brain chamber the heart mystery was given. Here the initiate for the first time truly comprehended the meaning of those immortal words: "As a man thinketh in his heart, so is he." As there are seven hearts in the brain so there are seven brains in the heart, but this is a matter of superphysics of which little can be said at the present time.

Proclus writes on this subject in the first book of *On the Theology of Plato*: "Indeed, Socrates in the (First) Alcibiades rightly observes, that the soul entering into herself will behold all other things, and deity itself. For verging to her own union, and to the centre of all life, laying aside multitude, and the variety of the all manifold powers which she contains, she ascends to the highest watchtower of beings. And as in the most holy of the mysteries, they say, that the mystics at first meet with the multiform, and many-shaped genera, which are hurled forth before the gods, but on entering the temple, unmoved, and guarded by the mystic rites, they genuinely receive in their bosom [heart] divine illumination, and divested of their garments, as they would say, participate of a divine nature; the same mode, as it appears to me, takes place in the speculation of wholes. For the soul when looking at things posterior to herself, beholds the shadows and images of beings, but when she converts herself to herself she evolves her own essence, and the reasons which she contains. And at first indeed, she only as it were beholds herself; but, when she penetrates more profoundly into the knowledge of herself, she finds in herself both intellect, and the orders of beings. When however, she proceeds into her interior recesses, and into the adytum as it were of the soul, she perceives with her eye closed [without the aid of the lower mind], the genus of the gods, and the unities of beings. For all things are in us psychically, and through this we are naturally capable of knowing all things, by exciting the powers and the images of wholes which we contain."

The initiates of old warned their disciples that an image is not a reality but merely the objectification of a subjective idea. The images of the gods were not designed to be objects of worship but were to be regarded merely as emblems or reminders of invisible powers and principles. Similarly, the body of man must not be considered as the individual but only as the house of the individual, in the same manner that the temple was the House of God. In a state of grossness and perversion man's body is the tomb or prison of a divine principle; in a state of unfoldment and regeneration it is the House or Sanctuary of the Deity by whose creative powers it was fashioned. "Personality is suspended upon a thread from the nature of Being," declares the secret work. Man is essentially a permanent and immortal principle; only his bodies pass through the cycle of birth and death. The immortal is the reality; the mortal is the unreality. During each period of earth life, reality thus dwells in unreality, to be liberated from it temporarily by death and permanently by illumination.

While generally regarded as polytheists, the pagans gained this reputation not because they worshiped more than one God but rather because they personified the attributes of this God, thereby creating a pantheon of posterior deities each manifesting a part of what the One God manifested as a whole. The various pantheons of ancient religious therefore actually represent the catalogued and personified attributes of Deity. In this respect they correspond to the hierarchies of the Hebrew Qabbalists. All the gods and goddesses of antiquity consequently have their analogies in the human body, as have also the elements, planets, and constellations which were assigned as proper vehicles for these celestials. Four body centers are assigned to the elements, the seven vital organs to the planets, the twelve principal parts and members to the zodiac, the invisible parts of man's divine nature to various supermundane deities, while the hidden God was declared to manifest through the marrow in the bones.

It is difficult for many to realize that they are actual universes; that their physical bodies are a visible nature through the structure of which countless waves of evolving life are unfolding their latent potentialities. Yet through man's physical body not only are a mineral, a plant, and an animal kingdom evolving, but also unknown classifications and divisions of invisible spiritual life. Just as cells are infinitesimal units in the structure of man, so man is an infinitesimal unit in the structure of the universe. A theology based upon the knowledge and appreciation of these relationships is as profoundly just as it is profoundly true.

As man's physical body has five distinct and important extremities—two legs, two arms, and a head, of which the last governs the first four—the number 5 has been accepted as the symbol of man. By its four corners the pyramid symbolizes the arms and legs, and by its apex the head, thus indicating that one rational power controls four irrational corners. The hands and feet are used to represent the four elements, of which the two feet are earth and water, and the two hands fire and air. The brain then symbolizes the sacred fifth element— æther—which controls and unites the other four. If the feet are placed together and the arms outspread, man then symbolizes the cross with the rational intellect as the head or upper limb.

The fingers and toes also have special significance. The toes represent the Ten Commandments of the physical law and the fingers the Ten Commandments of the spiritual law. The four fingers of each hand represent the four elements and the three phalanges of each finger represent the divisions of the element, so that in each hand there are twelve parts to the fingers, which are analogous to the signs of the zodiac, whereas the two phalanges and base of each thumb signify the threefold Deity. The first phalange corresponds to the creative aspect, the second to the preservative aspect, and the base to the generative and destructive aspect. When the hands are brought together, the result is the twenty-four Elders and the six Days of Creation.

In symbolism the body is divided vertically into halves, the right half being considered as light and the left half as darkness. By those unacquainted with the true meanings of light and darkness the light half was denominated spiritual and the left half material. Light is the symbol of objectivity; darkness of subjectivity. Light is a manifestation of life and is therefore posterior to life. That which is anterior to light is darkness, in which light exists temporarily but darkness permanently. As life precedes light, its only symbol is darkness, and darkness is considered as the veil which must eternally conceal the true nature of abstract and undifferentiated Being.

In ancient times men fought with their right arms and defended the vital centers with their left arms, on which was carried the protecting shield. The right half of the body was regarded therefore as offensive and the left half defensive.

For this reason also the right side of the body was considered masculine and the left side feminine. Several authorities are of the opinion that the present prevalent right-handedness of the race is the outgrowth of the custom of holding the left hand in restraint for defensive purposes. Furthermore, as the source of Being is in the primal darkness which preceded light, so the spiritual nature of man is in the dark part of his being, for the heart is on the left side.

Among the curious misconceptions arising from the false practice of associating darkness with evil is one by which several early nations used the right hand for all constructive labors and the left hand for only those purposes termed unclean and unfit for the sight of the gods. For the same reason black magic was often referred to as the left-hand path, and heaven was said to be upon the right and hell upon the left. Some philosophers further declared that there were two methods of writing: one from left to right, which was considered the exoteric method; the other from right to left, which was considered esoteric. The exoteric writing was that which was done out or away from the heart, while the esoteric writing was that which—like the ancient Hebrew—was written toward the heart.

The secret doctrine declares that every part and member of the body is epitomized in the brain and, in turn, that all that is in the brain is epitomized in the heart. In symbolism the human head is frequently used to represent intelligence and self-knowledge. As the human body in its entirety is the most perfect known product of the earth's evolution, it was employed to represent Divinity—the highest appreciable state or condition. Artists, attempting to portray Divinity, often show only a hand emerging from an impenetrable cloud. The cloud signifies the Unknowable Divinity concealed from man by human limitation. The hand signifies the Divine activity, the only part of God which is cognizable to the lower senses.

The face consists of a natural trinity: the eyes representing the spiritual power which comprehends; the nostrils representing the preservative and vivifying power; and the mouth and ears representing the material Demiurgic power of the lower world. The first sphere is eternally existent and is creative; the second sphere pertains to the mystery of the creative breath; and the third sphere to the creative word. By the Word of God the material universe was fabricated, and the seven creative powers, or vowel sounds—which had been brought into existence by the speaking of the Word—became the seven Elohim or Deities by whose power and ministration the lower world was organized. Occasionally the Deity is symbolized by an eye, an ear, a nose, or a mouth. By the first, Divine awareness is signified; by the second, Divine interest; by the third, Divine vitality; and by the fourth, Divine command.

The ancients did not believe that spirituality made men either righteous or rational, but rather that righteousness and rationality made men spiritual. The Mysteries taught that spiritual illumination was attained only by bringing the lower nature up to a certain standard of efficiency and purity. The Mysteries were therefore established for the purpose of unfolding the nature of man according to certain fixed rules which, when faithfully followed, elevated the human consciousness to a point where it was capable of cognizing its own constitution and the true purpose of existence. This knowledge of how man's manifold constitution could be most quickly and most completely regenerated to the point of spiritual illumination constituted the secret, or esoteric, doctrine of antiquity. Certain apparently physical organs and centers are in reality the veils or sheaths of spiritual centers. What these were and how they could be unfolded was never revealed to the unregenerate, for the philosophers realized that once he understands the complete working of any system, a man may accomplish a prescribed end without being qualified to manipulate and control the effects which he has produced. For this reason long periods of probation were imposed, so that the knowledge of how to become as the gods might remain the sole possession of the worthy.

Lest that knowledge be lost, however, it was concealed in allegories and myths which were meaningless to the profane but self-evident to those acquainted with that theory of personal redemption which was the foundation of philosophical theology. Christianity itself may be cited as an example. The entire New Testament is in fact an ingeniously concealed exposition of the secret processes of human regeneration. The characters so long considered as historical men and women are really the personification of certain processes which take place in the human body when man begins the task of consciously liberating himself from the bondage of ignorance and death.

The garments and ornamentations supposedly worn by the gods are also keys, for in the Mysteries clothing was considered as synonymous with form. The degree of spirituality or materiality of the organisms was signified by the quality, beauty, and value of the garments worn. Man's physical body was looked upon as the robe of his spiritual nature; consequently, the more developed were his supersubstantial powers the more glorious his apparel. Of course, clothing was originally worn for ornamentation rather than protection, and such practice still prevails among many primitive peoples. The Mysteries taught that man's only lasting adornments were his virtues and worthy characteristics; that he was clothed in his own accomplishments and adorned by his attainments. Thus the white robe was symbolic of purity, the red robe of sacrifice and love, and the blue robe of altruism and integrity. Since the body was said to be the robe of the spirit, mental or moral deformities were depicted as deformities of the body.

Considering man's body as the measuring rule of the universe, the philosophers declared that all things resemble in constitution—if not in form—the human body. The Greeks, for example, declared Delphi to be the navel of the earth, for the physical planet was looked upon as a gigantic human being twisted into the form of a ball. In contradistinction to the belief of Christendom that the earth is an inanimate thing, the pagans considered not only the earth but also all the sidereal bodies as individual creatures possessing individual intelligences. They even went so far as to view the various kingdoms of Nature as individual entities. The animal kingdom, for example, was looked upon as one being—a composite of all the creatures composing that kingdom. This prototypic beast was a mosaic embodiment of all animal propensities and within its nature the entire animal world existed as the human species exists within the constitution of the prototypic Adam.

In the same manner, races, nations, tribes, religions, states, communities, and cities were viewed as composite entities, each made up of varying numbers of individual units. Every community has an individuality which is the sum of the individual attitudes of its inhabitants. Every religion is an individual whose body is made up of a hierarchy and vast host of individual worshipers. The organization of any religion represents its physical body, and its individual members the cell life making up this organism. Accordingly, religions, races, and communities—like individuals—pass through Shakespeare's *Seven Ages,* for the life of man is a standard by which the perpetuity of all things is estimated.

According to the secret doctrine, man, through the gradual refinement of his vehicles and the ever-increasing sensitiveness resulting from that refinement, is gradually overcoming the limitations of matter and is disentangling himself from his mortal coil. When humanity has completed its physical evolution, the empty shell of materiality left behind will be used by other life waves as stepping-stones to their own liberation. The trend of man's evolutionary growth is ever toward his own essential Selfhood. At the point of deepest materialism, therefore, man is at the greatest distance from Himself. According to the Mystery teachings, not all the spiritual nature of man incarnates in matter. The spirit of man is diagrammatically shown as an equilateral triangle with one point downward. This lower point, which is one-third of the spiritual nature but in comparison to the dignity of the other two is much less than a third, descends into the illusion of material existence for a brief space of time. That which never clothes itself in the sheath of matter is the Hermetic *Anthropos*—the Overman—analogous to the Cyclops or guardian *dæmon* of the Greeks, the *angel* of Jakob Böhme, and the Oversoul of Emerson, "that Unity, that Oversoul, within which every man's particular being is contained and made one with all other."

At birth only a third part of the Divine Nature of man temporarily dissociates itself from its own immortality and takes upon itself the dream of physical birth and existence, animating with its own celestial enthusiasm a vehicle composed of material elements, part of and bound to the material sphere. At death this incarnated part awakens from the dream of physical existence and reunites itself once more with its eternal condition. This periodical descent of spirit into matter is termed the *wheel of life and death,* and the principles involved are treated at length by the philosophers under the subject of metempsychosis. By initiation into the Mysteries and a certain process known as operative theology, this law of birth and death is transcended, and during the course of physical existence that part of the spirit which is asleep in form is awakened without the intervention of death—the inevitable Initiator—and is consciously reunited with the *Anthropos,* or the overshadowing substance of itself. This is at once the primary purpose and the consummate achievement of the Mysteries: that man shall become aware of and consciously be reunited with the divine source of himself without tasting of physical dissolution.

The Hiramic Legend

hen Solomon—the beloved of God, builder of the Everlasting House, and Grand Master of the Lodge of Jerusalem— ascended the throne of his father David he consecrated his life to the erection of a temple to God and a palace for the kings of Israel. David's faithful friend, Hiram, King of Tyre, hearing that a son of David sat upon the throne of Israel, sent messages of congratulation and offers of assistance to the new ruler. In his *History of the Jews,* Josephus mentions that copies of the letters passing between the two kings were then to be seen both at Jerusalem and at Tyre. Despite Hiram's lack of appreciation for the twenty cities of Galilee which Solomon presented to him upon the completion of the temple, the two monarchs remained the best of friends. Both were famous for their wit and wisdom, and when they exchanged letters each devised puzzling questions to test the mental ingenuity of the other. Solomon made an agreement with Hiram of Tyre promising vast amounts of barley, wheat, corn, wine, and oil as wages for the masons and carpenters from Tyre who were to assist the Jews in the erection of the temple. Hiram also supplied cedars and other fine trees, which were made into rafts and floated down the sea to Joppa, whence they were taken inland by Solomon's workmen to the temple site.

Because of his great love for Solomon, Hiram of Tyre sent also the Grand Master of the Dionysiac Architects, CHiram Abiff, a Widow's Son, who had no equal among the craftsmen of the earth. CHiram is described as being "a Tyrian by birth, but of Israelitish descent," and "a second Bezaleel, honored by his king with the title of Father." *The Freemason's Pocket Companion* (published in 1771) describes CHiram as "the most cunning, skilful and curious workman that ever lived, whose abilities were not confined to building alone, but extended to all kinds of work, whether in gold, silver, brass or iron; whether in linen, tapestry, or

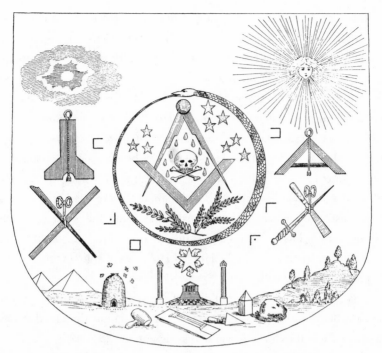

FROM AN EARLY HAND-PAINTED MASONIC APRON.

A MASONIC APRON WITH SYMBOLIC FIGURES.

While the mystic symbolism of Freemasonry decrees that the apron shall be a simple square of white lambskin with appropriate flap, Masonic aprons are frequently decorated with curious and impressive figures. "When silk, cotton, or linen is worn," writes Albert Pike, "the symbolism is lost. Nor is one clothed who blots, defaces, and desecrates the white surface with ornamentation, figuring, or colors of any kind." (See *Symbolism.*)

To Mars, the ancient planet of cosmic energy, the Atlantean and Chaldean "star gazers" assigned Aries as a diurnal throne and Scorpio as a nocturnal throne. Those not raised to spiritual life by initiation are described as "dead from the sting of the scorpion," for they wander in the night side of divine power. Through the mystery of the Paschal Lamb, or the attainment of the Golden Fleece, these souls are *raised* into the constructive day power of Mars in Aries—the symbol of the Creator.

When worn over the area related to the animal passions, the pure lambskin signifies the regeneration of the procreative forces and their consecration to the service of the Deity. The size of the apron, exclusive of the flap, makes it the symbol of salvation, for the Mysteries declare that it must consist of 144 square inches.

The apron shown above contains a wealth of symbolism: the beehive, emblematic of the Masonic lodge itself; the trowel, the mallet, and the trestleboard; the rough and trued ashlars; the pyramids and hills of Lebanon; the pillars, the Temple, and checkerboard floor; and the blazing star and tools of the Craft. The center of the apron is occupied by the compass and square, representative of the Macrocosm and the microcosm, and the alternately black and white serpent of astral light. Below is an acacia branch with seven sprigs, signifying the life centers of the superior and the inferior man. The skull and crossbones are a continual reminder that the spiritual nature attains liberation only after the *philosophical death* of man's sensuous personality.

embroidery; whether considered as an architect, statuary [*sic*], founder or designer, separately or together, he equally excelled. From his designs, and under his direction, all the rich and splendid furniture of the Temple and its several appendages were begun, carried on, and finished. Solomon appointed him, in his absence, to fill the chair, as Deputy Grand-Master; and in his presence, Senior Grand-Warden, Master of work, and general overseer of all artists, as well those whom David had formerly procured from Tyre and Sidon, as those Hiram should now send." (Modern Masonic writers differ as to the accuracy of the last sentence.)

Although an immense amount of labor was involved in its construction, Solomon's Temple—in the words of George Oliver—"was only a small building and very inferior in point of size to some of our churches." The number of buildings contiguous to it and the vast treasure of gold and precious stones used in its construction concentrated a great amount of wealth within the temple area. In the midst of the temple stood the Holy of Holies, sometimes called the Oracle. It was an exact cube, each dimension being twenty cubits, and exemplified the influence of Egyptian symbolism. The buildings of the temple group were ornamented with 1,453 columns of Parian marble, magnificently sculptured, and 2,906 pilasters decorated with capitals. There was a broad porch facing the east, and the *sanctum sanctorum* was upon the west. According to tradition, the various buildings and courtyards could hold in all 300,000 persons. Both the Sanctuary and the Holy of Holies were entirely lined with solid gold plates encrusted with jewels.

King Solomon began the building of the temple in the fourth year of his reign on what would be, according to modern calculation, the 21st day of April, and finished it in the eleventh year of his reign on the 23rd day of October. The temple was begun in the 480th year after the children of Israel had passed the Red Sea. Part of the labor of construction included the building of an artificial foundation on the brow of Mount Moriah. The stones for the temple were hoisted from quarries directly beneath Mount Moriah and were trued before being brought to the surface. The brass and golden ornaments for the temple were cast in molds in the clay ground between Succoth and Zeredatha, and the wooden parts were all finished before they reached the temple site. The building was put together, consequently, without sound and without instruments, all its parts fitting exactly "without the hammer of contention, the axe of division, or any tool of mischief."

Anderson's much-discussed *Constitutions of the Free-Masons,* published in London in 1723, and reprinted by Benjamin Franklin in Philadelphia in 1734, thus describes the division of the laborers engaged in the building of the Everlasting House:

"But Dagon's Temple, and the finest structures of Tyre and Sidon, could not be compared with the Eternal God's Temple at Jerusalem, * * * there were employed about it no less than 3,600 Princes, or Master-Masons, to conduct the work according to Solomon's directions, with 80,000 hewers of stone in the mountain, or Fellow Craftsmen, and 70,000 labourers, in all 153,600 besides the levy under Adoniram to work in the mountains of Lebanon by turns with the Sidonians, viz., 30,000, being in all 183,600." Daniel Sickels gives 3,300 overseers, instead of 3,600, and lists the three Grand Masters separately. The same author estimates the cost of the temple at nearly four thousand millions of dollars.

The Masonic legend of the building of Solomon's Temple does not in every particular parallel the Scriptural version, especially in those portions relating to CHiram Abiff. According to the Biblical account, this Master workman returned to his own country; in the Masonic allegory he is foully murdered. On this point A. E. Waite, in his *New Encycloaedia of Freemasonry,* makes the following explanatory comment:

"The legend of the Master-Builder is the great allegory of Masonry. It happens that his figurative story is grounded on the fact of a personality mentioned in Holy Scripture, but this historical background is of the accidents and not the essence; the significance is in the allegory and not in any point of history which may lie behind it."

CHiram, as Master of the Builders, divided his workmen into three groups, which were termed *Entered Apprentices, Fellow-Craftsmen,* and *Master Masons.* To each division he gave certain passwords and signs by which their respective excellence could be quickly determined. While all were classified according to their merits some were dissatisfied, for they desired a more exalted position than they were capable of filling. At last three Fellow-Craftsmen, more daring than their companions, determined to force CHiram to reveal to them the password of the Master's degree. Knowing that CHiram always went into the unfinished sanctum sanctorum at high noon to pray, these *ruffians*—whose names were Jubela, Jubelo, and Jubelum—lay in wait for him, one at each of the main gates of the temple. CHiram, about to leave the temple by the south gate, was suddenly confronted by Jubela armed with a twenty-four-inch gauge. Upon CHiram's refusal to reveal the Master's *Word,* the ruffian struck him on the throat with the rule, and the wounded Master then hastened to the west gate, where Jubelo, armed with a Square, awaited him and made a similar demand. Again CHiram was silent, and the second assassin struck him on the breast with the square. CHiram thereupon staggered to the east gate, only to be met there by Jubelum armed with a maul. When CHiram refused him the Master's *Word,* Jubelum struck the Master between the eyes with the mallet and CHiram fell dead.

The body of CHiram was buried by the murderers over the brow of Mount Moriah and a sprig of acacia placed upon the grave. The murderers then sought to escape punishment for their crime by embarking for Ethiopia, but the port was closed. All three were finally captured, and after admitting their guilt were duly executed. Parties of three were then sent out by King Solomon, and one of these groups discovered the newly made grave marked by the evergreen sprig. After the Entered Apprentices and the Fellow-Craftsmen had failed to resurrect their Master from the dead he was finally *raised* by the Master Mason with the "strong grip of a Lion's Paw."

To the initiated Builder the name *CHiram Abiff* signifies "My Father, the Universal Spirit, one in essence, three in aspect." Thus the murdered Master is a type of the Cosmic Martyr—the crucified Spirit of Good, the *dying god*—whose Mystery is celebrated throughout the world. Among the manuscripts of Dr. Sigismund Bacstrom, the initiated Rosicrucian, appears the following extract from von Welling concerning the true philosophic nature of the Masonic CHiram:

"The original word חירם, , CHiram, is a radical word consisting of three consonants ה ר and מ i.e. *Cheth, Resh* and *Mem*. (1) ה , *Cheth*, signifies *Chamah*, the Sun's light, i.e. the *Universal, invisible, cold fire of Nature* attracted by the Sun, manifested into *light* and sent down to us and to every planetary body belonging to the solar system. (2) ר , *Resh*, signifies רוח *Ruach*, i.e. *Spirit, air, wind*, as being the *Vehicle* which *conveys* and *collects the light* into numberless Foci, wherein the solar rays of light are agitated by a circular motion and manifested in *Heat* and *burning Fire*. (3) מ, or מ *Mem*, signifies *majim, water, humidity*, but rather the *mother of water*, i.e. *Radical Humidity* or a particular kind of *condensed air*. These three constitute the Universal Agent or fire of Nature in one word, חירם, , *CHiram*, not Hiram."

Albert Pike mentions several forms of the name *CHiram: Khirm, Khurm,* and *Khur-Om,* the latter ending in the sacred Hindu monosyllable *OM,* which may also be extracted from the names of the three murderers. Pike further relates the three ruffians to a triad of stars in the constellation of Libra and also calls attention to the fact that the Chaldean god Bal—metamorphosed into a demon by the Jews—appears in the name of each of the murderers, Ju*bel*a, Ju*bel*o, and Ju*bel*um. To interpret the Hiramic legend requires familiarity with both the Pythagorean and Qabbalistic systems of numbers and letters, and also the philosophic and astronomic cycles of the Egyptians, Chaldeans, and Brahmins. For example, consider the number 33. The first temple of Solomon stood for thirty-three years in its pristine splendor. At the end of that time it was pillaged by the Egyptian King Shishak, and finally (588 B.C.) it was completely destroyed by Nebuchadnezzar and the people of Jerusalem were led into captivity to Babylon. (See *General History of Freemasonry,* by Robert Macoy.) Also King David ruled for thirty-three years in Jerusalem; the Masonic Order is divided into thirty-three symbolic degrees; there are thirty-three segments in the human spinal column; and Jesus was crucified in the thirty-third year of His life.

The efforts made to discover the origin of the Hiramic legend show that, while the legend in its present form is comparatively modern, its underlying principles run back to remotest antiquity. It is generally admitted by modern Masonic scholars that the story of the martyred CHiram is based upon the Egyptian rites of Osiris, whose death and resurrection figuratively portrayed the *spiritual* death of man and his regeneration through initiation into the Mysteries. CHiram is also identified with Hermes through the inscription on the Emerald Table. From these associations it is evident that CHiram is to be considered as a prototype of humanity; in fact he is Plato's *Idea* (archetype) of man. As Adam after the Fall symbolizes the Idea of human degeneration, so CHiram through his resurrection symbolizes the Idea of human regeneration.

On the 19th day of March, 1314, Jacques de Molay, the last Grand Master of the Knights Templars, was burned on a pyre erected upon that point of the islet of the Seine, at Paris, where afterwards was erected the statue of King Henry IV. (See *The Indian Religions,* by Hargrave Jennings.) "It is mentioned as a tradition in some of the accounts of the burning," writes Jennings, "that Molay, ere he expired, summoned Clement, the Pope who had pronounced the bull of abolition against the Order and had condemned the Grand Master to the flames, to appear, within forty days, before the Supreme Eternal Judge, and Philip [the king] to the same awful tribunal within the space of a year. Both predictions were fulfilled." The close relationship between Freemasonry and the original Knights Templars has caused the story of CHiram to be linked with the martyrdom of Jacques de Molay. According to this interpretation, the three *ruffians* who cruelly slew their Master at the gates of the temple because he refused to reveal the secrets of his Order represent the Pope, the king, and the executioners. De Molay died maintaining his innocence and refusing to disclose the philosophical and magical arcana of the Templars.

Those who have sought to identify CHiram with the murdered King Charles the First conceive the Hiramic legend to have been invented for that purpose by Elias Ashmole, a mystical philosopher, who was probably a member of the Rosicrucian Fraternity. Charles was dethroned in 1647 and died on the block in 1649, leaving the Royalist party leaderless. An attempt has been made to relate the term "the Sons of the Widow" (an appellation frequently applied to members of the Masonic Order) to this incident in English history, for by the murder of her king England became a *Widow* and all Englishmen *Widow's Sons.*

To the mystic Christian Mason, CHiram represents the Christ who in three days (degrees) raised the temple of His body from its earthly sepulcher. His three murderers were Cæsar's agent (the state), the Sanhedrin (the church), and the incited populace (the mob). Thus considered, CHiram becomes the higher nature of man and the murderers are ignorance, superstition, and fear. The indwelling Christ can give expression to Himself in this world only through man's thoughts, feelings, and actions. Right thinking, right feeling, and right action—these are three gates through which the Christ power passes into the material world, there to labor in the erection of the Temple of Universal Brotherhood. Ignorance, superstition, and fear are three *ruffians* through whose agencies the Spirit of Good is murdered and a false kingdom, controlled by wrong thinking, wrong feeling, and wrong action, established in its stead. In the material universe evil appears ever victorious.

"In this sense," writes Daniel Sickels, "the myth of the Tyrian is perpetually repeated in the history of human affairs. Orpheus was murdered, and his body thrown into the Hebrus; Socrates was made to drink the hemlock; and, in all ages, we have seen Evil temporarily triumphant, and Virtue and Truth calumniated, persecuted, crucified, and slain. But Eternal Justice marches surely and swiftly through the world: the Typhons, the children of darkness, the plotters of crime, all the infinitely varied forms of evil, are swept into oblivion; and Truth and Virtue—for a time laid low—come forth, clothed with diviner majesty, and crowned with everlasting glory!" (See *General Ahiman Rezon.*)

If, as there is ample reason to suspect, the modern Freemasonic Order was profoundly influenced by, if it is not an actual outgrowth of, Francis Bacon's secret society, its symbolism is undoubtedly permeated with Bacon's two great ideals: universal education and universal democracy. The deadly enemies of universal education are ignorance, superstition, and fear, by which the human soul is held in bondage to the lowest part of its own constitution. The arrant enemies of universal democracy have ever been the crown, the tiara, and the torch. Thus CHiram symbolizes that ideal state of spiritual, intellectual, and physical emancipation which has ever been *sacrificed* upon the altar of human selfishness. CHiram is the Beautifier of the Eternal House. Modern utilitarianism, however, sacrifices the *beautiful* for the *practical,* in the same breath declaring the obvious lie that selfishness, hatred, and discord are practical.

Dr. Orville Ward Owen found a considerable part of the first thirty-two degrees of Freemasonic ritualism hidden in the text of the First Shakespeare Folio. Masonic emblems are to be observed also upon the title pages of nearly every book published by Bacon. Sir Francis Bacon considered himself as a living sacrifice upon the altar of human need; he was obviously *cut down* in the midst of his labors, and no student of his *New Atlantis* can fail to recognize the Masonic symbolism contained therein. According to the observations of Joseph Fort Newton, the Temple of Solomon described by Bacon in that utopian romance was not a house at all but the name of an ideal state. Is it not true that the Temple of Freemasonry is also emblematic of a condition of society? While, as before stated, the principles of the Hiramic legend are of the greatest antiquity, it is not impossible that its present form may be based upon incidents in the life of Lord Bacon, who passed through the philosophic death and was *raised* in Germany.

DIANA OF EPHESUS.

Crowned with a triple tower-like tiara and her form adorned with symbolic creatures representative of her spiritual powers, Diana stood for the source of that imperishable doctrine which, flowing from the bosom of the Great Multimammia, is the spiritual food of those aspiring men and women who have consecrated their lives to the contemplation of reality. As the physical body of man receives its nutriment from the Great Earth Mother, so the spiritual nature of man is fed from the never-failing fountains of Truth pouring outward from the invisible worlds.

In an old manuscript appears the statement that the Freemasonic Order was formed by alchemists and Hermetic philosophers who had banded themselves together to protect their secrets against the infamous methods used by avaricious persons to wring from them the secret of gold-making. The fact that the Hiramic legend contains an alchemical formula gives credence to this story. Thus the building of Solomon's Temple represents the consummation of the *magnum opus,* which cannot be realized without the assistance of CHiram, the Universal Agent. The Masonic Mysteries teach the initiate how to prepare within his own soul a miraculous *powder of projection* by which it is possible for him to transmute the base lump of human ignorance, perversion, and discord into an ingot of spiritual and philosophic gold.

Sufficient similarity exists between the Masonic CHiram and the *Kundalini* of Hindu mysticism to warrant the assumption that CHiram may be considered a symbol also of the Spirit Fire moving through the sixth ventricle of the spinal column. The exact science of human regeneration is the Lost Key of Masonry, for when the Spirit Fire is *lifted up* through the thirty-three degrees, or segments of the spinal column, and enters into the domed chamber of the human skull, it finally passes into the pituitary body (Isis), where it invokes Ra (the pineal gland) and demands the Sacred Name. Operative Masonry, in the fullest meaning of that term, signifies the process by which the Eye of Horus is opened. E. A. Wallis Budge has noted that in some of the papyri illustrating the entrance of the souls of the dead into the judgment hall of Osiris the deceased person has a pine cone attached to the crown of his head. The Greek mysteries also carried a symbolic staff, the upper end being in the form of a pine cone, which was called the *thyrsus* of Bacchus. In the human brain there is a tiny gland called the pineal body, which is the sacred eye of the ancients, and corresponds to the third eye of the Cyclops. Little is known concerning the function of the pineal body, which Descartes suggested (more wisely than he knew) might be the abode of the spirit of man. As its name signifies, the pineal gland is the sacred pine cone in man—the *eye single,* which cannot be opened until CHiram (the Spirit Fire) is *raised* through the sacred seals which are called the Seven Churches in Asia.

There is an Oriental painting which shows three sunbursts. One sunburst covers the head, in the midst of which sits Brahma with four heads, his body a mysterious dark color. The second sunburst—which covers the heart, solar plexus, and upper abdominal region—shows Vishnu sitting in the blossom of the lotus on a couch formed of the coils of the serpent of cosmic motion, its seven-hooded head forming a canopy over the god. The third sunburst is over the generative system, in the midst of which sits Shiva, his body a grayish white and the Ganges River flowing out of the crown of his head. This painting was the work of a Hindu mystic who spent many years subtly concealing great philosophical principles within these figures. The Christian legends could be related also to the human body by the same method as the Oriental, for the arcane meanings hidden in the teachings of both schools are identical.

As applied to Masonry, the three sunbursts represent the gates of the temple at which CHiram was struck, there being no gate in the north because the sun never shines from the northern angle of the heavens. The north is the symbol of the physical because of its relation to ice (crystallized water) and to the body (crystallized spirit). In man the light shines toward the north but never from it, because the body has no light of its own but shines with the reflected glory of the divine life-particles concealed within physical substance. For this reason the moon is accepted as the symbol of man's physical nature. CHiram is the mysterious fiery, airy water which must be raised through the three grand centers symbolized by the ladder with three rungs and the sunburst flowers mentioned in the description of the Hindu painting. It must also pass upward by means of the ladder of seven rungs—the seven plexuses proximate to the spine. The nine seg-

ments of the sacrum and coccyx are pierced by ten foramina, through which pass
the roots of the Tree of Life. Nine is the sacred number of man, and in the symbolism of the sacrum and coccyx a great mystery is concealed. That part of the
body from the kidneys downward was termed by the early Qabbalists the *Land of
Egypt* into which the children of Israel were taken during the captivity. Out of
Egypt, Moses (the illuminated mind, as his name implies) led the tribes of Israel
(the twelve faculties) by *raising* the brazen serpent in the wilderness upon the
symbol of the Tau cross. Not only CHiram but the god-men of nearly every pagan
Mystery ritual are personifications of the Spirit Fire in the human spinal cord.

The astronomical aspect of the Hiramic legend must not be overlooked.
The tragedy of CHiram is enacted annually by the sun during its passage
through the signs of the zodiac.

"From the journey of the Sun through the twelve signs," writes Albert Pike,
"come the legend of the twelve labors of Hercules, and the incarnations of
Vishnu and Buddha. Hence came the legend of the murder of Khurum, repre-
sentative of the Sun, by the three Fellow-Crafts, symbols of the Winter signs,
Capricornus, Aquarius, and Pisces, who assailed him at the three gates of
Heaven and slew him at the Winter Solstice. Hence the search for him by the
nine Fellow-Crafts, the other nine signs, his finding, burial, and resurrection."
(See *Morals and Dogma*.)

Other authors consider Libra, Scorpio, and Sagittarius as the three murderers of the sun, inasmuch as Osiris was murdered by Typhon, to whom were
assigned the thirty degrees of the constellation of Scorpio. In the Christian Mysteries also Judas signifies the Scorpion, and the thirty pieces of silver for which
he betrayed His Lord represent the number of degrees in that sign. Having been
struck by Libra (the state), Scorpio (the church), and Sagittarius (the mob), the
sun (CHiram) is secretly borne through the darkness by the signs of Capricorn,
Aquarius, and Pisces and buried over the brow of a hill (the vernal equinox).
Capricorn has for its symbol an old man with a scythe in his hand. This is Father
Time—a wayfarer—who is symbolized in Masonry as straightening out the
ringlets of a young girl's hair. If the Weeping Virgin be considered a symbol of
Virgo, and Father Time with his scythe a symbol of Capricorn, then the interval
of ninety degrees between these two signs will be found to correspond to that
occupied by the three murderers. Esoterically, the urn containing the *ashes* of
CHiram represents the human heart. Saturn, the old man who lives at the north
pole, and brings with him to the children of men a sprig of evergreen (the
Christmas tree), is familiar to the little folks under the name of *Santa Claus*, for
he brings each winter the gift of a new year.

The martyred sun is discovered by Aries, a Fellow-Craftsman, and at the vernal equinox the process of *raising* him begins. This is finally accomplished by the Lion of Judah, who in ancient times occupied the position of the keystone of the Royal Arch of Heaven. The precession of the equinoxes causes various signs to play the rôle of the murderers of the sun during the different ages of the world, but the principle involved remains unchanged. Such is the cosmic story of CHiram, the Universal Benefactor, the Fiery Architect of the Divine House, who carries with him to the grave that Lost Word which, when spoken, *raises* all life to power and glory. According to Christian mysticism, when the Lost Word is found it is discovered in a stable, surrounded by beasts and marked by a star. "After the sun leaves Leo," writes Robert Hewitt Brown, "the days begin to grow unequivocally shorter as the sun declines toward the autumnal equinox, to be again slain by the *three* autumnal months, lie dead through the *three* winter ones, and be raised again by the *three* vernal ones. Each year the great tragedy is repeated, and the glorious resurrection takes place." (See *Stellar Theology and Masonic Astronomy.*)

CHiram is termed *dead* because in the average individual the cosmic creative forces are limited in their manifestation to purely physical—and correspondingly materialistic—expression. Obsessed by his belief in the reality and permanence of physical existence, man does not correlate the material universe with the blank north wall of the temple. As the solar light symbolically is said to die as it approaches the winter solstice, so the physical world may be termed the winter solstice of the spirit. Reaching the winter solstice, the sun apparently stands still for three days and then, rolling away the stone of winter, begins its triumphal march north towards the summer solstice. The condition of ignorance may be likened to the winter solstice of philosophy; spiritual understanding to the summer solstice. From this point of view, initiation into the Mysteries becomes the vernal equinox of the spirit, at which time the CHiram in man crosses from the realm of mortality into that of eternal life. The autumnal equinox is analogous to the mythological *fall* of man, at which time the human spirit descended into the realms of Hades by being immersed in the illusion of terrestrial existence.

In *An Essay on the Beautiful,* Plotinus describes the refining effect of beauty upon the unfolding consciousness of man. Commissioned to decorate the Everlasting House, CHiram Abiff is the embodiment of the beautifying principle. Beauty is essential to the natural unfoldment of the human soul. The Mysteries held that man, in part at least, was the product of his environment. Therefore they considered it imperative that every person be surrounded by objects which would evoke the highest and noblest sentiments. They proved that it was possible to produce beauty in life by surrounding life with beauty. They discovered that symmetrical bodies were built by souls continuously in the presence of symmetrical bodies; that noble thoughts were produced by minds surrounded by examples of mental nobility. Conversely, if a man were forced to look upon an ignoble or asymmetrical structure it would arouse within him a sense of ignobility which would provoke him to commit ignoble deeds. If an ill-proportioned building were erected in the midst of a city there would be ill-proportioned children born in that community; and men and women, gazing upon the asymmetrical structure, would live inharmonious lives. Thoughtful men of antiquity realized that their great philosophers were the natural products of the æsthetic ideals of architecture, music, and art established as the standards of the cultural systems of the time.

The substitution of the discord of the fantastic for the harmony of the beautiful constitutes one of the great tragedies of every civilization. Not only were the Savior-Gods of the ancient world beautiful, but each performed a ministry of beauty, seeking to effect man's regeneration by arousing within him the love of the beautiful. A renaissance of the golden age of fable can be made possible only by the elevation of beauty to its rightful dignity as the all-pervading, idealizing quality in the religious, ethical, sociological, scientific, and political departments of life. The Dionysiac Architects were consecrated to the *raising* of their Master Spirit—Cosmic Beauty—from the sepulcher of material ignorance and selfishness by erecting buildings which were such perfect exemplars of symmetry and majesty that they were actually magical formulæ by which was evoked the spirit of the martyred Beautifier entombed within a materialistic world.

In the Masonic Mysteries the triune spirit of man (the light Delta) is symbolized by the three Grand Masters of the Lodge of Jerusalem. As God is the pervading principle of three worlds, in each of which He manifests as an active principle, so the spirit of man, partaking of the nature of Divinity, dwells upon three planes of being: the Supreme, the Superior, and the Inferior spheres of the Pythagoreans. At the gate of the Inferior sphere (the underworld, or dwelling place of mortal creatures) stands the guardian of Hades—the three-headed dog Cerberus, who is analogous to the three murderers of the Hiramic legend. According to this symbolic interpretation of the triune spirit, CHiram is the third, or incarnating, part—the Master Builder who through all ages erects living temples of flesh and blood as shrines of the Most High. CHiram comes forth as a flower and is cut down; he *dies* at the gates of matter; he is *buried* in the elements of creation, but—like Thor—he swings his mighty hammer in the fields of space, sets the primordial atoms in motion, and establishes order out of Chaos. As the potentiality of cosmic power within each human soul, CHiram lies waiting for man by the elaborate ritualism of life to transmute potentiality into divine potency. As the sense perceptions of the individual increase, however, man gains ever greater control over his various parts, and the spirit of life within gradually attains freedom. The three murderers represent the laws of the Inferior world— birth, growth, and decay—which ever frustrate the plan of the Builder. To the average individual, physical birth actually signifies the death of CHiram, and physical death the resurrection of CHiram. To the initiate, however, the resurrection of the spiritual nature is accomplished without the intervention of physical death.

The curious symbols found in the base of Cleopatra's Needle now standing in Central Park, New York, were interpreted as being of first Masonic significance by S. A. Zola, 33°, Past Grand Master of the Grand Lodge of Egypt. Masons' marks and symbols are to be found on the stones of numerous public buildings not only in England and on the Continent but also in Asia. In his *Indian Masons' Marks of the Moghul Dynasty,* A. Gorham describes scores of markings appearing on the walls of buildings such as the *Taj Mahal,* the *Jama Masjid,* and that famous Masonic structure, the *Kutab Minar.* According to those who regard Masonry as an outgrowth of the secret society of architects and builders which for thousands of years formed a caste of master craftsmen, CHiram Abiff was the Tyrian Grand Master of a world-wide organization of artisans, with headquarters in Tyre. Their philosophy consisted of incorporating into the measurements and ornamentation of temples, palaces, mausoleums, fortresses, and other public buildings their knowledge of the laws controlling the universe. Every initiated workman was given a hieroglyphic with which he marked the stones he trued to show to all posterity that he thus dedicated to the Supreme Architect of the Universe each perfected product of his labor. Concerning Masons' marks, Robert Freke Gould writes:

"It is very remarkable that these marks are to be found in all countries—in the chambers of the Great Pyramid at Gizeh, on the underground walls of Jerusalem, in Herculaneum and Pompeii, on Roman walls and Grecian temples, in Hindustan, Mexico, Peru, Asia Minor—as well as on the great ruins of England, France, Germany, Scotland, Italy, Portugal and Spain." (See *A Concise History of Freemasonry.*)

From this viewpoint the story of CHiram may well represent the incorporation of the divine secrets of architecture into the actual parts and dimensions of earthly buildings. The three degrees of the Craft *bury* the Grand Master (the

Great Arcanum) in the actual structure they erect, after first having *killed* him with the builders' tools, by reducing the dimensionless Spirit of Cosmic Beauty to the limitations of concrete form. These abstract ideals of architecture can be resurrected, however, by the Master Mason who, by meditating upon the structure, releases therefrom the divine principles of architectonic philosophy incorporated or *buried* within it. Thus the physical building is actually the tomb or embodiment of the Creative Ideal of which its material dimensions are but the shadow.

Moreover, the Hiramic legend may be considered to embody the vicissitudes of philosophy itself. As institutions for the dissemination of ethical culture, the pagan Mysteries were the architects of civilization. Their power and dignity were personified in CHiram Abiff—the Master Builder—but they eventually fell a victim to the onslaughts of that recurrent trio of state, church, and mob. They were desecrated by the state, jealous of their wealth and power; by the early church, fearful of their wisdom; and by the rabble or soldiery incited by both state and church. As CHiram when *raised* from his grave whispers the Master Mason's Word which was lost through his untimely death, so according to the tenets of philosophy the reestablishment or resurrection of the ancient Mysteries will result in the rediscovery of that secret teaching without which civilization must continue in a state of spiritual confusion and uncertainty.

When the mob governs, man is ruled by ignorance; when the church governs, he is ruled by superstition; and when the state governs, he is ruled by fear. Before men can live together in harmony and understanding, ignorance must be transmuted into wisdom, superstition into an illumined faith, and fear into love. Despite statements to the contrary, Masonry is a religion seeking to unite God and man by elevating its initiates to that level of consciousness whereon they can behold with clarified vision the workings of the Great Architect of the Universe. From age to age the vision of a perfect civilization is preserved as the ideal for mankind. In the midst of that civilization shall stand a mighty university wherein both the sacred and secular sciences concerning the mysteries of life will be freely taught to all who will assume the philosophic life. Here creed and dogma will have no place; the superficial will be removed and only the essential be preserved. The world will be ruled by its most illumined minds, and each will occupy the position for which he is most admirably fitted.

The great university will be divided into grades, admission to which will be through preliminary tests or initiations. Here mankind will be instructed in the most sacred, the most secret, and the most enduring of all Mysteries—*Symbolism.* Here the initiate will be taught that every visible object, every abstract thought, every emotional reaction is but the symbol of an eternal principle. Here mankind will learn that CHiram (Truth) lies buried in every atom of Kosmos; that every form is a symbol and every symbol the tomb of an eternal verity. Through education—spiritual, mental, moral, and physical—man will learn to release living truths from their lifeless coverings. The perfect government of the earth must be patterned eventually after that divine government by which the universe is ordered. In that day when perfect order is reestablished, with peace universal and good triumphant, men will no longer seek for happiness, for they shall find it welling up within themselves. Dead hopes, dead aspirations, dead virtues shall rise from their graves, and the Spirit of Beauty and Goodness repeatedly slain by ignorant men shall again be the Master of Work. Then shall sages sit upon the seats of the mighty and the gods walk with men.

XVII

The Pythagorean Theory of Music and Color

armony is a state recognized by great philosophers as the immediate prerequisite of beauty. A compound is termed *beautiful* only when its parts are in *harmonious* combination. The world is called beautiful and its Creator is designated the *Good* because good perforce must act in conformity with its own nature; and good acting according to its own nature is harmony, because the good which it accomplishes is harmonious with the good which it is. Beauty, therefore, is harmony manifesting its own intrinsic nature in the world of form.

The universe is made up of successive gradations of good, these gradations ascending from matter (which is the least degree of good) to spirit (which is the greatest degree of good). In man, his superior nature is the *summum bonum*. It therefore follows that his highest nature most readily cognizes good, because the good external to him in the world is in harmonic ratio with the good present in his soul. What man terms *evil* is therefore, in common with matter, merely the least degree of its own opposite. The least degree of good presupposes likewise the least degree of harmony and beauty. Thus deformity (evil) is really the least harmonious combination of elements naturally harmonic as individual units. Deformity is unnatural, for, the sum of all things being the *Good*, it is natural that all things should partake of the *Good* and be arranged in combinations that are harmonious. Harmony is the manifesting expression of the *Will* of the eternal *Good*.

The Philosophy of Music

It is highly probable that the Greek initiates gained their knowledge of the philosophic and therapeutic aspects of music from the Egyptians, who, in turn,

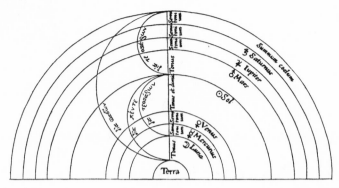

FROM STANLEY'S *THE HISTORY OF PHILOSOPHY*.

THE INTERVALS AND HARMONIES OF THE SPHERES.

In Pythagorean concept of the *music of the spheres*, the interval between the earth and the sphere of the fixed stars was considered to be a diapason—the most perfect harmonic interval. The following arrangement is most generally accepted for the musical intervals of the planets between the earth and the sphere of the fixed stars: From the sphere of the earth to the sphere of the moon, one tone; from the sphere of the moon to that of Mercury, one-half tone; from Mercury to Venus, one-half tone; from Venus to the sun, one and one-half tones; from the sun to Mars, one tone; from Mars to Jupiter, one-half tone; from Jupiter to Saturn, one-half tone; from Saturn to the fixed stars, one-half tone. The sum of these intervals equals the six whole tones of the octave.

considered Hermes the founder of the art. According to one legend, this god constructed the first lyre by stretching strings across the concavity of a turtle shell. Both Isis and Osiris were patrons of music and poetry. Plato, in describing the antiquity of these arts among the Egyptians, declared that songs and poetry had existed in Egypt for at least ten thousand years, and that these were of such an exalted and inspiring nature that only gods or godlike men could have composed them. In the Mysteries the lyre was regarded as the secret symbol of the human constitution, the body of the instrument representing the physical form, the strings the nerves, and the musician the spirit. Playing upon the nerves, the spirit thus created the harmonies of normal functioning, which, however, became discords if the nature of man were defiled.

While the early Chinese, Hindus, Persians, Egyptians, Israelites, and Greeks employed both vocal and instrumental music in their religious ceremonials, also to complement their poetry and drama, it remained for Pythagoras to raise the art to its true dignity by demonstrating its mathematical foundation. Although it is said that he himself was not a musician, Pythagoras is now generally credited with the discovery of the diatonic scale. Having first learned the divine theory of music from the priests of the various Mysteries into which he had been accepted, Pythagoras pondered for several years upon the laws governing consonance and dissonance. How he actually solved the problem is unknown, but the following explanation has been invented.

One day while meditating upon the problem of harmony, Pythagoras chanced to pass a brazier's shop where workmen were pounding out a piece of metal upon an anvil. By noting the variances in pitch between the sounds made by large hammers and those made by smaller implements, and carefully estimating the harmonies and discords resulting from combinations of these sounds, he gained his first clue to the musical intervals of the diatonic scale. He entered the shop, and after carefully examining the tools and making mental note of their weights, returned to his own house and constructed an arm of wood so that it extended out from the wall of his room. At regular intervals along this arm he attached four cords, all of like composition, size, and weight. To the first of these he attached a twelve-pound weight, to the second a nine-pound weight, to the third an eight-pound weight, and to the fourth a six-pound weight. These different weights corresponded to the sizes of the braziers' hammers.

Pythagoras thereupon discovered that the first and fourth strings when sounded together produced the harmonic interval of the octave, for doubling the weight had the same effect as halving the string. The tension of the first string being twice that of the fourth string, their ratio was said to be 2:1, or duple. By similar experimentation he ascertained that the first and third string produced the harmony of the diapente, or the interval of the fifth. The tension of the first string being half again as much as that of the third string, their ratio was said to be 3:2, or sesquialter. Likewise the second and fourth strings, having the same ratio as the first and third strings, yielded a diapente harmony. Continuing his investigation, Pythagoras discovered that the first and second strings produced the harmony of the diatessaron, or the interval of the third; and the tension of the first string being a third greater than that of the second string, their ratio was said to be 4:3, or sesquitertian. The third and fourth strings, having the same ratio as the first and second strings, produced another harmony of the diatessaron. According to Iamblichus, the second and third strings had the ratio of 8:9, or epogdoan.

The key to harmonic ratios is hidden in the famous Pythagorean *tetractys*, or pyramid of dots. The *tetractys* is made up of the first four numbers—1, 2, 3, and 4—which in their proportions reveal the intervals of the octave, the diapente, and the diatessaron. While the law of harmonic intervals as set forth above is true, it has been subsequently proved that hammers striking metal in the manner described will not produce the various tones ascribed to them. In all probability, therefore, Pythagoras actually worked out his theory of harmony from the monochord—a contrivance consisting of a single string stretched between two pegs and supplied with movable frets.

To Pythagoras music was one of the dependencies of the divine science of mathematics, and its harmonies were inflexibly controlled by mathematical proportions. The Pythagoreans averred that mathematics demonstrated the exact method by which the *Good* established and maintained its universe. Number therefore preceded harmony, since it was the immutable law that governs all harmonic proportions. After discovering these harmonic ratios, Pythagoras gradually initiated his disciples into this, the supreme arcanum of his Mysteries. He divided the multitudinous parts of creation into a vast number of planes or spheres, to each of which he assigned a tone, a harmonic interval, a number, a name, a color, and a form. He then proceeded to prove the accuracy of his deductions by demonstrating them upon the different planes of intelligence and substance ranging from the most abstract logical premise to the most concrete geometrical solid. From the common agreement of these diversified methods of proof he established the indisputable existence of certain natural laws.

Having once established music as an exact science, Pythagoras applied his newly found law of harmonic intervals to all the phenomena of Nature, even going so far as to demonstrate the harmonic relationship of the planets, constellations, and elements to each other. A notable example of modern corroboration of ancient philosophical teaching is that of the progression of the elements according to harmonic ratios. While making a list of the elements in the ascending order of their atomic weights, John A. Newlands discovered at every eighth element a distinct repetition of properties. This discovery is known as the *law of octaves* in modern chemistry.

Since they held that harmony must be determined not by the sense perceptions but by reason and mathematics, the Pythagoreans called themselves *Canonics,* as distinguished from musicians of the *Harmonic School,* who asserted taste and instinct to be the true normative principles of harmony. Recognizing, however, the profound effect of music upon the senses and emotions, Pythagoras did not hesitate to influence the mind and body with what he termed "musical medicine."

Pythagoras evinced such a marked preference for stringed instruments that he even went so far as to warn his disciples against allowing their ears to be defiled by the sounds of flutes or cymbals. He further declared that the soul could be purified from its irrational influences by solemn songs sung to the accompaniment of the lyre. In his investigation of the therapeutic value of harmonics, Pythagoras discovered that the seven modes—or keys—of the Greek system of music had the power to incite or allay the various emotions. It is related that while observing the stars one night he encountered a young man befuddled with strong drink and mad with jealousy who was piling faggots about his mistress' door with the intention of burning the house. The frenzy of the youth was accentuated by a flutist a short distance away who was playing a tune in the stirring Phrygian mode. Pythagoras induced the musician to change his air to the slow and rhythmic Spondaic mode, whereupon the intoxicated youth immediately became composed and, gathering up his bundles of wood, returned quietly to his own home.

There is also an account of how Empedocles, a disciple of Pythagoras, by quickly changing the mode of a musical composition he was playing, saved the life of his host, Anchitus, when the latter was threatened with death by the sword of one whose father he had condemned to public execution. It is also known that Esculapius, the Greek physician, cured sciatica and other diseases of the nerves by blowing a loud trumpet in the presence of the patient.

Pythagoras cured many ailments of the spirit, soul, and body by having certain specially prepared musical compositions played in the presence of the sufferer or by personally reciting short selections from such early poets as Hesiod and Homer. In his university at Crotona it was customary for the Pythagoreans to open and to close each day with songs—those in the morning calculated to clear the mind from sleep and inspire it to the activities of the coming day; those in the evening of a mode soothing, relaxing, and conducive to rest. At the vernal equinox, Pythagoras caused his disciples to gather in a circle around one of their number who led them in song and played their accompaniment upon a lyre.

The therapeutic music of Pythagoras is described by Iamblichus thus: "And there are certain melodies devised as remedies against the passions of the soul, and also against despondency and lamentation, which Pythagoras invented as things that afford the greatest assistance in these maladies. And again, he employed other melodies against rage and anger, and against every aberration of the soul. There is also another kind of modulation invented as a remedy against desires." (See *The Life of Pythagoras*.)

It is probable that the Pythagoreans recognized a connection between the Seven Greek modes and the planets. As an example, Pliny declares that Saturn moves in the Dorian mode and Jupiter in the Phrygian mode. It is also apparent that the temperaments are keyed to the various modes, and the passions likewise. Thus, anger—which is a fiery passion—may be accentuated by a fiery mode or its power neutralized by a watery mode.

The far-reaching effect exercised by music upon the culture of the Greeks is thus summed up by Emil Nauman: "Plato depreciated the notion that music was intended solely to create cheerful and agreeable emotions, maintaining rather that it should inculcate a love of all that is noble, and hatred of all that is mean, and that nothing could more strongly influence man's innermost feelings than melody and rhythm. Firmly convinced of this, he agreed with Damon of Athens, the musical instructor of Socrates, that the introduction of a new and presumably enervating scale would endanger the future of a whole nation, and that it was not possible to alter a key without shaking the very foundations of the State. Plato affirmed that music which ennobled the mind was of a far higher kind than that which merely appealed to the senses, and he strongly insisted that it was the paramount duty of the Legislature to suppress all music of an effeminate and lascivious character, and to encourage only that which was pure and dignified; that bold and stirring melodies were for men, gentle and soothing ones for women. From this it is evident that music played a considerable part in the education of the Greek youth. The greatest care was also to be taken in the selection of instrumental music, because the absence of words rendered its signification doubtful, and it was difficult to foresee whether it would exercise upon the people a benign or baneful influence. Popular taste, being always tickled by sensuous and meretricious effects, was to be treated with deserved contempt." (See *The History of Music*.)

Even today martial music is used with telling effect in times of war, and religious music, while no longer developed in accordance with the ancient theory, still profoundly influences the emotions of the laity.

The Music of the Spheres

The most sublime but least known of all the Pythagorean speculations was that of sidereal harmonics. It was said that of all men only Pythagoras heard *the music of the spheres*. Apparently the Chaldeans were the first people to conceive of the heavenly bodies joining in a cosmic chant as they moved in stately manner across the sky. Job describes a time "when the stars of the morning sang together," and in *The Merchant of Venice* the author of the Shakesperian plays writes: "There's not the smallest orb which thou behold'st but in his motion like an angel sings." So little remains, however, of the Pythagorean system of celestial music that it is only possible to approximate his actual theory.

Pythagoras conceived the universe to be an immense monochord, with its single string connected at its upper end to absolute spirit and at its lower end to absolute matter—in other words, a cord stretched between heaven and earth. Counting inward from the circumference of the heavens, Pythagoras, according to some authorities, divided the universe into nine parts; according to others, into twelve parts. The twelvefold system was as follows: The first division was called the *empyrean*, or the sphere of the fixed stars, and was the dwelling place of the immortals. The second to twelfth divisions were (in order) the spheres of Saturn, Jupiter, Mars, the sun, Venus, Mercury, and the moon, and fire, air, water, and earth. This arrangement of the seven planets (the sun and moon being regarded as planets in the old astronomy) is identical with the candlestick symbolism of the Jews—the sun in the center as the main stem with three planets on either side of it.

The names given by the Pythagoreans to the various notes of the diatonic scale were, according to Macrobius, derived from an estimation of the velocity and magnitude of the planetary bodies. Each of these gigantic spheres as it rushed endlessly through space was believed to sound a certain tone caused by its continuous displacement of the *æthereal diffusion*. As these tones were a manifestation of divine order and motion, it must necessarily follow that they partook of the harmony of their own source. "The assertion that the planets in their revolutions round the earth uttered certain sounds differing according to their respective 'magnitude, celerity and local distance,' was commonly made by the Greeks. Thus Saturn, the farthest planet, was said to give the gravest note, while the Moon, which is the nearest, gave the sharpest. 'These sounds of the seven planets, and the sphere of the fixed stars, together with that above us [Antichthon], are the nine Muses, and their joint symphony is called Mnemosyne.'" (See *The Canon.*) This quotation contains an obscure reference to the ninefold division of the universe previously mentioned.

The Greek initiates also recognized a fundamental relationship between the individual heavens or spheres of the seven planets, and the seven sacred vowels. The first heaven uttered the sound of the sacred vowel A (Alpha); the second heaven, the sacred vowel E (Epsilon); the third, H (Eta); the fourth, I (Iota); the fifth, O (Omicron); the sixth, Y (Upsilon); and the seventh heaven, the sacred vowel Ω (Omega). When these seven heavens sing together they produce a perfect harmony which ascends as an everlasting praise to the throne of the Creator. (See Irenæus' *Against Heresies.*) Although not so stated, it is probable that the planetary heavens are to be considered as ascending in the Pythagorean order, beginning with the sphere of the moon, which would be the first heaven.

Many early instruments had seven strings, and it is generally conceded that Pythagoras was the one who added the eighth string to the lyre of Terpander. The seven strings were always related both to their correspondences in the human body and to the planets. The names of God were also conceived to be formed from combinations of the seven planetary harmonies. The Egyptians confirmed their sacred songs to the seven primary sounds, forbidding any others to be uttered in their temples. One of their hymns contained the following invocation: "The seven sounding tones praise Thee, the Great God, the cease-less working Father of the whole universe." In another the Deity describes Him-self thus: "I am the great indestructible lyre of the whole world, attuning the songs of the heavens." (See Nauman's *History of Music*.)

The Pythagoreans believed that everything which existed had a voice and that all creatures were eternally singing the praise of the Creator. Man fails to hear these divine melodies because his soul is enmeshed in the illusion of mate-rial existence. When he liberates himself from the bondage of the lower world with its sense limitations, *the music of the spheres* will again be audible as it was in the Golden Age. Harmony recognizes harmony, and when the human soul regains its true estate it will not only hear the celestial choir but also join with it in an everlasting anthem of praise to that Eternal *Good* controlling the infinite number of parts and conditions of Being.

The Greek Mysteries included in their doctrines a magnificent concept of the relationship existing between music and form. The elements of architecture, for example, were considered as comparable to musical modes and notes, or as having a musical counterpart. Consequently when a building was erected in which a number of these elements were combined, the structure was then likened to a musical chord, which was harmonic only when it fully satisfied the mathematical requirements of harmonic intervals. The realization of this anal-ogy between sound and form led Goethe to declare that "architecture is crystal-lized music."

In constructing their temples of initiation, the early priests frequently demonstrated their superior knowledge of the principles underlying the phe-nomena known as vibration. A considerable part of the Mystery rituals con-sisted of invocations and intonements, for which purpose special sound chambers were constructed. A word whispered in one of these apartments was so intensified that the reverberations made the entire building sway and be filled with a deafening roar. The very wood and stone used in the erection of these sacred buildings eventually became so thoroughly permeated with the sound vibrations of the religious ceremonies that when struck they would reproduce the same tones thus repeatedly impressed into their substances by the rituals.

Every element in Nature has its individual keynote. If these elements are combined in a composite structure the result is a chord that, if sounded, will dis-integrate the compound into its integral parts. Likewise each individual has a keynote that, if sounded, will destroy him. The allegory of the walls of Jericho falling when the trumpets of Israel were sounded is undoubtedly intended to set forth the arcane significance of individual keynote or vibration.

The Philosophy of Color

"Light," writes Edwin D. Babbitt, "reveals the glories of the external world and yet is the most glorious of them all. It gives beauty, reveals beauty and is itself most beautiful. It is the analyzer, the truth-teller and the exposer of shams, for it shows things as they are. Its infinite streams measure off the universe and flow into our telescopes from stars which are quintillions of miles distant. On the other hand it descends to objects inconceivably small, and reveals through the microscope objects fifty millions of times less than can be seen by the naked eye. Like all other fine forces, its movement is wonderfully soft, yet penetrating and powerful. Without its vivifying influence, vegetable, animal, and human life must immediately perish from the earth, and general ruin take place. We shall do well, then, to consider this potential and beautiful principle of light and its component colors, for the more deeply we penetrate into its inner laws, the more will it present itself as a marvelous storehouse of power to vitalize, heal, refine, and delight mankind." (See *The Principles of Light and Color.*)

Since light is the basic physical manifestation of life, bathing all creation in its radiance, it is highly important to realize, in part at least, the subtle nature of this divine substance. That which is called *light* is actually a rate of vibration causing certain reactions upon the optic nerve. Few realize how they are walled in by the limitations of the sense perceptions. Not only is there a great deal more to light than anyone has ever seen but there are also unknown forms of light which no optical equipment will ever register. There are unnumbered colors which cannot be seen, as well as sounds which cannot be heard, odors which cannot be smelt, flavors which cannot be tasted, and substances which cannot be felt. Man is thus surrounded by a supersensible universe of which he knows nothing because the centers of sense perception within himself have not been developed sufficiently to respond to the subtler rates of vibration of which that universe is composed.

Among both civilized and savage peoples color has been accepted as a natural language in which to couch their religious and philosophical doctrines. The ancient city of Ecbatana as described by Herodotus, its seven walls colored according to the seven planets, revealed the knowledge of this subject possessed by the Persian Magi. The famous *zikkurat* or astronomical tower of the god Nebo at Borsippa ascended in seven great steps or stages, each step being painted in the key color of one of the planetary bodies. (See Lenormant's *Chaldean Magic.*) It is thus evident that the Babylonians were familiar with the concept of the spectrum in its relation to the seven Creative Gods or Powers. In

India, one of the Mogul emperors caused a fountain to be made with seven levels. The water pouring down the sides through specially arranged channels changed color as it descended, passing sequentially through all shades of the spectrum. In Tibet, color is employed by the native artists to express various moods. L. Austine Waddell, writing of Northern Buddhist art, notes that in Tibetan mythology "White and yellow complexions usually typify mild moods, while the red, blue, and black belong to fierce forms, though sometimes light blue, as indicating the sky, means merely celestial. Generally the gods are pictured white, goblins red, and devils black, like their European relative." (See *The Buddhism of Tibet*.)

In *Meno,* Plato, speaking through Socrates, describes color as "an effluence of form, commensurate with sight, and sensible." In *Theœtetus* he discourses more at length on the subject thus: "Let us carry out the principle which has just been affirmed, that nothing is self-existent, and then we shall see that every color, white, black, and every other color, arises out of the eye meeting the appropriate motion, and that what we term the substance of each color is neither the active nor the passive element, but something which passes between them, and is peculiar to each percipient; are you certain that the several colors appear to every animal—say a dog—as they appear to you?"

In the Pythagorean *tetractys*—the supreme symbol of universal forces and processes—are set forth the theories of the Greeks concerning color and music. The first three dots represent the threefold White Light, which is the Godhead containing potentially all sound and color. The remaining seven dots are the colors of the spectrum and the notes of the musical scale. The colors and tones are the active creative powers which, emanating from the First Cause, establish the universe. The seven are divided into two groups, one containing three powers and the other four—a relationship also shown in the *tetractys*. The higher group—that of three—becomes the spiritual nature of the created universe; the lower group—that of four—manifests as the irrational sphere, or inferior world.

In the Mysteries the seven *Logi,* or Creative Lords, are shown as streams of force issuing from the mouth of the Eternal One. This signifies the spectrum being extracted from the white light of the Supreme Deity. The seven Creators, or Fabricators, of the inferior spheres were called by the Jews the *Elohim.* By the Egyptians they were referred to as the *Builders* (sometimes as the *Governors*) and are depicted with great knives in their hands with which they carved the universe from its primordial substance. Worship of the planets is based upon their acceptation as the cosmic embodiments of the seven creative attributes of

God. The Lords of the planets were described as dwelling within the body of the sun, for the true nature of the sun, being analogous to the white light, contains the seeds of all the tone and color potencies which it manifests.

There are numerous arbitrary arrangements setting forth the mutual relationships of the planets, the colors, and the musical notes. The most satisfactory system is that based upon the *law of the octave.* The sense of hearing has a much wider scope than that of sight, for whereas the ear can register from nine to eleven octaves of sound the eye is restricted to the cognition of but seven fundamental color tones, or one tone short of the octave. Red, when posited as the lowest color tone in the sale of chromatics, thus corresponds to *do,* the first note of the musical scale. Continuing the analogy, orange corresponds to *re,* yellow to *mi,* green to *fa,* blue to *sol,* indigo to *la,* and violet to *si (ti).* The eighth color tone necessary to complete the scale should be the higher octave of red, the first color tone. The accuracy of the above arrangement is attested by two striking facts: (1) the three fundamental notes of the musical scale—the first, the third, and the fifth—correspond with the three primary colors—red, yellow, and blue; (2) the seventh, and least perfect, note of the musical scale corresponds with purple, the least perfect tone of the color scale.

In *The Principles of Light and Color,* Edwin D. Babbitt confirms the correspondence of the color and musical scales: "As C is at the bottom of the musical scale and made with the coarsest waves of air, so is red at the bottom of the chromatic scale and made with the coarsest waves of luminous ether. As the musical note B [the seventh note of the scale] requires 45 vibrations of air every time the note C at the lower end of the scale requires 24, or but little over half as many, so does extreme violet require about 800 trillions of vibrations of ether in a second, while extreme red requires only about 450 trillions, which also are but little more than half as many. When one musical octave is finished another one commences and progresses with just twice as many vibrations as were used in the first octave, and so the same notes are repeated on a finer scale. In the same way when the scale of colors visible to the ordinary eye is completed in the violet, another octave of finer invisible colors, with just twice as many vibrations, will commence and progress on precisely the same law."

When the colors are related to the twelve signs of the zodiac, they are arranged as the spokes of a wheel. To Aries is assigned pure red; to Taurus, red-orange; to Gemini, pure orange; to Cancer, orange-yellow; to Leo, pure yellow; to Virgo, yellow-green; to Libra, pure green; to Scorpio, green-blue; to Sagittarius, pure blue; to Capricorn, blue-violet; to Aquarius, pure violet; and to Pisces, violet-red.

In expounding the Eastern system of esoteric philosophy, H. P. Blavatsky relates the colors to the septenary constitution of man and the seven states of matter as follows:

COLOR	PRINCIPLES OF MAN	STATES OF MATTER
Violet	*Chaya*, or Etheric Double	Ether
Indigo	Higher *Manas*, or Spiritual Intelligence	Critical State called Air
Blue	Auric Envelope	Steam or Vapor
Green	Lower *Manas*, or Animal Soul	Critical State
Yellow	*Buddhi*, or Spiritual Soul	Water
Orange	*Prana*, or Life Principle	Critical State
Red	*Kama Rupa*, or Seat of Animal Life	Ice

This arrangement of the colors of the spectrum and the musical notes of the octave necessitates a different grouping of the planets in order to preserve their proper tone and color analogies. Thus *do* becomes Mars; *re*, the sun; *mi*, Mercury; *fa*, Saturn; *sol*, Jupiter; *la*, Venus; *si* (*ti*) the moon. (See *The E. S. Instructions.*)

XVIII

Fishes, Insects, Animals, Reptiles, and Birds

PART I

The creatures inhabiting the water, air, and earth were held in veneration by all races of antiquity. Realizing that visible bodies are only symbols of invisible forces, the ancients worshiped the Divine Power through the lower kingdoms of Nature, because those less evolved and more simply constituted creatures responded most readily to the creative impulses of the gods. The sages of old studied living things to a point of realization that God is most perfectly understood through a knowledge of His supreme handiwork—animate and inanimate Nature.

Every existing creature manifests some aspect of the intelligence or power of the Eternal One, who can never be known save through a study and appreciation of His numbered but inconceivable parts. When a creature is chosen, therefore, to symbolize to the concrete human mind some concealed abstract principle it is because its characteristics demonstrate this invisible principle in visible action. Fishes, insects, animals, reptiles, and birds appear in the religious symbolism of nearly all nations, because the forms and habits of these creatures and the media in which they exist closely relate them to the various generative and germinative powers of Nature, which were considered as prima-facie evidence of divine omnipresence.

The early philosophers and scientists, realizing that all life has its origin in water, chose the fish as the symbol of the life germ. The fact that fishes are most prolific makes the simile still more apt. While the early priests may not have possessed the instruments necessary to analyze the spermatozoon, they concluded by deduction that it resembled a fish.

Fishes were sacred to the Greeks and Romans, being connected with the worship of Aphrodite (Venus). An interesting survival of pagan ritualism is

FROM PICART'S *RELIGIOUS CEREMONIALS*.

THE FIRST INCARNATION, OR MATSYA AVATAR, OF VISHNU.

The fish has often been associated with the World Saviors. Vishnu, the Hindu Redeemer, who takes upon himself ten forms for the redemption of the universe, was expelled from the mouth of a fish in his first incarnation. Isis, while nursing the infant Horus, is often shown with a fish on her headdress. Oannes, the Chaldean Savior (borrowed from the Brahmins), is depicted with the head and body of a fish, from which his human form protrudes at various points. Jesus was often symbolized by a fish. He told His disciples that they should become "fishers of men." The sign of the fish was also the first monogram of the Christians. The mysterious Greek name of Jesus, ΙΧΘΥΣ, means "a fish." The fish was accepted as a symbol of the Christ by a number of early canonized church fathers. St. Augustine likened the Christ to a fish that had been broiled, and it was also pointed out that the flesh of that Fish was the food of righteous and holy men.

found in the custom of eating fish on Friday. *Freya,* in whose honor the day was named, was the Scandinavian Venus, and this day was sacred among many nations to the goddess of beauty and fecundity. This analogy further links the fish with the procreative mystery. Friday is also sacred to the followers of the Prophet Mohammed.

The word *nun* means both fish and growth, and as Inman says: "The Jews were led to victory by the Son of the Fish whose other names were Joshua and

Jesus (the Savior). *Nun* is still the name of a female devotee" of the Christian faith. Among early Christians three fishes were used to symbolize the Trinity, and the fish is also one of the eight sacred symbols of the great Buddha. It is also significant that the dolphin should be sacred to both Apollo (the Solar Savior) and Neptune. It was believed that this fish carried shipwrecked sailors to heaven on its back. The dolphin was accepted by the early Christians as an emblem of Christ, because the pagans had viewed this beautiful creature as a friend and benefactor of man. The heir to the throne of France, the *Dauphin,* may have secured his title from this ancient pagan symbol of the divine preservative power. The first advocates of Christianity likened converts to fishes, who at the time of baptism "returned again into the sea of Christ."

Primitive peoples believed the sea and land were inhabited by strange creatures, and early books on zoology contain curious illustrations of composite beasts, reptiles, and fishes, which did not exist at the time the mediæval authors compiled these voluminous books. In the ancient initiatory rituals of the Persian, Greek, and Egyptian Mysteries the priests disguised themselves as composite creatures, thereby symbolizing different aspects of human consciousness. They used birds and reptiles as emblems of their various deities, often creating forms of grotesque appearance and assigning to them imaginary traits, habits, and places of domicile, all of which were symbolic of certain spiritual and transcendental truths thus concealed from the profane. The *phœnix* made its nest of incense and flames. The *unicorn* had the body of a horse, the feet of an elephant, and the tail of a wild boar. The upper half of the *centaur*'s body was human and the lower half equine. The *pelican* of the Hermetists fed its young from its own breast, and to this bird were assigned other mysterious attributes which could have been true only allegorically.

Though regarded by many writers of the Middle Ages as actual living creatures, none of these—the pelican excepted—ever existed outside the symbolism of the Mysteries. Possibly they originated in rumors of animals then little known. In the temple, however, they became a reality, for there they signified the manifold characteristics of man's nature. The *mantichora* had certain points in common with the hyena; the *unicorn* may have been the single-horned rhinoceros. To the student of the secret wisdom these composite animals and birds simply represent various forces working in the invisible worlds. This is a point which nearly all writers on the subject of mediævel monsters seem to have overlooked. (See Vlyssis Aldrovandi's *Monstrorum Historia,* 1642, and *Physica Curiosa,* by P. Gaspare Schotto, 1697.)

There are also legends to the effect that long before the appearance of human beings there existed a race or species of composite creatures which was destroyed by the gods. The temples of antiquity preserved their own historical records and possessed information concerning the prehistoric world that has never been revealed to the uninitiated. According to these records, the human race evolved from a species of creature that partook somewhat of the nature of an amphibian, for at that time primitive man had the gills of a fish and was partly covered with scales. To a limited degree, the human embryo demonstrates the possibility of such a condition. As a result of the theory of man's origin in water, the fish was looked upon as the progenitor of the human family. This gave rise to the ichthyolatry of the Chaldeans, Phœnicians, and Brahmins. The American Indians believe that the waters of lakes, rivers, and oceans are inhabited by a mysterious people, the "Water Indians."

The fish has been used as an emblem of damnation; but among the Chinese it typified contentment and good fortune, and fishes appear on many of their coins. When Typhon, or Set, the Egyptian evil genius, had divided the body of the god Osiris into fourteen parts, he cast one part into the river Nile, where, according to Plutarch, it was devoured by three fishes—the *lepidotus* (probably the *lepidosiren*), the *phagrus,* and the *oxyrynchus* (a form of pike). For this reason the Egyptians would not eat the flesh of these fishes, believing that to do so would be to devour the body of their god. When used as a symbol of evil, the fish represented the earth (man's lower nature) and the tomb (the sepulcher of the Mysteries). Thus was Jonah three days in the belly of the "great fish," as Christ was three days in the tomb.

Several early church fathers believed that the "whale" which swallowed Jonah was the symbol of God the Father, who, when the hapless prophet was thrown overboard, accepted Jonah into His own nature until a place of safety was reached. The story of Jonah is really a legend of initiation into the Mysteries, and the "great fish" represents the darkness of ignorance which engulfs man when he is thrown over the side of the ship (is born) into the sea (life). The custom of building ships in the form of fishes or birds, common in ancient times, could give rise to the story, and mayhap Jonah was merely picked up by another vessel and carried into port, the pattern of the ship causing it to be called a "great fish." (*"Veritatis simplex oratio est!"*) More probably the "whale" of Jonah is based upon the pagan mythological creature, *hippocampus,* part horse and part dolphin, for the early Christian statues and carvings show the composite creature and not a true whale.

It is reasonable to suppose that the mysterious sea serpents which, according to the Mayan and Toltec legends, brought the gods to Mexico were Viking or Chaldean ships, built in the shape of composite sea monsters or dragons. H. P. Blavatsky advances the theory that the word *cetus,* the great whale, is derived from *keto,* a name for the fish god, Dagon, and that Jonah was actually confined in a cell hollowed out in the body of a gigantic statue of Dagon after he had been captured by Phœnician sailors and carried to one of their cities. There is no doubt a great mystery in the gigantic form of *cetus,* which is still preserved as a constellation.

FROM REDGROVE'S *BYGONE BELIEFS.*

THE MANTICHORA.

The most remarkable of allegorical creatures was the *mantichora,* which Ctesias describes as having a flame-colored body, lionlike in shape, three rows of teeth, a human head and ears, blue eyes, a tail ending in a series of spikes and stings, thorny and scorpionlike, and a voice which sounded like the blare of trumpets. This synthetic quadruped ambled into mediæval works on natural history, but, though seriously considered, had never been seen, because it inhabited inaccessible regions and consequently was difficult to locate.

According to many scattered fragments extant, man's lower nature was symbolized by a tremendous, awkward creature resembling a great sea-serpent, or dragon, called *leviathan.* All symbols having serpentine form or motion signify the solar energy in one of its many forms. This great creature of the sea therefore represents the solar life force imprisoned in water and also the divine energy coursing through the body of man, where, until transmuted, it manifests itself as a writhing, twisting monster—man's greeds, passions, and lusts. Among the symbols of Christ as the Savior of men are a number relating to the mystery of His divine nature concealed within the personality of the lowly Jesus.

The Gnostics divided the nature of the Christian Redeemer into two parts—the one Jesus, a mortal man; the other, Christos, a personification of *Nous,* the principle of Cosmic Mind. *Nous,* the greater, was for the period of three years (from baptism to crucifixion) using the fleshly garment of the mortal man (Jesus). In order to illustrate this point and still conceal it from the ignorant, many strange, and often repulsive, creatures were used whose rough exteriors concealed magnificent organisms. Kenealy, in his notes on the *Book of Enoch,* observes: "Why the caterpillar was a symbol of the Messiah is evident; because, under a lowly, creeping, and wholly terrestrial aspect, he conceals the beautiful butterfly-form, with its radiant wings, emulating in its varied colors the

Rainbow, the Serpent, the Salmon, the Scarab, the Peacock, and the dying Dolphin * * *."

Insects

In 1609 Henry Khunrath's *Amphitheatrum Sapientiæ Æternæ* was published. Eliphas Levi declared that within its pages are concealed all the great secrets of magical philosophy. A remarkable plate in this work shows the Hermetic sciences being attacked by the bigoted and ignorant pedagogues of the seventeenth century. In order to express his complete contempt for his slanderers, Khunrath made out of each a composite beast, adding donkey ears to one and a false tail to another. He reserved the upper part of the picture for certain petty backbiters to whom he gave appropriate forms. The air was filled with strange creatures— great dragon flies, winged frogs, birds with human heads, and other weird forms which defy description—heaping venom, gossip, spite, slander, and other forms of persecution upon the secret arcanum of the wise. The drawing indicated that their attacks were ineffectual. Poisonous insects were often used to symbolize the deadly power of the human tongue.

Insects of all kinds were also considered emblematic of the Nature spirits and dæmons, for both were believed to inhabit the atmosphere. Mediæval drawings showing magicians in the act of invoking spirits often portray the mysterious powers of the other world, which the conjurer has exorcised, as appearing to him in composite part-insect forms. The early philosophers apparently held the opinion that the diseases which swept through communities in the form of plagues were actually living creatures, but instead of considering a number of tiny germs they viewed the entire plague as one individuality and gave it a hideous shape to symbolize its destructiveness. The fact that plagues came in the air caused an insect or a bird to be used as their symbol.

Beautiful symmetrical forms were assigned to all natural benevolent conditions or powers, but to unnatural or malevolent powers were assigned contorted and abnormal figures. The Evil One was either hideously deformed or else of the nature of certain despised animals. A popular superstition during the Middle Ages held that the Devil had the feet of a rooster, while the Egyptians assigned to Typhon (Devil) the body of a hog.

The habits of the insects were carefully studied. Therefore the ant was looked upon as emblematic of industry and foresight, as it stored up supplies for the winter and also had strength to move objects many times its own weight. The locusts which swept down in clouds, and in some parts of Africa and Asia obscured the sun and destroyed every green thing, were considered fit emblems of passion, disease, hate, and strife; for these emotions destroy all that is good in the soul of man and leave a barren desert behind them. In the folklore of various nations, certain insects are given special significance, but the ones which have received world-wide veneration and considera-

tion are the scarab, the king of the insect kingdom; the scorpion, the great betrayer; the
butterfly, the emblem of metamorphosis; and
the bee, the symbol of industry.

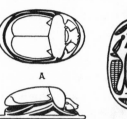

The Egyptian scarab is one of the most
remarkable symbolic figures ever conceived by
the mind of man. It was evolved by the erudi-

FROM HALL'S *CATALOGUE OF EGYPTIAN SCARABS, ETC., IN THE BRITISH MUSEUM.*

tion of the priestcraft from a simple insect

ROYAL EGYPTIAN SCARAB.

which, because of its peculiar habits and
appearance, properly symbolized the strength
of the body, the resurrection of the soul, and the
Eternal and Incomprehensible Creator in His
aspect as Lord of the Sun. E. A. Wallis Budge
says, in effect, of the worship of the scarab by
the Egyptians:

The flat under side of a scarab usually bears an inscription relating to the dynasty during which it was cut.
These scarabs were sometimes used as seals. Some
were cut from ordinary or precious stones; others were
made of clay, baked and glazed. Occasionally the
stone scarabs were also glazed. The majority of the
small scarabs are pierced as though originally used as
beads. Some are so hard that they will cut glass. In
the picture above, *A* shows top and side views of the
scarab, and *B* the under surface with the name of
Men-ka-Ra within the central cartouche.

"Yet another view held in primitive times
was that the sky was a vast meadow over which a huge beetle crawled, pushing the disk of the sun before him. This beetle was the Sky-god, and, arguing from the example of the beetle (*Scarabæus sacer*), which was observed to roll along with its hind legs a ball that was believed to contain its eggs, the early Egyptians thought that the ball of the Sky-god contained his egg and that the sun was his offspring. Thanks, however, to the investigations of the eminent entomologist, Monsieur J. H. Fabre, we now know that the ball which the *Scarabæus sacer* rolls along contains not its eggs, but dung that is to serve as food for its egg, which it lays in a carefully prepared place."

Initiates of the Egyptian Mysteries were sometimes called scarabs; again, lions and panthers. The scarab was the emissary of the sun, symbolizing light, truth, and regeneration. Stone scarabs, called heart scarabs, about three inches long, were placed in the heart cavity of the dead when that organ was removed to be embalmed separately as part of the process of mummifying. Some maintain that the stone beetles were merely wrapped in the winding cloths at the time of preparing the body for eternal preservation. The following passage concerning this appears in the great Egyptian book of initiation, *The Book of the Dead:* "And behold, thou shalt make a scarab of green stone, which shall be placed in the breast of a man, and it shall perform for him, 'the opening of the mouth.'" The funeral rites of many nations bear a striking resemblance to the initiatory ceremonies of their Mysteries.

Ra, the god of the sun, had three important aspects. As the Creator of the universe he was symbolized by the head of a scarab and was called *Khepera,* which signified the resurrection of the soul and a new life at the end of the mortal span. The mummy cases of the Egyptian dead were nearly always ornamented with scarabs. Usually one of these beetles, with outspread wings, was painted on the mummy case directly over the breast of the dead. The finding of such great numbers of small stone scarabs indicates that they were a favorite article of adornment among the Egyptians. Because of its relationship to the sun, the scarab symbolized the divine part of man's nature. The fact that its beautiful wings were concealed under its glossy shell typified the winged soul of man hidden within its earthly sheath. The Egyptian soldiers were given the scarab as their special symbol because the ancients believed that these creatures were all of the male sex and consequently appropriate emblems of virility, strength, and courage.

Plutarch noted the fact that the scarab rolled its peculiar ball of dung backwards, while the insect itself faced the opposite direction. This made it an especially fitting symbol for the sun, because this orb (according to Egyptian astronomy) was rolling from west to east, although apparently moving in the opposite direction. An Egyptian allegory states that the sunrise is caused by the scarab unfolding its wings, which stretch out as glorious colors on each side of its body—the solar globe—and that when it folds its wings under its dark shell at sunset, night follows. *Khepera,* the scarab-headed aspect of *Ra,* is often symbolized riding through the sea of the sky in a wonderful ship called the *Boat of the Sun.*

The scorpion is the symbol of both wisdom and self-destruction. It was called by the Egyptians the creature accursed; the time of year when the sun entered the sign of Scorpio marked the beginning of the rulership of Typhon. When the twelve signs of the zodiac were used to represent the twelve Apostles (although the reverse is true), the scorpion was assigned to Judas Iscariot—the betrayer.

The scorpion stings with its tail, and for this reason it has been called a backbiter, a false and deceitful thing. Calmet, in his *Dictionary of the Bible,* declares the scorpion to be a fit emblem of the wicked and the symbol of persecution. The dry winds of Egypt are said to be produced by Typhon, who imparts to the sand the blistering heat of the infernal world and the sting of the scorpion. This insect was also the symbol of the spinal fire which, according to the Egyptian Mysteries, destroyed man when it was permitted to gather at the base of his spine (the tail of the scorpion). The red star *Antares* in the back of the

THE FLEUR-DE-LIS.

The bee was used as a symbol of royalty by the immortal Charlemagne, and it is probable that the fleur-de-lis, or lily of France, is merely a conventionalized bee and not a flower. There is an ancient Greek legend to the effect that the nine Muses occasionally assumed the form of bees.

celestial scorpion was considered the worst light in the heavens. *Kalb al Akrab,* or the heart of the scorpion, was called by the ancients the lieutenant or deputy of Mars. (See footnote to Ptolemy's *Tetrabiblos.*) *Antares* was believed to impair the eyesight, often causing blindness if it rose over the horizon when a child was born. This may refer again to the sand storm, which was capable of blinding unwary travelers.

The scorpion was also the symbol of wisdom, for the fire which it controlled was capable of illuminating as well as consuming. Initiation into the Greater Mysteries among the pagans was said to take place only in the sign of the scorpion. In the papyrus of *Ani* (*The Book of the Dead*), the deceased likens his soul to a scorpion, saying: "I am a swallow, I am that scorpion, the daughter of Ra!" Elizabeth Goldsmith, in her treatise on *Sex Symbolism,* states that the scorpions were a "symbol of Selk, the Egyptian goddess of writing, and also [were] revered by the Babylonians and Assyrians as guardians of the gateway of the sun. Seven scorpions were said to have accompanied Isis when she searched for the remains of Osiris scattered by Set" (Typhon).

In his *Chaldean Account of the Genesis,* George Smith, copying from the cuneiform cylinders, in describing the wanderings of the hero *Izdubar* (Nimrod), throws some light on the scorpion god who guards the sun. The tablet which he translated is not perfect, but the meaning is fairly clear: " * * * who each day guard the rising sun. Their crown was at the lattice of heaven, under hell their feet were placed [the spinal column]. The scorpion man guarded the gate, burning with terribleness, their appearance was like death, the might of his fear shook the forest. At the rising of the sun and the setting of the sun, they guarded the sun; *Izdubar* saw them and fear and terror came into his face."

Among the early Latins there was a machine of war called the scorpion. It was used for firing arrows and probably obtained its name from a long beam, resembling a scorpion's tail, which flew up to hurl the arrows. The missiles discharged by this machine were also called scorpions.

The butterfly (under the name of *Psyche,* a beautiful maiden with wings of opalescent light) symbolizes the human soul because of the stages it passes through in order to unfold its power of flight. The three divisions through which the butterfly passes in its unfoldment resemble closely the three degrees of the Mystery School, which degrees are regarded as consummating the unfoldment of man by giving him emblematic wings by which he may soar to the skies. Unregenerate man, ignorant and helpless, is symbolized by the stage between ovum and larva; the disciple, seeking truth and dwelling in meditation, by the second stage, from larva to pupa, at which time the insect enters its chrysalis (the tomb of the Mysteries); the third stage, from pupa to imago (wherein the perfect butterfly comes forth), typifies the unfolded enlightened soul of the initiate rising from the tomb of his baser nature.

Night moths typify the secret wisdom, because they are hard to discover and are concealed by the darkness (ignorance). Some are emblems of death, as *Acherontia atropos,* the death's-head moth, which has a marking on its body somewhat like a human skull. The death-watch beetle, which was believed to give warning of approaching death by a peculiar ticking sound, is another instance of insects involved in human affairs.

Opinions differ concerning the spider. Its shape makes it an appropriate emblem of the nerve plexus and ganglia of the human body. Some Europeans consider it extremely bad luck to kill a spider—possibly because it is looked upon as an emissary of the Evil One, whom no person desires to offend. There is a mystery concerning all poisonous creatures, especially insects. Paracelsus taught that the spider was the medium for a powerful but evil force which the Black Magicians used in their nefarious undertakings.

Certain plants, minerals, and animals have been sacred among all the nations of the earth because of their peculiar sensitiveness to the astral fire—a mysterious agency in Nature which the scientific world has contacted through its manifestations as electricity and magnetism. Lodestone and radium in the mineral world and various parasitic growths in the plant kingdom are strangely susceptible to this cosmic electric fire, or universal life force. The magicians of the Middle Ages surrounded themselves with such creatures as bats, spiders, cats, snakes, and monkeys, because they were able to appropriate the life forces of these species and use them to the attainment of their own ends. Some ancient schools of wisdom taught that all poisonous insects and reptiles are germinated out of the evil nature of man, and that when intelligent human beings no longer breed hate in their own souls there will be no more ferocious animals, loathsome diseases, or poisonous plants and insects.

Among the American Indians is the legend of a "Spider Man," whose web connected the heaven worlds with the earth. The secret schools of India symbolize certain of the gods who labored with the universe during its making as connecting the realms of light with those of darkness by means of webs. Therefore the builders of the cosmic system who held the embryonic universe together with threads of invisible force were sometimes referred to as the Spider Gods and their ruler was designated The Great Spider.

The beehive is found in Masonry as a reminder that in diligence and labor for a common good true happiness and prosperity are found. The bee is a symbol of wisdom, for as this tiny insect collects pollen from the flowers, so men may extract wisdom from the experiences of daily life. The bee is sacred to the goddess Venus and, according to mystics, it is one of several forms of life which came to the earth from the planet Venus millions of years ago. Wheat and bananas are said to be of similar origin. This is the reason why the origin of these three forms of life cannot be traced. The fact that bees are ruled by queens is one reason why this insect is considered a sacred feminine symbol.

In India the god Prana—the personification of the universal life force—is sometimes shown surrounded by a circle of bees. Because of its importance in pollenizing flowers, the bee is the accepted symbol of the generative power. At one time the bee was the emblem of the French kings. The rulers of France wore robes embroidered with bees, and the canopies of their thrones were decorated with gigantic figures of these insects.

The fly symbolizes the tormentor, because of the annoyance it causes to animals. The Chaldean god Baal was often called Baal-Zebul, or the god of the dwelling place. The word *zebub,* or *zabab,* means a fly, and Baal-Zebul became Baalzebub, or Beezelbub, a word which was loosely translated to mean Jupiter's fly. The fly was looked upon as a form of the divine power, because of its ability to destroy decaying substances and thus promote health. The fly may have obtained its name *zebub* from its peculiar buzzing or humming. Inman believes that Baalzebub, which the Jews ridiculed as My Lord of Flies, really means My Lord Who Hums or Murmurs.

Inman recalls the singing Memnon on the Egyptian desert, a tremendous figure with an Æolian harp on the top of its head. When the wind blows strongly this great statue sighs, or hums. The Jews changed Baalzebub into Beelzebub, and made him their prince of devils by interpreting *dæmon* as "demon." Naudæus, in defending Virgil from accusations of sorcery, attempted a wholesale denial of the miracles supposedly performed by Virgil and produced enough evidence to convict the poet on all counts. Among other strange feats, Virgil fashioned a fly out of brass, and after certain mysterious ceremonies, placed it over one of the gates of Naples. As a result, no flies entered the city for more than eight years.

Reptiles

The serpent was chosen as the head of the reptilian family. Serpent worship in some form has permeated nearly all parts of the earth. The serpent mounds of the American Indian; the carved-stone snakes of Central and South America; the hooded cobras of India; Python, the great snake of the Greeks; the sacred serpents of the Druids; the Midgard snake of Scandinavia; the Nagas of Burma, Siam, and Cambodia; the brazen serpent of the Jews; the mystic serpent of Orpheus; the snakes at the oracle of Delphi twining themselves around the tripod upon which the Pythian priestess sat, the tripod itself being in the form of twisted serpents; the sacred serpents preserved in the Egyptian temples; the Uræus coiled upon the foreheads of the Pharaohs and priests;—all these bear witness to the universal veneration in which the snake was held. In the ancient Mysteries the serpent entwining a staff was the symbol of the physician. The serpent-wound staff of Hermes remains the emblem of the medical profession. Among nearly all these ancient peoples the serpent was accepted as the symbol of wisdom or salvation. The antipathy which Christendom feels towards the snake is based upon the little-understood allegory of the Garden of Eden.

The serpent is true to the principle of wisdom, for it tempts man to the knowledge of himself. Therefore the knowledge of self resulted from man's disobedience to the *Demiurgus*, Jehovah. How the serpent came to be in the garden of the Lord after God had declared that all creatures which He had made during the six days of creation were good has not been satisfactorily answered by the interpreters of Scripture. The tree that grows in the midst of the garden is the spinal fire; the knowledge of the use of that spinal fire is the gift of the great serpent. Notwithstanding statements to the contrary, the serpent is the symbol and prototype of the Universal Savior, who redeems the worlds by giving creation the knowledge of itself and the realization of good and evil. If this be not so, why did Moses raise a brazen serpent upon a cross in the wilderness that all who looked upon it might be saved from the sting of the lesser snakes? Was not the brazen serpent a prophecy of the crucified Man to come? If the serpent be only a thing of evil, why did Christ instruct His disciples to be as wise as serpents?

The accepted theory that the serpent is evil cannot be substantiated. It has long been viewed as the emblem of immortality. It is the symbol of reincarnation, or metempsychosis, because it annually sheds its skin, reappearing, as it were, in a new body. There is an ancient superstition to the effect that snakes never die except by violence and that, if uninjured, they would live forever. It was also believed that snakes swallowed themselves, and this resulted in their being considered emblematic of the Supreme Creator, who periodically reabsorbed His universe back into Himself.

In *Isis Unveiled,* H. P. Blavatsky makes this significant statement concerning the origin of serpent worship: "Before our globe had become egg-shaped or round it was a long trail of cosmic dust or fire-mist, moving and writhing like a serpent. This, say the explanations, was the Spirit of God moving on the chaos until its breath had incubated cosmic matter and made it assume the annular shape of a serpent with its tail in its mouth—emblem of eternity in its spiritual and of our world in its physical sense."

The seven-headed snake represents the Supreme Deity manifesting through His Elohim, or Seven Spirits, by whose aid He established His universe. The coils of the snake have been used by the pagans to symbolize the motion and also the orbits of the celestial bodies, and it is probable that the symbol of the serpent twisted around the egg—which was common to many of the ancient Mystery schools—represented both the apparent motion of the sun around the earth, and the bands of astral light, or the great magical agent, which move about the planet incessantly.

Electricity was commonly symbolized by the serpent because of its motion. Electricity passing between the poles of a spark gap is serpentine in its motion. Force projected through atmosphere was called The Great Snake. Being symbolic of universal force, the serpent was emblematic of both good and evil. Force can tear down as rapidly as it can build up. The serpent with its tail in its mouth is the symbol of eternity, for in this position the body of the reptile has neither beginning nor end. The head and tail represent the positive and negative poles of the cosmic life circuit. The initiates of the Mysteries were often referred to as serpents, and their wisdom was considered analogous to the divinely inspired power of the snake. There is no doubt that the title "Winged Serpents" (the Seraphim?) was given to one of the invisible hierarchies that labored with the earth during its early formation.

There is a legend that in the beginning of the world winged serpents rained upon the earth. These were probably the demigods which antedate the historical civilization of every nation. The symbolic relationship between the sun and the serpent found literal witness in the fact that life remains in the snake until sunset, even though it be cut into a dozen parts. The Hopi Indians consider the serpent to be in close communication with the Earth Spirit. Therefore, at the time of their annual snake dance they send their prayers to the Earth Spirit by first specially sanctifying large numbers of these reptiles and then liberating them to return to the earth with the prayers of the tribe.

The great rapidity of motion manifested by lizards has caused them to be associated with Mercury, the Messenger of the Gods, whose winged feet traveled infinite distances almost instantaneously. A point which must not be overlooked in connection with reptiles in symbolism is clearly brought out by the eminent scholar, Dr. H. E. Santee, in his *Anatomy of the Brain and Spinal Cord:* "In reptiles there are two pineal bodies, an anterior and a posterior, of which the posterior remains undeveloped but the anterior forms a rudimentary, cyclopean eye. In the Hatteria, a New Zealand lizard, it projects through the parietal foramen and presents an imperfect lens and retina and, in its long stalk, nerve fibers."

Crocodiles were regarded by the Egyptians both as symbols of Typhon and emblems of the Supreme Deity, of the latter because while under water the crocodile is capable of seeing—Plutarch asserts—though its eyes are covered by a thin membrane. The Egyptians declared that no matter how far away the crocodile laid its eggs, the Nile would reach up to them in its next inundation, this reptile being endowed with a mysterious sense capable of making known the extent of the flood months before it took place. There were two kinds of crocodiles. The larger and more ferocious was hated by the Egyptians, for they likened it to the nature of Typhon, their destroying demon. Typhon waited to devour all who failed to pass the Judgment of the Dead, which rite took place in the Hall of Justice between the earth and the Elysian Fields. Anthony Todd Thomson thus describes the good treatment accorded the smaller and tamer crocodiles, which the Egyptians accepted as personifications of good: "They were fed daily and occasionally had mulled wine poured down their throats. Their ears were ornamented with rings of gold and precious stones, and their forefeet adorned with bracelets."

To the Chinese the turtle was a symbol of longevity. At a temple in Singapore a number of sacred turtles are kept, their age recorded by carvings on their shells. The American Indians use the ridge down the back of the turtle shell as a symbol of the Great Divide between life and death. The turtle is a symbol of wisdom because it retires into itself and is its own protection. It is also a phallic symbol, as its relation to long life would signify. The Hindus symbolized the universe being supported on the backs of four great elephants who, in turn, are standing upon an immense turtle which is crawling continually through chaos.

The Egyptian sphinx, the Greek centaur, and the Assyrian man-bull have much in common. All are composite creatures combining human and animal members; in the Mysteries all signify the composite nature of man and subtly refer to the hierarchies of celestial beings that have charge of the destiny of mankind. These hierarchies are the *twelve holy animals* now known as constellations—star groups which are merely symbols of impersonal spiritual impulses. Chiron, the centaur, teaching the sons of men, symbolizes the intelligences of the constellation of Sagittarius, who were the custodians of the secret doctrine while (geocentrically) the sun was passing through the sign of Gemini. The five-footed Assyrian man-bull with the wings of an eagle and the head of a man is a reminder that the invisible nature of man has the wings of a god, the head of a man, and the body of a beast. The same concept was expressed through the sphinx—that armed guardian of the Mysteries who, crouching at the gate of the temple, denied entrance to the profane. Thus placed between man and his divine possibilities, the sphinx also represented the secret doctrine itself. Children's fairy stories abound with descriptions of symbolic monsters, for nearly all such tales are based upon the ancient mystic folklore.

Fishes, Insects, Animals, Reptiles, and Birds

PART II

s appropriate emblems of various human and divine attributes birds were included in religious and philosophic symbolism—that of pagans and of Christians alike. Cruelty was
signified by the buzzard; courage by the eagle; self-sacrifice
by the pelican; and pride by the peacock. The ability of
birds to leave the earth and fly aloft toward the source of light has resulted in
their being associated with aspiration, purity, and beauty. Wings were therefore
often added to various terrene creatures in an effort to suggest transcendency.
Because their habitat was among the branches of the sacred trees in the hearts of
ancient forests, birds were also regarded as the appointed messengers of the tree
spirits and Nature gods dwelling in these consecrated groves, and through their
clear notes the gods themselves were said to speak. Many myths have been fabricated to explain the brilliant plumage of birds. A familiar example is the story of
Juno's peacock, in whose tail feathers were placed the eyes of Argus. Numerous
American Indian legends also deal with birds and the origin of the various colors of feathers. The Navahos declare that when all living things climbed to the
stalk of a bamboo to escape the Flood, the wild turkey was on the lowest branch
and his tail feathers trailed in the water; hence the color was all washed out.

Gravitation, which is a law in the material world, is the impulse toward the
center of materiality; levitation, which is a law in the spiritual world, is the
impulse toward the center of spirituality. Seeming to be capable of neutralizing
the effect of gravity, the bird was said to partake of a nature superior to other terrestrial creation; and its feathers, because of their sustaining power, came to be

accepted as symbols of divinity, courage, and accomplishment. A notable example is the dignity attached to eagle feathers by the American Indians, among whom they are insignia of merit. Angels have been invested with wings because, like birds, they were considered to be the intermediaries between the gods and men and to inhabit the air or middle kingdom betwixt heaven and earth. As the dome of the heavens was likened to a skull in the Gothic Mysteries, so the birds which flew across the sky were regarded as thoughts of the Deity. For this reason Odin's two messenger ravens were called Hugin and Munin—*thought* and *memory*.

FROM LYCOSTHENES' *PRODIGIORUM AC OSTENTORUM CHRONICON.*

THE PHŒNIX ON ITS NEST OF FLAMES.

The phœnix is the most celebrated of all the symbolic creatures fabricated by the ancient Mysteries for the purpose of concealing the great truths of esoteric philosophy. Though modern scholars of natural history declare the existence of the phœnix to be purely mythical, Pliny describes the capture of one of these birds and its exhibition in the Roman Forum during the reign of the Emperor Claudius.

Among the Greeks and Romans, the eagle was the appointed bird of Jupiter and consequently signified the swiftly moving forces of the Demiurgus; hence it was looked upon as the mundane lord of the birds, in contradistinction to the phœnix, which was symbolic of the celestial ruler. The eagle typified the sun in its material phase and also the immutable Demiurgic law beneath which all mortal creatures must bend. The eagle was also the Hermetic symbol of sulphur, and signified the mysterious fire of Scorpio—the most profoundly significant sign of the zodiac and the *Gate of the Great Mystery.* Being one of the three symbols of Scorpio, the eagle, like the Goat of Mendes, was an emblem of the theurgic art and the secret processes by which the infernal fire of the scorpion was transmuted into the spiritual *light-fire* of the gods.

Among certain American Indian tribes the thunderbird is held in peculiar esteem. This divine creature is said to live above the clouds; the flapping of its wings causes the rumbling which accompanies storms, while the flashes from its eyes are the lightning. Birds were used to signify the vital breath; and among the Egyptians, mysterious hawklike birds with human heads, and carrying in their claws the symbol of immortality, are often shown hovering as emblems of the liberated soul over the mummified bodies of the dead. In Egypt the hawk was the sacred symbol of the sun; and Ra, Osiris, and Horus are often depicted with the heads of hawks. The cock, or rooster, was a symbol of Cashmala (Cadmillus) in the Samothracian Mysteries, and is also a phallic symbol sacred to the sun. It was accepted by the Greeks as the emblem of Ares (Mars) and typified watch-fulness and defense. When placed in the center of a weather vane it signifies the sun in the midst of the four corners of creation. The Greeks sacrificed a rooster to the gods at the time of entering the Eleusinian Mysteries. Sir Francis Bacon is supposed to have died as the result of stuffing a fowl with snow. May this not signify Bacon's initiation into the pagan Mysteries which still existed in his day?

Both the peacock and the ibis were objects of veneration because they destroyed the poisonous reptiles which were popularly regarded as the emis-saries of the infernal gods. Because of the myriad of eyes in its tail feathers the peacock was accepted as the symbol of wisdom, and on account of its general appearance it was often confused with the fabled phœnix of the Mysteries. There is a curious belief that the flesh of the peacock will not putrefy even though kept for a considerable time. As an outgrowth of this belief the peacock became the emblem of immortality, because the spiritual nature of man—like the flesh of this bird—is incorruptible.

The Egyptians paid divine honors to the ibis and it was a cardinal crime to kill one, even by accident. It was asserted that the ibis could live only in Egypt and that if transported to a foreign country it would die of grief. The Egyptians declared this bird to be the preserver of crops and especially worthy of venera-tion because it drove out the winged serpents of Libya which the wind blew into Egypt. The ibis was sacred to Thoth, and when its head and neck were tucked under its wing its body closely resembled a human heart. (See Montfaucon's *Antiquities.*) The black and white ibis was sacred to the moon; but all forms were revered because they destroyed crocodile eggs, the crocodile being a sym-bol of the detested Typhon.

Nocturnal birds were appropriate symbols of both sorcery and the secret divine sciences: sorcery because black magic cannot function in the light of truth (day) and is powerful only when surrounded by ignorance (night); and the divine sciences because those possessing the arcana are able to see through the darkness of ignorance and materiality. Owls and bats were consequently often associated with either witchcraft or wisdom. The goose was an emblem of the first primitive substance or condition from which and within which the worlds were fashioned. In the Mysteries, the universe was likened to an egg which the Cosmic Goose had laid in space. Because of its blackness the crow was the sym-bol of chaos or the chaotic darkness preceding the light of creation. The grace and purity of the swan were emblematic of the spiritual grace and purity of the initiate. This bird also represented the Mysteries which unfolded these qualities in humanity. This explains the allegories of the gods (the secret wisdom) incarnating in the body of a swan (the initiate).

Being scavengers, the vulture, the buzzard, and the condor signified that form of divine power which by disposing of refuse and other matter dangerous to the life and health of humanity cleanses and purifies the lower spheres. These birds were therefore adopted as symbols of the disintegrative processes which accomplish good while apparently destroying, and by some religions have been mistakenly regarded as evil.

PHŒNIX OR EAGLE, WHICH?

On the left is the bird's head from the first Great Seal of the United States (1782) and on the right the Great Seal of 1902. When the first Great Seal was actually cut, the bird represented upon it was very different from the eagle which now appears: the neck was much longer and the tuft of feathers at the upper back part of the head was quite noticeable; the beak bore little resemblance to that of the eagle; and the entire bird was much thinner and its wings shorter. It requires very little imagination to trace in this first so-called eagle the mythological phœnix of antiquity. What is more, there is every reason why a phœnix bird should be used to represent a new country rising out of an old, while as Benjamin Franklin caustically noted, the eagle was not even a bird of good moral character!

Birds such as the parrot and raven were accorded veneration because, being able to mimic the human voice, they were looked upon as links between the human and animal kingdoms.

The dove, accepted by Christianity as the emblem of the Holy Ghost, is an extremely ancient and highly revered pagan yonic emblem. In many of the ancient Mysteries it represented the third person of the Creative Triad, or the Fabricator of the world. As the lower worlds were brought into existence through a generative process, so the dove has been associated with those deities identified with the procreative functions. It is sacred to Astarte, Cybele, Isis, Venus, Juno, Mylitta, and Aphrodite. On account of its gentleness and devotion to its young, the dove was looked upon as the embodiment of the maternal instinct. The dove is also an emblem of wisdom, for it represents the power and order by which the lower worlds are maintained. It has long been accepted as a messenger of the divine will, and signifies the activity of God.

The name *dove* has been given to oracles and to prophets. "The true name of the dove was *Ionah* or *Iönas;* it was a very sacred emblem, and at one time almost universally received; it was adopted by the Hebrews; and the mystic Dove was regarded as a symbol from the days of Noah by all those who were of the Church of God. The prophet sent to Ninevah as God's messenger was called Jonah or the Dove; our Lord's forerunner, the Baptist, was called in Greek by the name of Ioannes; and so was the Apostle of Love, the author of the fourth Gospel and of the Apocalypse, named *Ioannes.*" (Bryant's *Analysis of Ancient Mythology.*)

In Masonry the dove is the symbol of purity and innocence. It is significant that in the pagan Mysteries the dove of Venus was crucified upon the four spokes of a great wheel, thus foreshadowing the mystery of the crucified Lord of Love. Although Mohammed drove the doves from the temple at Mecca, occasionally he is depicted with a dove sitting upon his shoulder as the symbol of divine inspiration. In ancient times the effigies of doves were placed upon the heads of scepters to signify that those bearing them were overshadowed by divine prerogative. In mediæval art, the dove frequently was pictured as an emblem of divine benediction.

The Phœnix

Clement, one of the ante-Nicæan Fathers, describes, in the first century after Christ, the peculiar nature and habits of the phœnix, in this wise: "There is a certain bird which is called a Phœnix. This is the only one of its kind and lives five hundred years. And when the time of its dissolution draws near that it must die, it builds itself a nest of frankincense, and myrrh, and other spices, into which, when the time is fulfilled, it enters and dies. But as the flesh decays a certain kind of worm is produced, which, being nourished by the juices of the dead bird, brings forth feathers. Then, when it has acquired strength, it takes up that nest in which are the bones of its parent, and bearing these it passes from the land of Arabia into Egypt, to the city called Heliopolis. And, in open day, flying in the sight of all men, it places them on the altar of the sun, and having done this, hastens back to its former abode. The priests then inspect the registers of the dates, and find that it has returned exactly as the five hundredth year was completed."

Although admitting that he had not seen the phœnix bird (there being only one alive at a time), Herodotus amplifies a bit the description given by Clement: "They tell a story of what this bird does, which does not seem to me to be credible: that he comes all the way from Arabia, and brings the parent bird, all plastered with myrrh, to the temple of the sun, and there buries the body. In order to bring him, they say, he first forms a ball of myrrh as big as he finds that he can carry; then he hollows out the ball, and puts his parent inside; after which he covers over the opening with fresh myrrh, and the ball is then of exactly the same weight as at first; so he brings it to Egypt, plastered over as I have said, and deposits it in the temple of the sun. Such is the story they tell of the doings of this bird."

Both Herodotus and Pliny noted the general resemblance in shape between the phœnix and the eagle, a point which the reader should carefully consider, for it is reasonably certain that the modern Masonic eagle was originally a phœnix. The body of the phœnix is described as having been covered with glossy purple feathers, while its long tail feathers were alternately blue and red. Its head was light in color and about its neck was a circlet of golden plumage. At the back of its head the phœnix had *a peculiar tuft of feathers,* a fact quite evident, although it has been overlooked by most writers and symbolists.

AN EGYPTIAN PHŒNIX.

The Egyptians occasionally represented the phœnix as having the body of a man and the wings of a bird. This biform creature had a tuft of feathers upon its head and its arms were upraised in an attitude of prayer. As the phœnix was the symbol of regeneration, the tuft of feathers on the back of its head might well symbolize the activity of the pineal gland, or third eye, the occult function of which was apparently well understood by the ancient priesthood.

The phœnix was regarded as sacred to the sun, and the length of its life (500 to 1000 years) was taken as a standard for measuring the motion of the heavenly bodies and also the cycles of time used in the Mysteries to designate the periods of existence. The diet of the bird was unknown. Some writers declare that it subsisted upon the atmosphere; others that it ate at rare intervals but never in the presence of man. Modern Masons should realize the special Masonic significance of the phœnix, for the bird is described as using sprigs of acacia in the manufacture of its nest.

The phœnix (which is the mythological Persian *roc*) is also the name of a Southern constellation, and therefore it has both an astronomical and an astrological significance. In all probability, the phœnix was the swan of the Greeks, the eagle of the Romans, and the peacock of the Far East. To the ancient mystics the phœnix was a most appropriate symbol of the immortality of the human soul, for just as the phœnix was reborn out of its own dead self seven times seven, so again and again the spiritual nature of man rises triumphant from his dead physical body.

Mediæval Hermetists regarded the phœnix as a symbol of the accomplishment of alchemical transmutation, a process equivalent to human regeneration. The name *phœnix* was also given to one of the secret alchemical formulæ. The familiar pelican of the Rose Croix degree, feeding its young from its own breast, is in reality a phœnix, a fact which can be confirmed by an examination of the head of the bird. The ungainly lower part of the pelican's beak is entirely missing, the head of the phœnix being far more like that of an eagle than of a pelican. In the Mysteries it was customary to refer to initiates as *phœnixes* or *men who had been born again,* for just as physical birth gives man consciousness in the physical world, so the neophyte, after nine degrees in the womb of the Mysteries, was born into a consciousness of the spiritual world. This is the mystery of the initiation to which Christ referred when he said, "Except a man be born again, he cannot see the kingdom of God" (John iii. 3). The phœnix is a fitting symbol of this spiritual birth.

FROM HUNT'S *HISTORY OF THE SEAL OF THE UNITED STATES*.

THE OBVERSE AND REVERSE OF THE GREAT SEAL OF THE UNITED STATES OF AMERICA.

The significance of the mystical number 13, which frequently appears upon the Great Seal of the United States, is not limited to the number of the original colonies. The sacred emblem of the ancient initiates, here composed of 13 stars, also appears above the head of the "eagle." The motto, *E Pluribus Unum*, contains 13 letters, as does also the inscription, *Annuit Cœptis*. The "eagle" clutches in its right talon a branch bearing 13 leaves and 13 berries and in its left a sheaf of 13 arrows. The face of the pyramid, exclusive of the panel containing the date, consists of 72 stones arranged in 13 rows.

European mysticism was not dead at the time the United States of America was founded. The hand of the Mysteries controlled in the establishment of the new government, for the signature of the Mysteries may still be seen on the Great Seal of the United States of America. Careful analysis of the seal discloses a mass of occult and Masonic symbols, chief among them the so-called American eagle—a bird which Benjamin Franklin declared unworthy to be chosen as the emblem of a great, powerful, and progressive people. Here again only the student of symbolism can see through the subterfuge and realize that the American eagle upon the Great Seal is but a conventionalized phœnix, a fact plainly discernible from an examination of the original seal. In his sketch of *The History of the Seal of the United States,* Gaillard Hunt unwittingly brings forward much material to substantiate the belief that the original seal carried the phœnix bird on its obverse surface and the Great Pyramid of Gizeh upon its reverse surface. In a colored sketch submitted as a design for the Great Seal by William Barton in 1782, an actual phœnix appears sitting upon a nest of flames. This itself demonstrates a tendency towards the use of this emblematic bird.

If any one doubts the presence of Masonic and occult influences at the time the Great Seal was designed, he should give due consideration to the comments of Professor Charles Eliot Norton of Harvard, who wrote concerning the unfinished pyramid and the All-Seeing Eye which adorned the reverse of the seal, as follows: "The device adopted by Congress is practically incapable of effective treatment; it can hardly (however artistically treated by the designer) look otherwise than as a dull emblem of a Masonic fraternity." (The *History of the Seal of the United States*.)

The eagles of Napoleon and Cæsar and the zodiacal eagle of Scorpio are really phœnixes, for the latter bird—not the eagle—is the symbol of spiritual victory and achievement. Masonry will be in a position to solve many of the secrets of its esoteric doctrine when it realizes that both its single- and double-headed eagles are phœnixes, and that to all initiates and philosophers the phœnix is the symbol of the transmutation and regeneration of the creative energy—commonly called the accomplishment of the Great Work. The double-headed phœnix is the prototype of an androgynous man, for according to the secret teachings there will come a time when the human body will have two spinal cords, by means of which vibratory equilibrium will be maintained in the body.

Not only were many of the founders of the United States Government Masons, but they received aid from a secret and august body existing in Europe, which helped them to establish this country for a peculiar and particular purpose known only to the initiated few. The Great Seal is the signature of this exalted body—unseen and for the most part unknown—and the unfinished pyramid upon its reverse side is a trestleboard setting forth symbolically the task to the accomplishment of which the United States Government was dedicated from the day of its inception.

Animals

The lion is the king of the animal family and, like the head of each kingdom, is sacred to the sun, whose rays are symbolized by the lion's shaggy mane. The allegories perpetuated by the Mysteries (such as the one to the effect that the lion opens the secret book) signify that the solar power opens the seed pods, releasing the spiritual life within. There was also a curious belief among the ancients that the lion sleeps with his eyes open, and for this reason the animal was chosen as a symbol of vigilance. The figure of a lion placed on either side of doors and gateways is an emblem of divine guardianship. King Solomon was often symbolized as a lion. For ages the feline family has been regarded with peculiar veneration. In several of the Mysteries—most notably the Egyptian— the priests wore the skins of lions, tigers, panthers, pumas, or leopards. Hercules and Samson (both Solar symbols) slew the lion of the constellation of Leo and robed themselves in his skin, thus signifying that they represented the sun itself when at the summit of the celestial arch.

At Bubastis in Egypt was the temple of the famous goddess Bast, the cat deity of the Ptolemies. The Egyptians paid homage to the cat, especially when its fur was of three shades or its eyes of different colors. To the priests the cat was symbolic of the magnetic forces of Nature, and they surrounded themselves with these animals for the sake of the astral fire which emanated from their bodies. The cat was also a symbol of eternity, for when it sleeps it curls up into a ball with its head and tail touching. Among the Greeks and Latins the cat was sacred to the goddess Diana. The Buddhists of India invested the cat with special significance, but for a different reason. The cat was the only animal absent at the death of the great Buddha, because it had stopped on the way to chase a mouse. That the symbol of the lower astral forces should not be present at the liberation of the Buddha is significant.

Regarding the cat, Herodotus says: "Whenever a fire breaks out, cats are agitated with a kind of divine motion, which they that keep them observe, neglecting the fire: The cats, however, in spite of their care, break from them, leaping even over the heads of their keepers to throw themselves into the fire. The Egyptians then make great mourning for their death. If a cat dies a natural death in a house, all they of that house shave their eyebrows: If a dog, they shave the head and all the body. They used to embalm their dead cats, and carry them to Bubastis to be interred in a sacred house." (Montfaucon's *Antiquities*.)

The most important of all symbolic animals was the Apis, or Egyptian bull of Memphis, which was regarded as the sacred vehicle for the transmigration of the soul of the god Osiris. It was declared that the Apis was conceived by a bolt of lightning, and the ceremony attendant upon its selection and consecration was one of the most impressive in Egyptian ritualism. The Apis had to be marked in a certain manner. Herodotus states that the bull must be black with a square white spot on his forehead, the form of an eagle (probably a vulture) on his back, a beetle upon (under) his tongue, and the hair of his tail lying two ways. Other writers declare that the sacred bull was marked with twenty-nine sacred symbols, his body was spotted, and upon his right side was a white mark in the form of a crescent. After its sanctification the Apis was kept in a stable adjacent to the temple and led in processionals through the streets of the city upon certain solemn occasions. It was a popular belief among the Egyptians that any child upon whom the bull breathed would become illustrious. After reaching a certain age (twenty-five years) the Apis was taken either to the river Nile or to a sacred fountain (authorities differ on this point) and drowned, amidst the lamentations of the populace. The mourning and wailing for his death continued until the new Apis was found, when it was declared that Osiris had reincarnated, whereupon rejoicing took the place of grief.

The worship of the bull was not confined to Egypt, but was prevalent in many nations of the ancient world. In India, Nandi—the sacred white bull of Siva—is still the object of much veneration; and both the Persians and the Jews accepted the bull as an important religious symbol. The Assyrians, Phœnicians, Chaldeans, and even the Greeks reverenced this animal, and Jupiter turned himself into a white bull to abduct Europa. The bull was a powerful phallic emblem signifying the paternal creative power of the Demiurgus. At his death he was frequently mummified and buried with the pomp and dignity of a god in a specially prepared sarcophagus. Excavations in the Serapeum at Memphis have uncovered the tombs of more than sixty of these sacred animals.

As the sign rising over the horizon at the vernal equinox constitutes the starry body for the annual incarnation of the sun, the bull not only was the celestial symbol of the Solar Man but, because the vernal equinox took place in the constellation of Taurus, was called the *breaker* or *opener* of the year. For this reason in astronomical symbolism the bull is often shown breaking the annular egg with his horns. The Apis further signifies that the God-Mind is incarnated in the body of a beast and therefore that the physical beast form is the sacred vehicle of divinity. Man's lower personality is the Apis in which Osiris incarnates. The result of the combination is the creation of Sor-Apis (Serapis)—the material soul as ruler of the irrational material body and involved therein. After a certain period (which is determined by the square of five, or twenty-five years), the body of the Apis is destroyed and the soul liberated by the water which drowns the material life. This was indicative of the washing away of the material nature by the baptismal waters of divine light and truth. The drowning of the Apis is the symbol of death; the resurrection of Osiris in the new bull is the symbol of eternal renovation. The white bull was also symbolically sacred as the appointed emblem of the initiates, signifying the spiritualized material bodies of both man and Nature.

When the vernal equinox no longer occurred in the sign of Taurus, the Sun God incarnated in the constellation of Aries and the ram then became the vehicle of the solar power. Thus the sun rising in the sign of the Celestial Lamb triumphs over the symbolic serpent of darkness. The lamb is a familiar emblem of purity because of its gentleness and the whiteness of its wool. In many of the pagan Mysteries it signified the Universal Savior, and in Christianity it is the favorite symbol of Christ. Early church paintings show a lamb standing upon a little hill, and from its feet pour four streams of living water signifying the four Gospels. The blood of the lamb is the solar life pouring into the world through the sign of Aries.

The goat is both a phallic symbol and also an emblem of courage or aspiration because of its surefootedness and ability to scale the loftiest peaks. To the alchemists the goat's head was the symbol of sulphur. The practice among the ancient Jews of choosing a scapegoat upon which to heap the sins of mankind is merely an allegorical depiction of the Sun Man who is the scapegoat of the world and upon whom are cast the sins of the twelve houses (tribes) of the celestial universe. Truth is the Divine Lamb worshiped throughout pagandom and slain for the sins of the world, and since the dawn of time the Savior Gods of all religions have been personifications of this Truth. The Golden Fleece sought by Jason and his Argonauts is the Celestial Lamb—the spiritual and intellectual sun. The secret doctrine is also typified by the Golden Fleece—the wool of the Divine Life, the rays of the Sun of Truth. Suidas declares the Golden Fleece to have been in reality a book, written upon skin, which contained the formulæ for the production of gold by means of chemistry. The Mysteries were institutions elected for the transmutation of base ignorance into precious illumination. The dragon of ignorance was the terrible creature set to guard the Golden Fleece, and represents the darkness of the old year which battles with the sun at the time of its equinoctial passage.

Deer were sacred in the Bacchic Mysteries of the Greeks; the Bacchantes were often clothed in fawnskins. Deer were associated with the worship of the moon goddess and the Bacchic orgies were usually conducted at night. The grace and speed of this animal caused it to be accepted as the proper symbol of esthetic abandon. Deer were objects of veneration with many nations. In Japan, herds of them are still maintained in connection with the temples.

The wolf is usually associated with the principle of evil, because of the mournful discordance of its howl and the viciousness of its nature. In Scandinavian mythology the Fenris Wolf was one of the sons of Loki, the infernal god of the fires. With the temple of Asgard in flames about them, the gods under the command of Odin fought their last great battle against the chaotic forces of evil. With frothing jowls the Fenis Wolf devoured Odin, the Father of the Gods, and thus destroyed the Odinic universe. Here the Fenris Wolf represents those mindless powers of Nature that overthrew the primitive creation.

The unicorn, or monoceros, was a most curious creation of the ancient initiates. It is described by Thomas Boreman as "a beast, which though doubted of by many writers, yet is by others thus described: He has but one horn, and that an exceedingly rich one, growing out of the middle of his forehead. His head resembles an hart's, his feet an elephant's, his tail a boar's, and the rest of his body an horse's. The horn is about a foot and half in length. His voice is like the lowing of an ox. His mane and hair are of a yellowish colour. His horn is as hard as iron, and as rough as any file, twisted or curled, like a flaming sword; very straight, sharp, and every where black, excepting the point. Great virtues are attributed to it, in expelling of poison and curing of several diseases. He is not a beast of prey." (See Redgrove's *Bygone Beliefs.*)

While the unicorn is mentioned several times in Scripture, no proof has yet been discovered of its existence. There are a number of drinking horns in various museums presumably fashioned from its spike. It is reasonably certain, however, that these drinking vessels were really made either from the tusks of some large mammal or the horn of a rhinoceros. J. P. Lundy believes that the horn of the unicorn symbolizes the horn of salvation mentioned by St. Luke which, pricking the hearts of men, turns them to a consideration of salvation through Christ. Mediæval Christian mystics employed the unicorn as an emblem of Christ, and this creature must therefore signify the spiritual life in man. The single horn of the unicorn may represent the pineal gland, or third eye, which is the spiritual cognition center in the brain. The unicorn was adopted by the Mysteries as a symbol of the illumined spiritual nature of the initiate, the horn with which it defends itself being the flaming sword of the spiritual doctrine against which nothing can prevail.

In the *Book of Lambspring,* a rare Hermetic tract, appears an engraving showing a deer and a unicorn standing together in a wood. The picture is accompanied by the following text: "The Sages say truly that two animals are in this forest: One glorious, beautiful, and swift, a great and strong deer; the other an unicorn. * * * If we apply the parable of our art, we shall call the forest the *body.* * * * The unicorn will be the *spirit* at all times. The deer desires no other name but that of the *soul;* * * *. He that knows how to tame and master them by art, to couple them together, and to lead them in and out of the forest, may justly be called a Master."

The Egyptian devil, Typhon, was often symbolized by the *Set* monster whose identity is obscure. It has a queer snoutlike nose and pointed ears, and may have been a conventional hyena. The *Set* monster lived in the sand storms and wandered about the world promulgating evil. The Egyptians related the howling of the desert winds with the moaning cry of the hyena. Thus when in the depths of the night the hyena sent forth its doleful wail it sounded like the last despairing cry of a lost soul in the clutches of Typhon. Among the duties of this evil creature was that of protecting the Egyptian dead against grave robbers.

Among other symbols of Typhon was the hippopotamus, sacred to the god Mars because Mars was enthroned in the sign of Scorpio, the house of Typhon. The ass was also sacred to this Egyptian demon. Jesus riding into Jerusalem upon the back of an ass has the same significance as Hermes standing upon the prostrate form of Typhon. The early Christians were accused of worshiping the head of an ass. A most curious animal symbol is the hog or sow, sacred to Diana, and frequently employed in the Mysteries as an emblem of the occult art. The wild boar which goared Atys shows the use of this animal in the Mysteries.

According to the Mysteries, the monkey represents the condition of man before the rational soul entered into his constitution. Therefore it typifies the irrational man. By some the monkey is looked upon as a species not ensouled by the spiritual hierarchies; by others as a fallen state wherein man has been deprived of his divine nature through degeneracy. The ancients, though evolutionists, did not trace man's ascent through the monkey; the monkey they considered as having separated itself from the main stem of progress. The monkey was occasionally employed as a symbol of learning. Cynocephalus, the dog-headed ape, was the Egyptian hieroglyphic symbol of writing, and was closely associated with Thoth. Cynocephalus is symbolic of the moon and Thoth of the planet Mercury. Because of the ancient belief that the moon followed Mercury about the heavens the dog-ape was described as the faithful companion of Thoth.

The dog, because of its faithfulness, denotes the relationship which should exist between disciple and master or between the initiate and his God. The shepherd dog was a type of the priestcraft. The dog's ability to sense and follow unseen persons for miles symbolized the transcendental power by which the philosopher follows the thread of truth through the labyrinth of earthly error. The dog is also the symbol of Mercury. The Dog Star, Sirius or Sothis, was sacred to the Egyptians because it presaged the annual inundations of the Nile.

As a beast of burden the horse was the symbol of the body of man forced to sustain the weight of his spiritual constitution. Conversely, it also typified the spiritual nature of man forced to maintain the burden of the material personality. Chiron, the centaur, mentor of Achilles, represents the primitive creation which was the progenitor and instructor of mankind, as described by Berossus. The winged horse and the magic carpet both symbolize the secret doctrine and the spiritualized body of man. The wooden horse of Troy, secreting an army for the capture of the city, represents man's body concealing within it those infinite potentialities which will later come forth and conquer his environment. Again, like Noah's Ark, it represents the spiritual nature of man as containing a host of latent potentialities which subsequently become active. The siege of Troy is a symbolic account of the abduction of the human soul (Helena) by the personality (Paris) and its final redemption, through persevering struggle, by the secret doctrine—the Greek army under the command of Agamemnon.

Flowers, Plants, Fruits, and Trees

The yoni and phallus were worshiped by nearly all ancient peoples as appropriate symbols of God's creative power. The Garden of Eden, the Ark, the Gate of the Temple, the Veil of the Mysteries, the *vesica piscis* or oval nimbus, and the Holy Grail are important yonic symbols; the pyramid, the obelisk, the cone, the candle, the tower, the Celtic monolith, the spire, the campanile, the Maypole, and the Sacred Spear are symbolic of the phallus. In treating the subject of Priapic worship, too many modern authors judge pagan standards by their own and wallow in the mire of self-created vulgarity. The Eleusinian Mysteries—the greatest of all the ancient secret societies—established one of the highest known standards of morality and ethics, and those criticizing their use of phallic symbols should ponder the trenchant words of King Edward III, *"Honi soit qui mal y pense."*

The obscene rites practiced by the later Bacchanalia and Dionysia were no more representative of the standards of purity originally upheld by the Mysteries than the orgies occasionally occurring among the adherents of Christianity till the eighteenth century were representative of primitive Christianity. Sir William Hamilton, British Minister at the Court of Naples, declares that in 1780, Isernia, a community of Christians in Italy, worshiped with phallic ceremonies the pagan god Priapus under the name of St. Cosmo. (See *Two Essays on the Worship of Priapus,* by Richard Payne Knight.)

Father, mother, and child constitute the natural trinity. The Mysteries glorified the home as the supreme institution consisting of this trinity functioning as a unit. Pythagoras likened the universe to the family, declaring that as the supreme fire of the universe was in the midst of its heavenly bodies, so, by analogy, the supreme fire of the world was upon its hearthstones. The Pythagorean and other schools of philosophy conceived the one divine nature of God to manifest itself in the threefold aspect of Father, Mother, and Child. These three constituted the Divine Family, whose dwelling place is creation and whose natural and peculiar symbol is the 47th problem of Euclid. God the Father is spirit, God the Mother is matter, and God the Child—the product of the two—represents the sum of living things born out of and constituting Nature. The seed of spirit is sown in the womb of matter, and by an immaculate (pure) conception the progeny is brought into being. Is not this the true mystery of the Madonna holding the Holy Babe in her arms? Who dares to say that such symbolism is improper? The mystery of life is the supreme mystery, revealed in all of its divine dignity and glorified as Nature's perfect achievement by the initiated sages and seers of all ages.

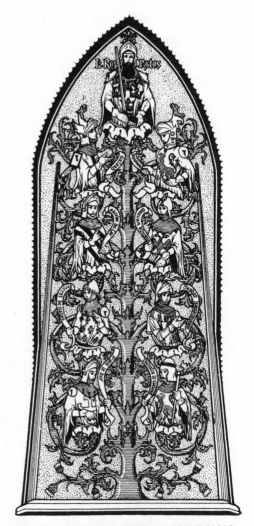

THE TREE OF THE KNIGHTS OF THE ROUND TABLE.

This remarkable example of the use of the tree in symbolism is from the Chateau de Pierrefonds in the little town of Pierrefonds in northern France. The eight side branches end in conventional cuplike flowers, from each of which rises the body of a knight carrying in his hand a ribbon bearing his name. The central stem is surmounted by a larger flower, from which emerges the body of King Arthur himself. The tree is a favorite motif in heraldry. The one trunk with its multitude of branches caused the tree to be frequently used in diagramming family lineage, from which practice has arisen the custom of terming such tables "family trees."

The prudery of today, however, declares this same mystery to be unfit for the consideration of holy-minded people. Contrary to the dictates of reason, a standard has been established which affirms that innocence bred of ignorance is more to be desired than virtue born of knowledge. Eventually, however, man will learn that he need never be ashamed of truth. Until he does learn this, he is false to his God, to his world, and to himself. In this respect, Christianity has woefully failed in its mission. While declaring man's body to be the living temple of the living God, in the same breath it asserts the substances and functions of this temple to be unclean and their study defiling to the sensitive sentiments of the righteous. By this unwholesome attitude, man's body—the house of God—is degraded and defamed. Yet the cross itself is the oldest of phallic emblems, and the lozenge-shaped windows of cathedrals are proof that yonic symbols have survived the destruction of the pagan Mysteries. The very structure of the church itself is permeated with phallicism. Remove from the Christian Church all emblems of Priapic origin and nothing is left, for even the earth upon which it stands was, because of its fertility, the first yonic symbol. As the presence of these emblems of the generative processes is either unknown or unheeded by the majority, the irony of the situation is not generally appreciated. Only those conversant with the secret language of antiquity are capable of understanding the divine significance of these emblems.

Flowers were chosen as symbols for many reasons. The great variety of flora made it possible to find some plant or flower which would be a suitable figure for nearly any abstract quality or condition. A plant might be chosen because of some myth connected with its origin, as the stories of Daphne and Narcissus; because of the peculiar environment in which it thrived, as the orchid and the fungus; because of its significant shape, as the passion flower and the Easter lily; because of its brilliance or fragrance, as the verbena and the sweet lavender; because it preserved its form indefinitely, as the everlasting flower; because of unusual characteristics, as the sunflower and heliotrope, which have long been sacred because of their affinity for the sun.

The plant might also be considered worthy of veneration because from its crushed leaves, petals, stalks, or roots could be extracted healing unctions, essences, or drugs affecting the nature and intelligence of human beings—such as the poppy and the ancient herbs of prophecy. The plant might also be regarded as efficacious in the cure of many diseases because its fruit, leaves, petals, or roots bore a resemblance in shape or color to parts or organs of the human body. For example, the distilled juices of certain species of ferns, also the hairy moss growing upon oaks, and the thistledown were said to have the power of growing hair; the *dentaria,* which resembles a tooth in shape, was said to cure the toothache; and the *palma Christi* plant, because of its shape, cured all afflictions of the hands.

The blossom is really the reproductive system of the plant and is therefore singularly appropriate as a symbol of sexual purity—an absolute requisite of the ancient Mysteries. Thus the flower signifies this ideal of beauty and regeneration which must ultimately take the place of lust and degeneracy.

Of all symbolic flowers the lotus blossom of India and Egypt and the rose of the Rosicrucians are the most important. In their symbolism these two flowers are considered identical. The esoteric doctrines for which the Eastern lotus stands have been perpetuated in modern Europe under the form of the rose. The rose and the lotus are yonic emblems, signifying primarily the maternal creative mystery, while the Easter lily is considered to be phallic.

The Brahmin and Egyptian initiates, who undoubtedly understood the secret systems of spiritual culture whereby the latent centers of cosmic energy in man may be stimulated, employed the lotus blossoms to represent the spinning vortices of spiritual energy located at various points along the spinal column and called *chakras,* or whirling wheels, by the Hindus. Seven of these *chakras* are of prime importance and have their individual correspondences in the nerve ganglia and plexuses. According to the secret schools, the sacral ganglion is called the four-petaled lotus; the prostatic plexus, the six-petaled lotus; the epigastric plexus and navel, the ten-petaled lotus; the cardiac plexus, the twelve-petaled lotus; the pharyngeal plexus, the sixteen-petaled lotus; the cavernous plexus, the two-petaled lotus; and the pineal gland or adjacent unknown center, the thousand-petaled lotus. The color, size, and number of petals upon the lotus are the keys to its symbolic import. A hint concerning the unfoldment of spiritual understanding according to the secret science of the Mysteries is found in the story of Aaron's rod that budded, and also in Wagner's great opera, *Tannhäuser,* where the budding staff of the Pope signifies the unfolding blossoms upon the sacred rod of the Mysteries—the spinal column.

The Rosicrucians used a garland of roses to signify the same spiritual vortices, which are referred to in the Bible as the seven lamps of the candlestick and the seven churches of Asia. In the 1642 edition of Sir Francis Bacon's *History of Henry the Seventh* is a frontispiece showing Lord Bacon with Rosicrucian roses for shoe buckles.

In the Hindu system of philosophy, each petal of the form bears a certain symbol which gives an added clue to the meaning of the flower. The Orientals also used the lotus plant to signify the growth of man through the three periods of human consciousness—ignorance, endeavor, and understanding. As the lotus exists in three elements (earth, water, and air) so man lives in three worlds—material, intellectual, and spiritual. As the plant, with its roots in the mud and the slime, grows upward through the water and finally blossoms forth in the light and air, so the spiritual growth of man is upward from the darkness of base action and desire into the light of truth and understanding, the water serving as a symbol of the ever-changing world of illusion through which the soul must pass in its struggle to reach the state of spiritual illumination. The rose and its Eastern equivalent, the lotus, like all beautiful flowers, represent spiritual unfoldment and attainment: hence, the Eastern deities are often shown seated upon the open petals of the lotus blossoms.

The lotus was also a universal motif in Egyptian art and architecture. The roofs of many temples were upheld by lotus columns, signifying the eternal wisdom; and the lotus-headed scepter—symbolic of self-unfoldment and divine prerogative—was often carried in religious processions. When the flower had nine petals, it was symbolic of man; when twelve, of the universe and the gods; when seven, of the planets and the law; when five, of the senses and the Mysteries; and when three, of the chief deities and the worlds. The heraldic rose of the Middle Ages generally has either five or ten petals, thereby showing its relationship to the spiritual mystery of man through the Pythagorean pentad and decad.

Cultus Arborum

The worship of trees as proxies of Divinity was prevalent throughout the ancient world. Temples were often built in the heart of sacred groves, and nocturnal ceremonials were conducted under the wide-spreading branches of great trees, fantastically decorated and festooned in honor of their patron deities. In many instances the trees themselves were believed to possess the attributes of divine power and intelligence, and therefore supplications were often addressed to them. The beauty, dignity, massiveness, and strength of oaks, elms, and cedars led to their adoption as symbols of power, integrity, permanence, virility, and divine protection.

Several ancient peoples—notably the Hindus and Scandinavians—regarded the Macrocosm, or Grand Universe, as a divine tree growing from a single seed sown in space. The Greeks, Persians, Chaldeans, and Japanese have legends describing the axle tree or reed upon which the earth revolves. Kapila declares the universe to be the eternal tree, Brahma, which springs from an imperceptible and intangible seed—the material monad. The mediæval Qabbalists represented creation as a tree with its roots in the reality of spirit and its branches in the illusion of tangible existence. The Sephirothic tree of the Qabbalah was therefore inverted, with its roots in heaven and its branches upon the earth. Madam Blavatsky notes that the Great Pyramid was considered to be a symbol of this inverted tree, with its root at the apex of the pyramid and its branches diverging in four streams towards the base.

The Scandinavian world-tree, Yggdrasil, supports on its branches nine spheres or worlds, which the Egyptians symbolized by the nine stamens of the persea or avocado. All of these are enclosed within the mysterious tenth sphere or cosmic egg—the definitionless Cipher of the Mysteries. The Qabbalistic tree of the Jews also consists of nine branches, or worlds, emanating from the First Cause or Crown, which surrounds its emanations as the shell surrounds the egg. The single source of life and the endless diversity of its expression has a perfect analogy in the structure of the tree. The trunk represents the single origin of all diversity; the roots, deeply imbedded in the dark earth, are symbolic of divine nutriment; and its multiplicity of branches spreading from the central trunk represent the infinity of universal effects dependent upon a single cause.

The tree has also been accepted as symbolic of the Microcosm, that is, man. According to the esoteric doctrine, man first exists potentially within the body of the world-tree and later blossoms forth into objective manifestation upon its branches. According to an early Greek Mystery myth, the god Zeus fabricated the third race of men from ash trees. The serpent so often shown wound around the trunk of the tree usually signifies the *mind*—the power of thought—and is the eternal tempter or urge which leads all rational creatures to the ultimate discovery of reality and thus overthrows the rule of the gods. The serpent hidden in the foliage of the universal tree represents the cosmic mind; and in the human tree, the individualized intellect.

The concept that all life originates from seeds caused grain and various plants to be accepted as emblematic of the human spermatozoon, and the tree was therefore symbolic of organized life unfolding from its primitive germ. The growth of the universe from its primitive seed may be likened to the growth of the mighty oak from the tiny acorn. While the tree is apparently much greater than its own source, nevertheless that source contains potentially every branch, twig, and leaf which will later be objectively unfolded by the processes of growth.

Man's veneration for trees as symbols of the abstract qualities of wisdom and integrity also led him to designate as *trees* those individuals who possessed these divine qualities to an apparently superhuman degree. Highly illumined philosophers and priests were therefore often referred to as *trees* or *tree men*—for example, the Druids, whose name, according to one interpretation, signifies *the men of the oak trees,* or the initiates of certain Syrian Mysteries who were called *cedars;* in fact it is far more credible and probable that the famous *cedars of Lebanon,* cut down for the building of King Solomon's Temple, were really illumined, initiated sages. The mystic knows that the true supports of God's Glorious House were not the logs subject to decay but the immortal and imperishable intellects of the *tree* hierophants.

Trees are repeatedly mentioned in the Old and New Testaments, and in the scriptures of various pagan nations. The Tree of Life and the Tree of the Knowledge of Good and Evil mentioned in Genesis, the burning bush in which the angel appeared to Moses, the famous vine and fig tree of the New Testament, the grove of olives in the Garden of Gethsemane where Jesus went to pray, and the miraculous tree of Revelation which bore twelve manners of fruit and whose leaves were for the healing of the nations, all bear witness to the esteem in which trees were held by the scribes of Holy Writ. Buddha received his illumination while under the *bodhi* tree, near Madras in India, and several of the Eastern gods are pictured sitting in meditation beneath the spreading branches of mighty trees. Many of the great sages and saviors carried wands, rods, or staves cut from the wood of sacred trees, as the rods of Moses and Aaron; Gungnir—the spear of Odin—cut from the Tree of Life; and the consecrated rod of Hermes, around which the fighting serpents entwined themselves.

The numerous uses which the ancients made of the tree and its products are factors in its symbolism. Its worship was, to a certain degree, based upon its usefulness. Of this J. P. Lundy writes: "Trees occupy such an important place in the economy of nature by way of attracting and retaining moisture, and shading the water-sources and the soil so as to prevent barrenness and desolation; they are so useful to man for shade, for fruit, for medicine, for fuel, for building houses and ships, for furniture, for almost every department of life, that it is no wonder that some of the more conspicuous ones, such as the oak, the pine, the palm, and the sycamore, have been made sacred and used for worship." (See *Monumental Christianity*.)

The early Fathers of the church sometimes used the tree to symbolize Christ. They believed that ultimately Christianity would grow up like a mighty oak and overshadow all other faiths of mankind. Because it annually discards its foliage, the tree was also looked upon as an appropriate emblem of resurrection and reincarnation, for though apparently dying each fall it blossomed forth again with renewed verdure each ensuing spring.

Under the appellations of the *Tree of Life* and the *Tree of the Knowledge of Good and Evil* is concealed the great arcanum of antiquity—the mystery of *equilibrium*. The *Tree of Life* represents the spiritual point of balance—the secret of immortality. The *Tree of the Knowledge of Good and Evil,* as its name implies, represents polarity, or unbalance—the secret of mortality. The Qabbalists reveal this by assigning the central column of their Sephirothic diagram to the *Tree of Life* and the two side branches to the *Tree of the Knowledge of Good and Evil.* "Unbalanced forces perish in the void," declares the secret work, and all is made known. The apple represents the knowledge of the procreative processes, by the awakening of which the material universe was established. The allegory of Adam and Eve in the Garden of Eden is a cosmic myth, revealing the methods of universal and individual establishment. The literal story, accepted for so many centuries by an unthinking world, is preposterous, but the creative mystery of which it is the symbol is one of Nature's profoundest verities. The Ophites (serpent worshipers) revered the Edenic snake because it was the cause of individual existence. Though humanity is still wandering in a world of good and evil, it will ultimately attain completion and eat of the fruit of the Tree of Life growing in the midst of the illusionary garden of worldly things. Thus the *Tree of Life* is also the appointed symbol of the Mysteries, and by partaking of its fruit man attains immortality.

The oak, the pine, the ash, the cypress, and the palm are the five trees of greatest symbolic importance. The Father God of the Mysteries was often worshiped under the form of an oak; the Savior God—frequently the World Martyr—in the form of a pine; the world axis and the divine nature in humanity in the form of an ash; the goddesses, or maternal principle, in the form of a cypress; and the positive pole of generation in the form of the inflorescence of the male date palm. The pine cone is a phallic symbol of remote antiquity. The thyrsus of Bacchus—a long wand or staff surmounted by a pine cone or cluster of grapes and entwined with ivy or grape-vine leaves, sometimes ribbons—signifies that the wonders of Nature may only be accomplished by the aid of solar virility, as symbolized by the cone or grapes. In the Phrygian Mysteries, Atys—the ever-present sun-savior—dies under the branches of the pine tree (an allusion to the solar globe at the winter solstice) and for this reason the pine tree was sacred to his cult. This tree was also sacred in the Mysteries of Dionysos and Apollo.

Among the ancient Egyptians and Jews the acacia, or tamarisk, was held in the highest religious esteem; and among modern Masons, branches of acacia, cypress, cedar, or evergreen are still regarded as most significant emblems. The shittim-wood used by the children of Israel in the construction of the Tabernacle and the Ark of the Covenant was a species of acacia. In describing this sacred tree, Albert Pike has written: "The genuine acacia, also, is the thorny tamarisk, the same tree which grew around the body of Osiris. It was a sacred tree among the Arabs, who made of it the idol Al-Uzza, which Mohammed destroyed. It is abundant as a bush in the desert of Thur; and of it the 'crown of thorns' was composed, which was set on the forehead of Jesus of Nazareth. It is a fit type of immortality on account of its tenacity of life; for it has been known, when planted as a door-post, to take root again and shoot out budding boughs above the threshhold." (See *Morals and Dogma.*)

It is quite possible that much of the veneration accorded the acacia is due to the peculiar attributes of the *mimosa,* or sensitive plant, with which it was often identified by the ancients. There is a Coptic legend to the effect that the sensitive plant was the first of all trees or shrubs to worship Christ. The rapid growth of the acacia and its beauty have also caused it to be regarded as emblematic of fecundity and generation.

The symbolism of the acacia is susceptible of four distinct interpretations: (1) it is the emblem of the vernal equinox—the annual resurrection of the solar deity; (2) under the form of the sensitive plant which shrinks from human touch, the acacia signifies purity and innocence, as one of the Greek meanings of its name implies; (3) it fittingly typifies human immortality and regeneration, and under the form of the evergreen represents that immortal part of man which survives the destruction of his visible nature; (4) it is the ancient and revered emblem of the Mysteries, and candidates entering the tortuous passageways in which the ceremonials were given carried in their hands branches of these sacred plants or small clusters of sanctified flowers.

Albert G. Mackey calls attention to the fact that each of the ancient Mysteries had its own peculiar plant sacred to the gods or goddesses in whose honor the rituals were celebrated. These sacred plants were later adopted as the symbols of the various degrees in which they were used. Thus, in the Mysteries of Adonis, lettuce was sacred; in the Brahmin and Egyptian rites, the lotus; among the Druids, the mistletoe; and among certain of the Greek Mysteries, the myrtle. (See *Encyclopædia of Freemasonry.*)

As the legend of CHiram Abiff is based upon the ancient Egyptian Mystery ritual of the murder and resurrection of Osiris, it is natural that the sprig of acacia should be preserved as symbolic of the resurrection of CHiram. The chest containing the body of Osiris was washed ashore near Byblos and lodged in the roots of a tamarisk, or acacia, which, growing into a mighty tree, enclosed within its trunk the body of the murdered god. This is undoubtedly the origin of the story that a sprig of acacia marks the grave of CHiram. The mystery of the evergreen marking the grave of the dead sun god is also perpetuated in the Christmas tree.

The apricot and quince are familiar yonic symbols, while the bunch of grapes and the fig are phallic. The pomegranate is the mystic fruit of the Eleusinian rites; by eating it, Prosperine bound herself to the realms of Pluto.

The fruit here signifies the sensuous life which, once tasted, temporarily deprives man of immortality. Also on account of its vast number of seeds the pomegranate was often employed to represent natural fecundity. For the same reason, Jacob Bryant in his *Ancient Mythology* notes that the ancients recognized in this fruit an appropriate emblem of the Ark of the Deluge, which contained the seeds of the new human race. Among the ancient Mysteries the pomegranate was also considered to be a divine symbol of such peculiar significance that its true explanation could not be divulged. It was termed by the Cabiri "the forbidden secret." Many Greek gods and goddesses are depicted holding the fruit or flower of the pomegranate in their hands, evidently to signify that they are givers of life and plenty. Pomegranate capitals were placed upon the pillars of Jachin and Boaz standing in front of King Solomon's Temple; and by the order of Jehovah, pomegranate blossoms were embroidered upon the bottom of the High Priest's ephod.

Strong wine made from the juice of the grape was looked upon as symbolic of the false life and false light of the universe, for it was produced by a false process— artificial fermentation. The rational faculties are clouded by strong drink, and the animal nature, liberated from bondage, controls the individual—facts which necessarily were of the greatest spiritual significance. As the lower nature is the eternal tempter seeking to lead man into excesses which inhibit the spiritual faculties, the grape and its product were used to symbolize the Adversary.

The juice of the grape was thought by the Egyptians to resemble human blood more closely than did any other substance. In fact, they believed that the grape secured its life from the blood of the dead who had been buried in the earth. According to Plutarch, "The priests of the sun at Heliopolis never carry any wine into their temples, * * * and if they made use of it at any time in their libations to the gods, it was not because they looked upon it as in its own nature acceptable to them; but they poured it upon their altars as the blood of those enemies who formerly had fought against them. For they look upon the vine to have first sprung out of the earth after it was fattened with the carcasses of those who fell in the wars against the gods. And this, say they, is the reason why drinking its juice in great quantities makes men mad and beside themselves, filling than as it were with the blood of their own ancestors. (See *Isis and Osiris.*)

Among some cults the state of intoxication was viewed as a condition somewhat akin to ecstasy, for the individual was believed to be possessed by the Universal Spirit of Life, whose chosen vehicle was the vine. In the Mysteries, the grape was often used to symbolize lust and debauchery because of its demoralizing effect upon the emotional nature. The fact was recognized, however, that fermentation was the certain evidence of the presence of the solar fire, hence the grape was accepted as the proper symbol of the Solar Spirit—the giver of divine enthusiasm. In a somewhat similar manner, Christians have accepted wine as the emblem of the blood of Christ, partaking of it in Holy Communion. Christ, the exoteric emblem of the Solar Spirit, said, "I am the vine." He was therefore worshiped with the wine of ecstasy in the same manner as were his pagan proto- types—Bacchus, Dionysos, Atys, and Adonis.

The *mandragora officinarum,* or mandrake, is accredited with possessing the most remarkable magical powers. Its narcotic properties were recognized by the Greeks, who employed it to deaden pain during surgical operations, and it has been identified also with *baaras,* the mystic herb used by the Jews for cast- ing out demons. In the *Jewish Wars,* Josephus describes the method of securing the *baaras,* which he declares emits flashes of lightning and destroys all who seek to touch it, unless they proceed according to certain rules supposedly for- mulated by King Solomon himself.

The occult properties of the mandrake, while little understood, have been responsible for the adoption of the plant as a talisman capable of increasing the value or quantity of anything with which it was associated. As a phallic charm, the mandrake was considered to be an infallible cure for sterility. It was one of the Pri- apic symbols which the Knights Templars were accused of worshiping. The root of the plant closely resembles a human body and often bore the outlines of the human head, arms, or legs. This striking similarity between the body of man and the man- dragora is one of the puzzles of natural science and is the real basis for the venera- tion in which this plant was held. In *Isis Unveiled,* Madam Blavatsky notes that the mandragora seems to occupy upon earth the point where the vegetable and animal kingdoms meet, as the zoophites and polypi do in the sea. This thought opens a vast field of speculation concerning the nature of this animal-plant.

According to a popular superstition, the mandrake shrank from being touched and, crying out with a human voice, clung desperately to the soil in which it was imbedded. Anyone who heard its cry while plucking it either immediately died or went mad. To circumvent this tragedy, it was customary to dig around the roots of the mandrake until the plant was thoroughly loosened and then to tie one end of a cord about the stalk and fasten the other end to a dog. The dog, obeying his master's call, thereupon dragged the root from the earth and became the victim of the mandragora curse. When once uprooted, the plant could be handled with immunity.

During the Middle Ages, mandrake charms brought great prices and an art was evolved by which the resemblance between the mandragora root and the human body was considerably accentuated. Like most superstitions, the belief in the peculiar powers of the mandrake was founded upon an ancient secret doctrine concerning the true nature of the plant. "It is slightly narcotic," says Elpihas Levi, "and an aphrodisiacal virtue was ascribed to it by the ancients, who represented it as being sought by Thessalian sorcerers for the composition of philtres. Is this root the umbilical vestige of our terrestrial origin, as a certain magical mysticism has suggested? We dare not affirm it seriously, but it is true all the same that man issued from the slime of earth and his first appearance must have been in the form of a rough sketch. The analogies of Nature compel us to admit the notion, at least as a possibility. The first men were, in this case, a family of gigantic, sensitive mandrogores, animated by the sun, who rooted themselves up from the earth." (See *Transcendental Magic.*)

The homely onion was revered by the Egyptians as a symbol of the universe because its rings and layers represented the concentric planes into which creation was divided according to the Hermetic Mysteries. It was also regarded as possessing great medicinal virtue. Because of peculiar properties resulting from its pungency, the garlic plant was a powerful agent in transcendental magic. To this day no better medium has been found for the treatment of obsession. Vampirism and certain forms of insanity—especially those resulting from mediumship and the influences of elemental larvæ—respond immediately to the use of garlic. In the Middle Ages, its presence in a house was believed to ward off all evil powers.

Trifoliate plants, such as the shamrock, were employed by many religious cults to represent the principle of the Trinity. St. Patrick is supposed to have used the shamrock to illustrate this doctrine of the triune Divinity. The reason for the additional sanctity conferred by a fourth leaf is that the fourth principle of the Trinity is man, and the presence of this leaf therefore signifies the redemption of humanity.

Wreaths were worn during initiation into the Mysteries and the reading of the sacred books to signify that these processes were consecrated to the deities. On the symbolism of wreaths, Richard Payne Knight writes: "Instead of beads, wreaths of foliage, generally of laurel, olive, myrtle, ivy, or oak, appear upon coins, sometimes encircling the symbolical figures, and sometimes as chaplets upon their heads. All these were sacred to some peculiar personifications of the deity, and significant of some particular attributes, and, in general, all evergreens were Dionysiac plants; that is, symbols of the generative power, signifying perpetuity of youth and vigor, as the circles of beads and diadems signify perpetuity of existence." (See *Symbolical Language of Ancient Art and Mythology.*)

XXI

Stones, Metals, and Gems

ach of the four primary elements as taught by the early philosophers has its analogue in the quaternary terrestrial constitution of man. The rocks and earth correspond to the bones and flesh; the water to the various fluids; the air to the gases; and the fire to the bodily heat. Since the bones are the framework that sustains the corporeal structure, they may be regarded as a fitting emblem of the spirit—that divine foundation which supports the composite fabric of mind, soul, and body. To the initiate, the skeleton of death holding in bony fingers the reaper's scythe denotes Saturn (Kronos), the father of the gods, carrying the sickle with which he mutilated Ouranos, his own sire.

In the language of the Mysteries, *the spirits of men are the powdered bones of Saturn.* The latter deity was always worshiped under the symbol of the base or footing, inasmuch as he was considered to be the substructure upholding creation. The myth of Saturn has its historical basis in the fragmentary records preserved by the early Greeks and Phœnicians concerning a king by that name who ruled over the ancient continent of Hyperborea. Polaris, Hyperborea, and Atlantis, because they lie buried beneath the continents and oceans of the modern world, have frequently been symbolized as rocks supporting upon their broad surfaces new lands, races, and empires. According to the Scandinavian Mysteries, the stones and cliffs were formed from the bones of Ymir, the primordial giant of the *seething clay,* while to the Hellenic mystics the rocks were the bones of the Great Mother, Gæa.

After the deluge sent by the gods to destroy mankind at the close of the Iron Age, only Deucalion and Pyrrha were left alive. Entering a ruined sanctuary to pray, they were directed by an oracle to depart from the temple and with heads veiled and garments unbound cast behind them the bones of their mother. Construing the cryptic message of the god to mean that the earth was the Great

Mother of all creatures, Deucalion picked up loose rocks and, bidding Pyrrha do likewise, cast them behind him. From these rocks there sprang forth a new and stalwart race of human beings, the rocks thrown by Deucalion becoming men and those thrown by Pyrrha becoming women. In this allegory is epitomized the mystery of human evolution; for spirit, by ensouling matter, becomes that indwelling power which gradually but sequentially raises the mineral to the states of the plant; the plant to the plane of the animal; the animal to the dignity of man; and man to the estate of the gods.

The solar system was organized by forces operating inward from the great ring of the Saturnian sphere; and since the beginnings of all things were under the control of Saturn, the most reasonable inference is that the first forms of worship were dedicated to him and his peculiar symbol—the stone. Thus the intrinsic nature of Saturn is synonymous with that spiritual rock which is the enduring foundation of the Solar Temple, and has its antitype or lower octave in that terrestrial rock—the planet Earth—which sustains upon its jagged surface the diversified genera of mundane life.

Although its origin is uncertain, litholatry undoubtedly constitutes one of the earliest forms of religious expression. "Throughout all the world," writes Godfrey Higgins, "the first object of Idolatry seems to have been a plain, unwrought stone, placed in the ground, as an emblem of the generative or procreative powers of nature." (See *The Celtic Druids*.) Remnants of stone worship are distributed over the greater part of the earth's surface, a notable example being the menhirs at Carnac, in Brittany, where several thousand gigantic uncut stones are arranged in eleven orderly rows. Many of these monoliths stand over twenty feet out of the sand in which they are embedded, and it has been calculated that some of the larger ones weigh as much as 250,000 pounds. By some it is believed that certain of the menhirs mark the location of buried treasure, but the most plausible view is that which regards Carnac as a monument to the astronomical knowledge of antiquity. Scattered throughout the British Isles and Europe, these cairns, dolmens, menhirs, and cistvaens stand as mute but eloquent testimonials to the existence and achievements of races now extinct.

Of particular interest are the rocking or logan stones, which evince the mechanical skill of these early peoples. These relics consist of enormous boulders poised upon one or two small points in such a manner that the slightest pressure will sway them, but the greatest effort is not sufficient to overthrow them. These were called *living* stones by the Greeks and Latins, the most famous one being the Gygorian stone in the Strait of Gibraltar. Though so perfectly balanced that it could be moved with the stalk of a daffodil, this rock could not be upset by the combined weight of many men. There is a legend that Hercules raised a rocking stone over the graves of the two sons of Boreas whom he had killed in combat. This stone was so delicately poised that it swayed back and forth with the wind, but no application of force could overturn it. A number of logan stones have been found in Britain, traces of one no longer standing having been discovered in Stonehenge. (See *The Celtic Druids*.) It is interesting to note that the green stones forming the inner ring of Stonehenge are believed to have been brought from Africa.

In many cases the monoliths are without carving or inscription, for they undoubtedly antedate both the use of tools and the art of writing. In some instances the stones have been trued into columns or obelisks, as in the runic monuments and the Hindu *lingams* and *sakti* stones; in other instances they are fashioned into rough likenesses of the human body, as in the Easter Island statues, or into the elaborately sculptured figures of the Central American Indians and the *Khmers* of Cambodia. The first rough-stone images can hardly be considered as effigies of any particular deity but rather as the crude effort of primitive man to portray in the enduring qualities of stone the procreative attributes of abstract Divinity. An instinctive recognition of the stability of Deity has persisted through all the intervening ages between primitive man and modern civilization. Ample proof of the survival of litholatry in the Christian faith is furnished by allusions to the *rock of refuge*, the *rock* upon which the church of Christ was to be founded, the *corner stone* which the builders rejected, Jacob's *stony pillow* which he set up and anointed with oil, the *sling stone* of David, the *rock Moriah* upon which the altar of King Solomon's Temple was erected, the *white stone* of Revelation, and the *Rock of Ages*.

Stones were highly venerated by prehistoric peoples primarily because of their usefulness. Jagged bits of stone were probably man's first weapons; rocky cliffs and crags constituted his first fortifications, and from these vantage points he hurled loose boulders down upon marauders. In caverns or rude huts fashioned from slabs of rock the first humans protected themselves from the rigors of the elements. Stones were set up as markers and monuments to primitive achievement; they were also placed upon the graves of the dead, probably as a precautionary measure to prevent the depredations of wild beasts. During migrations, it was apparently customary for primitive peoples to carry about with them stones taken from their original habitat. As the homeland or birthplace of a race was considered sacred, these stones were emblematic of that universal regard shared by all nations for the place of their geniture. The discovery that fire could be produced by striking together two pieces of stone augmented man's reverence for stones, but ultimately the hitherto unsuspected world of wonders opened by the newly discovered element of fire caused pyrolatry to supplant stone worship. The dark, cold Father—stone—gave birth out of itself to the bright, glowing Sun—fire; and the newly born flame, by displacing its parent, became the most impressive and mysterious of all religio-philosophic symbols, widespread and enduring through the ages.

The *body* of every thing was likened to a rock, trued either into a cube or more ornately chiseled to form a pedestal, while the *spirit* of every thing was likened to the elaborately carved figure surmounting it. Accordingly, altars were erected as a symbol of the lower world, and fires were kept burning upon them to represent that spiritual essence illuminating the body it surmounted. The square is actually one surface of a cube, its corresponding figure in plane geometry, and its proper philosophic symbol. Consequently, when considering the earth as an element and not as a body, the Greeks, Brahmins, and Egyptians always referred to its four corners, although they were fully aware that the planet itself was a sphere.

Because their doctrines were the sure foundation of all knowledge and the first step in the attainment of conscious immortality, the Mysteries were often represented as cubical or pyramidal stones. Conversely, these stories themselves became the emblem of that condition of self-achieved godhood. The unchangeability of the stone made it an appropriate emblem of God—the immovable and unchangeable Source of Existence—and also of the divine sciences—the eternal revelation of Himself to mankind. As the personification of the rational intellect, which is the true foundation of human life, Mercury, or Hermes, was symbolized in a like manner. Square or cylindrical pillars, surmounted by a bearded head of Hermes and called hermæ, were set up in public places. Terminus, a form of Jupiter and god of boundaries and highways, from whose name is derived the modern word *terminal,* was also symbolized by an upright stone, sometimes ornamented with the head of the god, which was placed at the borders of provinces and the intersections of important roads.

The *philosopher's stone* is really the *philosophical stone,* for philosophy is truly likened to a magic jewel whose touch transmutes base substances into priceless gems like itself. Wisdom is the alchemist's *powder of projection* which transforms many thousand times its own weight of gross ignorance into the precious substance of enlightenment.

The Tablets of the Law

While upon the heights of Mount Sinai, Moses received from Jehovah two tablets bearing the characters of the Decalogue traced by the very finger of Israel's God. These tables were fashioned from the divine sapphire, *Schethiyâ*, which the Most High, after removing from His own throne, had cast into the Abyss to become the foundation and generator of the worlds. This sacred stone, formed of heavenly dew, was sundered by the breath of God, and upon the two parts were drawn in black fire the figures of the Law. These precious inscriptions, aglow with celestial splendor, were delivered by the Lord on the Sabbath day into the hands of Moses, who was able to read the illumined letters from the reverse side because of the transparency of the great jewel. (See *The Secret Doctrine in Israel* or *The Zohar* for details of this legend.)

The Ten Commandments are the ten shining gems placed by the Holy One in the sapphire sea of Being, and in the depths of matter the reflections of these jewels are seen as the laws governing the sublunary spheres. They are the sacred ten by which the Supreme Deity has stamped His will upon the face of Nature. This same decad was celebrated by the Pythagoreans under the form of the tetractys—that triangle of spermatic points which reveals to the initiated the whole working of the cosmic scheme; for ten is the number of perfection, the key to creation, and the proper symbol of God, man, and the universe.

Because of the idolatry of the Israelites, Moses deemed the people unworthy to receive the sapphire tables; hence he destroyed them, that the Mysteries of Jehovah should not be violated. For the original set Moses substituted two tablets of rough stone into the surface of which he had cut ten ancient letters. While the former tables—partaking of the divinity of the Tree of Life—blazed forth eternal verities, the latter—partaking of the nature of the Tree of Good and Evil—revealed only temporal truths. Thus the ancient tradition of Israel returned again to heaven, leaving only its shadow with the children of the twelve tribes.

One of the two tables of stone delivered by the Lawgiver to his followers stood for the oral, the other for the written traditions upon which the Rabbinical School was founded. Authorities differ widely as to the size and substance of the inferior tables. Some describe them as being so small that they could be held in the hollow of a man's hand; others declare that each table was ten or twelve cubits in length and of enormous weight. A few even deny that the tables were of stone, maintaining that they were of a wood called *sedr,* which, according to the Mohammedans, grows profusely in Paradise.

The two tables signify respectively the superior and the inferior worlds—

the paternal and the maternal formative principles. In their undivided state they present the Cosmic Androgyne. The breaking of the tables signifies obscurely the separation of the superior and the inferior spheres and also the division of the sexes. In the religious processionals of the Greeks and Egyptians an ark or ship was carried which contained stone tablets, cones, and vessels of various shapes emblematic of the procreative processes. The Ark of the Israelites—which was patterned after the sacred chests of the Isiac Mysteries—contained three holy objects, each having an important phallic interpretation: the pot of manna, the rod that budded, and the Tablets of the Law—the first, second, and third Principles of the Creative Triad. The manna, the blossoming staff, and the stone tables are also appropriate images respectively of the Qabbalah, the Mishna, and the written law—the spirit, soul, and body of Judaism. When placed in King Solomon's Everlasting House, the Ark of the Covenant contained only the Tablets of the Law. Does this indicate that even at that early date the secret tradition had been lost and the letter of the revelation alone remained?

As representing the power that fabricated the lower, or Demiurgic, sphere, the tablets of stone were sacred to Jehovah in contradistinction to the tablets of sapphire that signified the potency that established the higher, or celestial, sphere. Without doubt the Mosaic tablets have their prototype in the stone pillars or obelisks placed on either side of the entrance to pagan temples. These columns may pertain to that remote time when men worshiped the Creator through His zodiacal sign of Gemini, the symbol of which is still the phallic pillars of the Celestial Twins. "The Ten Commandments," writes Hargrave Jennings, "are inscribed in two groups of five each, in columnar form. The five to the right (looking from the altar) mean the 'Law'; the five to the left mean the 'Prophets.' The right stone is masculine, the left stone is feminine. They correspond to the two disjoined pillars of stone (or towers) in the front of every cathedral, and of every temple in the heathen times." (See *The Rosicrucians: Their Rites and Mysteries.*) The same author states that the Law is masculine because it was delivered direct from the Deity, while the Prophets, or Gospels, were feminine because born through the nature of man.

The right Tablet of the Law further signifies *Jachin*—the white pillar of light; the left Tablet, *Boaz*—the shadowy pillar of darkness. These were the names of the two pillars cast from brass set up on the porch of King Solomon's Temple. They were eighteen cubits in height and beautifully ornamented with wreaths of chainwork, nets, and pomegranates. On the top of each pillar was a large bowl—now erroneously called a ball or globe—one of the bowls probably containing fire and the other water. The celestial globe (originally the bowl of fire), surmounting the right-hand column (Jachin), symbolized the divine man; the terrestrial globe (the bowl of water), surmounting the left-hand column (Boaz), signified the earthly man. These two pillars respectively connote also the active and the passive expressions of Divine Energy, the sun and the moon, sulphur and salt, good and bad, light and darkness. Between them is the door leading into the House of God, and standing thus at the gates of Sanctuary they are a reminder that Jehovah is both an androgynous and an anthropomorphic deity. As two parallel columns they denote the zodiacal signs of Cancer and Capricorn, which were formerly placed in the chamber of initiation to represent birth and death—the extremes of physical life. They accordingly signify the summer and the winter solstices, now known to Freemasons under the comparatively modern appellation of the "two St. Johns."

In the mysterious Sephirothic Tree of the Jews, these two pillars symbolize Mercy and Severity. Standing before the gate of King Solomon's Temple, these columns had the same symbolic import as the obelisks before the sanctuaries of Egypt. When interpreted Qabbalistically, the names of the two pillars mean "In strength shall My House be established." In the splendor of mental and spiritual illumination, the High Priest stood between the pillars as a mute witness to the perfect virtue of equilibrium—that hypothetical point equidistant from all extremes. He thus personified the divine nature of man in the midst of his compound constitution—the mysterious Pythagorean Monad in the presence of the Duad. On one side towered the stupendous column of the intellect; on the other, the brazen pillar of the flesh. Midway between these two stands the glorified wise man, but he cannot reach this high estate without first suffering upon the cross made by joining these pillars together. The early Jews occasionally represented the two pillars, Jachin and Boaz, as the legs of Jehovah, thereby signifying to the modern philosopher that Wisdom and Love, in their most exalted sense, support the whole order of creation—both mundane and supermundane.

The Holy Grail

Like the sapphire Schethiyâ, the *Lapis Exilis,* crown jewel of the Archangel Lucifer, fell from heaven. Michael, archangel of the sun and the Hidden God of Israel, at the head of the angelic hosts swooped down upon Lucifer and his legions of rebellious spirits. During the conflict, Michael with his flaming sword struck the flashing *Lapis Exilis* from the coronet of his adversary, and the green stone fell through all the celestial rings into the dark and immeasurable Abyss.

GROUP OF WORLD RELIGIONS.

A t the left of the plate stands Mohammed, holding aloft pages from the Koran, his left foot upon an image which he has overthrown. Behind Mohammed the Celestial Bull—signifying the constellation of Taurus—opens the "Egg of the Year" with his horns. At the lower right is a bas-relief of the Persian Sun God, Mithras, in an attitude signifying the conquest of the sun over the Celestial Bull at the ancient vernal equinox. In the center stands the High Priest of Israel, his right arm encircling the base of the seven-branched candlestick—the Mosaic symbol of the Planetary Governors of the world. To his right is the statue of the golden calf and to his left the robed figures of the Greek mystics bearing a tripod in which burns the sacrificial fire. Behind the bull Apis, crowned with the lunar globe, and Father Nile, bearing the horn of plenty and pouring the waters of life from his urn, loom the Pyramids—the great Egyptian temples of initiation. In the clouds at the left is the seated figure of Jupiter Ammon, brandishing a flaming thunderbolt and horned to signify that he partakes of the attributes of the zodiacal ram. In the heavens appears the mystery of the Apocalypse. The four creatures of Ezekiel's Vision surround an altar upon which is the Book of Seven Seals and the Lamb of God. At the upper left is the band of the zodiac. The constellations of Taurus, Aries, and Pisces represent the stellar influences which—according to the ancients—descending upon the earth, are responsible for the establishment of the religious and philosophical institutions herein set forth.

HERMES STANDING UPON THE BACK OF TYPHON.

Hermes, as the personification of Universal Wisdom, is here depicted with his foot upon the back of Typhon, the vanquished dragon of ignorance and perversion. To the Egyptian initiates Typhon, the devourer of souls, signified the lower world which swallows up the spiritual nature of the individual who, being imperfect, is forced to descend from the higher spheres and be reborn into the physical universe. To be swallowed by Typhon therefore signifies the process of rebirth, from which man can only release himself by vanquishing his mortal Adversary.

In one hand Hermes carries the Caduceus, a winged rod with two fighting serpents entwined about it; in the other, the immortal Emerald, upon whose surface was inscribed in raised letters the sum of philosophy. The figure wears the ancient Egyptian Masonic apron according to the pattern discovered by Belzoni, the eminent Egyptologist. The two small circles contain the forms and symbols most closely associated with Hermes. In the upper circle is the ibis, whose curious characteristics have caused it to be particularly associated with the medical art. In the initiation ceremonies the Egyptian priests wore masks in the form of the ibis head to signify that they represented the attributes of Thoth, or Hermes. The lower circle contains the dog, an animal always associated with Hermes because of its intelligence and devotion. Upon the forehead of Hermes appears the uræus, the secret symbol of the constellation of Scorpio, which represents the regeneration of the same power that in the form of a dragon lies helpless under his foot. The scarab over the heart of Hermes represents the presence of the spiritual and regenerative light within his own soul; the collar typifies by its circles the orbits of the heavenly bodies. The three points of the tail of Typhon which end in arrows indicate the three destructive expressions of universal energy—mental, moral, and physical perversion. The entire diagram signifies mastery through the regeneration of the body, the illumination of the mind, and the transmutation of the emotions.

AN IDEALISTIC DEPICTION OF THE ATLANTEAN MYSTERY TEMPLE.

In the Critias, Plato describes in detail the divine foundation of the Atlantean Empire, originally known as Poseidonis. The golden age preserved in myth and legend, when the gods walked with men, depicts the zenith of Atlantean civilization. The demigods of the ancient world were the Atlanteans, to whom every civilized nation owes an incalculable debt of gratitude. In the British Museum there is a remarkable document—known as the Troano manuscript—which was written over 3,500 years ago by the Mayas of Yucatan, containing an authentic account of the cataclysm which sank the continent of Atlantis. This priceless document contains the following statement according to the translation by Le Plongeon: "In the year 6 Kan, on the 11th Mulac in the month Zac, there occurred terrible earthquakes, which continued without interruption until the 13th Chuen. The country of the hills of Mud, the land of Mu, was sacrificed; being twice upheaved it suddenly disappeared during one night, the basin being continually shaken by volcanic forces. Being confined, these caused the land to sink and to rise several times and in various places. At last the surface gave away and ten countries were torn asunder and scattered; unable to stand the force of the convulsions, they sank with their 64,000,000 inhabitants."

Before the Atlantean continent was submerged, the initiates of the Atlantean Mysteries, carrying with them the secret doctrines entrusted to their keeping, immigrated into Egypt and other parts of the earth where they would be safe from the impending catastrophe. Thus their secret teaching—with its priceless value to subsequent ages—was preserved. They established centers of learning and promulgated the code, clothed in the language of symbolism, to such as they deemed worthy to receive it.

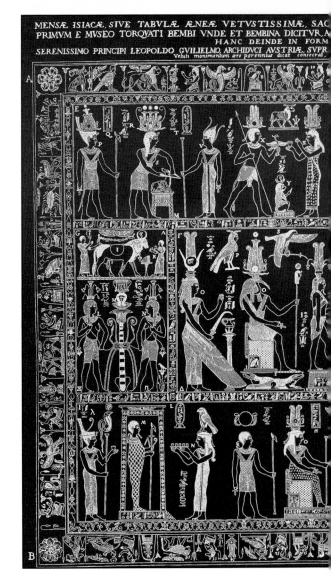

MENSÆ ISIACÆ, SIVE TABVLÆ ÆNEÆ VETVSTISSIMÆ, SAC
PRIMVM E MVSEO TORQVATI BEMBI VNDE ET BEMBINA DICITVR, A
HANC DEINDE IN FORM
SERENISSIMO PRINCIPI LEOPOLDO GVILIELMO ARCHIDVCI AVSTRIÆ, SVPR
Veluti monimentum ære perennius dicat consecrat.

THE BEMBINE TABLE OF ISIS.

C oncerning the theurgic or magic sense in which the Egyptian priests exhibited in the Bembine Table of Isis the philosophy of sacrifice, rites, and ceremonies by a system of occult symbols, Athanasius Kircher writes: "The early priests believed that a great spiritual power was invoked by correct and unabridged sacrificial ceremonies. If one feature were lacking, the whole was vitiated, says Iamblichus. Hence they were most careful in all details, for they considered it absolutely essential for the entire chain of logical connections to be exactly according to ritual. Certainly for no other reason did they prepare and prescribe for future use the manuals, as it were, for conducting the rites. They learned, too, what the first hieromancers—possessed, as it were, by a divine fury—devised as a system of symbolism for exhibiting their mysteries. These they placed in this Tablet of Isis, before the eyes of those admitted to the sanctum sanctorum in order to teach the natures of the Gods and the prescribed forms of sacrifice. Since each of the orders of Gods had its peculiar symbols, gestures, costumes, and ornaments, they thought it necessary to observe these in the whole apparatus of worship, as nothing was more efficacious in drawing the benign attention of the deities and genii. * * * Thus their temples, remote from the usual haunts of men, contained representations of nearly every form in nature. First, in the pavement, they symbolized the physical economy of the world, using minerals, stones, and other things suitable for ornaments, including little streams of water. The walls showed the starry world, and the dome the world of genii. In the center was the altar, to suggest the emanations of the Supreme Mind from its center. Thus the entire interior constituted a picture of the Universe of Worlds. The priests in making sacrifices wore raiment adorned with figures similar to those attributed to the Gods. Their bodies were partially bare like those of the deities, and they themselves were divested of all material cares and practiced the strictest chastity. * * * Their heads were veiled to indicate their charge of earthly things. Their heads and bodies where shaved, for they regarded hair as a useless excrescence. Upon the head they bore the same insignia as those attributed to the Gods. Thus arrayed, they regarded themselves to be transformed into

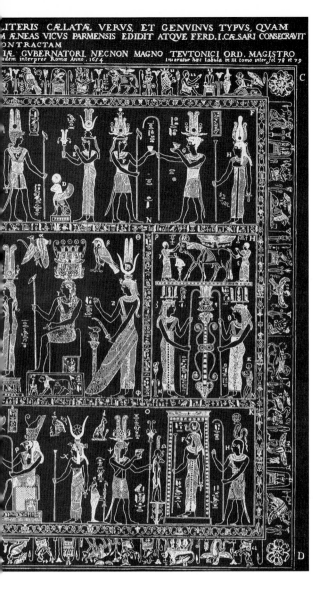

that intelligence with which they continuously desired to be identified. For example, in order to call down to the world the soul and spirit of the Universe, they stood before the image shown in the throne in the center of our Tablet, wearing the same symbols as that figure and its attendants, and offered sacrifices. By these and the accompanying singing of hymns they believed that they infallibly drew the God's attention to their prayer. And so they did in regard to the other regions of the Tablet, believing that of necessity the proper ritual properly carried out would evoke the deity desired. That this was the origin of the science of the oracles is apparent. As a touched chord produces a harmony of sound, likewise the adjoining chords respond though not touched. Similarly the idea they expressed by their concurrent acts while adoring the God came into accord with basic Idea and, by an intellectual union, it was returned to them deiformed, and they thus obtained the Idea of Ideas. Hence there sprang up in their souls, they thought, the gift of prophecy and divination, and they believed they could foretell future events, impeding evils, etc. For as in the Supreme Mind everything is simultaneous and spaceless, the future is therefore present in that Mind; and they thought that while the human mind was absorbed in the Supreme by contemplation, by that union they were enabled to know all the future. Nearly all that is represented in our Tablet consists of amulets which, by the analogy above described, would inspire them, under the described conditions, with the virtues of the Superior Power and enable them to receive good and avert evil. They also believed they could in this magical manner effect cures of diseases; that genii could be induced to appear to them during sleep and cure or teach them to cure the sick. In this belief they consulted the Gods about all sorts of doubts and difficulties, while adorned with the simulacra of the mystic rite and intently contemplating the Divine Ideas; and while so enraptured they believed the God by some sign, nod or gesture communicated with them, whether asleep or awake, concerning the truth or falsity of the matter in point." (See Œdipus Ægyptiacus.)

I, ISIS AM ALL THAT HAS BEEN, THAT IS OR SHALL BE; NO MORTAL MAN HATH EVER ME UNVEILED.

THE FRUIT WHICH I HAVE BROUGHT FORTH IS THE "SUN"

THE SAITIC ISIS.

"I am Isis, mistress of the whole land: I was instructed by Hermes, and with Hermes I invented the writings of the nations, in order that not all should write with the same letters. I gave mankind their laws, and ordained what no one can alter. I am the eldest daughter of Kronos. I am the wife and sister of the king Osiris. I am she who rises in the dog star. I am she who is called the goddess of women. * * * I am she who separated the heaven from the earth. I have pointed out their paths to the stars. I have invented seamanship. * * * I have brought together men and women. * * * I have ordained that the elders shall be beloved by the children. With my brother Osiris I made an end of cannibalism. I have instructed mankind in the mysteries. I have taught reverence of the divine statues. I have established the temple precincts. I have overthrown the dominion of the tyrants. I have caused men to love woman. I have made justice more powerful than silver and gold. I have caused truth to be considered beautiful." (See Erman's *Handbook of Egyptian Religion*.)

The face and form of Isis were covered with a veil of scarlet cloth, symbolic of ignorance and emotionalism which forever stand between man and Truth. Isis lifts her veil and discovers herself to the true and wise investigator who unselfishly, humbly, and earnestly seeks to understand the mysteries which surround him in the universe. Those to whom she reveals herself are warned to remain silent concerning the mysteries which they have seen. The great admonition of the Wise Men was: "If you know it, be silent." To the vulgar and profane, the infidel and disinterested one, she does not uncover her face, for they could not understand the secret processes of the invisible worlds.

CONSULTING THE ORACLE OF DELPHI.

While the tripod and its base as here shown differ from the description of several authors, an attempt has been made to follow as closely as possible the symbolism concealed within the allegory of the oracle. The Delphic Mysteries used the oracle as their chief symbol, and it is the spiritual esoteric mystery rather than the historical and consequently unimportant aspect with which the student of symbolism is interested.

While the spirit inhabiting the fumes which rose continuously from the fissure entered into the body of the priestess, the tripod vibrated as though struck severe and repeated blows. Loud clangings were heard, which echoed through the cavern. The din increased as the control of the dæmon over the priestess became more complete, and the rattling and crashing did not cease until the spirit released its hold upon the Pythia. The three legs of the tripod symbolize the three periods of time controlled by Apollo, namely, the past, the present, and the future. The space enclosed by the legs of the tripod forms the sacred Pythagorean tetrahedron with the prophetess seated upon its apex. As the priestess of Delphi is held aloft over the abyss of the oracle, supported only by three slender legs ending in claws, so the spiritual nature of man is suspended over the abyss of oblivion by three golden threads of Divine power. The face of Apollo appears upon the tripod, and around the base are coiled serpents to symbolize Python, whose decaying body lies beneath the Delphic shrine.

PYTHAGORAS OF CROTONA.

Though Pythagoras excelled Plato in the profundity of his philosophic deductions, the transcendental element in his doctrines has provoked the ridicule of a materialistic modern science. All too lightly the world has passed over the achievements of the first "philosopher" to whom it is indebted for so many of the basic theorems of mathematics, music, and astronomy. The twentieth century student of Greek philosophy has been taught to associate the name of Pythagoras with such puerile issues as his golden shin bone and his ban upon the eating of beans! It has also been held against Pythagoras that he delivered his discourses from behind a curtain, preached in allegories and enigmas, and revealed his scientific knowledge only to such initiated disciples as had spent many years in self-discipline. His sciolistic critics, however, have failed to consider the manner in which Pythagoras obtained his immense wealth of abstract learning. The Mysteries of Greece, Egypt, Persia, and India without exception bound their initiates to inviolable secrecy. Having accepted the obligations of these societies, Pythagoras had no honorable course other than to abide by their regulations. Iamblichus lists 218 men and 17 women among the most famous of the Pythagorean philosophers. It is thus evident that Pythagoras revealed his secrets to a considerable number of persons— probably all who he felt could understand and be benefited by his knowledge. The Pythagorean doctrine of mathematical philosophy may yet be accepted as the one system of thought able to cope with the riddle of existence.

THE ANCIENT OF THE ANCIENTS.

In the Greater Holy Assembly it is written of the Ancient of the Ancients that He is the Concealed of the Concealed Ones, the Eternal of the Eternal Ones, the Mystery of the Mysteries, and that in His symbols He is knowable and unknowable. In the *Zohar* His robes are said to be white, but they are here shown as red to signify that the garments of Divinity partake of the nature of cosmic activity. His face is declared to be the likeness of a face vast, luminous, and terrible. He sits upon a throne of flaming light and the flashes of the fire are subject to His will. The white light streaming from His head illumines four hundred thousand worlds. (Some texts read forty thousand superior worlds.) The glory of this light shall be given unto the just, who are called "the sacred fruits of the Tree of the Sephiroth."

Thirteen thousand myriads of worlds come into light from His skull, from which issues forth a mysterious dew having the power to awaken the spiritually dead into everlasting life. The length of "The Great Face" is declared to be three hundred and seventy thousand myriads of worlds; therefore it is called "The Long Face." The appearance of the Ancient of the Ancients is that of the Aged of the Aged, who has been before the beginning and whose throne stands upon the firmament. By the Aged of the Aged is willed "The Short Face," or creation, which is the chariot of the Most Holy of the Most Holy.

The hair and beard of the Ancient of the Ancients extend to the uttermost parts of the universe. From His skull hang down a thousand thousand myriads, seven thousand and five hundred curling hairs which are not mingled lest confusion exist; and in each curl are four hundred and ten locks of hair, and these hairs all and singular radiate into four hundred and ten worlds. In the hollow of His skull is the aerial membrane of the supreme hidden Wisdom and His brain extends and goes forth by thirty-two paths. From the beard of the Ancient of the Ancients flow thirteen fountains and from His hands pour the Mother and Father Rays, by which existence comes into being. The head of the Ancient of the Ancients is cleft like that of Zeus to permit wisdom in the form of Athena to emerge therefrom.

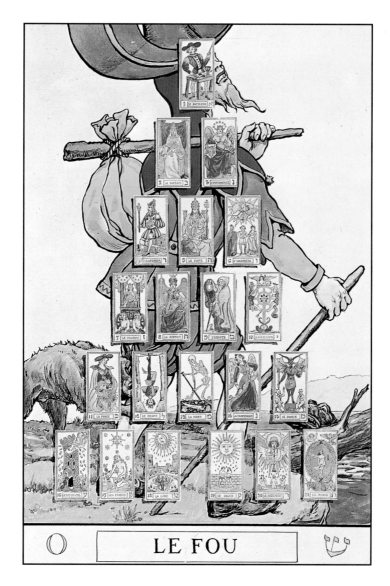

LE FOU

A LAYOUT OF MAJOR TAROT TRUMPS.

The Tarot consists of a deck of 78 curiously emblazoned cards of uncertain origin and date. The deck is divided into two general sections, of which the larger contains 56 cards—termed the minor trumps—and the smaller, 22 cards—termed the major trumps. The minor trumps are further divided into four suits—each containing 14 cards—somewhat similar to those of modern playing cards. The four suits are called Rods (Clubs), Swords (Spades), Cups (Hearts), and Coins (Diamonds). The pip cards of each suit ascend from the ace to the 10, and their denominations are shown by groups of their respective emblems, as 6 Rods, 4 Cups, 9 Coins, or 3 Swords. The court cards of each suit are four in number, termed King, Queen, Knight, and Page. The Kings and Queens are usually depicted seated, the Knights on horseback, and the Pages standing. Each holds the emblem of its suit. The major trumps are also divided into two sections, one of which is composed of 21 cards, usually numbered, and the other of a single card, either unnumbered or marked with a cipher. The accepted order of the 21 cards with their names is as follows. (1) the *Juggler*; (2) the *High Priestess*, or *Female Pope*; (3) the *Empress*; (4) the *Emperor*; (5) the *Pope*; (6) the *Lovers*, or *Marriage*; (7) the *Chariot*; (8) *Justice*; (9) the *Hermit*; (10) the *Wheel of Fortune*; (11) *Strength*; (12) the *Hanged Man*; (13) *Death*; (14) *Temperance*; (15) the *Devil*; (16) the *Fire from Heaven*; (17) the *Stars*; (18) the *Moon*; (19) the *Sun*; (20) the *Judgment*; and (21) the *World*. The unnumbered card upon which the others are spread is designated the *Fool*.

THE COURTYARD OF THE TABERNACLE.

While the religion of the early Israelites has been adversely criticized, its disparagers have failed to give consideration to the time and environment of which it was a natural and consistent product. It is impossible to judge one civilization by comparing it with another widely separated from it in point of time. The modern world looks upon many ancient practices as cruel and barbarous, but is guilty every day of offenses which would have proved equally revolting to the sensibilities of ancient peoples! At no time has the world been composed of a majority of thinking people. Only here and there is found an intellect actually seeking to solve not only the problems of its own destiny but also those of others. The esoteric, spiritual side of every religion is a beautiful, humanitarian, and transcendent code, to be understood only by those who have raised themselves above the plane of the prosaic and the conventional. For ages man has served the "letter of the law," not realizing that *"the letter killeth, but the spirit giveth life."*

To the true scholar and mystic, the Old Testament is an endless source of inspiration. To the intellectualist, it is a cause of ceaseless wrangling, and he argues over dates and places, overlooking entirely the sublime truths concealed under the crude allegories of Scripture. He who understands thoroughly the Mystery of the Tabernacle needs no other religion, for he will be at one with the seers of all ages. As he goes about his daily life, every man—unknown to himself—is a priest of the Tabernacle; for as priests were appointed by Jehovah to keep His house in order, so each individual is, in a like manner, appointed to keep his own little world in order. Nature is the Tabernacle, man is the priest, and the one God of all nations and all peoples dwells in every human soul behind the embroidered veil of the "Holy of Holies."

GRAND ROSICRUCIAN ALCHEMICAL FORMULA.

İn the heavens and surrounded by both an outer and an inner aureole and by hierarchies of celestial beings are the radiant symbols of the Holy Trinity: יהוה (the Father?), the Lamb (the Son), and the Dove (the Holy Ghost). The respective dignities of the heavenly host are determined by the number and arrangement of their wings. The glory of the Godhead and the invisible world is concealed from the inferior creation partly by a line and partly by the circle of the starry heavens, itself obscured by clouds. Five birds—a crow (Saturn, lead); a swan (Jupiter, tin); a cock (Mars, iron); a pelican (Venus, copper); and the phœnix (Mercury, quicksilver)—occupy the half circle directly within the band of the starry heavens. The upper half of the blue circle containing the five planetary signs is occupied by the zodiacal signs. In the green circle appear the words: "The solar year, the stellar year, and the year of winds"; in the yellow circle, "The mercury of the sages, corporeal mercury, and common, or visible, mercury"; in the orange circle, "Combustible sulphur, fixed sulphur, and volatile, or ethereal, sulphur"; in the red circle, "Elementary salt, earthly salt, and central salt"; and in the violet circle, "Four kinds of fire are requisite for the work." The white central triangle contains the figure of the solar mercury.

The entire upper section of the plate is an esoteric diagram of the constitution of the threefold spiritual sun. In the lower foreground is a hill upon which grow a number of trees, each bearing the symbol of an alchemical substance. (For details consult Basil Valentine's table of alchemical symbols in chapter XXXV.) At the lower right and represented by a nocturnal scene is the inferior world, while at the lower left and represented by a diurnal scene is the superior world. Thus water is symbolized by the right side of the plate and fire by the left side. Under the wings of the phœnix are two circles containing the symbols of fire and air; under the wings of the eagle are two other circles containing the symbols of earth and water. The human figures, one male and the other female, both attached to the superior wold by a golden chain and

Aquila

REDRAWN FROM *MUSEUM HERMETICUM REFORMATUM ET AMPLIFICATUM.*

bearing upon their bodies the symbols of the creative forces, stand for the divine (male) and human (female) principles in every creature. The spirit and will are represented by a lion rampant; the soul and intuition by a deer with twelve lights or stars upon its horns and bearing a trifoliate leaf symbolic of the threefold division of all natural things.

In the center of the picture is the figure of philosophic equilibrium and the accomplishment of the *magnum opus*. The double-bodied lion emphasizes to the initiated the necessity for the final union of all diversified parts; also that light and darkness (symbols of all natural opposites) are two bodies with a single head. Upon this strange creature which he has fabricated by his art and which symbolizes the reconciliation of apparently irreconcilable elements, stands the alchemistic philosopher. The stars upon his robe reveal the luminous nature of the purified and regenerated adept, and with the maces (the illumined intellect) he destroys the illusion of light and darkness and, uniting the various scattered parts of cosmos, fashions therefrom the philosophic androgyne. In the *Hermetic Museum* this plate is accompanied by the following quotation: "By the word of the Lord were the heavens established, and their hosts by the breath of His mouth. The Spirit of the Lord hath filled the wold. All things are satisfied with Thy goodness, O Lord. Thou turnest away Thy face, they are troubled. Thou turnest away Thy Spirit, they die and return again to their dust. Thou sendest forth Thy Spirit and they are created, and renewest the face of the earth. Thy glory is for everlasting." In the *Hermetic Museum* a free rendering of the Emerald Table of Hermes (q.v.) is also annexed to this plate.

Only by profound contemplation and familiarity with the principles of mediæval alchemy may the true spirit of chemical mysticism be discovered. In the above plate is set forth the complete key to the regeneration of the metals, the transmutation of earthliness into celestial splendor, and the mystery of generation which has been so sadly and ignorantly misinterpreted by the sciolists of the twentieth century.

PARSIFAL AND THE HOLY GRAIL.

In the great temple on Mount Salvat stands Parsifal, the third and last king of the Holy Grail, holding aloft the scintillating green Grail Cup and the sacred spear. From the tip of the spear trickles an endless stream of blood. Before Parsifal kneels Kundry (Kundalini), the temptress, who, released from the spell of the evil Klingsor, adores the sacred relics of the Passion. Of the Grail Mysteries, Hargrave Jennings writes: "The council of the Knights or Brothers of the Holy Grail, or Graël, was a reflex of the sacred bond sanctified by sacraments which held the majestic and mystic Rosicrucians together. These were really the guardians of the greater mysteries. In this sense of the mysterious and the sacred, the 'garter' of the 'Most noble the Order of the Garter'—the first of chivalry—is not a 'garter' at all, but the 'Garder,' or 'Keeper,' the sacredest and holiest guardian of the the supernatural chastity of none other than the most exalted feminine personality (of course in the abstract and miraculous sense), the very foundation of Christianity—the 'Cestus' or girdle of the blessed and immaculate Virgin Mary, the Queen of Heaven, with her victorious foot, for all the ages past and to come, trampling upon the Dragon, in her celestial purity, as the 'Mother of Christ.'" (See *Phallicism*.) The key to the Grail Mysteries will be apparent if in the sacred spear is recognized the pineal gland with its peculiar pointlike projection and in the Holy Grail the pituitary body containing the mysterious Water of Life. Mount Salvat is the human body; the domed temple upon its summit, the brain; and the castle of Klingsor in the dark valley below, the animal nature which lures the knights (brain energies) into the garden of illusion and perversion. Parsifal, as the purified candidate, becomes the Master of the holy relics and of the sacred science for which they stand; Kundry, having fulfilled the purpose of her existence, dies at the foot of the altar with the immortal words: "I serve!"

A ROSICRUCIAN CRUCIFIXION.

The solar crucifixion is an outstanding example of the astronomical knowledge possessed by the so-called prehistoric world. "In Herschel's ground-plan of the universe in human form," writes Albert Ross Parsons, "our solar system is located at the heart of the Divine Man of the skies. Hence, the catastrophe in our solar system, by which the ecliptic was sundered from the celestial equator, was a rupture or piercing of the heart of the Divine Man. The ecliptic and equator no longer coinciding, they formed a cross upon which the Divine Man was transfixed in space. This idea was familiar to the Hindus and to Plato. Hence arose the prehistoric Christianity, the religion of the lamb slain from the foundation of the world, of the Book of Revelation." (See *New Light from the Great Pyramid.*)

Ignoring the story of the crucifixion in its literal sense, the Gnostics considered only its cosmic import. In Rosicrucian mysticism, the Christ Spirit is said to have established a direct link with the earth through the blood which poured from the wounds in the hands, feet, and side of Jesus. Being the ancient symbol of the secret doctrine, the cross represents to the initiated that divine institution which, releasing the heavenly man from his animal part, launches the spiritual nature into the sphere of Reality. Therefore the cross may be said to be the emblem of philosophic death, and the Mysteries cannot achieve their end until they have caused each of their neophytes to pass victoriously through the cycle of suffering, death and resurrection. The entire procedure is concealed in the symbolism of the grape. As one author has perceived, the agony in the Garden of Gethsemane is analogous to the crushing of the grapes in the wine press. He who comprehends the mystery of the sacramental cup possesses the key to human regeneration. Man, crucified, passes through death upon the symbol of life and attains to life upon the symbol of death. The break between the Self and the not-self is thus complete and the spirit, emerging from its chrysalis, leaves the empty shell behind as the token of its attainment. The agony of the Savior, consequently, is not the agony of death but the agony of birth. Only to him who has found his life by losing it is the mystery comprehensible.

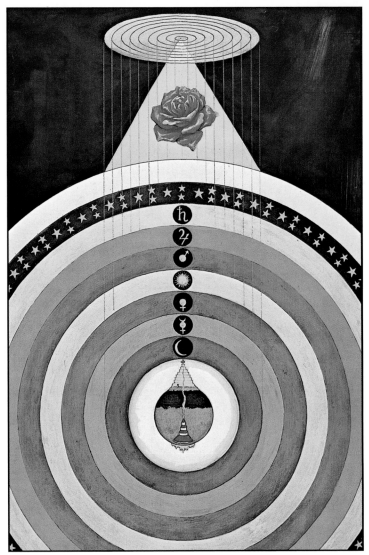

THE KEY TO DANTE'S DIVINE COMEDY.

I n his article on *The Topography of Dante's Spiritual World*, Charles Allen Dinsmore writes: "He [Dante] maintained the earth is round, having a hemisphere of land, in the centre of which stands Jerusalem. The other hemisphere originally contained land; but when Lucifer, hurled from Heaven, was about to fall upon it, the soil 'veiled itself with the sea' and came to the other side of the globe, making a hemisphere of land and a hemisphere of water. The interior of the earth also retreated before the descending Lucifer, leaving a vast conical-shaped cavity, which extended from the centre of the globe to the surface of the inhabited hemisphere. The void which evil made in the world is the abode of lost souls, and is divided into nine circles, of which the seventh is subdivided into three smaller circles, the eighth into ten ditches, and the ninth into four belts. At the centre of the earth, and thus at the point farthest from God, is Lucifer, with his head and body in one hemisphere, and his legs in the other, so that when Virgil and Dante turned upon his haunch, they passed the centre of gravity and emerged from one hemisphere into the other."

In the midst of the hemisphere of water stands a conical mountain, Purgatory, rising in seven steps. On its summit is the terrestrial Paradise or Garden of Eden where Dante met Beatrice. According to *The Divine Comedy*, as the soul climbs the seven steps of Purgatory it is cleansed of the seven mortal sins, and it then ascends through the seven spheres of the Ptolemaic universe. To each of the planets is assigned one of the seven virtues. In the eighth sphere the soul receives a knowledge of spiritual truths and in the ninth, or highest, it is absorbed into the celestial mysteries.

Out of Lucifer's radiant gem was fashioned the Sangreal, or Holy Grail, from which Christ is said to have drunk at the Last Supper.

Though some controversy exists as to whether the Grail was a cup or a platter, it is generally depicted in art as a chalice of considerable size and unusual beauty. According to the legend, Joseph of Arimathea brought the Grail Cup to the place of the crucifixion and in it caught the blood pouring from the wounds of the dying Nazarene. Later Joseph, who had become custodian of the sacred relics—the Sangreal and the Spear of Longinus—carried them into a distant country. According to one version, his descendants finally placed these relics in Glastonbury Abbey in England; according to another, in a wonderful castle on Mount Salvat, Spain, built by angels in a single night. Under the name of Prester John, Parsifal, the last of the Grail Kings, carried the Holy Cup with him into India, and it disappeared forever from the Western World. Subsequent search for the Sangreal was the motif for much of the knight-errantry of the Arthurian legends and the ceremonials of the Round Table. (See the *Morte d'Arthur.*)

No adequate interpretation has ever been given to the Grail Mysteries. Some believe the Knights of the Holy Grail to have been a powerful organization of Christian mystics perpetuating the Ancient Wisdom under the rituals and sacraments of the oracular Cup. The quest for the Holy Grail is the eternal search for truth, and Albert G. Mackey sees in it a variation of the Masonic legend of the Lost Word so long sought by the brethren of the Craft. There is also evidence to support the claim that the story of the Grail is an elaboration of an early pagan Nature myth which has been preserved by reason of the subtle manner in which it was engrafted upon the cult of Christianity. From this particular viewpoint, the Holy Grail is undoubtedly a type of the ark or vessel in which the life of the world is preserved and therefore is significant of the body of the Great Mother—Nature. Its green color relates it to Venus and to the mystery of generation; also to the Islamic faith, whose sacred color is green and whose Sabbath is Friday, the day of Venus.

The Holy Grail is a symbol both of the lower (or irrational) world and of the bodily nature of man, because both are receptacles for the living essences of the superior worlds. Such is the mystery of the redeeming blood which, descending into the condition of death, overcomes the last enemy by ensouling all substance with its own immortality. To the Christian, whose mystic faith especially emphasizes the *love* element, the Holy Grail typifies the heart in which continually swirls the living water of eternal life. Moreover, to the Christian, the search for the Holy Grail is the search for the real Self which, when found, is the consummation of the *magnum opus.*

The Holy Cup can be discovered only by those who have raised themselves above the limitations of sensuous existence. In his mystic poem, *The Vision of Sir Launfal,* James Russell Lowell discloses the true nature of the Holy Grail by showing that it is visible only to a *certain state of spiritual consciousness.* Only upon returning from the vain pursuit of haughty ambition did the aged and broken knight see in the transformed leper's cup the glowing chalice of his lifelong dream. Some writers trace a similarity between the Grail legend and the stories of the martyred Sun Gods whose blood, descending from heaven into the earth, was caught in the cup of matter and liberated therefrom by the initiatory rites. The Holy Grail may also be the seed pod so frequently employed in the ancient Mysteries as an emblem of germination and resurrection; and if the cuplike shape of the Grail be derived from the flower, it signifies the regeneration and spiritualization of the generative forces in man.

There are many accounts of stone images which, because of the substances entering into their composition and the ceremonials attendant upon their construction, were ensouled by the divinities whom they were created to resemble. To such images were ascribed various human faculties and powers, such as speech, thought, and even motion. While renegade priests doubtless resorted to trickery—an instance of which is related in a curious apocryphal fragment entitled *Bel and the Dragon* and supposedly deleted from the end of the *Book of Daniel*—many of the phenomena recorded in connection with sanctified statues and relics can hardly be explained unless the work of supernatural agencies be admitted.

History records the existence of stones which, when struck, threw all who heard the sound into a state of ecstasy. There were also echoing images which whispered for hours after the room itself had become silent, and musical stones productive of the sweetest harmonies. In recognition of the sanctity which the Greeks and Latins ascribed to stones, they placed their hands upon certain consecrated pillars when taking an oath. In ancient times stones played a part in determining the fate of accused persons, for it was customary for juries to reach their verdicts by dropping pebbles into a bag.

Divination by stones was often resorted to by the Greeks, and Helena is said to have foretold by lithomancy the destruction of Troy. Many popular superstitions about stones survive the so-called Dark Ages. Chief among these is the one concerning the famous black stone in the seat of the coronation chair in Westminster Abbey, which is declared to be the actual rock used by Jacob as a pillow. The black stone also appears several times in religious symbolism. It was called *Heliogabalus,* a word presumably derived from *Elagabal,* the Syro-Phœnician sun god. This stone was sacred to the sun and declared to possess great and diversified properties. The black stone in the Caaba at Mecca is still revered throughout

the Mohammedan world. It is said to have been white originally and of such brilliancy that it could be seen many days' journey from Mecca, but as ages passed it
became blackened by the tears of pilgrims and the sins of the world.

The Magic of Metals and Gems

According to the teachings of the Mysteries, the rays of the celestial bodies,
striking the crystallizing influences of the lower world, become the various elements. Partaking of the astral virtues of their source, these elements neutralize
certain unbalanced forms of celestial activity and, when properly combined,
contribute much to the well-being of man. Little is known today concerning
these magical properties, but the modern world may yet find it profitable to consider the findings of the early philosophers who determined these relationships
by extensive experimentation. Out of such research arose the practice of identi-
fying the metals with the bones of the various deities. For example, the Egyptians, according to Manetho, considered iron to be the bone of Mars and the
lodestone the bone of Horus. By analogy, lead would be the physical skeleton of
Saturn, copper of Venus, quicksilver of Mercury, gold of the sun, silver of the
moon, and antimony of the earth. It is possible that uranium will prove to be the
metal of Uranus and radium to be the metal of Neptune.

The four *Ages* of the Greek mystics—the Golden Age, the Silver Age, the
Bronze Age, and the Iron Age—are metaphoric expressions referring to the four
major periods in the life of all things. In the divisions of the day they signify
dawn, midday, sunset, and midnight; in the duration of gods, men, and universes, they denote the periods of birth, growth, maturity, and decay. The Greek
Ages also bear a close correspondence to the four *Yugas* of the Hindus: *Krita-
Yuga, Treta-Yuga, Dvapara-Yuga,* and *Kali-Yuga.* Their method of calculation
is described by Ullamudeian as follows; "In each of the 12 signs there are 1800
minutes; multiply this number by 12 you have 21600; e.g. $1800 \times 12=21600$.
Multiply this 21600 by 80 and it will give 1,728,000, which is the duration of
the first age, called *Krita-Yuga.* If the same number be multiplied by 60, it will
give 1,296,000, the years of the second age, *Treta-Yuga.* The same number multiplied by 40 gives 864,000, the length of the third age, *Dvapara-Yuga.* The
same multiplied by 20 gives 432,000, the fourth age, *Kali-Yuga.*" (It will be
noted that these multipliers decrease in inverse ratio to the Pythagorean tetractys: 1, 2, 3, and 4.)

H. P. Blavatsky declares that Orpheus taught his followers how to affect a
whole audience by means of a lodestone, and that Pythagoras paid particular

attention to the color and nature of precious stones. She adds: "The Buddhists assert that the sapphire produces peace of mind, equanimity, and chases all evil thoughts by establishing a healthy circulation in man. So does an electric battery, with its well-directed fluid, say our electricians. 'The sapphire,' say the Buddhists, 'will open barred doors and dwellings (for the spirit of man); it produces a desire for prayer, and brings with it more peace than any other gem; but he who would wear it must lead a pure and holy life.'" (See *Isis Unveiled.*)

Mythology abounds with accounts of magical rings and talismanic jewels. In the second book of his *Republic,* Plato describes a ring which, when the collet was turned inward, rendered its wearer invisible. With this Gyges, the shepherd, secured for himself the throne of Lydia. Josephus also describes magical rings designed by Moses and King Solomon, and Aristotle mentions one which brought love and honor to its possessor. In his chapter dealing with the subject, Henry Cornelius Agrippa not only mentions the same rings, but states, upon the authority of Philostratus Jarchus, that Apollonius of Tyana extended his life to over 130 years with the aid of seven magical rings presented to him by an East Indian prince.

FROM CARTARI'S *IMAGINI DEGLI DEI DEGLI ANTICHI.*

THE PYTHAGOREAN SIGNET RING.

The number five was peculiarly associated by the Pythagoreans with the art of healing, and the pentagram, or five-pointed star, was to them the symbol of health. The above figure represents a magical ring set with a talismanic gem bearing the *pentalpha,* or star formed by five different positions of the Greek *Alpha.* On this subject Albert Mackey writes: "The disciples of Pythagoras, who were indeed its real inventors, placed within each of its interior angles one of the letters of the Greek word ΥΓΕΙΑ, or the Latin one SALUS, both of which signify *health;* and thus it was made the talisman of health. They placed it at the beginning of their epistles as a greeting to invoke a secure health to their correspondent. But its use was not confined to the disciples of Pythagoras. As a talisman, it was employed all over the East as a charm to resist evil spirits."

Each of these seven rings was set with a gem partaking of the nature of one of the seven ruling planets of the week, and by daily changing the rings Apollonius protected himself against sickness and death by the intervention of the planetary influences. The philosopher also instructed his disciples in the virtues of these talismanic jewels, considering such information to be indispensable to the theurgist. Agrippa describes the preparation of magical rings as follows: "When any Star [Planet] ascends fortunately, with the fortunate aspect or conjunction of the Moon, we must take a stone and herb that is under that Star, and make a ring of the metal that is suitable to this Star, and in it fasten the stone, putting the herb or root under it—not omitting the inscriptions of images, names, and characters, as also the proper suffumigations." (See *Three Books of Occult Philosophy*.)

The ring has long been regarded as the symbol of attainment, perfection, and immortality—the last because the circlet of precious metal had neither beginning nor end. In the Mysteries, rings chased to resemble a serpent with its tail in its mouth were worn by the initiates as material evidence of the position reached by them in the order. Signet rings, engraved with certain secret emblems, were worn by the hierophants, and it was not uncommon for a messenger to prove that he was the official representative of a prince or other dignitary by bringing with his message either an impression from his master's ring or the signet itself. The wedding ring originally was intended to imply that in the nature of the one who wore it the state of equilibrium and completion had been attained. This plain band of gold therefore bore witness of the union of the Higher Self (God) with the lower self (Nature) and the ceremony consummating this indissoluble blending of Divinity and humanity in the one nature of the initiated mystic constituted the *hermetic marriage* of the Mysteries.

In describing the regalia of a magician, Eliphas Levi declares that on Sunday (the day of the sun) he should carry in his right hand a golden wand, set with a ruby or chrysolite; on Monday (the day of the moon) he should wear a collar of three strands consisting of pearls, crystals, and selenites; on Tuesday (the day of Mars) he should carry a wand of magnetized steel and a ring of the same metal set with an amethyst; on Wednesday (the day of Mercury) he should wear a necklace of pearls or glass beads containing mercury, and a ring set with an agate; on Thursday (the day of Jupiter) he should carry a wand of glass or resin and wear a ring set with an emerald or a sapphire; on Friday (the day of Venus) he should carry a wand of polished copper and wear a ring set with a turquoise and a crown or diadem decorated with lapis lazuli and beryl; and on Saturday (the day of Saturn) he should carry a wand ornamented with onyx stone and wear a ring set with onyx and a chain about the neck formed of lead. (See *The Magical Ritual of the Sanctum Regnum*.)

Paracelsus, Agrippa, Kircher, Lilly, and numerous other magicians and astrologers have tabulated the gems and stones corresponding to the various planets and zodiacal signs. The following list has been compiled from their writings. To the sun is assigned the carbuncle, ruby, garnet—especially the pyrope—and other fiery stones, sometimes the diamond; to the moon, the pearl, selenite, and other forms of crystal; to Saturn, the onyx, jasper, topaz, and sometimes the lapis lazuli; to Jupiter, the sapphire, emerald, and marble; to Mars, the amethyst, hyacinth, lodestone, sometimes the diamond; to Venus, the turquoise, beryl, emerald, and sometimes the pearl, alabaster, coral, and carnelian; to Mercury, the chrysolite, agate, and variegated marble.

To the zodiac the same authorities assigned the following gems and stones: To Aries the sardonyx, bloodstone, amethyst, and diamond; to Taurus the carnelian, turquoise, hyacinth, sapphire, moss agate, and emerald; to Gemini the topaz, agate, chrysoprase, crystal, and aquamarine; to Cancer the topaz, chalcedony, black onyx, moonstone, pearl, cat's-eye, crystal, and sometimes the emerald; to Leo the jasper, sardonyx, beryl, ruby, chrysolite, amber, tourmaline, sometimes the diamond; to Virgo the emerald, carnelian, jade, chrysolite, and sometimes the pink jasper and hyacinth; to Libra, the beryl, sardius, coral, lapis lazuli, opal, and sometimes the diamond; to Scorpio the amethyst, beryl, sardonyx, aquamarine, carbuncle, lodestone, topaz, and malachite; to Sagittarius the hyacinth, topaz, chrysolite, emerald, carbuncle, and turquoise; to Capricorn the chrysoprase, ruby, malachite, black onyx, white onyx, jet, and moonstone; to Aquarius the crystal, sapphire, garnet, zircon, and opal; to Pisces the sapphire, jasper, chrysolite, moonstone, and amethyst.

Both the magic mirror and the crystal ball are symbols little understood. Woe to that benighted mortal who accepts literally the stories circulated concerning them! He will discover—often at the cost of sanity and health—that sorcery and philosophy, while often confused, have nothing in common. The Persian Magi carried mirrors as an emblem of the material sphere which reflects Divinity from its every part. The crystal ball, long misused as a medium for the cultivation of psychical powers, is a threefold symbol: (1) it signifies the crystalline *Universal Egg* in whose transparent depths creation exists; (2) it is a proper figure of Deity previous to Its immersion in matter; (3) it signifies the ætheric sphere of the world in whose translucent essences is impressed and preserved the perfect image of all terrestrial activity.

Meteors, or *rocks from heaven*, were considered tokens of divine favor and enshrined as evidence of a pact between the gods and the community in which they fell. Curiously marked or chipped natural stones are occasionally found. In China there is a slab of marble the grain of which forms a perfect likeness of the Chinese dragon. The Oberammergau stone, chipped by Nature into a close resemblance to the popular conception of the face of Christ, is so remarkable that even the crowned heads of Europe requested the privilege of beholding it. Stones of such nature were held in the highest esteem among primitive peoples and even today exert a wide influence upon the religiously-minded.

XXII

Ceremonial Magic
and Sorcery

eremonial magic is the ancient art of invoking and control-
ling spirits by a scientific application of certain formulæ. A
magician, enveloped in sanctified vestments and carrying a
wand inscribed with hieroglyphic figures, could by the
power vested in certain words and symbols control the
invisible inhabitants of the elements and of the astral world. While the elaborate
ceremonial magic of antiquity was not necessarily evil, there arose from its perversion several false schools of sorcery, or *black magic*.

Egypt, a great center of learning and the birthplace of many arts and sciences, furnished an ideal environment for transcendental experimentation.
Here the black magicians of Atlantis continued to exercise their superhuman
powers until they had completely undermined and corrupted the morals of the
primitive Mysteries. By establishing a sacerdotal caste they usurped the position
formerly occupied by the initiates, and seized the reins of spiritual government.
Thus black magic dictated the state religion and paralyzed the intellectual and
spiritual activities of the individual by demanding his complete and unhesitat-
ing acquiescence in the dogma formulated by the priestcraft. The Pharaoh
became a puppet in the hands of the Scarlet Council—a committee of archsor-
cerers elevated to power by the priesthood.

These sorcerers then began the systematic destruction of all keys to the
ancient wisdom, so that none might have access to the knowledge necessary to
reach adeptship without first becoming one of their order. They mutilated the
rituals of the Mysteries while professing to preserve them, so that even though
the neophyte passed through the degrees he could not secure the knowledge to
which he was entitled. Idolatry was introduced by encouraging the worship of

FROM LEVI'S *TRANSCENDENTAL MAGIC*.

BAPHOMET, THE GOAT OF MENDES.

The practice of magic—either *white* or *black*—depends upon the ability of the adept to control the universal life force—that which Eliphas Levi calls the *great magical agent* or the *astral light*. By the manipulation of this fluidic essence the phenomena of transcendentalism are produced. The famous hermaphroditic Goat of Mendes was a composite creature formulated to symbolize this *astral light*. It is identical with Baphomet, the mystic *pantheos* of those disciples of ceremonial magic, the Templars, who probably obtained it from the Arabians.

the images which in the beginning the wise had erected solely as symbols for study and meditation. False interpretations were given to the emblems and figures of the Mysteries, and elaborate theologies were created to confuse the minds of their devotees. The masses, deprived of their birthright of understanding and groveling in ignorance, eventually became the abject slaves of the spiritual impostors. Superstition universally prevailed and the black magicians completely dominated national affairs, with the result that humanity still suffers from the sophistries of the priestcrafts of Atlantis and Egypt.

Fully convinced that their Scriptures sanctioned it, numerous mediæval Qabbalists devoted their lives to the practice of ceremonial magic. The transcendentalism of the Qabbalists is founded upon the ancient and magical formula of King Solomon, who has long been considered by the Jews as the prince of ceremonial magicians.

Among the Qabbalists of the Middle Ages were a great number of black magicians who strayed from the noble concepts of the *Sepher Yetzirah* and became enmeshed in demonism and witchcraft. They sought to substitute magic mirrors, consecrated daggers, and circles spread around posts of coffin nails, for the living of that virtuous life which, without the assistance of complicated rituals or submundane creatures, unfailingly brings man to the state of true individual completion.

Those who sought to control elemental spirits through ceremonial magic did so largely with the hope of securing from the invisible worlds either rare knowledge or supernatural power. The little red demon of Napoleon Bonaparte and the infamous oracular heads of de Medici are examples of the disastrous results of permitting elemental beings to dictate the course of human procedure. While the learned and godlike dæmon of Socrates seems to have been an exception, this really proves that the intellectual and moral status of the magician has much to do with the type of elemental he is capable of invoking. But even the dæmon of Socrates deserted the philosopher when the sentence of death was passed.

Transcendentalism and all forms of phenomenalistic magic are but blind alleys—outgrowths of Atlantean sorcery; and those who forsake the straight path of philosophy to wander therein almost invariably fall victims to their imprudence. Man, incapable of controlling his own appetites, is not equal to the task of governing the fiery and tempestuous elemental spirits.

Many a magician has lost his life as the result of opening a way whereby submundane creatures could become active participants in his affairs. When Eliphas Levi invoked the spirit of Apollonius of Tyana, what did he hope to accomplish? Is the gratification of curiosity a motive sufficient to warrant the devotion of an entire lifetime to a dangerous and unprofitable pursuit? If the living Apollonius refused to divulge his secrets to the profane, is there any probability that after death he would disclose them to the curious-minded? Levi himself did not dare to assert that the specter which appeared to him was actually the great philosopher, for Levi realized only too well the proclivity of elementals to impersonate those who have passed on. The majority of modern mediumistic apparitions are but elemental creatures masquerading through bodies composed of thought substance supplied by the very persons desiring to behold these wraiths of decarnate beings.

The Theory and Practice of Black Magic

Some understanding of the intricate theory and practice of ceremonial magic may be derived from a brief consideration of its underlying premises.

First. The visible universe has an invisible counterpart, the higher planes of which are peopled by good and beautiful spirits; the lower planes, dark and foreboding, are the habitation of evil spirits and demons under the leadership of the Fallen Angel and his ten Princes.

Second. By means of the secret processes of ceremonial magic it is possible to contact these invisible creatures and gain their help in some human undertaking. Good spirits willingly lend their assistance to any worthy enterprise, but the evil spirits serve only those who live to pervert and destroy.

Third. It is possible to make contracts with spirits whereby the magician becomes for a stipulated time the master of an elemental being.

Fourth. True black magic is performed with the aid of a demoniacal spirit, who serves the sorcerer for the length of his earthly life, with the understanding that after death the magician shall become the servant of his own demon. For this reason a black magician will go to inconceivable ends to prolong his physical life, since there is nothing for him beyond the grave.

The most dangerous form of black magic is the scientific perversion of occult power for the gratification of personal desire. Its less complex and more universal form is human selfishness, for selfishness is the fundamental cause of all worldly evil. A man will barter his eternal soul for temporal power, and down through the ages a mysterious process has been evolved which actually enables him to make this exchange. In its various branches the black art includes nearly all forms of ceremonial magic, necromancy, witchcraft, sorcery, and vampirism. Under the same general heading are also included mesmerism and hypnotism, except when used solely for medical purposes, and even then there is an element of risk for all concerned.

Though the demonism of the Middle Ages seems to have disappeared, there is abundant evidence that in many forms of modern thought—especially the so-called "prosperity" psychology, "will-power-building" metaphysics, and systems of "high-pressure" salesmanship—black magic has merely passed through a metamorphosis, and although its name be changed its nature remains the same.

A well-known magician of the Middle Ages was Dr. Johannes Faustus, more commonly known as Dr. Faust. By a study of magical writings he was enabled to bind to his service an elemental who served him for many years in various capacities. Strange legends are told concerning the magical powers possessed by Dr. Faust. Upon one occasion the philosopher, being apparently in a playful mood, threw his mantle over a number of eggs in a market-woman's basket, causing them to hatch instantly. At another time, having fallen overboard from a small boat, he was picked up and returned to the craft with his clothes still dry. But, like nearly all other magicians, Dr. Faust came at length to disaster; he was found one morning with a knife in his back, and it was commonly believed that his familiar spirit had murdered him. Although Goethe's Dr. Faust is generally regarded as merely a fictional character, this old magician actually lived during the sixteenth century. Dr. Faust wrote a book describing his experiences with spirits, a section of which is reprinted below. (Dr. Faust must not be confused with Johann Fust, the printer.)

Extract from the Book of Dr. Faust, Wittenberg, 1524

(An abridged translation from the original German of a book ordered destroyed.)

"From my youth I followed art and science and was tireless in my reading of books. Among those which came to my hand was a volume containing all kinds of invocations and magical formulæ. In this book I discovered information to the effect that a spirit, whether he be of the fire, the water, the earth or the air, can be compelled to do the will of a magician capable of controlling him. I also discovered that according as one spirit has more power than another, each is adapted for a different operation and each is capable of producing certain supernatural effects.

"After reading this wonderful book, I made several experiments, desiring to test the accuracy of the statements made therein. At first I had little faith that what was promised would take place. But at the very first invocation which I attempted a mighty spirit manifested to me, desiring to know why I had invoked him. His coming so amazed me that I scarcely knew what to say, but finally asked him if he would serve me in my magical investigations. He replied that if certain conditions were agreed upon he would. The conditions were that I should make a pact with him. This I did not desire to do, but as in my ignorance I had not protected myself with a circle and was actually at the mercy of the spirit, I did not dare to refuse his request and resigned myself to the inevitable, considering it wisest to turn my mantle according to the wind.

"I then told him that if he would be serviceable to me according to my desires and needs for a certain length of time, I would sign myself over to him.

After the pact had been arranged, this mighty spirit, whose name was *Asteroth,* introduced me to another spirit by the name of *Marbuel,* who was appointed to be my servant. I questioned *Marbuel* as to his suitability for my needs. I asked him how quick he was, and he answered, 'As swift as the winds.' This did not satisfy me, so I replied, 'You cannot become my servant. Go again whence you have come.' Soon another spirit manifested itself, whose name was *Aniguel.* Upon asking him the same question he answered that he was swift as a bird in the air, I said, 'You are still too slow for me. Go whence you came.' In the same moment another spirit by the name of *Aciel* manifested himself. For the third time I asked my question and he answered, 'I am as swift as human thought.' 'You shall serve me,' I replied. This spirit was faithful for a long time, but to tell you how he served me is not possible in a document of this length and I will here only indicate how spirits are to be invoked and how the circles for protection are to be prepared. There are many kinds of spirits which will permit themselves to be invoked by man and become his servant. Of these I will list a few:

FROM *THE COMPLETE BOOK OF MAGIC SCIENCE* (UNPUBLISHED).

A MAGIC CIRCLE.

The above figure is a complete and faithful representation of a magic circle as designed by mediæval conjurers for the invocation of spirits. The magician accompanied by his assistant takes his place at the point formed by the crossing of the central lines marked MAGISTER. The words about the circle are the names of the invisible intelligences, and the small crosses mark points at which certain prayers and invocations are recited. The small circle outside is prepared for the spirit to be invoked, and while in use has the signature of the desired intelligence traced within the triangle.

"*Aciel:* The mightiest among those who serve men. He manifests in pleasing human form about three feet high. He must be invoked three times before he will come forth into the circle prepared for him. He will furnish riches and will instantly fetch things from a great distance, according to the will of the magician. He is as swift as human thought.

"*Aniguel:* Serviceable and most useful, and comes in the form of a ten-year-old boy. He must be invoked three times. His special power is to discover treasures and minerals hidden in the ground, which he will furnish to the magician.

"*Marbuel:* A true lord of the mountains and swift as a bird on the wing. He is an opposing and troublesome spirit, hard to control. You must invoke him four times. He appears in the person of Mars [a warrior in heavy armor]. He will furnish the magician those things which grow above and under the earth. He is particularly the lord of the *spring-root.* [The *spring-root* is a mysterious herb, possibly of a reddish color, which mediæval magicians asserted had the property of drawing forth or opening anything it touched. If placed against a locked door, it would open the door. The Hermetists believed that the red-capped woodpecker was specially endowed with the faculty of discovering *spring-root,* so they followed this bird to its nest, and then stopped up the hole in the tree where its young were. The red-crested woodpecker went at once in quest of the *spring-root,* and, discovering it, brought it to the tree. It immediately drew forth the stopper from the entrance to the nest. The magician then secured the root from the bird. It was also asserted that because of its structure, the etheric body of the *spring-root* was utilized as a vehicle of expression by certain elemental spirits which manifested through the proclivity of drawing out or opening things.]

"*Aciebel:* A mighty ruler of the sea, controlling things both upon and under the water. He furnishes things lost or sunk in rivers, lakes, and oceans, such as sunken ships and treasures. The more sharply you invoke him, the swifter he is upon his errands.

"*Machiel:* Comes in the form of a beautiful maiden and by her aid the magician is raised to honor and dignity. She makes those she serves worthy and noble, gracious and kindly, and assists in all matters of litigation and justice. She will not come unless invoked twice.

"*Baruel:* The master of all arts. He manifests as a master workman and comes wearing an apron. He can teach a magician more in a moment than all the master workmen of the world combined could accomplish in twenty years. He must be invoked three times.

"These are the spirits most serviceable to man, but there are numerous others which, for lack of space, I am unable to describe. Now, if you desire the aid of the spirit to get this or that, then you must first draw the sign of the spirit whom you desire to invoke. The drawing must be made just in front of a circle made before sunrise, in which you and your assistants will stand. If you desire financial assistance, then you must invoke the spirit *Aciel.* Draw his sign in front of the circle. If you need other things, then draw the sign of the spirit capable of furnishing them. On the place where you intend to make the circle, you must first draw a great cross with a large sword with which no one ever has been hurt.

Then you must make three concentric circles. The innermost circle is made of a long narrow strip of virgin parchment and must be hung upon twelve crosses made of the wood of *cross-thorn.* Upon the parchment you must write the names and symbols according to the figure which follows. Outside this first circle make the second as follows:

"First secure a thread of red silk that has been spun or twisted to the left instead of the right. Then place in the ground twelve crosses made of laurel leaves, and also prepare a long strip of new white paper. Write with an unused pen the characters and symbols as seen on the second circle. Wind this latter strip of paper around with the red silken thread and pin them upon the twelve crosses of laurel leaves. Outside this second circle make a third one which is also of virgin parchment and pinned upon twelve crosses of consecrated palm. When you have made these three circles, retire into them until at last you stand in the center upon a pentagram drawn in the midst of the great cross first drawn. Now, to insure success, do everything according to the description, and when you have read off the sacred invocation pronounce the name of the spirit which you desire to appear. It is essential that you pronounce the name very distinctly. You must also note the day and the hour, for each spirit can only be invoked at certain times."

While the black magician at the time of signing his pact with the elemental demon may be fully convinced that he is strong enough to control indefinitely the powers placed at his disposal, he is speedily undeceived. Before many years elapse he must turn all his energies to the problem of self-preservation. A world of horrors to which he has attuned himself by his own covetousness looms nearer every day, until he exists upon the edge of a seething maelstrom, expecting momentarily to be sucked down into its turbid depths. Afraid to die— because he will become the servant of his own demon—the magician commits crime after crime to prolong his wretched earthly existence. Realizing that life is maintained by the aid of a mysterious universal life force which is the common property of all creatures, the black magician often becomes an occult vampire, stealing this energy from others. According to mediæval superstition, black magicians turned themselves into werewolves and roamed the earth at night, attacking defenseless victims for the life force contained in their blood.

Modus Operandi for the Invocation of Spirits

The following condensed extract from an ancient manuscript is reproduced herewith as representative of the ritualism of ceremonial magic. The extract is from *The Complete Book of Magic Science,* an unpublished manuscript (original in the British Museum), with pentacles in colors, mentioned by Francis Barrett in his *Magus.*

"OPENING PRAYER

"Omnipotent and Eternal God who hath ordained the whole creation for thy praise and glory and for the salvation of man, I earnestly beseech thee that thou wouldst send one of thy spirits of the order of Jupiter, one of the messengers of *Zadkiel* whom thou hast appointed governor of thy firmament at the present time, most faithfully, willingly, and readily to show me these things which I shall ask, command or require of him, and truly execute my desires. Nevertheless, O Most Holy God, thy will and not mine be done through JC, thine only begotten Son our Lord. Amen.

FROM LEVI'S *TRANSCENDENTAL MAGIC.*

THE PENTAGRAM.

The pentagram is the figure of the microcosm— the magical formula of man. It is the one rising out of the four—the human soul rising from the bondage of the animal nature. It is the true light—the "Star of the morning." It marks the location of five mysterious centers of force, the awakening of which is the supreme secret of white magic.

"THE INVOCATION.

[The magician, having properly consecrated his vestments and utensils and being protected by his circle, now calls upon the spirits to appear and accede to his demands.]

"Spirits, whose assistance I require, behold the sign and the very Hallowed Names of God full of power. Obey the power of this our pentacle; go out your hidden caves and dark places; cease your hurtful occupations to those unhappy mortals whom without ceasing you torment; come into this place where the Divine Goodness has assembled us; be attentive to our orders and known to our just demands; believe not that your resistance will cause us to abandon our operations. Nothing can dispense with your obeying us. We command you by the Mysterious Names *Elohe Agla Elohim Adonay Gibort.* Amen.

"I call upon thee, *Zadkiel,* in the Name of the Father, and of the Son, and of the Holy Ghost, blessed Trinity, unspeakable Unity.

"I invoke and intreat thee, *Zadkiel,* in this hour to attend to the words and conjurations which I shall use this day by the Holy Names of God *Elohe El Elohim Elion Zebaoth Escerehie lah Adonay Tetragrammaton.*

"I conjure thee, I exorcise thee, thou Spirit *Zadkiel,* by these Holy Names *Hagios O Theos Iscyros Athanatos Paracletus Agla on Alpha et Omega Ioth Aglan-*

broth Abiel Anathiel Tetragrammaton: And by all other great and glorious, holy and unspeakable, mysterious, mighty, powerful, incomprehensible Names of God, that you attend unto the words of my mouth, and send unto me *Pabiel* or other of your ministering, serving Spirits, who may show me such things as I shall demand of him in the Name of the Father, and of the Son, and of the Holy Ghost. Amen.

"I intreat thee, *Pabiel,* by the whole Spirit of Heaven, Seraphim, Cherubim, Thrones, Dominations, Witnesses, Powers, Principalities, Archangels, and Angels, by the holy, great, and glorious Angels *Orphaniel Tetra-Dagiel Salamla Acimoy pastor poti,* that thou come forthwith, readily show thyself that we may see you and audibly hear you, speak unto us and fulfil our desires, and by your star which is Jupiter, and by all the constellations of Heaven, and by whatsoever you obey, and by your character which you have given, proposed, and confirmed, that you attend unto me according to the prayer and petitions which I have made unto Almighty God, and that you forthwith send me one of your ministering Spirits, who may willingly, truly, and faithfully fulfil all my desires, and that you command him to appear unto me in the form of a beautiful Angel, gently, courteously, affably, and meekly, entering into communication with me, and that he neither permitting any evil Spirit to approach in any sort of hurt, terrify or affright me in any way nor deceiving me in any wise. Through the virtue of Our Lord JC, in whose Name I attend, wait for, and expect thy appearance. Fiat, fiat, fiat. Amen, Amen, Amen.

"INTERROGATORIES.

[Having summoned the spirit unto his presence, the magician shall question him as follows:]

"'Comest thou in peace in the Name of the Father and of the Son and of the Holy Ghost?' [And the spirit shall answer:] 'Yes.'

"'Thou art welcome, noble Spirit. What is thy Name?' [And the spirit shall answer:] *'Pabiel.'*

"'I have called thee in the Name of Jesus of Nazareth at whose Name every knee doth bow in heaven, earth, and hell, and every tongue shall confess there is no name like unto the Name of Jesus, who hath given power unto man to bind and to loose all things in his most Holy Name, yea even unto those that trust in his salvation.

"'Art thou the messenger of Zadkiel?' [And the spirit shall answer:] 'Yes.'

"'Wilt thou confirm thyself unto me at this time and henceforth reveal all things unto me that I shall desire to know, and teach me how I may increase in wisdom and knowledge and show unto me all the secrets of the Magic Art, and of all liberal sciences, that I may thereby set forth the glory of Almighty God?' [And the spirit shall answer:] 'Yes.'

"'Then I pray thee give and confirm thy character unto me whereby I may call thee at all times, and also swear unto me this oath and I will religiously keep my vow and covenant unto Almighty God and will courteously receive thee at all times where thou dost appear unto me.'

"LICENSE TO DEPART.

"'Forasmuch as thou comest in peace and quietness and hath answered unto my petitions, I give humble and hearty thanks unto Almighty God in whose Name I called and thou camest, and now thou mayest depart in peace unto thine orders and return unto me again at what time soever I shall call thee by thine oath, or by thy name or by thine order, or by thine office which is granted thee from the Creator, and the power of God be with me and thee and upon the whole issue of God, Amen.

"'Glory be to the Father, and to the Son, and to the Holy Ghost.'

[Note.] "It would be advisable for the invocant to remain in the circle for a few minutes after reciting the license, and if the place of operation be in the open air, let him destroy all traces of the circle, et cetera, and return quietly to his home. But should the operation be performed in a retired part of a house, et cetera, the circle may remain, as it might serve in a like future operation, but the room or building must be locked up to avoid the intrusion of strangers."

The agreement set forth above is purely ceremonial magic. In the case of black magic, it is the magician and not the demon who must sign the pact. When the black magician binds an elemental to his service, a battle of wits ensues, which the demon eventually wins. With his own blood the magician signs the pact between himself and the demon, for in the arcanum of magic it is declared that "he controls the soul who controls the blood of another." As long as the magician does not fail, the elemental will fulfil to the letter his obligation under the pact, but the demon will try in every possible way to prevent the magician from carrying out his part of the contract. When the conjurer, ensconced within his circle, has evoked the spirit he desires to control and has made known his intention, the spirit will answer somewhat as follows: "I cannot accede to your request nor fulfil it, unless after fifty years, you give yourself to me, body and soul, to do with as I may please."

If the magician refuses, other terms will be discussed. The spirit may say: "I will remain in your service as long as on every Friday morning you will go forth upon the public street giving alms in the name of Lucifer. The first time you fail in this you belong to me."

If the magician still refuses, realizing that the demon will make it impossible for him to fulfil his contract, other terms will be discussed, until at last a pact is agreed upon. It may read as follows: "I hereby promise the Great Spirit Lucifuge, Prince of Demons, that each year I will bring unto him a human soul to do with as it may please him, and in return Lucifuge promises to bestow upon me the treasures of the earth and fulfil my every desire for the length of my natural life. If I fail to bring him each year the offering specified above, then my own soul shall be forfeit to him. Signed . . . ." [Invocant signs pact with his own blood.]

The Pentagram

In symbolism, an inverted figure always signifies a perverted power. The average person does not even suspect the occult properties of emblematic pentacles. On this subject the great Paracelsus has written: "No doubt many will scoff at the seals, their characters and their uses, which are described in these books, because it seems incredible to them that metals and characters which are dead should have any effect. Yet no one has ever proved that the metals and also the characters as we know them are dead, for the salts, sulphur, and quintessences of metals are the highest preservatives of human life and are far superior to all other simples." (Translated from the original German.)

The black magician cannot use the symbols of white magic without bringing down upon himself the forces of white magic, which would be fatal to his schemes. He must therefore distort the hierograms so that they typify the occult fact that he himself is distorting the principles for which the symbols stand. Black magic is not a fundamental art; it is the misuse of an art. Therefore it has no symbols of its own. It merely takes the emblematic figures of white magic, and by inverting and reversing them signifies that it is left-handed.

A good instance of this practice is found in the pentagram or five-pointed star, made of five connected lines. This figure is the time-honored symbol of the magical arts, and signifies the five properties of the Great Magical Agent, the five senses of man, the five elements of nature, the five extremities of the human body. By means of the pentagram within his own soul, man not only may master and govern all creatures inferior to himself, but may demand consideration at the hands of those superior to himself.

The pentagram is used extensively in black magic, but when so used its form always differs in one of three ways: The star may be broken at one point by not permitting the converging lines to touch; it may be inverted by having one point down and two up; or it may be distorted by having the points of varying lengths. When used in black magic, the pentagram is called the "sign of the cloven hoof," or the footprint of the Devil. The star with two points upward is also called the "Goat of Mendes," because the inverted star is the same shape as a goat's head. When the upright star turns and the upper point falls to the bottom, it signifies the fall of the Morning Star.

XXIII

The Elements and Their Inhabitants

For the most comprehensive and lucid exposition of occult pneumatology (the branch of philosophy dealing with spiritual substances) extant, mankind is indebted to Philippus Aureolus Paracelsus (Theophrastus Bombastus von Hohenheim), prince of alchemists and Hermetic philosophers and true possessor of the *Royal Secret* (the Philosopher's Stone and the Elixir of Life). Paracelsus believed that each of the four primary elements known to the ancients (earth, fire, air, and water) consisted of a subtle, vaporous principle and a gross corporeal substance.

Air is, therefore, twofold in nature—tangible atmosphere and an intangible, volatile substratum which may be termed *spiritual air*. Fire is visible and invisible, discernible and indiscernible—a spiritual, ethereal flame manifesting through a material, substantial flame. Carrying the analogy further, water consists of a dense fluid and a potential essence of a fluidic nature. Earth has likewise two essential parts—the lower being fixed, terreous, immobile; the higher, rarefied, mobile, and virtual. The general term *elements* has been applied to the lower, or physical, phases of these four primary principles, and the name *elemental essences* to their corresponding invisible, spiritual constitutions. Minerals, plants, animals, and men live in a world composed of the gross side of these four elements, and from various combinations of them construct their living organisms.

Henry Drummond, in *Natural Law in the Spiritual World,* describes this process as follows: "If we analyse this material point at which all life starts, we shall find it to consist of a clear structureless, jelly-like substance resembling albumen or white of egg. It is made of Carbon, Hydrogen, Oxygen and Nitro-

gen. Its name is protoplasm. And it is
not only the structural unit with which
all living bodies start in life, but with
which they are subsequently built up.
'Protoplasm,' says Huxley, 'simple or
nucleated, is the formal basis of all life.
It is the clay of the Potter.'"

The *water* element of the ancient
philosophers has been metamorphosed into the hydrogen of modern
science; the *air* has become oxygen;
the *fire,* nitrogen; the *earth,* carbon.

Just as visible Nature is populated
by an infinite number of living creatures, so, according to Paracelsus, the
invisible, spiritual counterpart of visible Nature (composed of the tenuous
principles of the visible elements) is
inhabited by a host of peculiar beings,
to whom he has given the name *elementals,* and which have later been

FROM PARCELSUS' *AUSLEGUNG VON 30 MAGISCHEN FIGUREN.*

A SALAMANDER, ACCORDING TO PARACELSUS.

The Egyptians, Chaldeans, and Persians often mistook the salamanders for gods, because of their radiant splendor and great power. The
Greeks, following the example of earlier nations, deified the fire spirits and in their honor kept incense and altar fires burning perpetually.

termed the Nature spirits. Paracelsus divided these people of the elements into
four distinct groups, which he called *gnomes, undines, sylphs,* and *salamanders.*
He taught that they were really living entities, many resembling human beings in
shape, and inhabiting worlds of their own, unknown to man because his undeveloped senses were incapable of functioning beyond the limitations of the
grosser elements.

The civilizations of Greece, Rome, Egypt, China, and India believed
implicitly in satyrs, sprites, and goblins. They peopled the sea with mermaids,
the rivers and fountains with nymphs, the air with fairies, the fire with Lares and
Penates, and the earth with fauns, dryads, and hamadryads. These Nature spirits were held in the highest esteem, and propitiatory offerings were made to
them. Occasionally, as the result of atmospheric conditions or the peculiar sensitiveness of the devotee, they became visible. Many authors wrote concerning
them in terms which signify that they had actually beheld these inhabitants of
Nature's finer realms. A number of authorities are of the opinion that many of
the gods worshiped by the pagans were elementals, for some of these *invisibles*
were believed to be of commanding stature and magnificent deportment.

The Greeks gave the name *dæmon* to some of these elementals, especially those of the higher orders, and worshiped them. Probably the most famous of these *dæmons* is the mysterious spirit which instructed Socrates, and of whom that great philosopher spoke in the highest terms. Those who have devoted much study to the invisible constitution of man realize that it is quite probable the dæmon of Socrates and the angel of Jakob Böhme were in reality not elementals, but the overshadowing divine natures of these philosophers themselves. In his notes to *Apuleius on the God of Socrates,* Thomas Taylor says:

"As the dæmon of Socrates, therefore, was doubtless one of the highest order, as may be inferred from the intellectual superiority of Socrates to most other men, Apuleius is justified in calling this dæmon a God. And that the dæmon of Socrates indeed was divine, is evident from the testimony of Socrates himself in the First Alcibiades: for in the course of that dialogue he clearly says, 'I have long been of the opinion that the God did not as yet direct me to hold any conversation with you.' And in the Apology he most unequivocally evinces that this dæmon is allotted a divine transcendency, considered as ranking in the order of dæmons."

The idea once held, that the invisible elements surrounding and interpenetrating the earth were peopled with living, intelligent beings, may seem ridiculous to the prosaic mind of today. This doctrine, however, has found favor with some of the greatest intellects of the world. The sylphs of Facius Cardan, the philosopher of Milan; the salamander seen by Benvenuto Cellini; the pan of St. Anthony; and *le petit homme rouge* (the little red man, or gnome) of Napoleon Bonaparte, have found their places in the pages of history.

Literature has also perpetuated the concept of Nature spirits. The mischievous Puck of Shakespeare's *Midsummer Night's Dream;* the elementals of Alexander Pope's Rosicrucian poem, *The Rape of the Lock;* the mysterious creatures of Lord Lytton's *Zanoni;* James Barrie's immortal Tinker Bell; and the famous bowlers that Rip Van Winkle encountered in the Catskill Mountains, are well-known characters to students of literature. The folklore and mythology of all peoples abound in legends concerning these mysterious little figures who haunt old castles, guard treasures in the depths of the earth, and build their homes under the spreading protection of toadstools. Fairies are the delight of childhood, and most children give them up with reluctance. Not so very long ago the greatest minds of the world believed in the existence of fairies, and it is still an open question as to whether Plato, Socrates, and Iamblichus were wrong when they avowed their reality.

Paracelsus, when describing the substances which constitute the bodies of the elementals, divided flesh into two kinds, the first being that which we have all inherited through Adam. This is the visible, corporeal flesh. The second was that flesh which had not descended from Adam and, being more attenuated, was not subject to the limitations of the former. The bodies of the elementals were composed of this transubstantial flesh. Paracelsus stated that there is as much difference between the bodies of men and the bodies of the Nature spirits as there is between matter and spirit.

"Yet," he adds, "the Elementals are not spirits, because they have flesh, blood and bones; they live and propagate offspring; they eat and talk, act and sleep, &c., and consequently they cannot be properly called 'spirits.' They are beings occupying a place between men and spirits, resembling men and spirits, resembling men and women in their organization and form, and resembling spirits in the rapidity of their locomotion." (*Philosophia Occulta,* translated by Franz Hartmann.) Later the same author calls these creatures *composita,* inasmuch as the substance out of which they are composed seems to be a composite of spirit and matter. He uses color to explain the idea. Thus, the mixture of blue and red gives purple, a new color, resembling neither of the others yet composed of both. Such is the case with the Nature spirits; they resemble neither spiritual creatures nor material beings, yet are composed of the substance which we may call *spiritual matter,* or ether.

Paracelsus further adds that whereas man is composed of several natures (spirit, soul, mind, and body) combined in one unit, the elemental has but one *principle,* the ether out of which it is composed and in which it lives. The reader must remember that by *ether* is meant the spiritual essence of one of the four elements. There are as many ethers as there are elements and as many distinct families of Nature spirits as there are ethers. These families are completely isolated in their own ether and have no intercourse with the denizens of the other ethers; but, as man has within his own nature centers of consciousness sensitive to the impulses of *all* the four ethers, it is possible for any of the elemental kingdoms to communicate with him under proper conditions.

The Nature spirits cannot be destroyed by the grosser elements, such as material fire, earth, air, or water, for they function in a rate of vibration higher than that of earthy substances. Being composed of only one element or principle (the ether in which they function), they have no immortal spirit and at death merely disintegrate back into the element from which they were originally individualized. No individual consciousness is preserved after death, for there is no superior vehicle present to contain it. Being made of but one substance, there is no friction between vehicles: thus there is little wear or tear incurred by their bodily functions, and they therefore live to great age. Those composed of earth ether are the shortest lived; those composed of air ether, the longest. The average length of life is between three hundred and a thousand years. Paracelsus maintained that they live in conditions similar to our earth environments, and are somewhat subject to disease. These creatures are thought to be incapable of spiritual development, but most of them are of a high moral character.

Concerning the elemental ethers in which the Nature spirits exist, Paracelsus wrote: "They live in the four elements: the Nymphæ in the element of water, the Sylphes in that of the air, the Pigmies in the earth, and the Salamanders in fire. They are also called Undinæ, Sylvestres, Gnomi, Vulcani, &c. Each species moves only in the element to which it belongs, and neither of them can go out of its appropriate element, which is to them as the air is to us, or the water to fishes; and none of them can live in the element belonging to another class. To each elemental being the element in which it lives is transparent, invisible and respirable, as the atmosphere is to ourselves." (*Philosophia Occulta,* translated by Franz Hartmann.)

The reader should be careful not to confuse the Nature spirits with the true life waves evolving through the invisible worlds. While the elementals are composed of only one etheric (or atomic) essence, the angels, archangels, and other superior, transcendental entities have composite organisms, consisting of a spiritual nature and a chain of vehicles to express that nature not unlike those of men, but not including the physical body with its attendant limitations.

To the philosophy of Nature spirits is generally attributed an Eastern origin, probably Brahmanic; and Paracelsus secured his knowledge of them from Oriental sages with whom he came in contact during his lifetime of philosophical wanderings. The Egyptians and Greeks gleaned their information from the same source. The four main divisions of Nature spirits must now be considered separately, according to the teachings of Paracelsus and the Abbé de Villars and such scanty writings of other authors as are available.

The Gnomes

The elementals who dwell in that attenuated body of the earth which is called the terrreous ether are grouped together under the general heading of *gnomes.* (The name is probably derived from the Greek *genomus,* meaning earth dweller. See *New English Dictionary.*)

Just as there are many types of human beings evolving through the objective physical elements of Nature, so there are many types of gnomes evolving through the subjective ethereal body of Nature. These earth spirits work in an element so close in vibratory rate to the material earth that they have immense power over its rocks and flora, and also over the mineral elements in the animal and human kingdoms. Some, like the pygmies, work with the stones, gems, and metals, and are supposed to be the guardians of hidden treasures. They live in caves, far down in what the Scandinavians called the Land of the Nibelungen. In Wagner's wonderful opera cycle, The *Ring of the Nibelungen,* Alberich makes himself King of the Pygmies and forces these little creatures to gather for him the treasures concealed beneath the surface of the earth.

CONVENTIONAL GNOMES.

The type of gnome most frequently seen is the brownie, or elf, a mischievous and grotesque little creature from twelve to eighteen inches high, usually dressed in green or russet brown. Most of them appear as very aged, often with long white beards, and their figures are inclined to rotundity. They can be seen scampering out of holes in the stumps of trees and sometimes they vanish by actually dissolving into the tree itself.

Besides the pygmies there are other gnomes, who are called tree and forest sprites. To this group belong the sylvestres, satyrs, pans, dyrads, hamadryads, durdalis, elves, brownies, and little old men of the woods. Paracelsus states that the gnomes build houses of substances resembling in their constituencies alabaster, marble, and cement, but the true nature of these materials is unknown, having no counterpart in physical nature. Some families of gnomes gather in communities, while others are indigenous to the substances with and in which they work. For example, the hamadryads live and die with the plants or trees of which they are a part. Every shrub and flower is said to have its own Nature spirit, which often uses the physical body of the plant as its habitation. The ancient philosophers, recognizing the principle of intelligence manifesting itself in every department of Nature alike, believed that the quality of natural selection exhibited by creatures not possessing organized mentalities expressed in reality the decisions of the Nature spirits themselves.

C. M. Gayley, in *The Classic Myths,* says: "It was a pleasing trait in the old paganism that it loved to trace in every operation of nature the agency of deity. The imagination of the Greeks peopled the regions of earth and sea with divinities, to whose agency it attributed the phenomena that our philosophy ascribes to the operation of natural law." Thus, in behalf of the plant it worked with, the elemental accepted and rejected food elements, deposited coloring matter therein, preserved and protected the seed, and performed many other beneficent offices. Each species was served by a different but appropriate type of Nature spirit. Those working with poisonous shrubs, for example, were offensive in their appearance. It is said the Nature spirits of poison hemlock resemble closely tiny human skeletons, thinly covered with a semi-transparent flesh. They live in and through the hemlock, and if it be cut down remain with the broken shoots until both die, but while there is the slightest evidence of life in the shrub it shows the presence of the elemental guardian.

Great trees also have their Nature spirits, but these are much larger than the elementals of smaller plants. The labors of the pygmies include the cutting of the crystals in the rocks and the development of veins of ore. When the gnomes are laboring with animals or human beings, their work is confined to the tissues corresponding with their own natures. Hence they work with the bones, which belong to the mineral kingdom, and the ancients believed the reconstruction of broken members to be impossible without the cooperation of the elementals.

The gnomes are of various sizes—most of them much smaller than human beings, though some of them have the power of changing their stature at will. This is the result of the extreme mobility of the element in which they function. Concerning them Abbé de Villars wrote: "The earth is filled well nigh to its center with Gnomes, people of slight stature, who are the guardians of treasures, minerals and precious stones. They are ingenious, friends of man, and easy to govern."

Not all authorities agree concerning the amiable disposition of the gnomes. Many state that they are of a tricky and malicious nature, difficult to manage, and treacherous. Writers agree, however, that when their confidence is won they are faithful and true. The philosophers and initiates of the ancient world were instructed concerning these mysterious little people and were taught how to communicate with them and gain their cooperation in undertakings of importance. The magi were always warned, however, never to betray the trust of the elementals, for if they did, the invisible creatures, working through the subjective nature of man, could cause them endless sorrow and probably ultimate destruction. So long as the mystic served others, the gnomes would save him, but if he sought to use their aid selfishly to gain temporal power they would turn upon him with unrelenting fury. The same was true if he sought to deceive them.

The earth spirits meet at certain times of the year in great conclaves, as Shakespeare suggests in his *Midsummer Night's Dream,* where the elementals all gather to rejoice in the beauty and harmony of Nature and the prospects of an excellent harvest. The gnomes are ruled over by a king, whom they greatly love and revere. His name is *Gob;* hence his subjects are often called *goblins.* Mediæval mystics gave a corner of creation (one of the cardinal points) to each of the four kingdoms of Nature spirits, and because of their earthy character the gnomes were assigned to the North—the place recognized by the ancients as the source of darkness and death. One of the four main divisions of human disposition was also assigned to the gnomes, and because so many of them dwelt in the darkness of caves and the gloom of forests their temperament was said to be melancholy, gloomy and despondent. By that it is not meant that they themselves are of such disposition, but rather that they have special control over elements of similar consistency.

The gnomes marry and have families, and the female gnomes are called *gnomides*. Some wear clothing woven of the element in which they live. In other instances their garments are part of themselves and grow with them, like the fur of animals. The gnomes are said to have insatiable appetites, and to spend a great part of the time eating, but they earn their food by diligent and conscientious labor. Most of them are of a miserly temperament, fond of storing things away in secret places. There is abundant evidence of the fact that small children often see the gnomes, inasmuch as their contact with the material side of Nature is not yet complete and they still function more or less consciously in the invisible worlds.

According to Paracelsus, "Man lives in the exterior elements and the Elementals live in the interior elements. The latter have dwellings and clothing, manners and customs, languages and governments of their own, in the same sense as the bees have their queens and herds of animals their leaders." (*Philosophia Occulta*, translated by Franz Hartmann.)

Paracelsus differs somewhat from the Greek mystics concerning the environmental limitations imposed on the Nature spirits. The Swiss philosopher constitutes them of subtle invisible ethers. According to this hypothesis they would be visible only at certain times and only to those *en rapport* with their ethereal vibrations. The Greeks, on the other hand, apparently believed that many Nature spirits had material constitutions capable of functioning in the physical world. Often the recollection of a dream is so vivid that, upon awakening, a person actually believes that he has passed through a physical experience. The difficulty of accurately judging as to the end of physical sight and the beginning of ethereal vision may account for these differences of opinion.

Even this explanation, however, does not satisfactorily account for the satyr which, according to St. Jerome, was captured alive during the reign of Constantine and exhibited to the people. It was of human form with the horns and feet of a goat. After its death it was preserved in salt and taken to the Emperor that he might testify to its reality. (It is within the bounds of probability that this curiosity was what modern science knows as *monstrosity*.)

The Undines

As the gnomes were limited in their function to the elements of the earth, so the *undines* (a name given to the family of water elementals) function in the invisible, spiritual essence called humid (or liquid) ether. In its vibratory rate this is close to the element water, and so the undines are able to control, to a great degree, the course and function of this fluid in Nature. Beauty seems to be the keynote of the water spirits. Wherever we find them pictured in art or sculpture, they abound in symmetry and grace. Controlling the water element—which has always been a feminine symbol—it is natural that the water spirits should most often be symbolized as female.

FROM LYCOSTHENES' *PRODIGIORUM AC OSTENTORUM CHRONICON.*

A MERMAID.

Probably the most famous of the undines were the mythological mermaids, with which early mariners peopled the Seven Seas. Belief in the existence of these creatures, the upper half of their bodies human in form and the lower half fishlike, may have been inspired by flocks of penguins seen at a great distance, or possibly seals. In mediæval descriptions of the mermaids, it was also stated that their hair was green like seaweed and that they wore wreaths twisted from the blossoms of subaqueous plants and sea anemones.

There are many groups of undines. Some inhabit waterfalls, where they can be seen in the spray; others are indigenous to swiftly moving rivers; some have their habitat in dripping, oozing fens or marshes; while other groups dwell in clear mountain lakes. According to the philosophers of antiquity, every fountain had its nymph; every ocean wave its oceanid. The water spirits were known under such names as oreades, nereides, limoniades, naiades, water sprites, sea maids, mermaids, and potamides. Often the water nymphs derived their names from the streams, lakes, or seas in which they dwelt.

In describing them, the ancients agreed on certain salient features. In general, nearly all the undines closely resembled human beings in appearance and size, though the ones inhabiting small streams and fountains were of correspondingly lesser proportions. It was believed that these water spirits were occasionally capable of assuming the appearance of normal human beings and actually associating with men and women. There are many legends about these spirits and their adoption by the families of fishermen, but in nearly every case the undines heard the call of the waters and returned to the realm of Neptune, the King of the Sea.

Practically nothing is known concerning the male undines. The water spirits did not establish homes in the same way that the gnomes did, but lived in coral caves under the ocean or among the reeds growing on the banks of rivers or the shores of lakes. Among the Celts there is a legend to the effect that Ireland was peopled, before the coming of its present inhabitants, by a strange race of semidivine creatures; with the coming of the modern Celts they retired into the marshes and fens, where they remain even to this day. Diminutive undines lived under lily pads and in little houses of moss sprayed by waterfalls. The undines worked with the vital essences and liquids in plants, animals, and human beings, and were present in everything containing water. When seen, the undines generally resembled the goddess of Greek statuary. They rose from the water draped in mist and could not exist very long apart from it.

There are many families of undines, each with its peculiar limitations. It is impossible to consider them here in detail. Their ruler, *Necksa,* they love and honor, and serve untiringly. Their temperament is said to be vital, and to them has been given as their throne the western corner of creation. They are rather emotional beings, friendly to human life and fond of serving mankind. They are sometimes pictured riding on dolphins or other great fish and seem to have a special love of flowers and plants, which they serve almost as devotedly and intelligently as the gnomes. Ancient poets have said that the songs of the undines were heard in the West Wind and that their lives were consecrated to the beautifying of the material earth.

The Salamanders

The third group of elementals is the salamanders, or spirits of fire, who live in that attenuated, spiritual ether which is the invisible fire element of Nature. Without them material fire cannot exist; a match cannot be struck nor will flint and steel give off their spark without the assistance of a salamander, who immediately appears (so the mediæval mystics believed), evoked by friction. Man is unable to communicate successfully with the salamanders, owing to the fiery element in which they dwell, for everything is resolved to ashes that comes into their presence. By specially prepared compounds of herbs and perfumes the philosophers of the ancient world manufactured many kinds of incense. When incense was burned, the vapors which arose were especially suitable as a medium for the expression of these elementals, who, by borrowing the ethereal effluvium from the incense smoke, were able to make their presence felt.

The salamanders are as varied in their grouping and arrangement as either the undines or the gnomes. There are many families of them, differing in appearance, size, and dignity. Sometimes the salamanders were visible as small balls of light. Paracelsus says: "Salamanders have been seen in the shapes of fiery balls, or tongues of fire, running over the fields or peering in houses." (*Philosophia Occulta,* translated by Franz Hartmann.)

Mediæval investigators of the Nature spirits were of the opinion that the most common form of salamander was lizard-like in shape, a foot or more in length, and visible as a glowing Urodela, twisting and crawling in the midst of the fire. Another group was described as huge flaming giants in flowing robes, protected with sheets of fiery armor. Certain mediæval authorities, among them the Abbé de Villars, held that Zarathustra (Zoroaster) was the son of Vesta (believed to have been the wife of Noah) and the great salamander Oromasis. Hence, from that time onward, undying fires have been maintained upon the Persian altars in honor of Zarathustra's flaming father.

One most important subdivision of the salamanders was the Acthnici. These creatures appeared only as indistinct globes. They were supposed to float over water at night and occasionally to appear as forks of flame on the masts and rigging of ships (St. Elmo's fire). The salamanders were the strongest and most powerful of the elementals, and had as their ruler a magnificent flaming spirit called *Djin,* terrible and awe-inspiring in appearance. The salamanders were dangerous and the sages were warned to keep away from them, as the benefits derived from studying them were often not commensurate with the price paid. As the ancients associated heat with the South, this corner of creation was assigned to the salamanders as their throne, and they exerted special influence over all beings of fiery or tempestuous temperament. In both animals and men, the salamanders work through the emotional nature by means of the body heat, the liver, and the blood stream. Without their assistance there would be no warmth.

The Sylphs

While the sages said that the fourth class of elementals, or sylphs, lived in the element of air, they meant by this not the natural atmosphere of the earth, but the invisible, intangible, spiritual medium—an ethereal substance similar in composition to our atmosphere, but far more subtle. In the last discourse of Socrates, as preserved by Plato in his *Phædo,* the condemned philosopher says:

"And upon the earth are animals and men, some in a middle region, others [elementals] dwelling about the air as we dwell about the sea; others in islands which the air flows round, near the continent; and in a word, the air is used by them as the water and the sea are by us, and the ether is to them what the air is to us. Moreover, the temperament of their seasons is such that they have no disease [Paracelsus disputes this], and live much longer than we do, and have sight and hearing and smell, and all the other senses, in far greater perfection, in the same degree that air is purer than water or the ether than air. Also they have temples and sacred places in which the gods really dwell, and they hear their voices and receive their answers, and are conscious of them and hold converse with them, and they see the sun, moon, and stars as they really are, and their other blessedness is of a piece with this." While the sylphs were believed to live among the clouds and in the surrounding air, their true home was upon the tops of mountains.

In his editorial notes to the *Occult Sciences* of Salverte, Anthony Todd Thomson says: "The Fayes and Fairies are evidently of Scandinavian origin, although the name of Fairy is supposed to be derived from, or rather [is] a modification of the Persian Peri, an imaginary benevolent being, whose province it was to guard men from the maledictions of evil spirits; but with more probability it may be referred to the Gothic Fagur, as the term Elves is from Alfa, the general appellation for the whole tribe. If this derivation of the name of Fairy be admitted, we may date the commencement of the popular belief in British Fairies to the period of the Danish conquest. They were supposed to be diminutive aerial beings, beautiful, lively, and beneficent in their intercourse with mortals, inhabiting a region called Fairy Land, Alf-heinner; commonly appearing on earth at intervals—when they left traces of their visits, in beautiful green-rings, where the dewy sward had been trodden in their moonlight dances."

To the sylphs the ancients gave the labor of modeling the snowflakes and gathering clouds. This latter they accomplished with the cooperation of the undines who supplied the moisture. The winds were their particular vehicle and the ancients referred to them as the spirits of the air. They are the highest of all the elementals, their native element being the highest in vibratory rate. They live hundreds of years, often attaining to a thousand years and never seeming to grow old. The leader of the sylphs is called *Paralda,* who is said to dwell on the highest mountain of the earth. The female sylphs were called *sylphids.*

It is believed that the sylphs, salamanders, and nymphs had much to do with the oracles of the ancients; that in fact they were the ones who spoke from the depths of the earth and from the air above.

The sylphs sometimes assume human form, but apparently for only short periods of time. Their size varies, but in the majority of cases they are no larger than human beings and often considerably smaller. It is said that the sylphs have accepted human beings into their communities and have permitted them to live there for a considerable period; in fact, Paracelsus wrote of such an incident, but of course it could not have occurred while the human stranger was in his physical body. By some, the Muses of the Greeks are believed to have been sylphs, for these spirits are said to gather around the mind of the dreamer, the poet, and the artist, and inspire him with their intimate knowledge of the beauties and workings of Nature. To the sylphs were given the eastern corner of creation. Their temperament is mirthful, changeable, and eccentric. The peculiar qualities common to men of genius are supposedly the result of the cooperation of sylphs, whose aid also brings with it the sylphic inconsistency. The sylphs labor with the gases of the human body and indirectly with the nervous system, where their inconstancy is again apparent. They have no fixed domicile, but wander about from place to place—elemental nomads, invisible but ever-present powers in the intelligent activity of the universe.

General Observations

Certain of the ancients, differing with Paracelsus, shared the opinion that the elemental kingdoms were capable of waging war upon one another, and they recognized in the battlings of the elements disagreements among these kingdoms of Nature spirits. When lightning struck a rock and splintered it, they believed that the salamanders were attacking the gnomes. As they could not attack one another on the plane of their own peculiar etheric essences, owing to the fact that there was no vibratory correspondence between the four ethers of which these kingdoms are composed, they had to attack through a common denominator, namely, the material substance of the physical universe over which they had a certain amount of power.

Wars were also fought within the groups themselves; one army of gnomes would attack another army, and civil war would be rife among them. Philosophers of long ago solved the problems of Nature's apparent inconsistencies by individualizing and personifying all its forces, crediting them with having temperaments not unlike the human and then expecting them to exhibit typical human inconsistencies. The four fixed signs of the zodiac were assigned to the four kingdoms of elementals. The gnomes were said to be of the nature of Taurus; the undines, of the nature of Scorpio; the salamanders exemplified the constitution of Leo; while the sylphs manipulated the emanations of Aquarius.

The Christian Church gathered all the elemental entities together under the title of *demon*. This is a misnomer with far-reaching consequences, for to the average mind the word *demon* means an evil thing, and the Nature spirits are essentially no more malevolent than are the minerals, plants, and animals. Many of the early Church Fathers asserted that they had met and debated with the elementals.

As already stated, the Nature spirits are without hope of immortality, although some philosophers have maintained that in isolated cases immortality was conferred upon them by adepts and initiates who understood certain subtle principles of the invisible worlds. As disintegration takes place in the physical world, so it takes place in the ethereal counterpart of physical substance. Under normal conditions at death, a Nature spirit is merely resolved back into the transparent primary essence from which it was originally individualized. Whatever evolutionary growth is made is recorded solely in the consciousness of that primary essence, or element, and not in the temporarily individualized entity of the elemental. Being without man's compound organism and lacking his spiritual and intellectual vehicles, the Nature spirits are subhuman in their rational intelligence, but from their functions—limited to one element—has resulted a specialized type of intelligence far ahead of man in those lines of research peculiar to the element in which they exist.

The terms *incubus* and *succubus* have been applied indiscriminately by the Church Fathers to elementals. The incubus and succubus, however, are evil and unnatural creations, whereas *elementals* is a collective term for all the inhabitants of the four elemental essences. According to Paracelsus, the incubus and succubus (which are male and female respectively) are parasitical creatures subsisting upon the evil thoughts and emotions of the astral body. These terms are also applied to the superphysical organisms of sorcerers and black magicians. While these *larvæ* are in no sense imaginary beings, they are, nevertheless, the offspring of the imagination. By the ancient sages they were recognized as the invisible cause of vice because they hover in the ethers surrounding the morally weak and continually incite them to excesses of a degrading nature. For this reason they frequent the atmosphere of the dope den, the dive, and the brothel, where they attach themselves to those unfortunates who have given themselves up to iniquity. By permitting his senses to become deadened through indulgence in habit-forming drugs or alcoholic stimulants, the individual becomes temporarily *en rapport* with these denizens of the astral plane. The *houris* seen by the hasheesh or opium addict and the lurid monsters which torment the victim of delirium tremens are examples of submundane beings, visible only to those whose evil practices are the magnet for their attraction.

Differing widely from the elementals and also the incubus and succubus is the vampire, which is defined by Paracelsus as the astral body of a person either living or dead (usually the latter state). The vampire seeks to prolong existence upon the physical plane by robbing the living of their vital energies and misappropriating such energies to its own ends.

In his *De Ente Spirituali* Paracelsus writes thus of these malignant beings: "A healthy and pure person cannot become obsessed by them, because such Larvæ can only act upon men if the latter make room for them in their minds. A healthy mind is a castle that cannot be invaded without the will of its master; but if they are allowed to enter, they excite the passions of men and women, they create cravings in them, they produce bad thoughts which act injuriously upon the brain; they sharpen the animal intellect and suffocate the moral sense. Evil spirits obsess only those human beings in whom the animal nature is predominating. Minds that are illuminated by the spirit of truth cannot be possessed; only those who are habitually guided by their own lower impulses may become subjected to their influences." (See *Paracelsus,* by Franz Hartmann.)

A strange concept, and one somewhat at variance with the conventional, is that evolved by the Count de Gabalis concerning the *immaculate conception,* namely, that it represents the union of a human being with an elemental. Among the offspring of such unions he lists Hercules, Achilles, Æneas, Theseus, Melchizedek, the divine Plato, Apollonius of Tyana, and Merlin the Magician.

Hermetic Pharmacology, Chemistry, and Therapeutics

he art of healing was originally one of the secret sciences of the priestcraft, and the mystery of its source is obscured by the same veil which hides the genesis of religious belief. All higher forms of knowledge were originally in the possession of the sacerdotal castes. The temple was the cradle of civilization. The priests, exercising their divine prerogative, made the laws and enforced them; appointed the rulers and controlled them; ministered to the needs of the living, and guided the destinies of the dead. All branches of learning were monopolized by the priesthood, who admitted into their ranks only those intellectually and morally qualified to perpetuate their arcanum. The following quotation from Plato's *Statesman* is apropos of the subject: "* * * in Egypt, the King himself is not allowed to reign, unless he have priestly powers; and if he should be one of another class, and have obtained the throne by violence, he must get enrolled in the priestcraft."

Candidates aspiring to membership in the religious orders underwent severe tests to prove their worthiness. These ordeals were called *initiations.* Those who passed them successfully were welcomed as *brothers* by the priests and were instructed in the secret teachings. Among the ancients, philosophy, science, and religion were never considered as separate units: each was regarded as an integral part of the whole. Philosophy was scientific and religious; science was philosophic and religious; religion was philosophic and scientific. Perfect wisdom was considered unattainable save as the result of harmonizing all three of these expressions of mental and moral activity.

While modern physicians accredit Hippocrates with being the father of medicine, the ancient *therapeutæ* ascribed to the immortal Hermes the distinction of being the founder of the art of healing. Clemens Alexandrinus, in describing the books purported to be from the stylus of Hermes, divided the sacred writings into six general classifications, one of which, the *Pastophorus,* was devoted to the science of medicine. The *Smaragdine,* or Emerald Tablet, found in the valley of Ebron and generally accredited to Hermes, is in reality a chemical formula of a high and secret order.

Hippocrates, the famous Greek physician, during the fifth century before Christ, dissociated the healing art from the other sciences of the temple and thereby established a precedent for separateness. One of the consequences is the present widespread crass scientific materialism. The ancients realized the interdependence of the sciences. The moderns do not; and as a result, incomplete systems of learning are attempting to maintain isolated individualism. The obstacles which confront present-day scientific research are largely the result of prejudicial limitations imposed by those who are unwilling to accept that which transcends the concrete perceptions of the five primary human senses.

The Paracelsian System of Medical Philosophy

During the Middle Ages the long-ignored axioms and formulæ of Hermetic wisdom were assembled once more, and chronicled, and systematic attempts were made to test their accuracy. To Theophrastus of Hohenheim, who called himself *Paracelsus* (a name meaning "greater than Celsus"), the world is indebted for much of the knowledge it now possesses of the ancient systems of medicine. Paracelsus devoted his entire life to the study and exposition of Hermetic philosophy. Every notion and theory was grist to his mill, and, while members of the medical fraternity belittle his memory now as they opposed his system then, the occult world knows that he will yet be recognized as the greatest physician of all times. While the heterodox and exotic temperament of Paracelsus has been held against him by his enemies, and his wanderlust has been called vagabondage, he was one of the few minds who intelligently sought to reconcile the art of healing with the philosophic and religious systems of paganism and Christianity.

In defending his right to seek knowledge in all parts of the earth, and among all classes of society, Paracelsus wrote: "Therefore I consider that it is for me a matter of praise, not of blame, that I have hitherto and worthily pursued my wanderings. For this will I bear witness respecting nature: he who will investigate her ways must travel her books with his feet. That which is written is investigated not through its letters, but nature from land to land—as often a land so

often a leaf. Thus is the Codex of Nature, thus must its leaves be turned."
(*Paracelsus,* by John Maxson Stillman.)

Paracelsus was a great observationalist, and those who knew him best
have called him "The Second Hermes" and "The Trismegistus of Switzerland."
He traveled Europe from end to end, and may have penetrated Eastern lands
while running down superstitions and ferreting out supposedly lost doctrines.
From the gypsies he learned much concerning the uses of simples, and apparently from the Arabians concerning the making of talismans and the
influences of the heavenly bodies. Paracelsus felt that the healing of the sick
was of far greater importance than the maintaining of an orthodox medical
standing, so he sacrificed what might otherwise have been a dignified medical
career and at the cost of lifelong persecution bitterly attacked the therapeutic
systems of his day.

Uppermost in his mind was the hypothesis that everything in the universe is
good for something—which accounts for his cutting fungus from tombstones
and collecting dew on glass plates at midnight. He was a true explorer of
Nature's arcanum. Many authorities have held the opinion that he was the discoverer of mesmerism, and that Mesmer evolved the art as the result of studying
the writings of this great Swiss physician.

The utter contempt which Paracelsus felt for the narrow systems of medicine in vogue during his lifetime, and his conviction of their inadequacy, are best
expressed in his own quaint way: "But the number of diseases that originate
from some unknown causes is far greater than those that come from mechanical
causes, and for such diseases our physicians know no cure because not knowing
such causes they cannot remove them. All they can prudently do is to observe
the patient and make their guesses about his condition; and the patient may rest
satisfied if the medicines administered to him do no serious harm, and do not
prevent his recovery. The best of our popular physicians are the ones that do
least harm. But, unfortunately, some poison their patients with mercury, others
purge them or bleed them to death. There are some who have learned so much
that their learning has driven out all their common sense, and there are others
who care a great deal more for their own profit than for the health of their
patients. A disease does not change its state to accommodate itself to the knowledge of the physician, but the physician should understand the causes of the disease. A physician should be a servant of Nature, and not her enemy; he should
be able to guide and direct her in her struggle for life and not throw, by his
unreasonable interference, fresh obstacles in the way of recovery." (From the
Paragranum, translated by Franz Hartmann.)

The belief that nearly all diseases have their origin in the invisible nature of man (the Astrum) is a fundamental precept of Hermetic medicine, for while Hermetists in no way disregarded the physical body, they believed that man's material constitution was an emanation from, or an objectification of, his invisible spiritual principles. A brief, but it is believed fairly comprehensive, résumé of the Hermetic principles of Paracelsus follows.

There is one vital substance in Nature upon which all things subsist. It is called *archæus,* or *vital life force,* and is synonymous with the *astral light* or *spiritual air* of the ancients. In regard to this substance, Eliphas Levi has written: "Light, that creative agent, the vibrations of which are the movement and life of all things; light, latent in the universal ether, radiating about absorbing centres, which, being saturated thereby, project movement and life in their turn, so forming creative currents; light, astralized in the stars, animalized in animals, humanized in human beings; light, which vegetates all plants, glistens in metals, produces all forms of Nature and equilibrates all by the laws of universal sympathy—this is the light which exhibits the phenomena of magnetism, divined by Paracelsus, which tinctures the blood, being released from the air as it is inhaled and discharged by the hermetic bellows of the lungs." (*The History of Magic.*)

This vital energy has its origin in the spiritual body of the earth. Every created thing has two bodies, one visible and substantial, the other invisible and transcendent. The latter consists of an ethereal counterpart of the physical form; it constitutes the vehicle of *archæus,* and may be called a *vital body.* This etheric *shadow sheath* is not dissipated by death, but remains until the physical form is entirely disintegrated. These "etheric doubles," seen around graveyards, have given rise to a belief in ghosts. Being much finer in its substances than the earthly body, the etheric double is far more susceptible to impulses and inharmonies. It is derangements of this astral light body that cause much disease. Paracelsus taught that a person with a morbid mental attitude could poison his own etheric nature, and this infection, diverting the natural flow of *vital life force,* would later appear as a physical ailment. All plants and minerals have an invisible nature composed of this "archæus," but each manifests it in a different way.

Concerning the astral-light bodies of flowers, James Gaffarel, in 1650, wrote the following: "I answer, that though they be chopt in pieces, brayed in a Mortar, and even burnt to Ashes; yet do they neverthelesse retaine, (by a certaine Secret, and wonderfull Power of Nature), both in the Juyce, and in the Ashes, the selfe same Forme, and Figure, that they had before: and though it be not there Visible, yet it may by Art be drawne forth, and made Visible to the Eye, by an Artist. This perhaps will seem a Ridiculous story to those, who reade only the Titles of Bookes: but, those that please, may see this truth confirmed, if they but have recourse to the Workes of M. du Chesne, S. de la Violette, one of the best Chymists that our Age hath produced; who affirmes, that himselfe saw an Excellent Polich Physician of Cracovia, who kept, in Glasses, the Ashes of almost all the Hearbs that are knowne: so that, when any one, out of Curiosity, had a desire to see any of them, as (for example) a Rose, in one of his Glasses, he tooke That where the Ashes of a Rose were preserved; and holding it over a lighted Candle, so soone as it ever began to feele the Heat, you should presently see the Ashes begin to Move; which afterwards rising up, and dispersing themselves about the Glasse, you should immediately observe a kind of little Dark Cloud; which dividing it selfe into many parts, it came at length to represent a Rose; but so Faire, so Fresh, and so Perfect a one, that you would have thought it to have been as Substancial, & as Odoriferous a Rose, as growes on the Rose-tree." (*Unheard-of Curiosities Concerning Talismanical Sculpture of the Persians.*)

Paracelsus, recognizing derangements of the etheric double as the most important cause of disease, sought to reharmonize its substances by bringing into contact with it other bodies whose vital energy could supply elements needed, or were strong enough to overcome the diseased conditions existing in the aura of the sufferer. Its invisible cause having been thus removed, the ailment speedily vanished.

The vehicle for the *archæus,* or vital life force, Paracelsus called the *mumia*. A good example of a physical mumia is vaccine, which is the vehicle of a semi-astral virus. Anything which serves as a medium for the transmission of the archæus, whether it be organic or inorganic, truly physical or partly spiritualized, was termed a mumia. The most universal form of the mumia was ether, which modern science has accepted as a hypothetical substance serving as a medium between the realm of vital energy and that of organic and inorganic substance.

The control of universal energy is virtually impossible, save through one of its vehicles (the mumia). A good example of this is food. Man does not secure nourishment from dead animal or plant organisms, but when he incorporates their structures into his own body he first gains control over the mumia, or etheric double, of the animal or plant. Having obtained this control, the human organism then diverts the flow of the archæus to its own uses. Paracelsus says: "That which constitutes life is contained in the Mumia, and by imparting the Mumia we impart life." This is the secret of the remedial properties of talismans and amulets, for the mumia of the substances of which they are composed serves as a channel to connect the person wearing them with certain manifestations of the universal vital life force.

According to Paracelsus, in the same way that plants purify the atmosphere by accepting into their constitutions the carbon dioxide exhaled by animals and humans, so may plants and animals accept disease elements transferred to them by human beings. These lower forms of life, having organisms and needs different from man, are often able to assimilate these substances without ill effect. At other times, the plant or animal dies, sacrificed in order that the more intelligent, and consequently more useful, creature may survive. Paracelsus discovered that in either case the patient was gradually relieved of his malady. When the lower life had either completely assimilated the foreign mumia from the patient, or had itself died and disintegrated as the result of its inability to do so, complete recovery resulted. Many years of investigation were necessary to determine which herb or animal most readily accepted the mumia of each of various diseases.

Paracelsus discovered that in many cases plants revealed by their shape the particular organs of the human body which they served most effectively. The medical system of Paracelsus was based on the theory that by removing the diseased etheric mumia from the organism of the patient and causing it to be accepted into the nature of some distant and disinterested thing of comparatively little value, it was possible to divert from the patient the flow of the archæus which had been continually revitalizing and nourishing the malady. Its vehicle of expression being transplanted, the archæus necessarily accompanied its mumia, and the patient recovered.

The Hermetic Theory Concerning the Causations of Disease

According to the Hermetic philosophers, there were seven primary causes of disease. The first was *evil spirits*. These were regarded as creatures born of degenerate actions, subsisting on the vital energies of those to whom they attached themselves. The second cause was a *derangement of the spiritual nature and the material nature:* these two, failing to coordinate, produced mental and physical subnormality. The third was an *unhealthy or abnormal mental attitude.* Melancholia, morbid emotions, excess of feeling, such as passions, lusts, greeds, and hates, affected the mumia, from which they reacted into the physical body, where they resulted in ulcers, tumors, cancers, fevers, and tuberculosis. The ancients viewed the disease germ as a unit of mumia which had been impregnated with the emanations from evil influences which it had contacted. In other words, germs were minute creatures born out of man's evil thoughts and actions.

The fourth cause of disease was what the Orientals called *Karma,* that is, the Law of Compensation, which demanded that the individual pay in full for the indiscretions and delinquencies of the past. A physician had to be very careful how he interfered with the workings of this law, lest he thwart the plan of Eternal Justice. The fifth cause was the *motion and aspects of the heavenly bodies.* The stars did not *compel* the sickness but rather *impelled* it. The Hermetists taught that a strong and wise man ruled his stars, but that a negative, weak person was ruled by them. These five causes of disease are all superphysical in nature. They must be estimated by inductive and deductive reasoning and a careful consideration of the life and temperament of the patient.

The sixth cause of disease was a *misuse of faculty, organ, or function,* such as overstraining a member or overtaxing the nerves. The seventh cause was the *presence in the system of foreign substances, impurities, or obstructions.* Under this heading must be considered diet, air, sunlight, and the presence of foreign bodies. This list does not include accidental injuries; such do not belong under the heading of disease. Frequently they are methods by which the Law of Karma expresses itself.

According to the Hermetists, disease could be prevented or successfully combated in seven ways. First, by spells and invocations, in which the physician ordered the evil spirit causing the disease to depart from the patient. This procedure was probably based on the Biblical account of the man possessed of devils whom Jesus healed by commanding the devils to leave the man and enter into a herd of swine. Sometimes the evil spirits entered a patient at the bidding of someone desiring to injure him. In these cases the physician commanded the spirits to return to the one who sent them. It is recorded that in some instances the evil spirits departed through the mouth in the form of clouds of smoke; sometimes from the nostrils as flames. It is even averred that the spirits might depart in the form of birds and insects.

The second method of healing was by vibration. The inharmonies of the bodies were neutralized by chanting spells and intoning the sacred names or by playing upon musical instruments and singing. Sometimes articles of various colors were exposed to the sight of the sick, for the ancients recognized, at least in part, the principle of color therapeutics, now in the process of rediscovery.

The third method was with the aid of talismans, charms, and amulets. The ancients believed that the planets controlled the functions of the human body and that by making charms out of different metals they could combat the malignant influences of the various stars. Thus, a person who is anæmic lacks iron. Iron was believed to be under the control of Mars. Therefore, in order to bring the influence of Mars to the sufferer, around his neck was hung a talisman made of iron and bearing upon it certain secret instructions reputed to have the power of invoking the spirit of Mars. If there was too much iron in the system, the patient was subjected to the influence of a talisman composed of the metal corresponding to some planet having an antipathy to Mars. This influence would then offset the Mars energy and thus aid in restoring normality.

The fourth method was by the aid of herbs and simples. While they used metal talismans, the majority of the ancient physicians did not approve of mineral medicine in any form for internal use. Herbs were their favorite remedies. Like the metals, each herb was assigned to one of the planets. Having diagnosed by the stars the sickness and its cause, the doctors then administered the herbal antidote.

The fifth method of healing disease was by prayer. All ancient peoples believed in the compassionate intercession of the Deity for the alleviation of human suffering. Paracelsus said that faith would cure all disease. Few persons, however, possess a sufficient degree of faith.

The sixth method—which was prevention rather than cure—was regulation of the diet and daily habits of life. The individual, by avoiding the things which caused illness, remained well. The ancients believed that health was the normal state of man; disease was the result of man's disregard of the dictates of Nature.

The seventh method was "practical medicine," consisting chiefly of bleeding, purging, and similar lines of treatment. These procedures, while useful in moderation, were dangerous in excess. Many a useful citizen has died twenty-five or fifty years before his time as the result of drastic purging or of having all the blood drained out of his body.

Paracelsus used all seven methods of treatment, and even his worst enemies admitted that he accomplished results almost miraculous in character. Near his old estate in Hohenheim, the dew falls very heavily at certain seasons of the year, and Paracelsus discovered that by gathering the dew under certain configurations of the planets he obtained a water possessing marvelous medicinal virtue, for it had absorbed the properties of the heavenly bodies.

Hermetic Herbalism and Pharmacology

The herbs of the fields were sacred to the early pagans, who believed that the gods had made plants for the cure of human ills. When properly prepared and applied, each root and shrub could be used for the alleviation of suffering, or for the development of spiritual, mental, moral, or physical powers. In *The Mistletoe and Its Philosophy,* P. Davidson pays the following beautiful tribute to the plants: "Books have been written on the language of flowers and herbs, the poet from the earliest ages has held the sweetest and most loving converse with them, kings are even glad to obtain their essences at second hand to perfume themselves; but to the true physician—Nature's High-Priest—they speak in a far higher and more exalted strain. There is not a plant or mineral which has disclosed the last of its properties to the scientists. How can they feel confident that for every one of the discovered properties there may not be many powers concealed in the inner nature of the plant? Well have flowers been called the 'Stars of Earth,' and why should they not be beautiful? Have they not from the time of their birth smiled in the splendor of the sun by day, and slumbered under the brightness of the stars by night? Have they not come from another and more spiritual world to our earth, seeing that God made 'every plant of the field BEFORE it was in the earth, and every herb of the field BEFORE IT GREW'?"

Many primitive peoples used herbal remedies, with many remarkable cures. The Chinese, Egyptians, and American Indians cured with herbs diseases for which modern science knows no remedy. Doctor Nicholas Culpeper, whose useful life ended in 1654, was probably the most famous of herbalists. Finding that the medical systems of his day were unsatisfactory in the extreme, Culpeper turned his attention to the plants of the fields, and discovered a medium of healing which gained for him national renown.

In Doctor Culpeper's correlation of astrology and herbalism, each plant was under the jurisdiction of one of the planets or luminaries. He believed that disease was also controlled by celestial configurations. He summed up his system of treatment as follows: "You may oppose diseases by Herbs of the planet opposite to the planet that causes them: as diseases of Jupiter by Herbs of Mercury, and the contrary; diseases of the Luminaries by the Herbs of Saturn, and the contrary; diseases of Mars by Herbs of Venus and the contrary. * * * There is a way to cure diseases sometimes by Sympathy, and so every planet cures his own disease; as the Sun and Moon by their Herbs cure the Eyes, Saturn the Spleen, Jupiter the Liver, Mars the Gall and diseases of choler, and Venus diseases in the Instruments of Generation." (*The Complete Herbal.*)

Mediæval European herbalists rediscovered only in part the ancient Hermetic secrets of Egypt and Greece. These earlier nations evolved the fundamentals of nearly all modern arts and sciences. At that time the methods used in healing were among the secrets imparted to initiates of the Mysteries. Unctions, collyria, philters, and potions were concocted to the accompaniment of strange rites. The effectiveness of these medicines is a matter of historical record. Incenses and perfumes were also much used.

Barrett in his *Magus* describes the theory on which they worked, as follows:

"For, because our spirit is the pure, subtil, lucid, airy and unctuous vapour of the blood, nothing, therefore, is better adapted for collyriums than the like vapours which are more suitable to our spirit in substance; for then, by reason of their likeness, they do more stir up, attract and transform the spirit."

Poisons were thoroughly studied, and in some communities extracts of deadly herbs were administered to persons sentenced to death—as in the case of Socrates. The infamous Borgias of Italy developed the art of poisoning to its highest degree. Unnumbered brilliant men and women were quietly and efficiently disposed of by the almost superhuman knowledge of chemistry which for many centuries was preserved in the Borgia family.

Egyptian priests discovered herb extracts by means of which temporary clairvoyance could be induced, and they made use of these during the initiatory rituals of their Mysteries. The drugs were sometimes mixed with the food given to candidates, and at other times were presented in the form of sacred potions, the nature of which was explained. Shortly after the drugs were administered to him, the neophyte was attacked by a spell of dizziness. He found himself floating through space, and while his physical body was absolutely insensible (being guarded by priests that no ill should befall it) the candidate passed through a number of weird experiences, which he was able to relate after regaining consciousness. In the light of present-day knowledge, it is difficult to appreciate an art so highly developed that by means of draughts, perfumes, and incenses any mental attitude desired could be induced almost instantaneously, yet such an art actually existed among the priestcraft of the early pagan world.

Concerning this subject, H. P. Blavatsky, the foremost occultist of the nineteenth century, has written: "Plants also have like mystical properties in a most wonderful degree, and the secret of the herbs of dreams and enchantments are only lost to European science, and useless to say, too, are unknown to it, except in a few marked instances, such as opium and hashish. Yet, the psychical effects of even these few upon the human system are regarded as evidences of a temporary mental disorder. The women of Thessaly and Epirus, the female hierophants of the rites of Sabazius, did not carry their secrets away with the downfall of their sanctuaries. They are still preserved, and those who are aware of the nature of Soma, know the properties of other plants as well." (*Isis Unveiled.*)

Herbal compounds were used to cause temporary clairvoyance in connection with the oracles, especially the one at Delphi. Words spoken while in these imposed trances were regarded as prophetic. Modern mediums, while under control as the result of partly self-imposed catalepsy, give messages somewhat similar to those of the ancient prophets, but in the majority of cases their results are far less accurate, for the soothsayers of today lack the knowledge of Nature's hidden forces.

The Mysteries taught that during the higher degrees of initiation the gods themselves took part in the instruction of candidates or at least were present, which was in itself a benediction. As the deities dwelt in the invisible worlds and came only in their spiritual bodies, it was impossible for the neophyte to cognize them without the assistance of drugs which stimulated the clairvoyant center of his consciousness (probably the pineal gland). Many initiates in the ancient Mysteries stated emphatically that they had conversed with the immortals, and had beheld the gods.

When the standards of the pagans became corrupted, a division took place in the Mysteries. The band of truly enlightened ones separated themselves from the rest and, preserving the most important of their secrets, vanished without leaving a trace. The rest slowly drifted, like rudderless ships, on the rocks of degeneracy and disintegration. Some of the less important of the secret formulæ fell into the hands of the profane, who perverted them—as in the case of the Bacchanalia, during which drugs were mixed with wine and became the real cause of the orgies.

In certain parts of the earth it was maintained that there were natural wells, springs, or fountains, in which the water (because of the minerals through which it coursed) was tinctured with sacred properties. Temples were often built near these spots, and in some cases natural caves which chanced to be in the vicinity were sanctified to some deity.

"The aspirants to initiation, and those who came to request prophetic dreams of the Gods, were prepared by a fast, more or less prolonged, after which they partook of meals expressly prepared; and also of mysterious drinks, such as the water of Lethe, and the water of Mnemosyne in the grotto of Trophonius; or of the Ciceion in the mysteries of the Eleusinia. Different drugs were easily mixed up with the meats or introduced into the drinks, according to the state of mind or body into which it was necessary to throw the recipient, and the nature of the visions he was desirous of procuring." (Salverte's *The Occult Sciences.*) The same author states that certain sects of early Christianity were accused of using drugs for the same general purposes as the pagans.

The sect of the Assassins, or the Yezidees as they are more generally known, demonstrated a rather interesting aspect of the drug problem. In the eleventh century this order, by capturing the fortress of Mount Alamont, established itself at Irak. Hassan Sabbah, the founder of the order, known as the "Old Man of the Mountain," is suspected of having controlled his followers by the use of narcotics. Hassan made his followers believe that they were in Paradise, where they would be forever if they implicitly obeyed him while they were alive. De Quincey, in his *Confessions of an Opium Eater,* describes the peculiar psychological effects produced by this product of the poppy, and the use of a similar drug may have given rise to the idea of Paradise which filled the minds of the Yezidees.

The philosophers of all ages have taught that the visible universe was but a fractional part of the whole, and that by analogy the physical body of man is in reality the least important part of his composite constitution. Most of the medical systems of today almost entirely ignore the superphysical man. They pay but scant attention to causes, and concentrate their efforts on ameliorating effects. Paracelsus, noting the same proclivity on the part of physicians during his day, aptly remarked: "There is a great difference between the power that removes the invisible causes of disease, and which is Magic, and that which causes merely external effects [to] disappear, and which is Physic, Sorcery, and Quackery." (Translated by Franz Hartmann.)

Disease is unnatural, and is evidence that there is a maladjustment within or between organs or tissues. Permanent health cannot be regained until harmony is restored. The outstanding virtue of Hermetic medicine was its recognition of spiritual and psychophysical derangements as being largely responsible for the condition which is called physical disease. Suggestive therapy was used with marked success by the priest-physicians of the ancient world. Among the American Indians, the *Shamans*—or "Medicine Men"—dispelled sickness with the aid of mysterious dances, invocations, and charms. The fact that in spite of their ignorance of modern methods of medical treatment these sorcerers effected innumerable cures, is well worthy of consideration.

The magic rituals used by the Egyptian priests for the curing of disease were based upon a highly developed comprehension of the complex workings of the human mind and its reactions upon the physical constitution. The Egyptian and Brahmin worlds undoubtedly understood the fundamental principle of vibrotherapeutics. By means of chants and mantras, which emphasized certain vowel and consonant sounds, they set up vibratory reactions which dispelled congestions and assisted Nature in reconstructing broken members and depleted organisms. They also applied their knowledge of the laws governing vibration to the spiritual constitution of man; by their intonings, they stimulated latent centers of consciousness and thereby vastly increased the sensitiveness of the subjective nature.

In the *Book of Coming Forth by Day,* many of the Egyptian secrets have been preserved to this generation. While this ancient scroll has been well translated, only a few understand the secret significance of its magical passages. Oriental races have a keen realization of the dynamics of sound. They know that every spoken word has tremendous power and that by certain arrangements of words they can create vortices of force in the invisible universe about them and thereby profoundly influence physical substance. The *Sacred Word* by which the world was established, the *Lost Word* which Masonry is still seeking, and the threefold Divine Name symbolized by *A. U. M.*—the creative tone of the Hindus—all are indicative of the veneration accorded the principle of sound.

The so-called "new discoveries" of modern science are often only rediscoveries of secrets well known to the priests and philosophers of ancient pagandom. Man's inhumanity to man has resulted in the loss of records and formulæ which, had they been preserved, would have solved many of the greatest problems of this civilization. With sword and firebrand, races obliterate the records of their predecessors, and then inevitably meet with an untimely fate for need of the very wisdom they have destroyed.

The Qabbalah, the Secret Doctrine of Israel

lbert Pike, quoting from *Transcendental Magic*, thus sums up the importance of Qabbalism as a key to Masonic esotericism: "One is filled with admiration, on penetrating into the Sanctuary of the Kabalah, at seeing a doctrine so logical, so simple, and at the same time so absolute. The necessary union of ideas and signs, the consecration of the most fundamental realities by the primitive characters; the Trinity of Words, Letters, and Numbers; a philosophy simple as the alphabet, profound and infinite as the Word; theorems more complete and luminous than those of Pythagoras; a theology summed up by counting on one's fingers; an Infinite which can be held in the hollow of an infant's hand; ten ciphers and twenty-two letters, a triangle, a square, and a circle,—these are all the elements of the Kabalah. These are the elementary principles of the written Word, reflection of that spoken Word that created the world!" (*Morals and Dogma.*)

Hebrew theology was divided into three distinct parts. The first was *the law*, the second was *the soul of the law*, and the third was *the soul of the soul of the law*. The law was taught to all the children of Israel; the *Mishna*, or the soul of the law, was revealed to the Rabbins and teachers; but the *Qabbalah*, the soul of the soul of the law, was cunningly concealed, and only the highest initiates among the Jews were instructed in its secret principles.

According to certain Jewish mystics, Moses ascended Mount Sinai three times, remaining in the presence of God forty days each time. During the first forty days the tables of the written law were delivered to the prophet; during the second forty days he received the soul of the law; and during the last forty days God instructed him in the mysteries of the Qabbalah, the soul of the soul of the law. Moses concealed in the first four books of the Pentateuch the secret instructions that God had given him, and for centuries students of Qabbalism have sought therein the secret doctrine of Israel. As the spiritual nature of man is concealed in his physical body, so the unwritten law—the *Mishna* and the *Qabbalah*—is concealed within the written teachings of the Mosaic code. *Qabbalah* means the *secret or hidden tradition, the unwritten law,* and according to an early Rabbi, it was delivered to man in order that through the aid of its abstruse principles he might learn to understand the mystery of both the universe about him and the universe within him.

The origin of Qabbalism is a legitimate subject for controversy. Early initiates of the Qabbalistic Mysteries believed that its principles were first taught by God to a school of His angels before the fall of man. The angels later communicated the secrets to Adam, so that through the knowledge gained from an understanding of its principles fallen humanity might regain its lost estate. The Angel Raziel was dispatched from heaven to instruct Adam in the mysteries of the Qabbalah. Different angels were employed to initiate the succeeding patriarchs in this difficult science. Tophiel was the teacher of Shem, Raphael of Isaac, Metatron of Moses, and Michael of David. (See *Faiths of the World.*)

Christian D. Ginsburg has written: "From Adam it passed over to Noah, and then to Abraham, the friend of God, who emigrated with it to Egypt, where the patriarch allowed a portion of this mysterious doctrine to ooze out. It was in this way that the Egyptians obtained some knowledge of it, and the other Eastern nations could introduce it into their philosophical systems. Moses, who was learned in all the wisdom of Egypt, was first initiated into it in the land of his birth, but became most proficient in it during his wanderings in the wilderness, when he not only devoted to it the leisure hours of the whole forty years, but received lessons in it from one of the angels. * * * Moses also initiated the seventy Elders into the secrets of this doctrine and they again transmitted them from hand to hand. Of all who formed the unbroken line of tradition, David and Solomon were most initiated into the Kabbalah." (See *The Kabbalah.*)

According to Eliphas Levi, the three greatest books of Qabbalism are the *Sepher Yetzirah,* The Book of Formation; the *Sepher ha Zohar,* The Book of Splendor; and the *Apocalypse,* The Book of Revelation. The dates of the writing of these books are by no means thoroughly established. Qabbalists declare that the *Sepher Yetzirah* was written by Abraham. Although it is by far the oldest of the Qabbalistic books, it was probably from the pen of the Rabbi Akiba, A.D. 120.

The *Sepher ha Zohar* presumably was written by Simeon ben Jochai, a disciple of Akiba. Rabbi Simeon was sentenced to death about A.D. 161 by Lucius

Verus, co-regent of the Emperor Marc Aurelius Antoninus. He escaped with his son and, hiding in a cave, transcribed the manuscript of the *Zohar* with the assistance of Elias, who appeared to them at intervals. Simeon was twelve years in the cave, during which time he evolved the complicated symbolism of the "Greater Face" and the "Lesser Face." While discoursing with disciples Rabbi Simeon expired, and the "Lamp of Israel" was extinguished. His death and burial were accompanied by many supernatural phenomena. The legend goes on to relate that the secret doctrines of Qabbalism had been in existence since the beginning of the world, but that Rabbi Simeon was the first man permitted to reduce them to writing. Twelve hundred years later the books which he had compiled were discovered and published for the benefit of humanity by Moses de León. The probability is that Moses de León himself compiled the *Zohar* about A.D. 1305, drawing his material from the unwritten secrets of earlier Jewish mystics. The *Apocalypse,* accredited to St. John the Divine, is also of uncertain date, and the identity of its author has never been satisfactorily proved.

Because of its brevity and because it is the key to Qabbalistic thought, the *Sepher Yetzirah* is reproduced in full in this chapter. So far as is known, the *Sepher ha Zohar* has never been completely translated into English, but it can be obtained in French. (S. L. MacGregor-Mathers translated three books of the *Zohar* into English.) The *Zohar* contains a vast number of philosophical tenets, and a paraphrase of its salient points is embodied in this work.

Few realize the influence exerted by Qabbalism over mediæval thought, both Christian and Jewish. It taught that there existed within the sacred writings a hidden doctrine which was the key to those writings. This is symbolized by the crossed keys upon the papal crest. Scores of learned minds began to search for those arcane truths by which the race should be redeemed; and that their labor was not without its reward, their subsequent writings have demonstrated.

The theories of Qabbalism are inextricably interwoven with the tenets of alchemy, Hermeticism, Rosicrucianism, and Freemasonry. The words *Qabbalism* and *Hermeticism* are now considered as synonymous terms covering all the arcana and esotericism of antiquity. The simple Qabbalism of the first centuries of the Christian Era gradually evolved into an elaborate theological system, which became so involved that it was next to impossible to comprehend its dogma.

The Qabbalists divided the uses of their sacred science into five sections. The *Natural Qabbalah* was used solely to assist the investigator in his study of Nature's mysteries. The *Analogical Qabbalah* was formulated to exhibit the relationship which exists between all things in Nature, and it revealed to the

wise that all creatures and substances were one in essence, and that man—
the Little Universe—was a replica in miniature of God—the Great Universe. The
Contemplative Qabbalah was evolved for the purpose of revealing through the
higher intellectual faculties the mysteries of the celestial spheres. By its aid

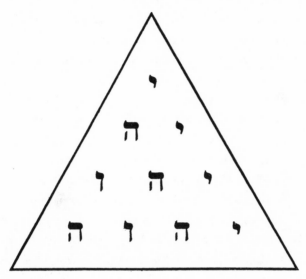

THE TETRAGRAMMATON.

By arranging the four letters of the Great Name, ה ו ה י (I H V H), in the form of the Pythagorean Tetractys, the 72 powers of the
Great Name of God are manifested. The key to the problem is as follows:

•	=	I	=	10	=	10
• •	=	H I	=	5+10	=	15
• • •	=	V H I	=	6+5+10	=	21
• • • •	=	H V H I	=	5+6+5+10	=	26
		The Great Name of God	=	72		

the abstract reasoning faculties cognized the measureless planes of infinity and
learned to know the creatures existing within them. The *Astrological Qabbalah*
instructed those who studied its lore in the power, magnitude, and actual substance of the sidereal bodies, and also revealed the mystical constitution of the
planet itself. The fifth, or *Magical Qabbalah,* was studied by such as desired to
gain control over the demons and subhuman intelligences of the invisible
worlds. It was also highly valued as a method of healing the sick by talismans,
amulets, charms, and invocations.

The *Sepher Yetzirah,* according to Adolph Franck, differs from other sacred
books in that it does not explain the world and the phenomena of which it is the
stage by leaning on the idea of God or by setting itself up as the interpreter of the
supreme will. This ancient work rather reveals God by estimating His manifold
handiwork. In preparing the *Sepher Yetzirah* for the consideration of the reader,

five separate English translations have been compared. The resulting form, while it embodies the salient features of each, is not a direct translation from any one Hebrew or Latin text. Although the purpose was to convey the spirit rather than the letter of the ancient document, there are no wide deviations from the original rendition. So far as known, the first translation of the *Sepher Yetzirah* into English was made by the Rev. Dr. Isidor Kalisch, in 1877. (See Arthur Edward Waite.) In this translation the Hebrew text accompanies the English words. The work of Dr. Kalisch has been used as the foundation of the following interpretation, but material from other authorities has been incorporated and many passages have been rewritten to simplify the general theme.

At hand also was a manuscript copy in English of the *Book of the Cabalistick Art,* by Doctor John Pistor. The document is undated; but judging from the general type of the writing, the copy was made during the eighteenth century. The third volume used as a reference was the *Sepher Yetzirah,* by the late Wm. Wynn Westcott, Magus of the Rosicrucian Society of England. The fourth was the *Sepher Yetzirah,* or The Book of Creation, according to the translation in the *Sacred Books and Early Literature of the East,* edited by Prof. Charles F. Horne. The fifth was a recent publication, *The Book of Formation,* by Knut Stenring, containing an introduction by Arthur Edward Waite. At hand also were four other copies—two German, one Hebrew, and one Latin. Certain portions of the *Sepher Yetzirah* are considered older and more authentic than the rest, but the controversy regarding them is so involved and nonproductive that it is useless to add further comment. The doubtful passages are therefore included in the document at the points where they would naturally fall.

The Sepher Yetzirah, the Book of Formation

CHAPTER ONE

1. YAH, the Lord of Hosts, the living Elohim, King of the Universe, Omnipotent, the Merciful and Gracious God, Supreme and Extolled, Dweller in the Height whose habitation is Eternity, who is Sublime and Most-Holy, engraved His name and ordained (formed) and created the Universe in thirty-two mysterious paths (stages) of wisdom (science), by three Sepharim, namely, Numbers, Letters, and Sounds, which are in Him one and the same.

2. Ten Sephiroth (ten properties from the Ineffable One) and twenty-two letters are the Foundation of all things. Of these twenty-two letters three are called "Mothers," seven "Double," and twelve "Simple."

3. The ten numbers (Sephiroth) out of Nothing are analogous to the ten fingers and the ten toes: five over against five. In the center between them is the covenant with the Only One God. In the spiritual world it is the covenant of the voice (the Word), and in the corporeal world the circumcision of the flesh (the rite of Abraham).

4. Ten are the numbers (of the Sephiroth) out of Nothing, ten—not nine; ten—not eleven. Comprehend this great wisdom, understand this knowledge and be wise. Inquire into the mystery and ponder it. Examine all things by means of the ten Sephiroth. Restore the Word to Its Creator and lead the Creator back to His throne again. He is the only Formator and beside Him there is no other. His attributes are ten and are without limit.

5. The ten ineffable Sephiroth have ten infinitudes, which are as follows:

> The infinite beginning and the infinite end;
> The infinite good and the infinite evil;
> The infinite height and the infinite depth;
> The infinite East and the infinite West;
> The infinite North and the infinite South;

and over them is the Lord Superlatively One, the faithful King. He rules over all in all from His holy habitation for ages of ages.

6. The appearance of the ten spheres (Sephiroth) out of Nothing is as a flash of lightning or a sparkling flame, and they are without beginning or end. The Word of God is in them when they go forth and when they return. They run by His order like a whirlwind and prostrate themselves before His throne.

7. The ten Sephiroth have their end linked to their beginning and their beginning linked to their end, cojoined as the flame is wedded to the live coal, for the Lord is Superlatively One and to Him there is no second. Before One what can you count?

8. Concerning the number (10) of the spheres of existence (Sephiroth) out of Nothing, seal up your lips and guard your heart as you consider them, and if your mouth opens for utterance and your heart turns towards thought, control them, returning to silence. So it is written: "And the living creatures ran and returned." (Ezekiel i. 14.) And on this wise was the covenant made with us.

9. These are the ten emanations of number out of Nothing:

1st. The spirit of the living Elohim, blessed and more than blessed be the living Elohim of ages. His Voice, His Spirit, and His Word are the Holy Spirit.

2nd. He produced air from the spirit and in the air He formed and established twenty-two sounds—the letters. Three of them were fundamental, or mothers; seven were double; and twelve were simple (single); but the spirit is the first one and above all.

3rd. Primordial water He extracted from the air. He formed therein twenty-two letters and established them out of mud and loam, making them like a border, putting them up like a wall, and surrounding them as with a rampart. He poured snow upon them and it became earth, as it reads: "He said to the snow be thou earth." (Job. xxxvii. 6.)

4th. Fire (ether) He drew forth from the water. He engraved and established by it the Throne of Glory. He fashioned the Seraphim, the Ophanim, and the Holy Living Creatures (Cherubim?), as His ministering angels; and with (of) these three he formed His habitation, as it reads: "Who made His angels spirits, His ministers a flaming fire." (Psalms civ. 4.)

5th. He selected three consonants (I, H, V) from the simple ones— a secret belonging to the three mothers, or first elements; א מ ש (A, M, Sh), air, water, fire (ether). He sealed them with His spirit and fashioned them into a Great Name and with this sealed the universe in six directions. He turned towards the above and sealed the height with יהו (I, H, V).

6th. He turned towards the below and sealed the depth with היו (H, I, V).

7th. He turned forward and sealed the East with ויה (V, I, H).

8th. He turned backward and sealed the West with והי (V, H, I).

9th. He turned to the right and sealed the South with יוה (I, V, H).

10th. He turned to the left and sealed the North with הוי (H, V, I).

Note. This arrangement of the letters of the Great Name is according to the Rev. Dr. Isidor Kalisch.

10. These are the ten ineffable existences out of nothing: From the spirit of the Living God emanated air; from the air, water; from the water, fire (ether); from the fire, the height and the depth, the East and the West, the North and the South.

CHAPTER TWO

1. There are twenty-two basic (sounds and) letters. Three are the first elements (water, air, fire), fundamentals, or mothers; seven are double letters; and

THE HEBREW LETTERS ACCORDING TO THE SEPHER YETZIRAH.

In the central triangle are the three Mother Letters from which come forth the seven Double Letters—the planets and the heavens. Surrounding the black star are the signs of the zodiac symbolized by the twelve Simple Letters. In the midst of this star is the Invisible Throne of the Most Ancient of the Ancients—the Supreme Definitionless Creator.

twelve are simple letters. The three fundamental letters אמש have as their basis the balance. At one end of the scale are the virtues and at the other the vices, placed in equilibrium by the tongue. Of the fundamental letters מ (M) is mute like the water, ש (Sh) hissing like fire, א (A) a reconciling breath between them.

2. The twenty-two basic letters having been designed, appointed, and established by God, He combined, weighed, and exchanged them (each with the others), and formed by them all beings which are in existence, and all which will be formed in time to come.

3. He established twenty-two basic letters, formed by the voice and impressed upon the air by the breath. He set them to be audibly uttered in five different parts of the human mouth: namely, Gutturals, א ה ח ע;; Palatals, ג י כ ק; ; Linguals, ד ט ל נ ת; Dentals, ז ש ס ר צ; Lal; Labials, ב ו מ פ.

4. He fixed the twenty-two basic letters in a ring (sphere) like a wall with two hundred and thirty-one gates, and turned the sphere forward and backward. Turned forward, the sphere signified good; when reversed, evil. Three letters may serve for an illustration: There is nothing better than ‫ע נ ג‬ (O, N, G), pleasure (joy), and nothing worse than ‫נ ג ע‬ (N, G, O), plague (sorrow).

5. How was it all accomplished? He combined, weighed, and changed: the ‫א‬ (A) with all the other letters in succession, and all the others again with ‫א‬ (A), and all again with ‫ב‬ (B); and so with the whole series of letters. Hence it follows that there are two hundred and thirty-one formations, or gates, through which the powers of the letters go forth; every creature and every language proceeded from One Name and the combinations of its letters.

6. He created a reality out of Nothing. He called the nonentity into existence and hewed colossal pillars from intangible air. This has been shown by the example of combining the letter ‫א‬ (A) with all the other letters, and all the other letters with ‫א‬ (A). By speaking He created every creature and every word by the power of One Name. As an illustration, consider the twenty-two elementary substances from the primitive substance of ‫א‬ (A). The production of every creature from the twenty-two letters is proof that they are in reality the twenty-two parts of one living body.

Chapter Three

1. The first three elements (the Mother letters, ‫א מ ש‬) resemble a balance, in one scale virtue and in the other vice, placed in equilibrium by the tongue.

2. These three Mothers, ‫א מ ש‬, enclose a great, wonderful, and unknown mystery, and are sealed by six wings (or elementary circles), namely, air, water, fire—each divided into an active and a passive power. The Mothers, ‫א מ ש‬, gave birth to the Fathers (the progenitors), and these gave birth to the generations.

3. God appointed and established three Mothers, ‫א מ ש‬, combined, weighed, and exchanged them, forming by them three Mothers, ‫א מ ש‬, in the universe, in the year, and in man (male and female).

4. The three Mothers, ‫א מ ש‬,, in the universe are: air, water, and fire. Heaven was created from the elementary fire (or ether), ‫ש‬; the earth, comprising sea and land, from the elementary water, ‫מ‬; and the atmospheric air from the

elementary air, or spirit, א, which establishes the balance among them. Thus were all things produced.

5. The three Mothers, א מ ש, produce in the year heat, coldness, and the temperate state. Heat was created from fire, coldness from water, and the temperate state from air, which equilibrates them.

6. The three Mothers, א מ ש, produce in man (male and female) breast, abdomen, and head. The head was formed from the fire, ש; the abdomen from the water, מ; and the breast (thorax) from air, א, which places them in equilibrium.

7. God let the letter א (A) predominate in primordial air, crowned it, combined it with the other two, and sealed the air in the universe, the temperate state in the year, and the breast in man (male and female).

8. He let the letter מ (M) predominate in primordial water, crowned it, combined it with the other two, and sealed the earth in the universe (including land and sea), coldness in the year, and the abdomen in man (male and female).

9. He let the letter ש (Sh) predominate in primordial fire, crowned it, combined it with the other two, and sealed heaven in the universe, heat in the year, and the head of man (male and female).

Chapter Four

1. The seven double letters, ב ג ד כ פ ר ת (B, G, D, K, P, R, Th), have a duplicity of pronunciation (two voices), aspirated and unaspirated, namely: ב ב, ג ג, ד ד, כ כ, פ פ, ר ר, ת ת. They serve as a model of softness and hardness, strength and weakness.

2. The seven double letters symbolize wisdom, riches, fertility life, power, peace, and grace.

3. The seven double letters also signify the antitheses to which human life is exposed. The opposite of wisdom is foolishness; of riches, poverty; of fertility, sterility; of life, death; of power, servitude; of peace, war; and of beauty, deformity.

4. The seven double letters point out the six dimensions, height, depth, East and West, North and South, and the Holy Temple in the center, which sustains them all.

5. The double letters are seven and not six, they are seven and not eight; reflect upon this fact, search into it and reveal its hidden mystery and place the Creator on His throne again.

6. The seven double letters having been designed, established, purified, weighed, and exchanged by God, He formed of them seven planets in the universe, seven days in the Year, and seven gateways of the senses in man (male and female). From these seven He also produced seven heavens, seven earths, and seven Sabbaths. Therefore He loved seven more than any other number beneath His throne.

7. The seven planets in the universe are: Saturn, Jupiter, Mars, Sun, Venus, Mercury, and Moon. The seven days in the Year are the seven days of the week (possibly the seven creative days are meant). The seven gateways in man (male and female) are two eyes, two ears, two nostrils, and the mouth.

8. *Note.* Knut Stenring differs from other authorities in his arrangement of the planets and days of the week in the following seven stanzas. Kircher has still a different order. Rev. Dr. Isidor Kalisch, Wm. Wynn Westcott, and *The Sacred Books and Early Literature of the East* adopt the following arrangement.

    1st. He caused the letter ב (B) to predominate in wisdom, crowned it, combined each with the others, and formed by them the Moon in the universe, the first day in the year, and the right eye in man (male and female).

    2nd. He caused the letter ג (G) to predominate in riches, crowned it, combined each with the others, and formed by them Mars in the universe, the second day in the year, and the right ear in man (male and female).

    3rd. He caused the letter ד (D) to predominate in fertility, crowned it, combined each with the others, and formed by them the Sun in the universe, the third day in the year, and the right nostril in man (male and female).

    4th. He caused the letter כ (K) to predominate in life, crowned it, combined each with the others, and formed by them Venus in its the universe, the fourth day in the year, and the left eye in man (male and female).

    5th. He caused the letter פ (P) to predominate in power, crowned it, combined each with the others, and formed by them Mercury in the universe, the fifth day in the year, and the left ear in man (male and female).

    6th. He caused the letter ר (R) to predominate in peace, crowned it, combined each with the others, and formed by them Saturn in the universe, the sixth day in the year, and the left nostril in man (male and female).

7th. He caused the letter ת (Th) to predominate in grace, crowned it, combined each with the others, and formed by them Jupiter in the universe, the seventh day in the year, and the mouth of man (male and female).

9. With the seven double letters He also designed seven earths, seven heavens, seven continents, seven seas, seven rivers, seven deserts, seven days, seven weeks (from Passover to Pentecost), and in the midst of them His Holy Palace. There is a cycle of seven years and the seventh is the release year, and after seven release years is the Jubilee. For this reason God loves the number seven more than any other thing under the heavens.

10. In this manner God joined the seven double letters together. Two stones build two houses, three stones build six houses, four stones build twenty-four houses, five stones build 120 houses, six stones build 720 houses, and seven stones build 5,040 houses. Make a beginning according to this arrangement and reckon further than the mouth can express or the ear can hear.

CHAPTER FIVE

1. The twelve simple letters ק צ ע ס נ ל י ט ח ז ו ה (H, V, Z, Ch, T, I, L, N, S, O, Tz, Q) symbolize the twelve fundamental properties: speech, thought, movement, sight, hearing, work, coition, smell, sleep, anger, taste (or swallowing), and mirth.

2. The simple letters correspond to twelve directions: east height, northeast, east depth; south height, southeast, south depth; west height, southwest, west depth; north height, northwest, north depth. They diverge to all eternity and are the arms of the universe.

3. The simple letters having been designed, established, weighed, and exchanged by God, He produced by them twelve zodiacal signs in the universe, twelve months in the year, and twelve chief organs in the human body (male and female).

4. The signs of the zodiac are: Aries, Taurus, Gemini, Cancer, Leo, Virgo, Libra, Scorpio, Sagittarius, Capricorn, Aquarius, and Pisces. The months of the year are: Nisan, Ijar, Sivan, Tammuz, Ab, Elul, Tisri, Marcheshvan, Kislev, Tebet, Sebat, and Adar. The organs of the human body are: two hands, two feet, two kidneys, gall, small intestine, liver, esophagus, stomach, and spleen.

5. *Note.* In the following twelve stanzas, Knut Stenring again differs, this time as to the arrangement of properties:

1st. God used the letter ה (H) to predominate in speech, crowned it, combined it with the others, and fashioned by them Aries (the Ram) in the universe, the month Nisan in the year, and the right foot of the human body (male and female).

2nd. He used the letter ו (V) to predominate in thought, crowned it, combined it with the others, and fashioned by them Taurus (the Bull) in the universe, the month Ijar in the year, and the right kidney of the human body (male and female).

3rd. He caused the letter ז (Z) to predominate in movement, crowned it, combined it with the others, and fashioned by them Gemini (the Twins) in the universe, the month Sivan in the year, and the left foot of the human body (male and female).

4th. He caused the letter ח (Ch) to predominate in sight, crowned it, combined it with the others, and fashioned by them Cancer (the Crab) in the universe, the month Tammuz in the year, and the right hand of the human body (male and female).

5th. He caused the letter ט (T) to predominate in hearing, crowned it, combined it with the others, and fashioned by them Leo (the Lion) in the universe, the month Ab in the year, and the left kidney of the human body (male and female).

6th. He caused the letter י (I) to predominate in work, crowned it, combined it with the others, and fashioned by them Virgo (the Virgin) in the universe, the month Elul in the year, and the left hand of the human body (male and female).

7th. He caused the letter ל (L) to predominate in coition, crowned it, combined it with the others, and fashioned by them Libra (the Balance) in the universe, the month Tisri in the year, and the gall of the human body (male and female).

8th. He caused the letter נ (N) to predominate in smell, crowned it, combined it with the others, and fashioned by them Scorpio (the Scorpion) in the universe, the month Marcheshvan in the year, and the small intestine in the human body (male and female).

9th. He caused the letter ס (S) to predominate in sleep, crowned it, combined it with the others, and fashioned by them Sagittarius (the Archer) in the universe, the month Kislev in the year, and the stomach in the human body (male and female).

10th. He caused the letter ע (O) to predominate in anger, crowned it, combined it with the others, and fashioned by them Capricorn (the Goat) in the universe, the month Tebet in the year, and the liver in the human body (male and female).

11th. He caused the letter צ (Tz) to predominate in taste (or swallowing), crowned it, combined it with the others, and fashioned by them Aquarius (the Water Bearer) in the universe, the month Sebat in the year, and the esophagus in the human body (male and female).

12th. He caused the letter ק (Q) to predominate in mirth, crowned it, combined it with the others, and fashioned by them Pisces (the Fishes) in the universe, the month Adar in the year, and the spleen in the human body (male and female).

6. He made them as a conflict, He arranged them as provinces and drew them up like a wall. He armed them and set one against another as in warfare. (The Elohim did likewise in the other spheres.)

CHAPTER SIX

1. There are three Mothers or first elements, א מ ש (A, M, Sh), from which emanated three Fathers (progenitors)—primordial (spiritual) air, water, and fire—from which issued the seven planets (heavens) with their angels, and the twelve oblique points (zodiac).

2. To prove this there are three faithful witnesses: the universe, the year, and man. There are the twelve, the balance, and the seven. Above is the Dragon, below is the world, and lastly the heart of man; and in the midst is God who regulates them all.

3. The first elements are air, water, and fire; the fire is above, the water is below, and a breath of air establishes balance between them. The token is: the fire carries the water. The letter מ (M) is mute; ש (Sh) is hissing like fire; there is א (A) among them, a breath of air which reconciles the two.

4. The Dragon (Tali) is in the universe like a king upon his throne; the celestial sphere is in the year like a king in his empire; and the heart is in the body of men like a king in warfare.

5. God also set the opposites against each other: the good against the evil, and the evil against the good. Good proceeds from good, evil from evil; the good

purifies the bad, the bad the good. The good is reserved for the good, and the evil for the wicked.

6. There are three of which each stands by itself: one is in the affirmative (filled with good), one is in the negative (filled with evil), and the third equilibrates them.

7. There are seven divided three against three, and one in the midst of them (balance). Twelve stand in warfare: three produce love and three hatred; three are life-givers and three are destroyers.

8. The three that cause love are the heart and the two ears; the three that produce hatred are the liver, the gall, and the tongue; the three life-givers are the two nostrils and the spleen; and the three destroyers are the mouth and the two lower openings of the body. Over all these rules God, the faithful king, from His holy habitation in all eternity. God is One above three, three are above seven, seven are above twelve, yet all are linked together.

9. There are twenty-two letters by which the I AM (YAH), the Lord of Hosts, Almighty and Eternal, designed and created by three Sepharim (Numbers, Letters, and Sounds) His universe, and formed by them all creatures and all those things that are yet to come.

10. When the Patriarch Abraham had comprehended the great truths, meditated upon them, and understood them perfectly, the Lord of the Universe (the Tetragrammaton) appeared to him, called him His friend, kissed him upon the head, and made with him a covenant. First, the covenant was between the ten fingers of his hands, which is the covenant of the tongue (spiritual); second, the covenant was between the ten toes of his feet, which is the covenant of circumcision (material); and God said of him, "Before I formed thee * * * I knew thee." (Jeremiah i. 5.)

Abraham bound the spirit of the twenty-two letters (the Thora) upon his tongue and God disclosed to him their secrets. God permitted the letters to be immersed in water, He burned them in the fire and imprinted them upon the winds. He distributed them among the seven planets and gave them to the twelve zodiacal signs.

XXVI

Fundamentals of Qabbalistic Cosmogony

he Qabbalists conceive of the Supreme Deity as an In-comprehensible Principle to be discovered only through the process of eliminating, in order, all its cognizable attri-butes. That which remains—when every knowable thing has been removed—is AIN SOPH, the eternal state of *Being*. Although indefinable, the Absolute permeates all space. Abstract to the degree of inconceivability, AIN SOPH is the *unconditioned state of all things*. Substances, essences, and intelligences are manifested out of the inscrutability of AIN SOPH, but the Absolute itself is without substance, essence, or intelli-gence. AIN SOPH may be likened to a great field of rich earth out of which rises a myriad of plants, each different in color, formation, and fragrance, yet each with its roots in the same dark loam—which, however, is unlike any of the forms nurtured by it. The "plants" are universes, gods, and man, all nourished by AIN SOPH and all with their source in one definitionless essence; all with their spir-its, souls, and bodies fashioned from this essence, and doomed, like the plant, to return to the black ground—AIN SOPH, the only Immortal—whence they came.

AIN SOPH was referred to by the Qabbalists as *The Most Ancient of all the Ancients*. It was always considered as sexless. Its symbol was a closed eye. While it may be truly said of AIN SOPH that to define It is to defile It, the Rabbis pos-tulated certain theories regarding the manner in which AIN SOPH projected creations out of Itself, and they also assigned to this Absolute Not-Being certain symbols as being descriptive, in part at least, of Its powers. The nature of AIN SOPH they symbolize by a circle, itself emblematic of eternity. This hypotheti-cal circle encloses a dimensionless area of incomprehensible life, and the circu-lar boundary of this life is abstract and measureless infinity.

THE HEBREW TRIAD.

The Qabbalists used the letter ש, *Shin*, to signify the trinity of the first three Sephiroth. The central circle slightly above the other two is the first Sephira—*Kether,* the White Head, the Crown. The other two circles represent *Chochmah,* the Father, and *Binah,* the Mother. From the union of the Divine Father and the Divine Mother are produced the worlds and the generations of living things. The three flame-like points of the letter ש have long been used to conceal this Creative Triad of the Qabbalists.

According to this concept, God is not only a Center but also Area. Centralization is the first step towards limitation. Therefore, centers which form in the substances of AIN SOPH are finite because they are predestined to dissolution back into the Cause of themselves, while AIN SOPH Itself is infinite because It is the ultimate condition of all things. The circular shape given to AIN SOPH signifies that space is hypothetically enclosed within a great crystal-like globe, outside of which there is nothing, not even a vacuum. Within this globe—symbolic of AIN SOPH—creation and dissolution take place. Every element and principle that will ever be used in the eternities of Kosmic birth, growth, and decay is within the transparent substances of this intangible sphere. It is the Kosmic Egg which is not broken till the great day "Be With Us," which is the end of the Cycle of Necessity, when all things return to their ultimate cause.

In the process of creation the diffused life of AIN SOPH retires from the circumference to the center of the circle and establishes a point, which is the first manifesting One—the primitive limitation of the all-pervading O. When the Divine Essence thus retires from the circular boundary to the center, It leaves behind the Abyss, or, as the Qabbalists term it, the Great Privation. Thus, in AIN SOPH is established a twofold condition where previously had existed but one. The first condition is the central point—the primitive objectified radiance of the eternal, subjectified life. About this radiance is darkness caused by the deprivation of the life which is drawn to the center to create the first point, or universal germ. The universal AIN SOPH, therefore, no longer shines through space, but rather upon space from an established first point. Isaac Myer describes this process as follows: "The Ain Soph at first was filling All and then made an absolute concentration into Itself which produced the Abyss, Deep, or Space, the Aveer Qadmon or Primitive Air, the Azoth; but this is not considered in the Qabbalah as a perfect void or vacuum, a perfectly empty Space, but is thought of as the Waters or Crystalline Chaotic Sea, in which was a certain degree of Light inferior to that by which all the created [worlds and hierarchies] were made." (See *The Qabbalah.*)

In the secret teachings of the Qabbalah it is taught that man's body is enveloped in an ovoid of bubble-like iridescence, which is called the Auric Egg. This is the causal sphere of man. It bears the same relationship to man's physical body that the globe of AIN SOPH bears to Its treated universes. In fact, this Auric Egg is the AIN SOPH sphere of the entity called man. In reality, therefore, the supreme consciousness of man is in this aura, which extends in all directions and completely encircles his lower bodies. As the consciousness in the Kosmic Egg is withdrawn into a central point, which is then called God—the Supreme One—so the consciousness in the Auric Egg of man is concentrated, thereby causing the establishment of a point of consciousness called the Ego. As the universes in Nature are formed from powers latent in the Kosmic Egg, so everything used by man in all his incarnations throughout the kingdoms of Nature is drawn from the latent powers within his Auric Egg. Man never passes from this egg; it remains even after death. His births, deaths, and rebirths all take place within it, and it cannot be broken until the lesser day "Be With Us," when mankind—like the universe—is liberated from the Wheel of Necessity.

The Qabbalistic System of Worlds

On the accompanying circular chart, the concentric rings represent diagrammatically the forty rates of vibration (called by the Qabbalists *Spheres*) which emanate from AIN SOPH. The circle X 1 is the outer boundary of space. It circumscribes the area of AIN SOPH. The nature of AIN SOPH Itself is divided into three parts, represented by the spaces respectively between X 1 and X 2, X 2 and X 3, X 3 and A 1; thus:

X 1 to X 2, אין , AIN, the vacuum of pure spirit.

X 2 to X 3, אין סוף , AIN SOPH, the Limitless and Boundless.

X 3 to A 1, אין סוף אור , AIN SOPH AUR, the Limitless Light.

It should be borne in mind that in the beginning the Supreme Substance, AIN, alone permeated the area of the circle; the inner rings had not yet come into manifestation. As the Divine Essence concentrated Itself, the rings X 2 and X 3 became apprehensible, for AIN SOPH is a limitation of AIN, and AIN SOPH AUR, or Light, is a still greater limitation. Thus the nature of the Supreme One is considered to be threefold, and from this threefold nature the powers and elements of creation were reflected into the Abyss left by the motion of AIN SOPH towards the center of Itself. The continual motion of AIN SOPH towards the center of Itself resulted in the establishment of the dot in the circle. The dot was called God, as being the supreme individualization of the Universal Essence. Concerning this the Zohar says:

"When the concealed of the Concealed wished to reveal Himself He first made a single point: the Infinite was entirely unknown, and diffused no light before this luminous point violently broke through into vision."

The name of this point is I AM, called by the Hebrews *Eheieh.* The Qabbalists gave many names to this dot. On this subject Christian D. Ginsberg writes, in substance: The dot is called the first crown, because it occupies the highest position. It is called the aged, because it is the first emanation. It is called the primordial or smooth point. It is called the white head, the *Long Face*—Macroprosophus—and the inscrutable height, because it controls and governs all the other emanations.

When the white shining point had appeared, it was called *Kether,* which means the *Crown,* and out of it radiated nine great globes, which arranged themselves in the form of a tree. These nine together with the first crown constituted the first system of *Sephiroth.* These ten were the first limitation of ten abstract points within the nature of AIN SOPH Itself. The power of AIN SOPH did not descend into these globes but rather was reflected upon them as the light of the sun is reflected upon the earth and planets. These ten globes were called the shining sapphires, and it is believed by many Rabbins that the word *sapphire* is the basis of the word *Sephira* (the singular of Sephiroth). The great area which had been privated by the withdrawal of AIN SOPH into the central point, *Kether,* was now filled by four concentric globes called worlds, or spheres, and the light of the ten Sephiroth was reflected down through each of these in turn. This resulted in the establishment of four symbolical trees, each bearing the reflections of the ten Sephirothic globes.

The 40 spheres of creation out of AIN SOPH are divided into four great world chains, as follows:

A 1 to A 10, *Atziluth,* the Boundless World of Divine Names.

B 1 to B 10, *Briah,* the Archangelic World of Creations.

C 1 to C 10, *Yetzirah,* the Hierarchal World of Formations.

D 1 to D 10, *Assiah,* the Elemental World of Substances.

Each of these worlds has ten powers, or spheres—a parent globe and nine others which come out of it as emanations, each globe born out of the one preceding. On the plane of *Atziluth* (A 1 to A 10), the highest and most divine of all the created worlds, the unmanifested AIN SOPH established His first point or dot in the Divine Sea—the three spheres of X. This dot—A 1—contains all creation within it, but in this first divine and uncontaminated state the dot, or first manifested God, was not considered as a personality by the Qabbalists but rather as a divine establishment or foundation. It was called the *First Crown* and from it issued the other circles of the *Atziluthic* World: A 2, A 3, A 4, A 5, A 6, A 7, A 8, A 9, and A 10. In the three lower worlds these circles are intelligences, planets, and elements, but in this first divine world they are called the *Rings of the Sacred Names.*

The first ten great circles (or globes) of light which were manifested out of AIN SOPH and the ten names of God assigned to them by the Qabbalists are as follows:

From AIN SOPH came A 1, the First Crown, and the name of the first power of God was *Eheieh,* which means *I Am* [*That I Am*].

From A 1 came A 2, the first Wisdom, and the name of the second power of God was *Jehovah,* which means *Essence of Being.*

From A 2 came A 3, the first Understanding, and the name of the third power of God was *Jehovah Elohim,* which means *God of Gods.*

From A 3 came A 4, the first Mercy, and the name of the fourth power of God was *El,* which means *God the Creator.*

From A 4 came A 5, the first Severity, and the name of the fifth power of God was *Elohim Gibor,* which means *God the Potent.*

From A 5 came A 6, the first Beauty, and the name of the sixth power of God was *Eloah Vadaath,* which means *God the Strong.*

From A 6 came A 7, the first Victory, and the name of the seventh power of God was *Jehovah Tzaboath,* which means *God of Hosts.*

From A 7 came A 8, the first Glory, and the name of the eighth power of God was *Elohim Tzaboath,* which means *Lord God of Hosts.*

From A 8 came A 9, the first Foundation, and the name of the ninth power of God was *Shaddai, El Chai,* which means *Omnipotent.*

From A 9 came A 10, the first Kingdom, and the name of the tenth power of God was *Adonai Melekh,* which means *God.*

From A 10 came B 1, the Second Crown, and the World of *Briah* was established.

The ten emanations from A 1 to A 10 inclusive are called the foundations of all creations. The Qabbalists designate them the ten roots of the Tree of Life. They are arranged in the form of a great human figure called Adam Qadmon—the man made from the fire mist (red dirt), the prototypic Universal Man. In the *Atziluthic* World, the powers of God are most purely manifested. These ten pure and perfect radiations do not descend into the lower worlds and take upon themselves forms, but are reflected upon the substances of the inferior spheres. From the first, or *Atziluthic,* World they are reflected into the second, or *Briatic,* World. As the reflection always lacks some of the brilliancy of the original image, so in the *Briatic* World the ten radiations lose part of their infinite power. A reflection is always like the thing reflected, but smaller and fainter.

In the second world, B 1 to B 10, the order of the spheres is the same as in the *Atziluthic* World, but the ten circles of light are less brilliant and more tangible, and are here referred to as ten great Spirits—divine creatures who assist in the establishment of order and intelligence in the universe. As already noted, B 1 is born out of A 10 and is included within all the spheres superior to itself. Out of B 1 are taken nine globes—B 2, B 3, B 4, B 5, B 6, B 7, B 8, B 9, and B 10—which constitute the World of *Briah.* These ten subdivisions, however, are really the ten *Atziluthic* powers reflected into the substance of the *Briatic* World. B 1 is the ruler of this world, for it contains all the other rings of its own world and also the rings of the third and fourth worlds, C and D. In the World of *Briah* the ten spheres of light are called the *Archangels of Briah.* Their order and powers are as follows:

From A 10 came B 1, the Second Crown; it is called *Metatron,* the Angel of the Presence.

From B 1 came B 2, the second Wisdom; it is called *Raziel,* the Herald of Deity who revealed the mysteries of Qabbalah to Adam.

From B 2 came B 3, the second Understanding; it is called *Tsaphkiel,* the Contemplation of God.

From B 3 came B 4, the second Mercy; it is called *Tsadkiel,* the Justice of God.

From B 4 came B 5, the second Severity; it is called *Samael,* the Severity of God.

From B 5 came B 6, the second Beauty; it is called *Michael,* Like Unto God.

From B 6 came B 7, the second Victory; it is called *Haniel,* the Grace of God.

From B 7 came B 8, the second Glory; it is called *Raphael,* the Divine Physician.

From B 8 came B 9, the second Foundation; it is called *Gabriel,* the Man-God.

From B 9 came B 10, the second Kingdom; it is called *Sandalphon,* the Messias.

From B 10 came C 1, the Third Crown, and the World of *Yetzirah* was established.

The ten Archangels of *Briah* are conceived to be ten great spiritual beings, whose duty is to manifest the ten powers of the Great Name of God existent in the *Atziluthic* World, which surrounds and interpenetrates the entire world of creation. All things manifesting in the lower worlds exist first in the intangible rings of the upper spheres, so that creation is, in truth, the process of making tangible the intangible by extending the intangible into various vibratory rates. The ten globes of *Briatic* power, while themselves reflections, are mirrored downward into the third or *Yetziratic* World, where still more limited in their expression they become the spiritual and invisible zodiac which is behind the visible band of constellations. In this third world the ten globes of the original *Atziluthic* World are greatly limited and dimmed, but they are still infinitely powerful in comparison with the state of substance in which man dwells. In the third world, C 1 to C 10, the globes become hierarchies of celestial creatures, called the *Choirs of Yetzirah*. Here again, all are included within the ring C 1, the power which controls the *Yetziratic* World and which includes within itself and controls the entire world D. The order of the globes and the names of the hierarchies composing them are as follows:

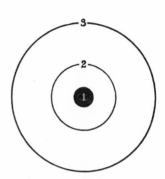

THE PLAN OF DIVINE ACTIVITY.

According to the Qabbalists, the life of the Supreme Creator permeates all substance, all space, and all time, but for diagrammatic purposes the Supreme, All-Inclusive Life is limited by Circle 3, which may be called "the boundary line of Divine existence." The Divine Life permeating the area bounded by Circle 3 is focused at Point 1, which thus becomes the personification of the impersonal life and is termed "the First Crown." The creative forces pouring through Point 1 come into manifestation as the objective universe in the intermediate space, Circle 2.

From B 10 came C 1, the Third Crown; the Hierarchy is the Cherubim, *Chaioth Ha Kadosh,* the Holy Animals.

From C 1 came C 2, the third Wisdom; the Hierarchy is the Cherubim, *Orphanim,* the Wheels.

From C 2 came C 3, the third Understanding; the Hierarchy is the Thrones, *Aralim,* the Mighty Ones.

From C 3 came C 4, the third Mercy; the Hierarchy is the Dominations, *Chashmalim,* the Brilliant Ones.

From C 4 came C 5, the third Severity; the Hierarchy is the Powers, *Seraphim,* the Flaming Serpents.

From C 5 came C 6, the third Beauty; the Hierarchy is the Virtues, *Melachim,* the Kings.

From C 6 came C 7, the third Victory; the Hierarchy is the Principalities, *Elohim,* the Gods.

From C 7 came C 8, the third Glory; the Hierarchy is the Archangels, *Ben Elohim,* the Sons of God.

From C 8 came C 9, the third Foundation; the Hierarchy is the Angels, *Cherubim,* the Seat of the Sons.

From C 9 came C 10, the third Kingdom; the Hierarchy is Humanity, the *Ishim,* the Souls of Just Men.

From C 10 came D 1, the Fourth Crown, and the World of *Assiah* was established.

From the *Yetziratic* World the light of the ten spheres is reflected into the World of *Assiah,* the lowest of the four. The ten globes of the original *Atziluthic* World here take upon themselves forms of physical matter and the sidereal system is the result. The World of *Assiah,* or the elemental world of substance, is the one into which humanity descended at the time of Adam's fall. The Garden of Eden is the three upper worlds, and for his sins man was forced into the sphere of substance and assumed coats of skin (bodies). All of the spiritual forces of the upper worlds, A, B, C, when they strike against the elements of the lower world, D, are distorted and perverted, resulting in the creation of hierarchies of demons to correspond with the good spirits in each of the higher worlds. In all the ancient Mysteries, matter was regarded as the source of all evil and spirit the source of all good, for matter inhibits and limits, often so clogging the inner perceptions that man is unable to recognize his own divine potentialities. Since matter thus prevents humanity from claiming its birthright, it is called the *Adversary,* the power of evil. The fourth world, D, is the world of solar systems, comprising not only the one of which the earth is a part but all the solar systems in the universe.

Opinions differ as to the arrangement of the globes of this last world, D 1 to D 10 inclusive. The ruler of the fourth world is D 1, called by some the *Fiery Heaven;* by others the *Primum Mobile,* or the *First Motion.* From this whirling fire emanates the material starry zodiac, D 2, in contradistinction to the invisible spiritual zodiac of the *Yetziratic* World. From the zodiac, D 2, are differentiated the spheres of the planets in concatenate order. The ten spheres of the World of *Assiah* are as follows:

From C 10 came D 1, the Fourth Crown; *Rashith Ha-Galagalum,* the Primum Mobile, the fiery mist which is the beginning of the material universe.

From D 1 came D 2, the fourth Wisdom; *Masloth,* the Zodiac, the Firmament of the Fixed Stars.

From D 2 came D 3, the fourth Understanding; *Shabbathai,* the sphere of Saturn.

From D 3 came D 4, the fourth Mercy; *Tzedeg,* the sphere of Jupiter.

From D 4 came D 5, the fourth Severity; *Madim,* the sphere of Mars.

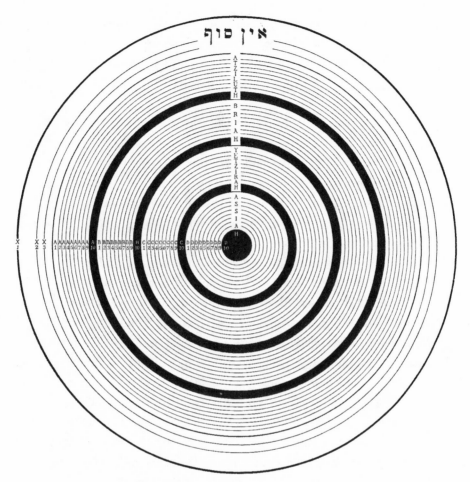

אין סוף

ATZILUTH
BRIAH
YETZIRAH
ASSIAH

THE QABBALISTIC SCHEME OF THE FOUR WORLDS.

In the above chart the dark line between X3 and A1 constitutes the boundary of the original dot, while the concentric circles within this heavier line symbolize the emanations and worlds which came forth from the dot. As this dot is contained within the outer rings X 1, X 2, and X 3, and represents the first establishment of individualized existence, so the lower universe symbolized by the forty concentric circles within the dot represents the lower creation evolved out of and yet contained within the nature of the first Crown, which may be called God, within whom the divine powers, the celestial beings, the sidereal worlds, and man, live and move and have their being. It is highly important that all the rings within A1 be considered as being enclosed by the primitive dot, which is itself encircled by the great ring X1, or the Auric Egg of AIN SOPH.

Each ring includes within its own nature all the rings within itself and is included within the natures of all the rings outside of itself. Thus, A 1—the primitive dot—controls and contains the thirty-nine rings which it encloses, all of these partaking of its nature in varying degrees according to their respective dignities. Consequently, the entire area from A 1 to D 10 inclusive is the original dot, and the rings symbolize the divisions which took place within it and the emanations which poured out from it after its establishment in the midst of the abstract nature of AIN SOPH. The powers of the rings decrease towards the center of the diagram, for power is measured by the number of things controlled, and each ring controls the rings within it and is controlled by the rings outside of it. Thus, while A 1 controls thirty-nine rings besides itself, B 1 controls only twenty-nine rings besides its own. Therefore, A 1 is more powerful than B 1. As the greatest spiritual solidity, or permanence, is at the circumference and the greatest material density, or impermanence, is at the center of the diagram, the rings as they decrease in power become more material and substantial until the center sphere, D 10, symbolizes the actual chemical elements of the earth. The rates of vibration are also lower as the rings approach the center. Thus, the vibration of A 2 is lower than A 1 but higher than A 3, and so on in decreasing scale towards the center, A 1 being the highest and D 10 the lowest sphere of creation. While A 1, the ruler of creation, controls the circles marked A, B, C, and D, it is less than the three rings of AIN SOPH—X 1, X 2, and X 3—and therefore bows before the throne of the ineffable Creator from whose substances it was individualized.

From D 5 came D 6, the fourth Beauty; *Shemesh,* the sphere of the Sun.

From D 6 came D 7, the fourth Victory; *Nogah,* the sphere of Venus.

From D 7 came D 8, the fourth Glory; *Kokab,* the sphere of Mercury.

From D 8 came D 9, the fourth Foundation; *Levanah,* the sphere of the Moon.

From D 9 came D 10, the Fourth Kingdom; *Cholom Yosodoth,* the sphere of the Four Elements.

By inserting a sphere (which he calls the *Empyrean*) before the *Primum Mobile,* Kircher moves each of the other spheres down one, resulting in the elimination of the sphere of the elements and making D 10 the sphere of the Moon.

In the World of *Assiah* are to be found the demons and tempters. These are likewise reflections of the ten great globes of *Atziluth,* but because of the distortion of the images resulting from the base substances of the World of *Assiah* upon which they are reflected, they become evil creatures, called *shells* by the Qabbalists. There are ten hierarchies of these demons to correlate with the ten hierarchies of good spirits composing the *Yetziratic* World. There are also ten Archdemons, corresponding to the ten Archangels of *Briah.* The black magicians use these inverted spirits in their efforts to attain their nefarious ends, but in time the demon destroys those who bind themselves to it. The ten orders of demons and the ten Archdemons of the World of *Assiah* are as follows:

D 1, the evil Crown; the hierarchy is called *Thaumiel,* the doubles of God, the Two-headed; the Archdemons are *Satan* and *Moloch.*

From D 1 came D 2, the evil Wisdom; the hierarchy is called *Chaigidiel,* those who obstruct; the Archdemon is *Adam Belial.*

From D 2 came D 3, the evil Understanding; the hierarchy is called *Satharial,* the concealment of God; the Archdemon is *Lucifuge.*

From D 3 came D 4, the evil Mercy; the hierarchy is called *Gamchicoth,* the disturber of things; the Archdemon is *Astaroth.*

From D 4 came D 5, the evil Severity; the hierarchy is called *Golab,* incendiarism and burning; the Archdemon is *Asmodeus.*

From D 5 came D 6, the evil Beauty; the hierarchy is called *Togarini,* the wranglers; the Archdemon is *Belphegor.*

From D 6 came D 7, the evil Victory; the hierarchy is called *Harab Serap,* the dispensing Raven; the Archdemon is *Baal Chanan.*

From D7 came D8, the evil Glory; the hierarchy is called *Samael,* the embroiler; the Archdemon is *Adramelek.*

From D 8 came D 9, the evil Foundation; the hierarchy is called *Gamaliel,* the obscene; the Archdemon is *Lilith.*

From D 9 came D 10, the evil Kingdom; the hierarchy is called *Nahemoth*, the impure; the Archdemon is *Nahema*.

The Qabbalists declare that the worlds, intelligences, and hierarchies were established according to the vision of Ezekiel. By the man of Ezekiel's vision is symbolized the World of *Atziluth;* by the throne, the World of *Briah;* by the firmament, the World of *Yetzirah;* and by the living creatures the World of *Assiah*. These spheres are the wheels within wheels of the prophet. The Qabbalists next established a human figure in each of the four worlds: A 1 was the head and A 10 the feet of the man of *Atziluth;* B 1 was the head and B 10 the feet of the man of *Briah;* C 1 was the head and C 10 the feet of the man of *Yetzirah;* D 1 was the head and D 10 the feet of the man of *Assiah*. These four are called the *World Men*. They are considered androgynous and are the prototypes of humanity.

The human body, like that of the universe, is considered to be a material expression of ten globes or spheres of light. Therefore man is called the *Microcosm*—the little world, built in the image of the great world of which he is a part. The Qabbalists also established a mysterious universal man with his head at A 1 and his feet at D 10. This is probably the secret significance of the great figure of Nebuchadnezzar's dream, with its head in the World of *Atziluth*, its arms and hands in the World of *Briah*, its generative system in the World of *Yetzirah*, and its legs and feet in the World of *Assiah*. This is the *Grand Man of the Zohar*, of whom Eliphas Levi writes:

"It is not less astonishing to observe at the beginning of the Zohar the profundity of its notions and the sublime simplicity of its images. It is said as follows: 'The science of equilibrium is the key of occult science. Unbalanced forces perish in the void. So passed the kings of the elder world, the princes of the giants. They have fallen like trees without roots, and their place is found no more. Through the conflict of unbalanced forces, the devastated earth was void and formless, until the Spirit of God made for itself a place in heaven and reduced the mass of waters. All the aspirations of Nature were directed then towards unity of form, towards the living synthesis of equilibrated forces; the face of God, crowned with light, rose over the vast sea and was reflected in the waters thereof. His two eyes were manifested, radiating with splendour, darting two beams of light which crossed with those of the reflection. The brow of God and His eyes formed a triangle in heaven, and its reflection formed a second triangle in the waters. So was revealed the number six, being that of universal creation.' The text, which would be unintelligible in a literal version, is translated here by way of interpretation. The author makes it plain that the human form which he ascribes to Deity is only an image of his meaning and that God is beyond expression by human thought or representation by any figure. Pascal said that God is a circle, of which the center is everywhere and the circumference nowhere. But how is one to imagine a circle apart from its circumference? The Zohar adopts the antithesis of this paradoxical image and in respect of the circle of Pascal would say rather that the circumference is everywhere, while that which is nowhere is the center. It is however to a balance and not to a circle that it compares the universal equilibrium of things. It affirms that equilibrium is everywhere and so also is the central point where the balance hangs in suspension. We find that the Zohar is thus more forcible and more profound than Pascal. * * * The Zohar is a genesis of light; the Sepher Yetzirah is a ladder of truth. Therein are expounded the two-and-thirty absolute symbols of speech—being numbers and letters. Each letter produces a number, an idea and a form, so that mathematics are applicable to forms and ideas, even as to numbers, in virtue of an exact proportion, and a perfect correspondence. By the science of the Sepher Yetzirah, the human mind is rooted in truth and in reason; it accounts for all progress possible to intelligence by means of the evolution of numbers. Thus does the Zohar represent absolute truth, while the Sepher Yetzirah furnishes the method of its acquisition, its discernment and application." (*History of Magic.*)

By placing man himself at the point D 10, his true constitution is revealed. He exists upon four worlds, only one of which is visible. It is then made evident that his parts and members upon the material plane are, by analogy, hierarchies and intelligences in the higher worlds. Here, again, the law of interpenetration is evidenced. Although within man is the entire universe (the 43 spheres interpenetrating D 10), he is ignorant of its existence because he cannot exercise control over that which is superior to or greater than himself. Nevertheless, all these higher spheres exercise control over him, as his functions and activities demonstrate. If they did not, he would be an inert mass of substance. Death is merely the result of deflecting the life impulses of the higher rings away from the lower body.

The control of the transubstantial rings over their own material reflection is called *life,* and the spirit of man is, in reality, a name given to this great host of intelligences, which are focused upon substance through a point called the *ego,* established in the midst of themselves. X 1 is the outside boundary of the human Auric Egg, and the entire diagram becomes a cross section of the constitution of man, or a cross section of the Kosmic constitution, if correlated with the universe. By the secret culture of the Qabbalistic School, man is taught how to climb the rings (unfold his consciousness) until at last he returns to AIN SOPH. The process by which this is accomplished is called the *Fifty Gates of*

Light. Kircher, the Jesuit Qabbalist, declares that Moses passed through forty-nine of the gates, but that Christ alone passed the fiftieth gate.

To the third edition of the *Sepher Yetzirah* translated from the Hebrew by Wm. Wynn Westcott are appended the Fifty Gates of Intelligence emanating from *Binah,* the second Sephira. The source of this information is Kircher's *Œdipus Ægyptiacus.* The gates are divided into six orders, of which the first four have each ten subdivisions, the fifth nine, and the sixth only one.

The first order of gates is termed *Elementary* and its divisions are as follows: (1) Chaos, Hyle, the First Matter; (2) Formless, void, lifeless; (3) The Abyss; (4) Origin of the Elements; (5) Earth (no seed germs); (6) Water; (7) Air; (8) Fire; (9) Differentiation of qualities; (10) Mixture and combination.

The second order of gates is termed *Decad of Evolution* and its divisions are as follows: (11) Minerals differentiate; (12) Vegetable principles appear; (13) Seeds germinate in moisture; (14) Herbs and Trees; (15) Fructification in vegetable life; (16) Origin of low forms of animal life; (17) Insects and Reptiles appear; (18) Fishes, vertebrate life in the waters; (19) Birds, vertebrate life in the air; (20) Quadrupeds, vertebrate earth animals.

The third order of gates is termed *Decad of Humanity* and its divisions are as follows: (21) Appearance of Man; (22) Material human body; (23) Human Soul conferred; (24) Mystery of Adam and Eve; (25) Complete Man as the Microcosm; (26) Gift of five human faces acting exteriorly; (27) Gift of five powers to the soul; (28) Adam Kadmon, the Heavenly Man; (29) Angelic beings; (30) Man in the image of God.

The fourth order of gates is termed *World of Spheres* and its divisions are as follows: (31) The Heaven of the Moon; (32) The Heaven of Mercury; (33) The Heaven of Venus; (34) The Heaven of the Sun; (35) The Heaven of Mars; (36) The Heaven of Jupiter; (37) The Heaven of Saturn; (38) The Firmament; (39) The Primum Mobile; (40) The Empyrean Heaven.

The fifth order of gates is termed *The Angelic World* and its divisions are as follows: (41) Ishim—Sons of Fire; (42) Orphanim—Cherubim; (43) Aralim—Thrones; (44) Chashmalim—Dominions; (45) Seraphim—Virtues; (46) Melachim—Powers; (47) Elohim—Principalities; (48) Ben Elohim—Angels; (49) Cherubim—Archangels. [The order of the Angels is a matter of controversy, the arrangement above differing from that accepted in other sections of this volume. The Rabbins disagree fundamentally as to the proper sequence of the Angelic names.]

The sixth order is termed *The Archetype* and consists of but one gate: (50) God, AIN SOPH, He whom no mortal eye hath seen. The fiftieth gate leads from creation into the Creative Principle and he who passes through it returns into the unlimited and undifferentiated condition of ALL. The fifty gates reveal a certain evolutionary process and it was declared by the Rabbins that he who would attain to the highest degree of understanding must pass sequentially through all of these orders of life, each of which constituted a gate in that the spirit, passing from the lower to the higher, found in each more responsive organism new avenues of self-expression.

XXVII

The Tree of the Sephiroth

he Tree of the Sephiroth may be considered an invaluable compendium of the secret philosophy which originally was the spirit and soul of Chasidism. The Qabbalah is the priceless heritage of Israel, but each year those who comprehend its true principles become fewer in number. The Jew of today, if he lacks a realization of the profundity of his people's doctrines, is usually permeated with that most dangerous form of ignorance, modernism, and is prone to regard the Qabbalah either as an evil to be shunned like the plague or as a ridiculous superstition which has survived the black magic of the Dark Ages. Yet without the key which the Qabbalah supplies, the spiritual mysteries of both the Old and the New Testament must remain unsolved by Jew and Gentile alike.

The Sephirothic Tree consists of ten globes of luminous splendor arranged in three vertical columns and connected by 22 channels or paths. The ten globes are called the *Sephiroth* and to them are assigned the numbers 1 to 10. The three columns are called *Mercy* (on the right), *Severity* (on the left), and, between them, *Mildness,* as the reconciling power. The columns may also be said to represent *Wisdom, Strength,* and *Beauty,* which form the triune support of the universe, for it is written that the foundation of all things is the *Three.* The 22 channels are the letters of the Hebrew alphabet and to them are assigned the major trumps of the Tarot deck of symbolic cards.

Eliphas Levi declared that by arranging the Tarot cards according to a definite order man could discover all that is knowable concerning his God, his universe, and himself. When the ten numbers which pertain to the globes (Sephiroth) are combined with the 22 letters relating to the channels, the resultant sum is 32—the number peculiar to the Qabbalistic Paths of Wisdom. These Paths, occasionally referred to as the 32 teeth in the mouth of the *Vast*

ᏟXXIII

REPRESENTATION CONTAINING THE SUM TOTAL OF THE CABALA FOR INSERTION
IN VOL.,II, BOOK IV, CONCERNING CABALA OF THE HEBREWS

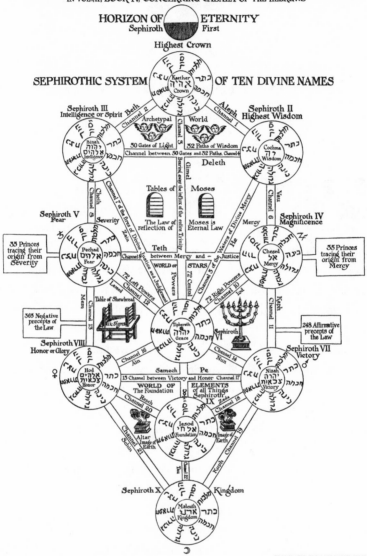

TRANSLATED FROM KIRCHER'S *ŒDIPUS ÆGYPTIACUS.*

THE SEPHIROTHIC TREE OF THE LATER QABBALISTS.

Having demonstrated that the Qabbalists divided the universe into four worlds, each consisting of ten spheres, it is necessary to consider next how the ten spheres of each world were arranged into what is called the "Sephirothic Tree." This Tree is composed of ten circles, representing the numbers 1 to 10 and connected together by twenty-two canals—the twenty-two letters of the Hebrew alphabet. The ten numbers plus the twenty-two letters result in the occult number 32, which, according to the *Mishna*, signifies the Thirty-two Paths of Wisdom. Letters and numbers, according to the Qabbalists, are the keys to all knowledge, for by a secret system of arranging them the mysteries of creation are revealed. For this reason they are called "the Paths of Wisdom." This occult fact is carefully concealed in the 32nd degree of Freemasonry.

There are four trees, one in each of the four worlds described in the preceding chapter. The first is in the Atziluthic World, the ten circles being the ten globes of light established in the midst of AIN SOPH. The powers and attributes of this Tree are reflected into each of the three lower worlds, the form of the Tree remaining the same but its power diminishing as it descends. To further complicate their doctrine, the Qabbalists created another tree, which was a composite of all four of the world trees but consisted of only ten globes. In this single tree were condensed all the arcana previously scattered through the voluminous archives of Qabbalistic literature.

Countenance or as the 32 nerves that branch out from the Divine Brain, are analogous to the first 32 degrees of Freemasonry, which elevate the candidate to the
dignity of a Prince of the Royal Secret. Qabbalists also consider it extremely significant that in the original Hebrew Scriptures the name of God should occur
32 times in the first chapter of Genesis. (In the English translations of the Bible
the name appears 33 times.) In the mystic analysis of the human body, according
to the Rabbins, 32 spinal segments lead upward to the Temple of Wisdom—the
skull.

The four Qabbalistic Trees described in the preceding chapter were combined by later Jewish scholars into one all-inclusive diagram and termed by
them not only the Sephirothic but also the *Archetypal,* or *Heavenly, Adam.*
According to some authorities, it is this Heavenly Adam, and not a terrestrial
man, whose creation is described in the opening chapters of Genesis. Out of the
substances of this divine man the universe was formed; in him it remains and
will continue even after dissolution shall resolve the spheres back into their own
primitive substance. The Deity is never conceived of as actually contained in the
Sephiroth, which are purely hypothetical vessels employed to define the limits
of the Creative Essence. Adolph Franck rather likens the Sephiroth to varicolored, transparent glass bowls filled with pure light, which apparently assumes
the color of its containers but whose essential nature remains ever unchanged
and unchangeable.

The ten Sephiroth composing the body of the prototypic Adam, the numbers related to them, and the parts of the universe to which they correspond are
as follows:

No.	The Sephiroth	The Universe	Alternative
1	Kether—the Crown	Primum Mobile	The Fiery Heavens
2	Chochmah—Wisdom	The Zodiac	The First Motion
3	Binah—Understanding	Saturn	The Zodiac
4	Chesed—Mercy	Jupiter	Saturn
5	Geburah—Severity	Mars	Jupiter
6	Tiphereth—Beauty	Sun	Mars
7	Netsah—Victory	Venus	Sun
8	Hod—Glory	Mercury	Venus

| 9 | Jesod—the Foundation | Moon | Mercury |
| 10 | Malchuth— the Kingdom | Elements | Moon |

It must continually be emphasized that the Sephiroth and the properties assigned to them, like the *tetractys* of the Pythagoreans, are merely symbols of the cosmic system with its multitude of parts. The truer and fuller meaning of these emblems may not be revealed by writing or by word of mouth, but must be divined as the result of study and meditation. In the *Sepher ha Zohar* it is written that there is a *garment*—the written doctrine—which every man may see. Those with understanding do not look upon the *garment* but at the body beneath it— the intellectual and philosophical code. The wisest of all, however, the servants of the Heavenly King, look at nothing save the soul—the spiritual doctrine—which is the eternal and ever-springing root of the law. Of this great truth Eliphas Levi also writes declaring that none can gain entrance to the secret House of Wisdom unless he wear the voluminous *cape* of Apollonius of Tyana and carry in his hand the *lamp* of Hermes. The cape signifies the qualities of self-possession and self-reliance which must envelope the seeker as a cloak of strength, while the ever-burning lamp of the sage represents the illumined mind and perfectly balanced intellect without which the mystery of the ages can never be solved.

The Sephirothic Tree is sometimes depicted as a human body, thus more definitely establishing the true identity of the first, or Heavenly, Man—*Adam Kadmon*—the *Idea* of the Universe. The ten divine globes (Sephiroth) are then considered as analogous to the ten sacred members and organs of the *Proto-gonos,* according to the following arrangement. Kether is the crown of the Proto-typic Head and perhaps refers to the pineal gland; Chochmah and Binah are the right and left hemispheres respectively of the Great Brain; Chesed and Geburah (Pechad) are the right and left arms respectively, signifying the active creative members of the Grand Man; Tiphereth is the heart, or, according to some, the entire viscera; Netsah and Hod are the right and left legs respectively, or the supports of the world; Jesod is the generative system, or the foundation of form; and Malchuth represents the two feet, or the base of being. Occasionally Jesod is considered as the male and Malchuth as the female generative power. The Grand Man thus conceived is the gigantic image of Nebuchadnezzar's dream, with head of gold, arms and chest of silver, body of brass, legs of iron, and feet of clay. The mediæval Qabbalists also assigned one of the Ten Commandments and a tenth part of the Lord's Prayer in sequential order to each of the ten Sephiroth.

Concerning the emanations from Kether which establish themselves as three triads of Creative Powers—termed in the *Sepher ha Zohar* three heads each with three faces—H. P. Blavatsky writes: "This [Kether] was the first Sephiroth, containing in herself the other nine ספירות Sephiroth, or intelligences. In their totality and unity they represent the archetypal man, Adam Kadmon, the πρωτόγονος, who in his individuality or unity is yet dual, or bisexual, the Greek *Didumos,* for he is the prototype of all humanity. Thus we obtain three trinities, each contained in a 'head.' In the first head, or face (the three-faced Hindu Trimurti), we find *Sephira* [Kether], the first androgyne, at the apex of the upper triangle, emitting *Hachama* [Chochmah], or Wisdom, a masculine and active potency—also called Jah, יה—and *Binah,* בינה, or Intelligence, a female and passive potency, also represented by the name Jehovah יהוה.. These three form the first trinity or 'face' of the Sephiroth. This triad emanated *Hesed,* חסד, or Mercy, a masculine active potency, also called *El,* from which emanated *Geburah* גבורה, or Justice, also called Eloha, a feminine passive potency; from the union of these two was produced *Tiphereth* תפארת, Beauty, Clemency, the Spiritual Sun, known by the divine name *Elohim;* and the second triad, 'face,' or 'head,' was formed. These emanating, in their turn, the masculine potency *Netzah,* נצח, Firmness, or Jehovah Sabaoth, who issued the feminine passive potency *Hod,* הוד, Splendor, or Elohim Sabaoth; the two produced *Jesod,* יסוד, Foundation, who is the mighty living one *El-Chai,* thus yielding the third trinity or 'head.' The tenth Sephiroth is rather a duad, and is represented on the diagrams as the lowest circle. It is Malchuth or Kingdom, מלכות, and Shekinah שכינה, also called Adonai, and *Cherubim* among the angelic hosts. The first 'Head' is called the Intellectual world; the second 'Head' is the Sensuous, or the world of Perception, and the third is the material or Physical world." (See *Isis Unveiled.*)

Among the later Qabbalists there is also a division of the Sephirothic Tree into five parts, in which the distribution of the globes is according to the following order:

(1) *Macroprosophus,* or the *Great Face,* is the term applied to Kether as the first and most exalted of the Sephiroth and includes the nine potencies or Sephiroth issuing from Kether.

(2) *Abba,* the *Great Father,* is the term generally applied to Chochmah—Universal Wisdom—the first emanation of Kether, but, according to Ibn Gebirol, Chochmah represents the Son, the Logos or the Word born from the union of Kether and Binah.

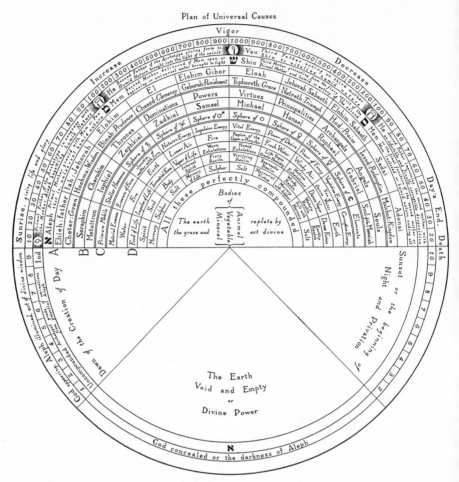

A TABLE OF SEPHIROTHIC CORRESPONDENCES.

FROM FLUDD'S *COLLECTIO OPERUM.*

The above diagram has been specially translated from the Latin as being of unique value to students of Qabbalism and also as an example of Robert Fludd's unusual ability in assembling tables of correspondences. Robert Fludd ranks among the most eminent Rosicrucians and Freemasons; in fact, he has often been called "the first English Rosicrucian." He has written several valuable documents directly bearing upon the Rosicrucian enigma. It is significant that the most important of his works should be published at the same time as those of Bacon, Shakespeare, and the first Rosicrucian authors.

(3) *Aima,* the *Great Mother,* is the name by which Binah, or the third Sephira, is generally known. This is the Holy Ghost, from whose body the generations issue forth. Being the third person of the Creative Triad, it corresponds to Jehovah, the Demiurgus.

(4) *Microprosophus,* or the *Lesser Face,* is composed of the six Sephiroth—Chesed, Geburah, Tiphereth, Netsah, Hod, and Jesod. The *Microprosophus* is commonly called the *Lesser Adam,* or *Zauir Anpin,* whereas the *Macroprosophus,* or *Superior Adam,* is *Arikh Anpin.* The *Lesser Face* is properly symbolized by the six-pointed star or interlaced triangles of Zion and also by

the six faces of the cube. It represents the directions north, east, south, west, up, and down, and also the first six days of Creation. In his list of the parts of the *Microprosophus,* MacGregor-Mathers includes Binah as the first and superior part of the *Lesser Adam,* thus making his constitution septenary. If *Microprosophus* be considered as sexpartite, then his globes (Sephiroth) are analogous to the six days of Creation, and the tenth globe, Malchuth, to the Sabbath of rest.

(5) The Bride of *Microprosophus* is the Malchuth—the epitome of the Sephiroth, its quaternary constitution being composed of blendings of the four elements. This is the divine Eve that is taken out of the side of *Microprosophus* and combines the potencies of the entire Qabbalistic Tree in one sphere, which may be termed man.

According to the mysteries of the Sephiroth, the order of the Creation, or the Divine Lightning Flash which zigzags through the four worlds according to the order of the divine emanations, is thus described: From AIN SOPH, the Nothing and All, the Eternal and Unconditioned Potency, issues *Macroprosophus,* the *Long Face,* of whom it is written, "Within His skull exist daily thirteen thousand myriads of worlds which draw their existence from Him and by Him are upheld." (See *The Greater Holy Assembly.*) *Macroprosophus,* the directionalized will of AIN SOPH, corresponding to Kether, the Crown of the Sephiroth, gives birth out of Himself to the nine lesser spheres of which He is the sum and the overbrooding cause. The 22 letters of the Hebrew alphabet, by the various combinations of which the laws of the universe are established, constitute the scepter of *Macroprosophus* which He wields from His flaming throne in the Atziluthic World.

From this eternal and ancient androgyne—Kether—come forth Chochmah, the *Great Father,* and Binah, the *Great Mother.* These two are usually referred to as *Abba* and *Aima* respectively—the first male and the first female, the prototypes of sex. These correspond to the first two letters of the sacred name, Jehovah, יהוה,, *IHVH.* The Father is the י, or *I,* and the Mother is the ה,, or *H.* *Abba* and *Aima* symbolize the creative activities of the universe, and are established in the creative world of Briah. In the *Sepher ha Zohar* it is written, "And therefore are all things established in the equality of male and female; for were it not so, how could they subsist? This beginning is the Father of all things; the Father of all Fathers; and both are mutually bound together, and the one path shineth into the other—Chochmah, Wisdom, as the Father; Binah, Understanding, as the Mother."

There is a difference of opinion concerning certain of the relationships of the parts of the first triad. Some Qabbalists, including Ibn Gebirol, consider Kether as the Father, Binah as the Mother, and Chochmah as the Son. In this later arrangement, Wisdom, which is the attribute of the Son, becomes the creator of the lower spheres. The symbol of Binah is the dove, a proper emblem for the brooding maternal instinct of the Universal Mother.

Because of the close similarity of their creative triad to the Christian Trinity, the later Qabbalists rearranged the first three Sephiroth and added a mysterious point called *Daath*—a hypothetical eleventh Sephira. This is located where the horizontal line connecting Chochmah and Binah crosses the vertical line joining Kether and Tiphereth. While *Daath* is not mentioned by the first Qabbalists, it is a highly important element and its addition to the Sephirothic Tree was not made without full realization of the significance of such action. If Chochmah be considered the active, intelligent energy of Kether, and Binah the receptive capacity of Kether, then *Daath* becomes the *thought* which, created by Chochmah, flows into Binah. The postulation of *Daath* clarifies the problem of the Creative Trinity, for here it is diagrammatically represented as consisting of Chochmah (the Father), Binah (the Mother, or Holy Ghost), and *Daath,* the Word by which the worlds were established. Isaac Myer discounts the importance of *Daath,* declaring it a subterfuge to conceal the fact that Kether, and not Chochmah, is the true Father of the Creative Triad. He makes no attempt to give a satisfactory explanation for the symbolism of this hypothetical Sephira.

According to the original conception, from the union of the Divine Father and the Divine Mother is produced *Microprosophus*—the *Short Face* or the *Lesser Countenance,* which is established in the Yetziratic World of formation and corresponds to the letter ו, or *V,* in the Great Name. The six powers of *Microprosophus* flow from and are contained in their own source, which is Binah, the Mother of the *Lesser Adam.* These constitute the spheres of the sacred planets; their name is *Elohim,* and they move upon the face of the deep. The tenth Sephira—Malchuth, the Kingdom—is described as the Bride of the *Lesser Adam,* created back to back with her lord, and to it is assigned the final ה, or *H,* the last letter of the Sacred Name. The dwelling place of Malchuth is in the fourth world—Assiah—and it is composed of all the superior powers reflected into the elements of the terrestrial sphere. Thus it will be seen that the Qabbalistic Tree extends through four worlds, with its branches in matter and its roots in the Ancient of Ancients—*Macroprosophus.*

Three vertical columns support the universal system as typified by the Sephirothic Tree. The central pillar has its foundation in Kether, the Eternal

One. It passes downward through the hypothetical Sephira, *Daath,* and then through Tiphereth and Jesod, with its lower end resting upon the firm foundation of Malchuth, the last of the globes. The true import of the central pillar is equilibrium. It demonstrates how the Deity always manifests by emanating poles of expression from the midst of Itself but remaining free from the illusion of polarity. If the numbers of the four Sephiroth connected by this column be added together (1 + 6 + 9 + 10), the sum is 26, the number of Jehovah. (See chapter on *Pythagorean Mathematics.*)

The column on the right, which is called *Jachin,* has its foundation on Chochmah, the outpouring Wisdom of God; the three globes suspended from it are all masculine potencies. The column at the left is called *Boaz.* The three globes upon it are feminine and receptive potencies, for it is founded in Understanding, a receptive and maternal potency. *Wisdom,* it will be noted, is considered as radiant or outpouring, and *Understanding* as receptive, or something which is filled by the flowing of *Wisdom.* The three pillars are ultimately united in Malchuth, in which all the powers of the superior worlds are manifested.

The four globes upon the central column reveal the function of the creative power in the various worlds. In the first world the creative power is *Will*—the one Divine Cause; in the second world, the hypothetical *Daath*—the Word coming forth from the Divine Thought; in the third world, Tiphereth—the Sun, or focal point between God and Nature; in the fourth world it is twofold, being the positive and negative poles of the reproductive system, of which Jesod is the male and Malchuth the female.

In Kircher's Sephirothic Tree it should be especially noted that the ornaments of the Tabernacle appear in the various parts of the diagram. These indicate a direct relationship between the sacred House of God and the universe—a relationship which must always be considered as existing between the Deity through whose activity the world is produced and the world itself, which must be the house or vehicle of that Deity. Could the modern scientific world but sense the true profundity of these philosophical deductions of the ancients, it would realize that those who fabricated the structure of the Qabbalah possessed a knowledge of the celestial plan comparable in every respect with that of the modern savant.

The *Tetragrammaton,* or the four-lettered Name of God, written thus יהוה, is pronounced Jehovah. The first letter is י, , *Yod,* the Germ, the Life, the Flame, the Cause, the One, and the most fundamental of the Jewish phallic emblems. Its numerical value is 10, and it is to be considered as the 1 containing the 10. In the Qabbalah it is declared that the *Yod* is in reality three *Yods,* of which the first is the *beginning,* the second is the *center,* and the third is the *end.* Its throne is the Sephira Chochmah (according to Ibn Gebirol, Kether), from which it goes forth to impregnate Binah, which is the first ה, *He.* The result of this union is Tiphereth, which is the ו, *Vau,* whose power is 6 and which symbolizes the six members of the *Lesser Adam.* The final ה, *He,* is Malchuth, the *Inferior Mother,* partaking in part of the potencies of the *Divine Mother,* the first *He.* By placing the four letters of the *Tetragrammaton* in a vertical column, a figure closely resembling the human body is produced, with *Yod* for the head, the first *He* for the arms and shoulders, *Vau* for the trunk of the body, and the final *He* for the hips and legs. If the Hebrew letters be exchanged for their English equivalents, the form is not materially changed or the analogy altered. It is also extremely significant that by inserting the letter ש, *Shin,* in the middle of the name *Jehovah,* the word *Jehoshua,* or *Jesus,* is formed thus:

יהשוה

In the Qabbalistic Mysteries, according to Eliphas Levi, the name *Jehovah* is occasionally written by connecting together 24 dots—the 24 powers before the throne—and it is believed that the name of the Power of Evil is the sign of Jehovah reversed or inverted. (See *Transcendental Magic.*) Of the Great Word, Albert Pike writes: "The True Word of a Mason is to be found in the concealed and profound meaning of the Ineffable Name of Deity, communicated by God to Moses; and which meaning was long lost by the very precautions taken to conceal it. The true pronunciation of that name was in truth a secret, in which, however, was involved the far more profound secret of its meaning. In that meaning is included all the truth that can be known by us, in regard to the nature of God." (See *Morals and Dogma.*)

XXVIII

Qabbalistic Keys to the Creation of Man

enrie Stephen, in *A World of Wonders,* published in 1607, mentions a monk of St. Anthony who declared that while in Jerusalem the patriarch of that city had shown him not only one of the ribs of the *Word made flesh* and some rays from the Star of Bethlehem, but also the snout of a seraph, a finger nail of a cherub, the horns of Moses, and a casket containing the breath of Christ! To a people believing implicitly in a seraph sufficiently tangible to have its proboscis preserved, the more profound issues of Judaistic philosophy must necessarily be incomprehensible. Nor is it difficult to imagine the reaction taking place in the mind of some ancient sage should he hear that a cherub—which, according to St. Augustine, signifies the Evangelists; according to Philo Judæus, the outermost circumference of the entire heavens; and according to several of the Church Fathers, the wisdom of God—had sprouted finger nails. The hopeless confusion of divine principles with the allegorical figures created to represent them to the limited faculties of the uninitiated has resulted in the most atrocious misconceptions of spiritual truths. Concepts well-nigh as preposterous as these, however, still stand as adamantine barriers to a true understanding of Old and New Testament symbolism; for, until man disentangles his reasoning powers from the web of venerated absurdities in which his mind has lain ensnared for centuries, how can Truth ever be discovered?

The Old Testament—especially the Pentateuch—contains not only the traditional account of the creation of the world and of man, but also, locked within it, the secrets of the Egyptian initiators of *Moses* concerning the genesis of the god-man (the initiate) and the mystery of his rebirth through philosophy. While the Lawgiver of Israel is known to have compiled several works other than those

FROM THE "BEAR" BIBLE.

THE VISION OF EZEKIEL.

This plate, which is from the first Protestant Bible published in Spanish, shows the *Mercavah*, or chariot of Jehovah, which appeared to Ezekiel by the river Chebar. The prophet beheld four strange creatures (E), each having four heads, four wings, and brazen hoofs like those of a calf. And there were four wheels (F) filled with eyes. Where the cherubim went the wheels went also. The space between the cherubim and the wheels was filled with coals of fire. Upon the top of the chariot was a throne, upon which sat the likeness of a man (H). Ezekiel fell upon his knees when he beheld the Mercavah surrounded by a whirlwind of clouds and flames (A, B, C). A hand (K) reached out from the clouds and the prophet was ordered to eat of a scroll which the hand held forth.

According to the mystics, the wheels supporting the throne of God represent the orbits of the planets, and the entire solar system is properly the Mercavah, or chariot of God. One of the divisions of the Qabbalah—that dealing wtih the arts and sciences of those planes which are under the heavens—is called the Mercavah. In the Zohar it is written that the celestial throne of Ezekiel's vision signifies the traditional law; the appearance of a man sitting upon the throne represents the written law. Philo Judæus in describing the cherubim upon the Ark of the Covenant declares that the figures are an intimation of the revolutions of the whole heavens, one of the cherubim representing the outer circumference and the other the inner sphere. Facing each other, they represent the two hemispheres of the world. The flaming sword of the cherubim of Genesis is the central motion and agitation of the heavenly bodies. In all probability it also represents the solar ray.

generally attributed to him, the writings now commonly circulated as the purported sixth and seventh books of Moses are in reality spurious treatises on black magic foisted on the credulous during the Middle Ages. Out of the hundreds of millions of pious and thoughtful students of Holy Writ, it is almost inconceivable that but a mere handful have sensed the sublimity of the esoteric teachings of Sod (the Jewish Mysteries of Adonai). Yet familiarity with the three Qabbalistical processes termed *Gematria, Notarikon,* and *Temurah* makes possible the discovery of many of the profoundest truths of ancient Jewish superphysics.

By Germatria is meant not only the exchange of letters for their numerical equivalents but also the method of determining by an analysis of its measurements the mystic purpose for which a building or other object was constructed. S. L. MacGregor-Mathers, in *The Kabbalah Unveiled,* gives this example of the application of Gematria: "Thus also the passage, Gen. xviii. 2 VHNH SHLSHH, *Vehenna Shalisha,* 'And lo, three men,' equals in numerical value ALV MIKAL GBRIAL VRPAL, *Elo Mikhael Gabriel Ve-Raphael,* 'These are Mikhael, Gabriel and Raphael;' for each phrase=701." Assuming the sides of a scalene to be 11, 9, and 6 inches, a triangle of such dimensions would then be an appropriate symbol of Jehovah, for the sum of its three sides would be 26, the numerical value of the Hebrew word IHVH. Gematria also includes the system of discovering the arcane meaning of a word by analyzing the size and arrangement of the strokes employed in the formation of its various letters. Gematria was employed by the Greeks as well as the Jews. The books of the New Testament—particularly those attributed to St. John—contain many examples of its use. Nicephorus Callistus declared the Gospel according to St. John to have been discovered in a cavern under the Temple at Jerusalem, the volume having been secreted "long anterior to the Christian æra." The existence of interpolated material in the fourth Gospel substantiates the belief that the work *was originally written without any specific reference to the man Jesus,* the statements therein accredited to Him being originally mystical discourses delivered by the personification of the Universal Mind. The remaining Johannine writings—the Epistles and the Apocalypse—are enshrouded by a similar veil of mystery.

By Notarikon each letter of a word may become the initial character of a new word. Thus from BRASHITH, first word in the book of Genesis, are extracted six words which mean that "in the beginning the Elohim saw that Israel would accept the law." Mr. MacGregor-Mathers also gives six additional examples of Notarikon formed from the above word by Solomon Meir Ben Moses, a mediæval Qabbalist. From the famous acrostic ascribed to the Erythræan Sibyl, St. Augustine derived the word IXΘYΣ, which by Notarikon was expanded into the phrase, "Jesus Christ, Son of God, Savior." By another use of Notarikon, directly the reverse of the first, the initial, last, or middle letters of the words of a sentence may be joined together to form a new word or words. For example, the name *Amen,* ἀμήν, may be extracted from ארנימלרנאמז, "the Lord is the faithful King." Because they had embodied these cryptic devices in their sacred writings, the ancient priests admonished their disciples never to translate, edit, or rewrite the contents of the sacred books.

Under the general heading of *Temurah* several systems may be grouped and explained in which various letters are substituted for other letters according to prearranged tables or certain mathematical arrangements of letters, regular or irregular. Thus the alphabet may be broken into two equal parts and written in horizontal lines so that the letters of the lower row can be exchanged for those of the upper row, or vice versa. By this procedure the letters of the word *Kuzu* may be exchanged for those of IHVH, the *Tetragrammaton.* In another form of Temurah the letters are merely rearranged. שתיה is the stone which is found in the center of the world, from which point the earth spread out on all sides. When broken in two the stone is שת יה, which means "the placing of God." (See *Pekudei Rakov,* 71, 72.) Again, Temurah may consist of a simple anagram, as in the English word *live,* which reversed becomes *evil.* The various systems of Temurah are among the most complicated and profound devices of the ancient Rabbins.

Among theological scholars there is a growing conviction that the hitherto accepted translations of the Scriptural writings do not adequately express the spirit of the original documents.

"After the first copy of the *Book of God,*" writes H. P. Blavatsky, "has been edited and launched on the world by Hilkiah, this copy disappears, and Ezra has to make a *new Bible,* which Judas Maccabeus finishes; * * * when it was copied from the horned letters into square letters, it was corrupted beyond recognition; * * * the Masorah completed the work of destruction; finally, we have a text, not 900 years old, abounding with omissions, interpolations, and premeditated perversions." (See *Isis Unveiled.*)

Prof. Crawford Howell Toy of Harvard notes: "Manuscripts were copied and recopied by scribes who not only sometimes made errors in letters and words, but permitted themselves to introduce new material into the text, or to combine in one manuscript, without mark of division, writings composed by different men; instances of these sorts of procedure are found especially in Micah and Jeremiah, and the groups of prophecies which go under the names of Isaiah and Zachariah." (See *Judaism and Christianity.*)

Does the mutilated condition of the Holy Bible—in part accidental—represent none the less a definite effort to confuse the uninitiated reader and thus better conceal the secrets of the Jewish *Tannaim?* Never has the Christian world been in possession of those hidden scrolls which contain the secret doctrine of Israel, and if the Qabbalists were correct in their assumption that the lost books of the Mosaic Mysteries have been woven into the fabric of the *Torah,* then the Scriptures are veritably books within books. In rabbinical circles the opinion is prevalent that Christendom never has understood the Old Testament and probably never will. In fact, the feeling exists—in some quarters, at least—that the Old Testament is the exclusive possession of the Jewish faith; also that Christianity, after its unrelenting persecution of the Jew, takes unwarranted liberties when it includes strictly Jewish writings in its sacred canon. But, as noted by one rabbi, if Christianity *must* use the Jewish Scriptures, it should at least strive to do so with some degree of intelligence!

In the opening chapter of Genesis it is stated that after creating light and separating it from darkness, the seven Elohim divided the waters which were under the firmament from the waters which were above the firmament. Having thus established the inferior universe in perfect accord with the esoteric teachings of the Hindu, Egyptian, and Greek Mysteries, the Elohim next turned their attention to the production of flora and fauna and lastly man. "And God said, Let *us* make man in *our* image, after *our* likeness. * * * So God created man in *his* own image, in the image of God created *he him; male* and *female* created *he them.* And God blessed *them,* and God said unto *them,* Be fruitful, and multiply, and *re*plenish the earth, * * *."

Consider in thoughtful silence the startling use of pronouns in the above extract from "the most perfect example of English literature." When the plural and androgynous Hebrew word *Elohim* was translated into the singular and sexless word *God,* the opening chapters of Genesis were rendered comparatively meaningless. It may have been feared that had the word been correctly translated as "the male and female creative agencies," the Christians would have been justly accused of worshiping a plurality of gods in the face of their repeated claims to monotheism! The plural form of the pronouns *us* and *our* reveals unmistakably, however, the pantheistic nature of Divinity. Further, the androgynous constitution of the Elohim (God) is disclosed in the next verse, where *he* (referring to God) is said to have created man in *his* own image, *male* and *female;* or, more properly, as the division of the sexes had not yet taken place, *male-female.* This is a deathblow to the time-honored concept that God is a masculine potency as portrayed by Michelangelo on the ceiling of the Sistine Chapel. The Elohim then order these androgynous beings *to be fruitful.* Note that neither the masculine nor the feminine principle as yet existed in a separate state!

And, lastly, note the word "*re*plenish." The prefix *re* denotes "back to an original or former state or position," or "repetition or restoration." (See *Webster's International Dictionary,* 1926.) This definite reference to a humanity existing prior to the "creation of man" described in Genesis must be evident to the most casual reader of Scripture.

An examination of Bible dictionaries, encyclopedias, and commentaries discloses the plural form of the word *Elohim* to be beyond the comprehension of their respected authors and editors. *The New Schaff-Herzog Encyclopedia of Religious Knowledge* thus sums up the controversy over the plural form of the word Elohim: "Does it now or did it originally signify plurality of divine being?" *A Dictionary of the Bible,* edited by James Hastings, contains the following conclusion, which echoes the sentiments of more critical etymologists of the Bible: "The use of the plur. Elohim is also difficult to explain." Dr. Havernick considers the plural form Elohim to signify the abundance and super-richness existing in the Divine Being. His statement, which appears in *The Popular and Critical Bible Encyclopædia,* is representative of the efforts made to circumvent this extremely damaging word. The *International Standard Bible Dictionary* considers the explanations offered by modern theologians—of which Dr. Havernick's is a fair example—to be too ingenious to have been conceived by the early Hebrews and maintains that the word represents the survival of a polytheistic stage of Semitic thought. *The Jewish Encyclopedia* supports the latter assumption with the following concise statement: "As far as epigraphic material, traditions, and folk-lore throw light on the question, the Semites are shown to be of polytheistic leanings."

Various schools of philosophy, both Jewish and Gentile, have offered explanations erudite and otherwise of the identity of Adam. In this primordial man the Neo-Platonists recognized the Platonic *Idea* of humanity—the archetype or pattern of the *genus homo.* Philo Judæus considered Adam to represent the human mind, which could understand (and hence give names to) the creatures about it, but could not comprehend (and hence left nameless) the mystery of its own nature. Adam was also likened to the Pythagorean *monad* which by virtue of its state of perfect unity could dwell in the Edenic sphere. When through a process akin to fission the monad became the *duad*—the proper symbol of discord and delusion—the creature thus formed was exiled from its celestial home. Thus the twofold man was driven from the Paradise belonging to the undivided creation and cherubim and a flaming sword were placed on guard at the gates of the Causal World. Consequently, only after the reestablishment of unity within himself can man regain his primal spiritual state.

According to the Isarim, the secret doctrine of Israel taught the existence of four Adams, each dwelling in one of the four Qabbalistic worlds. The first, or heavenly, Adam dwelt alone in the Atziluthic sphere and within his nature existed all spiritual and material potentialities. The second Adam resided in the sphere of Briah. Like the first Adam, this being was androgynous and the tenth division of its body (its heel, *Malchuth*) corresponded to the church of Israel that shall bruise the serpent's head. The third Adam—likewise androgynous— was clothed in a body of light and abode in the sphere of Yetzirah. The fourth Adam was merely the third Adam after the *fall* into the sphere of Assiah, at which time the spiritual man took upon himself the animal shell or *coat of skins.* The fourth Adam was still considered as a single individual, though division had taken place within his nature and two shells or physical bodies existed, in one of which was incarnated the masculine and in the other the feminine potency. (For further details consult Isaac Myer.)

The universal nature of Adam is revealed in the various accounts concerning the substances of which he was formed. It was originally ordained that the "dirt" to be used in fashioning him was to be derived from the seven worlds. As these planes, however, refused to give of their substances, the Creator wrenched from them by force the elements to be employed in the Adamic constitution. St. Augustine discovered a Notarikon in the name of Adam. He showed that the four letters, A-D-A-M, are the first letters of the four words *Anatole Dysis Arktos Mesembria,* the Greek names for the four corners of the world. The same author also sees in Adam a prototype of Christ, for he writes: "Adam sleeps that Eve may be formed: Christ dies, that the Church may be formed. While Adam sleeps, Eve is formed from his side. When Christ is dead, His side is smitten with a spear, that there flow forth sacraments to form the church. * * * Adam himself was the figure of Him that was to come."

In his recent work, *Judaism,* George Foote Moore thus describes the proportions of the Adamic man: "He was a huge mass that filled the whole world to all the points of the compass. The dust of which his body was formed was gathered from every part of the world, or from the site of the future altar. Of greater interest is the notion that man was created androgynous, because it is probably a bit of foreign lore adapted to the first pair in Genesis. R. Samuel bar Nahman (third century), said, when God created Adam, He created him facing both ways (דיו פרצופים); then He sawed him in two and made two backs, one for each figure."

The Zohar holds the concept of two Adams: the first a divine being who, stepping forth from the highest original darkness, created the second, or earthly,

Adam in His own image. The higher, or celestial, man was the Causal sphere with its divine potencies and potentialities considered as a gigantic personality; its members, according to the Gnostics, being the basic elements of existence. This Adam may have been symbolized as facing both ways to signify that with one face it looked upon the proximate Cause for itself and with the other face looked upon the vast sea of Cosmos into which it was to be immersed.

Philosophically, Adam may be regarded as representative of the full spiritual nature of man—androgynous and not subject to decay. Of this fuller nature the mortal man has little comprehension. Just as spirit contains matter within itself and is both the source and ultimate of the state denominated *matter,* so Eve represents the lower, or mortal, portion that is taken out of, or has temporal existence in, the greater and fuller *spiritual creation.* Being representative of the inferior part of the individual, Eve is the temptress who, conspiring with the serpent of mortal knowledge, caused Adam to sink into a trancelike condition in which he was unconscious of his own higher Self. When Adam seemingly awoke, he actually sank into sleep, for he no longer was in the spirit but in the body; division having taken place within him, the true Adam rested in Paradise while his lesser part incarnated in a material organism (Eve) and wandered in the darkness of mortal existence.

The followers of Mohammed apparently sensed more accurately than the uninitiated of other sects the true mystic import of Paradise, for they realized that prior to his *fall* the dwelling place of man was not in a physical garden in any particular part of the earth but rather in a higher sphere (the angelic world) watered by four mystical streams of life. After his banishment from Paradise, Adam alighted on the Island of Ceylon, and this spot is sacred to certain Hindu sects who recognize the old Island of Lanka—once presumably connected with the mainland by a bridge—as the actual site of the Garden of Eden from which the human race migrated. According to the *Arabian Nights* (Sir Richard Burton's translation), Adam's footprint may still be seen on the top of a Ceylonese mountain. In the Islamic legends, Adam was later reunited with his wife and after his death his body was brought to Jerusalem subsequent to the Flood for burial by Melchizedek. (See the *Koran.*)

The word ADM signifies a species or race and only for lack of proper understanding has Adam been considered as an individual. As the Macrocosm, Adam is the gigantic Androgyne, even the Demiurgus; as the Microcosm, he is the chief production of the Demiurgus and within the nature of the Microcosm the Demiurgus established all the qualities and powers which He Himself possessed. The Demiurgus, however, did not possess immortality and, therefore, could not bestow it upon Adam. According to legend, the Demiurgus strove to keep man from learning the incompleteness of his Maker. The Adamic man consequently partook of the qualities and characteristics of the angels who were the ministers of the Demiurgus. It was affirmed by the Gnostic Christians that the redemption of humanity was assured through the descent of *Nous* (Universal Mind), who was a great spiritual being superior to the Demiurgus and who, entering into the constitution of man, conferred conscious immortality upon the Demiurgic fabrications.

That phallic symbolism occupies an important place in early Jewish mysticism is indisputable. Hargrave Jennings sees in the figure of Adam a type of the lingam of Shiva, which was a stone representative of the creative power of the World Generator. "In Gregorie's works * * *," writes Jennings, "is a passage to the effect that 'Noah daily prayed in the Ark before the *Body of Adam,*' i.e., before the Phallus—Adam being the primitive Phallus, great procreator of the human race. 'It may possibly seem strange,' he says, 'that this orison should be daily said before the body of Adam,' but 'it is a most confessed tradition among the eastern men that Adam was commanded by God that his dead body should be kept above ground till a fullness of time should come to commit it פדכבאלאוע to the *middle of the earth* by a priest of the Most High God.' This means Mount Moriah, the Meru of India. 'This body of Adam was embalmed and transmitted from father to son, till at last it was delivered up by Lamech into the hands of Noah.'" (See *Phallicism.*)

This interpretation somewhat clarifies the Qabbalistic assertion that in the first Adam were contained all the souls of the Israelites. (See *Sod.*) Though according to the *Aurea Legenda* Adam was buried with the three seeds of the Tree of Knowledge in his mouth, it should be borne in mind that apparently conflicting myths were often woven around a single individual. One of the profound mysteries of Qabbalism is that set forth in the Notarikon based upon the letters of the name Adam (ADM). These three letters form the initials of the names *Adam, David,* and the *Messiah,* and these three personalities were said to contain one soul. As this soul represents the World Soul of humanity, Adam signifies the involving soul, the Messiah the evolving soul, and David that condition of the soul termed *epigenesis.*

In common with certain philosophic institutions of Asia, the Jewish Mysteries contained a strange doctrine concerning the *shadows of the Gods.* Gazing down into the Abyss, the Elohim beheld their own shadows and from these shadows patterned the inferior creation. "In the dramatic representation of the creation of man in the Mysteries," writes the anonymous Master of Balliol College, "the Aleim [Elohim] were represented by men who, when sculpturing the form of an Adamite being, of a man, traced the outline of it on their own shadow, or modelled it on their own shadow traced on the wall. This is how the art of drawing originated in Egypt, and the hieroglyphic figures carved on the Egyptian monuments have so little relief that they still resemble a shadow."

In the ritualism of the early Jewish Mysteries the pageantry of creation was enacted, the various actors impersonating the Creative Agencies. The *red dirt* from which the Adamic man was fashioned may signify fire, particularly since Adam is related to the *Yod,* or fire flame, which is the first letter of the sacred name *Jehovah.* In John ii. 20 it is written that the Temple was forty and six years in the building, a statement in which St. Augustine sees a secret and sacred Gematria; for, according to the Greek philosophy of numbers, the numerical value of the name *Adam* is 46. Adam thus becomes the type of the Temple, for the House of God—like primitive man—was a microcosm or epitome of the universe.

In the Mysteries, Adam is accredited with having the peculiar power of spiritual generation. Instead of reproducing his kind by the physical generative processes, he caused to issue from himself—or, more correctly, to be reflected upon substance—a shadow of himself. This shadow he then ensouled and it became a living creature. These shadows, however, remain only as long as the original figure of which they are the reflections endures, for with the removal of the original the host of likenesses vanish with it. Herein is the key to the allegorical creation of Eve out of the side of Adam; for Adam, representative of the *idea* or pattern, is reflected into the material universe as a multitude of ensouled images which collectively are designated *Eve.* According to another theory, the division of the sexes took place in the archetypal sphere; hence the shadows in the lower world were divided into two classes consistent with the orders established in the Archetype. In the apparently incomprehensible attraction of one sex for the other Plato recognized a cosmic urge toward reunion of the severed halves of this archetypal Being.

Exactly what is to be inferred by the division of the sexes as symbolically described in Genesis is a much-debated question. That man was primarily androgynous is quite universally conceded and it is a reasonable presumption that he will ultimately regain this bisexual state. As to the manner in which this will be accomplished two opinions are advanced. One school of thought affirms that the human soul was actually divided into two parts (male and female) and that man remains an unperfected creature until these parts are reunited through the emotion which man calls *love.* From this concept has grown the much-abused doctrine of "soul mates" who must quest through the ages until the complementary part of each severed soul is discovered. The modern concept of marriage is to a certain degree founded upon this ideal.

According to the other school, the so-called division of the sexes resulted from suppression of one pole of the androgynous being in order that the vital energies manifesting through it might be diverted to development of the rational faculties. From this point of view man is still actually androgynous and spiritually complete, but in the material world the feminine part of man's nature and the masculine part of woman's nature are quiescent. Through spiritual unfoldment and knowledge imparted by the Mysteries, however, the latent element in each nature is gradually brought into activity and ultimately the human being thus regains sexual equilibrium. By this theory woman is elevated from the position of being man's errant part to one of complete equality. From this point of view, marriage is regarded as a companionship in which two complete individualities manifesting opposite polarities are brought into association that each may thereby awaken the qualities latent in the other and thus assist in the attainment of individual completeness. The first theory may be said to regard marriage as an end; the second as a means to an end. The deeper schools of philosophy have leaned toward the latter as more adequately acknowledging the infinite potentialities of divine completeness in both aspects of creation.

The Christian Church is fundamentally opposed to the theory of marriage, claiming that the highest degree of spirituality is achievable only by those preserving the virginal state. This concept seemingly originated among certain sects of the early Gnostic Christians, who taught that to propagate the human species was to increase and perpetuate the power of the Demiurgus; for the lower world was looked upon as an evil fabrication created to ensnare the souls of all born into it—hence it was a crime to assist in bringing souls to earth. When, therefore, the unfortunate father or mother shall stand before the Final Tribunal, all their offspring will also appear and accuse them of being the cause of those miseries attendant upon physical existence. This view is strengthened by the allegory of Adam and Eve, whose *sin* through which humanity has been brought low is universally admitted to have been concerned with the mystery of generation. Mankind, owing to Father Adam its physical existence, regards its progenitor as the primary cause of its misery; and in the Judgment Day, rising up as a mighty progeny, will accuse its common paternal ancestor.

Those Gnostic sects maintaining a more rational attitude on the subject declared the very existence of the lower worlds to signify that the Supreme Creator had a definite purpose in their creation; to doubt his judgment was, therefore, a grievous error. The church, however, seemingly arrogated to itself the astonishing prerogative of correcting God in this respect, for wherever possible it continued to impose celibacy, a practice resulting in an alarming number of neurotics. In the Mysteries, celibacy is reserved for those who have reached a certain degree of spiritual unfoldment. When advocated for the mass of unenlightened humanity, however, it becomes a dangerous heresy, fatal alike to both religion and philosophy. As Christendom in its fanaticism has blamed every individual Jew for the crucifixion of Jesus, so with equal consistency it has maligned every member of the feminine sex. In vindication of Eve philosophy claims that the allegory signifies merely that man is tempted by his emotions to depart from the sure path of reason.

Many of the early Church Fathers sought to establish a direct relationship between Adam and Christ, thereby obviously discounting the extremely sinful nature of man's common ancestor, since it is quite certain that when St. Augustine likens Adam to Christ and Eve to the church he does not intend to brand the latter institution as the direct cause of the fall of man. For some inexplicable reason, however, religion has ever regarded intellectualism—in fact every form of knowledge—as fatal to man's spiritual growth. The Ignorantine Friars are an outstanding example of this attitude.

In this ritualistic drama—possibly derived from the Egyptians—Adam, banished from the Garden of Eden, represents man philosophically exiled from the sphere of Truth. Through ignorance man falls; through wisdom he redeems himself. The Garden of Eden represents the House of the Mysteries (see *The Vision of Enoch*) in the midst of which grew both the Tree of Life and the Tree of the Knowledge of Good and Evil.

Man, the banished Adam, seeks to pass from the outer court of the Sanctuary (the exterior universe) into the *sanctum sanctorum,* but before him rises a vast creature armed with a flashing sword that, moving slowly but continually, sweeps clear a wide circle, and through this "Ring Pass Not" the Adamic man cannot break.

The cherubim address the seeker thus: "Man, thou art dust and to dust thou shalt return. Thou wert fashioned by the Builder of Forms; thou belongest to the sphere of form, and the breath that was breathed into thy soul was the breath of form and like a flame it shall flicker out. More than thou art thou canst not be. Thou art a denizen of the outer world and it is forbidden thee to enter this inner place."

And the Adam replies: "Many times have I stood within this courtyard and begged admission to my Father's house and thou hast refused it me and sent me back to wander in darkness. True it is that I was fashioned out of the dirt and that my Maker could not confer upon me the boon of immortality. But no more shalt thou send me away; for, wandering in the darkness, I have discovered that the Almighty hath decreed my salvation because He hath sent out of the most hidden Mystery His Only Begotten who didst take upon Himself the world fashioned by the Demiurgus. Upon the elements of that world was He crucified and from Him hath poured forth the blood of my salvation. And God, entering into His creation, hath quickened it and established therein a road that leadeth to Himself. While my Maker could not give me immortality, immortality was inherent in the very dust of which I was composed, for before the world was fabricated and before the Demiurgus became the Regent of Nature the Eternal Life had impressed itself upon the face of Cosmos. This is its sign—the *Cross*. Do you now deny me entrance, I who have at last learned the mystery of myself?"

And the voice replies: "He who is aware, *IS!* Behold!"

Gazing about him, Adam finds himself in a radiant place, in the midst of which stands a tree with flashing jewels for fruit and entwined about its trunk a flaming, winged serpent crowned with a diadem of stars. It was the voice of the serpent that had spoken.

"Who art thou?" demands the Adam.

"I," the serpent answers, "am Satan who was stoned; I am the Adversary— the Lord who is against you, the one who pleads for your destruction before the Eternal Tribunal. I was your enemy upon the day that you were formed; I have led you into temptation; I have delivered you into the hands of evil; I have maligned you; I have striven ever to achieve your undoing. I am the guardian of the Tree of Knowledge and I have sworn that none whom I can lead astray shall partake of its fruits."

The Adam replies: "For uncounted ages have I been thy servant. In my ignorance I listened to thy words and they led me into paths of sorrow. Thou hast placed in my mind dreams of power, and when I struggled to realize those dreams they brought me naught but pain. Thou hast sowed in me the seeds of desire, and when I lusted after the things of the flesh agony was my only recompense. Thou hast sent me false prophets and false reasoning, and when I strove to grasp the magnitude of Truth I found thy laws were false and only dismay rewarded my strivings. I am done with thee forever, O artful Spirit! I have tired of thy world of illusions. No longer will I labor in thy vineyards of iniquity. Get thee behind me, tempter, and the host of thy temptations. There is no happiness, no peace, no good, no future in the doctrines of selfishness, hate, and passion preached by thee. All these things do I cast aside. Renounced is thy rule forever!"

And the serpent makes answer: "Behold, O Adam, the nature of thy Adversary!" The serpent disappears in a blinding sunburst of radiance and in its place stands an angel resplendent in shining, golden garments with great scarlet wings that spread from one corner of the heavens to the other. Dismayed and awestruck, the Adam falls before the divine creature.

"I am the Lord who is against thee and thus accomplishes thy salvation," continues the voice. "Thou hast hated me, but through the ages yet to be thou shalt bless me, for I have led thee out of the sphere of the Demiurgus; I have turned thee against the illusion of worldliness; I have weaned thee of desire; I have awakened in thy soul the immortality of which I myself partake. Follow me, O Adam, for I am the Way, the Life, and the Truth!"

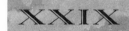

An Analysis of the Tarot Cards

pinions of authorities differ widely concerning the origin of playing cards, the purpose for which they were intended, and the time of their introduction into Europe. In his *Researches into the History of Playing Cards,* Samuel Weller Singer advances the opinion that cards reached Southern Europe from India by way of Arabia. It is probable that the Tarot cards were part of the magical and philosophical lore secured by the Knights Templars from the Saracens or one of the mystical sects then flourishing in Syria. Returning to Europe, the Templars, to avoid persecution, concealed the arcane meaning of the symbols by introducing the leaves of their magical book ostensibly as a device for amusement and gambling. In support of this contention, Mrs. John King Van Rensselaer states:

"That cards were brought by the home-returning warriors, who imported many of the newly acquired customs and habits of the Orient to their own countries, seems to be a well-established fact; and it does not contradict the statement made by some writers who declared that the gypsies—who about that time began to wander over Europe—brought with them and introduced cards, which they used, as they do at the present day, for divining the future." (See *The Devil's Picture Books.*)

Through the Gypsies the Tarot cards may be traced back to the religious symbolism of the ancient Egyptians. In his remarkable work, *The Gypsies,* Samuel Roberts presents ample proof of their Egyptian origin. In one place he writes: "When Gypsies originally arrived in England is very uncertain. They are first noticed in our laws, by several statutes against them in the reign of Henry VIII, in which they are described as 'an outlandish people, calling themselves

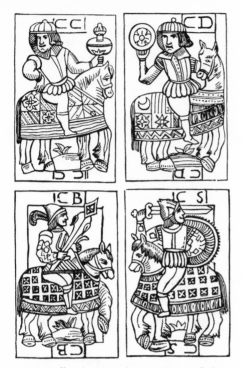

FROM CHATTO'S *ORIGIN AND HISTORY OF PLAYING CARDS.*

EARLY PORTUGUESE CARDS.

In writing of the deck from which the four cavaliers (jacks) here reproduced were taken, William Andrew Chatto notes: "Some of the specimens of Portuguese cards given in the 'Jeux de Cartes Tarots et de Cartes Numérales' have very much the appearance of having been originally suggested by, if not copied from, an Oriental type; more especially in the suits of Danari and Bastoni,—Money and Clubs. In those cards the circular figure, generally understood as representing Danari, or Money, is certainly much more like the Chakra, or quoit of Vichnou [Vishnu], as seen in Hindostanee drawings, than a piece of coin; while on the top of the Club there is a diamond proper, which is another of the attributes of the same deity." Also worthy of note are the Rosicrucian and Masonic emblems appearing on various mediæval decks. As the secrets of these organizations were often concealed in cryptic engravings, it is very probable that the enigmatic diagrams upon various decks of cards were used both to conceal and to perpetuate the political and philosophical arcana of these orders. The frontispiece of Mr. Chatto's book shows a knave of hearts bearing a shield emblazoned with a crowned Rosicrucian rose.

Egyptians; who do not profess any craft or trade, but go about in great numbers, * * *.'" A curious legend relates that after the destruction of the Serapeum in Alexandria, the large body of attendant priests banded themselves together to preserve the secrets of the rites of Serapis. Their descendants (Gypsies) carrying with them the most precious of the volumes saved from the burning library—the Book of Enoch, or Thoth (the Tarot)—became wanderers upon the face of the earth, remaining a people apart with an ancient language and a birthright of magic and mystery.

Count de Gébelin believed the word *Tarot* itself to be derived from two Egyptian words, *Tar,* meaning "road," and *Ro,* meaning "royal." Thus the Tarot constitutes the *royal road to wisdom.* (See *Le Monde Primitif.*) In his *History of Magic,* P. Christian, the mouthpiece of a certain French secret society, presents a fantastic account of a purported initiation into the Egyptian Mysteries wherein the 22 major Tarots assume the proportions of trestleboards of immense size and line a great gallery. Stopping before each card in turn, the initiator described its symbolism to the candidate. Edouard Schuré, whose source of information was similar to that of Christian's, hints at the same ceremony in his chapter on initiation into the Hermetic Mysteries. (See *The Great Initiates.*) While the Egyptians may well have employed the Tarot cards in their rituals, these French mystics present no evidence other than their own assertions to support this theory. The validity also of the so-called Egyptian Tarots now in circulation has never been satisfactorily established. The drawings are not only quite modern but the symbolism itself savors of French rather than Egyptian influence.

The Tarot is undoubtedly a vital element in Rosicrucian symbolism, possibly the very book of universal knowledge which the members of the order claimed to possess. The *Rota Mundi* is a term frequently occurring in the early manifestoes of the Fraternity of the Rose Cross. The word *Rota* by a rearrangement of its letters becomes *Taro,* the ancient name of these mysterious cards. W.F.C. Wigston has discovered evidence that Sir Francis Bacon employed the Tarot symbolism in his ciphers. The numbers 21, 56, and 78, which are all directly related to the divisions of the Tarot deck, are frequently involved in Bacon's cryptograms. In the great Shakespearian Folio of 1623 the Christian name of Lord Bacon appears 21 times on page 56 of the Histories. (See *The Columbus of Literature.*)

Many symbols appearing upon the Tarot cards have definite Masonic interest. The Pythagorean numerologist will also find an important relationship to exist between the numbers on the cards and the designs accompanying the numbers. The Qabbalist will be immediately impressed by the significant sequence of the cards, and the alchemist will discover certain emblems meaningless save to one versed in the divine chemistry of transmutation and regeneration. As the Greeks placed the letters of their alphabet—with their corresponding numbers—upon the various parts of the body of their humanly represented *Logos,* so the Tarot cards have an analogy not only in the parts and members of the universe but also in the divisions of the human body. They are in fact the key to the magical constitution of man.

The Tarot cards must be considered (1) as separate and complete hieroglyphs, each representing a distinct principle, law, power, or element in Nature; (2) in relation to each other as the effect of one agent operating upon another; and (3) as vowels and consonants of a philosophic alphabet. The laws governing all phenomena are represented by the symbols upon the Tarot cards, whose numerical values are equal to the numerical equivalents of the phenomena. As every structure consists of certain elemental parts, so the Tarot cards represent the components of the structure of philosophy. Irrespective of the science or philosophy with which the student is working, the Tarot cards can be identified with the essential constituents of his subject, each card thus being related to a specific part according to mathematical and philosophical laws. "An imprisoned person," writes Eliphas Levi, "with no other book than the Tarot, if he knew how to use it, could in a few years acquire universal knowledge, and would be able to speak on all subjects with unequalled learning and inexhaustible eloquence." (See *Transcendental Magic.*)

The diverse opinions of eminent authorities on the Tarot symbolism are quite irreconcilable. The conclusions of the scholarly Court de Gébelin and the bizarre Grand Etteila—the first authorities on the subject—not only are at radical variance but both are equally discredited by Levi, whose arrangement of the Tarot trumps was rejected in turn by Arthur Edward Waite and Paul Case as being an effort to mislead students. The followers of Levi—especially Papus, Christian, Westcott, and Schuré—are regarded by the "reformed Tarotists" as honest but benighted individuals who wandered in darkness for lack of Pamela Coleman Smith's new deck of Tarot cards with revisions by Mr. Waite.

Most writers on the Tarot (Mr. Waite a notable exception) have proceeded upon the hypothesis that the 22 major trumps represent the letters of the Hebrew alphabet. This supposition is based upon nothing more substantial than the coincidence that both consist of 22 parts. That Postel, St. Martin, and Levi all wrote books divided into sections corresponding to the major Tarots is an interesting sidelight on the subject. The major trump cards portray incidents from the Book of Revelation; and the Apocalypse of St. John is also divided into 22 chapters. Assuming the Qabbalah to hold the solution to the Tarot riddle, seekers have often ignored other possible lines of research. The task, however, of discovering the proper relationship sustained by the Tarot trumps to the letters of the Hebrew alphabet and the Paths of Wisdom thus far has not met with any great measure of success. The major trumps of the Tarot and the 22 letters of the Hebrew alphabet cannot be synchronized without first fixing the correct place of the unnumbered, or zero, card—Le Mat, the Fool. Levi places this card between the 20th and 21st Tarots, assigning to it the Hebrew letter Shin (ש). The same order is followed by Papus, Christian, and Waite, the last, however, declaring this arrangement to be incorrect. Westcott makes the zero card the 22nd of the Tarot major trumps. On the other hand, both Court de Gébelin and Paul Case place the unnumbered card before the first numbered card of the major trumps, for if the natural order of the numbers (according to either the Pythagorean or Qabbalistic system) be adhered to, the zero card must naturally precede the number 1.

This does not dispose of the problem, however, for efforts to assign a Hebrew letter to each Tarot trump in sequence produce an effect far from convincing. Mr. Waite, who reedited the Tarot, expresses himself thus: "I am not to be included among those who are satisfied that there is a valid correspondence between Hebrew letters and Tarot Trump symbols." (See introduction to *The Book of Formation* by Knut Stenring.) The real explanation may be that the major Tarots no longer are in the same sequence as when they formed the leaves of Hermes' sacred book, for the Egyptians—or even their Arabian successors—could have purposely confused the cards so that their secrets might be better preserved. Mr. Case has developed a system, which, while superior to most, depends largely upon two debatable points, namely, the accuracy of Mr. Waite's revised Tarot and the justification for assigning the first letter of the Hebrew alphabet to the unnumbered, or zero, card. Since *Aleph* (the first Hebrew letter) has the numerical value of 1, its assignment to the zero card is equivalent to the statement that zero is equal to the letter *Aleph* and therefore synonymous with the number 1.

With rare insight, Court de Gébelin assigned the zero card to AIN SOPH, the Unknowable First Cause. As the central panel of the Bembine Table represents the Creative Power surrounded by seven triads of manifesting divinities, so may the zero card represent that Eternal Power of which the 21 surrounding or manifesting aspects are but limited expressions. If the 21 major trumps be considered as limited forms existing in the abstract substance of the zero card, it then becomes their common denominator. Which letter, then, of the Hebrew alphabet is the origin of all the remaining letters? The answer is apparent: *Yod.* In the presence of so many speculations, one more may not offend. The zero card—*Le Mat,* the Fool—has been likened to the material universe because the mortal sphere is the world of unreality. The lower universe, like the mortal body of man, is but a garment, a motley costume, well likened to cap and bells. Beneath the garments of the fool is the divine substance, however, of which the jester is but a shadow; this world is a Mardi Gras—a pageantry of divine sparks masked in the garb of fools. Was not this zero card (the Fool) placed in the Tarot deck to deceive all who could not pierce the veil of Illusion?

The Tarot cards were entrusted by the illumined hierophants of the Mysteries into the keeping of the foolish and the ignorant, thus becoming playthings—in many instances even instruments of vice. Man's evil habits therefore actually became the unconscious perpetrators of his philosophical precepts. "We must admire the wisdom of the Initiates," writes Papus, "who utilized vice and made it produce more beneficial results than virtue." Does not this act of the ancient priests itself afford proof that the entire mystery of the Tarot is wrapped up in the symbolism of its zero card? If knowledge was thus entrusted to fools, should it not be sought for in this card?

If *Le Mat* be placed before the first card of the Tarot deck and the others laid out in a horizontal line in sequence from left to right, it will be found that the Fool is walking toward the other trumps as though about to pass through the various cards. Like the spiritually hoodwinked and bound neophyte, *Le Mat* is about to enter upon the supreme adventure—that of passage through the gates of the Divine Wisdom. If the zero card be considered as extraneous to the major trumps, this destroys the numerical analogy between these cards and the Hebrew letters by leaving one letter without a Tarot correspondent. In this event it will be necessary to assign the missing letter to a hypothetical Tarot card called the *elements,* assumed to have been broken up to form the 56 cards of the minor trumps. It is possible that each of the major trumps may be subject to a similar division.

The first numbered major trump is called *Le Bateleur,* the Juggler, and according to Court de Géblein, indicates the entire fabric of creation to be but a dream, existence a juggling of divine elements, and life a perpetual game of hazard. The seeming miracles of Nature are but feats of cosmic legerdemain. Man is like the little ball in the hands of the juggler, who waves his wand and, presto! the ball vanishes. The world looking on does not realize that the vanished article is still cleverly concealed by the juggler in the hollow of his hand. This is also the Adept whom Omar Khayyam calls "the master of the show." His message is that the wise direct the phenomena of Nature and are never deceived thereby.

The magician stands behind a table on which are spread out a number of objects, prominent among them a cup—the Holy Grail and the cup placed by Joseph in Benjamin's sack; a coin—the tribute money and the wages of a Master Builder; and a sword—that of Goliath and also the mystic blade of the philosopher which divides the false from the true. The magician's hat is in the form of the cosmic lemniscate, signifying the first motion of creation. His right hand points to the earth; his left holds aloft the wand symbolic of his mastership over the terrestrial universe—the objects on the table. The wand is the rod of Jacob and also the staff that budded—the human spine crowned with the globe of creative intelligence. In the pseudo-Egyptian Tarot the magician wears a *uræus* or golden band about his forehead, the table before him is in the form of a perfect cube, and his girdle is the serpent of eternity devouring its own tail.

The second numbered major trump is called *La Papesse,* the Female Pope, and has been associated with a curious legend of the only woman who ever sat in the pontifical chair. Pope Joan is supposed to have accomplished this by masquerading in male attire, and was stoned to death when her subterfuge was discovered. This card portrays a seated woman crowned with a tiara surmounted by a lunar crescent. In her lap is the *Tora,* or book of the Law (usually partly closed), and in her left hand are the keys to the secret doctrine, one gold and the other silver. Behind her rise two pillars (Jachin and Boaz) with a multicolored veil stretched between. Her throne stands upon a checkerboard floor. A figure called *Juno* is occasionally substituted for *La Papesse.* Like the female hierophant of the Mysteries of Cybele, this symbolic figure personifies the *Shekinah*, or Divine Wisdom. In the pseudo-Egyptian Tarot the priestess is veiled, a reminder that the full countenance of truth is not revealed to uninitiated man. A veil also covers one-half of her book, thus intimating that but one-half of the mystery of being can be comprehended.

The third numbered major trump is called *L'Impératrice*, the Empress, and has been likened to the "woman clothed with the sun" described in the Apocalypse. On this card appears the winged figure of a woman seated upon a throne, supporting with her right hand a shield emblazoned with a phœnix and holding in her left a scepter surmounted by an orb or trifoliate flower. Beneath her left foot is sometimes shown the crescent. Either the Empress is crowned or her head is surrounded by a diadem of stars; sometimes both. She is called *Generation*, and represents the threefold spiritual world out of which proceeds the fourfold material world. To the graduate of the College of the Mysteries she is the *Alma Mater* out of whose body the initiate has been "born again." In the pseudo-Egyptian Tarot the Empress is shown seated upon a cube filled with eyes and a bird is balanced upon the forefinger of her left hand. The upper part of her body is surrounded by a radiant golden nimbus. Being emblematic of the power from which emanates the entire tangible universe, *L'Impératrice* is frequently symbolized as pregnant.

The fourth numbered major trump is called *L'Empereur*, the Emperor, and by its numerical value is directly associated with the great Deity revered by the Pythagoreans under the form of the *tetrad*. His symbols declare the Emperor to be the *Demiurgus*, the Great King of the inferior world. The Emperor is dressed in armor and his throne is a cube stone, upon which a phœnix is also clearly visible. The king has his legs crossed in a most significant manner and carries either a scepter surmounted by an orb or a scepter in his right hand and an orb in his left. The orb itself is evidence that he is supreme ruler of the world. Upon his right and left breasts respectively appear the symbols of the sun and moon, which in symbolism are referred to as the eyes of the Great King. The position of the body and legs forms the symbol of sulphur, the sign of the ancient alchemical monarch. In the pseudo-Egyptian Tarot the figure is in profile. He wears a Masonic apron and the skirt forms a right-angled triangle. Upon his head is the Crown of the North and his forehead is adorned with the coiled *uræus*.

The fifth numbered major trump is called *Le Pape*, the Pope, and represents the high priest of a pagan or Christian Mystery school. In this card the hierophant wears the tiara and carries in his left hand the triple cross surmounting the globe of the world. His right hand, bearing upon its back the stigmata, makes "the ecclesiastic sign of esotericism," and before him kneel two suppliants or acolytes. The back of the papal throne is in the form of a celestial and a terrestrial column. This card signifies the initiate or master of the mystery of life and, according to the Pythagoreans, the spiritual physician. The illusionary universe in the form of two figures (polarity) kneels before the throne upon which sits the initiate who has elevated his consciousness to the plane of spiritual understanding and reality. In the pseudo-Egyptian Tarot the Master wears the *uræus*. A white and a black figure—life and death, light and darkness, good and evil—kneel before him. The initiate's mastery over unreality is indicated by the tiara and the triple cross, emblems of rulership over the three worlds which have issued from the Unknowable First Cause.

The sixth numbered major trump is called *L'Amoureux,* the Lovers. There are two distinct forms of this Tarot. One shows a marriage ceremony in which a priest is uniting a youth and a maiden (Adam and Eve?) in holy wedlock. Sometimes a winged figure above transfixes the lovers with his dart. The second form of the card portrays a youth with a female figure on either side. One of these figures wears a golden crown and is winged, while the other is attired in the flowing robes of the bacchante and on her head is a wreath of vine leaves. The maidens represent the twofold soul of man (spiritual and animal), the first his guardian angel and the second his ever-present demon. The youth stands at the beginning of mature life, "the Parting of the Ways," where he must choose between virtue and vice, the eternal and the temporal. Above, in a halo of light, is the genius of Fate (his star), mistaken for Cupid by the uninformed. If youth chooses unwisely, the arrow of blindfolded Fate will transfix him. In the pseudo-Egyptian Tarot the arrow of the genius points directly to the figure of vice, thereby signifying that the end of her path is destruction. This card reminds man that the price of free will—or, more correctly, the power of choice—is responsibility.

The seventh numbered major trump is called *Le Chariot,* the Chariot, and portrays a victorious warrior crowned and riding in a chariot drawn by black and white sphinxes or horses. The starry canopy of the chariot is upheld by four columns. This card signifies the Exalted One who rides in the chariot of creation. The vehicle of the solar energy being numbered seven reveals the arcane truth that the seven planets are the chariots of the solar power which rides victorious in their midst. The four columns supporting the canopy represent the four Mighty Ones who uphold the worlds represented by the star-strewn drapery. The figure carries the scepter of the solar energy and its shoulders are ornamented with lunar crescents—the Urim and Thummim. The sphinxes drawing the chariot represent the secret and unknown power by which the victorious ruler is moved continuously through the various parts of his universe. In certain Tarot decks the victor signifies the regenerated man, for the body of the chariot is a cubic stone. The man in armor is not standing in the chariot but is rising out of the cube, thus typifying the ascension of the 3 out of the 4—the turning upward of the flap of the Master Mason's apron. In the pseudo-Egyptian Tarot the warrior carries the curved sword of Luna, is bearded to signify maturity, and wears the collar of the planetary orbits. His scepter (emblematic of the threefold universe) is crowned with a square upon which is a circle surmounted by a triangle.

The eighth numbered major trump is called *La Justice,* Justice, and portrays a seated figure upon a throne, the back of which rises in the form of two columns. Justice is crowned and carries in her right hand a sword and in her left a pair of scales. This card is a reminder of the judgment of the soul in the hall of Osiris. It teaches that only balanced forces can endure and that eternal Justice destroys with the sword that which is unbalanced. Sometimes Justice is depicted with a braid of her own hair twisted around her neck in a manner resembling a hangman's knot. This may subtly imply that man is the cause of his own undoing, his actions (symbolized by his hair) being the instrument of

FROM TAYLOR'S *THE HISTORY OF PLAYING CARDS.*

A CARD FROM THE MANTEGNA PACK.

Among the more curious examples of playing cards are those of the Mantegna deck. In 1820, a perfect deck of fifty cards brought the then amazing price of eighty pounds. The fifty subjects composing the Mantegna deck, each of which is represented by an appropriate figure, are: (1) A beggar; (2) A page; (3) A goldsmith; (4) A merchant; (5) A gentleman; (6) A knight; (7) The Doge; (8) A king; (9) An emperor; (10) The Pope; (11) Calliope; (12) Urania; (13) Terpsichore; (14) Erato; (15) Polyhymnia; (16) Thalia; (17) Melpomene; (18) Euterpe; (19) Clio; (20) Apollo; (21) Grammar; (22) Logic; (23) Rhetoric; (24) Geometry; (25) Arithmetic; (26) Music; (27) Poetry; (28) Philosophy; (29) Astrology; (30) Theology; (31) Astronomy; (32) Chronology; (33) Cosmogony; (34) Temperance; (35) Prudence; (36) Fortitude; (37) Justice; (38) Charity; (39) Hope; (40) Faith; (41) the Moon; (42) Mercury; (43) Venus; (44) the Sun; (45) Mars; (46) Jupiter; (47) Saturn; (48) the eighth Sphere; (49) the Primum Mobile; (50) the First Cause. The Qabbalistic significance of these cards is apparent, and it is possible that they have a direct analogy to the fifty gates of light referred to in Qabbalistic writings.

his annihilation. In the pseudo-Egyptian Tarot the figure of Justice is raised upon a dais of three steps, for Justice can be fully administered only by such as have been elevated to the third degree. Justice is blindfolded, that the visible shall in no way influence its decision. (For reasons he considers beyond his readers' intelligence, Mr. Waite reversed the eighth and eleventh major trumps.)

The ninth numbered major trump is called *L'Hermite,* the Hermit, and portrays an aged man, robed in a monkish habit and cowl, leaning upon a staff. This card was popularly supposed to represent Diogenes in his quest for an honest man. In his right hand the recluse carries a lamp which he partly conceals within the folds of his cape. The hermit thereby personifies the secret organizations which for uncounted centuries have carefully concealed the light of the Ancient Wisdom from the profane. The staff of the hermit is knowledge, which is man's main and only enduring support. Sometimes the mystic rod is divided by knobs into seven sections, a subtle reference to the mystery of the seven sacred centers along the human spine. In the pseudo-Egyptian Tarot the hermit shields the lamp behind a rectangular cape to emphasize the philosophic truth that wisdom, if exposed to the fury of ignorance, would be destroyed like the tiny flame of a lamp unprotected from the storm. Man's bodies form a cloak through which his divine nature is faintly visible like the flame of the partly covered lantern. Through renunciation—the Hermetic life—man attains depth of character and tranquillity of spirit.

The tenth numbered major trump is called *La Roue de Fortune,* the Wheel of Fortune, and portrays a mysterious wheel with eight spokes—the familiar Buddhist symbol of the Cycle of Necessity. To its rim cling Anubis and Typhon—the principles of good and evil. Above sits the immobile sphinx, carrying the sword of Justice and signifying the perfect equilibrium of Universal Wisdom. Anubis is shown rising and Typhon descending; but when Typhon reaches the bottom, evil ascends again, and when Anubis reaches the top good wanes once more. The Wheel of Fortune represents the lower universe as a whole with Divine Wisdom (the sphinx) as the eternal arbiter between good and evil. In India, the *chakra,* or wheel, is associated with the life centers either of a world or of an individual. In the pseudo-Egyptian Tarot the sphinx is armed with a javelin, and Typhon is being thrown from the wheel. The vertical columns, supporting the wheel and so placed that but one is visible, represent the axis of the world with the inscrutable sphinx upon its northern pole. Sometimes the wheel with its supports is in a boat upon the water. The water is the Ocean of Illusion, which is the sole foundation of the Cycle of Necessity.

The eleventh numbered major trump is called *La Force,* Strength, and portrays a girl wearing a hat in the form of a lemniscate, with her hands upon the mouth of an apparently ferocious lion. Considerable controversy exists as to whether the maid is closing or opening the lion's mouth. Most writers declare her to be closing the jaws of the beast, but a critical inspection conveys the opposite impression. The young woman symbolizes spiritual strength and the lion either the animal world which the girl is mastering or the Secret Wisdom over which she is mistress. The lion also signifies the summer solstice and the girl, Virgo, for when the sun enters this constellation, the Virgin robs the lion of his strength. King Solomon's throne was ornamented with lions and he himself was likened to the king of beasts with the key of wisdom between its teeth. In this sense, the girl may be opening the lion's mouth to find the key contained therein, for courage is a prerequisite to the attainment of knowledge. In the pseudo-Egyptian Tarot the symbolism is the same except that the maiden is represented as a priestess wearing an elaborate crown in the form of a bird surmounted by serpents and an ibis.

The twelfth numbered major trump is called *Le Pendu,* the Hanged Man, and portrays a young man hanging by his left leg from a horizontal beam, the latter supported by two tree trunks from each of which six branches have been removed. The right leg of the youth is crossed in back of the left and his arms are folded behind his back in such a way as to form a cross surmounting a downward pointing triangle. The figure thus forms an inverted symbol of sulphur and, according to Levi, signifies the accomplishments of the *magnum opus.* In some decks the figure carries under each arm a money bag from which coins are escaping. Popular tradition associates this card with Judas Iscariot, who is said to have gone forth and hanged himself, the money bags representing the payment he received for his crime.

Levi likens the hanged man to Prometheus, the Eternal Sufferer, further declaring that the upturned feet signify the spiritualization of the lower nature. It is also possible that the inverted figure denotes the loss of the spiritual faculties, for the head is below the level of the body. The stumps of the twelve branches are the signs of the zodiac divided into two groups—positive and negative. The picture therefore depicts polarity temporarily triumphant over the spiritual principle of equilibrium. To attain the heights of philosophy, therefore, man must reverse (or invert) the order of his life. He then loses his sense of personal possession because he renounces the rule of gold in favor of the golden rule. In the pseudo-Egyptian Tarot the hanged man is suspended between two palm trees and signifies the Sun God who dies perennially for his world.

The thirteenth numbered major trump is called *La Mort,* Death, and portrays a reaping skeleton with a great scythe cutting off the heads, hands, and feet rising out of the earth about it. In the course of its labors the skeleton has apparently cut off one of its own feet. Not all Tarot decks show this peculiarity, but this point well emphasizes the philosophic truth that unbalance and destructiveness are synonymous. The skeleton is the proper emblem of the first and supreme

Deity because it is the foundation of the body, as the Absolute is the foundation of creation. The reaping skeleton physically signifies death but philosophically that irresistible impulse in Nature which causes every being to be ultimately absorbed into the divine condition in which it existed before the illusionary universe had been manifested. The blade of the scythe is the moon with its crystallizing power. The field in which death reaps is the universe, and the card discloses that all things growing out of the earth shall be cut down and return to earth again.

Kings, queens, courtesans, and knaves are alike to death, the master of the visible and apparent parts of all creatures. In some Tarot decks death is symbolized as a figure in armor mounted on a white horse which tramples under foot old and young alike. In the pseudo-Egyptian Tarot a rainbow is seen behind the figure of death, thus signifying that the mortality of the body of itself achieves the immortality of the spirit. Death, though it destroys form, can never destroy life, which continually renews itself. This card is the symbol of the constant renovation of the universe—disintegration that reintegration may follow upon a higher level of expression.

The fourteenth numbered major trump is called *La Temperance,* Temperance, and portrays an angelic figure with the sun upon her forehead. She carries two urns, one empty and the other full, and continually pours the contents of the upper into the lower. In some Tarot decks the flowing water takes the form of the symbol of Aquarius. Not one drop, however, of the living water is lost in this endless transference between the superior vessel and the inferior. When the lower urn is filled the vases are reversed, thus signifying that life pours first from the invisible into the visible, then from the visible back into the invisible. The spirit controlling this flow is an emissary of the great Jehovah, Demiurgus of the world. The sun, or light cluster, upon the woman's forehead controls the flow of water, which, being drawn upward into the air by the solar rays, descends upon the earth as rain, to be drawn up and fall again *ad infinitum.* Herein is also shown the passage of the human life forces back and forth between the positive and negative poles of the creative system. In the pseudo-Egyptian Tarot the symbolism is the same, except that the winged figure is male instead of female. It is surrounded by a solar nimbus and pours water from a golden urn into a silver one, typifying the descent of the celestial forces into the sublunary spheres.

The fifteenth numbered major trump is called *Le Diable,* the Devil, and portrays a creature resembling Pan with the horns of a ram or deer, the arms and body of a man, and the legs and feet of a goat or dragon. The figure stands upon a cubic stone, to a ring in the front of which are chained two satyrs. For a scepter this so-called demon carries a lighted torch or candle. The entire figure is symbolic of the magic powers of the astral light, or universal mirror, in which the divine forces are reflected in an inverted, or infernal, state. The demon is winged like a bat, showing that it pertains to the nocturnal, or shadowy, inferior sphere. The animal natures of man, in the form of a male and a female elemental, are chained to its footstool. The torch is the false light which guides unillumined souls to their own undoing. In the pseudo-Egyptian Tarot appears Typhon—a winged creature composed of a hog, a man, a bat, a crocodile, and a hippopotamus—standing in the midst of its own destructiveness and holding aloft the firebrand of the incendiary. Typhon is created by man's own misdeeds, which, turning upon their maker, destroy him.

The sixteenth numbered major trump is called *Le Feu du Ciel,* the Fire of Heaven, and portrays a tower the battlements of which, in the form of a crown, are being destroyed by a bolt of lightning *issuing from the sun.* The crown, being considerably smaller than the tower which it surmounts, possibly indicates that its destruction resulted from its insufficiency. The lightning bolt sometimes takes the form of the zodiacal sign of Scorpio and the tower may be considered a phallic emblem. Two figures are falling from the tower, one in front and the other behind. This Tarot card is popularly associated with the traditional fall of man. The divine nature of humanity is depicted as a tower. When his crown is destroyed, man falls into the lower world and takes upon himself the illusion of materiality. Here also is a key to the mystery of sex. The tower is supposedly filled with gold coins which, showering out in great numbers from the rent made by the lightning bolt, suggest potential powers. In the pseudo-Egyptian Tarot the tower is a pyramid, its apex shattered by a lightning bolt. Here is a reference to the missing capstone of the Universal House. In support of Levi's contention that this card is connected with the Hebrew letter *Ayin,* the falling figure in the foreground is similar in general appearance to the sixteenth letter of the Hebrew alphabet.

The seventeenth numbered major trump is called *Les Etoiles,* the Stars, and portrays a young girl kneeling with one foot in water and the other on land, her body somewhat suggesting the swastika. She has two urns, the contents of which she pours upon the land and sea. Above the girl's head are eight stars, one of which is exceptionally large and bright. Court de Gébelin considers the great star to be Sothis, or Sirius; the other seven are the sacred planets of the ancients. He believes the female figure to be Isis in the act of causing the inundations of the Nile which accompanied the rising of the Dog Star. The unclothed figure of Isis may well signify that Nature does not receive her garment of verdure until the rising of the Nile waters releases the germinal life of plants and flowers. The bush and bird (or butterfly) signify the growth and resurrection which accompany the rising of the waters. In the pseudo-Egyptian Tarot the great star contains a diamond composed of a black and white triangle, and the flowering bush is a tall plant with a trifoliate head upon which a butterfly alights. Here Isis is in the form of an upright triangle and the vases have become shallow cups. The elements of water and earth under her feet represent the opposites of Nature sharing impartially in the divine abundance.

The eighteenth numbered major trump is called *La Lune*, the Moon, and portrays Luna rising between two towers—one light and the other dark. A dog and a wolf are baying at the rising moon, and in the foreground is a pool of water from which emerges a crawfish. Between the towers a path winds, vanishing in the extreme background. Court de Gébelin sees in this card another reference to the rising of the Nile and states on the authority of Pausanius that the Egyptians believed the inundations of the Nile to result from the tears of the moon goddess which, falling into the river, swelled its flow. These tears are seen dropping from the lunar face. Court de Gébelin also relates the towers to the Pillars of Hercules, beyond which, according to the Egyptians, the luminaries never passed. He notes also that the Egyptians represented the tropics as dogs who as faithful doorkeepers prevented the sun and moon from penetrating too near the poles. The crab or crawfish signifies the retrograde motion of the moon.

This card also refers to the path of wisdom. Man in his quest of reality emerges from the pool of illusion. After mastering the guardians of the gates of wisdom he passes between the fortresses of science and theology and follows the winding path leading to spiritual liberation. His way is faintly lighted by human reason (the moon), which is but a reflection of divine wisdom. In the pseudo-Egyptian Tarot the towers are pyramids, the dogs are black and white respectively, and the moon is partly obscured by clouds. The entire scene suggests the dreary and desolate place in which the Mystery dramas of the Lesser Rites were enacted.

The nineteenth numbered major trump is called *Le Soleil*, the Sun, and portrays two children—probably Gemini, the Twins—standing together in a garden surrounded by a magic ring of flowers. One of these children should be shown as male and the other female. Behind them is a brick wall apparently enclosing the garden. Above the wall the sun is rising, in rays alternately straight and curved. Thirteen teardrops are falling from the solar face. Levi, seeing in the two children Faith and Reason, which must coexist as long as the temporal universe endures, writes: "Human equilibrium requires two feet, the worlds gravitate by means of two forces, generation needs two sexes. Such is the meaning of the arcanum of Solomon, represented by the two pillars of the temple, Jakin and Bohas." (See *Transcendental Magic.*) The sun of Truth is shining into the garden of the world over which these two children, as personifications of eternal powers, preside. The harmony of the world depends upon the coordination of two qualities symbolized throughout the ages as the mind and the heart. In the pseudo-Egyptian Tarot the children give place to a youth and a maiden. Above them in a solar nimbus is the phallic emblem of generation—a line piercing a circle. Gemini is ruled by Mercury and the two children personify the serpents entwined around the *caduceus.*

The twentieth numbered major trump is called *Le Jugement,* the Judgment, and portrays three figures rising apparently from their tombs, though but one coffin is visible. Above them in a blaze of glory is a winged figure (presumably the Angel Gabriel) blowing a trumpet. This Tarot represents the liberation of man's threefold spiritual nature from the sepulcher of his material constitution. Since but one-third of the spirit actually enters the physical body, the other two-thirds constituting the Hermetic *anthropos* or *overman,* only one of the three figures is actually rising from the tomb. Court de Gébelin believes that the coffin may have been an afterthought of the card makers and that the scene actually represents creation rather than resurrection. In philosophy these two words are practically synonymous. The blast of the trumpet represents the Creative Word, by the intoning of which man is liberated from his terrestrial limitations. In the pseudo-Egyptian Tarot it is evident that the three figures signify the parts of a single being, for three mummies are shown emerging from one mummy case.

The twenty-first numbered major trump is called *Le Monde,* the World, and portrays a female figure draped with a scarf which the wind blows into the form of the Hebrew letter *Kaph.* Her extended hands—each of which holds a wand— and her left leg, which crosses behind the right, cause the figure to assume the form of the alchemical symbol of sulphur. The central figure is surrounded by a wreath in the form of a *vesica piscis* which Levi likens to the Qabbalistic crown *Kether.* The Cherubim of Ezekiel's vision occupy the corners of the card. This Tarot is called the Microcosm and the Macrocosm because in it are summed up every agency contributing to the structure of creation. The figure in the form of the emblem of sulphur represents the divine fire and the heart of the Great Mystery. The wreath is Nature, which surrounds the fiery center. The Cherubim represent the elements, worlds, forces, and planes issuing out of the divine fiery center of life. The wreath again signifies the crown of the initiate which is given to those who master the four guardians and enter into the presence of unveiled Truth. In the pseudo-Egyptian Tarot the Cherubim surround a wreath composed of twelve trifoliate flowers—the decanates of the zodiac. A human figure kneels below this wreath, playing upon a harp of three strings, for the spirit must create harmony in the triple constitution of its inferior nature before it can gain for itself the solar crown of immortality.

The four suits of the minor trumps are considered as analogous to the four elements, the four corners of creation, and the four worlds of Qabbalism. The key to the lesser Tarots is presumably the *Tetragrammaton,* or the four-letter name of Jehovah, IHVH. The four suits of the minor trumps represent also the major divisions of society: *cups* are the priesthood, *swords* the military, *coins* the tradesmen, and *rods* the farming class. From the standpoint of what Court de Gébelin calls "political geography," *cups* represent the northern countries, *swords* the Orient, *coins* the Occident, and *rods* the southern countries. The ten pip cards of each suit represent the nations composing each of these grand divisions. The *kings* are their governments, the *queens* their religions, the *knights* their histories and national characteristics, and the *pages* their arts and sciences. Elaborate treatises have been written concerning the use of the Tarot cards in divination, but as this practice is contrary to the primary purpose of the Tarot no profit can result from its discussion.

Many interesting examples of early playing cards are found in the museums of Europe, and there are also noteworthy specimens in the cabinets of various private collectors. A few hand-painted decks exist which are extremely artistic. These depict various important personages contemporary with the artists. In some instances, the court cards are portraitures of the reigning monarch and his family. In England engraved cards became popular, and in the British Museum are also to be seen some extremely quaint stenciled cards. Heraldic devices were employed; and Chatto, in his *Origin and History of Playing Cards,* reproduces four heraldic cards in which the arms of Pope Clement IX adorn the king of clubs. There have been philosophical decks with emblems chosen from Greek and Roman mythology, also educational decks ornamented with maps or pictorial representations of famous historic places and incidents. Many rare examples of playing cards have been found bound into the covers of early books. In Japan there are card games the successful playing of which requires familiarity with nearly all the literary masterpieces of that nation. In India there are circular decks depicting episodes from Oriental myths. There are also cards which in one sense of the word are not cards, for the designs are on wood, ivory, and even metal. There are comic cards caricaturing disliked persons and places, and there are cards commemorating various human achievements. During the American Civil War a patriotic deck was circulated in which stars, eagles, anchors, and American flags were substituted for the suits and the court cards were famous generals.

Modern playing cards are the minor trumps of the Tarot, from each suit of which the *page,* or *valet,* has been eliminated, leaving 13 cards. Even in its abridged form, however, the modern deck is of profound symbolic importance, for its arrangement is apparently in accord with the divisions of the year. The two colors, red and black, represent the two grand divisions of the year—that during which the sun is north of the equator and that during which it is south of the equator. The four suits represent the seasons, the *ages* of the ancient Greeks, and the *Yugas* of the Hindus. The twelve court cards are the signs of the zodiac arranged in triads of a Father, a Power, and a Mind according to the upper section of the Bembine Table. The ten pip cards of each suit represent the Sephirothic trees existing in each of the four worlds (the suits). The 13 cards of each suit are the 13 lunar months in each year, and the 52 cards of the deck are the 52 weeks in the year. Counting the number of pips and reckoning the jacks, queens, and kings as 11, 12, and 13 respectively, the sum for the 52 cards is 364. If the *joker* be considered as one point, the result is 365, or the number of days in the year. Milton Pottenger believed that the United States of America was laid out according to the conventional deck of playing cards, and that the government will ultimately consist of 52 States administered by a 53rd undenominated division, the District of Columbia.

The court cards contain a number of important Masonic symbols. Nine are full face and three are profile. Here is the broken "Wheel of the Law," signifying the nine months of the prenatal epoch and the three degrees of spiritual unfoldment necessary to produce the perfect man. The four armed kings are the Egyptian Ammonian Architects who gouged out the universe with knives. They are also the cardinal signs of the zodiac. The four queens, carrying eight-petaled flowers symbolic of the Christ, are the fixed signs of the zodiac. The four jacks, two of whom bear acacia sprigs—the jack of hearts in his hand, the jack of clubs in his hat—are the four common signs of the zodiac. It should be noted also that the court cards of the spade suit will not look upon the pip in the corner of the card but face away from it as though fearing this emblem of death. The Grand Master of the Order of the Cards is the king of clubs, who carries the orb as emblematic of his dignity.

In its symbolism chess is the most significant of all games. It has been called "the royal game"—the pastime of kings. Like the Tarot cards, the chessmen represent the elements of life and philosophy. The game was played in India and

China long before its introduction into Europe. East Indian princes were wont to sit on the balconies of their palaces and play chess with living men standing upon a checkerboard pavement of black and white marble in the courtyard below. It is popularly believed that the Egyptian Pharaohs played chess, but an examination of their sculpture and illuminations has led to the conclusion that the Egyptian game was a form of draughts. In China, chessmen are often carved to represent warring dynasties, as the Manchu and the Ming. The chessboard consists of 64 squares alternately black and white and symbolizes the floor of the House of the Mysteries. Upon this field of existence or thought move a number of strangely carved figures, each according to fixed law. The white king is Ormuzd; the black king, Ahriman; and upon the plains of Cosmos the great war between Light and Darkness is fought through all the ages. Of the philosophical constitution of man, the kings represent the spirit; the queens the mind; the bishops the emotions; the knights the vitality; the castles, or rooks, the physical body. The pieces upon the kings' side are positive; those upon the queens' side, negative. The pawns are the sensory impulses and perceptive faculties—the eight parts of the soul. The white king and his suite symbolize the Self and its vehicles; the black king and his retinue, the not-self—the false Ego and its legion. The game of chess thus sets forth the eternal struggle of each part of man's compound nature against the shadow of itself. The nature of each of the chessmen is revealed by the way in which it moves; geometry is the key to their interpretation. For example: The castle (the body) moves on the square; the bishop (the emotions) moves on the slant; the king, being the spirit, cannot be captured, but loses the battle when so surrounded that it cannot escape.

The Tabernacle in
the Wilderness

here is no doubt that much of the material recorded in the first five books of the Old Testament is derived from the initiatory rituals of the Egyptian Mysteries. The priests of Isis were deeply versed in occult lore, and the Israelites during their captivity in Egypt learned from them many things concerning the significance of Divinity and the manner of worshiping It. The authorship of the first five books of the Old Testament is generally attributed to Moses, but whether or not he was the actual writer of them is a matter of controversy. There is considerable evidence to substantiate the hypothesis that the Pentateuch was compiled at a much later date, from oral traditions. Concerning the authorship of these books, Thomas Inman makes a rather startling statement: "It is true that we have books which purport to be the books of Moses; so there are, or have been, books purporting to be written by Homer, Orpheus, Enoch, Mormon, and Junius; yet the existence of the writings, and the belief that they were written by those whose name they bear, are no real evidences of the men or the genuineness of the works called by their names. It is true also that Moses is spoken of occasionally in the time of the early Kings of Jerusalem; but it is clear that these passages are written by a late hand, and have been introduced into the places where they are found, with the definite intention of making it appear that the lawgiver was known to David and Solomon." (See *Ancient Faiths Embodied in Ancient Names*.)

While this noted scholar undoubtedly had much evidence to support his belief, it seems that this statement is somewhat too sweeping in character. It is apparently based upon the fact that Thomas Inman doubted the historical existence of Moses. This doubt was based upon the etymological resemblance of

THE ANCIENT OF DAYS.

It is in this form that Jehovah is generally pictured by the Qabbalists. The drawing is intended to represent the Demiurgus of the Greeks and Gnostics, called by the Greeks "Zeus," the Immortal Mortal, and by the Hebrews "IHUH."

the word *Moses* to an ancient name for the sun. As the result of these deductions, Inman sought to prove that the Lawgiver of Israel was merely another form of the omnipresent solar myth. While Inman demonstrated that by transposing two of the ancient letters the word *Moses* (משה) became *Shemmah* (שמה), an appellation of the celestial globe, he seems to have overlooked the fact that in the ancient Mysteries the initiates were often given names synonymous with the sun, to symbolize the fact that the redemption and regeneration of the solar power had been achieved within their own natures. It is far more probable that the man whom we know as Moses was an accredited representative of the secret schools, laboring—as many other emissaries have labored—to instruct primitive races in the mysteries of their immortal souls.

The true name of the Grand Old Man of Israel who is known to history as Moses will probably never be ascertained. The word *Moses,* when understood in its esoteric Egyptian sense, means one who has been admitted into the Mystery Schools of Wisdom and has gone forth to teach the ignorant concerning the will of the gods and the mysteries of life, as these mysteries were explained within the temples of Isis, Osiris, and Serapis. There is much controversy concerning the nationality of Moses. Some assert that he was a Jew, adopted and educated by the ruling house of Egypt; others hold the opinion that he was a full-blooded Egyptian. A few even believe him to be identical with the immortal Hermes, for both these illustrious founders of religious systems received tablets from heaven supposedly written by the finger of God. The stories told concerning Moses, his discovery in the ark of bulrushes by Pharaoh's daughter, his adoption into the royal family of Egypt, and his later revolt against Egyptian autocracy coincide exactly with certain ceremonies through which the candidates of the Egyptian Mysteries passed in their ritualistic wanderings in search of truth and understanding. The analogy can also be traced in the movements of the heavenly bodies.

It is not strange that the erudite Moses, initiated in Egypt, should teach the Jews a philosophy containing the more important principles of Egyptian esotericism. The religions of Egypt at the time of the Israelitic captivity were far older than even the Egyptian priests themselves realized. Histories were difficult to compile in those days, and the Egyptians were satisfied to trace their race back to a mythological period when the gods themselves walked the earth and with their own power established the Double Empire of the Nile. The Egyptians did not dream that these divine progenitors were the Atlanteans, who, forced to abandon their seven islands because of volcanic cataclysms, had immigrated into Egypt—then an Atlantean colony—where they established a great philosophic and literary center of civilization which was later to influence profoundly the religions and sciences of unnumbered races and peoples. Today Egypt is forgotten, but things Egyptian will always be remembered and revered. Egypt is dead—yet it lives immortal in its literature, philosophy, and architectonics.

As Odin founded his Mysteries in Scandinavia, and Quexalcoatl in Mexico, so Moses, laboring with the then nomadic people of Israel's twelve tribes, established in the midst of them his secret and symbolic school, which has come to be known as *The Tabernacle Mysteries.* The Tabernacle of the Jews was merely a temple patterned after the temples of Egypt, and transportable to meet the needs of that roving disposition for which the Israelites were famous. Every part of the Tabernacle and the enclosure which surrounded it was symbolic of some great natural or philosophic truth. To the ignorant it was but a place to which to bring offerings and in which to make sacrifice; to the wise it was a temple of learning, sacred to the Universal Spirit of Wisdom.

While the greatest minds of the Jewish and Christian worlds have realized that the Bible is a book of allegories, few seem to have taken the trouble to investigate its symbols and parables. When Moses instituted his Mysteries, he is said to have given to a chosen few initiates certain oral teachings which could never be written but were to be preserved from one generation to the next by word-of-mouth transmission. Those instructions were in the form of philosophical keys, by means of which the allegories were made to reveal their hidden significance. These mystic keys to their sacred writings were called by the Jews the *Qabbalah* (*Cabala, Kaballah*).

The modern world seems to have forgotten the existence of those unwritten teachings which explained satisfactorily the apparent contradictions of the written Scriptures, nor does it remember that the pagans appointed their two-faced Janus as custodian of the key to the Temple of Wisdom. Janus has been metamorphosed into St. Peter, so often symbolized as holding in his hand the key to the gate of heaven. The gold and silver keys of "God's Vicar on Earth," the Pope, symbolize this "secret doctrine" which, when properly understood, unlocks the treasure chest of the Christian and Jewish Qabbalah.

The temples of Egyptian mysticism (from which the Tabernacle was copied) were—according to their own priests—miniature representations of the universe. The solar system was always regarded as a great temple of initiation, which candidates entered through the gates of birth; after threading the tortuous passageways of earthly existence, they finally approached the veil of the Great Mystery—Death—through whose gate they vanished back into the invisible world. Socrates subtly reminded his disciples that Death was, in reality, the great initiation, for his last words were: "Crito, I owe a cock to Asclepius; will you remember to pay the debt?" (As the rooster was sacred to the gods and the sacrifice of this bird accompanied a candidate's introduction into the Mysteries, Socrates implied that he was about to take his great initiation.)

Life is the great mystery, and only those who pass successfully through its tests and trials, interpreting them aright and extracting the essence of experience therefrom, achieve true understanding. Thus, the temples were built in the form of the world and their rituals were based upon life and its multitudinous problems. Not only was the Tabernacle itself patterned according to Egyptian mysticism; its utensils were also of ancient and accepted form. The Ark of the Covenant itself was an adaptation of the Egyptian Ark, even to the kneeling figures upon its lid. Bas-reliefs on the Temple of Philæ show Egyptian priests carrying their Ark—which closely resembled the Ark of the Jews—upon their shoulders by means of staves like those described in Exodus.

The following description of the Tabernacle and its priests is based upon the account of its construction and ceremonies recorded by Josephus in the Third Book of his *Antiquities of the Jews*. The Bible references are from a "Breeches" Bible (famous for its rendering of the seventh verse of the third chapter of Genesis), printed in London in 1599, and the quotations are reproduced in their original spelling and punctuation.

The Building of the Tabernacle

Moses, speaking for Jehovah, the God of Israel, appointed two architects to superintend the building of the Tabernacle. They were Besaleel, the son of Uri, of the tribe of Judah, and Aholiab, the son of Ahisamach, of the tribe of Dan. Their popularity was so great that they were also the unanimous choice of the people. When Jacob upon his deathbed blessed his sons (see Genesis xlix), he assigned to each a symbol. The symbol of Judah was a lion; that of Dan a serpent or a bird (possibly an eagle). The lion and the eagle are two of the four beasts of the Cherubim (the fixed signs of the zodiac); and the Rosicrucian alchemists maintained that the mysterious Stone of the Wise (the Soul) was compounded with the aid of the Blood of the Red Lion and the Gluten of the White Eagle. It seems probable that there is a hidden mystic relationship between fire (the Red Lion), water (the White Eagle), as they were used in occult chemistry, and the representatives of these two tribes whose symbols were identical with these alchemical elements.

As the Tabernacle was the dwelling place of God among men, likewise the soul body in man is the dwelling place of his divine nature, round which gathers a twelvefold material constitution in the same manner that the tribes of Israel camped about the enclosure sacred to Jehovah. The idea that the Tabernacle was really symbolic of an invisible spiritual truth outside the comprehension of the Israelites is substantiated by a statement made in the eighth chapter of Hebrews: "Who serve unto the paterne and shadowe of heavenly things, as Moses was warned by God, when he was about to finish the Tabernacle." Here we find the material physical place of worship called a "shadow" or symbol of a spiritual institution, invisible but omnipotent.

The specifications of the Tabernacle are described in the book of Exodus, twenty-fifth chapter: "Then the Lord spake unto Moses, saying, Speake unto the children of Israel that they receive an offering for me: of every man, whose heart giveth it freely, ye shall take the offering for me. And this is the offering which ye shall take of them, gold and silver, and brass, and blue silke, and purple, and scarlet, and fine linnen and goats haire. And rammes skinnes coloured red, and the skinnes of badgers, and the wood Shittim, oyle for the light, spices for anoynting oyle, and for the perfume of sweet favour, onix stones, and stones to be set in the Ephod, and in the breastplate. Also they shall make me a Sanctuary, that I may dwell among them. According to all that I shew thee, even so shall ye make the forme of the Tabernacle, and the fashion of all the instruments thereof."

The court of the Tabernacle was an enclosed area, fifty cubits wide and one hundred cubits long, circumscribed by a wall of linen curtains hung from brazen pillars five cubits apart. (The cubit is an ancient standard of measurement, its length being equal to the distance between the elbow and the extreme end of the index finger, approximately eighteen inches.) There were twenty of these pillars on each of the longer sides and ten on the shorter. Each pillar had a base of brass and a capital of silver. The Tabernacle was always laid out with the long sides facing north and south and the short sides facing east and west, with the entrance to the east, thus showing the influence of primitive sun worship.

The outer court served the principal purpose of isolating the tent of the Tabernacle proper, which stood in the midst of the enclosure. At the entrance to the courtyard, which was in the eastern face of the rectangle, stood the Altar of Burnt Offerings, made of brass plates over wood and ornamented with the horns of bulls and rams. Farther in, but on a line with this altar, stood the Laver of Purification, a great vessel containing water for priestly ablutions. The Laver was twofold in its construction, the upper part being a large bowl, probably covered, which served as a source of supply for a lower basin in which the priests bathed themselves before participating in the various ceremonials. It is supposed that this Laver was encrusted with the metal mirrors of the women of the twelve tribes of Israel.

The dimensions of the Tabernacle proper were as follows: "Its length, when it was set up, was thirty cubits, and its breadth was ten cubits. The one of its walls was on the south, and the other was exposed to the north, and on the back part of it remained the west. It was necessary that its height should be equal to its breadth (ten cubits)." (Josephus.)

It is the custom of bibliologists to divide the interior of the Tabernacle into two rooms: one room ten cubits wide, ten cubits high, and twenty cubits long, which was called the Holy Place and contained three special articles of furniture, namely, the Seven-Branched Candlestick, the Table of the Shewbread, and the Altar of Burnt Incense; the other room ten cubits wide, ten cubits high, and ten cubits long, which was called the Holy of Holies and contained but one article of furniture—the Ark of the Covenant. The two rooms were separated from each other by an ornamental veil upon which were embroidered many kinds of flowers, but no animal or human figures.

Josephus hints that there was a third compartment which was formed by subdividing the Holy Place, at least hypothetically, into two chambers. The Jewish historian is not very explicit in his description of this third room, and the majority of writers seem to have entirely overlooked and neglected this point, although Josephus emphatically states that Moses himself divided the inner tent into three sections. The veil separating the Holy Place from the Holy of Holies was hung across four pillars, which probably indicated in a subtle way the four elements, while at the entrance to the tent proper the Jews placed seven pillars, referring to the seven senses and the seven vowels of the Sacred Name. That later only five pillars are mentioned may be accounted for by the fact that at the present time man has only five developed senses and five active vowels. The early Jewish writer of *The Baraitha* treats of the curtains as follows:

"There were provided ten curtains of blue, of purple, and scarlet, and fine-twined linen. As is said, 'Moreover thou shall make the tabernacle with ten curtains of fine-twined linen, and blue, and purple, and scarlet.' * * * There were provided eleven curtains of goats' hair, and the length of every one of them was thirty cubits, * * *. Rabbi Judah said, 'There were two covers—the lower one of rams' skins dyed red, and the upper one of badgers' skins.'"

Calmet is of the opinion that the Hebrew word translated "badger" really means "dark purple" and therefore did not refer to any particular animal, but probably to a heavily woven waterproof fabric of dark and inconspicuous color. During the time of Israel's wanderings through the wilderness, it is supposed that a pillar of fire hovered over the Tabernacle at night, while a column of smoke traveled with it by day. This cloud was called by the Jews the *Shechinah* and was symbolic of the presence of the Lord. In one of the early Jewish books rejected at the time of the compiling of the Talmud the following description of the *Shechinah* appears:

"Then a cloud covered the tent of the congregation, and the glory of the Lord filled the Tabernacle. And that was one of the clouds of glory, which served the Israelites in the wilderness forty years. One on the right hand, and one on the left, and one before them, and one behind them. And one over them, and a cloud dwelling in their midst (and the cloud, the Shechinah which was in the tent), and the pillar of cloud which moved before them, making low before them the high places, and making high before them the low places, and killing serpents and scorpions, and burning thorns and briars, and guiding them in the straight way." (From *The Baraitha*, the Book of the Tabernacle.)

The Furnishings of the Tabernacle

There is no doubt that the Tabernacle, its furnishings and ceremonials, when considered esoterically, are analogous to the structure, organs, and functions of the human body. At the entrance to the outer court of the Tabernacle stood the Altar of Burnt Offerings, five cubits long and five cubits wide but only three cubits high. Its upper surface was a brazen grill upon which the sacrifice was placed, while beneath was a space for the fire. This altar signified that a candidate, when first entering the precincts of sanctuary, must offer upon the brazen altar not a poor unoffending bull or ram but its correspondence within his own nature. The bull, being symbolic of earthiness, represented his own gross constitution which must be burned up by the fire of his Divinity. (The sacrificing of beasts, and in some cases human beings, upon the altars of the pagans was the result of their ignorance concerning the fundamental principle underlying sacrifice. They did not realize that their offerings must come from within their own natures in order to be acceptable.)

Farther westward, in line with the Brazen Altar, was the Laver of Purification already described. It signified to the priest that he should cleanse not only his body but also his soul from all stains of impurity, for none who is not clean in both body and mind can enter into the presence of Divinity and live. Beyond the Laver of Purification was the entrance to the Tabernacle proper, facing the east, so that the first rays of the rising sun might enter and light the chamber. Between the encrusted pillars could be seen the Holy Place, a mysterious chamber, its walls hung with magnificent drapes embroidered with the faces of Cherubs.

Against the wall on the southern side of the Holy Place stood the great Candlestick, or lampstand, of cast gold, which was believed to weigh about a hundred pounds. From its central shaft branched out six arms, each ending in a cup-shaped depression in which stood an oil lamp. There were seven lamps, three on the arms at each side and one on the central stem. The Candlestick was ornamented with seventy-two almonds, knops, and flowers. Josephus says seventy, but wherever this round number is used by the Hebrews it really means seventy-two. Opposite the Candlestick, against the northern wall, was a table bearing twelve loaves of Shewbread in two stacks of six loaves each. (Calmet is of the opinion that the bread was not stacked up but spread out on the table in two rows, each containing six loaves.) On this table also stood two lighted incensories, which were placed upon the tops of the stacks of Shewbread so that the smoke of the incense might be an acceptable aroma to the Lord, bearing with it in its ascent the soul of the Shewbread.

In the center of the room, almost against the partition leading into the Holy of Holies, stood the Altar of Burnt Incense, made of wood overlaid with golden plates. Its width and length were each a cubit and its height was two cubits. This altar was symbolic of the human larynx, from which the words of man's mouth ascend as an acceptable offering unto the Lord, for the larynx occupies the position in the constitution of man between the Holy Place, which is the trunk of his body, and the Holy of Holies, which is the head with its contents.

Into the Holy of Holies none might pass save the High Priest, and he only at certain prescribed times. The room contained no furnishings save the Ark of the

Covenant, which stood against the western wall, opposite the entrance. In Exodus the dimensions of the Ark are given as two and a half cubits for its length, one cubit and a half its breadth and one cubit and a half its height. It was made of shittim-wood, gold plated within and without, and contained the sacred tablets of the Law delivered to Moses upon Sinai. The lid of the Ark was in the form of a golden plate upon which knelt two mysterious creatures called Cherubim, facing each other, with wings arched overhead. It was upon this mercy seat between the wings of the celestials that the Lord of Israel descended when He desired to communicate with His High Priest.

The furnishings of the Tabernacle were made conveniently portable. Each altar and implement of any size was supplied with staves which could be put through rings; by this means it could be picked up and carried by four or more bearers. The staves were never removed from the Ark of the Covenant until it was finally placed in the Holy of Holies of the Everlasting House, King Solomon's Temple.

There is no doubt that the Jews in early times realized, at least in part, that their Tabernacle was a symbolic edifice. Josephus realized this and while he has been severely criticized because he interpreted the Tabernacle symbolism according to Egyptian and Grecian paganism, his description of the secret meanings of its drapes and furnishings is well worthy of consideration. He says:

"When Moses distinguished the tabernacle into three parts, and allowed two of them to the priests, as a place accessible and common, he denoted the land and the sea, these being of general access to all; but he set apart the third division for God, because heaven is inaccessible to men. And when he ordered twelve loaves to be set on a table, he denoted the year, as distinguished into so many months. By branching out the candlestick into seventy parts, he secretly intimated the Decani, or seventy divisions of the planets; and as to the seven lamps upon the candlesticks, they referred to the course of the planets, of which that is the number. The veils too, which were composed of four things, they declared the four elements; for the plain linen was proper to signify the earth, because the flax grows out of the earth; the purple signified the sea, because that color is dyed by the blood of a sea shell-fish; the blue is fit to signify the air; and the scarlet will naturally be an indication of fire.

"Now the vestment of the high-priest being made of linen, signified the earth; the blue denoted the sky, being like lightning in its pomegranates, and in the noise of the bells resembling thunder. And for the Ephod, it showed that God had made the universe of four (elements); and as for the gold interwoven, * * * it related to the splendor by which all things are enlightened. He also appointed the breastplate to be placed in the middle of the Ephod, to resemble the earth, for that has the very middle place of the world. And the girdle which encompassed the high-priest round signified the ocean, for that goes round about and includes the universe. Each of the sardonyxes declares to us the sun

FROM CALMET'S *DICTIONARY OF THE HOLY BIBLE*.

THE ARK WITH ITS CHERUBIM.

Josephus tells us that the Cherubim were flying creatures but different in appearance from anything to be seen on earth; therefore impossible to describe. Moses is supposed to have seen these beings kneeling at the footstool of God when he was picked up and brought into the presence of Jehovah. It is probable that they resembled, at least in general appearance, the famous Cherubim of Ezekiel.

and the moon, those, I mean, that were in the nature of buttons on the high-priest's shoulders. And for the twelve stones, whether we understand by them the months, or whether we understand the like number of the signs of that circle which the Greeks call the Zodiac, we shall not be mistaken in their meaning. And for the mitre, which was of a blue colour, it seems to me to mean heaven; for how otherwise could the name of God be inscribed upon it? That it was also illustrated with a crown, and that of gold also, is because of that splendour with which God is pleased." It is also symbolically significant that the Tabernacle was built in seven months and dedicated to God at the time of the new moon.

The metals used in the building of the Tabernacle were all emblematic. Gold represents spirituality, and the golden plates laid over the shittim-wood were emblems of the spiritual nature which glorifies the human nature symbolized by the wood. Mystics have taught that man's physical body is surrounded by a series of invisible bodies of diverse colors and great splendor. In the majority of people the spiritual nature is concealed and imprisoned in the material nature, but in a few this internal constitution has been objectified and the spiritual nature is outside, so that it surrounds man's personality with a great radiance.

Silver, used as the capitals for the pillars, has its reference to the moon, which was sacred to the Jews and the Egyptians alike. The priests held secret ritualistic ceremonies at the times of the new and the full moon, both of which periods were sacred to Jehovah. Silver, so the ancients taught, was gold with its sun-ray turned inward instead of objectified. While gold symbolized the spiritual soul, silver represented the purified and regenerated human nature of man.

The brass used in the outer altars was a composite substance consisting of an alloy of precious and base metals. Thus, it represented the constitution of the average individual, who is a combination of both the higher and the lower elements.

The three divisions of the Tabernacle should have a special interest to Freemasons, for they represent the three degrees of the Blue Lodge, while the three orders of priests who served the Tabernacle are preserved to modern Masonry as the Entered Apprentice, the Fellow Craftsman, and the Master Mason. The Hawaiian Islanders built a Tabernacle not unlike that of the Jews, except that their rooms were one above another and not one behind another, as in the case of the Tabernacle of the Israelites. The three rooms are also the three important chambers of the Great Pyramid of Gizeh.

The Robes of Glory

As explained in the quotation from Josephus, the robes and adornments of the Jewish priests had a secret significance, and even to this day there is a religious cipher language concealed in the colors, forms, and uses of sacred garments, not only among the Christian and Jewish priests but also among pagan religions. The vestments of the Tabernacle priests were called *Cahanææ;* those of the High Priest were termed *Cahanææ Rabbæ.* Over the *Machanese,* an undergarment resembling short trousers, they wore the *Chethone,* a finely woven linen robe, which reached to the ground and had long sleeves tied to the arms of the wearer. A brightly embroidered sash, twisted several times around the waist (a little higher than is customary), with one end pendent in front, and a closely fitting linen cap, designated *Masnaemphthes,* completed the costume of the ordinary priest.

The vestments of the High Priest were the same as those of the lesser degrees, except that certain garments and adornments were added. Over the specially woven white linen robe the High Priest wore a seamless and sleeveless habit, sky-blue in color and reaching nearly to his feet. This was called the *Meeir* and was ornamented with a fringe of alternated golden bells and pomegranates. In Ecclesiasticus (one of the books rejected from the modern Bible), these bells and their purpose are described in the following words: "And he compassed him with pomegranates, and with many golden bells round about, that as he went, there might be a sound and a noise that might be heard in the temple, for a memorial to the children of his people." The *Meeir* was also bound in with a variegated girdle finely embroidered and with gold wire inserted through the embroidery.

The *Ephod,* a short vestment described by Josephus as resembling a coat or jacket, was worn over the upper part of the *Meeir.* The threads of which the *Ephod* was woven were of many colors, probably red, blue, purple, and white, like the curtains and coverings of the Tabernacle. Fine gold wires were also woven into the fabric. The *Ephod* was fastened at each shoulder with a large onyx in the form of a button, and the names of the twelve sons of Jacob were engraven upon these two stones, six on each. These onyx buttons were supposed to have oracular powers, and when the High Priest asked certain questions, they emitted a celestial radiance. When the onyx on the right shoulder was illuminated, it signified that Jehovah answered the question of the High Priest in the affirmative, and when the one on the left gleamed, it indicated a negative answer to the query.

In the middle of the front surface of the *Ephod* was a space to accommodate the *Essen,* or *Breastplate of Righteousness and Prophecy,* which, as its name signifies, was also an oracle of great power. This pectoral was roughly square in shape and consisted of a frame of embroidery into which were set twelve stones, each held in a socket of gold. Because of the great weight of its stones, each of which was of considerable size and immense value, the breastplate was held in position by special golden chains and ribbons. The twelve stones of the breastplate, like the onyx stones at the shoulders of the *Ephod,* had the mysterious power of lighting up with Divine glory and so serving as oracles. Concerning the strange power of these flashing symbols of Israel's twelve tribes, Josephus writes:

"Yet will I mention what is still more wonderful than this: For God declared beforehand, by those twelve stones which the High Priest bare upon his breast and which were inserted into his breastplate, when they should be victorious in battle; for so great a splendor shone forth from them before the army began to march, that all the people were sensible of God's being present for their assistance. Whence it came to pass that those Greeks, who had a veneration for our laws, because they could not possibly contradict this, called the breastplate 'the Oracle'." The writer then adds that the stones ceased to light up and gleam some two hundred years before he wrote his history, because the Jews had broken the laws of Jehovah and the God of Israel was no longer pleased with His chosen people.

The Jews learned astronomy from the Egyptians, and it is not unlikely that the twelve jewels of the breastplate were symbolic of the twelve constellations of the zodiac. These twelve celestial hierarchies were looked upon as jewels adorning the breastplate of the Universal Man, the Macroprosophus, who is referred to in the Zohar as The Ancient of Days. The number *twelve* frequently occurs among ancient peoples, who in nearly every case had a pantheon consisting of twelve demigods and goddesses presided over by The Invincible One, who was Himself subject to the Incomprehensible All-Father. This use of the number *twelve* is especially noted in the Jewish and Christian writings. The twelve prophets, the twelve patriarchies, the twelve tribes, and the twelve Apostles— each group has a certain occult significance, for each refers to the Divine Duodecimo, or Twelvefold Deity, whose emanations are manifested in the tangible created Universe through twelve individualized channels. The secret doctrine also taught the priests that the jewels represented centers of life within their own constitutions, which when unfolded according to the esoteric instructions of the Temple, were capable of absorbing into themselves and radiating forth again the Divine light of the Deity. (The East Indian lotus blossoms have a similar meaning.) The Rabbis have taught that each twisted linen thread used in weaving the Tabernacle curtains and ornamentations consisted of twenty-four separate strands, reminding the discerning that the experience gained during the twenty-four hours of the day (symbolized in Masonry by the twenty-four-inch rule) becomes the threads from which are woven the Garments of Glory.

The Urim and Thummim

In the reverse side of the *Essen,* or breastplate, was a pocket containing mysterious objects—the *Urim* and *Thummim.* Aside from the fact that they were used in divination, little is now known about these objects. Some writers contend that they were small stones (resembling the fetishes still revered by certain aboriginal peoples) which the Israelites had brought with them out of Egypt because of their belief that they possessed divine power. Others believe that the *Urim* and *Thummim* were in the form of dice, used for deciding events by being cast upon the ground. A few have maintained that they were merely sacred names, written on plates of gold and carried as talismans. "According to some, the Urim and the Thummim signify 'lights and perfections,' or 'light and truth' which last present a striking analogy to the two figures of Re (Ra) and Themi in the breastplate worn by the Egyptians." (Gardner's *The Faiths of the World.*)

Not the least remarkable of the vestments of the High Priest was his bonnet, or headdress. Over the plain white cap of the ordinary priest this dignitary wore an outer cloth of blue and a crown of gold, the crown consisting of three bands, one above the other like the triple miter of the Persian Magi. This crown symbolized that the High Priest was ruler not only over the three worlds which the ancients had differentiated (heaven, earth, and hell), but also over the threefold divisions of man and the universe—the spiritual, intellectual, and material worlds. These divisions were also symbolized by the three apartments of the Tabernacle itself.

At the peak of the headdress was a tiny cup of gold, made in the form of a flower. This signified that the nature of the priest was receptive and that he had a vessel in his own soul which, cuplike, was capable of catching the eternal waters of life pouring upon him from the heavens above. This flower over the crown of his head is similar in its esoteric meaning to the rose growing out of a skull, so famous in Templar symbology. The ancients believed that the spiritual nature escaping from the body passed upward through the crown of the head; therefore, the flowerlike calyx, or cup, symbolized also the spiritual consciousness. On the front of the golden crown were inscribed in Hebrew, *Holiness unto the Lord.*

Though robes and ornaments augmented the respect and veneration of the Israelites for their High Priest, such trappings meant nothing to Jehovah. Therefore, before entering the Holy of Holies, the High Priest removed his earthly finery and entered into the presence of the Lord God of Israel unclothed. There he could be robed only in his own virtues, and his spirituality must adorn him as a garment.

There is a legend to the effect that any who chanced to enter the Holy of Holies unclean were destroyed by a bolt of Divine fire from the Mercy Seat. If the High Priest had but one selfish thought, he would be struck dead. As no man knows when an unworthy thought may flash through his mind, precautions had to be taken in case the High Priest should be struck dead while in the presence of Jehovah. The other priests could not enter the sanctuary; therefore, when their leader was about to go in and receive the commands of the Lord, they tied a chain around one of his feet so that if he were struck down while behind the veil they could drag the body out.

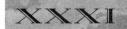

The Fraternity of the Rose Cross

ho were the Rosicrucians? Were they an organization of profound thinkers rebelling against the inquisitional religious and philosophical limitations of their time or were they isolated transcendentalists united only by the similarity of their viewpoints and deductions? Where was the "House of the Holy Spirit," in which, according to their manifestoes, they met once a year to plan the future activities of their Order? Who was the mysterious person referred to as "Our Illustrious Father and Brother C.R.C."? Did those three letters actually stand for the words "Christian Rosie Cross"? Was Christian Rosencreutz, the supposed author of the *Chymical Nuptials,* the same person who with three others founded "The Society of the Rose Cross"?

What relationship existed between Rosicrucianism and mediæval Freemasonry? Why were the destinies of these two organizations so closely interwoven? Is the "Brotherhood of the Rose Cross" the much-sought-after link connecting the Freemasonry of the Middle Ages with the symbolism and mysticism of antiquity, and are its secrets being perpetuated by modern Masonry? Did the original Rosicrucian Order disintegrate in the latter part of the eighteenth century, or does the Society still exist as an organization, maintaining the same secrecy for which it was originally famous? What was the true purpose for which the "Brotherhood of the Rose Cross" was formed? Were the Rosicrucians a religious and philosophic brotherhood, as they claimed to be, or were their avowed tenets a blind to conceal the true object of the Fraternity, which possibly was the political control of Europe? These are some of the problems involved in the study of Rosicrucianism.

There are four distinct theories regarding the Rosicrucian enigma. Each is the result of a careful consideration of the evidence by scholars who have spent their lives ransacking the archives of Hermetic lore. The conclusions reached demonstrate clearly the inadequacy of the records available concerning the genesis and early activities of the "Brethren of the Rose Cross."

The First Postulate

It is assumed that the Rosicrucian Order existed historically in accordance with the description of its foundation and subsequent activities published in its manifesto, the *Fama Fraternitatis,* which is believed to have been written in the year 1610, but apparently did not appear in print until 1614, although an earlier edition is suspected by some authorities. Intelligent consideration of the origin of Rosicrucianism requires a familiarity with the contents of the first and most important of its documents. The *Fama Fraternitatis* begins with a reminder to all the world of God's goodness and mercy, and it warns the intelligentsia that their egotism and covetousness cause them to follow after false prophets and to ignore the true knowledge which God in His goodness has revealed to them. Hence, a reformation is necessary, and God has raised up philosophers and sages for this purpose.

In order to assist in bringing about the reformation, a mysterious person called "The Highly Illuminated Father C.R.C.," a German by birth, descended of a noble family, but himself a poor man, instituted the "Secret Society of the Rose Cross." C.R.C. was placed in a cloister when only five years of age, but later becoming dissatisfied with its educational system, he associated himself with a brother of Holy Orders who was setting forth on a pilgrimage to the Holy Land. They started out together, but the brother died at Cyprus and C.R.C. continued alone to Damascus. Poor health prevented him from reaching Jerusalem, so he remained at Damascus, studying with the philosophers who dwelt there.

While pursuing his studies, he heard of a group of mystics and Qabbalists abiding in the mystic Arabian city of Damcar. Giving up his desire to visit Jerusalem, he arranged with the Arabians for his transportation to Damcar. C.R.C. was but sixteen years of age when he arrived at Damcar. He was received as one who had been long expected, a comrade and a friend in philosophy, and was instructed in the secrets of the Arabian adepts. While there, C.R.C. learned the Arabic tongue and translated the sacred book *M* into Latin, and upon returning to Europe he brought this important volume with him.

After studying three years in Damcar, C.R.C. departed for the city of Fez, where the Arabian magicians declared further information would be given him. At Fez he was instructed how to communicate with the Elementary inhabitants [probably the Nature spirits], and these disclosed to him many other great secrets of Nature. While the philosophers in Fez were not so great as those in Damcar, the previous experiences of C.R.C. enabled him to distinguish the true from the false and thus add greatly to his store of knowledge.

After two years in Fez, C.R.C. sailed for Spain, carrying with him many treasures, among them rare plants and animals accumulated during his wanderings. He fondly hoped that the learned men of Europe would receive with gratitude the rare intellectual and material treasures which he had brought for their consideration. Instead he encountered only ridicule, for the so-called wise were afraid to admit their previous ignorance lest their prestige be impaired. At this point in the narrative is an interpolation stating that Paracelsus, while not a member of the "Fraternity of the Rose Cross," had read the book *M* and from a consideration of its contents had secured information which made him the foremost physician of mediæval Europe.

Tired, but not discouraged, as the result of the fruitlessness of his efforts, C.R.C. returned to Germany, where he built a house in which he could quietly carry on his study and research. He also manufactured a number of rare scientific instruments for research purposes. While he could have made himself famous had he cared to commercialize his knowledge, he preferred the companionship of God to the esteem of men.

After five years of retirement he decided to renew his struggle for a reformation of the arts and sciences of his day, this time with the aid of a few trusted friends. He sent to the cloister where his early training had been received and called to himself three brethren, whom he bound by an oath to preserve inviolate the secrets he should impart and to write down for the sake of posterity the information he should dictate. These four founded the "Fraternity of the Rose Cross." They prepared its secret cipher language and, according to the *Fama,* a great dictionary in which all forms of wisdom were classified to the glorification of God. They also began the work of transcribing the book *M,* but found the task too difficult because of the demands of the great numbers of sick who came to them for healing.

Having completed a newer and larger building, which they called the "House of the Holy Spirit," they decided to include four new members in the Fraternity, thus increasing the number to eight, seven of whom were German. All were unmarried. Working industriously together, they speedily completed the arduous labor of preparing the documents, instructions, and arcana of the Order. They also put the house called "Sancti Spiritus" in order.

They then decided to separate and visit the other countries of the earth, not only that their wisdom might be given to others who deserved it but also that they might check and correct any mistakes existing in their own system. Before separating, the Brethren prepared six rules, or by-laws, and each bound himself to obey them. The first rule was that they should take to themselves no other dignity or credit than that they were willing to heal the sick without charge. The second was that from that time on forever they should wear no special robe or garment, but should dress according to the custom of the country wherein they dwelt. The third stated that every year upon a certain day they should meet in the "House of the Holy Spirit," or, if unable to do so, should be represented by an epistle. The fourth decreed that each member should search for a worthy person to succeed him at his own demise. The fifth stated that the letters "R.C." should be their seal, mark, and character from that time onward. The sixth specified that the Fraternity should remain unknown to the world for a period of one hundred years.

THE CRUCIFIED ROSE.

The original symbol of the Rosicrucian Fraternity was a hieroglyphic rose crucified upon a cross. The cross was often raised upon a three-stepped Calvary. Occasionally the symbol of a cross rising from a rose was used in connection with their activities. The Rosicrucian rose was drawn upon the Round Table of King Arthur, and is the central motif for the links forming the chain from which the "Great George" is suspended among the jewels of The Order of the Garter. Hargrave Jennings suspects this Order of having some connection with the Rosicrucians.

After they had sworn to this code five of the Brothers departed to distant lands, and a year later two of the others also went their way, leaving Father C.R.C. alone in the "House of the Holy Spirit." Year after year they met with great joy, for they had quietly and sincerely promulgated their doctrines among the wise of the earth.

When the first of the Order died in England, it was decided that the burial places of the members should be secret. Soon afterward Father C.R.C. called the remaining six together, and it is supposed that then he prepared his own symbolic tomb. The *Fama* records that none of the Brothers alive at the time of its writing knew when Father C.R.C. died or where he was buried. His body was accidentally discovered 120 years after his death when one of the Brothers, who possessed considerable architectural skill, decided to make some alterations in the "House of the Holy Spirit." [It is only suspected that the tomb was in this building.]

While making his alterations, the Brother discovered a memorial tablet upon which were inscribed the names of the early members of the Order. This he decided to transfer to a more imposing chapel, for at that time no one knew in what country Father C.R.C. had died, this information having been concealed by the original members. In attempting to remove the memorial tablet, which was held in place by a large nail, some stones and plastering were broken from the wall, disclosing a door concealed in the masonry. The members of the Order immediately cleared away the rest of the débris and uncovered the entrance to a vault. Upon the door in large letters were the words: POST CXX ANNOS PATEBO. This, according to the mystic interpretation of the Brethren, meant, "In 120 years I shall come forth."

The following morning the door was opened and the members entered a vault with seven sides and seven corners, each side five feet broad and eight feet high. Although the sun never penetrated this tomb, it was brilliantly illuminated by a mysterious light in the ceiling. In the center was a circular altar, upon which were brass plates engraved with strange characters. In each of the seven sides was a small door which, upon being opened, revealed a number of boxes filled with books, secret instructions, and the supposedly lost arcanum of the Fraternity.

Upon moving the altar to one side a brass cover was disclosed. Lifting this revealed a body, presumably that of C.R.C., which, although it had lain there 120 years, was as well preserved as though it had just been interred. It was ornamented and attired in the robes of the Order, and in one hand was clasped a mysterious parchment which, next to the Bible, was the most valued possession of the Society. After thoroughly investigating the contents of the secret chamber, the brass plate and altar were put back in place, the door of the vault was again sealed, and the Brothers went their respective ways, their spirits raised and their faith increased by the miraculous spectacle which they had beheld.

The document ends by saying in effect, "In accordance with the will of Father C.R.C., the *Fama* has been prepared and sent forth to the wise and learned of all Europe in five languages, that all may know and understand the secrets of the august Fraternity. All of sincere soul who labor for the glory of God are invited to communicate with the Brethren and are promised that their appeal shall be heard, regardless of where they are or how the messages are sent. At the same time, those of selfish and ulterior motives are warned that only sorrow and misery will attend any who attempt to discover the Fraternity without a clean heart and a pure mind."

Such, in brief, is the story of the *Fama Fraternitatis.* Those who accept it literally regard Father C.R.C. as the actual founder of the Brotherhood, which he is believed to have organized about 1400. The fact that historical corroboration of the important points of the *Fama* has never been discovered is held against this theory. There is no proof that Father C.R.C. ever approached the learned men of Spain. The mysterious city of Damcar cannot be found, and there is no record that anywhere in Germany there existed a place where great numbers of the halt and sick came and were mysteriously healed. A. E. Waite's *The Secret Tradition in Freemasonry* contains a picture of Father C.R.C. showing him with a long beard upon his breast, sitting before a table upon which burns a candle. One hand is supporting his head and the other is resting the tip of its index finger on the temple of a human skull. The picture, however, proves nothing. Father C.R.C. was never seen by other than members of his own Order, and they did not preserve a description of him. That his name was Christian Rosencreutz is most improbable, as the two were not even associated until the writing of the *Chymical Nuptials.*

The Second Postulate

Those Masonic brethren who have investigated the subject accept the historical existence of the "Brotherhood of the Rose Cross" but are divided concerning the origin of the Order. One group holds the society originated in mediæval Europe as an outgrowth of alchemical speculation. Robert Macoy, *33°*, believes that Johann Valentin Andreæ, a German theologian, was the true founder, and he also believes it possible that this divine merely reformed and amplified an existing society which had been founded by Sir Henry Cornelius Agrippa. Some believe that Rosicrucianism represented the first European invasion of Buddhist and Brahmin culture. Still others hold the opinion that the "Society of the Rose Cross" was founded in Egypt during the philosophic supremacy of that empire, and that it also perpetuated the Mysteries of ancient Persia and Chaldea.

In his *Anacalypsis,* Godfrey Higgins writes: "The Rosicrucians of Germany are quite ignorant of their origin; but, by tradition, they suppose themselves descendants of the ancient Egyptians, Chaldeans, Magi, and Gymnosophists." (The last was a name given by the followers of Alexander the Great to a caste of naked Wise Men whom they found meditating along the river banks in India.) The consensus among these factions is that the story of Father C.R.C., like the Masonic legend of Hiram Abiff, is an allegory and should not be considered literally. A similar problem has confronted students of the Bible, who have found not only difficult, but in the majority of cases impossible, their efforts to substantiate the historical interpretation of the Scriptures.

Admitting the existence of the Rosicrucians as a secret society with both philosophic and political ends, it is remarkable that an organization with members in all parts of Europe could maintain absolute secrecy throughout the centuries. Nevertheless, the "Brothers of the Rose Cross" were apparently able to accomplish this. A great number of scholars and philosophers, among them Sir Francis Bacon and Wolfgang von Goethe, have been suspected of affiliation with the Order, but their connection has not been established to the satisfaction of prosaic historians. Pseudo-Rosicrucians abounded, but the true members of the "Ancient and Secret Order of The Unknown Philosophers" have successfully lived up to their name; to this day they remain unknown.

During the Middle Ages a number of tracts appeared, purporting to be from the pens of Rosicrucians. Many of them, however, were spurious, being issued for their self-aggrandizement by unscrupulous persons who used the revered and magic name *Rosicrucian* in the hope of gaining religious or political power. This has greatly complicated the work of investigating the Society. One group of pseudo-Rosicrucians went so far as to supply its members with a black cord by which they were to know each other, and warned them that if they broke their vow of secrecy the cord would be used to strangle them. Few of the principles of Rosicrucianism have been preserved in literature, for the original Fraternity published only fragmentary accounts of its principles and activities.

In his *Secret Symbols of the Rosicrucians,* Dr. Franz Hartmann describes the Fraternity as "A secret society of men possessing superhuman—if not supernatural—powers; they were said to be able to prophesy future events, to penetrate into the deepest mysteries of Nature, to transform Iron, Copper, Lead, or Mercury into Gold, to prepare an *Elixir of Life,* or *Universal Panacea,* by the use of which they could preserve their youth and manhood; and moreover it was believed that they could command the *Elemental Spirits* of Nature, and knew the secret of the *Philosopher's Stone,* a substance which rendered him who possessed it all-powerful, immortal, and supremely wise."

The same author further defines a Rosicrucian as "A person who by the process of spiritual awakening has attained a *practical* knowledge of the secret significance of the *Rose* and the *Cross.* * * * To call a person a Rosicrucian does not make him one, nor does the act of calling a person a Christian make him a Christ. The real Rosicrucian or Mason cannot be made; he must grow to be one by the expansion and unfoldment of the divine power within his own heart. The inattention to this truth is the cause that many churches and secret societies are far from being that which their names express."

The symbolic principles of Rosicrucianism are so profound that even today they are little appreciated. Their charts and diagrams are concerned with weighty cosmic principles which they treat with a philosophic understanding decidedly refreshing when compared with the orthodox narrowness prevalent in their day. According to the available records, the Rosicrucians were bound together by mutual aspirations rather than by the laws of a fraternity. The "Brothers of the Rose Cross" are believed to have lived unobtrusively, laboring industriously in trades and professions, disclosing their secret affiliation to no one—in many cases not even to their own families. After the death of C.R.C., most of the Brethren apparently had no central meeting place. Whatever initiatory ritual the Order possessed was so closely guarded that it has never been revealed. Doubtless it was couched in chemical terminology.

Efforts to join the Order were apparently futile, for the Rosicrucians always chose their disciples. Having agreed on one who they believed would do honor to their illustrious fraternity, they communicated with him in one of many mysterious ways. He might receive a letter, either anonymous or with a peculiar seal, usually bearing the letters "C.R.C." or "R.C." upon it. He would be instructed to go to a certain place at an appointed time. What was disclosed to him he never revealed, although in many cases his later writings showed that a new influence had come into his life, deepening his understanding and broadening his intellect. A few have written allegorically concerning what they beheld when in the august presence of the "Brethren of the Rose Cross."

FROM *GEHEIME FIGUREN DER ROSENKREUZER.*

THE ROSICRUCIAN ROSE.

The rose is a yonic symbol associated with generation, fecundity, and purity. The fact that flowers blossom by unfolding has caused them to be chosen as symbolic of spiritual unfoldment. The red color of the rose refers to the blood of Christ, and the golden heart concealed within the midst of the flower corresponds to the spiritual gold concealed within the human nature. The number of its petals being ten is also a subtle reminder of the perfect Pythagorean number. The rose symbolizes the heart, and the heart has always been accepted by Christians as emblematic of the virtues of love and compassion, as well as the nature of Christ—the personification of these virtues. The rose as a religious emblem is of great antiquity. It was accepted by the Greeks as the symbol of the sunrise, or the coming of dawn. In his *Metamorphosis, or Golden Ass,* Apuleius, turned into a donkey because of his foolishness, regained his human shape by eating a sacred rose given him by the Egyptian priests.

The presence of a hieroglyphic rose upon the escutcheon of Martin Luther has been the basis of much speculation as to whether any connection existed between his Reformation and the secret activities of the Brothers of the Rose Cross.

Alchemists were sometimes visited in their laboratories by mysterious strangers, who delivered learned discourses concerning the secret processes of the Hermetic arts and, after disclosing certain processes, departed, leaving no trace. Others declared that the "Brothers of the Rose Cross" communicated with them through dreams and visions, revealing the secrets of Hermetic wisdom to them while they were asleep. Having been instructed, the candidate was bound to secrecy not only concerning the chemical formulæ which had been disclosed to him but also concerning the method by which he had secured them. While these nameless adepts were suspected of being "Brothers of the Rose Cross," it could never be proved who they were, and those visited could only conjecture.

Many suspect the Rosicrucian rose to be a conventionalization of the Egyptian and Hindu lotus blossom, with the same symbolic meaning as this more ancient symbol. *The Divine Comedy* stamps Dante Alighieri as being familiar with the theory of Rosicrucianism. Concerning this point, Albert Pike in his *Morals and Dogma* makes this significant statement: "His Hell is but a negative Purgatory. His heaven is composed of a series of Kabalistic circles, divided by a cross, like the Pantacle of Ezekiel. In the center of this cross blooms a rose, and we see the symbol of the Adepts of the Rose-Croix for the first time publicly expounded and almost categorically explained."

Doubt has always existed as to whether the name *Rosicrucian* came from the symbol of the rose and cross, or whether this was merely a blind to deceive the uninformed and further conceal the true meaning of the Order. Godfrey Higgins believes that the word *Rosicrucian* is not derived from the flower but from the word *Ros,* which means *dew.* It is also interesting to note that the word *Ras* means *wisdom,* while *Rus* is translated *concealment.* Doubtless all of these meanings have contributed to Rosicrucian symbolism.

A. E. Waite holds with Godfrey Higgins that the process of forming the Philosopher's Stone with the aid of dew is the secret concealed within the name Rosicrucian. It is possible that the dew referred to is a mysterious substance within the human brain, closely resembling the description given by alchemists of the dew which, falling from heaven, redeemed the earth. The cross is symbolic of the human body, and the two symbols together—the rose on the cross—signify that the soul of man is crucified upon the body, where it is held by three nails.

It is probable that Rosicrucian symbolism is a perpetuation of the secret tenets of the Egyptian Hermes, and that the Society of Unknown Philosophers is the true link connecting modern Masonry, with its mass of symbols, to ancient Egyptian Hermeticism, the source of that symbolism. In his *Doctrine and Literature of the Kabalah,* A. E. Waite makes this important observation: "There are certain indications which point to a possible connection between Masonry and

Rosicrucianism, and this, if admitted, would constitute the first link in its connection with the past. The evidence is, however, inconclusive, or at least unextricated. Freemasonry *per se,* in spite of the affinity with mysticism which I have just mentioned, has never exhibited any mystic character, nor has it a clear notion how it came by its symbols."

Many of those connected with the development of Freemasonry were suspected of being Rosicrucians; some, as in the case of Robert Fludd, even wrote defenses of this organization. Frank C. Higgins, a modern Masonic symbolist, writes: "Doctor Ashmole, a member of this fraternity [Rosicrucian], is revered by Masons as one of the founders of the first Grand Lodge in London." (See *Ancient Freemasonry.*) Elias Ashmole is but one of many intellectual links connecting Rosicrucianism with the genesis of Freemasonry. The *Encyclopædia Britannica* notes that Elias Ashmole was initiated into the Freemasonic Order in 1646, and further states that he was "the first gentleman, or amateur, to be 'accepted'."

On this same subject, Papus, in his *Tarot of the Bohemians,* has written: "We must not forget that the Rosicrucians were the Initiators of Leibnitz, and the founders of actual Freemasonry through Ashmole." If the founders of Freemasonry were initiated into the Great Arcanum of Egypt—and the symbolism of modern Masonry would indicate that such was the case—then it is reasonable to suppose that they secured their information from a society whose existence they admitted and which was duly qualified to teach them these symbols and allegories.

One theory concerning the two Orders is to the effect that Freemasonry was an outgrowth of Rosicrucianism; in other words, that the "Unknown Philosophers" became known through an organization which they created to serve them in the material world. The story goes on to relate that the Rosicrucian adepts became dissatisfied with their progeny and silently withdrew from the Masonic hierarchy, leaving behind their symbolism and allegories, but carrying away the keys by which the locked symbols could be made to give up their secret meanings. Speculators have gone so far as to state that, in their opinion, modern Freemasonry has completely absorbed Rosicrucianism and succeeded it as the world's greatest secret society. Other minds of equal learning declare that the Rosicrucian Brotherhood still exists, preserving its individuality as the result of having withdrawn from the Masonic Order.

According to a widely accepted tradition, the headquarters of the Rosicrucian Order is near Carlsbad, in Austria (see Doctor Franz Hartmann). Another version has it that a mysterious school, resembling in general principles the

Rosicrucian Fraternity, which calls itself "The Bohemian Brothers," still maintains its individuality in the *Schwarzwald* (Black Forest) of Germany. One thing is certain: with the rise of Freemasonry, the Rosicrucian Order in Europe practically disappeared, and notwithstanding existing statements to the contrary, it is certain that the 18th degree (commonly known as the Rose-Croix) perpetuates many of the symbols of the Rosicrucian Fire Alchemists.

In an anonymous unpublished manuscript of the eighteenth century bearing the earmarks of Rosicrucian Qabbalism appears this statement: "Yet will I now give the over-wise world a paradox to be solved, namely, that some illuminated men have undertaken to found Schools of Wisdom in Europe and these for some peculiar reason have called themselves *Fratres Rosæ Crucis.* But soon afterwards came false schools into existence and corrupted the good intentions of these wise men. Therefore, the Order no longer exists as most people would understand existence, and as this Fraternity of the *Seculo Fili* call themselves *Brothers of the Rosie Cross,* so also will they in the *Seculo Spiritus Sancti* call themselves *Brothers of the Lily Cross* and the *Knights of the White Lion.* Then will the Schools of Wisdom begin again to blossom, but why the first one chose their name and why the others shall also choose theirs, only those can solve who have understanding grounded in Nature."

Political aspirations of the Rosicrucians were expressed through the activities of Sir Francis Bacon, the Comte de St.-Germain, and the Comte di Cagliostro. The last named is suspected of having been an emissary of the Knights Templars, a society deeply involved in transcendentalism, as Eliphas Levi has noted. There is a popular supposition to the effect that the Rosicrucians were at least partial instigators of the French Revolution. (Note particularly the introduction to Lord Bulwer-Lytton's Rosicrucian novel *Zanoni.*)

The Third Postulate

The third theory takes the form of a sweeping denial of Rosicrucianism, asserting that the so-called original Order never had any foundation in fact but was entirely a product of imagination. This viewpoint is best expressed by a number of questions which are still being asked by investigators of this elusive group of metaphysicians. Was the "Brotherhood of the Rose Cross" merely a mythical institution created in the fertile mind of some literary cynic for the purpose of deriding the alchemical and Hermetic sciences? Did the "House of the Holy Spirit" ever exist outside the imagination of some mediæval mystic? Was the whole Rosicrucian story a satire to ridicule the gullibility of scholastic Europe?

Was the mysterious Father C.R.C. a product of the literary genius of Johann Valentin Andreæ, or another of similar mind, who, attempting to score alchemical and Hermetic philosophy, unwittingly became a great power in furthering the cause of its promulgation? That at least one of the early documents of the Rosicrucians was from the pen of Andreæ there is little doubt, but for just what purpose he compiled it still remains a matter of speculation. Did Andreæ himself receive from some unknown person, or persons, instructions to be carried out? If he wrote the *Chymical Nuptials of Christian Rosencreutz* when only fifteen years old, was he overshadowed in the preparation of that book?

To these vital questions no answers are forthcoming. A number of persons accepted the magnificent imposture of Andreæ as absolute truth. It is maintained by many that, as a consequence, numerous psuedo-societies sprang up, each asserting that it was the organization concerning which the *Fama Fraternitatis* and the *Confessio Fraternitatis* were written. Beyond doubt there are many spurious orders in existence today; but few of them can offer valid claims that their history dates back farther than the beginning of the nineteenth century.

The mystery associated with the Rosicrucian Fraternity has resulted in endless controversy. Many able minds, notable among them Eugenius Philalethes, Michael Maier, John Heydon, and Robert Fludd, defended the concrete existence of "The Society of Unknown Philosophers." Others equally qualified have asserted it to be of fraudulent origin and doubtful existence. Eugenius Philalethes, while dedicating books to the Order, and himself writing an extended exposition of its principles, disclaims all personal connection with it. Many others have done likewise.

Some are of the opinion that Sir Francis Bacon had a hand in the writing of the *Fama* and *Confessio Fraternitatis,* on the basis that the rhetorical style of these works is similar to that of Bacon's *New Atlantis.* They also contend that certain statements in the latter work point to an acquaintance with Rosicrucian symbology. The elusiveness of the Rosicrucians has caused them to be favorite subjects for literary works. Outstanding among the romances which have been woven around them is *Zanoni.* The author, Lord Bulwer-Lytton, is regarded by some as a member of the Order, while others assert that he applied for membership but was rejected. Pope's *Rape of the Lock,* the *Comte de Gabalis* by Abbé de Villars, and essays by De Quincey, Hartmann, Jennings, Mackenzie, and others, are examples of Rosicrucian literature. Although the existence of these mediæval Rosicrucians is difficult to prove, sufficient evidence is at hand to make it extremely probable that there existed in Germany, and afterwards in France, Italy, England, and other European countries, a secret society of illuminated savants who made contributions of great import to the sum of human knowledge, while maintaining absolute secrecy concerning their personalities and their organization.

The Fourth Postulate

The apparent incongruities of the Rosicrucian controversy have also been accounted for by a purely transcendental explanation. There is evidence that early writers were acquainted with such a supposition—which, however, was popularized only after it had been espoused by Theosophy. This theory asserts that the Rosicrucians actually possessed all the supernatural powers with which they were credited; that they were in reality citizens of two worlds: that, while they had physical bodies for expression on the material plane, they were also capable, through the instructions they received from the Brotherhood, of functioning in a mysterious ethereal body not subject to the limitations of time or distance. By means of this "astral form" they were able to function in the invisible realm of Nature, and in this realm, beyond reach of the profane, their temple was located.

According to this viewpoint, the true Rosicrucian Brotherhood consisted of a limited number of highly developed adepts, or initiates, those of the higher degrees being no longer subject to the laws of mortality; candidates were accepted into the Order only after long periods of probation; adepts possessed the secret of the Philosopher's Stone and knew the process of transmuting the base metals into gold, but taught that these were only allegorical terms concealing the true mystery of human regeneration through the transmutation of the "base elements" of man's lower nature into the "gold" of intellectual and spiritual realization. According to this theory, those who have sought to record the events of importance in connection with the Rosicrucian controversy have invariably failed because they approached their subject from a purely physical or materialistic angle.

These adepts were believed to have been able to teach man how to function away from his physical body at will by assisting him to remove the "rose from the cross." They taught that the spiritual nature was attached to the material form at certain points, symbolized by the "nails" of the crucifixion; but by three alchemical initiations which took place in the spiritual world, in the true Temple of the Rose Cross, they were able to "draw" these nails and permit the divine nature of man to come down from its cross. They concealed the processes by which this was accomplished under three alchemical metaphoric expressions:

"The Casting of the Molten Sea," "The Making of the Rose Diamond," and "The Achieving of the Philosopher's Stone."

While the intellectualist flounders among contradictory theories, the mystic treats the problem in an entirely different manner. He believes that the true Rosicrucian Fraternity, consisting of a school of supermen (not unlike the fabled Mahatmas of India), is an institution existing not in the visible world but in its spiritual counterpart, which he sees fit to call the "inner planes of Nature"; that the Brothers can be reached only by those who are capable of transcending the limitations of the material world. To substantiate their viewpoint, these mystics cite the following significant statement from the *Confessio Fraternitatis:* "A thousand times the unworthy may clamour, a thousand times may present themselves, yet God hath commanded our ears that they should hear none of them, and hath so compassed us about with His clouds that unto us, His servants, no violence can be done; wherefore now no longer are we beheld by human eyes, unless they have received strength borrowed from the eagle." In mysticism the eagle is a symbol of initiation (the spinal Spirit Fire), and by this is explained the inability of the unregenerated world to understand the Secret Order of the Rose Cross.

Those professing this theory regard the Comte de St.-Germain as their highest adept and assert that he and Christian Rosencreutz were one and the same individual. They accept fire as their universal symbol because it was the one element by means of which they could control the metals. They declared themselves the descendants of Tubal-cain and Hiram Abiff, and that the purpose of their existence was to preserve the spiritual nature of man through ages of materiality. "The Gnostic sects, the Arabs, Alchemists, Templars, Rosicrucians, and lastly the Freemasons, form the Western chain in the transmission of occult science." (See *The Tarot of the Bohemians* translated by A. E. Waite from the French of Papus.)

Max Heindel, the Christian mystic, described the Rosicrucian Temple as an "etheric structure" located in and around the home of a European country gentleman. He believed that this invisible building would ultimately be moved to the American continent. Mr. Heindel referred to the Rosicrucian Initiates as so advanced in the science of life that "death had forgotten them."

XXXII

Rosicrucian Doctrines
and Tenets

rustworthy information is unavailable concerning the actual philosophical beliefs, political aspirations, and humanitarian activities of the Rosicrucian Fraternity. Today, as of old, the mysteries of the Society are preserved inviolate by virtue of their essential nature; and attempts to interpret Rosicrucian philosophy are but speculations, anything to the contrary notwithstanding.

Evidence points to the probable existence of two distinct Rosicrucian bodies: an inner organization whose members never revealed their identity or teachings to the world, and an outer body under the supervision of the inner group. In all probability, the symbolic tomb of Christian Rosencreutz, Knight of the Golden Stone, was in reality this outer body, the spirit of which is in a more exalted sphere. For a period of more than a century subsequent to 1614, the outer body circulated tracts and manifestoes under either its own name or the names of various initiated members. The purpose of these writings was apparently to confuse and mislead investigators, and thus effectively to conceal the actual designs of the Fraternity.

When Rosicrucianism became the philosophical "fad" of the seventeenth century, numerous documents on the subject were also circulated for purely commercial purposes by impostors desirous of capitalizing its popularity. The cunningly contrived artifices of the Fraternity itself and the blundering literary impostures of charlatans formed a double veil behind which the inner organization carried on its activities in a manner totally dissimilar to its purposes and principles as publicly disseminated. The *Fratres Rosæ Crucis* naïvely refer to the misunderstandings which they have for obvious reasons permitted to exist concerning themselves as being "clouds" within which they labor and behind which they are concealed.

An inkling of the substance of Rosicrucianism—its esoteric doctrines—can be gleaned from an analysis of its shadow—its exoteric writings. In one of the most important of their "clouds," the *Confessio Fraternitatis*, the Brethren of the Fraternity of R.C. seek to justify their existence and explain (?) the purposes and activities of their Order. In its original form the *Confessio* is divided into fourteen chapters, which are here epitomized.

Confessio Fraternitatis R.C. ad Eruditos Europæ

Chapter I. Do not through hasty judgment or prejudice misinterpret the statements concerning our Fraternity published in our previous manifesto—the *Fama Fraternitatis.* Jehovah, beholding the decadence of civilization, seeks to redeem humanity by revealing to the willing and by thrusting upon the reluctant those secrets which previously He had reserved for His elect. By this wisdom the godly shall be saved, but the sorrows of the ungodly shall be multiplied. While the true purpose of our Order was set forth in the *Fama Fraternitatis,* misunderstandings have arisen through which we have been falsely accused of heresy and treason. In this document we hope so to clarify our position that the learned of Europe will be moved to join with us in the dissemination of divine knowledge according to the will of our illustrious founder.

Chapter II. While it is alleged by many that the philosophic code of our day is sound, we declare it to be false and soon to die of its own inherent weakness. Just as Nature, however, provides a remedy for each new disease that manifests itself, so our Fraternity has provided a remedy for the infirmities of the world's philosophic system. The secret philosophy of the R.C. is founded upon that knowledge which is the sum and head of all faculties, sciences, and arts. By our divinely revealed system—which partakes much of theology and medicine but little of jurisprudence—we analyze the heavens and the earth; but mostly we study man himself, within whose nature is concealed the supreme secret. If the learned of our day will accept our invitation and join themselves to our Fraternity, we will reveal to them undreamed-of secrets and wonders concerning the hidden workings of Nature.

Chapter III. Do not believe that the secrets discussed in this brief document are lightly esteemed by us. We cannot describe fully the marvels of our Fraternity lest the uninformed be overwhelmed by our astonishing declarations and the vulgar ridicule the mysteries which they do not comprehend. We also fear that many will be confused by the unexpected generosity of our proclamation, for not understanding the wonders of this sixth age they do not realize the great changes which are to come. Like blind men living in a world full of light, they discern only through the sense of feeling. [By *sight* is implied spiritual cognition: by *feeling,* the material senses.]

Chapter IV. We firmly believe that through deep meditation on the inventions of the human mind and the mysteries of life, through the cooperation of the angels and spirits, and through experience and long observation, our loving Christian Father C.R.C. was so fully illumined with God's wisdom that were all the books and writings of the world lost and the foundations of science overturned, the Fraternity of R.C. could reestablish the structure of world thought upon the foundation of divine truth and integrity. Because of the great depth and perfection of our knowledge, those desiring to understand the mysteries of the Fraternity of R.C. cannot attain to that wisdom immediately, but must grow in understanding and knowledge. Therefore, our Fraternity is divided into grades through which each must ascend step by step to the Great Arcanum. Now that it has pleased God to lighten unto us His sixth candelabrum, is it not better to seek truth in this way than to wander through the labyrinths of worldly ignorance?

Furthermore, those who receive this knowledge shall become masters of all arts and crafts; no secret shall be hidden from them; and all good works of the past, present, and future shall be accessible to them. The whole world shall become as one book and the contradictions of science and theology shall be reconciled. Rejoice, O humanity! for the time has come when God has decreed that the number of our Fraternity shall be increased, a labor that we have joyously undertaken. The doors of wisdom are now open to the world, but only to those who have earned the privilege may the Brothers present themselves, for it is forbidden to reveal our knowledge even to our own children. The right to receive spiritual truth cannot be inherited: it must be evolved within the soul of man himself.

Chapter V. Though we may be accused of indiscretion in offering our treasures so freely and promiscuously—without discriminating between the godly, the wise, the prince, the peasant—we affirm that we have not betrayed our trust; for although we have published our *Fama* in five languages, only those understand it who have that right. Our Society is not to be discovered by curiosity seekers, but only by serious and consecrated thinkers; nevertheless we have circulated our *Fama* in five mother tongues so that the righteous of all nations may have an opportunity to know of us, even though they be not scholars. A thousand times the unworthy may present themselves and clamor at the gates, but God has forbidden us of the Fraternity of R.C. to hear their voices, and He has surrounded us with His clouds and His protection so that no harm may come to us, and God has decreed that we of the Order of R.C. can no longer be seen by mortal eyes unless they have received strength borrowed from the eagle. We further affirm that we shall reform the governments of Europe and pattern them according to the system applied by the philosophers of Damcar. All men desirous of securing knowledge shall receive as much as they are capable of understanding. The rule of false theology shall be overthrown and God shall make His will known through His chosen philosophers.

Chapter VI. Because of the need of brevity, it is enough to say that our Father C.R.C. was born in the year 1378 and departed at the age of 106, leaving to us the labor of spreading the doctrine of philosophic religion to the entire world. Our Fraternity is open to all who sincerely seek for truth; but we publicly warn the false and impious that they cannot betray or injure us, for God has protected our Fraternity, and all who seek to do it harm shall have their evil designs return and destroy them, while the treasures of our Fraternity shall remain untouched, to be used by the Lion in the establishment of his kingdom.

Chapter VII. We declare that God, before the end of the world, shall create a great flood of spiritual light to alleviate the sufferings of humankind. Falsehood and darkness which have crept into the arts, sciences, religions, and governments of humanity—making it difficult for even the wise to discover the path of reality—shall be forever removed and a single standard established, so that all may enjoy the fruitage of truth. We shall not be recognized as those responsible for this change, for people shall say that it is the result of the progressiveness of the age. Great are the reforms about to take place; but we of the Fraternity of R.C. do not arrogate to ourselves the glory for this divine reformation, since many there are, not members of our Fraternity but honest, true and wise men, who by their intelligence and their writings shall hasten its coming. We testify that sooner the stones shall rise up and offer their services than that there shall be any lack of righteous persons to execute the will of God upon earth.

Chapter VIII. That no one may doubt, we declare that God has sent messengers and signs in the heavens, namely, the new stars in *Serpentarius* and *Cygnus,* to show that a great Council of the Elect is to take place. This proves that God reveals in visible nature—for the discerning few—signs and symbols of all things that are coming to pass. God has given man two eyes, two nostrils, and two ears, but only one tongue. Whereas the eyes, the nostrils, and the ears admit the wisdom of Nature into the mind, the tongue alone may give it forth. In various ages there have been illumined ones who have seen, smelt, tasted, or heard the will of God, but it will shortly come to pass that those who have seen, smelt, tasted, or heard shall speak, and truth shall be revealed. Before this revelation of righteousness is possible, however, the world must sleep away the intoxication of her poisoned chalice (filled with the false life of the theological vine) and, opening her heart to virtue and understanding, welcome the rising sun of Truth.

Chapter IX. We have a magic writing, copied from that divine alphabet with which God writes His will upon the face of celestial and terrestrial Nature. With this new language we read God's will for all His creatures, and just as astronomers predict eclipses so we prognosticate the obscurations of the church and how long they shall last. Our language is like unto that of Adam and Enoch before the Fall, and though we understand and can explain our mysteries in this our sacred language, we cannot do so in Latin, a tongue contaminated by the confusion of Babylon.

Chapter X. Although there are still certain powerful persons who oppose and hinder us—because of which we must remain concealed—we exhort those who would become of our Fraternity to study unceasingly the Sacred Scriptures, for such as do this cannot be far from us. We do not mean that the Bible should be continually in the mouth of man, but that he should search for its true and eternal meaning, which is seldom discovered by theologians, scientists, or mathematicians because they are blinded by the opinions of their sects. We bear witness that never since the beginning of the world has there been given to man a more excellent book than the Holy Bible. Blessed is he who possesses it, more blessed he who reads it, most blessed he who understands it, and most godlike he who obeys it.

Chapter XI. We wish the statements we made in the *Fama Fraternitatis* concerning the transmutation of metals and the universal medicine to be rightly understood. While we realize that both these works are attainable by man, we fear that many really great minds may be led away from the true quest of knowledge and understanding if they permit themselves to limit their investigation to the transmutation of metals. When to a man is given power to heal disease, to overcome poverty, and to reach a position of worldly dignity, that man is beset by numerous temptations and unless he possess true knowledge and full understanding he will become a terrible menace to mankind. The alchemist who attains to the art of transmuting base metals can do all manner of evil unless his understanding be as great as his self-created wealth. We therefore affirm that man must first gain knowledge, virtue, and understanding; then all other things may be added unto him. We accuse the Christian Church of the great sin of possessing power and using it unwisely; therefore we prophesy that it shall fall by the weight of its own iniquities and its crown shall be brought to naught.

Chapter XII. In concluding our *Confessio,* we earnestly admonish you to cast aside the worthless books of pseudo-alchemists and philosophers (of whom there are many in our age), who make light of the Holy Trinity and deceive the credulous with meaningless enigmas. One of the greatest of these is a stage player, a man with sufficient ingenuity for imposition. Such men are mingled by the Enemy of human welfare among those who seek to do good, thus making Truth more difficult of discovery. Believe us, Truth is simple and unconcealed, while falsehood is complex, deeply hidden, proud, and its fictitious worldly knowledge, seemingly aglitter with godly luster, is often mistaken for divine wisdom. You that are wise will turn from these false teachings and come to us, who seek not your money but freely offer you our greater treasure. We desire not your goods, but that you should become partakers of our goods. We do not deride parables, but invite you to understand all parables and all secrets. We do not ask you to receive us, but invite you to come unto our kingly homes and palaces, not because of ourselves but because we are so ordered by the Spirit of God, the desire of our most excellent Father C.R.C., and the need of the present moment, which is very great.

Chapter XIII. Now that we have made our position clear: that we sincerely confess Christ; disavow the Papacy; devote our lives to true philosophy and worthy living; and daily invite and admit into our Fraternity the worthy of all nations, who thereafter share with us the Light of God: will you not join yourselves with us to the perfection of yourselves, the development of all the arts, and the service of the world? If you will take this step, the treasures of every part of the earth shall be at one time given unto you, and the darkness which envelopes human knowledge and which results in the vanities of material arts and sciences shall be forever dispelled.

Chapter XIV. Again we warn those who are dazzled by the glitter of gold or those who, now upright, might be turned by great riches to a life of idleness and pomp, not to disturb our sacred silence with their clamorings; for though there be a medicine which will cure all diseases and give unto all men wisdom, yet it is against the will of God that men should attain to understanding by any means other than virtue, labor, and integrity. We are not permitted to manifest ourselves to any man except it be by the will of God. Those who believe that they can partake of our spiritual wealth against the will of God or without His sanction will find that they shall sooner lose their lives in seeking us than attain happiness by finding us.

Fraternitas R.C.

Johann Valentin Andreæ is generally reputed to be the author of the *Confessio*. It is a much-mooted question, however, whether Andreæ did not permit his name to be used as a pseudonym by Sir Francis Bacon. Apropos of this subject are two extremely significant references occurring in the introduction to that remarkable potpourri, *The Anatomy of Melancholy*. This volume first appeared in 1621 from the pen of Democritus Junior, who was afterwards identified as Robert Burton, who, in turn, was a suspected intimate of Sir Francis Bacon. One reference archly suggests that at the time of publishing *The Anatomy of Melancholy* in 1621 the founder of the Fraternity of R.C. was still alive. This statement—concealed from general recognition by its textual involvement—has escaped the notice of most students of Rosicrucianism. In the same work there also appears a short footnote of stupendous import. It contains merely the words: "Joh. Valent. Andreas, Lord Verulam." This single line definitely relates Johann Valentin Andreæ to Sir Francis Bacon, who was Lord Verulam, and by its punctuation intimates that they are one and the same individual.

FROM THE *TURBÆ PHILOSOPHORUM.*

THE ALCHEMICAL ANDROGYNE.

The *Turbæ Philosophorum* is one of the earliest known documents on alchemy in the Latin tongue. Its exact origin is unknown. It is sometimes referred to as *The Third Pythagorical Synod.* As its name implies, it is an assembly of the sages and sets forth the alchemical viewpoints of many of the early Greek philosophers. The symbol reproduced above is from a rare edition of the *Turbæ Philosophorum* published in Germany in 1750, and represents by a hermaphroditic figure the accomplishment of the *magnum opus*. The active and passive principles of Nature were often depicted by male and female figures, and when these two principles were harmoniously conjoined in any one nature or body it was customary to symbolize this state of perfect equilibrium by the composite figure above shown.

Prominent among Rosicrucian apologists was John Heydon, who inscribes himself "A Servant of God, and a Secretary of Nature." In his curious work, *The Rosie Cross Uncovered*, he gives an enigmatic but valuable description of the Fraternity of R.C. in the following language:

"Now there are a kind of men, as they themselves report, named *Rosie Crucians,* a divine fraternity that inhabit the suburbs of heaven, and these are the officers of the *Generalissimo* of the world, that are as the eyes and ears of the great King, seeing and hearing all things: they say these *Rosie Crucians* are seraphically illuminated, as *Moses* was, according to this order of the elements, earth refin'd to water, water to air, air to fire." He further declares that these mysterious Brethren possessed polymorphous powers, appearing in any desired form at will. In the preface of the same work, he enumerates the strange powers of the Rosicrucian adepts:

"I shall here tell you what *Rosie Crucians* are, and that *Moses* was their Father, and he was Θεοῦ παῖς; some say they were of the order of Elias, some say the Disciples of Ezekiel; * * * For it should seem *Rosie Crucians* were not only initiated into the Mosaical Theory, but have arrived also to the power of working miracles, as *Moses, Elias, Ezekiel,* and the succeeding Prophets did, as being transported where they please, as *Habakkuk* was from *Jewry* to Babylon, or as Philip, after he had baptized the *Eunuch to* Azorus, and one of these went from me to a friend of mine in *Devonshire,* and came and brought me an answer to *London* the same day, which is four days journey; they taught me excellent predictions of Astrology and Earthquakes; they slack the Plague in Cities; they silence the violent Winds and Tempests; they calm the rage of the Sea and Rivers; they walk in the Air, they frustrate the malicious aspects of Witches; they cure all Diseases."

The writings of John Heydon are considered a most important contribution to Rosicrucian literature. John Heydon was probably related to Sir Christopher Heydon, "a Seraphically Illuminated Rosie Crucian," whom the late F. Leigh Gardner, Hon. Secretary Soc. Ros. in Anglia, believes to have been the source of his Rosicrucian knowledge. In his *Bibliotheca Rosicruciana* he makes the following statement concerning John Heydon: "On the whole, from the internal evidence of his writings, he appears to have gone through the lower grade of the R.C. Order and to have given out much of this to the world." John Heydon traveled extensively, visiting Arabia, Egypt, Persia, and various parts of Europe, as related in a biographical introduction to his work, *The Wise-Mans Crown, Set with Angels, Planets, Metals, etc., or The Glory of the Rosie Cross*—a work declared by him to be a translation into English of the mysterious book *M* brought from Arabia by Christian Rosencreutz.

Thomas Vaughan (Eugenius Philalethes), another champion of the Order, corroborates the statement of John Heydon concerning the ability of the Rosicrucian initiates to make themselves invisible at will: "The Fraternity of R.C. can move in this white mist. 'Whosoever would communicate with us must be able to see in this light, or us he will never see—unless by our own will.'"

The Fraternity of R.C. is an august and sovereign body, arbitrarily manipulating the symbols of alchemy, Qabbalism, astrology, and magic to the attainment of its own peculiar purposes, but entirely independent of the cults whose terminology it employs. The three major objects of the Fraternity are:

1. *The abolition all monarchical forms of government and the substitution therefor of the rulership of the philosophic elect.* The present democracies are the direct outgrowth of Rosicrucian efforts to liberate the masses from the domination of despotism. In the early part of the eighteenth century the Rosicrucians turned their attention to the new American Colonies, then forming the nucleus of a great nation in the New World. The American War of Independence represents their first great political experiment and resulted in the establishment of a national government founded upon the fundamental principles of divine and natural law. As an imperishable reminder of their *sub rosa* activities, the Rosicrucians left the Great Seal of the United States. The Rosicrucians were also the instigators of the French Revolution, but in this instance were not wholly successful, owing to the fact that the fanaticism of the revolutionists could not be controlled and the Reign of Terror ensued.

2. *The reformation of science, philosophy, and ethics.* The Rosicrucians declared that the material arts and sciences were but shadows of the divine wisdom, and that only by penetrating the innermost recesses of Nature could man attain to reality and understanding. Though calling themselves Christians, the Rosicrucians were evidently Platonists and also profoundly versed in the deepest mysteries of early Hebrew and Hindu theology. There is undeniable evidence that the Rosicrucians desired to reestablish the institutions of the ancient Mysteries as the foremost method of instructing humanity in the secret and eternal doctrine. Indeed, being in all probability the perpetuators of the ancient Mysteries, the Rosicrucians were able to maintain themselves against the obliterating forces of dogmatic Christianity only by absolute secrecy and the subtlety of their subterfuges. They so carefully guarded and preserved the Supreme Mystery—the identity and interrelationship of the *Three Selves*—that no one to whom they did not of their own accord reveal themselves has ever secured any satisfactory information regarding either the existence or the purpose of the Order. The Fraternity of R.C., through its outer organization, is gradually creating an environment or body in which the Illustrious Brother C.R.C. may ultimately incarnate and consummate for humanity the vast spiritual and material labors of the Fraternity.

3. *The discovery of the Universal Medicine, or panacea, for all forms of disease.* There is ample evidence that the Rosicrucians were successful in their quest

for the Elixir of Life. In his *Theatrum Chemicum Britannicum,* Elias Ashmole states that the Rosicrucians were not appreciated in England, but were
welcomed on the Continent. He also states that Queen Elizabeth was twice
cured of the smallpox by the Brethren of the Rosy Cross, and that the Earl of
Norfolk was healed of leprosy by a Rosicrucian physician. In the quotations
that follow it is hinted by John Heydon that the Brothers of the Fraternity
possessed the secret of prolonging human existence indefinitely, but not
beyond the time appointed by the will of God:

"And at last they could restore by the same course every Brother that died
to life again, and so continue many ages; the rules you find in the fourth book.
* * * After this manner began the Fraternity of the Rosie Cross, first by four
persons, who died and rose again until Christ, and then they came to worship as
the Star guided them to Bethlehem of Judea, where lay our Saviour in his
mother's arms; and then they opened their treasure and presented unto him
gifts, gold, frankincense, and myrrh, and by the commandment of God went
home to their habitation. These four waxing young again successively many
hundreds of years, made a magical language and writing, with a large dictionary,
which we yet daily use to God's praise and glory, and do find great wisdom
therein. * * * Now whilst Brother C.R. was in a proper womb quickening, they
concluded to draw and receive yet others more into their Fraternity."

The *womb* herein referred to was apparently the glass casket, or container,
in which the Brothers were buried. This was also called the *philosophical egg.*
After a certain period of time the philosopher, breaking the shell of his egg, came
forth and functioned for a prescribed period, after which he retired again into
his shell of glass. The Rosicrucian medicine for the healing of all human infirmities may be interpreted either as a chemical substance which produces the physical effects described or as spiritual understanding—the true healing power
which, when a man has partaken of it, reveals truth to him. Ignorance is the
worst form of disease, and that which heals ignorance is therefore the most
potent of all medicines. The perfect Rosicrucian medicine was for the healing of
nations, races, and individuals.

In an early unpublished manuscript, an unknown philosopher declares
alchemy, Qabbalism, astrology, and magic to have been divine sciences originally, but that through perversion they had become false doctrines, leading seekers after wisdom ever farther from their goal. The same author gives a valuable
key to esoteric Rosicrucianism by dividing the path of spiritual attainment into

three steps, or schools, which he calls *mountains.* The first and lowest of these mountains is *Mount Sophia;* the second, *Mount Qabbalah;* and the third, *Mount Magia.* These three mountains are sequential stages of spiritual growth. The unknown author then states:

"By philosophy is to be understood the knowledge of the workings of Nature, by which knowledge man learns to climb to those higher mountains above the limitations of sense. By Qabbalism is to be understood the language of the angelic or celestial beings, and he who masters it is able to converse with the messengers of God. On the highest of the mountains is the School of Magia (Divine Magic, which is the language of God) wherein man is taught the true nature of all things by God Himself."

There is a growing conviction that if the true nature of Rosicrucianism were divulged, it would cause consternation, to say the least. Rosicrucian symbols have many meanings, but the Rosicrucian meaning has not yet been revealed. The mount upon which stands the House of the Rosy Cross is still concealed by clouds, in which the Brethren hide both themselves and their secrets. Michael Maier writes: "What is contained in the *Fama* and *Confessio* is true. It is a very childish objection that the brotherhood have promised so much and performed so little. With them, as elsewhere, many are called but few are chosen. The masters of the order hold out the rose as the remote prize, but they impose the cross on those who are entering." (See *Silentium post Clamores,* by Maier, and *The Rosicrucians and the Freemasons,* by De Quincey.)

The rose and the cross appear upon the stained glass windows of Lichfield Chapter House, where Walter Conrad Arensberg believes Lord Bacon and his mother to have been buried. A crucified rose within a heart is watermarked into the dedication page of the 1628 edition of Robert Burton's *Anatomy of Melancholy.*

The fundamental symbols of the Rosicrucians were the rose and the cross; the rose female and the cross male, both universal phallic emblems. While such learned gentlemen as Thomas Inman, Hargrave Jennings, and Richard Payne Knight have truly observed that the rose and the cross typify the generative processes, these scholars seem unable to pierce the veil of symbolism; they do not realize that the creative mystery in the material world is merely a shadow of the divine creative mystery in the spiritual world. Because of the phallic significance of their symbols, both the Rosicrucians and the Templars have been falsely accused of practicing obscene rites in their secret cremonials. While it is quite true that the alchemical retort symbolizes the womb, it also has a far more significant meaning concealed under the allegory of the second birth. As generation is the key to material existence, it is natural that the Fraternity of R.C. should adopt as its characteristic symbols those exemplifying the reproductive processes. As regeneration is the key to spiritual existence, they therefore founded their symbolism upon the rose and the cross, which typify the redemption of man through the union of his lower temporal nature with his higher eternal nature. The rosy cross is also a hieroglyphic figure representing the formula of the Universal Medicine.

XXXIII

Fifteen Rosicrucian and Qabbalistic Diagrams

I n his well-known work, *The Rosicrucians, Their Rites and Mysteries,* Hargrave Jennings reproduces five Qabbalistic charts which he declares to be genuine Rosicrucian drawings. He gives no information concerning their origin nor does he attempt an elucidation of their symbolism. A recent writer who reproduced one of these charts correlated it to the emblematic tomb of Father C.R.C., thus exposing the true nature of Christian Rosencreutz.

The five plates reproduced in Hargrave Jennings' book are part of a series of fifteen diagrams which appear in *The Magical, Qabbalistical, and Theosophical Writings of Georgius von Welling, on the Subject of Salt, Sulphur, and Mercury.* This extremely rare volume was published at Frankfort and Leipzig in 1735 and 1760. The numbers and figures on the charts refer to the chapters and sections of the *Writings.* These fifteen charts constitute a remarkable and invaluable addition to the few other known admittedly authentic Qabbalistic and Rosicrucian diagrams.

Lucifer is the greatest mystery of symbolism. The secret knowledge of the Rosicrucians concerning Lucifer is nowhere so plainly set forth as in these plates, which virtually reveal his true identity, a carefully guarded secret about which little has been written. Lucifer is represented by the number 741.

Von Welling does not give a complete exposition of the fifteen charts; to have done so would have been contrary to the principles of Qabbalistic philosophy. The deeper significance of the symbols is revealed only by profound study and contemplation.

Table I, Figures 1–11. Figure 1 is a Ptolemaic chart showing the true relationship existing between the primordial elements. Its secret significance is as

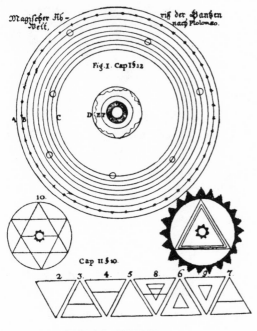

TABLE I, FIGURES 1–11.

follows: The outer ring enclosed by the lines *A* and *B* is the region of *Schamayim*, a Qabbalistic name for the Supreme Deity, signifying the expanse of the heavens, or a spiritual fiery water. Schamayim is "The Ocean of Spirit," within which all created and uncreated things exist and by the life of which they are animated. In the lower worlds Schamayim becomes the astral light.

The space between *B* and *C* marks the orbits or planes of the seven Spiritual Intelligences called the Divine Planets (not the visible planets). According to the Mysteries, the souls of men enter the lower worlds through ring *B*, the fixed stars. All creation reflects the glory of Schamayim, the energy that filters into the spheres of the elements through the windows of the stars and planets. Between *C* and *D* lies the region of the subtle, spiritual air, a subdivision of ether. *D* to *E* marks the surface of the earth and sea, by which are also meant grades of ether. *E* to *F* marks the lower region, called "The Gathering of the Waters and the Production of the Virgin Earth," or "Ares." The alchemists called this "quicksand," the true mystic foundation of the solid earth. *F* to *G* marks the circle of the subterranean air, which is more dense and coarse than that in the outer space, *C* to *D*. In this denser atmosphere the stellar influences and celestial impulses are crystallized into corporeal spirits, thus forming the multitude of forms which exist without knowledge of their own fiery source. *G* is the region of the central fire of the element earth, a coarse fire in contradistinction to the divine fiery Schamayim. The sphere of the starry heavens likewise has its opposite in the sphere of the subterranean air; and the sphere of the upper air (or subtle vaporous water) has its opposite in the sphere *E* to *F.* The focal point, *D* to *E,* between the three higher and the three lower spheres, is called "The Reservoir." It receives impressions from both the superior and the inferior regions and is common to both.

Figure 2 is the Qabbalistic symbol of elemental water; Figure 9 represents the spiritual invisible water. Figure 3 is the Qabbalistic symbol of elemental air;

Figure 7 represents the spiritual and invisible air. Figure 4 is the Qabbalistic sign of the elemental earth; Figure 8 represents the spiritual and invisible earth. Figure 5 is the Qabbalistic sign of the elemental fire; Figure 6 represents the spiritual and invisible fire. Figures 6, 7, 8, and 9 symbolize the four elements before the descent of Lucifer. They are the four rivers spoken of in Genesis, having their source in the one river, Figure 10, which represents the elements superimposed on one another. The golden ball in the center is Schamayim, the fiery source of all elements. Figure 11 is the emblem of the beginning and the end of all creatures. From it all things proceed and to it all must return again, to become one with the fiery water of divine understanding.

Table II, Figures 12–51. Figures 12, 13, 14 demonstrate the sphere as a symbol of motion to be emblematic of fire, water, and air; and the cube as a symbol of weight to be emblematic of earth. The sphere rests upon a point, the cube upon a surface; the sphere is therefore used to symbolize spirit, and the cube, matter. Figure 14 demonstrates that atmosphere rushing in behind a falling object increases its velocity and apparently adds to its weight. The essential nature of each element is occultly signified by the peculiar symbol and character assigned to it.

Of Figure 15, the symbol of salt, von Welling writes, in substance: The cube has six sides, corresponding to the six days of creation, with the point of rest (the seventh day) in the center of the cube. On each surface of the cube appear the signs of the four elements [triangles]. The alchemists declared that salt was the first created substance produced by the fire (Schamayim) which flowed out of God. In salt all creation is concentrated; in salt are the beginning and end of all things. The cube, furthermore, is composed of twelve bodies, each of which has six sides. These bodies are the twelve fundamental pillars of the true invisi-

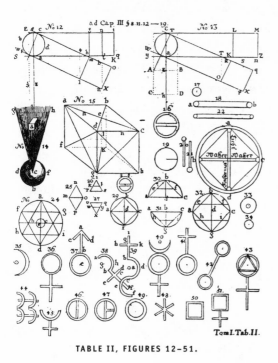

TABLE II, FIGURES 12–51.

ble church, and when these twelve bodies are multiplied by their six sides the magical number 72 results. The wise have said that nothing is perfect until it has been dissolved, separated, and again united so that it becomes a body composed of twelve bodies, like the cube. The cube also consists of six pyramids with the six surfaces of the cube as their bases. The points of these six pyramids meet at the center of the cube. These six pyramids, each consisting of four triangles, signify the elements, and produce the magical number 24, which refers to the Elders before the Throne. The six surfaces and the point constitute the magical number 7. If 7 be multiplied by 7 and the product by 7 again, and so on 7 times, the answer will reveal the method used by the ancients for measuring the periods of eternity; thus: (1) $7 \times 7 = 49$; (2) $49 \times 7 = 343$; (3) $343 \times 7 = 2,401$; (4) $2,401 \times 7 = 16,807$; (5) $16,807 \times 7 = 117,649$; (6) $117,649 \times 7 = 823,543$; (7) $823,543 \times 7 = 5,764,801$. (This is not to be taken as earth years or times.) The 5,000,000 represents the great hall year; the 700,000 the great Sabbath year, wherein all human beings gradually gain true understanding and become heirs to their original and eternal inheritance, which was lost when they were enmeshed in the lower elements. The 64,800 is the number of the fallen angels, and the last one year signifies the liberation of Lucifer and return to his original estate.

Figure 16 is another symbol of salt, while Figure 17 (the dot) is the sign of spirit, gold, the sun, or the germ of life. If the dot be moved before itself it becomes a line, Figure 18. This motion of the dot is the first motion. The beginning and end of every line is a dot. Figure 19 is the circle. It is the second motion and the most perfect of all lines. Out of it are formed all figures and bodies imaginable. Figure 20 represents the outpouring of the upper and spiritual life into manifestation. Figure 21 represents darkness, for it is the loosening of the subterrene destructive principle. Figure 20 is also the symbol of day, and Figure 21 of night.

Figure 22 is a symbol of water; Figure 23 is the complete universal character of light and darkness. The upright triangle represents Schamayim; the inverted triangle the dark earth which imprisons the infernal subterranean fire. It is "The First Day of Creation," or the time of the separation of Schamayim and Ares. Figure 24 represents the six days of creation and proves that the elements are an outflow of the Divine Fire which, breaking up, becomes the substances of the tangible universe, as signified in Figure 25.

Figure 26 is the character of the air, showing that air is born out of the Eternal Light and the ethereal water. Figure 27 is the character of water. It is the inversion of Figure 26, indicating that its origin is from the lower fire and not the higher. Its upper part signifies that water does not lack the Divine element, but as a universal mirror reflects the heavenly influences. Figures 28 and 29 are symbols of salt, showing that it is both fire and water in one. Figure 30 is the character of fire in all its attributes, and Figure 31 (the same inverted), water in all its powers. Figure 32 is the character of salt in all its attributes. Figure 33 represents both gold and the sun. Their essential natures are identical, being formed from the first fire out of Schamayim. They are perfect, as can be seen from their symbol, for no more perfect form can be produced out of the dot than the circle.

Figure 34 is the character of the greater and lesser worlds; as the dot is surrounded by its circumference, this world is surrounded by Schamayim. Man (the Little World) is included in this symbol because his inner nature is potential gold (Aphar Min Haadamah), which gold is his eternal indestructible spiritual body. Gold is the masculine principle of the universe.

Figure 35 is the character of silver and the moon. It signifies that silver (like gold) is a perfect metal, except that the red part of its nature is turned inward. Silver is the feminine principle of the universe.

Figure 36 is the character of copper and Venus; Figure 37, of iron and Mars; Figure 38, of tin and Jupiter; Figure 39, of lead and Saturn; Figure 40, of Mercury (both the planet and the element); Figure 41, of antimony, the key metal of the earth itself; Figure 42, of arsenic; Figure 43, of sulphur; Figure 44, of cinnabar; Figure 45 of quicklime; Figure 46, of nitre; and Figure 47, of vitriol. Figure 48 is the character of sal ammoniac, which element derives its name from the Temple of Jupiter Ammon in an Egyptian desert, where it was found. Figure 49 is the character of alum; Figure 50, of alkali, a name of Arabian origin; and Figure 51, of sal tartar, a substance possessing great occult virtue.

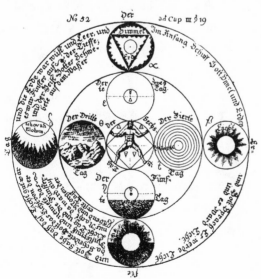

TABLE III, FIGURE 52.

Table III, Figure 52. The eight globes and the central square represent the seven days of creation. The three worlds wherein creation occurs are symbolized by three concentric rings. The German words in the outer ring are extracts from the first chapter of

Genesis. The words around the outside of the outer ring are *The First Day.* The four small globes inside the outer ring deal with the abstract phases of creation. The upper globe containing the triangle encloses the words *Heaven* and *Earth.* The globe to the right contains the word *Light,* and the one to the left, *Jehovah Elohim* in the upper part and *Darkness* in the lower part. The globe at the bottom contains the word *Day* in the upper half and *Night* in the lower.

The four globes within the second ring depict the second, third, fourth, and fifth days of creation. The white globe above divided by a dotted line is designated *The Second Day;* the globe to the left with the mountains, *The Third Day;* the globe to the right with the planetary rings, *The Fourth Day;* and the globe below bisected by a dotted line, *The Fifth Day.* The square in the central ring containing the human form is marked *The Sixth Day.* This chart is a diagrammatic exposition of the three layers of the macrocosmic and microcosmic auric eggs, showing the forces active within them.

Table IV, Figure 53. Figure 53 has been designated the symbolic tomb of Christian Rosencreutz. The upper circle is the first world—the Divine Sphere of God. The triangle in the center is the throne of God. The small circles at the points of the star symbolize the seven great Spirits before the throne, mentioned in the Book of Revelation, in the midst of which walks the Alpha and Omega— the Son of God. The central triangle contains three flames—the Divine Trinity. From the lowest of these flames proceeds the first divine outflow, shown by two parallel lines descending through the throne of Saturn (the Spirit *Orifelis,* through whom God manifested Himself). Passing through the boundary of the celestial universe and the 22 spheres of the lower system, the lines end at point *B,* the throne of Lucifer, in whom the divine outpouring is concentrated and reflected. From him the divine light irradiates in succession to *d* (Capricorn), *e* (Gemini),

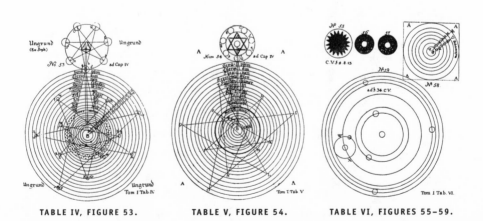

TABLE IV, FIGURE 53.   TABLE V, FIGURE 54.   TABLE VI, FIGURES 55–59.

f (Libra), *g* (Taurus), *h* (Pisces), *i* (Aquarius), *k* (Cancer), *l* (Virgo), *m* (Aries), *n* (Leo), *o* (Scorpio), *p* (Sagittarius), thence back to *d.* The zodiacal circles represent twelve orders of great and beneficent Spirits, and the smaller circles within the ring of fixed stars mark the orbits of the sacred planets.

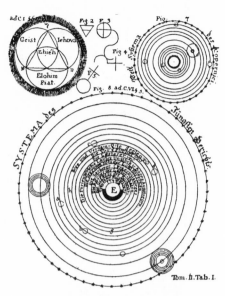

TABLE VII, FIGURES 1–5, 7, AND 8.

Table V, Figure 54. Figure 54 is similar to Figure 53, but represents the universe at the time God manifested Himself through the character of Jupiter, the Spirit *Sachasiel.* Von Welling gives no reason for the change in the order of influx into the twelve orders of spirits, for the third world, for the adding of another circle and the interlaced triangles in the upper world, or for the letters *Y* and *Z.* In the upper triangle, *A* represents the Father Principle, *F* the divine outflow, *G* the point of influx into the twelve orders of spirits (probably Sagittarius). The letters *H, I, J, K, L, M, N, O, P, Q R, S,* and *T* denote the sequential points of irradiations to each other; *W* and *X,* the World of the Sons of God; and *B, C, D,* and *E,* the World of Lucifer. This plate shows the universe after the descent of Lucifer into matter. According to von Welling, when Lucifer wanted to control power, the influx of the divine light instantly ceased. Lucifer's world (which later became the solar system), with all its legions of spirits (who in their essence were Schamayim) reflecting his ideas and inverting the divine light, was turned into darkness. Lucifer's Schamayim thereupon became a contracted disc, a tangible substance; and Chaos came into existence.

Table VI, Figures 55–59. Figure 55 symbolizes the Chaos of Lucifer; Figure 56, the separation of light from darkness; Figure 57, the light in the midst of the darkness; and Figure 58, the regions of the elements and their inhabitants. The four *A*'s signify the Abyss surrounding all things. The *A B* is the fiery throne of Lucifer. The plane of *g* is the subterranean air; *f,* the subterranean water; *c,* the earth region; *d,* the outer water; *e,* the outer air; *W* and *X* the region of Schamayim. The elemental inhabitants of the planes differ in goodness according to their proximity to the center of wickedness; (*A B*). The earth's surface (*c*) divides the subterranean elementals from those of the outer water, air, and fire (*d, e,* and *X*). The elementals of the upper strata (the upper half of *c,* and all of

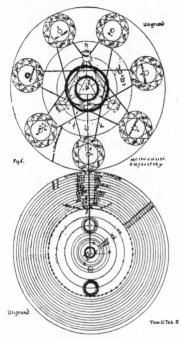

TABLE VIII, FIGURE 6.

a, e, and *X*) represent an ascending scale of virtue, while those of the lower strata (the lower half of *c,* and all of *f, g,* and *A B*) represent a descending scale of depravity.

The region of air (*e*) is a partial exception to this order. While air is close to the light and filled with beautiful spirits, it is also the habitation of Beelzebub, the Evil Spirit of the air, with his legion of elemental demons. Upon the subtle element of air are impressed the influences of the stars; the thoughts, words, and deeds of man; and a myriad of mysterious influences from the various planes of Nature. Man inhales these impressions, and they produce diverse effects upon his mind. In air are suspended also the seed germs by which water is impregnated and made capable of bringing forth forms of organic and inorganic life. The grotesque figures seen in crystal caves and frost pictures upon windows are caused by these aerial impressions. While the air elementals are great and wise, they are treacherous and confused because amenable to both good and evil impressions. The mighty elemental beings who inhabit the watery light fire of the region *X* cannot be deceived by the spirits of darkness. They love the creatures of the waters, for the watery element (*d*) proceeded from the fiery water (*X*). Mortal man cannot endure the society of these fiery spirits, but gains wisdom from them through the creatures of the waters in which they continually mirror themselves. Figure 59 represents this solar system, with *W* and *X* as the locality of the Garden of Eden.

Table VII, Figures 1–5, 7, 8. (Table VIII has Figure 6.) Figure 1 is the triune divine sulphur, the All-Perfect out of the All-Perfect, the Soul of creatures. The threefold Divine One is symbolized by three interlaced circles designated alchemically *salt, sulphur,* and

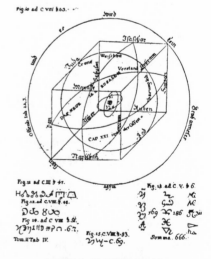

TABLE X, FIGURES 10–15.

mercury. In the central triangle is the divine name *Ehieh.* *Geist* means spirit. The other words require no translation. Figure 2 is common destructive sulphur. A bar placed in the triangle makes it the character of earth. Figure 3 is true oil of vitriol, composed of a circle with two diameters and two reversed half-circles hanging below. In this are hidden the characters of all metals. Tin is symbolized by Figure 4 and iron by Figure 5. Figure 7 is the solar system according to Copernicus. Figure 8 is the

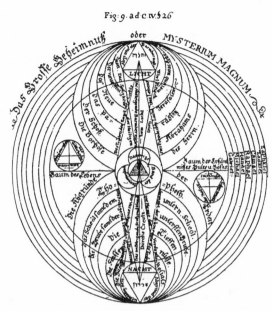

TABLE IX, FIGURE 9.

last judgment. The sun is removed from the center of the solar system and replaced by the earth. This changes the respective positions of all the other planets except Mars, Jupiter, and Saturn, which retain their respective circles.

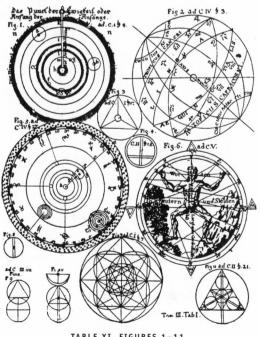

TABLE XI, FIGURES 1–11.

The letter *a* signifies the circle of the sun; *b*, that of Mercury; *c*, that of Venus; *d*, (sic) that of the moon; and *E*, that of the earth. Inward from the sphere *h* are the great circles of damnation.

Table VIII, Figure 6. In Figure 6 the letter *a* marks the center of eternity. The motion of the rays toward *b, d,* and *c* was the first divine manifestation and is symbolized by the equilateral triangle, *b, d, c*. The eternal world within the inner circle became manifest in the water (salt), the light (mercury), and the fire (sulphur) of the archetypal world, represented by the three circles (*f, e, g*) within the triangle of complete equality (*h, i, k*), which is in turn surrounded by the circle of the high throne. The circle *f* is named *understanding; e, wisdom; g, reason.* In circle *i* is the word *Father;* in circle *h, Son;* in circle *k, Spirit.* The seven outer circles are the seven spirits before the throne. The lower part of the figure is similar to Figures 53 and 54. The outer circles are the angelic world ending in the cognizable world of the Sons of God. Then comes the circle of the visible constellations and fixed stars; within this is the solar system with the sun as the center (*l*). *Ungrund* means the Abyss.

Table IX, Figure 9. Figure 9 is a synthesis of the Old and New Testaments and represents the interblending planes of being. In the right margin the seven outer circles contain the names of the planetary angels. The words in the graduated circles from the top triangle downward read: (1) *Abyss of Compassion;* (2) *Zion;* (3) *The New Heaven and the New Earth;* (4) *The New Jerusalem;* (5) *Paradise;* (6) *The Bosom of Abraham;* (7) *The Outer Courts of the Lord.* From below the circles of darkness reach upward, each divine principle being opposed by an infernal opposite. The small circle on the left containing a triangle and cross is named *The Tree of Life,* and that on the right *The Tree of the Knowledge of Good and Evil.* In the center of the diagram is the Trinity, joined with the superior and inferior planes by lines of activity.

Table X, Figures 10–15. Figure 10 shows the New Jerusalem in form of a cube, with the names of the twelve tribes of Israel written on the twelve lines of the cube. In the center is the eye of God. The words round the outer circle are from the Book of Revelation. Figures 11, 12, 13, 14, and 15 possibly are cipher symbols of the angels of the plagues, the name of the Antichrist, the signature of the beast of Babylon, and the name of the woman riding on the beast of blasphemy.

Table XI, Figures 1–11. Figure 1 is the solar system according to Genesis. The *o* on top of the radius of the circle is the dot of Eternity—the Beginning of Beginnings. The whole diameter is the outflow of God, manifesting first in the heaven of heavens—the Schamayim, in which region human understanding cannot function. The space from *k* to *i* contains the heavens of Saturn, Jupiter, and Mars; *l* to *m*, the heavens of Venus and Mercury; *m* to *h*, the heavens of the sun. The letter *e* is the moon, the circle of the earth.

Figure 2 is the globe of the earth, showing the houses and signs of the zodiac. Figure 3 is the character of the Universal Mercury (Divine Life) in its triune aspect of *mercury, sulphur,* and *salt.* Figure 4 is true saltpetre purified with quicklime and alkali. Figure 5 shows the exact degree or angle of the planets' places as well as the individual fixed stars in the zodiac. The letter *a* is the sun and *b* is the earth. From *k* to *i* are the circles of Mercury and Venus; *g* to *h*, the circles of earth and moon; *f* to *e* and *e* to *c*, of Jupiter and Saturn; *c* to *d*, the starry belt or zodiac. Figure 6 is the Microcosm, with the planets and signs of the zodiac corresponding to the different parts of its form. The words upon the figure read: *Know thyself. In words, herbs, and stones lies a great power.* Figure 7 is the

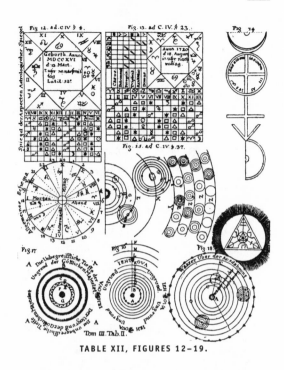

TABLE XII, FIGURES 12–19.

universal character from which all characters have been taken. Figures 8, 9, and 10 are left to the solution of the reader. Figure 11 is the radiating Universal Mercury.

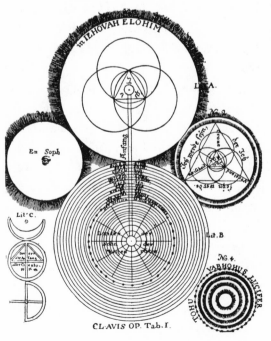

TABLE XIII, FIGURES 1–4.

Table XII, Figures 12–19. Figure 12 is called *A Mirror of Astrological Aspects.* Below it is an astrologer's wheel. Figure 13 is similar to Figure 12. Figure 14 is a secret alchemical formula. The words around the circle read: *Out of one in all is all.* Figure 15 is an unsatisfactory attempt to show the comparative sizes of the suns and planets and their distances from each other. Figure 16 is the solar system with its internal and spiritual heavens. *A B* is the solar system; *C* is the sphere of fixed stars; *D, E, F, G* are the systems of the spiritual worlds; *H* is the throne of the living God; *J, K, L, M,* and *N* are the Great Beyond, unmeasurable.

Figure 17 shows the creation of the solar system out of the ring of the Divine Eternity. The four *A*'s are the Abyss, *B* is the first revelation of God out of the Abyss, and from this revelation *C, D, E, F,* and *G* were created. *C* and *D* represent the spiritual hierarchies; *D* and *E,* the upper worlds, or constellations; *E* and *F,* the distance from Jupiter to the upper worlds; *F* and *G,* the solar system with its planets and their heavens; *B* and *C,* the throne of Christ.

Figure 18 describes the division according to Genesis of the waters above the heavens (*D*) from the waters below (*A, B,* and *C*). Figure 19 is the mercury of the philosophers, essential to material existence.

Table XIII, Figures 1–4. Figure 1 is *Ain Soph,* the Incomprehensible Abyss of Divine Majesty, an endless welling up, limitless in time and space. Figure 2 symbolizes the three Divine Principles—Father, Son, and Holy Ghost. Around the triangle is written: *I Shall Be That I Shall Be.* At the apex of the triangle is the word *Crown;* in the left point, *Wisdom;* in the right point, *Understanding.* Figure 3 represents the Trinity with its outflow. The words above the upper sphere are *Revelation of the Divine Majesty in Jehovah Elohim.* The lower circles contain the names of the Hierarchies controlling the lower worlds. The words within the circle of stars read: *Lucifer the Son of the Aurora of the morning.* The letter *C* represents the Universal Mercury. The words within the circle read: *The first beginning of all creatures.* Figure 4 represents the abode of Lucifer and his angels, the Chaos spoken of in Genesis.

Table XIV, Figures 5, 7, 8. Figure 5 shows the triangle of triune Divinity in the midst of a cross. At the left is a small triangle containing the words *The Secrets of Elohim,* and at the right is another inscribed *The Secrets of Nature.* On the horizontal arms of the cross are the words *The Tree of Life* and *The Tree of the Knowledge of Good and Evil.* The plate explains the interblending of the spiritual and infernal powers in the creation of the universe. Figure 7 is called *The Road to Paradise.* It probably indicates the positions of the sun, moon, and planets at the moment of their genesis. Figure 8 is the earth before the flood, when it was watered by a mist or vapor. The words at the left are *The Tree of Life;* those at the right, *The Tree of the Knowledge of Good and Evil.* The diagram with the symbol of Mars is devoted to a consideration of the rainbow.

Table XV, Figures 6, 9, 10. Figure 6 is similar to Figure 5 and is called *The Secret of Nature.* An interesting diagram is shown on either side of the central figure, each consisting of a triangle with circles radiating from its points. The

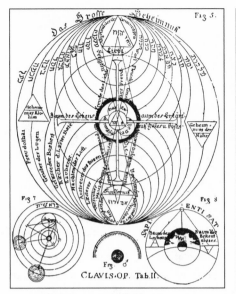

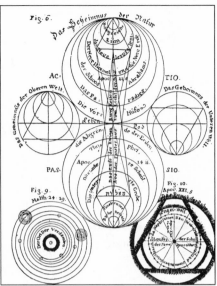

TABLE XIV, FIGURES 5, 7, AND 8.   **TABLE XV, FIGURES 6, 9, AND 10.**

diagram on the left is called *The Secrets of the Upper World,* and the one on the right *The Secrets of the Underworld.*

Figure 9 is the solar system. Around the central part are the words *The Place of the Damned.* Figure 10 shows the dot, or point of rest, surrounded by a triangle enclosing a circle containing the names of the twelve tribes of Israel. It represents completion of the process of regeneration and the consummation of the Great Work.

XXXIV

Alchemy and Its Exponents

 s the transmutation of base metals into gold possible? Is the idea one at which the learned of the modern world can afford to scoff? Alchemy was more than a speculative art: it was also an operative art. Since the time of the immortal Hermes, alchemists have asserted (and not without substantiating evidence) that they could manufacture gold from tin, silver, lead, and mercury. That the galaxy of brilliant philosophic and scientific minds who, over a period of two thousand years, affirmed the actuality of metallic transmutation and multiplication, could be completely sane and rational on all other problems of philosophy and science, yet hopelessly mistaken on this one point, is untenable. Nor is it reasonable that the hundreds declaring to have seen and performed transmutations of metals could all have been dupes, inbeciles, or liars.

Those assuming that all alchemists were of unsound mentality would be forced to put in this category nearly all the philosophers and scientists of the ancient and mediæval worlds. Emperors, princes, priests, and common townsfolk have witnessed the apparent miracle of metallic metamorphosis. In the face of existing testimony, anyone is privileged to remain unconvinced, but the scoffer elects to ignore evidence worthy of respectful consideration. Many great alchemists and Hermetic philosophers occupy an honored niche in the Hall of Fame, while their multitudinous critics remain obscure. To list all these sincere seekers after Nature's great arcanum is impossible, but a few will suffice to acquaint the reader with the superior types of intellect who interested themselves in this abstruse subject.

Among the more prominent names are those of Thomas Norton, Isaac of Holland, Basil Valentine (the supposed discoverer of antimony), Jean de Meung, Roger Bacon, Albertus Magnus, Quercetanus Gerber (the Arabian who

EFFIGIES PHILIPPI
THEOPHRASTI AB HO
HENHEIM : ÆTATIS SUÆ. XLVIL

PHILIPPUS
THEOPHRASTUS
BOMBAST

HOHENHEIMENSIS:
SVEVORVM.
ex Panægyris Nobilium
ARPINAS:
Confœderatorum Eremi
EREMITA:

PHILOSOPHUS
PARADOXUS.

MYSTERIARCHA

ARTIUM MAGISTER,
MEDICINARUM PROFESSOR,
Mufarum Mechanicarum

TRISMEGISTVS.
GERMANUS,

FROM *THE COMPLETE WRITINGS OF PARACELSUS OF HOHENHEIM.*

PARACELSUS.

In his *Biographia Antiqua,* Francis Barrett appends to the name of Paracelsus the followng titles of distinction: "The Prince of Physicians and Philosophers by Fire; Grand Paradoxical Physician; The Trismegistus of Switzerland; First Reformer of Chymical Philosophy; Adept in Alchymy, Cabala, and Magic; Nature's Faithful Secretary; Master of the Elixir of Life and The Philosopher's Stone," and the "Great Monarch of Chymical Secrets."

brought the knowledge of alchemy to Europe through his writings), Paracelsus, Nicholas Flammel, John Frederick Helvetius, Raymond Lully, Alexander Sethon, Michael Sendivogius, Count Bernard of Treviso, Sir George Ripley, Picus de Mirandola, John Dee, Henry Khunrath, Michael Maier, Thomas Vaughan, J. B. von Helmont, John Heydon, Lascaris, Thomas Charnock, Synesius (Bishop of Ptolemais), Morieu, the Comte di Cagliostro, and the Comte de St.-Germain. There are legends to the effect that King Solomon and Pythagoras were alchemists and that the former manufactured by alchemical means the gold used in his temple.

Albert Pike takes sides with the alchemical philosopher by declaring that the gold of the Hermetists was a reality. He says: "The Hermetic Science, like all the *real* sciences, is mathematically demonstrable. Its results, even material, are as rigorous as that of a correct equation. The Hermetic Gold is not only a true dogma, a light without Shadow, a Truth without alloy of falsehood; it is also a material gold, real, pure, the most precious that can be found in the mines of the earth." So much for the Masonic angle.

William and Mary jointly ascended the throne of England in 1689, at which time alchemists must have abounded in the kingdom, for during the first year of their reign they repealed an Act made by King Henry IV in which that sovereign declared the *multiplying of metals* to be a crime against the crown. In Dr. Sigmund Bacstrom's *Collection of Alchemical Manuscripts* is a handwritten copy of the Act passed by William and Mary, copied from Chapter 30 of Statutes at Large for the first year of their reign. The Act reads as follows: "An Act to repeal the Statute made in the 5th year of King Henry IV, late king of England, [wherein] it was enacted, among other things, in these words, or to this effect, namely: 'that none from henceforth should use to multiply Gold or Silver or use the craft of multiplication, and if any the same do they shall incur the pain of felony.' And whereas, since the making of the said statute, divers persons have by their study, industry and learning, arrived to great skill & perfection in the art of melting and refining of metals, and otherwise improving and *multiplying* them and their ores, which very much abound in this realm, and extracting gold and silver out of the same, but dare not to exercise their said skill within this realm, for fear of falling under the penalty of the said statute, but exercise the said art in foreign parts, to the great loss and detriment of this realm: Be it therefore enacted by the King's and Queen's most excellent Majesties, by and with the advice and consent of the Lords spiritual and temporal and Commons in this present parliament assembled, that from henceforth the aforesaid branch, article, or sentence, contained in the said act, and every word, matter and thing contained in the said branch or sentence, shall be repealed, annulled, revoked, and for ever made void, any thing in the said act to the contrary in any wise whatsoever notwithstanding. Provided always, and be it enacted by the authority aforesaid, that all the gold and silver that shall be extracted by the aforesaid art of melting or refining of metals, and otherwise improving and *multiplying* of them and their ores, as before set forth, be from henceforth employed for no other use or uses whatsoever but for the increase of monies; and that the place hereby appointed for the disposal thereof shall be their Majesties mint, within the Tower of London, at which place they are to receive the full and true value of their gold and silver, so procured, from time to time, according to the assay and fineness thereof, and so for any greater or less weight, and that none of that metal of gold and silver so refined and procured be permitted to be used or disposed of in any other place or places within their Majesties dominions." After this repealing measure had become effective, William and Mary encouraged the further study of alchemy.

Dr. Franz Hartmann has collected reliable evidence concerning four different alchemists who transmuted base metals into gold not once but many times. One of these accounts concerns a monk of the Order of St. Augustine named Wenzel Seiler, who discovered a small amount of mysterious red powder in his convent. In the presence of Emperor Leopold I, King of Germany, Hungary, and Bohemia, he transmuted quantities of tin into gold. Among other things which he dipped into his mysterious essence was a large silver medal. That part of the medal which came in contact with the gold-producing substance was transmuted into the purest quality of the more precious metal. The rest remained silver. With regard to this medal, Dr. Hartmann writes:

"The most indisputable proof (if appearances can prove anything) of the possibility of transmuting base metals into gold, may be seen by everyone who visits Vienna; it being a medal preserved in the Imperial treasury chamber, and it is stated that this medal, consisting originally of silver, has been partly transformed into gold, by alchemical means, by the same Wenzel Seiler who was afterwards made a knight by the Emperor Leopold I. and given the title Wenzeslaus Ritter von Reinburg." (*In the Pronaos of the Temple of Wisdom.*)

Space limitations preclude a lengthy discussion of the alchemists. A brief sketch of the lives of four should serve to show the general principles on which they worked, the method by which they obtained their knowledge, and the use which they made of it. These four were Grand Masters of this secret science; and the stories of their wanderings and strivings, as recorded by their own pens and by contemporaneous disciples of the Hermetic art, are as fascinating as any romance of fiction.

Paracelsus of Hohenheim

The most famous of alchemical and Hermetic philosophers was Philippus Aureolus Theophrastus Bombastus von Hohenheim. This man, who called himself *Paracelsus,* declared that some day all the doctors of Europe would turn from the other schools and, following him, revere him above every other physician. The accepted date of the birth of Paracelsus is December 17, 1493. He was an only child. Both his father and mother were interested in medicine and chemistry. His father was a physician and his mother the superintendent of a hospital. While still a youth, Paracelsus became greatly interested in the writings of Isaac of Holland, and determined to reform the medical science of his day.

When twenty years old he began a series of travels which continued for about twelve years. He visited many European countries, including Russia. It is possible that he penetrated into Asia. It was in Constantinople that the great secret of the Hermetic arts was bestowed upon him by Arabian adepts. His knowledge of the Nature spirits and the inhabitants of the invisible worlds he probably secured from the Brahmins of India with whom he came in contact either directly or through their disciples. He became an army physician, and his understanding and skill brought him great success.

Upon his return to Germany, he began his long-dreamed-of reformation of the medical arts and sciences. He was opposed on every hand and criticized unmercifully. His violent temper and tremendously strong personality undoubtedly precipitated many storms upon his head which might have been avoided had he been of a less caustic disposition. He flayed the apothecaries, asserting that they did not use the proper ingredients in their prescriptions and did not consider the needs of their patients, desiring only to collect exorbitant fees for their concoctions.

The remarkable cures which Paracelsus effected only made his enemies hate him more bitterly, for they could not duplicate the apparent miracles which he wrought. He not only treated the more common diseases of his day but is said to have actually cured leprosy, cholera, and cancer. His friends claimed for him that he all but raised the dead. His systems of healing were so heterodox, however, that slowly but surely his enemies overwhelmed him and again and again forced him to leave the fields of his labors and seek refuge where he was not known.

There is much controversy concerning the personality of Paracelsus. That he had an irascible disposition there is no doubt. His hatred for physicians and for women amounted to a mania; for them he had nothing but abuse. As far as can be learned, there was never a love affair in his life. His peculiar appearance and immoderate system of living were always held against him by his adversaries. It is believed that his physical abnormalities may have been responsible for much of the bitterness against society which he carried with him throughout all his intolerant and tempestuous life.

His reputed intemperance brought upon him still more persecution, for it was asserted that even during the time of his professorship in the University of

Basel he was seldom sober. Such an accusation is difficult to understand in view of the marvelous mental clarity for which he was noted at all times. The vast amount of writing which he accomplished (the Strassburg Edition of his collected works is in three large volumes, each containing several hundred pages) is a monumental contradiction of the tales regarding his excessive use of alcoholics.

No doubt many of the vices of which he is accused were sheer inventions by his enemies, who, not satisfied with hiring assassins to murder him, sought to besmirch his memory after they had revengefully ended his life. The manner in which Paracelsus met his death is uncertain, but the most credible account is that he died as the indirect result of a scuffle with a number of assassins who had been hired by some of his professional enemies to make away with the one who had exposed their chicanery.

Few manuscripts are extant in the handwriting of Paracelsus, for he dictated the majority of his works to his disciples, who wrote them down. Professor John Maxson Stillman, of Stanford University, pays the following tribute to his memory: "Whatever be the final judgment as to the relative importance of Paracelsus in the upbuilding of medical science and practice, it must be recognized that he entered upon his career at Basel with the zeal and the self-assurance of one who believed himself inspired with a great truth, and destined to effect a great advance in the science and practice of medicine. By nature he was a keen and open-minded observer of whatever came under his observation, though probably also not a very critical analyst of the observed phenomena. He was evidently an unusually self-reliant and independent thinker, though the degree of originality in his thought may be a matter of legitimate differences of opinion. Certainly once having, from whatever combination of influences, made up his mind to reject the sacredness of the authority of Aristotle, Galen and Avicenna, and having found what to his mind was a satisfactory substitute for the ancient dogmas in his own modification of the neo-Platonic philosophy, he did not hesitate to burn his ships behind him.

"Having cut loose from the dominant Galenism of his time, he determined to preach and teach that the basis of the medical science of the future should be the study of nature, observation of the patient, experiment and experience, and not the infallible dogmas of authors long dead. Doubtless in the pride and self-confidence of his youthful enthusiasm he did not rightly estimate the tremendous force of conservatism against which he directed his assaults. If so, his experience in Basel surely undeceived him. From that time on he was to be a wanderer again, sometimes in great poverty, sometimes in moderate comfort, but manifestly disillusioned as to the immediate success of his campaign though never in doubt as to its ultimate success—for to his mind his new theories and practice of medicine were at one with the forces of nature, which were the expression of God's will, and eventually they must prevail."

FROM JOVIUS' *VITAE ILLUSTRIUM VIRORUM.*

ALBERTUS MAGNUS.

Albert de Groot was born about 1206 and died at the age of 74. It has been said of him that he was "magnus in magia, major in philosophia, maximus in theologia." He was a member of the Dominican order and the mentor of St. Thomas Aquinas in alchemy and philosophy. Among other positions of dignity occupied by Albertus Magnus was that of Bishop of Regensburg. He was beatified in 1622. Albertus was an Aristotelian philosopher, an astrologer, and a profound student of medicine and physics. During his youth, he was considered of deficient mentality, but his sincere service and devotion were rewarded by a vision in which the Virgin Mary appeared to him and bestowed upon him great philosophical and intellectual powers. Having become master of the magical sciences, Albertus began the construction of a curious automaton, which he invested with the powers of speech and thought. The *Android*, as it was called, was composed of metals and unknown substances chosen according to the stars and endowed with spiritual qualities by magical formulæ and invocations, and the labor upon it consumed over thirty years. St. Thomas Aquinas, thinking the device to be a diabolical mechanism, destroyed it, thus frustrating the labor of a lifetime. In spite of this act, Albertus Magnus left to St. Thomas Aquinas his alchemical formulæ, including (according to legend) the secret of the Philosopher's Stone.

On one occasion Albertus Magnus invited William II, Count of Holland and King of the Romans, to a garden party in midwinter. The ground was covered with snow, but Albertus had prepared a sumptuous banquet in the open grounds of his monastery at Cologne. The guests were amazed at the imprudence of the philosopher, but as they sat down to eat Albertus uttered a few words, and the snow disappeared, the garden was filled with flowers and singing birds, and the air was warm with the breezes of summer. As soon as the feast was over, the snow returned, much to the amazement of the assembled nobles. (For details, see *The Lives of Alchemystical Philosophers.*)

This strange man, his nature a mass of contradictions, his stupendous genius shining like a star through the philosophic and scientific darkness of mediæval Europe, struggling against the jealousy of his colleagues as well as against the irascibility of his own nature, fought for the good of the many against the domination of the few. He was the first man to write scientific books in the language of the common people so that all could read them.

Even in death Paracelsus found no rest. Again and again his bones were dug up and reinterred in another place. The slab of marble over his grave bears the following inscription: *"Here lies buried Philip Theophrastus the famous Doctor of Medicine who cured Wounds, Leprosy, Gout, Dropsy and other incurable Maladies of the Body, with wonderful Knowledge and gave his Goods to be divided and distributed to the Poor. In the Year 1541 on the 24th day of September he exchanged Life for Death. To the Living Peace, to the Sepulchred Eternal Rest."*

A. M. Stoddart, in her *Life of Paracelsus,* gives a remarkable testimonial of the love which the masses had for the great physician. Referring to his tomb, she writes: "To this day the poor pray there. Hohenheim's memory has 'blossomed in the dust' to sainthood, for the poor have canonized him. When cholera threatened Salzburg in 1830, the people made a pilgrimage to his monument and prayed him to avert it from their homes. The dreaded scourge passed away from them and raged in Germany and the rest of Austria." It was supposed that one early teacher of Paracelsus was a mysterious alchemist who called himself Solomon Trismosin. Concerning this person nothing is known save that after some years of wandering he secured the formula of transmutation and claimed to have made vast amounts of gold. A beautifully illuminated manuscript of this author, dated 1582 and called *Splendor Solis,* is in the British Museum. Trismosin claimed to have lived to the age of 150 as the result of his knowledge of alchemy. One very significant statement appears in his *Alchemical Wanderings,* which work is supposed to narrate his search for the Philosopher's Stone: "Study what thou art, whereof thou art a part, what thou knowest of this art, this is really what thou art. All that is without thee also is within, thus wrote Trismosin."

Raymond Lully

This most famous of all the Spanish alchemists was born about the year 1235. His father was seneschal to James the First of Aragon, and young Raymond was brought up in the court surrounded by the temptations and profligacy abounding in such places. He was later appointed to the position which his father had occupied. A wealthy marriage ensured Raymond's financial position, and he lived the life of a grandee.

One of the most beautiful women at the court of Aragon was Donna Ambrosia Eleanora Di Castello, whose virtue and beauty had brought her great renown. She was at that time married and was not particularly pleased to discover that young Lully was rapidly developing a passion for her. Wherever she went Raymond followed, and at last over a trivial incident he wrote some very amorous verses to her, which produced an effect quite different from what he had expected. He received a message inviting him to visit the lady. He responded with alacrity. She told him that it was only fair that he should behold more of the beauty concerning which he wrote such appealing poems and, drawing aside part of her garments, disclosed that one side of her body was nearly eaten away by a cancer. Raymond never recovered from the shock. It turned the entire course of his life. He renounced the frivolities of the court and became a recluse.

Some time afterwards while doing penance for his worldly sins a vision appeared to him in which Christ told him to follow in the direction in which He should lead. Later the vision was repeated. Hesitating no longer, Raymond divided his property among his family and retired to a hut on the side of a hill, where he devoted himself to the study of Arabic, that he might go forth and convert the infidels. After six years in this retreat he set out with a Mohammedan servant, who, when he learned that Raymond was about to attack the faith of his people, buried his knife in his master's back. Raymond refused to allow his would-be assassin to be executed, but later the man strangled himself in prison.

When Raymond regained his health he became a teacher of the Arabic language to those who intended traveling in the Holy Land. It was while so engaged that he came in contact with Arnold of Villa Nova, who taught him the principles of alchemy. As a result of this training, Raymond learned the secret of the transmutation and multiplication of metals. His life of wandering continued, and during the course of it he arrived at Tunis, where he began to debate with the Mohammedan teachers, and nearly lost his life as the result of his fanatical attacks upon their religion. He was ordered to leave the country and never to return again upon pain of death. Notwithstanding their threats he made a second visit to Tunis, but the inhabitants instead of killing him merely deported him to Italy.

An unsigned article appearing in *Household Words,* No. 273, a magazine conducted by Charles Dickens, throws considerable light on Lully's alchemical ability. "Whilst at Vienna he [Lully] received flattering letters from Edward the Second, King of England, and from Robert Bruce, King of Scotland, entreating him to visit them. He had also, in the course of his travels, met with John Cremer, Abbot of Westminster, with whom he formed a strong friendship; and it was more to please him than the king, that Raymond consented to go to

England. [A tract by John Cremer appears in the Hermetic Museum, but there is no record in the annals of Westminster of anyone by that name.] Cremer had an intense desire to learn the last great secret of alchemy—to make the powder of transmutation—and Raymond, with all his friendship, had never disclosed it. Cremer, however, set to work very cunningly; he was not long in discovering the object that was nearest to Raymond's heart—the conversion of the infidels. He told the king wonderful stories of the gold Lully had the art to make; and he worked upon Raymond by the hope that King Edward would be easily induced to raise a crusade against the Mahommedans, if he had the means.

"Raymond had appealed so often to popes and kings that he had lost all faith in them; nevertheless, as a last hope, he accompanied his friend Cremer to England. Cremer lodged him in his abbey, treating him with distinction; and there Lully at last instructed him in the powder, the secret of which Cremer had so long desired to know. When the powder was perfected, Cremer presented him to the king, who received him as a man may be supposed to receive one who could give him boundless riches. Raymond made only one condition; that the gold he made should not be expended upon the luxuries of the court or upon a war with any Christian king; and that Edward himself should go in person with an army against the infidels. Edward promised everything and anything.

"Raymond had apartments assigned him in the Tower, and there he tells us he transmuted fifty thousand pounds weight of quicksilver, lead, and tin into pure gold, which was coined at the mint into six million of nobles, each worth about three pounds sterling at the present day. Some of the pieces said to have been coined out of this gold are still to be found in antiquarian collections. [While desperate attempts have been made to disprove these statements, the evidence is still about equally divided.] To Robert Bruce he sent a little work entitled *Of the Art of Transmuting Metals.* Dr. Edmund Dickenson relates that when the cloister which Raymond occupied at Westminster was removed, the workmen found some of the powder, with which they enriched themselves.

"During Lully's residence in England, he became the friend of Roger Bacon. Nothing, of course, could be further from King Edward's thoughts than to go on a crusade. Raymond's apartments in the Tower were only an honorable prison; and he soon perceived how matters were. He declared that Edward would meet with nothing but misfortune and misery for his breach of faith. He made his escape from England in 1315, and set off once more to preach to the infidels. He was now a very old man, and none of his friends could ever hope to see his face again.

"He went first to Egypt, then to Jerusalem, and thence to Tunis a third time. There he at last met with the martyrdom he had so often braved. The people fell upon him and stoned him. Some Genoese merchants carried away his body, in which they discerned some feeble signs of life. They carried him on board their vessel; but, though he lingered awhile, he died as they came in sight of Majorca, on the 28th of June, 1315 at the age of eighty-one. He was buried with great honour in his family chapel at St. Ulma, the viceroy and all the principal nobility attending."

Nicholas Flammel

In the latter part of the fourteenth century there lived in Paris one whose business was that of illuminating manuscripts and preparing deeds and documents. To Nicholas Flammel the world is indebted for its knowledge of a most remarkable volume, which he bought for a paltry sum from some bookdealer with whom his profession of scrivener brought him in contact. The story of this curious document, called the *Book of Abraham the Jew*, is best narrated in his own words as preserved in his *Hieroglyphical Figures:* "Whilst therefore, I Nicholas Flammel, Notary, after the decease of my parents, got my living at our art of writing, by making inventories, dressing accounts, and summing up the expenses of tutors and pupils, there fell into my hands for the sum of two florins, a guilded book, very old and large. It was not of paper, nor of parchment, as other books be, but was only made of delicate rinds (as it seemed to me) of tender young trees. The cover of it was of brass, well bound, all engraven with letters, or strange figures; and for my part I think they might well be Greek characters, or some such like ancient language. Sure I am. I could not read them, and I know well they were not notes nor letters of the Latin nor of the Gaul, for of them we understand a little.

"As for that which was within it, the leaves of bark or rind, were engraven and with admirable diligence written, with a point of iron, in fair and neat Latin letters colored. It contained thrice seven leaves, for so were they counted in the top of the leaves, and always every seventh leaf there was painted a virgin and serpent swallowing her up. In the second seventh, a cross where a serpent was crucified; and the last seventh, there were painted deserts, or wildernesses, in the midst whereof ran many fair fountains, from whence there issued out a number of serpents, which ran up and down here and there. Upon the first of the leaves, was written in great capital letters of gold, *Abraham the Jew, Prince, Priest, Levite, Astrologer, and Philosopher, to the Nation of the Jews, by the*

Wrath of God dispersed among the Gauls, sendeth Health. After this it was filled with great execrations and curses (with this word *Maranatha,* which was often repeated there) against every person that should cast his eyes upon it, if he were not Sacrificer or Scribe.

"He that sold me this book knew not what it was worth nor more than I when I bought it; I believe it had been stolen or taken from the miserable Jews, or found in some part of the ancient place of their abode. Within the book, in the second leaf, he comforted his nation, counselling them to fly vices, and above all idolatry, attending with sweet patience the coming of the Messias, Who should vanquish all the kings of the earth and should reign with His people in glory eternally. Without doubt this had been some very wise and understanding man.

"In the third leaf, and in all the other writings that followed, to help his captive nation to pay their tributes unto the Roman emperors, and to do other things, which I will not speak of, he taught them in common words the transmutation of metals; he painted the vessels by the sides, and he advertised them of the colors, and of all the rest, saving of the first agent, of the which he spake not a word, but only (as he said) in the fourth and fifth leaves entire he painted it, and figured it with very great cunning and workmanship: for although it was well and intelligibly figured and painted, yet no man could ever have been able to understand it, without being well skilled in their Cabala, which goeth by tradition, and without having well studied their books.

"The fourth and fifth leaves therefore, were without any writing, all full of fair figures enlightened, or as it were enlightened, for the work was very exquisite. First he painted a young man with wings at his ancles, having in his hand a Caducean rod, writhen about with two serpents, wherewith he struck upon a helmet which covered his head. He seemed to my small judgment, to be the God Mercury of the pagans: against him there came running and flying with open wings, a great old man, who upon his head had an hour glass fastened, and in his hand a book (or sythe) like death, with the which, in terrible and furious manner, he would have cut off the feet of Mercury. On the other side of the fourth leaf, he painted a fair flower on the top of a very high mountain which was sore shaken with the North wind; it had the foot blue, the flowers white and red, the leaves shining like fine gold: and round about it the dragons and griffons of the North made their nests and abode.

"On the fifth leaf there was a fair rose tree flowered in the midst of a sweet garden, climbing up against a hollow oak; at the foot whereof boiled a fountain of most white water, which ran headlong down into the depths, notwithstanding it first passed among the hands of infinite people, who digged in the earth seeking for it; but because they were blind, none of them knew it, except here and there one who considered the weight. On the last side of the fifth leaf there was a king with a great fauchion, who made to be killed in his presence by some soldiers a great multitude of little infants, whose mothers wept at the feet of the unpitiful soldiers: the blood of which infants was afterwards by other soldiers gathered up, and put in a great vessel, wherein the sun and the moon came to bathe themselves.

"And because that this history did represent the more part of that of the innocents slain by Herod, and that in this book I learned the greatest part of the art, this was one of the causes why I placed in their church-yard these Hiero-glyphic Symbols of this secret science. And thus you see that which was in the first five leaves.

"I will not represent unto you that which was written in good and intelligible Latin in all the other written leaves, for God would punish me, because I should commit a greater wickedness, than he who (as it is said) wished that all the men of the World had but one head that he might cut it off with one blow. Having with me therefore this fair book, I did nothing else day nor night, but study upon it, understanding very well all the operations that it showed, but not knowing with what matter I should begin, which made me very heavy and soli-tary, and caused me to fetch many a sigh. My wife Perrenella, whom I loved as myself, and had lately married was much astonished at this, comforting me, and earnestly demanding, if she could by any means deliver me from this trouble. I could not possibly hold my tongue, but told her all, and showed this fair book, whereof at the same instant that she saw it, she became as much enamoured as myself, taking extreme pleasure to behold the fair cover, gravings, images, and portraits, whereof notwithstanding she understood as little as I: yet it was a great comfort to me to talk with her, and to entertain myself, what we should do to have the interpretation of them."

Nicholas Flammel spent many years studying the mysterious book. He even painted the pictures from it all over the walls of his house and made numerous copies which he showed to the learned men with whom he came in contact, but none could explain their secret significance. At last he determined to go forth in quest of an adept, or wise man, and after many wanderings he met a physician— by name Master Canches—who was immediately interested in the diagrams and asked to see the original book. They started forth together for Paris, and on the way the physician adept explained many of the principles of the hieroglyphics to Flammel, but before they reached their journey's end Master Canches was taken ill and died. Flammel buried him at Orleans, but having meditated deeply on the information he had secured during their brief acquaintance, he was able, with the assistance of his wife, to work out the formula for transmuting base metals into gold. He performed the experiment several times with perfect success, and before his death caused a number of hieroglyphic figures to be painted upon an arch of St. Innocent's churchyard in Paris, wherein he concealed the entire formula as it had been revealed to him from the *Book of Abraham the Jew*.

Count Bernard of Treviso

Of all those who sought for the Elixir of Life and the Philosopher's Stone, few passed through the chain of disappointments that beset Count Bernard of Treviso, who was born in Padua in 1406 and died in 1490. His search for the Philosopher's Stone and the secret of the transmutation of metals began when he was but fourteen years of age. He spent not only a lifetime but also a fortune in his quest. Count Bernard went from one alchemist and philosopher to another, each of whom unfolded some pet theorem which he eagerly accepted and experimented with but always without the desired result. His family believed him to be mad and declared that he was disgracing his house by his experiments, which were rapidly reducing him to a state of penury. He traveled in many countries, hoping that in distant places he would find wise men capable of assisting him. At last as he was approaching his seventy-sixth year, he was rewarded with success. The great secrets of the Elixir of Life, the Philosopher's Stone, and the transmutation of metals were revealed to him. He wrote a little book describing the results of his labors, and while he lived only a few years to enjoy the fruitage of his discovery he was thoroughly satisfied that the treasure he had found was worth the lifetime spent in search of it. An example of the industry and perseverance displayed by him is to be found in one of the processes which some foolish pretender coaxed him to attempt and which resulted in his spending twenty years calcining egg shells and nearly an equal period distilling alcohol and other substances. In the history of alchemical research there never was a more patient and persevering disciple of the Great Arcanum.

Bernard declared the process of dissolution, accomplished not with fire but with mercury, to be the supreme secret of alchemy.

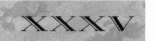
The Theory and
Practice of Alchemy

PART I

lchemy, the secret art of the land of Khem, is one of the two oldest sciences known to the world. The other is astrology. The beginnings of both extend back into the obscurity of prehistoric times. According to the earliest records extant, alchemy and astrology were considered as divinely revealed to man so that by their aid he might regain his lost estate. According to old legends preserved by the Rabbins, the angel at the gate of Eden instructed Adam in the mysteries of Qabbalah and of alchemy, promising that when the human race had thoroughly mastered the secret wisdom concealed within these inspired arts, the curse of the forbidden fruit would be removed and man might again enter into the Garden of the Lord. As man took upon himself "coats of skins" (physical bodies) at the time of his fall, so these sacred sciences were brought by him into the lower worlds incarnated in dense vehicles, through which their spiritual transcendental natures could no longer manifest themselves. Therefore they were considered as being dead or lost.

The earthly body of alchemy is chemistry, for chemists do not realize that half of *The Book of Torah* is forever concealed behind the veil of Isis (see the *Tarot*), and that so long as they study only material elements they can at best discover but half of the mystery. Astrology has crystallized into astronomy, whose votaries ridicule the dreams of ancient seers and sages, deriding their symbols as meaningless products of superstition. Nevertheless, the intelligentsia of the modern world can never pass behind the veil which divides the seen from the unseen except in the way appointed—*the Mysteries.*

What is *life?* What is *intelligence?* What is *force?* These are the problems to the solution of which the ancients consecrated their temples of learning. Who shall say that they did not answer those questions? Who would recognize the answers if given? Is it possible that under the symbols of alchemy and astrology lies concealed a wisdom so abstruse that the mind of this race is not qualified to conceive its principles?

The Chaldeans, Phœnicians, and Babylonians were familiar with the principles of alchemy, as were many early Oriental races. It was practiced in Greece and Rome; was the master science of the Egyptians. *Khem* was an ancient name for the land of Egypt; and both the words al*chemy* and *chemistry* are a perpetual reminder of the priority of Egypt's scientific knowledge. According to the fragmentary writings of those early peoples, alchemy was to them no speculative art. They implicitly believed in the multiplication of metals; and in the face of their reiterations both the scholar and the materialist should be more kindly in their consideration of alchemical theorems. Evolutionists trace the unfoldment of the arts and sciences up through the growing intelligence of the prehistoric man, while others, of a transcendental point of view, like to consider them as being direct revelations from God.

Many interesting solutions to the riddle of alchemy's origin have been

REDRAWN FROM AN ORIGINAL MANUSCRIPT DATED 1577.

THE LEAVES OF HERMES' SACRED TREE.

In his *Key to Alchemy,* Samuel Norton divides into fourteen parts the processes or states through which the alchemical substances pass from the time they are first placed in the test tube until ready as medicines for plants, minerals, or men:

1. *Solution,* the act of passing from a gaseous or solid condition into one of liquidity.
2. *Filtration,* the mechanical separation of a liquid from the undissolved particles suspended in it.
3. *Evaporation,* the changing or converting from a liquid or solid state into a vaporous state with the aid of heat.
4. *Distillation,* an operation by which a volatile liquid may be separated from substances which it holds in solution.
5. *Separation,* the operation of disuniting or decomposing substances.
6. *Rectification,* the process of refining or purifying any substance by repeated distillation.
7. *Calcination,* the conversion into a powder or calx by the action of heat; expulsion of the volatile substance from a matter.
8. *Commixtion,* the blending of different ingredients into one compound or mass.
9. *Purification* (through putrefaction), disintegration by spontaneous decomposition; decay by artificial means.
10. *Inhibition,* the process of holding back or restraining.
11. *Fermentation,* the conversion of organic substances into new compounds in the presence of a ferment.
12. *Fixation,* the act or process of ceasing to be a fluid and becoming firm; state of being fixed.
13. *Multiplication,* the act or process of multiplying or increasing in number; the state of being multiplied.
14. *Projection,* the process of transmuting the base metals into gold.

advanced. One is that alchemy was revealed to man by the mysterious Egyptian demigod Hermes Trismegistus. This sublime figure, looking through the mists of time and bearing in his hand the immortal Emerald, is credited by the Egyptians as being the author of all the arts and sciences. In honor of him all scientific knowledge was gathered under the general title of *The Hermetic Arts.* When the body of Hermes was interred in the Valley of Ebron (or Hebron), the divine Emerald was buried with it. Many centuries afterward the Emerald was discovered—according to one version, by an Arabian initiate; according to another, by Alexander the Great, King of Macedon. By means of the power of this Emerald, upon which were the mysterious inscriptions of the Thrice Great Hermes— thirteen sentences in all—Alexander conquered all the then known world. Not having conquered himself, however, he ultimately failed. Regardless of his glory and power, the prophecies of the talking trees were fulfilled, and Alexander was cut down in the midst of his triumph. (There are persistent rumors to the effect that Alexander was an initiate of high order who failed because of his inability to withstand the temptations of power.)

E. Y. Kenealy, quoting from the *Cosmodromium of Doctor Gobelin Persona,* describes the incident of Alexander and the talking trees, into the presence of which the King of Macedon is said to have been brought while on his campaign in India: "And now Alexander marched into other quarters equally dangerous; at one time over the tops of mountains, at another through dark valleys, in which his army was attacked by serpents and wild beasts, until after three hundred days he came into a most pleasant mountain, on whose sides hung chains or ropes of gold. This mountain had two thousand and fifty steps all of purest sapphire, by which one could ascend to the summit, and near this Alexander encamped. And on a day, Alexander with his Twelve Princes, ascended by the aforenamed steps to the top of the Mountain, and found there a Palace marvellously beautiful, having Twelve Gates, and seventy windows of the purest gold, and it was called the Palace of the Sun, and there was in it a Temple all of gold, before whose gates were vine trees bearing bunches of carbuncles and pearls, and Alexander and his Princes having entered the Palace, found there a Man lying on a golden bedstead; he was very stately and beautiful in appearance, and his head and beard were white as snow. Then Alexander and his princes bent the knee to the Sage who spake thus: 'Alexander, thou shalt now see what no earthly man hath ever before seen or heard.' To whom Alexander made answer: 'O, Sage, most happy, how dost thou know me?' He replied: 'Before the wave of the Deluge covered the face of the earth I knew thy works.' He added: 'Wouldst thou behold the most hallowed Trees of the Sun and Moon, which announce all future things?' Alexander made answer: 'It is well, my lord; greatly do we long to see them.' * * *

"Then the Sage said: 'Put away your rings and ornaments, and take off your shoes, and follow me.' And Alexander did so, and choosing out three from the Princes, and leaving the rest to await his return, he followed the Sage, and came to the Trees of the Sun and Moon. The Tree of the Sun has leaves of red gold, the Tree of the Moon has leaves of silver, and they are very great, and Alexander, at the suggestion of the Sage questioned the Trees, asking if he should return in triumph to Macedon? to which the Trees gave answer, No, but that he should live yet another year and eight months, after which he should die by a poisoned cup. And when he inquired, Who was he who should give him that poison? he received no reply, and the Tree of the Moon said to him, that his Mother, after a most shameful and unhappy death, should lie long unburied, but that happiness was in store for his sisters." (See *The Book of Enoch, The Second Messenger of God.*)

In all probability, the so-called talking trees were merely strips of wood with tables of letters upon them, by means of which oracles were evoked. At one time books written upon wood were called "talking trees." The difficulty in deciding the origin of alchemy is directly due to ignoring the lost continent of Atlantis. The Great Arcanum was the most prized of the secrets of the Atlantean priest-craft. When the land of Atlas sank, hierophants of the Fire Mystery brought the formula to Egypt, where it remained for centuries in the possession of the sages and philosophers. It gradually moved into Europe, where its secrets are still preserved intact. Those disagreeing with the legend of Hermes and his Emerald Tablet see in the two hundred angels who descended upon the mountains, as described by the Prophet Enoch, the first instructors in the alchemical art. Regardless of its originator, it was left to the Egyptian priests to preserve alchemy for the modern world. Egypt, because of the color of its earth, was called "the black empire" and is referred to in the Old Testament as "the land of darkness." By reason of its possible origin there, alchemy has long been known as "the black art," not in the sense of evil but in the sense of that darkness which has always enshrouded its secret processes.

During the Middle Ages, alchemy was not only a philosophy and a science but also a religion. Those who rebelled against the religious limitations of their day concealed their philosophic teachings under the allegory of gold-making. In this way they preserved their personal liberty and were ridiculed rather than persecuted. Alchemy is a threefold art, its mystery well symbolized by a triangle. Its symbol is 3 times 3—three elements or processes in three worlds or spheres. The

3 times 3 is part of the mystery of the 33rd degree of Freemasonry, for 33 is 3 times 3, which is 9, the number of esoteric man and the number of emanations from the root of the Divine Tree. It is the number of worlds nourished by the four rivers that pour out of the Divine Mouth as the *verbum fiat*. Beneath the so-called symbolism of alchemy is concealed a magnificent concept, for this ridiculed and despised craft still preserves intact the triple key to the gates of eternal life. Realizing, therefore, that alchemy is a mystery in three worlds—the divine, the human, and the elemental—it can easily be appreciated why the sages and philosophers created and evolved an intricate allegory to conceal their wisdom.

Alchemy is the science of multiplication and is based upon the natural phenomenon of growth. "Nothing from nothing comes," is an extremely ancient adage. Alchemy is not the process of making something from nothing; it is the process of increasing and improving that which already exists. If a philosopher were to state that a living man could be made from a stone, the unenlightened would probably exclaim, "Impossible!" Thus would they reveal their ignorance, for to the wise it is known that in every stone is the seed of man. A philosopher might declare that a universe could be made out of a man, but the foolish would regard this as an impossibility, not realizing that a man is a seed from which a universe may be brought forth.

God is the "within" and the "without" of all things. The Supreme One manifests Himself through growth, which is an urge from within outward, a struggle for expression and manifestation. There is no greater miracle in the growing and multiplication of gold by the alchemist than in a tiny mustard seed producing a bush many thousands of times the size of the seed. If a mustard seed produces a hundred thousand times its own size and weight when planted in an entirely different substance (the earth), why should not the seed of gold be multiplied a hundred thousand times by art when that seed is planted in its earth (the base metals) and nourished artificially by the secret process of alchemy?

Alchemy teaches that God is in everything; that He is One Universal Spirit, manifesting through an infinity of forms. God, therefore, is the spiritual seed planted in the dark earth (the material universe). By art it is possible so to grow and expand this seed that the entire universe of substance is *tinctured* thereby and becomes like unto the seed—pure gold. In the spiritual nature of man this is termed *regeneration;* in the material body of the elements it is called *transmutation.* As it is in the spiritual and material universes, so it is in the intellectual world. Wisdom cannot be imparted to an idiot because the seed of wisdom is not within him, but wisdom may be imparted to an ignorant person, however ignorant he may be, because the seed of wisdom exists in him and can be developed by art and culture. Hence a philosopher is only an ignorant man within whose nature a *projection* has taken place.

Through *art* (the process of learning) the whole mass of base metals (the mental body of ignorance) was transmuted into pure gold (wisdom), for it was *tinctured* with understanding. If, then, through faith and proximity to God the consciousness of man may be transmuted from base animal desires (represented by the masses of the planetary metals) into a pure, golden, and godly consciousness, illumined and redeemed, and the manifesting God within that one increased from a tiny spark to a great and glorious Being; if also the base metals of mental ignorance can, through proper endeavor and training, be transmuted into transcendent genius and wisdom, why is the process in two worlds or spheres of application not equally true in the third? If both the spiritual and mental elements of the universe can be multiplied in their expression, then by the law of analogy the material elements of the universe can also be multiplied, if the necessary process can be ascertained.

That which is true in the *superior* is true in the *inferior*. If alchemy be a great spiritual fact, then it is also a great material fact. If it can take place in the universe, it can take place in man; if it can take place in man, it can take place in the plants and minerals. If one thing in the universe grows, than everything in the universe grows. If one thing can be multiplied, then all things can be multiplied, "for the superior agrees with the inferior and the inferior agrees with the superior." But as the way for the redemption of the soul is concealed by the Mysteries, so the secrets for the redemption of the metals are also concealed, that they may not fall into the hands of the profane and thereby become perverted.

If any would grow metals, he must first learn the secrets of the metals: he must realize that all metals—like all stones, plants, animals, and universes—grow from seeds, and that these seeds are already in the body of Substance (the womb of the World Virgin); for the seed of man is in the universe before he is born (or grows), and as the seed of the plant exists for all time though the plant live but a part of that time, so the seeds of spiritual gold and material gold are ever present in all things. The metals grow throughout the ages, because life is imparted to them from the sun. They grow imperceptibly, in form like tiny shrubs, for everything grows in some way. Only the methods of growth differ, according to kind and magnitude.

One of the great axioms is, "Within everything is the seed of everything," although by the simple processes of Nature it may remain latent for many centuries, or its growth may be exceedingly slow. Therefore, every grain of sand contains not only the seed of the precious metals as well as the seed of the price-

FROM VALENTINE'S *THE LAST WILL AND TESTAMENT*.

A TABLE OF MEDIÆVAL ALCHEMICAL SYMBOLS.

Hermetists used the curious symbols shown in this rare table to represent various chemical elements and alchemical processes. The full meaning of these strange characters has never been revealed, the characters concealing effectually within their own forms the occult secrets regarding the spiritual nature of the metals and elements which they represent.

In their allegories the alchemists also used human, animal, and plant emblems; sometimes weird composite figures, such as the dragon, the winged serpent, the unicorn, and the phœnix. In almost every case they symbolized gold as a king with a crown on his head and often with a scepter in his hand. Sometimes they depicted him with the face of the solar disc surrounded by rays. Silver was personified as a woman, whom they called the queen. She wore no crown but often stood upon a lunar crescent, much after the fashion of the Madonna. Mercury was typified as a youth with wings, often with two heads, carrying serpents or sometimes the caduceus. Lead they symbolized by an old man with a scythe in his hand; iron by a soldier dressed in armor. To *aqua fortis* was given the curious name "the ostrich's stomach," and to the attainment of the "Great Work" they assigned the symbol of the phœnix sitting upon a nest of fire. The union of elements they symbolized by a marriage, the process of putrefaction by a skull, antimony by a dragon.

less gems, but also the seeds of sun, moon, and stars. As within the nature of man is reflected the entire universe in miniature, so in each grain of sand, each drop of water, each tiny particle of cosmic dust, are concealed all the parts and elements of cosmos in the form of tiny seed germs so minute that even the most powerful microscope cannot detect them. Trillions of times smaller than the ion or electron, these seeds—unrecognizable and incomprehensible—await the time assigned them for growth and expression. (Consider the *monads* of Leibnitz.)

There are two methods whereby growth may be accomplished. The first is by Nature, for Nature is an alchemist forever achieving the apparently impossible. The second is by *art*, and through *art* is produced in a comparatively short time that which requires Nature almost endless periods to duplicate. The true philosopher, desiring to accomplish the *Magnum Opus*, patterns his conduct according to the laws of Nature, recognizing that the *art* of alchemy is merely a method copied from Nature but with the aid of certain secret formulæ greatly shortened by being correspondingly intensified. Nature, in order to achieve her miracles, must work through either extensiveness or intensiveness. The extensive processes of Nature are such as are used in the transmutation of the pitch of black carbon into diamonds, requiring millions of years of natural hardening. The intensive process is *art*, which is ever the faithful servant of Nature (as Dr. A. Dee says), supplementing her every step and cooperating with her in all her ways. "So, in this philosophical work, Nature and *Art* ought so lovingly to embrace each other, as that *Art* may not require what Nature denies, nor Nature deny what may be perfected by *Art*. For Nature assenting, she demeans herself obediently to every artist, whilst by their industry she is helped, not hindered." (Dr. A. Dee in his *Chemical Collections*.)

By means of this *art* the seed which is within the soul of a stone may be made to germinate so intensively that in a few moments a diamond is grown from the seed of itself. If the seed of the diamond were not in the marble, granite, and sand, a diamond could not be grown therefrom. But as the seed is within all these things, a diamond may be grown out of any other substance in the universe. In some substances, however, it is easier to perform this miracle because in them these germs have already been long fertilized and are thus more nearly prepared for the vivifying process of the *art*. Likewise, to teach some men wisdom is easier than to teach others, for some already have a foundation upon which to work, while in others the thinking faculties are entirely dormant. Alchemy, therefore, should be regarded as the *art* of increasing and bringing into perfect flower with the greatest possible expedition. Nature may accomplish her desired end or, because of the destructiveness exercised by one element over another, she may not; but with the aid of the true *art*, Nature always accomplishes her end, for this *art* is not subject either to the wastings of time or to the vandalism of elemental reactions.

In his *History of Chemistry*, James Campbell Brown, late professor of chemistry in the University of Liverpool, sums up the ends which alchemists sought to achieve, in the following paragraphs:

"This, therefore, was the general aim of the alchemists—to carry out in the laboratory, as far as possible, the process which Nature carried out in the interior of the earth. Seven leading problems occupied their attention:—

"1. The preparation of a compound named elixir, magisterium medicine, or philosopher's stone, which possessed the property of transmuting the baser metals into gold and silver, and of performing many other marvelous operations. * * *

"2. The creation of *homunculi*, or living beings, of which many wonderful but incredible tales are told.

"3. The preparation of the alcahest or universal solvent, which dissolved every substance which was immersed in it. * * *

"4. Palingenesis, or the restoration of a plant from its ashes. Had they succeeded in this, they would have hoped to be able to raise the dead. [Professor Brown takes a great deal for granted.]

"5. The preparation of *spiritus mundi*, a mystic substance possessing many powers, the principal of which was its capacity of dissolving gold.

"6. The extraction of the quintessence or active principle of all substances.

"7. The preparation of *aurum potabile*, liquid gold, a sovereign remedy, because gold being itself perfect could produce perfection in the human frame."

Alchemical Symbolism

In alchemy there are three symbolic substances: mercury, sulphur, and salt. To these was added a fourth mysterious life principle called *Azoth*. Concerning the first three, Herr von Welling has written: "There are three basic chemical substances which are called by the philosophers salt, sulphur, and mercury, but which are not to be confounded in any way with the crude salt, sulphur, and mercury taken from the earth or secured from the apothecary. Salt, sulphur, and mercury each has a triune nature, for each of these substances contains, in reality, also the other two substances, according to the secret arcanum of the wise. The body of salt is, therefore, threefold, namely salt, sulphur, and mercury; but in the body of salt one of the three (salt) predominates. Mercury is likewise composed of salt, sulphur, and mercury with the latter element predominating. Sulphur, similarly, is actually salt, sulphur, and mercury, with sulphur predominating. These nine divisions—3 times 3, plus *Azoth* (the mysterious universal life force), equals 10, the sacred decad of Pythagoras. Concerning the nature of *Azoth* there is much controversy. Some view it as the invisible, eternal fire; others as electricity; still others as magnetism. Transcendentalists refer to it as the astral light.

"The universe is surrounded by the sphere of the stars. Beyond that sphere is the sphere of *Schamayim,* which is the Divine fiery water, the first outflow of the Word of God, the flaming river pouring from the presence of the Eternal. *Schamayim,* the fiery androgynous water, divides. The fire becomes the solar fire and the water becomes the lunar water. *Schamayim* is the universal mercury—sometimes called *Azoth*—the measureless spirit of life. The spiritual fiery original water—*Schamayim*—comes through Eden (in Hebrew, *vapor*) and pours itself into four main rivers [the elements]. This is the river of living water—*Azoth* [the fiery mercurial essence] that flows out from the throne of God and the Lamb. In this Eden [vaporous essence or mist] is the spiritual earth [incomprehensible and intangible], or the dust *Aphar,* out of which God formed *Adam min Haadamah,* the spiritual body of man, which body must sometime become revealed."

In another part of his writings von Welling also says that there was no material universe until Lucifer, attempting to perform the cosmic alchemy, misused the *Schamayim,* or the Divine Fire. In order to reestablish the *Schamayim* which Lucifer had perverted, this universe was formed as a means of liberating it from the dark cloud within which it was locked by the failure of Lucifer's attempt to control it. These statements clearly emphasize the fact that the early philosophers recognized in the Bible a book of chemical and alchemical formulæ. It is essential that this point be kept in mind at all times. Woe to that seeker who accepts as literal the rambling allegories of the alchemists. Such a one can never enter the inner sanctuary of truth. Elias Ashmole in his *Theatrum Chemicum Britannicum* thus describes the methods employed by the alchemists to conceal their true doctrines: "Their chiefest study was to wrap up their *Secrets* in *Fables,* and spin out their *Fancies* in *Vailes* and *shadows,* whose *Radii* seems to extend every way, yet so, that they meet in a *Common Center,* and point onely at One thing."

The fact that the Scriptures reveal a hidden knowledge, if considered allegorically, is clearly demonstrated by a parable describing King Solomon, his wives, concubines, and virgins, which parable occurs in *Geheime Figuren der Rosenkreuzer,* published in Ultona in 1785. Dr. Hartmann, who translated part of this work into English, declared that the wives of Solomon represented the arts, the concubines the sciences, and the virgins the still unrevealed secrets of Nature. By order of the King the virgins were forced to remove their veils, thus signifying that by means of wisdom (Solomon) the mystic arts were forced to disclose their hidden parts to the philosopher, while to the uninitiated world only the outside garments were visible. (Such is the mystery of the veil of Isis.)

As the alchemist must do his work in four worlds simultaneously if he would achieve the *Magnum Opus,* a table showing the analogies of the three principles in the four worlds may clarify the relationship which the various parts bear to each other. The early masters of the art of alchemical symbolism did not standardize either their symbols or their terms. Thus it required great familiarity with the subject combined with considerable intuitive power to unravel some of their enigmatical statements. The third and fourth divisions of the following table are given alternative renderings, owing to the fact that some authors did not draw a clear line between *spirit* and *soul.* According to the Scriptures, *spirit* is indestructible, but *soul* is destructible. Obviously, then, they are not synonymous. It is clearly stated that "the soul that sinneth, it shall die," but "the spirit shall return unto God who gave it." The table of analogies, as nearly as they can be established, is as follows:

THE TRIUNE POWER IN FOUR WORLDS

WORLD OF	FATHER	SON	MOTHER
1. God	Father	Son	Holy Ghost
2. Man	Spirit	Soul	Body
3. Elements	Air	Fire	Water
4. Chemicals	Mercury	Sulphur	Salt

The alternative renderings of 3 and 4 are:

WORLD OF	FATHER	SON	MOTHER
3. Elements	Fire	Air	Water
4. Chemicals	Sulphur	Mercury	Salt

Paracelsus made a different arrangement, somewhat Aristotelian, in which the three phases of the Triune God are omitted, combining only the elements of the second, third, and fourth worlds:

World of	Father	Son	Mother
2. Man	Spirit	Soul	Body
3. Elements	Air	Water	Earth
4. Chemicals	Sulphur	Mercury	Salt

The main point, however, is proved: the alchemical philosophers used the symbols of salt, sulphur, and mercury to represent not only chemicals but the spiritual and invisible principles of God, man, and the universe. The three substances (salt, sulphur, and mercury) existing in four worlds, as shown in the table, sum up to the sacred number 12. As these 12 are the foundations of the *Great Work,* they are called in Revelation the twelve foundation stones of the sacred city. In line with the same idea Pythagoras asserted that the dodecahedron, or twelve-faced symmetrical geometric solid, was the foundation of the universe. May there not be a relation also between this mysterious 3 times 4 and the four parties of three which in the legend of the third degree of Freemasonry go forth to the four angles of the cherubim, the composite creature of four parts?

The following table shows the angles to which the parties of three (salt, sulphur, and mercury) go in search of *CHiram:*

The Four "Corners" of Creation	East	South	West	North
The Fixed Signs of the Zodiac	Aquarius	Leo	Scorpio	Taurus
The Parts of the Cherubim	Man	Lion	Eagle	Bull
The Four Seasons	Spring	Summer	Autumn	Winter
The Ages of Man	Childhood	Youth	Maturity	Age
The Stages of Existence	Birth	Growth	Maturity	Decay
The Parts of Man's Constitution	Spirit	Soul	Mind	Body
The Four Elements	Air	Fire	Water	Earth

One more table should prove of interest to Masonic scholars: one showing the relationship existing between the three substances, salt, sulphur, and mercury, and certain symbols with which Masons are familiar. This table also has an alternative rendering, based on the interblending of philosophic principles, which are difficult—if not impossible—to separate into chronological order.

1. The Three Lights	Stellar Fire	Solar Fire	Lunar Fire
2. The Three Grand Masters	Hiram	Solomon	Hiram of Tyre
3. The Geometric Solids	Sphere	Pyramid	Cube
4. Alchemical Substances	Mercury	Sulphur	Salt

The alternative rendering of No. 2 is:

2. The Three Grand Masters	Solomon	Hiram	Hiram of Tyre

In alchemy is found again the perpetuation of the Universal Mystery; for as surely as Jesus died upon the cross, Hiram (*CHiram*) at the west gate of the Temple, Orpheus on the banks of the river Hebros, Christna on the banks of the Ganges, and Osiris in the coffin prepared by Typhon, so in alchemy, unless the elements first die, the *Great Work* cannot be achieved. The stages of the alchemical processes can be traced in the lives and activities of nearly all the world Saviors and teachers, and also among the mythologies of several nations. It is said in the Bible that "except a man be born again, he cannot see the kingdom of God." In alchemy it is declared that without putrefaction the *Great Work* cannot be accomplished. What is it that dies on the cross, is buried in the tomb of the Mysteries, and that dies also in the retort and becomes black with putrefaction? Also, what is it that does this same thing in the nature of man, that he may rise again, phœnix-like, from his own ashes (*caput mortuum*)?

The solution in the alchemical retort, if digested a certain length of time, will turn into a red elixir, which is called the *universal medicine.* It resembles a fiery water and is luminous in the dark. During the process of digestion it passes through many colors which has given rise to its being called the *peacock* because of its iridescence during one of the periods of its digestion. If the augmentations of its power be carried too far, the test tube containing the substance will explode and vanish as dust. This commonly occurs and is the greatest danger involved in the preparation of the medicine for men and metals. If developed too far, it will also seep through the glass, for there is no physical container sufficiently strong to hold it. The reason for this is that it is no longer a substance but a divine essence partaking of the interpenetrative power of Divinity. When it is properly developed, this universal solvent in liquid form will dissolve into itself all other metals. In this high state the universal salt is a liquid fire. This salt dissolved with the proper amount of any metal and run through the different stages of digestion and rotations of augmentations will eventually become a medicine for the transmuting of inferior metals.

The True Way of Nature by Hermes Trismegistus, given out by a genuine Freemason, I.C.H., describes the danger of over-augmenting the universal salt: "But this multiplication cannot be carried on ad infinitum but it attains completeness in the ninth rotation. For when this tincture has been rotated nine times it cannot be exalted any further because it will not permit any further separation. For as soon as it perceives only the smallest degree of material fire it goes instantly into a flux and passes through the glass like hot oil through paper."

In classifying the processes through which the chemical elements must pass before the Hermetic medicine is produced, lack of uniformity in terminology is evidenced, for in *The True Way of Nature* seven stages are given, while in the *Dictionnaire Mytho-Hermétique* twelve are noted. These twelve are linked with the signs of the zodiac in a manner worthy of consideration.

1. Aries, Calcination	5. Leo, Digestion	9. Sagittarius, Incineration
2. Taurus, Congelation	6. Virgo, Distillation	10. Capricorn, Fermentation
3. Gemini, Fixation	7. Libra, Sublimation	11. Aquarius, Multiplication
4. Cancer, Dissolution	8. Scorpio, Separation	12. Pisces, Projection

This arrangement opens an interesting field of speculation which may be of great service if intelligently carried out. These twelve "steps" leading up to the accomplishment of the *Magnum Opus* are a reminder of the twelve degrees of the ancient Rosicrucian Mysteries. To a certain degree, Rosicrucianism was chemistry theologized and alchemy philosophized. According to the Mysteries, man was redeemed as the result of his passage in rotation through the twelve mansions of the heavens. The twelve processes by means of which the "secret essence" may be discovered remind the student forcibly of the twelve Fellow Craftsmen who are sent forth in search of the murdered Builder of the Universe, the Universal Mercury.

According to Solomon Trismosin, the stages through which matter passes in its journey towards perfection are divided into twenty-two parts, each of which is represented by an appropriate drawing. There is an important connection between the twenty-two emblems of Trismosin, the twenty-two major cards of the *Tarot*, and the twenty-two letters of the Hebrew alphabet. These mysterious *Tarot* cards are themselves an alchemical formula, if properly interpreted. As if to substantiate the claims of mediæval philosophers that King Solomon was a master of alchemy, Dr. Franz Hartmann has noted that the much-abused and misunderstood *Song of Solomon* is in reality an alchemical formula. The student of natural philosophy will immediately recognize the "dark maid of Jerusalem," not as a person but as a *material* sacred to the sages. Dr. Hartmann writes: "The '*Song of Solomon*,' in the *Old Testament*, is a description of the processes of Alchemy. In this *Song* the *Subjectum* is described in *Cant. i.*, 5; the *Lilium artis* in *C. ii.*, 1; the *Preparation and Purification* in *C. ii.*, 4; the *Fire* in *C. ii.*, 7, and *C. iv.*, 16; the *Putrefaction* in *C. iii.*, 1; *Sublimation* and *Distillation* in *C. iii.*, 6; *Coagulation* and *Change of Colors, C. v.*, 9 to 14; *Fixation, C. ii.*, 12, and *C. viii.*, 4; *Multiplication, C. vi.*, 7; *Augmentation and Projection, C. viii.*, 8, etc., etc."

A tiny particle of the Philosopher's Stone, if cast upon the surface of water, will, according to an appendix to the work on the universal salt by Herr von Welling, immediately begin a process of recapitulating in miniature the history of the universe, for instantly the tincture—like the Spirits of Elohim—moves upon the face of the waters. A miniature universe is formed which the philosophers have affirmed actually rises out of the water and floats in the air, where it passes through all the stages of cosmic unfoldment and finally disintegrates into dust again. Not only is it possible to prepare a medicine for metals; it is also possible to prepare a tincture for minerals by means of which pieces of granite and marble can be turned into precious stones; also stones of inferior quality may be improved.

As one of the great alchemists fittingly observed, man's quest for gold is often his undoing, for he mistakes the alchemical processes, believing them to be purely material. He does not realize that the Philosopher's Gold, the Philosopher's Stone, and the Philosopher's Medicine exist in each of the four worlds and that the consummation of the experiment cannot be realized until it is successfully carried on in four worlds simultaneously according to one formula. Furthermore, one of the constituents of the alchemical formula exists only within the nature of man himself, without which his chemicals will not combine, and though he spend his life and fortune in chemical experimentation, he will not produce the desired end. The paramount reason why the material scientist is incapable of duplicating the achievements of the mediæval alchemists—although he follow every step carefully and accurately—is that the subtle element which comes out of the nature of the illuminated and regenerated alchemical philosopher is missing in his experimentation.

On this subject Dr. Franz Hartmann in a footnote to his translation of extracts from *Paracelsus* clearly expresses the conclusions of a modern investigator of alchemical lore: "I wish to warn the reader, who might be inclined to try any of the alchemical prescriptions * * *, not to do so unless he is an alchemist, because, although I know from personal experience that these prescriptions are not only allegorically but literally true, and will prove successful in the hands of an alchemist, they would only cause a waste of time and money in the hands of one who has not the necessary qualifications. A person who wants to be an alchemist must have in himself the 'magnesia', which means, the magnetic power to attract and 'coagulate' invisible astral elements."

In considering the formulæ on the following pages, it must be recognized that the experiments cannot be successfully conducted unless the one who performs them be himself a *Magus*. If two persons, one an initiate and the other unilluminated in the supreme *art*, were to set to work, side by side, using the same vessels, the same substances, and exactly the same *modus operandi*, the initiate would produce his "gold" and the uninitiated would not. Unless the greater alchemy has first taken place within the soul of man, he cannot perform the lesser alchemy in the retort. This is an invariable rule, although it is cunningly hidden in the allegories and emblems of Hermetic philosophy. Unless a man be "born again" he cannot accomplish the *Great Work*, and if the student of alchemical formulæ will remember this, it will save him much sorrow and disappointment. To speak of that part of the mystery which is concerned with the secret life principle within the actual nature of man, is forbidden, for it is decreed by the Masters of the *art* that each shall discover that for himself on this subject it is unlawful to speak at greater length.

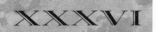
The Theory and
Practice of Alchemy

PART II

ll true philosophers of the natural or Hermetic sciences begin their labors with a prayer to the Supreme Alchemist of the Universe, beseeching His assistance in the consummation of the *Magnum Opus.* The prayer that follows, written in a provincial German centuries ago by an adept now unknown, is representative:

"O holy and hallowed Trinity, Thou undivided and triple Unity! Cause me to sink into the abyss of Thy limitless eternal Fire, for only in that Fire can the mortal nature of man be changed into humble dust, while the new body of the salt union lies in the light. Oh, melt me and transmute me in this Thy holy Fire, so that on the day at Thy command the fiery waters of the Holy Spirit draw me out from the dark dust, giving me new birth and making me alive with His breath. May I also be exalted through the humble humility of Thy Son, rising through His assistance out of the dust and ashes and changing into a pure spiritual body of rainbow colors like unto the transparent, crystal-like, paradisiacal gold, that my own nature may be redeemed and purified like the elements before me in these glasses and bottles. Diffuse me in the waters of life as though I were in the wine cellar of the eternal Solomon. Here the fire of Thy love will receive new fuel and will blaze forth so that no streams can extinguish it. Through the aid of this divine fire, may I in the end be found worthy to be called into the illumination of the righteous. May I then be sealed up with the light of the new world that I may also attain unto the immortality and glory where there shall be no more alternation of light and darkness. Amen."

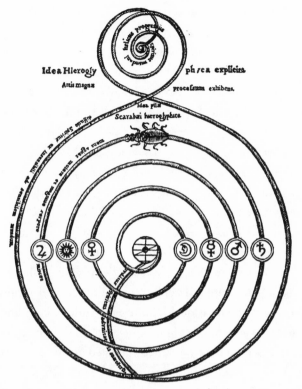

FROM KIRCHER'S *ŒDIPUS ÆGYPTIACUS.*

THE KEY TO ALCHEMY ACCORDING TO THE EGYPTIANS.

The priests of Egypt not only used the scarab as a symbol of regeneration but also discovered in its habits many analogies to the secret processes whereby base metals could be transmuted into gold. They saw in the egg of the scarab the seed of the metals, and the above figure shows the path of this seed through the various planetary bodies until, finally reaching the center, it is perfected and then returns again to its source. The words in the small spiral at the top read: "The spiral progress of the mundane spirit." After the scarab has wound its way around the spiral to the center of the lower part of the figure, it returns to the upper world along the path bearing the words: "Return of the spirit to the center of unity."

The Origin of Alchemical Formulæ

Apparently but few of the mediæval alchemists discovered the Great Arcanum without aid, some authors declaring that none of them attained the desired end without the assistance of a Master or Teacher. In every instance the identity of these Masters has been carefully concealed, and even during the Middle Ages speculation ran rife concerning them. It was customary to call such illuminated sages *adepts,* a title which indicated that they possessed the true secrets of transmutation and multiplication. These adepts were polyonymous individuals who unexpectedly appeared and disappeared again, leaving no trace of their whereabouts. There are indications that a certain degree of organization existed among them. The most powerful of the alchemical organizations were the Rosicrucians, the Illuminati, and certain Arabian and Syrian sects.

In the documents which follow, references are made to the "Brethren" or "Brothers." These are to signify that those who had actually accomplished the *Magnum Opus* were banded together and known to each other by cipher codes and secret signs or symbols. Apparently a number of these illuminated adepts dwelt in Arabia, for several of the great European alchemists were initiated in Asia Minor. When a disciple of the alchemical arts had learned the supreme secret, he guarded it jealously, revealing to no man his priceless treasure. He was not permitted to disclose it even to the members of his immediate family.

As the years passed, one who had discovered the secret—or, more properly, one to whom it had been revealed—sought for some younger man worthy to be entrusted with the formulæ. To this one, and to this one only, as a rule, the philosopher was permitted to disclose the arcanum. The younger man then became the "philosophical son" of the old sage, and to him the latter bequeathed his secrets. Occasionally, however, an adept, on finding a sincere and earnest seeker, would instruct him in the fundamental principles of the art, and if the disciple persisted, he was quietly initiated into the august fraternity of the Brethren. In such manner the alchemical processes were preserved, but the number of those who knew them did not increase rapidly.

During the sixteenth, seventeenth, and eighteenth centuries a considerable number of alchemical adepts made their way from place to place throughout Europe, appearing and disappearing apparently at will. According to popular tradition, these adepts were immortal, and kept themselves alive by means of the mysterious medicine that was one of the goals of alchemical aspiration. It is asserted that some lived hundreds of years, taking no food except this elixir, a few drops of which would preserve their youth for a long period of time. That such mysterious men did exist there can be little doubt, as their presence is attested by scores of reliable witnesses.

It is further asserted that they are still to be found by those who have qualified themselves to contact them. The philosophers taught that like attracts like, and that when the disciple has developed a virtue and integrity acceptable to the adepts they will appear to him and reveal those parts of the secret processes which cannot be discovered without such help. "Wisdom is as a flower from which the bee its honey makes and the spider poison, each according to its own nature." (By an unknown adept.)

The reader must bear in mind at all times that the formulæ and emblems of alchemy are to be taken primarily as allegorical symbols; for until their esoteric significance has been comprehended, their literal interpretation is valueless. Nearly every alchemical formula has one element purposely omitted, it being decided by the mediæval philosophers that those who could not with their own intelligence discover that missing substance or process were not qualified to be entrusted with secrets which could give them control over great masses of humanity and likewise subject to their will the elemental forces of Nature.

The Emerald Tablet of Hermes

The oldest and most revered of all the alchemical formulæ is the sacred Emerald Tablet of Hermes. Authorities do not agree as to the genuineness of this Table, some declaring it to be a post-Christian fraud, but there is much evidence that, regardless of its author, the Table is of great antiquity. While the symbol of the Emerald Table is of special Masonic import—relating as it does to the personality of *CHiram* (Hiram)—it is first and fundamentally an alchemical formula, relating both to the alchemy of the base metals and the divine alchemy of human regeneration.

In Dr. Sigismund Bacstrom's collection of alchemical manuscripts is a section devoted to the translations and interpretations of this remarkable Tablet, which was known to the ancients as the *Tabula Smaragdina.* Dr. Bacstrom was initiated into the Brotherhood of the Rose Cross on the island of Mauritius by one of those unknown adepts who at that time called himself *Comte de Chazal.* Dr. Bacstrom's translations and notes on the Emerald Tablet are, in part, as follows, the actual text being reproduced in capital letters:

"*The Emerald Table, the Most Ancient Monument of the Chaldeans concerning the Lapis Philosophorum* (the stone of the philosophers).

"The Emerald Table furnishes the origin of the allegorical history of King *Hiram* (rather *Chiram*). The Chaldeans, Egyptians, and Hebrews in what concerns *Chiram* have taken their knowledge from one and the same fountain; *Homerus,* who relates this history in a different manner, followed that original, and *Virgil* followed *Homerus,* as *Hesiodus* took the subject for his Theogony likewise from thence, which *Ovidius* took afterwards for a pattern for his Metamorphosis. The knowledge of Nature's secret operations constitutes the principal sense of all these ancient writings, but ignorance framed out of it that external or veiled mythology and the lower class of people turned it into idolatry.

"*The Genuine Translation from the Original Very Ancient Chaldee is as Follows:*

"THE SECRET WORKS OF *CHIRAM ONE* IN ESSENCE, BUT THREE IN ASPECT.

"(The two first large words mean *the Secret Work.*)

"(The second line in large letters, reads: *Chiram Telat Machasot,* i.e. *Chiram the Universal Agent, One in Essence but three in aspect.*)

"IT IS TRUE, NO LIE, CERTAIN, AND TO BE DEPENDED UPON, THE SUPERIOR AGREES WITH THE INFERIOR, AND THE INFERIOR WITH THE SUPERIOR, TO EFFECT THAT ONE TRULY WONDERFUL WORK. AS ALL THINGS OWE THEIR EXISTENCE TO THE WILL OF THE *ONLY ONE,* SO ALL THINGS OWE THEIR ORIGIN TO THE *ONE ONLY THING,* THE MOST HIDDEN, BY THE ARRANGEMENT OF *THE ONLY GOD.* THE FATHER OF THAT *ONE ONLY THING* IS *THE SUN,* ITS MOTHER IS *THE MOON,* THE WIND CARRIES IT IN ITS BELLY; BUT ITS NOURSE IS *A SPIRITUOUS EARTH.* THAT *ONE ONLY THING* (after God) IS THE FATHER OF ALL THINGS IN THE UNIVERSE. ITS POWER IS PERFECT, AFTER IT HAS BEEN UNITED TO A SPIRITUOUS EARTH.

"(Process—First Distillation.) SEPARATE THAT SPIRITUOUS EARTH FROM THE DENSE OR CRUDE BY MEANS OF A GENTLE HEAT, WITH MUCH ATTENTION.

"(Last Digestion.) IN GREAT MEASURE IT ASCENDS *FROM THE EARTH* UP TO HEAVEN, AND DESCENDS AGAIN, NEWBORN, ON THE EARTH, AND THE SUPERIOR AND THE INFERIOR ARE INCREASED IN POWER. The Azoth ascends from the Earth, from the bottom of the Glass, and redescends in Veins and drops into the Earth and by this continual circulation the Azoth is more and more subtilized, *Volatilizes Sol* and carries the volatilized Solar atoms along with it and thereby becomes a *Solar Azoth,* i.e. *our third, and genuine Sophic Mercury,* and this circulation of the Solar Azoth must continue until it ceases of itself, and the Earth has sucked it all in, when it must become the black pitchy matter, the *Toad* [the substances in the alchemical retort and also the lower elements in the body of man], which denotes complete putrefaction or *Death of the Compound.*

"BY THIS THOU WILT PARTAKE OF THE HONOURS OF THE WHOLE WORLD. Without doubt as the black, pitchy matter will and must of necessity become *White* and *Red,* and the Red having been carried to perfection, *medicinally* and for Metals, is then fully capable to preserve *mentem sanam in carpore sano* until the natural period of Life and promise us ample means, in infinitum multipliable, to be benevolent and charitable without any diminution of our inexhaustible resources, therefore well may it be called the *Glory* [Honours] *of the Whole World,* as truly the study and contemplation of the L. P. [*Lapis Philosophorum*], harmonising with Divine Truths, elevates the mind to God our Creator and merciful Father, and if He should permit us to possess it practically must eradicate the very principle of Avarice, Envy, and Evil Inclinations, and cause our hearts to melt in gratitude toward Him that has been so kind to us! Therefore the Philosophers say with great Truth, that the L. P. either finds a good man or makes one.

"AND DARKNESS WILL FLY FROM THEE. By invigorating the Organs the Soul makes use of for communicating with exterior objects, the Soul must acquire greater powers not only for conception but also for retention, and therefore if we wish to obtain still more knowledge, the organs and secret springs of physical life being wonderfully strengthened and invigorated, the Soul must acquire new powers for conceiving and retaining, especially if we pray to God for knowledge, and confirm our prayers by faith, all Obscurity must vanish of course. That this has not been the case with all possessors, was their own fault, as they contented themselves merely with the Transmutation of Metals.

"(Use.) THIS IS THE STRENGTH OF ALL POWERS. This is a very strong figure, to indicate that the L. P. positively does possess all the Powers concealed in Nature, not for destruction but for exaltation and regeneration of matter, in the three Departments of Nature.

"WITH ALL THIS THOU WILT BE ABLE TO OVERCOME ALL THINGS, AND TO TRANSMUTE ALL *WHAT IS FINE* ([ART]) AND WHAT IS *COARSE* ([ART]). It will conquer every subtil Thing, of course, as it refixes the most subtil Oxygen into its own *fiery Nature* and that with more power, penetration and virtue, in a tenfold ratio, at every multiplication, and each time in a much shorter period, until its power becomes incalculable, which multiplied power also penetrates [overcomes] every *Solid Thing,* such as *unconquerable Gold and Silver,* the otherwise *unalterable Mercury,* Crystals and Glass Fluxes, to which it is able to give natural hardness and fixity, as *Philaletha* does attest, and is proved by an artificial Diamond, in my father's time, in possession of *Prince Lichtenstein in Vienna,* valued at Five Hundred Thousand Ducats, fixed by the Lapis [Philosopher's Stone].

"IN THIS MANNER THE WORLD WAS CREATED; THE ARRANGEMENTS TO FOLLOW THIS ROAD ARE HIDDEN. FOR THIS REASON I AM CALLED *CHIRAM TELAT MECHASOT, ONE IN ESSENCE,* BUT *THREE IN ASPECT.* IN THIS TRINITY IS HIDDEN

THE WISDOM OF THE WHOLE WORLD (i.e., in *Chiram* and *its Use*). It is thought that *Hermes* was *Moses* or *Zoroaster,* otherwise Hermes signifies a *Serpent,* and the Serpent used to be *an Emblem of Knowledge* or *Wisdom.* The *Serpent* is met with everywhere amongst the Hieroglyphics of the ancient Egyptians, so is *the Globe with Wings, the Sun* and *Moon, Dragons* and *Griffins,* whereby the Egyptians denoted their sublime knowledge of the Lapis Philosophorum, according to Suidas, the hints in the Scriptures, and even *De Non* where he speaks of the sanctuaries of the ancient Egyptian Temples.

"IT IS ENDED NOW, WHAT I HAVE SAID CONCERNING THE EFFECTS OF THE SUN. FINISH OF THE TABULA SMARAGDINA. What I have said or taught of the *Solar* Work, is now finished. The *perfect Seed,* fit for multiplication.

"This I know is acknowledged to be the genuine *Tabula Smaragdina Hermetis.*"

A Letter from the Brothers of R. C. (Rose Cross)

Although Eugenius Philalethes disclaimed membership in the Rosicrucian Fraternity, it is believed that for a number of years he was the head of that Order. In a little work called *Lumen de Lumine, or A New Magical Light Discovered and Communicated to the World,* published in London in 1651, Eugenius Philalethes gives a remarkable letter, presumably from the Rosicrucian Order. Accompanying the letter is an emblematic figure setting forth in symbolic form the processes and formulæ of the Philosopher's Stone. This epistle is an excellent example of the Rosicrucian system of combining abstract theological speculations with concrete chemical formulæ. With the aid of the material contained in various parts of this present book the student would do well to set himself the task of solving the riddle contained in this hieroglyph.

"*A Letter from the Brothers of R. C. Concerning the Invisible, Magical Mountain, And the Treasure therein Contained.*

"Every man naturally desires a superiority, to have treasures of Gold and Silver [intellect and soul], and to seem great in the eyes of the world. God indeed created all things for the use of man, that he might rule over them, and acknowledge therein the singular goodness and omnipotence of God, give Him thanks for His benefits, honor Him and praise Him. But there is no man looks after these things, otherwise than by spending his days idly; they would enjoy them without any previous labor and danger; neither do they look them out of that place where God hath treasured them up, Who expects also that man should seek for them there, and to those that seek will He give them. But there is not any that labors for a possession in that place, and therefore these riches are not found: For the way to this place, and the place itself hath been unknown for a long time, and it is hidden from the greatest part of the world. But notwithstanding it be difficult and laborious to find out this way and place, yet the place should be sought after.

"But it is not the will of God to conceal anything from those that are His, and therefore in this last age, before the final judgment comes, all these things shall be manifested to those that are worthy: As He Himself (though obscurely, lest it should be manifested to the unworthy) hath spoken in a certain place: There is nothing covered that shall not be revealed, and hidden that shall not be known. We therefore being moved by the Spirit of God, do declare the will of God to the world, which we have also already performed and published in several languages. But most men either revile, or contemne that, our Manifesto, (the *Fama* and *Confessio Fraternitatis*) or else waiving the Spirit of God, they expect the proposals thereof from us, supposing we will straightway teach them how to make gold by Art, or furnish them with ample treasures, whereby they may live pompously in the face of the world, swagger, and make wars, turn usurers, gluttons, and drunkards, live unchastely, and defile their whole life with several other sins, all which things are contrary to the blessed will of God. These men should have learned from those Ten Virgins (whereof five that were foolish demanded oil for their lamps, from those five that were wise) how that the case is much otherwise.

"It is expedient that every man should labor for this treasure by the assistance of God, and his own particular search and industry. But the perverse intentions of these fellows we understand out of their own writings, by the singular grace and revelation of God. We do stop our ears, and wrap ourselves as it were in clouds, to avoid the bellowings and howlings of those men, who in vain cry out for gold. And hence indeed it comes to pass that they brand us with infinite calumnies and slanders, which notwithstanding we do not resent but God in His good time will judge them for it. But after that we had well known (though unknown to you) and perceived also by your writing how diligently you are to peruse the Holy Scripture, and seek the true knowledge of God: we have also above many thousands, thought you worthy of some answer, and we signify this much to you by the will of God and the admonition of the Holy Ghost.

"There is a mountain situated in the midst of the earth, or center of the world, which is both small and great. It is soft, also above measure hard and stony. It is far off, and near at hand, but by the providence of God, invisible. In it are hidden most ample treasures, which the world is not able to value. This mountain by envy of the devil, who always opposeth the glory of God and the happiness of man, is compassed about with very cruel beasts and other [*sic*] ravenous birds, which make the way thither both difficult and dangerous; and therefore hitherto, because the time is not yet come, the way thither could not be sought after nor found out. But now at last the way is to be found by those that are worthy, but notwithstanding by every man's self-labor and endeavors.

"To this mountain you shall go in a certain night (when it comes) most long and most dark, and see that you prepare yourselves by prayer. Insist upon the way that leads to the mountain, but ask not of any man where the way lies: only follow your Guide, who will offer himself to you, and will meet you in the way but you shall not know him. This Guide will bring you to the mountain at midnight, when all things are silent and dark. It is necessary that you arm yourselves with a resolute heroic courage, lest you fear those things that will happen, and so fall back. You need no sword, nor any other bodily weapons, only call upon God sincerely and heartily.

"When you have discovered the mountain, the first miracle that will appear is this. A most vehement and very great wind, that will shake the mountain and shatter the rocks to pieces. You shall be encountered also by lions and dragons and other terrible beasts, but fear not any of these things. Be resolute and take heed that you return not, for your Guide who brought you thither will not suffer any evil to befall you. As for the treasure, it is not yet discovered but it is very near. After this wind will come an earthquake, that will overthrow those things which the wind hath left and make all flat. But be sure that you fall not off.

"The earthquake being past, there shall follow a fire, that will consume the earthly rubbish, and discover the treasure, but as yet you cannot see it. After all these things and near the daybreak there shall be a great calm, and you shall see the Day-Star arise and the dawning will appear, and you shall perceive a great treasure. The chiefest thing in it, and the most perfect, is a certain exalted tincture, with which the world (if it served God and were worthy of such gifts) might be tinged and turned into most pure gold.

"This tincture being used, as your Guide shall teach you, will make you young when you are old, and you shall perceive no disease in any part of your bodies. By means of this tincture also you shall find pearls of that excellency which cannot be imagined. But do not you arrogate anything to yourself because of your present power, but be contented with that which your Guide shall communicate to you. Praise God perpetually for this His gift, and have a special care that you use it not for worldly pride, but employ it in such works which are contrary to the world. Use it rightly and enjoy it so, as if you had it not. Live a temperate life, and beware of all sin, otherwise your Guide will forsake you, and you shall be deprived of this happiness. For know this of a truth, whosoever abuseth this tincture and lives not exemplarly, purely, and devoutly before men he shall lose this benefit, and scarce any hope will there be left ever to recover it afterwards."

If, as transcendentalists believe, the initiations into the Fraternity of the Rose Cross were given in the invisible worlds which surround and interpenetrate the visible universe, it is not beyond the range of possibility that this allegory is to be considered in the light of an initiatory ritual as well as an alchemical formula.

As has been noted, it is difficult to secure a complete formula for any of the alchemical operations. The one presented here is the most nearly complete of any available. The collecting of the rays and energies of the celestial bodies as precipitated in dew is a process which Paracelsus used with great success. Bear constantly in mind that these processes are only for those who have been properly instructed in the secret *art*.

"A TRUE REVELATION OF THE MANUAL OPERATION FOR THE UNIVERSAL MEDICINE COMMONLY CALLED 'THE PHILOSOPHER'S STONE.' By the celebrated philosopher of Leyden, as attested upon his deathbed with his own Blood, Anno Domini 1662. To my Loving Cousin and Son, the True Hermetic Philosopher—

"Dear Loving Cousin and Son:

"Although I had resolved never to give in writing to any person the secret of the Ancient Sages, yet notwithstanding out of peculiar affection and love to you, I have taken it upon me, to which the nearness of our relation obliges me, and especially because this temporal life is short, and Art is very dark and you may therefore not attain the wished for end;—but my Son because so precious a jewel belongs not to swine; and also this so great a gift of God may be treated carefully and Christianlike, in consideration thereof I do so largely declare myself to thee.

"I conjure thee with hand and mouth sacredly;

"1st. That most especially thou faithfully keep the same from all wicked, lustful and criminal persons.

"2dly. That thou exalt not thyself in any way.

"3dly. That thou seek to advance the honor of thy Creator of all things and the good of thy neighbor, preserve it sacredly that thy Lord may not have cause to complain of thee at the last day. I have written here in this treatise such a part of the Kingdom of Heaven, just as I myself have worked this treasure and finished it with my fingers, therefore I have subscribed all this work with my blood, lying on my deathbed in Leyden.

"*THE PROCESS*—In the Name of God, take of the purest and cleanest salt, sea salt, so as it is made by the sun itself, if such as is brought by shipping from Spain, (I used salt that came from St. Uber) let it be dried in a warm stove, grind it in a stone mortar, as fine as possible to a powder, that it may be so much the easier dissolved and taken up by our *Dew-water,* which is thus to be had in the months of May or June: When the Moon is at the full, observe when the *dew* falls with an East or South East wind. Then you must have sticks about one and a half feet high above the ground when driven in the Earth. Upon two or three such sticks, lay some four square plates of glass, and as the dew falls it easily fastens on the glass like a vapour, then have glass Vessels in readiness, let the dew drain from the sides of the glasses into your vessels. Do this until you have enough. The full of the Moon is a good season, afterwards it will be hard."

The solar rays descending from the sun carry with them solar sulphur—the Divine Fire. These rays are crystallized by contact with the lunar rays. The solar rays are also met by the emanations pouring upward from the earth's surface and are thus still further crystallized into a partly tangible substance, which is soluble in pure water. This substance is the "Magical Mountain of the Moon" referred to in the R. C. letter. The crystallization of the solar and lunar rays in water (dew) produces the virgin earth—a pure, invisible substance, uncontaminated by material matter. When the virgin earth crystals are wet, they appear green; when dry, white.

Von Welling makes a suggestion for the extraction of the solar life from stagnant water, but is reticent both as to naming the essence extracted and also as to the various processes through which it must pass to be refined and increased in power. His hint, however, is both valuable and unusual:

"Take sweet clean water and seal it in a large bottle, leaving about one-fourth empty. Place the bottle in the sun for some weeks until it rots, showing a precipitation in the bottom. This precipitation, when properly manipulated by distillation, will produce a clear, fiery, burning oil, the constituents and use of which are only known to the wise."

The philosopher of Leyden continues: "Now when you have enough of your dew close your glasses exactly, and keep it till you use it, that none of its spirits may evaporate, which may easily happen. Set it therefore in a cool place, that no warmth may come to it, or else the subtle spirit will rise and be gone;

which will not so happen if after you have filled your glasses with Dew quite full, you close them very well with wax.

"Now in the Name of God, take of this Dew-water as much as thou wilt, put in a clean dissolving glass, then cast a little of your forementioned powdered salt into it to be dissolved, and continue to put it in till your Dew-water will dissolve no more or till the salt lies in it four days without being dissolved, then it has enough, and unto your Dew is given its proper powder. Of this compounded water, take as much as thou wilt, I took about a pound and a half, and put it into a round vial with a short neck, fill it with our water and lute it with a good lute, a cover and stopple that fits it well, that the subtle and living spirit of the dew may not fume away, for if they should the soul of the salt will never be stirred up, nor the work ever brought to a right end. Let the lute dry very well of itself, and set it in the furnace of B. M. to putrefy. Make a slow fire and let it digest for forty days or fifty, and that the fume of the water be continually round about it, and you will see your matter grow black, which is a token of its putrefaction.

"As soon as you have taken it out, have your dry furnace ready. Set your glass with the matter into an inner globe to coagulate, give it a slow degree of fire, continue it equally for twelve or fifteen days, and your matter will begin to coagulate and to fasten round about your glass like a gray salt, which as soon as you see and before it be two days, slacken the fire that it may cool leisurely. Then have in readiness your putrefying furnace as before. Set your glass therein and give the same degree of fire as before. Let it stand twelve days, and again you will see the matter resolve and open as before, and open itself, but you must every time see that the lute and your glass is not hurt. When you set your glass in the putrefying furnace, take care that the neck of your glass is covered with a wooden or glass stopper that fits it exactly, that the moisture of the water may not come at it.

"When you see it black set your glass as before to coagulate and when it begins to be of a grayish color and whitish, set it in a third time to putrefy, and coagulate to the fifth time, until you see that your water in its dissolution is clean, pellucid and clear, and that it appears in its Calcination of a fine white like Snow. Then it is prepared and becomes a Salt fixed which will melt on hot Silver plate like wax; but before you set this your Salt out, set it again [in] the furnace of putrefaction that it may dissolve of itself, then let it cool, open your Glass and you will find your Matter lessened a third part. But instead of your former Salt Water you will have a fine Sweet and very penetrating Water which the Philosophers have hid under very wonderful Names—It is the Mercury of all true Philosophers, the Water out of which comes Gold and

Silver, for they say its Father is Gold and its Mother is Silver. Thus hast thou the strength of both these Luminaries conjoined in this Water, most true, in its right Pondus.

"*Prescription.* 5 Drops of this Water taken inwardly strengthens the understanding and memory, and opens to us most wonderful and sweet things, of which no man hath heard, and of which I dare not further write, because of the Oath I made God to the contrary. Time and the holy use of this blessed Water will teach us, as soon as you have taken it inwardly such influence will happen to thee as if the whole heavens and all the stars with their powers are working in thee. All Knowledge and secret Arts will be opened to thee as in a dream, but the most excellent of all is, you will perfectly learn rightly to know all creatures in their Nature, and by means thereof, the true understanding of God, the Creator of us, Heaven and Earth, like David and Moses and all the Saints of God, for the wisdom of our fountain of living Water will instruct thee as it did Solomon and the Brethren of our fraternity."

In his rare treatise on *Salt, Sulphur and Mercury,* von Welling discloses a secret not generally revealed in alchemical writings, namely, that the alchemists were concerned not only with the transmutation of metals but had a complete cosmological and philosophical system based upon the Qabbalah.

According to von Welling, the universal salt (in watery form) is a positive cure for all the physical ailments of mankind; it is in every living thing, but from some things it is more easily secured than from others: especially is this true of virgin earth; it is the universal solvent, the alkahest. The same writer also states that in the first stages of its preparation this salt will cure any and all diseases of the heart. The anonymous philosopher of Leyden continues:

"Would you now proceed further with our blessed Water to the forementioned intention of preparing a Tincture for Metals, hearken my Son—

"Take in the NAME of the Lord, of thy Paradisiacal Water, of heavenly Water of Mercury, as much as thou wilt, put it into a Glass to dissolve, and set it in a slow heat of Ashes, that it may just feel the warmth, then have ready well purified Gold for the Red, or Silver for the White Elixir, for in both the Processes are the same. Let your Gold or Silver be beaten as thin as leaf Gold, cast it by degrees into your dissolving Glass, that contains your blessed Water, as you did in the beginning with your Salt, and it will melt like Ice in Warm Water, and continue so to do till your Gold or Silver lie therein four days without dissolving, then it has received its due Pondus. Then put this dissolution as before into a round Glass, fill it two thirds parts full, seal it hermetically as before, let your Sigillum be well dried. Set it in the furnace of Balneum Vapori, make a fire and let it remain forty days, as before, then will the Gold or Silver be dissolved radically and will turn of the deepest black in the world, which as soon as you see, have your other drying furnace in readiness."

Continuing: "Philosophers say there is no true solution of the body without a proceeding coagulation of the spirit, for they are interchangeably mixed in a due proportion, whereby the bodily essence becomes of a spiritual penetrating nature. On the other hand, the incomprehensible spiritual essential virtue is also made corporeal by the fire, because there is made between them so near a relation or friendship, like as the heavens operate to the very Depth of Earth, and producing from thence all the treasures and riches of the whole World.

"*Admirandum Naturæ Operationem in Archidoxes Cognitam.*

"*With this Powder*—You may as follows project on metals. Take five parts of fine Gold or Silver according as you work, and melt it in a Crucible. Wrap up your Medicine in Wax, cast it therein, give a strong fire for an hour, then take the Crucible out, as it were, calcined, then cast one part on ten parts of imperfect metals, be it what it will, and the same will be immediately changed into purer Metal, than what is brought out of the Mines and produced by Melting; and when you augment it in strength and virtue by resolving and coagulating, the fifth time it will resolve itself in three days and be coagulated in twenty-four hours time, to an incredible and most highly pellucid Stone or Red Shining burning Coal. For the white work it will become like a white stream of Lightning.

"Of this last coagulation take one part, cast it upon five thousand of melted Gold or Silver as before. It changes the same into perfect Medicine, one part whereof will tinge one hundred thousand parts of melted imperfect Metals into the very finest Gold or Silver. So far I have brought and further I would not come, for as I would set in the matter [to distill] six times in twelve hours, it subtilized so highly that the most part (like somewhat most wonderful to behold) past through the Glass causing an inexpressible odoriferous Smell. Take heed that it happens not to you.

"Many more wonders of this holy Art might be added, namely how to prepare therewith all sorts of precious Stones, and other most admirable things, but it would require too great a book to express the whole as it ought to be, especially as the Art is endless and not to be apprehended with one view, and my purpose has been, Loving Cousin and Son, devoutly to lead thee into the Mysteries of Nature and this holy Science, and I have faithfully performed it."

In conclusion, the letter states: "Go thou to work as I have done before thee, fear God, Love thy neighbour from the bottom of thy Soul sincerely. So will in the Manual operation, everything to thee, and when thou art at work therein many of our brethren will reveal themselves to thee, of our holy order, privately; For I have on my part by the Eternal God wrote the truth which I found out by prayer and searching into Nature, which work I have seen with my eyes, and with my hands extracted. Therefore also I have subscribed this Testament with my own blood, the last day of my Life on my deathbed. Actum Leyden, 27 March 1662."

XXXVII

The Chemical Marriage

he self-admitted author of *The Chemical Marriage*, Johann Valentin Andreæ, born in Württemberg in 1586, was twenty-eight years of age when that work was first published. It was presumably written about twelve years prior to its publication—or when the author was fifteen or sixteen years old. The fact is almost incredible that one so young could produce a volume containing the wealth of symbolic thought and philosophy hidden between the lines of *The Chemical Marriage*. This book makes the earliest known reference to Christian Rosencreutz, and is generally regarded as the third of the series of original Rosicrucian manifestoes. As a symbolic work, the book itself is hopelessly irreconcilable with the statements made by Andreæ concerning it. The story of *The Chemical Marriage* relates in detail a series of incidents occurring to an aged man, presumably the Father C.R.C. of the *Fama* and *Confessio*. If Father C.R.C. was born in 1378, as stated in the *Confessio*, and is identical with the Christian Rosencreutz of *The Chemical Marriage*, he was elevated to the dignity of a Knight of the Golden Stone in the eighty-first year of his life (1459). In the light of his own statements, it is inconceivable that Andreæ could have been Father Rosy Cross.

Many figures found in the various books on symbolism published in the early part of the seventeenth century bear a striking resemblance to the characters and episodes in *The Chemical Marriage*. The alchemical wedding may prove to be the key to the riddle of Baconian Rosicrucianism. The presence in the German text of *The Chemical Marriage* of some words in English indicates its author to have been conversant also with that language. The following summary of the main episodes of the seven days of *The Chemical Marriage* will give the reader a fairly comprehensive idea of the profundity of its symbolism.

The First Day

Christian Rosencreutz, having prepared in his heart the Paschal Lamb together with a small unleavened loaf, was disturbed while at prayer one evening before Easter by a violent storm which threatened to demolish not only his little house but the very hill on which it stood. In the midst of the tempest he was touched on the back and, turning, he beheld a glorious woman with wings filled with eyes, and robed in sky-colored garments spangled with stars. In one hand she held a trumpet and in the other a bundle of letters in every language. Handing a letter to C.R.C., she immediately ascended into the air, at the same time blowing upon her trumpet a blast which shook the house. Upon the seal of the letter was a curious cross and the words *In hoc signo vinces*. Within, traced in letters of gold on an azure field, was an invitation to a royal wedding.

C.R.C. was deeply moved by the invitation because it was the fulfillment of a prophecy which he had received seven years before, but so unworthy did he feel that he was paralyzed with fear. At length, after resorting to prayer, he sought sleep. In his dreams he found himself in a loathsome dungeon with a multitude of other men, all bound and fettered with great chains. The grievousness of their sufferings was increased as they stumbled over each other in the darkness. Suddenly from above came the sound of trumpets; the cover of the dungeon was lifted, and a ray of light pierced the gloom. Framed in the light stood a hoary-headed man who announced that a rope would be lowered seven times and whoever could cling to the rope would be drawn up to freedom.

Great confusion ensued. All sought to grasp the rope and many were pulled away from it by others. C.R.C. despaired of being saved, but suddenly the rope swung towards him and, grasping it, he was raised from the dungeon. An aged woman called the "Ancient Matron" wrote in a golden yellow book the names of those drawn forth, and each of the redeemed was given for remembrance a piece of gold bearing the symbol of the sun and the letters *D L S*. C.R.C., who had been injured while clinging to the rope, found it difficult to walk. The aged woman bade him not to worry, but to thank God who had permitted him to come into so high a light. Thereupon trumpets sounded and C.R.C. awoke, but so vivid was the dream that he was still sensible of the wounds received while asleep.

With renewed faith C.R.C. arose and prepared himself for the *Hermetic Marriage*. He donned a white linen coat and bound a red ribbon crosswise over his shoulders. In his hat he stuck four roses and for food he carried bread, water, and salt. Before leaving his cottage, he knelt and vowed that whatever knowledge was revealed to him he would devote to the service of his neighbor. He then departed from his house with joy.

The Second Day

As he entered the forest surrounding his little house, it seemed to C.R.C. that all Nature had joyously prepared for the wedding. As he proceeded singing merrily, he came to a green heath in which stood three great cedars, one bearing a tablet with an inscription describing the four paths that led to the palace of the King: the first short and dangerous, the second circuitous, the third a pleasant and royal road, and the fourth suitable only for incorruptible bodies. Weary and perplexed, C.R.C. decided to rest and, cutting a slice of bread, was about to partake thereof when a white dove begged it from him. The dove was at once attacked by a raven, and in his efforts to separate the birds C.R.C. unknowingly ran a considerable distance along one of the four paths—that leading southward. A terrific wind preventing him from retracing his steps, the wedding guest resigned himself to the loss of his bread and continued along the road until he espied in the distance a great gate. The sun being low, he hastened towards the portal, upon which, among other figures, was a tablet bearing the words *Procul hinc procul ite profani.*

A gatekeeper in sky-colored habit immediately asked C.R.C. for his letter of invitation and, on receiving it, bade him enter and requested that he purchase a token. After describing himself as a Brother of the Red Rosie Cross, C.R.C. received in exchange for his water bottle a golden disk bearing the letters *S C.* Night drawing near, the wanderer hastened on to a second gate, guarded by a lion, and to which was affixed a tablet with the words *Date et dabitur volis,* where he presented a letter given him by the first gatekeeper. Being urged to purchase a token bearing the letters *S M,* he gave his little package of salt and then hastened on to reach the palace gates before they were locked for the night.

A beautiful virgin called *Virgo Lucifera* was extinguishing the castle lights as C.R.C. approached, and he was barely able to squeeze through the closing gates. As they closed they caught part of his coat, which he was forced to leave behind. Here his name was written in the Lord Bridegroom's little vellum book and he was presented with a new pair of shoes and also a token bearing the letters *S P N.* He was then conducted by pages to a small chamber where the "icegrey locks" were cut from the crown of his head by invisible barbers, after which he was ushered into a spacious hall where a goodly number of kings, princes, and commoners were assembled. At the sound of trumpets each seated himself at the table, taking a position corresponding to his dignity, so that C.R.C. received a very humble seat. Most of the pseudo-philosophers present being vain pretenders, the banquet became an orgy, which, however, suddenly ceased at the sound of stately and inspired music. For nearly half an hour no one spoke. Then amidst a great sound the door of the dining hall swung open and thousands of lighted tapers held by invisible hands entered. These were followed by the two pages lighting the beautiful *Virgo Lucifera* seated on a self-moving throne. The white-and-gold-robed Virgin then rose and announced that to prevent the admission of unworthy persons to the mystical wedding a set of scales would be erected the following day upon which each guest would be weighed to determine his integrity: Those unwilling to undergo this ordeal she stated should remain in the dining hall. She then withdrew, but many of the tapers stayed to accompany the guests to their quarters for the night.

Most of those present were presumptuous enough to believe that they could be safely weighed, but nine—including C.R.C.—felt their shortcomings so deeply that they feared the outcome and remained in the hall while the others were led away to their sleeping chambers. These nine were bound with ropes and left alone in darkness. C.R.C. then dreamed that he saw many men suspended over the earth by threads, and among them flew an aged man who, cutting here and there a thread, caused many to fall to earth. Those who in arrogance had soared to lofty heights accordingly fell a greater distance and sustained more serious injury than the more humble ones who, falling but a short distance, often landed without mishap. Considering this dream to be a good omen, C.R.C. related it to a companion, continuing in discourse with him until dawn.

The Third Day

Soon after dawn the trumpets sounded and the *Virgo Lucifera,* arrayed in red velvet, girded with a white sash, and crowned with a laurel wreath, entered accompanied by two hundred men in red and-white livery. She intimated to C.R.C. and his eight companions that they might fare better than the other, self-satisfied guests. Golden scales were then hung in the midst of the hall and near them were placed seven weights, one good-sized, four small, and two very large. The men in livery, each carrying a naked sword and a strong rope, were divided into seven groups and from each group was chosen a captain, who was given charge of one of the weights. Having remounted her high throne, *Virgo Lucifera* ordered the ceremony to begin. The first to step on the scales was an emperor so virtuous that the balances did not tip until six weights had been placed upon the opposite end. He was therefore turned over to the sixth group. The rich and poor alike stood upon the scales, but only a few passed the test successfully. To these were given velvet robes and wreaths of laurel, after which they were seated upon the steps of *Virgo Lucifera's* throne. Those who failed were ridiculed and scourged.

The "inquisition" being finished, one of the captains begged *Virgo Lucifera* to permit the nine men who had declared themselves unworthy also to be weighed, and this caused C.R.C. anguish and fear. Of the first seven one succeeded and was greeted with joy. C.R.C. was the eighth and he not only withstood all the weights but even when three men hung on the opposite end of the beam he could not be moved. A page cried out: "THAT IS HE!" C.R.C. was quickly set at liberty and permitted to release one of the captives. He chose the first emperor. *Virgo Lucifera* then requested the red roses that C.R.C. carried, which he immediately gave her. The ceremony of the scales ended about ten o'clock in the forenoon.

After agreeing upon the penalties to be imposed upon those whose shortcomings had been thus exposed, a dinner was served to all. The few successful "artists," including C.R.C., were given the chief seats, after which the Golden Fleece and a Flying Lion were bestowed upon them in the name of the Bridegroom. *Virgo Lucifera* then presented a magnificent goblet to the guests, stating that the King had requested all to share its contents. Following this, C.R.C. and his companions were taken out upon a scaffolding where they beheld the various penalties suffered by those who failed. Before leaving the palace, each of the rejected guests was given a draught of forgetfulness. The elect then returned to the castle, where to each was assigned a learned page, who conducted them through the various parts of the edifice. C.R.C. saw many things his companions were not privileged to behold, including the Royal Sepulcher, where he learned "more than is extant in all books." He also visited a magnificent library and an observatory containing a great globe thirty feet in diameter and with all the countries of the world marked upon it.

At supper the various guests propounded enigmas and C.R.C. solved the riddle which *Virgo Lucifera* asked concerning her own identity. Then entered the dining hall two youths and six virgins beautifully robed, followed by a seventh virgin wearing a coronet. The latter was called the Duchess, and was mistaken for the Hermetic Bride. The Duchess told C.R.C. that he had received more than the others, therefore should make a greater return. The Duchess then asked each of the virgins to pick up one of the seven weights which still remained in the great room. To *Virgo Lucifera* was given the heaviest weight, which was hung in the Queen's chamber during the singing of a hymn. In the second chamber the first virgin hung her weight during a similar ceremony; thus they proceeded from room to room until the weights had been disposed of. The Duchess then presented her hand to C.R.C. and his companions and, followed by her virgins, withdrew. Pages then conducted the guests to their sleeping chambers. The one assigned to C.R.C. was hung with rare tapestries and with beautiful paintings.

The Fourth Day

After washing and drinking in the garden from a fountain which bore several inscriptions—among them one reading, "Drink, brothers, and live"—the guests, led by *Virgo Lucifera,* ascended the 365 steps of the royal winding stairs. The guests were given wreaths of laurel and, a curtain being raised, found themselves in the presence of the King and Queen. C.R.C. was awestruck by the glory of the throne room and especially by the magnificence of the Queen's robes, which were so dazzling that he could not gaze upon them. Each guest was presented to the King by one of the virgins and after this ceremony the *Virgo Lucifera* made a short speech in which she recited the achievements of the honest "artists" and begged that each be questioned as to whether she had properly fulfilled her duty. Old Atlas then stepped forward and in the name of their Royal Majesties greeted the intrepid band of philosophers and assured *Virgo Lucifera* that she should receive a royal reward.

The length of the throne room was five times its width. To the west was a great porch in which stood three thrones, the central one elevated. On each throne sat two persons: on the first an ancient king with a young consort; on the third a black king with a veiled matron beside him; and on the central throne two young persons over whose heads hung a large and costly crown, about which hovered a little Cupid who shot his arrows first at the two lovers and then about the hall. Before the Queen a book bound in black velvet lay on a small altar, on which were golden decorations. Beside this were a burning candle, a celestial globe, a small striking-watch, a little crystal pipe from which ran a stream of clear blood-red liquor, and a skull with a white serpent crawling in and out of the orbits. After their presentations, the guests retired down the winding stairs to the great hall.

Later the *Virgo Lucifera* announced that a comedy was to be performed for the benefit of the six royal guests in a building called the House of the Sun.

C.R.C. and his companions formed part of the royal procession, which after a considerable walk arrived at the theater. The play was in seven acts, and after its happy ending all returned through the garden and up the winding stairs to the throne room. C.R.C. noticed the young King was very sad and that at the banquet following he often sent meat to the white serpent in the skull. The feast over, the young King, holding in his hand the little black book from the altar, asked the guests if they would all be true to him through prosperity and adversity, and when they tremblingly agreed he asked that each should sign his name in the little black book as proof of his fealty. The royal persons then drank from the little crystal fountain, the others afterwards doing likewise. This was called the "Draught of Silence." The royal persons then sadly shook hands with all present. Suddenly a little bell tinkled and immediately the kings and queens took off their white garments and donned black ones, the room was hung in sable draperies, and the tables were removed. The eyes of the royal persons were bound with six black taffeta scarfs and six coffins were placed in the center of the room. An executioner, a Moor, robed in black and bearing an axe, entered, and beheaded in turn each of the six royal persons. The blood of each was caught in a golden goblet, which was placed in the coffins with the body. The executioner was also decapitated and his head placed in a small chest.

The *Virgo Lucifera,* after assuring C.R.C. and his companions that all should be well if they were faithful and true, ordered the pages to conduct them to their rooms for the night while she remained to watch with the dead. About midnight C.R.C. awakened suddenly and, looking from his window, beheld seven ships sailing upon a lake. Above each hovered a flame; these he believed to be the spirits of the beheaded. When the ships reached shore, the *Virgo Lucifera* met them and on each of six of the vessels was placed a covered coffin. As soon as the coffins had been thus disposed of, the lights were extinguished and the flames passed back over the lake so that there remained but one light for a watch in each ship. After beholding this strange ceremony, C.R.C. returned to his bed and slept till morning.

The Fifth Day

Rising at daybreak and entreating his page to show him other treasures of the palace, C.R.C. was conducted down many steps to a great iron door bearing a curious inscription, which he carefully copied. Passing through, he found himself in the royal treasury, the light in which came entirely from some huge carbuncles. In the center stood the triangular sepulcher of Lady Venus. Lifting a copper door in the pavement, the page ushered C.R.C. into a crypt where stood a great bed upon which, when his guide had raised the coverlets, C.R.C. beheld the body of Venus. Led by his page, C.R.C. then rejoined his companions, saying nothing to them of his experience.

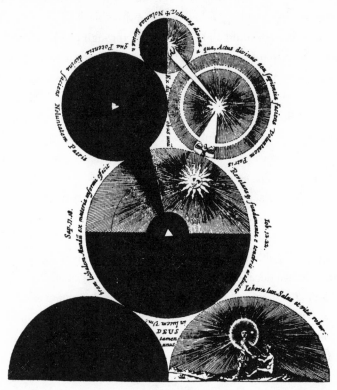

FROM FLUDD'S *PHILOSOPHIA MOSAICA.*

THE UNIVERSE CREATED BY THE DUAL PRINCIPLE OF LIGHT AND DARKNESS.

The Supreme Deity is symbolized by the small globe at the top, which is divided into two hemispheres, the dark half representing the divine darkness with which the Deity surrounds Himself and which serves as His hiding place. The radiant hemisphere signifies the divine light which is in God and which, pouring forth, manifests as the objective creative power. The large dark globe to the left and beneath the dark half of the upper sphere signifies the potential darkness which was upon the face of the primordial deep and within which moved the Spirit of God. The light globe to the right is the Deity who is revealed out of the darkness. Here the shining Word has dissipated the shadows and a glorious universe has been formed. The divine power of this radiant globe is cognizable to man as the sun. The large central sphere divided horizontally into a light and a dark section represents the created universe partaking of the light and darkness which are in the nature of the Creator. The dark half represents the Deep, or Chaos, the Eternal Waters pouring forth out of the Deity; the light half, the power of God which animates the waters and establishes order in Chaos. The light half-circle containing the figure of Apollo represents the diurnal hemisphere of the world, which the ancient Mysteries was ruled over by Apollo. The dark half-circle is the nocturnal hemisphere ruled over by Dionysius (Dionysos), whose figure is faintly visible in the gloom.

Virgo Lucifera, robed in black velvet and accompanied by her virgins, then led the guests out into the courtyard where stood six coffins, each with eight pall-bearers. C.R.C. was the only one of the group of "artists" who suspected the royal bodies were no longer in these coffins. The coffins were lowered into graves and great stones rolled over them. The *Virgo Lucifera* then made a short oration in which she exhorted each to assist in restoring the royal persons to life, declaring that they should journey with her to the Tower of Olympus, where the medicines necessary to the resurrection of the six royal persons could alone be found. C.R.C. and his companions followed *Virgo Lucifera* to the seashore, where all embarked on seven ships disposed according to a certain strange order. As the ships sailed across the lake and through a narrow channel into the open sea, they were attended by sirens, nymphs, and sea goddesses, who in honor of the wedding presented a great and beautiful pearl to the royal couple. When the ships came in sight of the Tower of Olympus, *Virgo Lucifera* ordered the discharge of cannon to signal their approach. Immediately a white flag appeared upon the tower and a small gilded pinnace, containing an ancient man—the warden of the tower—with his white-clad guards came out to meet the ships.

The Tower of Olympus stood upon an island which was exactly square and was surrounded by a great wall. Entering the gate, the group was led to the bottom of the central tower, which contained an excellent laboratory where the guests were fain to beat and wash plants, precious stones, and all sorts of things, extract their juice and essence, and put these latter into glasses. *Virgo Lucifera* set the "artists" to work so arduously that they felt they were mere drudges. When the day's work was finished, each was assigned a mattress on the stone floor. Being unable to sleep, C.R.C. wandered about contemplating the stars. Chancing upon a flight of steps leading to the top of the wall, he climbed up and looked out upon the sea. Remaining here for some time, about midnight he beheld seven flames which, passing over the sea towards him, gathered themselves on the top of the spire of the central tower. Simultaneously the winds arose, the sea became tempestuous, and the moon was covered with clouds. With some fear C.R.C. ran down the stairs and returned to the tower and, lying down on his mattress, was lulled to sleep by the sound of a gently flowing fountain in the laboratory.

The Sixth Day

The next morning the aged warden of the tower, after examining the work performed by the wedding guests in the laboratory and finding it satisfactory, caused ladders, ropes, and large wings to be brought forth, and addressed the assembled "artists" thus: "My dear sons, one of these three things must each of you this day constantly bear about with him." Lots were cast and to C.R.C., much to his chagrin, fell a heavy ladder. Those who secured wings had them fastened to their backs so cunningly that it was impossible to detect that they were artificial. The aged warden then locked the "artists" in the lower room of the tower, but in a short time a round hole was uncovered in the ceiling and *Virgo Lucifera* invited all to ascend. Those with wings flew at once through the opening, those with ropes had many difficulties, while C.R.C. with his ladder made reasonable speed. On the second floor the wedding guests, musicians, and *Virgo Lucifera* gathered about a fountain-like contrivance containing the bodies of the six royal persons.

Virgo Lucifera then placed the Moor's head in a kettle-like receptacle in the upper part of the fountain and poured upon it the substances prepared on the previous day in the laboratory. The virgins placed lamps beneath. These substances when they boiled passed out through holes in the sides of the kettle and, falling upon the bodies in the fountain below, dissolved them. The six royal bodies having been reduced thus to a liquid state, a tap was opened in the lower end of the fountain and the fluid drained into an immense golden globe, which, when filled, was of great weight. All but the wedding guests then retired and shortly a hole in the ceiling opened as before and the guests ascended pell-mell to the third floor. Here the globe were suspended by a strong chain. The walls of the apartment were of glass, and mirrors were so arranged that the sun's rays were concentrated upon the central globe, thus causing it to become very hot. Later the sun's rays were deflected and the globe permitted to cool, after which it was cut open with a diamond, revealing a beautiful white egg. Carrying this with her, *Virgo Lucifera* departed.

The guests, having ascended through another trap door, found themselves upon the fourth floor, where stood a square kettle filled with silver sand warmed by a gentle fire. The great white egg was placed upon the warm sand to mature. In a short time it cracked and there emerged an ugly, ill-tempered bird, which was fed with the blood of the beheaded royal persons diluted with prepared water. At each feeding its feathers changed color; from black they turned to white and at last they became varicolored, the disposition of the bird improving the while. Dinner was then served, after which *Virgo Lucifera* departed with the bird. The guests ascended with ropes, ladders, and wings to the fifth floor, when a bath colored with fine white powder had been prepared for the bird, which enjoyed bathing in it until the lamps placed beneath the bath caused the water to become uncomfortably warm. When the heat had removed all the bird's feathers it was taken out, but the fire continued until nothing remained in the bath save a sediment in the form of a blue stone. This was later pounded up and made into a pigment; with this, all of the bird except the head was painted.

The guests thereupon ascended to the sixth floor, where stood a small altar resembling that in the King's throne room. The bird drank from the little fountain and was fed with the blood of the white serpent which crawled through the openings in the skull. The sphere by the altar revolved continuously. The watch struck one, two, and then three, at which time the bird, laying its neck upon the book, suffered itself to be decapitated. Its body was burned to ashes, which were placed in a box of cypress wood. *Virgo Lucifera* told C.R.C. and three of his comrades that they were lazy and sluggish "labourators" and would therefore be excluded from the seventh room. Musicians were sent for, who with cornets were to "blow" the four in ridicule from the chamber. C.R.C. and his three companions were disheartened until the musicians told them to be of good cheer and led them up a winding stair to the eighth floor of the tower directly beneath the roof. Here the old warden, standing upon a little round furnace, welcomed them and congratulated them upon being chosen by *Virgo Lucifera* for this greater work. *Virgo Lucifera* then entered, and after laughing at the perplexity of her guests, emptied the ashes of the bird into another vessel, filling the cypress box with useless matter. She thereupon returned to the seventh floor, presumably to mislead those assembled there by setting them to work upon the false ashes in the box.

C.R.C. and his three friends were set to work moistening the bird's ashes with specially prepared water until the mixture became of doughlike consistency, after which it was heated and molded into two miniature forms. Later these were opened, disclosing two bright and almost transparent human images about four inches high (homunculi), one male and the other female. These tiny forms were laid upon satin cushions and fed drop by drop with the blood of the bird until they grew to normal size and of great beauty. Though the bodies had the consistency of flesh, they showed no signs of life, for the soul was not in them. The bodies were next surrounded with torches and their faces covered with silk. *Virgo Lucifera* then appeared, bearing two curious white garments. The virgins also entered, among them six bearing great trumpets. A trumpet was placed upon the mouth of one of the two figures and C.R.C. saw a tiny hole open in the dome of the tower and a ray of light descend through the tube of the trumpet and enter the body. This process was repeated three times on each body. The two newly ensouled forms were then removed upon a traveling couch. In about half an hour the young King and Queen awakened and the *Virgo Lucifera* presented them with the white garments. These they donned and the King in his own person most graciously returned thanks to C.R.C. and his companions, after which the royal persons departed upon a ship. C.R.C. and his three privileged friends then rejoined the other "artists," making no mention of that which they had seen. Later the entire party were assigned handsome chambers, where they rested till morning.

The Seventh Day

In the morning *Virgo Lucifera* announced that each of the wedding guests had become a "Knight of the Golden Stone." The aged warden then presented each man with a gold medal, bearing on one side the inscription "Ar. Nat. Mi." and on the other, "Tem. Na. F." The entire company returned in twelve ships to the King's palace. The flags on the vessels bore the signs of the zodiac, and C.R.C. sat under that of Libra. As they entered the lake, many ships met them and the King and Queen, together with their lords, ladies, and virgins, rode forth on a golden barge to greet the returning guests. Atlas then made a short oration in the King's behalf, also asking for the royal presents. In reply the aged warden delivered to Cupid, who hovered about the royal pair, a small, curious-shaped casket. C.R.C. and the old lord, each bearing a snow-white ensign with a red cross on it, rode in the carriage with the King. At the first gate stood the porter with blue clothes, who, upon seeing C.R.C., begged him to intercede with the King to release him from that post of servitude. The King replied that the porter was a famous astrologer who was forced to keep the gate as a punishment for the crime of having gazed upon Lady Venus reposing upon her couch. The King further declared that the porter could be released only when another was found who had committed the same crime. Upon hearing this, C.R.C.'s heart sank, for he realized himself to be the culprit, but he remained silent at that time.

The newly created Knights of the Golden Stone were obliged to subscribe to five articles drawn up by His Royal Highness: (1) That they would ascribe their Order only to God and His handmaid, Nature. (2) That they should abominate all uncleanness and vice. (3) That they should always be ready to assist the worthy and needy. (4) That they should not use their knowledge and power for the attainment of worldly dignity. (5) That they should not desire to live longer than God had decreed. They were then duly installed as Knights, which ceremony was ratified in a little chapel where C.R.C. hung up his Golden Fleece and his hat for an eternal memorial, and here he inscribed the following: *Summa Scientia nihil Scire,* Fr. Christianus Rosencreutz. *Eques aurei Lapidis.* Anno 1459.

After the ceremony, C.R.C. admitted that he was the one who had beheld Venus and consequently must become the porter of the gate. The King embraced him fondly and he was assigned to a great room containing three beds—one for himself, one for the aged lord of the tower, and the third for old Atlas.

The Chemical Marriage here comes to an abrupt end, leaving the impression that C.R.C. was to assume his duties as porter on the following morning. The book ends in the middle of a sentence, with a note in italics presumably by the editor.

Under the symbolism of an alchemical marriage, mediæval philosophers concealed the secret system of spiritual culture whereby they hoped to coordinate the *disjecta membra* of both the human and social organisms. Society, they maintained, was a threefold structure and had its analogy in the triune constitution of man, for as man consists of spirit, mind, and body, so society is made up of the church, the state, and the populace. The bigotry of the church, the tyranny of the state, and the fury of the mob are the three murderous agencies of society which seek to destroy Truth as recounted in the Masonic legend of Hiram Abiff. The first six days of *The Chemical Marriage* set forth the processes of philosophical "creation" through which every organism must pass. The three kings are the threefold spirit of man and their consorts the corresponding vehicles of their expression in the lower world. The executioner is the mind, the higher part of which—symbolized by the head—is necessary to the achievement of the philosophical labor. Thus the parts of man—by the alchemists symbolized as planets and elements—when blended together according to a certain Divine formula result in the creation of two philosophic "babes" which, fed upon the blood of the alchemical bird, become rulers of the world.

From an ethical standpoint, the young King and Queen resurrected at the summit of the tower and ensouled by Divine Life represent the forces of Intelligence and Love which must ultimately guide society. Intelligence and Love are the two great ethical luminaries of the world and correspond to enlightened spirit and regenerated body. The bridegroom is *reality* and the bride the regenerated being who attains perfection by becoming one with *reality* through a cosmic marriage wherein the mortal part attains immortality by being united with its own immortal Source. In the *Hermetic Marriage* divine and human consciousness are united in holy wedlock and he in whom this sacred ceremony takes place is designated as "Knight of the Golden Stone"; he thereby becomes a divine philosophic *diamond* composed of the quintessence of his own sevenfold constitution.

Such is the true interpretation of the mystical process of becoming "a bride of the Lamb." The Lamb of God is signified by the Golden Fleece that Jason was forced to win before he could assume his kingship. The Flying Lion is illumined will, an absolute prerequisite to the achievement of the Great Work. The episode of weighing the souls of men has its parallel in the ceremony described in the Egyptian *Book of the Dead.* The walled city entered by C.R.C. represents the sanctuary of wisdom wherein dwell the real rulers of the world—the initiated philosophers.

Like the ancient Mysteries after which it was patterned, the Order of the Rose Cross possessed a secret ritual which was lived by the candidate for a prescribed number of years before he was eligible to the inner degrees of the society. The various floors of the Tower of Olympus represent the orbits of the planets. The ascent of the philosophers from one floor to another also parallels certain rituals of the Eleusinian Mysteries and the rites of Mithras wherein the candidate ascended the seven rungs of a ladder or climbed the seven steps of a pyramid in order to signify release from the influences of the Planetary Governors. Man becomes master of the seven spheres only when he transmutes the impulses received from them. He who masters the seven worlds and is reunited with the Divine Source of his own nature consummates the *Hermetic Marriage.*

XXXVIII

Bacon, Shakspere, and the Rosicrucians

he present consideration of the Bacon-Shakspere-Rosicrucian controversy is undertaken not for the vain purpose of digging up dead men's bones but rather in the hope that a critical analysis will aid in the rediscovery of that knowledge lost to the world since the oracles were silenced. It was W.F.C. Wigston who called the Bard of Avon "phantom Captain Shakespeare, the Rosicrucian mask." This constitutes one of the most significant statements relating to the Bacon-Shakspere controversy.

It is quite evident that William Shakspere could not, unaided, have produced the immortal writings bearing his name. He did not possess the necessary literary culture, for the town of Stratford where he was reared contained no school capable of imparting the higher forms of learning reflected in the writings ascribed to him. His parents were illiterate, and in his early life he evinced a total disregard for study. There are in existence but six known examples of Shakspere's handwriting. All are signatures, and three of them are in his will. The scrawling, uncertain method of their execution stamps Shakspere as unfamiliar with the use of a pen, and it is obvious either that he copied a signature prepared for him or that his hand was guided while he wrote. No autograph manuscripts of the "Shakespearian" plays or sonnets have been discovered, nor is there even a tradition concerning them other than the fantastic and impossible statement appearing in the foreword of the *Great Folio*.

A well-stocked library would be an essential part of the equipment of an author whose literary productions demonstrate him to be familiar with the literature of all ages, yet there is no record that Shakspere ever possessed a library, nor does he make any mention of books in his will. Commenting on the known

FROM SHAKESPEARE'S *KING RICHARD THE SECOND,*
QUARTO OF 1597.

HEADPIECE SHOWING LIGHT AND SHADED A'S.

The ornamental headpiece shown above has long been considered a
Baconian or Rosicrucian signature. The light and the dark *A's* appear in
several volumes published by emissaries of the Rosicrucians. If the
above figure be compared with that from *Alciati Emblemata* on the following page, the cryptic use of the two *A's* will be further demonstrated.

illiteracy of Shakspere's daughter
Judith, who at twenty-seven could only
make her mark, Ignatius Donnelly
declares it to be unbelievable that
William Shakspere if he wrote the plays
bearing his name would have permitted
his own daughter to reach womanhood
and marry without being able to read
one line of the writings that made her
father wealthy and locally famous.

The query also has been raised, "Where did William Shakspere secure his
knowledge of modern French, Italian, Spanish, and Danish, to say nothing of classical Latin and Greek?" For, in spite of the rare discrimination with which Latin is
used by the author of the Shakespearian plays, Ben Jonson, who knew Shakspere
intimately, declared that the Stratford actor understood "small Latin and less
Greek"! It is not also more than strange that no record exists of William
Shakspere's having ever played a leading rôle in the famous dramas he is supposed
to have written or in others produced by the company of which he was a number?
True, he may have owned a small interest in the Globe Theatre or Blackfriars, but
apparently the height of his thespian achievements was the Ghost in *Hamlet!*

In spite of his admitted avarice, Shakspere seemingly made no effort during
his lifetime to control or secure remuneration from the plays bearing his name,
many of which were first published anonymously. As far as can be ascertained,
none of his heirs were involved in any manner whatsoever in the printing of the
First Folio after his death, nor did they benefit financially therefrom. Had he
been their author, Shakspere's manuscripts and unpublished plays would certainly have constituted his most valued possessions, yet his will—while making
special disposition of his second-best and his "broad silver gilt bowl"—neither
mentions nor intimates that he possessed any literary productions whatsoever.

While the *Folios* and *Quartos* usually are signed "William Shakespeare," all
the known autographs of the Stratford actor read "William Shakspere." Does
this change in spelling contain any significance heretofore generally overlooked? Furthermore, if the publishers of the *First Shakespearian Folio* revered
their fellow actor as much as their claims in that volume would indicate, why did
they, as if in ironical allusion to a hoax which they were perpetrating, place an
evident caricature of him on the title page?

Certain absurdities also in Shakspere's private life are irreconcilable. While
supposedly at the zenith of his literary career, he was actually engaged in buying

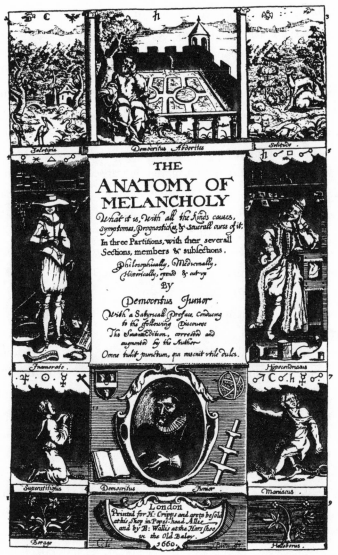

FROM BURTON'S *ANATOMY OF MELANCHOLY.*

THE TITLE PAGE OF BURTON'S *ANATOMY OF MELANCHOLY.*

Baconian experts declare Burton's *Anatomy of Melancholy* to be in reality Francis Bacon's scrapbook in which he gathered strange and rare bits of knowledge during the many years of his eventful life. This title page has long been supposed to contain a cryptic message. The key to this cipher is the pointing figure of the maniac in the lower right-hand corner of the design. According to Mrs. Elizabeth Wells Gallup, the celestial globe at which the maniac is pointing is a cryptic symbol of Sir Francis Bacon. The planetary signs which appear in the clouds opposite the marginal figures 4, 5, 6, and 7 signify the planetary configurations which produce the forms of mania depicted. The seated man, with his head resting upon his hand, is declared by Baconian enthusiasts to represent Sir Francis Bacon.

malt, presumably for a brewing business! Also picture the immortal Shakspere—the reputed author of *The Merchant of Venice*—as a moneylender! Yet among those against whom Shakspere brought action to collect petty sums was a fellow townsman—one Philip Rogers—whom he sued for an unpaid loan of two shillings, or about forty-eight cents! In short, there is nothing known in the life of Shakspere that would justify the literary excellence imputed to him.

The philosophic ideals promulgated throughout the Shakespearian plays distinctly demonstrate their author to have been thoroughly familiar with certain doctrines and tenets peculiar to Rosicrucianism; in fact the profundity of the Shakespearian productions stamps their creator as one of the illuminati of the ages. Most of those seeking a solution for the Bacon-Shakspere controversy have been intellectualists. Notwithstanding their scholarly attainments, they have overlooked the important part played by transcendentalism in the philosophic achievements of the ages. The mysteries of superphysics are inexplicable to the materialist, whose training does not equip him to estimate the extent of their ramifications and complexities. Yet who but a Platonist, a Qabbalist, or a Pythagorean could have written *The Tempest, Macbeth, Hamlet,* or *The Tragedy of Cymbeline?* Who but one deeply versed in Paracelsian lore could have conceived *A Midsummer Night's Dream?*

Father of modern science, remodeler of modern law, editor of the modern Bible, patron of modern democracy, and one of the founders of modern Freemasonry, Sir Francis Bacon was a man of many aims and purposes. He was a Rosicrucian, some have intimated *the* Rosicrucian. If not actually the Illustrious Father C.R.C. referred to in the Rosicrucian manifestoes, he was certainly a high initiate of the Rosicrucian Order, and it is his activities in connection with this secret body that are of prime importance to students of symbolism, philosophy, and literature.

Scores of volumes have been written to establish Sir Francis Bacon as the real author of the plays and sonnets popularly ascribed to William Shakspere. An impartial consideration of these documents cannot but convince the openminded of the verisimilitude of the Baconian theory. In fact those enthusiasts who for years have struggled to identify Sir Francis Bacon as the true "Bard of Avon" might long since have won their case had they emphasized its most important angle, namely, that Sir Francis Bacon, the Rosicrucian initiate, wrote into the Shakespearian plays the secret teachings of the Fraternity of R.C. and the true rituals of the Freemasonic Order, of which order it may yet be discovered that he was the actual founder. A sentimental world, however, dislikes to give up a traditional hero, either to solve a controversy or to right a wrong. Nevertheless, if it can be proved that by raveling out the riddle there can be discovered information of practical value to mankind, then the best minds of the world will cooperate in the enterprise. The Bacon-Shakspere controversy, as its most able advocates realize, involves the most profound aspects of science, religion, and ethics; he who solves its mystery may yet find therein the key to the suppos-edly lost wisdom of antiquity.

It was in recognition of Bacon's intellectual accomplishments that King James turned over to him the translators' manuscripts of what is now known as the King James Bible for the presumable purpose of checking, editing, and revising them. The documents remained in his hands for nearly a year, but no information is to be had concerning what occurred in that time. Regarding this work, William T. Smedley writes: "It will eventually be proved that the whole scheme of the Authorised Version of the Bible was Francis Bacon's." (See *The Mystery of Francis Bacon.*) The first edition of the King James Bible contains a cryptic Baconian headpiece. Did Bacon cryptographically conceal in the Authorized Bible that which he dared not literally reveal in the text—the secret Rosicrucian key to mystic and Masonic Christianity?

Sir Francis Bacon unquestionably possessed the range of general and philo-sophical knowledge necessary to write the Shakespearian plays and sonnets, for it is usually conceded that he was a composer, lawyer, and linguist. His chaplain, Doctor William Rawley, and Ben Jonson both attest his philosophic and poetic accomplishments. The former pays Bacon this remarkable tribute: "I have been enduced to think that if there were a beame of knowledge derived from God upon any man in these modern times, it was upon him. For though he was a great reader of books; yet he had not his knowledge from books but from some grounds and notions from within himself." (See Introduction to the *Resuscitatio.*)

Sir Francis Bacon, being not only an able barrister but also a polished courtier, also possessed that intimate knowledge of parliamentary law and the etiquette of the royal court revealed in the Shakespearian plays which could scarcely have been acquired by a man in the humble station of the Stratford actor. Lord Verulam furthermore visited many of the foreign countries forming the background for the plays and was therefore in a position to create the authentic local atmosphere contained therein, but there is no record of William Shakspere's ever having traveled outside of England.

The magnificent library amassed by Sir Francis Bacon contained the very volumes necessary to supply the quotations and anecdotes incorporated into the Shakespearian plays. Many of the plays, in fact, were taken from plots in ear-lier writings of which there was no English translation at that time. Because of his scholastic acquirements, Lord Verulam could have read the original books; it is most unlikely that William Shakspere could have done so.

Abundant cryptographic proof exists that Bacon was concerned in the pro-duction of the Shakespearian plays. Sir Francis Bacon's cipher number was 33.

FROM BACON'S *ADVANCEMENT OF LEARNING*.

FRANCIS BACON, BARON VERULAM, VISCOUNT ST. ALBANS.

Lord Bacon was born in 1561 and history records his death in 1626. There are records in existence, however, which would indicate the probability that his funeral was a mock funeral and that, leaving England, he lived for many years under another name in Germany, there faithfully serving the secret society to the promulgation of whose doctrines he had consecrated his life. Little doubt seems to exist in the minds of impartial investigators that Lord Bacon was the legitimate son of Queen Elizabeth and the Earl of Leicester.

In the *First Part of King Henry the Fourth,* the word "Francis" appears 33 times upon one page. To attain this end, obviously awkward sentences were required, as: "Anon Francis? No Francis, but tomorrow Francis: or Francis, on Thursday: or indeed Francis when thou wilt. But Francis."

Mr. WILLIAM

SHAKESPEARES

COMEDIES,
HISTORIES, &
TRAGEDIES.

Publifhed according to the True Originall Copies.

Martin Droeshout Sculpsit London

L O N D O N
Printed by Ifaac Iaggard, and Ed. Blount. 1623.

FROM SHAKESPEARE'S *GREAT FOLIO OF 1623.*

THE DROESHOUT PORTRAIT OF SHAKSPERE.

There are no authentic portraits of Shakspere in existence. The dissimilarities in the Droeshout, Chandos, Janssen, Hunt, Ashbourne, Soest, and Dunford portraits prove conclusively that the artists were unaware of Shakspere's actual features. An examination of the Droeshout portrait discloses several peculiarities. Baconian enthusiasts are convinced that the face is only a caricature, possibly the death mask of Francis Bacon. A comparison of the Droeshout Shakspere with portraits and engravings of Francis Bacon demonstrates the identity of the structure of the two faces, the difference in expression being caused by lines of shading. Note also the peculiar line running from the ear down to the chin. Does this line subtly signify that the face itself is a mask, ending at the ear? Notice also that the head is not connected with the body, but is resting on the collar. Most strange of all is the coat: one-half is on backwards. In drawing the jacket, the artist has made the left arm correctly, but the right arm has the back of the shoulder to the front. Frank Woodward has noted that there are 157 letters on the title page. This is a Rosicrucian signature of first importance. The date, 1623, plus the two letters "ON" from the word "LONDON," gives the cryptic signature of Francis Bacon, by a simple numerical cipher. By merely exchanging the 26 letters of the alphabet for numbers, 1 becomes A, 6 becomes F, 2 becomes B, and 3 becomes C, giving AFBC. To this is added the ON from LONDON, resulting in AFBCON, which rearranged forms F. BACON.

Throughout the Shakespearian *Folios* and *Quartos* occur scores of acrostic signatures. The simplest form of the acrostic is that whereby a name—in these instances Bacon's—was hidden in the first few letters of lines. In *The Tempest*, Act I, Scene 2, appears a striking example of the Baconian acrostic:

"Begun to tell me what I am, but stopt
And left me to a bootelesse Inquisition,
Concluding, stay: not yet."

The first letters of the first and second lines together with the first three letters of the third line form the word *BACon*. Similar acrostics appear frequently in Bacon's acknowledged writings.

The tenor of the Shakespearian dramas politically is in harmony with the recognized viewpoints of Sir Francis Bacon, whose enemies are frequently caricatured in the plays. Likewise their religious, philosophic, and educational undercurrents all reflect his personal opinions. Not only do these marked similarities of style and terminology exist in Bacon's writings and the Shakespearian plays, but there are also certain historical and philosophical inaccuracies common to both, such as identical misquotations from Aristotle.

Evidently realizing that futurity would unveil his full genius, Lord Verulam in his will bequeathed his soul to God above by the oblations of his Savior, his body to be buried obscurely, his name and memory to men's charitable speeches, to foreign nations, to succeeding ages, *and to his own countrymen after some time had elapsed.* That portion appearing in italics Bacon deleted from his will, apparently fearing that he had said too much.

That Sir Francis Bacon's subterfuge was known to a limited few during his lifetime is quite evident. Accordingly, stray hints regarding the true author of the Shakespearian plays may be found in many seventeenth century volumes. On page 33 (Bacon's cipher number) of the 1609 edition of Robert Cawdry's *Treasure or Storehouse of Similes* appears the following significant allusion: "Like as men would laugh at a poore man, if having precious garments lent him to act and play the part of some honourable personage upon a stage, when the play were at an ende he should keepe them as his owne, and bragge up and downe in them."

Repeated references to the word *hog* and the presence of cryptographic statements on page 33 of various contemporary writings demonstrate that the keys to Bacon's ciphers were his own name, words playing upon it, or its numerical equivalent. Notable examples are the famous statement of Mistress Quickly in *The Merry Wives of Windsor:* "Hang-hog is latten for Bacon, I warrant you"; the title pages of *The Countess of Pembroke's Arcadia* and Edmund Spenser's *Faerie Queene;* and the emblems appearing in the works of Alciatus and Wither. Furthermore, the word *honorificabilitudinitatibus* appearing in the fifth act of *Love's Labour's Lost* is a Rosicrucian signature, as its numerical equivalent (287) indicates.

Again, on the title page of the first edition of Sir Francis Bacon's *New Atlantis,* Father Time is depicted bringing a female figure out of the darkness of a cave. Around the device is a Latin inscription: "In time the secret truth shall be revealed." The catchwords and printer's devices appearing in volumes published especially during the first half of the seventeenth century were designed, arranged, and in some cases mutilated according to a definite plan.

It is evident also that the mispaginations in the Shakespearian *Folios* and other volumes are keys to Baconian ciphers, for re-editions—often from new type and by different printers—contain the same mistakes. For example, the *First* and *Second Folios* of Shakespeare are printed from entirely different type and by different printers nine years apart, but in both editions page 153 of the *Comedies* is numbered 151, and pages 249 and 250 are numbered 250 and 251 respectively. Also in the 1640 edition of Bacon's *The Advancement and Proficience of Learning,* pages 353 and 354 are numbered 351 and 352 respectively, and in the 1641 edition of *Du Bartas' Divine Weeks* pages 346 to 350 inclusive are entirely missing, while page 450 is numbered 442. The frequency with which pages ending in numbers 50, 51, 52, 53, and 54 are involved will be noted.

The requirements of Lord Verulam's biliteral cipher are fully met in scores of volumes printed between 1590 and 1650 and in some printed at other times. An examination of the verses by L. Digges, dedicated to the memory of the deceased "Author Maister W. Shakespeare," reveals the use of two fonts of type for both capital and small letters, the differences being most marked in the capital *T*'s, *N*'s, and *A*'s. (See the *First Folio.*) The cipher has been deleted from subsequent editions.

The presence of hidden material in the text is often indicated by needless involvement of words. On the sixteenth unnumbered page of the 1641 edition of *Du Bartas' Divine Weeks* is a boar surmounting a pyramidal text. The text is meaningless jargon, evidently inserted for cryptographic reasons and marked with Bacon's signature—the hog. The year following publication of the *First Folio* of Shakespeare's plays in 1623, there was printed in "Lunæburg" a remarkable volume on cryptography, avowedly by Gustavus Selenus. It is considered extremely probable that this volume constitutes the cryptographic key to the *Great Shakespearian Folio.*

Peculiar symbolical head- and tailpieces also mark the presence of cryptograms. While such ornaments are found in many early printed books, certain emblems are peculiar to volumes containing Baconian Rosicrucian ciphers. The light and dark shaded *A* is an interesting example. Bearing in mind the frequent recurrence in Baconian symbolism of the light and dark shaded *A* and the hog, the following statement by Bacon in his *Interpretation of Nature* is highly significant: "If the sow with her snout should happen to imprint the letter *A* upon the ground, wouldst thou therefore imagine that she could write out a whole tragedy as one letter?"

The Rosicrucians and other secret societies of the seventeenth century used watermarks as mediums for the conveyance of cryptographic references, and books presumably containing Baconian ciphers are usually printed upon paper bearing Rosicrucian or Masonic watermarks; often there are several symbols in one book, such as the Rose Cross, urns, bunches of grapes, and others.

At hand is a document which may prove a remarkable key to a cipher beginning in *The Tragedy of Cymbeline.* So far as known it has never been published and is applicable only to the 1623 Folio of the Shakespearian plays. The cipher is a line-and-word count involving punctuation, especially the long and short exclamation points and the straight and slanting interrogation points. This code was discovered by Henry William Bearse in 1900, and after it has been thoroughly checked its exact nature will be made public.

No reasonable doubt remains that the Masonic Order is the direct outgrowth of the secret societies of the Middle Ages, nor can it be denied that Freemasonry is permeated by the symbolism and mysticism of the ancient and mediæval worlds. Sir Francis Bacon knew the true secret of Masonic origin and there is reason to suspect that he concealed this knowledge in cipher and cryptogram. Bacon is not to be regarded solely as a man but rather as the focal point between an invisible institution and a world which was never able to distinguish between the messenger and the message which he promulgated. This secret society, having rediscovered the lost wisdom of the ages and fearing that the knowledge might be lost again, perpetuated it in two ways: (1) by an organization (Freemasonry) to the initiates of which it revealed its wisdom in the form of symbols; (2) by embodying its arcana in the literature of the day by means of cunningly contrived ciphers and enigmas.

Evidence points to the existence of a group of wise and illustrious *Fratres* who assumed the responsibility of publishing and preserving for future generations the choicest of the secret books of the ancients, together with certain other documents which they themselves had prepared. That future members of their fraternity might not only identify these volumes but also immediately note the significant passages, words, chapters, or sections therein, they created a symbolic alphabet of hieroglyphic designs. By means of a certain key and order, the discerning few were thus enabled to find that wisdom by which a man is "raised" to an illumined life.

FROM *ALCIATI EMBLEMATA.*

A BACONIAN SIGNATURE.

The curious volume from which this figure is taken was published in Paris in 1618. The attention of the Baconian student is immediately attracted by the form of the hog in the foreground. Bacon often used this animal as a play upon his own name, especially because the name *Bacon* was derived from the word *beech* and the nut of this tree was used to fatten hogs. The two pillars in the background have considerable Masonic interest. The two *A's* nearly in the center of the picture—one light and one shaded—are alone almost conclusive proof of Baconian influence. The most convincing evidence, however, is the fact that 17 is the numerical equivalent of the letters of the Latin form of Bacon's name (F. Baco) and there are 17 letters in the three words appearing in the illustration.

The tremendous import of the Baconian mystery is daily becoming more apparent. Sir Francis Bacon was a link in that great chain of minds which has perpetuated the secret doctrine of antiquity from its beginning. This secret doctrine is concealed in his cryptic writings. The search for this divine wisdom is the only legitimate motive for the effort to decode his cryptograms.

Masonic research might discover much of value if it would turn its attention to certain volumes published during the sixteenth and seventeenth centuries which bear the stamp and signet of that secret society whose members first established modern Freemasonry but themselves remained as an intangible group controlling and directing the activities of the outer body. *The unknown history and lost rituals of Freemasonry may be rediscovered in the symbolism and cryptograms of the Middle Ages.* Freemasonry is the bright and glorious son of a mysterious and hidden father. It cannot trace its parentage because that origin is obscured by the veil of the superphysical and the mystical. The *Great Folio* of 1623 is a veritable treasure house of Masonic lore and symbolism, and the time is at hand when that great work should be accorded the consideration which is its due.

Though Christianity shattered the material organization of the pagan Mysteries, it could not destroy the knowledge of supernatural power which the pagans possessed. Therefore it is known that the Mysteries of Greece and Egypt were secretly perpetuated through the early centuries of the church, and later, by being clothed in the symbolism of Christianity, were accepted as elements of faith. Sir Francis Bacon was one of those who had been entrusted with the perpetuation and dissemination of the arcana of the superphysical originally in the possession of the pagan hierophants, and to attain that end either formulated the Fraternity of R.C. or was admitted into an organization already existing under that name and became one of its principal representatives.

FROM RALEGH'S *HISTORY OF THE WORLD.*

A CRYPTIC HEADPIECE.

Many documents influenced by Baconian philosophy—or intended to conceal Baconian or Rosicrucian cryptograms—use certain conventional designs at the beginning and end of chapters, which reveal to the initiated the presence of concealed information. The above ornamental scroll has long been accepted as proof of the presence of Baconian influence and is to be found only in a certain number of rare volumes, all of which contain Baconian cryptograms. These cipher messages were placed in the books either by Bacon himself or by contemporaneous and subsequent authors belonging to the same secret society which Bacon served with his remarkable knowledge of ciphers and enigmas. Variants of this headpiece adorn the Great Shakespearian *Folio* (1623); Bacon's *Novum Organum* (1620); the St. James Bible (1611); Spenser's *Faerie Queene* (1611); and Sir Walter Ralegh's *History of the World* (1614). (See *American Baconiana.*)

For some reason not apparent to the uninitiated there has been a continued and consistent effort to prevent the unraveling of the Baconian skein. Whatever the power may be which continually blocks the efforts of the investigators, it is as unremitting now as it was immediately following Bacon's death, and those attempting to solve the enigma still feel the weight of its resentment.

A misunderstanding world has ever persecuted those who understood the secret workings of Nature, seeking in every conceivable manner to exterminate the custodians of this divine wisdom. Sir Francis Bacon's political prestige was finally undermined and Sir Walter Ralegh met a shameful fate because their transcendental knowledge was considered dangerous.

The forging of Shakspere's handwriting; the foisting of fraudulent portraits and death masks upon a gullible public; the fabrication of spurious biographies; the mutilation of books and documents; the destruction or rendering illegible of tablets and inscriptions containing cryptographic messages, have all compounded the difficulties attendant upon the solution of the Bacon-Shakspere-Rosicrucian riddle. The Ireland forgeries deceived experts for years.

According to material available, the supreme council of the Fraternity of R.C. was composed of a certain number of individuals who had died what is known as the "philosophic death." When the time came for an initiate to enter upon his labors for the Order, he conveniently "died" under somewhat mysterious circumstances. In reality he changed his name and place of residence, and a box of rocks or a body secured for the purpose was buried in his stead. It is believed that this happened in the case of Sir Francis Bacon who, like all servants of the Mysteries, renounced all personal credit and permitted others to be considered as the authors of the documents which he wrote or inspired.

The cryptic writings of Francis Bacon constitute one of the most powerful tangible elements in the mysteries of transcendentalism and symbolic philosophy. Apparently many years must yet pass before an uncomprehending world will appreciate the transcending genius of that mysterious man who wrote the *Novum Organum,* who sailed his little ship far out into the unexplored sea of learning through the Pillars of Hercules, and whose ideals for a new civilization are magnificently expressed in the Utopian dream of *The New Atlantis.* Was Sir Francis Bacon a second Prometheus? Did his great love for the people of the world and his pity for their ignorance cause him to bring the divine fire from heaven concealed within the contents of a printed page?

In all probability, the keys to the Baconian riddle will be found in classical mythology. He who understands the secret of the Seven-Rayed God will comprehend the method employed by Bacon to accomplish his monumental labor. Aliases were assumed by him in accordance with the attributes and order of the members of the planetary system. One of the least known—but most important—keys to the Baconian enigma is the Third, or 1637, Edition, published in Paris, of *Les Images ou Tableaux de platte peinture des deux Philostrates sophistes grecs et les statues de Callistrate,* by Blaise de Vigenere. The title page of this volume—which, as the name of the author when properly deciphered indicates, was written by or under the direction of Bacon or his secret society—is one mass of important Masonic or Rosicrucian symbols. On page 486 appears a plate entitled "Hercules Furieux," showing a gigantic figure shaking a spear, the ground before him strewn with curious emblems. In his curious work, *Das Bild des Speershüttlers die Lösung des Shakespeare-Rätsels,* Alfred Freund attempts to explain the Baconian symbolism in the *Philostrates.* Bacon he reveals as the philosophical Hercules, whom time will establish as the true "Spear-Shaker" (Shakespeare).

The Cryptogram as a Factor in Symbolic Philosophy

o treatise which deals with symbolism would be complete without a section devoted to the consideration of cryptograms. The use of ciphers has long been recognized as indispensable in military and diplomatic circles, but the modern world has overlooked the important rôle played by cryptography in literature and philosophy.

If the art of deciphering cryptograms could be made popular, it would result in the discovery of much hitherto unsuspected wisdom possessed by both ancient and mediæval philosophers. It would prove that many apparently verbose and rambling authors were wordy for the sake of concealing words. Ciphers are hidden in the most subtle manner: they may be concealed in the watermark of the paper upon which a book is printed; they may be bound into the covers of ancient books; they may be hidden under imperfect pagination; they may be extracted from the first letters of words or the first words of sentences; they may be artfully concealed in mathematical equations or in apparently unintelligible characters; they may be extracted from the jargon of clowns or revealed by heat as having been written in sympathetic ink; they may be word ciphers, letter ciphers, or apparently ambiguous statements whose meaning could be understood only by repeated careful readings; they may be discovered in the elaborately illuminated initial letters of early books or they may be revealed by a process of counting words or letters. If those interested in Freemasonic research would give serious consideration to this subject, they might find in books and manuscripts of the sixteenth and seventeenth centuries the information necessary to bridge the gap in Masonic history that now exists between the Mysteries of the ancient world and the Craft Masonry of the last three centuries.

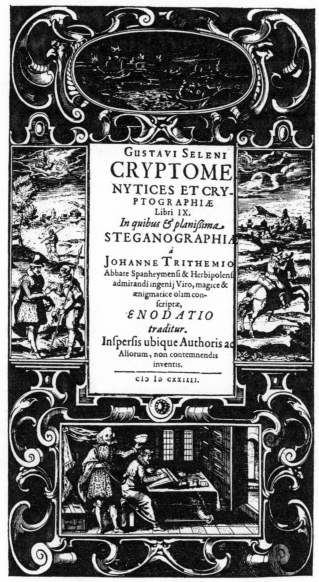

FROM SELENUS' *CRYPTOMENYTICES ET CRYPTOGRAPHICÆ.*

A FAMOUS CRYPTIC TITLE PAGE.

One year after the publication of the first Great "Shakespearian" Folio, a remarkable volume on cryptograms and ciphers was published. The title page of the work is reproduced above. The year of its publication (1624) was during the Rosicrucian controversy. The translation of the title page is as follows: "The Cryptomenysis and Cryptography of Gustavus Selenus in nine books, to which is added a clear explanation of the System of Steganography of John Trithemius, Abbot of Spanheim and Herbipolis, a man of admirable genius. Interspersed with worthy inventions of the Author and others, 1624."

The author of this volume was believed to be Augustus, Duke of Brunswick. The symbols and emblems ornamenting the title page, how-ever, are conclusive evidence that the fine hand of the Rosicrucians was behind its publication. At the bottom of the picture is a nobleman (Bacon?) placing his hat on another man's head. In the oval at the top of the plate, it is possible that the lights are *beacons,* or a play upon the name *Bacon.* In the two side panels are striking and subtle "Shakespearian" allusions. On the left is a nobleman (possibly Bacon) handing a paper to another man of mean appearance who carries in his hand a spear. At the right, the man who previously carried the spear is shown in the costume of an actor, wearing spurs and blowing a horn. The allusion to the actor blowing his horn and the figure carrying the spear suggest much, especially as *spear* is the last syllable of the name *"Shakespeare."*

Wisdom and understanding
are more to be
desired than riches

AN EXAMPLE OF BILITERAL WRITING.

In the above sentence note carefully the formation of the letters. Compare each letter with the two types of letters in the biliteral alphabet table reproduced from Lord Bacon's *De Augmentis Scientiarum.* A comparison of the "d" in "wisdom" with the "d" in "and" discloses a large loop at the top of the first, while the second shows practically no loop at all. Contrast the "i" in "wisdom" with the "i" in "understanding." In the former the lines are curved and in the latter angular. A similar analysis of the two "e's" in "desired" reveals obvious differences. The "o" in "more" differs only from the "o" in "wisdom" in that a tiny line continues from the top over towards the "r." The "a" in "than" is thinner and more angular than the "a" in "are," while the "r" in "riches" differs from that in "desired" in that the final upright stroke terminates in a ball instead of a sharp point. These minor differences disclose the presence of the two alphabets employed in writing the sentence.

The arcana of the ancient Mysteries were never revealed to the profane except through the media of symbols. Symbolism fulfilled the dual office of concealing the sacred truths from the uninitiated and revealing them to those qualified to understand the symbols. Forms are the symbols of formless divine principles; symbolism is the language of Nature. With reverence the wise pierce the veil and with clearer vision contemplate the reality; but the ignorant, unable to distinguish between the false and the true, behold a universe of symbols. It may well be said of Nature—the Great Mother—that she is ever tracing strange characters upon the surface of things, but only to her eldest and wisest sons as a reward for their faith and devotion does she reveal the cryptic alphabet which is the key to the import of these tracings.

The temples of the ancient Mysteries evolved their own sacred languages, known only to their initiates and never spoken save in the sanctuary. The illumined priests considered it sacrilege to discuss the sacred truths of the higher worlds or the divine verities of eternal Nature in the same tongue as that used by the vulgar for wrangling and dissension. A sacred science must needs be couched in a sacred language. Secret alphabets also were invented, and whenever the secrets of the wise were committed to writing, characters meaningless to the uninformed were employed. Such forms of writing were called sacred or Hermetic alphabets. Some—such as the famous *angelic writing*—are still retained in the higher degrees of Masonry.

Secret alphabets were not entirely satisfactory, however, for although they rendered unintelligible the true nature of the writings, their very presence disclosed the fact of concealed information—which the priests also sought to conceal. Through patience or persecution, the keys to these alphabets were eventually acquired and the contents of the documents revealed to the unworthy. This necessitated employment of more subtle methods for concealing the divine truths. The result was the appearance of cryptic systems of writing designed to conceal the presence of both the message and the cryptogram. Having thus devised a method of transmitting their secrets to posterity, the illuminati encouraged the circulation of certain documents specially prepared through incorporating into them ciphers containing the deepest secrets of mysticism and philosophy. Thus mediæval philosophers disseminated their theories throughout Europe without evoking suspicion, since volumes containing these cryptograms could be subjected to the closest scrutiny without revealing the presence of the hidden message.

During the Middle Ages scores of writers—members of secret political or religious organizations—published books containing ciphers. Secret writing became a fad; every European court had its own diplomatic cipher, and the intelligentsia vied with one another in devising curious and complicated cryptograms. The literature of the fifteenth, sixteenth, and seventeenth centuries is permeated with ciphers, few of which have ever been decoded. Many of the magnificent scientific and philosophic intellects of this period dared not

FROM BACON'S *DE AUGMENTIS SCIENTIARUM.*

THE BILITERAL ALPHABET.

This plate is reproduced from Bacon's *De Augmentis Scientiarum,* and shows the two alphabets as designed by him for the purpose of his cipher. Each capital and small letter has two distinct forms which are designated "a" and "b." The biliteral system did not in every instance make use of two alphabets in which the differences were as perceptible as in the example here given, but two alphabets were always used; sometimes the variations are so minute that it requires a powerful magnifying glass to distinguish the difference between the "a" and the "b" types of letters.

publish their findings, because of the religious intolerance of their day. In order to preserve the fruitage of their intellectual labors for mankind, these pioneers of progress concealed their discoveries in ciphers, trusting that future generations, more kindly than their own, would discover and appreciate their learning.

Many churchmen, it is interesting to note, used cryptograms, fearing excommunication or a worse fate should their scientific researches be suspected. Only recently an intricate cipher of Roger Bacon's has been unraveled, revealing the fact that this early scientist was well versed in the cellular theory. Lecturing before the American Philosophical Society, Dr. William Romaine Newbold, who translated the cipher manuscript of the friar, declared: "There are drawings which so accurately portray the actual appearance of certain objects that it is difficult to resist the inference that Bacon had seen them with the microscope. * * * These are spermatozoa, the body cells and the seminiferous tubes, the ova, with their nuclei distinctly indicated. There are nine large drawings, of which one at least bears considerable resemblance to a certain stage of development of fertilized cell." (See *Review of Reviews,* July, 1921.) Had Roger Bacon failed to conceal this discovery under a complicated cipher, he would have been persecuted as a heretic and would probably have met the fate of other early liberal thinkers. In spite of the rapid progress made by science in the last two hundred and fifty years, it still remains ignorant concerning many of the original discoveries made by mediæval investigators. The only record of these important findings is that contained in the cryptograms of the volumes which they published.

FROM BACON'S *DE AUGMENTIS SCIENTIARUM.*

THE KEY TO THE BILITERAL CIPHER.

After the document to be deciphered has been reduced to its "a" and "b" equivalents, it is then broken up into five-letter groups and the message read with the aid of the above table.

While many authors have written on the subject of cryptography, the books most valuable to students of philosophy and religion are: *Polygraphia* and *Steganographia,* by Trithemius, Abbot of Spanheim; *Mercury, or The Secret and Swift Messenger,* by John Wilkins, Bishop of Chester; *Œdipus Ægyptiacus* and other works by Athanasius Kircher, Society of Jesus; and *Cryptomenytices et Cryptographiæ,* by Gustavus Selenus.

To illustrate the basic differences in their construction and use, the various forms of ciphers are here grouped under seven general headings:

1. The *literal* cipher. The most famous of all literal cryptograms is the famous biliteral cipher described by Sir Francis Bacon in his *De Augmentis Scientiarum.* Lord Bacon originated the system while still a young man residing in Paris. The biliteral cipher requires the use of two styles of type, one an ordinary face and the other specially cut. The differences between the two fonts are in many cases so minute that it requires a powerful magnifying glass to detect them. Originally, the cipher messages were concealed only in the italicized words, sentences, or paragraphs, because the italic letters, being more ornate than the Roman letters, offered greater opportunity for concealing the slight but necessary variations. Sometimes the letters vary a trifle in size; at other times in thickness or in their ornamental flourishes. Later, Lord Bacon is believed to have had two Roman alphabets specially prepared in which the differences were so trivial that it is almost impossible for experts to distinguish them.

A careful inspection of the first four "Shakespeare" folios discloses the use throughout the volumes of several styles of type differing in minute but distinguishable details. It is possible that all the "Shakespeare" folios contain ciphers running through the text. These ciphers may have been added to the original plays, which are much longer in the folios than in the original quartos, full scenes having been added in some instances.

The biliteral cipher was not confined to the writings of Bacon and "Shakespeare," however, but appears in many books published during Lord Bacon's lifetime and for nearly a century after his death. In referring to the biliteral cipher, Lord Bacon terms it *omnia per omnia.* The cipher may run through an entire book and be placed therein at the time of printing without the knowledge of the original author, for it does not necessitate the changing of either words or punctuation. It is possible that this cipher was inserted for political purposes into many documents and volumes published during the seventeenth century. It is well known that ciphers were used for the same reason as early as the Council of Nicæa.

A MODERN WHEEL, OR DISC, CIPHER.

The above diagram shows a wheel cipher. The smaller, or inner, alphabet moves around so that any one of its letters may be brought opposite any one of the letters on the larger, or outer, alphabet. In some cases the inner alphabet is written backwards, but in the present example, both alphabets read the same way.

The Baconian biliteral cipher is difficult to use today, owing to the present exact standardization of type and the fact that so few books are now hand set. Accompanying this chapter are facsimiles of Lord Bacon's biliteral alphabet as it appeared in the 1640 English translation of *De Augmentis Scientiarum.* There are four alphabets, two for the capital and two for the small letters. Consider carefully the differences between these four and note that each alphabet has the power of either the letter *a* or the letter *b,* and that when reading a word its letters are divisible into one of two groups: those which correspond to the letter *a* and those which correspond to the letter *b.* In order to employ the biliteral cipher, a document must contain five times as many letters as there are in the cipher message to be concealed, for it requires five letters to conceal one. The biliteral cipher somewhat resembles a telegraph code in which letters are changed into dots and dashes; according to the biliteral system, however, the dots and dashes are represented respectively by *a*'s and *b*'s. The word *biliteral* is derived from the fact that all letters of the alphabet may be reduced to either *a* or *b.* An example of biliteral writing is shown in one of the accompanying diagrams. In order to demonstrate the working of this cipher, the message concealed within the words "Wisdom and understanding are more to be desired than riches" will now be deciphered.

The first step is to discover the letters of each alphabet and replace them by their equivalent *a* or *b* in accordance with the key given by Lord Bacon in his biliteral alphabet (*q.v.*). In the word *wisdom*, the *W* is from the *b* alphabet; therefore it is replaced by a *b*. The *i* is from the *a* alphabet; therefore an *a* is put in its place. The *s* is also from the *a* alphabet, but the *d* belongs to the *b* alphabet. The *o* and the *m* both belong to the *a* alphabet; hence each is replaced by *a*. By this process the word WISDOM therefore becomes *baabaa*. Treating the remaining words of the sentence in a similar manner, AND becomes *aba;* UNDERSTANDING, *aaabaaaaaabab;* ARE, *aba;* MORE, *abbb;* TO, *ab;* BE, *ab;* DESIRED, *abaabaa;* THAN, *aaba;* RICHES, *aaaaaa.*

The next step is to run all the letters together; thus: *baabaaabaaaa baaaaaaabababaabbbabababaabaaaabaaaaaaa.* All the combinations used in the Baconian biliteral cipher consist of groups containing five letters each. Therefore the solid line of letters must be broken into groups of five in the following manner: *baaba aabaa aabaa aaaab ababa abbba babab aabaa aabaa aaaaa.* Each of these groups of five letters now represents one letter of the cipher, and the actual letter can now be determined by comparing the groups with the alphabetical table, *The Key to the Biliteral Cipher,* from *De Augmentis Scientiarum* (*q.v.*); *baaba = T; aabaa = E; aabaa = E; aaaab = B; ababa = L; abbba = P; babab = X; aabaa = E; aabaa = E; aaaaa = A;* but the last five letters of the word *riches* being set off by a period from the initial *r,* the last five *a*'s do not count in the cipher. The letters thus extracted are now brought together in order, resulting in TEEBLPXEE.

At this point the inquirer might reasonably expect the letters to make intelligible words; but he will very likely be disappointed, for, as in the case above, the letters thus extracted are themselves a cryptogram, doubly involved to discourage those who might have a casual acquaintance with the biliteral system. The next step is to apply the nine letters to what is commonly called a wheel (or disc) cipher (*q.v.*), which consists of two alphabets, one revolving around the other in such a manner that numerous transpositions of letters are possible. In the accompanying cut the *A* of the inner alphabet is opposite the *H* of the outer alphabet, so that for cipher purposes these letters are interchangeable. The *F* and *M,* the *R* and *Y,* the *W* and *D,* in fact all the letters, may be transposed as shown by the two circles. The nine letters extracted by the biliteral cipher may thus be exchanged for nine others by the wheel cipher. The nine letters are considered as being on the inner circle of the wheel and are exchanged for the nine letters on the outer circle which are opposite the inner letters. By this process the *T* becomes *A;* the two *E*'s become two *L*'s; the *B* becomes *I;* the *L* becomes

S; the *P* becomes *W;* the *X* becomes *E;* and the two *E*'s become two *L*'s. The result is ALLISWELL, which, broken up into words, reads: "All is well."

Of course, by moving the inner disc of the wheel cipher, many different combinations in addition to the one given above can be made of the letters, but this is the only one which will produce sense, and the cryptogrammatist must keep on experimenting until he discovers a logical and intelligible message. He may then feel reasonably sure that he has deciphered the system. Lord Bacon involved the biliteral cipher in many different ways. There are probably a score of different systems used in the "Shakespeare" folio alone, some so intricate that they may forever baffle all attempts at their decipherment. In those susceptible of solution, sometimes the *a*'s and *b*'s have to be exchanged; at other times the concealed message is written backwards; again only every other letter is counted; and so on.

There are several other forms of the literal cipher in which letters are substituted for each other by a prearranged sequence. The simplest form is that in which two alphabets are written thus:

A	B	C	D	E	F	G	H	I	K	L	M	N
Z	Y	X	W	U	T	S	R	Q	P	O	N	M
O	P	Q	R	S	T	U	W	X	Y	Z		
L	K	I	H	G	F	E	D	C	B	A		

By substituting the letters of the lower alphabet for their equivalents in the upper one, a meaningless conglomeration results, the hidden message being decoded by reversing the process. There is also a form of the literal cipher in which the actual cryptogram is written in the body of the document, but unimportant words are inserted between important ones according to a prearranged order. The literal cipher also includes what are called acrostic signatures—that is, words written down the column by the use of the first letter of each line—and also more complicated acrostics in which the important letters are scattered through entire paragraphs or chapters. The two accompanying alchemical cryptograms illustrate another form of the literal cipher involving the first letter of each word. Every cryptogram based upon the arrangement or combination of the letters of the alphabet is called a literal cipher.

2. The *pictorial* cipher. Any picture or drawing with other than its obvious meaning may be considered a pictorial cryptogram. Instances of pictorial cipher are frequently found in Egyptian symbolism and early religious art. The diagrams of alchemists and Hermetic philosophers are invariably pictorial ciphers.

In addition to the simple pictorial cipher, there is a more technical form in which words or letters are concealed by the number of stones in a wall, by the spread of birds' wings in flight, by ripples on the surface of water, or by the length and order of lines used in shading. Such cryptograms are not obvious, and must be decoded with the aid of an arbitrary measuring scale, the length of the lines determining the letter or word concealed. The shape and proportion of a building, the height of a tower, the number of bars in a window, the folds of a man's garments—even the proportions or attitude of the human body—were used to conceal definite figures or characters which could be exchanged for letters or words by a person acquainted with the code.

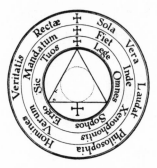

FROM BROWN'S *HISTORY OF CHEMISTRY.*

AN ALCHEMICAL CRYPTOGRAM.

James Campbell Brown reprints a curious cipher from Kircher. The capital letters of the seven words in the outer circle, when read clockwise, form the word SVLPHVR. From the five words in the second circle, when read in a similar manner, is derived FIXVM. The capitals of the six words in the inner circle, when properly arranged, also read EST SOL. The following cipher is thus extracted: "Sulphur Fixum Est Sol," which when translated is: "Fixed sulphur is gold."

Initial letters of names were secreted in architectural arches and spans. A notable example of this practice is found on the title page of Montaigne's *Essays,* third edition, where an initial *B* is formed by two arches and an *F* by a broken arch. Pictorial cryptograms are sometimes accompanied by the key necessary for their decipherment. A figure may point toward the starting point of the cipher or carry in its hand some implement disclosing the system of measurement used. There are also frequent instances in which the cryptographer purposely distorted or improperly clothed some figure in his drawing by placing the hat on backwards, the sword on the wrong side, or the shield on the wrong arm, or by employing some similar artifice. The much-discussed fifth finger on the Pope's hand in Raphael's *Sistine Madonna* and the sixth toe on Joseph's foot in the same artist's *Marriage of the Virgin* are cunningly concealed cryptograms.

3. The *acroamatic* cipher. The religious and philosophical writings of all nations abound with acroamatic cryptograms, that is, parables and allegories. The acroamatic is unique in that the document containing it may be translated or reprinted without affecting the cryptogram. Parables and allegories have been used since remote antiquity to present moral truths in an attractive and understandable manner. The acroamatic cryptogram is a pictorial cipher drawn in words and its symbolism must be so interpreted. The Old and New Testaments of the Jews, the writings of Plato and Aristotle, Homer's *Odyssey* and *Iliad,* Virgil's *Æneid, The Metamorphosis* of Apuleius, and *Æsop's Fables* are outstanding

examples of acroamatic cryptography in which are concealed the deepest and most sublime truths of ancient mystical philosophy.

The acroamatic cipher is the most subtle of all, for the parable or allegory is susceptible of several interpretations. Bible students for centuries have been confronted by this difficulty. They are satisfied with the moral interpretation of the parable and forget that each parable and allegory is capable of seven interpretations, of which the seventh—the highest—is complete and all-inclusive, whereas the other six (and lesser) interpretations are fragmentary, revealing but part of the mystery. The creation myths of the world are acroamatic cryptograms, and the deities of the various pantheons are only cryptic characters which, if properly understood, become the constituents of a divine alphabet. The initiated few comprehend the true nature of this alphabet, but the uninitiated many worship the letters of it as gods.

4. The *numerical* cipher. Many cryptograms have been produced in which numbers in various sequences are substituted for letters, words, or even complete thoughts. The reading of numerical ciphers usually depends upon the possession of specially arranged tables of correspondences. The numerical cryptograms of the Old Testament are so complicated that only a few scholars versed in rabbinical lore have ever sought to unravel their mysteries. In his *Œdipus Ægyptiacus,* Athanasius Kircher describes several Arabian Qabbalistic theorems, and a great part of the Pythagorean mystery was concealed in a secret method in vogue among Greek mystics of substituting letters for numbers.

The most simple numerical cipher is that in which the letters of the alphabet are exchanged for numbers in ordinary sequence. Thus *A* becomes 1, *B* 2, *C* 3, and so on, counting both *I* and *J* as 9 and both *U* and *V* as 20. The word *yes* by this system would be written 23-5-18. This cipher can be made more difficult by reversing the alphabet so that *Z* becomes 1, *Y* 2, *X* 3, and so on. By inserting a non-significant, or uncounted, number after each of the significant numbers the cipher is still more effectively concealed, thus: 23-16-5-9-18. The word *yes* is found by eliminating the second and fourth numbers. By adding 23, 5, and 18 together the sum 46 results. Therefore 46 is the numerical equivalent of the word *yes*. According to the simple numerical cipher, the sum 138 is equal to the words *Note carefully.* Therefore in a book using this method, line 138, page 138, or paragraph 138 may contain the concealed message. In addition to this simple numerical cipher there are scores of others so complicated that no one without the key can hope to solve them.

Authors sometimes based their cryptograms upon the numerical value of their own names; for example, Sir Francis Bacon repeatedly used the cryptic number 33—the numerical equivalent of his name. Numerical ciphers often involve the pagination of a book. Imperfect pagination, though generally attributed to carelessness, often conceals important secrets. The mispaginations found in the 1623 folio of "Shakspeare" and the consistent recurrence of similar errors in various volumes printed about the same period have occasioned considerable thought among scholars and cryptogrammatists. In Baconian cryptograms, all page numbers ending in 89 seem to have a special significance. The 89th page of the *Comedies* in the 1623 folio of "Shakespeare" shows an error of type in the pagination, the "9" being from a considerably smaller font than the "8." The 189th page is entirely missing, there being two pages numbered 187; and page 188 shows the second "8" scarcely more than half the size of the first one. Page 289 is correctly numbered and has no unusual features, but page 89 of the *Histories* is missing. Several volumes published by Bacon show similar errors, page 89 being often involved.

There are also numerical ciphers from which the cryptic message may be extracted by counting every tenth word, every twentieth word, or every fiftieth word. In some cases the count is irregular. The first important word may be found by counting 100, the second by counting 90, the third by counting 80, and so on until the count of 10 is reached. The count then returns to 100 and the process is repeated.

5. The *musical* cipher. John Wilkins, afterwards Bishop of Chester, in 1641 circulated an anonymous essay entitled *Mercury, or the Secret and Swift Messenger*. In this little volume, which was largely derived from the more voluminous treatises of Trithemius and Selenus, the author sets forth a method whereby musicians can converse with each other by substituting musical notes for the letters of the alphabet. Two persons understanding the code could converse with each other by merely playing certain notes upon a piano or other instrument. Musical cryptograms can be involved to an inconceivable point; by certain systems it is possible to take an already existing musical theme and conceal in it a cryptogram without actually changing the composition in any way. The pennants upon the notes may conceal the cipher, or the actual sounds of the notes may be exchanged for syllables of similar sound. This latter method is effective but its scope is somewhat limited. Several musical compositions by Sir Francis Bacon are still in existence. An examination of them might reveal musical cryptograms, for it is quite certain that Lord Bacon was well acquainted with the manner of their construction.

6. The *arbitrary* cipher. The system of exchanging letters of the alphabet for hieroglyphic figures is too easily decoded to be popular. Albert Pike

describes an arbitrary cipher based upon the various parts of the Knights Templars' cross, each angle representing a letter. The many curious alphabets that have been devised are rendered worthless, however, by the table of recurrence. According to Edgar Allan Poe, a great cryptogrammatist, the most common letter of the English language is *E;* the other letters in their order of frequency are as follows: *A, O, I, D, H, N, R, S, T, U, Y, C, F, G, L, M, W, B, K, P, Q, X, Z.* Other authorities declare the table of frequency to be: *E, T, A, O, N, I, R, S, H, D, L, C, W, U, M, F, Y, G, P, B, V, K, X, Q, J, Z.* By merely counting the number of times each character appears in the message, the law of recurrence discloses the English letter for which the arbitrary character stands. Further help is also rendered by the fact that if the cryptogram be split up into words there are only three single letters which may form words: *A, I, O.* Thus any single character set off from the rest of the text must be one of these three letters. For details of this system see *The Gold Bug,* by Edgar Allan Poe.

FROM *GEHEIME FIGUREN DER ROSENKREUZER.*

AN ALCHEMICAL CRYPTOGRAM.

Beginning with the word VISITA and reading clockwise, the seven initial letters of the seven words inscribed in the outer circle read: VITRIOL. This is a very simple alchemical enigma, but is a reminder that those studying works on Hermeticism, Rosicrucianism, alchemy, and Freemasonry should always be on the lookout for concealed meanings hidden either in parables and allegories or in cryptic arrangements of numbers, letters, and words.

To render more difficult the decoding of arbitrary ciphers, however, the characters are seldom broken up into words, and, further, the table of recurrence is partly nullified by assigning two or more different characters to each letter, thereby making it impossible to estimate accurately the frequency of recurrence. Therefore, the greater the number of arbitrary characters used to represent any single letter of the alphabet, the more difficult it is to decipher an arbitrary cryptogram. The secret alphabets of the ancients are comparatively easy to decode, the only requisites being a table of frequency, a knowledge of the language in which the cryptogram was originally written, a moderate amount of patience, and a little ingenuity.

7.   The *code* cipher. The most modern form of cryptogram is the code system. Its most familiar form is the Morse code for use in telegraphic and wireless communication. This form of cipher may be complicated somewhat by embodying dots and dashes into a document in which periods and colons are dots, while commas and semicolons are dashes. There are also codes used by the business world which can be solved only by the use of a private code book. Because they furnish an economical and efficient method of transmitting confi-

dential information, the use of such codes is far more prevalent than the average person has any suspicion.

In addition to the foregoing classifications there are a number of miscellaneous systems of secret writing, some employing mechanical devices, others

FROM BARRETT'S *MAGUS*.

QABBALISTIC AND MAGIC ALPHABETS.

Curious alphabets were invented by the early and medieval philosophers to conceal their doctrines and tenets from the profane. Some of these alphabets are still used to a limited extent in the higher degrees of Freemasonry. Probably the most famous is the *angelic writing,* termed in the above plate "The Writing called Malachim." Its figures are supposedly derived from the constellations. Advanced students of occult philosophy will come upon many valuable documents in which these figures are used. Under each letter of the first alphabet above is its equivalent in English.

Above each letter of the other three alphabets is its Hebrew letter equivalent.

colors. A few make use of sundry miscellaneous objects to represent words and even complete thoughts. But as these more elaborate devices were seldom employed by the ancients or by the mediæval philosophers and alchemists, they have no direct bearing upon religion and philosophy. The mystics of the Middle Ages, borrowing the terminology of the various arts and sciences, evolved a system of cryptography which concealed the secrets of the human soul under terms generally applied to chemistry, biology, astronomy, botany, and physiology. Ciphers of this nature can only be decoded by individuals versed in the deep philosophic principles upon which these mediæval mystics based their theories of life. Much information relating to the invisible nature of man is concealed under what seem to be chemical experiments or scientific speculations. Every student of symbolism and philosophy, therefore, should be reasonably well acquainted with the underlying principles of cryptography; in addition to serving him well in his researches, this art furnishes a fascinating method of developing the acuteness of the mental faculties. Discrimination and observation are indispensable to the seeker after knowledge, and no study is equal to cryptography as a means of stimulating these powers.

Freemasonic Symbolism

n several early Masonic manuscripts—for example, the Harleian, Sloane, Lansdowne, and Edinburgh-Kilwinning—it is stated that the craft of initiated builders existed before the Deluge, and that its members were employed in the building of the Tower of Babel. A Masonic Constitution dated 1701 gives the following naïve account of the origin of the sciences, arts, and crafts from which the major part of Masonic symbolism is derived:

"How this worthy Science was first begunne, I shall tell. Before Noah's Flood, there was a man called Lameck as it is written in the 4 Chap. of Gen.: and this Lameck had two Wives. The one was called Adah, and the other Zillah; by the first wife Adah he gott two Sons, the one called Jaball, and the other Juball, and by the other wife Zillah he got a Son and Daughter, and the four children found the beginning of all Crafts in the world. This Jaball was the elder Son, and he found the Craft of Geometrie, and he parted flocks, as of Sheep and Lambs in the fields, and first wrought Houses of Stone and Tree, as it is noted in the Chap^e aforesaid, and his Brother Juball found the crafte of Musick, of Songs, Organs and Harp. The Third Brother [Tubal-cain] found out Smith's craft to work Iron and steel, and their sister Naamah found out the art of Weaving. These children did know thatt God would take Vengeance for Sinne, either by fire or water, wherefor they wrote these Sciences which they had found in Two Pillars of stone, thatt they might be found after the Flood. The one stone was called Marbell—cannott burn with Fire, and the other was called Laturus [brass?], thatt cannott drown in the Water." The author of this Constitution thereupon declares that one of these pillars was later discovered by Hermes, who communicated to mankind the secrets thereon inscribed.

In his *Antiquities of the Jews,* Josephus writes that Adam had forewarned his descendants that sinful humanity would be destroyed by a deluge. In order to preserve their science and philosophy, the children of Seth therefore raised two pillars, one of brick and the other of stone, on which were inscribed the keys to their knowledge. The Patriarch Enoch—whose name means the Initiator—is evidently a personification of the sun, since he lived 365 years. He also constructed an underground temple consisting of nine vaults, one beneath the other, placing in the deepest vault a triangular tablet of gold bearing upon it the absolute and ineffable Name of Deity. According to some accounts, Enoch made two golden *deltas*. The larger he placed upon the white cubical altar in the lowest vault and the smaller he gave into the keeping of his son, Methusaleh, who did the actual construction work of the brick chambers according to the pattern revealed to his father by the Most High. In the form and arrangement of these vaults Enoch epitomized the nine spheres of the ancient Mysteries and the nine sacred strata of the earth through which the initiate must pass to reach the flaming Spirit dwelling in its central core.

According to Freemasonic symbolism, Enoch, fearing that all knowledge of the sacred Mysteries would be lost at the time of the Deluge, erected the two columns mentioned in the quotation. Upon the metal column in appropriate allegorical symbols he engraved the secret teaching and upon the marble column placed an inscription stating that a short distance away a priceless treasure would be discovered in a subterranean vault. After having thus faithfully completed his labors, Enoch was translated from the brow of Mount Moriah. In time the location of the secret vaults was lost, but after the lapse of ages there came another builder—an initiate after the order of Enoch—and he, while laying the foundations for another temple to the Great Architect of the Universe, discovered the long-lost vaults and the secrets contained within.

John Leylande was appointed by King Henry VIII to go through the archives of the various religious institutions dissolved by the king and remove for preservation any books or manuscripts of an important character. Among the documents copied by Leylande was a series of questions and answers concerning the mystery of Masonry written by King Henry VI. In answer to the question, "How came Masonry into England?" the document states that Peter Gower, a Grecian, traveled for knowledge in Egypt, Syria, and every land where the Phœnicians had planted Masonry; winning entrance in all lodges of Masons, he learned much, and returning, dwelt in Greater Greece. He became renowned for his wisdom, formed a great lodge at Groton, and made many Masons, some of whom journeyed in France, spreading Masonry there; from France in the course of time the order passed into England.

To even the superficial student of the subject it must be evident that the name of *Peter Gower,* the Grecian, is merely an Anglicized form of *Pythagoras;* consequently Groton, where he formed his lodge, is easily identified with Crotona. A link is thus established between the philosophic Mysteries of Greece and mediæval Freemasonry. In his notes on King Henry's questions and answers, William Preston enlarges upon the vow of secrecy as it was practiced by the ancient initiates. On the authority of Pliny he describes how Anaxarchus, having been imprisoned in order to extort from him some of the secrets with which he had been entrusted, bit out his own tongue and threw it in the face of Nicocreon, the tyrant of Cyprus. Preston adds that the Athenians revered a brazen statue that was represented without a tongue to denote the sanctity with which they regarded their oath-bound secrets. It is also noteworthy that, according to King Henry's manuscript, Masonry had its origin in the East and was the carrier of the arts and sciences of civilization to the primitive humanity of the western nations.

Conspicuous among the symbols of Freemasonry are the seven liberal arts and sciences. By *grammar* man is taught to express in noble and adequate language his innermost thoughts and ideals; by *rhetoric* he is enabled to conceal his ideals under the protecting cover of ambiguous language and figures of speech; by *logic* he is trained in the organization of the intellectual faculties with which he has been endowed; by *arithmetic* he not only is instructed in the mystery of universal order but also gains the key to multitude, magnitude, and proportion; by *geometry* he is inducted into the mathematics of form, the harmony and rhythm of angles, and the philosophy of organization; by *music* he is reminded that the universe is founded upon the laws of celestial harmonics and that harmony and rhythm are all-pervading; by *astronomy* he gains an understanding of the immensities of time and space, of the proper relationship between himself and the universe, and of the awesomeness of that Unknown Power which is driving the countless stars of the firmament through illimitable space. Equipped with the knowledge conferred by familiarity with the liberal arts and sciences, the studious Freemason therefore finds himself confronted by few problems with which he cannot cope.

The Dionysiac Architects

The most celebrated of the ancient fraternities of artisans was that of the Dionysiac Architects. This organization was composed exclusively of initiates of the Bacchus-Dionysos cult and was peculiarly consecrated to the science of building and the art of decoration. Acclaimed as being the custodians of a secret and sacred knowledge of architectonics, its members were entrusted with the design and erection of public buildings and monuments. The superlative excellence of their handiwork elevated the members of the guild to a position of surpassing dignity; they were regarded as the master craftsmen of the earth. Because of the first dances held in honor of Dionysos, he was considered the founder and patron of the theater, and the Dionysians specialized in the construction of buildings adapted for the presentation of dramatic performances. In the circular or semicircular orchestra they invariably erected an altar to Dionysos, and the rites of the Mysteries usually formed the motif for the tragedies and comedies enacted. It is related of Æschylus, the famous Greek poet, that while appearing in one of his own plays he was suspected by a mob of angry spectators of revealing one of the profound secrets of the Mysteries and was forced to seek refuge at the altar of Dionysos.

So carefully did the Dionysiac Architects safeguard the secrets of their craft that only fragmentary records exist of their esoteric teachings. John A. Weisse thus sums up the meager data available concerning the order:

"They made their appearance certainly not later than 1000 B.C., and appear to have enjoyed particular privileges and immunities. They also possessed secret means of recognition, and were bound together by specialties only known to themselves. The richer of this fraternity were bound to provide for their poorer brethren. They were divided into communities, governed by a Master and Wardens, and called γυνοικιαι (connected houses). They held a grand festival annually, and were held in high esteem. Their ceremonials were regarded as sacred. It has been claimed that Solomon, at the instance of Hiram, King of Tyre, employed them at his temple and palaces. They were also employed at the construction of the Temple of Diana at Ephesus. They had means of intercommunication all over the then known world, and from them, doubtless, sprang the guilds of the Traveling Masons known in the Middle Ages." (See *The Obelisk and Freemasonry*.)

The fraternity of the Dionysiac Architects spread throughout all of Asia Minor, even reaching Egypt and India. They established themselves in nearly all the countries bordering on the Mediterranean, and with the rise of the Roman Empire found their way into Central Europe and even into England. The most stately and enduring buildings in Constantinople, Rhodes, Athens, and Rome were erected by these inspired craftsmen. One of the most illustrious of their number was Vitruvius, the great architect, renowned as the author of *De Architectura Libri Decem*. In the various sections of his book Vitruvius gives several hints as to the philosophy underlying the Dionysiac concept of the principle of symmetry applied to the science of architecture, as derived from a consideration of the proportions established by Nature between the parts and members of the human body. The following extract from Vitruvius on the subject of symmetry is representative:

"The design of a temple depends on symmetry, the principles of which must be most carefully observed by the architect. They are due to proportion, in ἀναλογία. Proportion is a correspondence among the measures of the members of an entire work, and of the whole to a certain part selected as standard. From this result the principles of symmetry. Without symmetry and proportion there can be no principles in the design of any temple; that is, if there is no precise relation between its members, as in the case of those of a well shaped man. For the human body is so designed by nature that the face, from the chin to the top of the forehead and the lowest roots of the hair, is a tenth part of the whole height; the open hand from the wrist to the tip of the middle finger is just the same; the head from the chin to the crown is an eighth, and with the neck and shoulder from the top of the breast to the lowest roots of the hair is a sixth; from the middle of the breast to the summit of the crown is a fourth. If we take the height of the face itself, the distance from the bottom of the chin to the under side of the nostrils [and from that point] to a line between the eyebrows is the same; from there to the lowest roots of the hair is also a third, comprising the forehead. The length of the foot is one sixth of the height of the body; of the forearm, one fourth; and the breadth of the breast is also one fourth. The other members, too, have their own symmetrical proportions, and it was by employing them that the famous painters and sculptors of antiquity attained to great and endless renown."

The edifices raised by the Dionysiac Builders were indeed "sermons in stone." Though unable to comprehend fully the cosmic principles thus embodied in these masterpieces of human ingenuity and industry, even the uninitiated were invariably overwhelmed by the sense of majesty and symmetry resulting from the perfect coordination of pillars, spans, arches, and domes. By variations in the details of size, material, type, arrangement, ornamentation, and color, these inspired builders believed it possible to provoke in the nature of the onlooker certain distinct mental or emotional reactions. Vitruvius, for example, describes the disposition of bronze vases about a room so as to produce certain definite changes in the tone and quality of the human voice. In like manner, each chamber in the Mysteries through which the candidate passed had its own peculiar acoustics. Thus in one chamber the voice of the priest was amplified until his words caused the very room to vibrate, while in another the voice was diminished and softened to such a degree that it sounded like the distant tinkling of silver bells. Again, in some of the underground passageways the candidate was apparently bereft of the power of speech, for though he shouted at the top of his voice not even a whisper was audible to his ears. After progressing a few feet, however, he would discover that his softest sigh would be reechoed a hundred times.

The supreme ambition of the Dionysiac Architects was the construction of buildings which would create distinct impressions consistent with the purpose for which the structure itself was designed. In common with the Pythagoreans, they believed it possible by combinations of straight lines and curves to induce any desired mental attitude or emotion. They labored, therefore, to the end of producing a building perfectly harmonious with the structure of the universe itself. They may have even believed that an edifice so constructed—because it was in no respect at variance with any existing reality—would not be subject to dissolution but would endure throughout the span of mortal time. As a logical deduction from their philosophic trend of thought, such a building—*en rapport* with Cosmos—would also have become an oracle. Certain early works on magical philosophy hint that the Ark of the Covenant was oracular in character because of specially prepared chambers in its interior. These by their shape and arrangement were so attuned to the vibrations of the invisible world that they caught and amplified the voices of the ages imprinted upon and eternally existent in the substance of the astral light.

Unskilled in these ancient subtleties of their profession, modern architects often create architectural absurdities which would cause their creators to blush with shame did they comprehend their actual symbolic import. Thus, phallic emblems are strewn in profusion among the adornments of banks, office buildings, and department stores. Christian churches also may be surmounted with Brahmin or Mohammedan domes or be designed in a style suitable for a Jewish synagogue or a Greek temple to Pluto. These incongruities may be considered trivial in importance by the modern designer, but to the trained psychologist the purpose for which a building was erected is frustrated in large measure by the presence of such architectural discordances. Vitruvius thus defines the principle of propriety as conceived and applied by the Dionysians:

"Propriety is that perfection of style which comes when a work is authoritatively constructed on approved principles. It arises from prescription (Greek θεματισμῷ), from usage, or from nature. From prescription, in the case of hypæthral edifices, open to the sky, in honour of Jupiter Lightning, the Heaven, the Sun, or the Moon: for these are gods whose semblances and manifestations we behold before our very eyes in the sky when it is cloudless and bright. The temples of Minerva, Mars, and Hercules will be Doric, since the virile strength of these gods makes daintiness entirely inappropriate to their houses. In temples to Venus, Flora, Proserpine, Spring-Water, and the Nymphs, the Corinthian order will be found to have peculiar significance, because these are delicate divinities and so its rather slender outlines, its flowers, leaves, and ornamental volutes will lend propriety where it is due. The construction of temples of the Ionic order to Juno, Diana, Father Bacchus, and the other gods of that kind, will be in keeping with the middle position which they hold; for the building of such will be an appropriate combination of the severity of the Doric and the delicacy of the Corinthian."

In describing the societies of Ionian artificers, Joseph Da Costa declares the Dionysiac rites to have been founded upon the science of astronomy, which by the initiates of this order was correlated to the builder's art. In various documents dealing with the origin of architecture are found hints to the effect that the great buildings erected by these initiated craftsmen were based upon geometrical patterns derived from the constellations. Thus, a temple might be planned according to the constellation of Pegasus or a court of judgment modeled after the constellation of the Scales. The Dionysians evolved a peculiar code by which they were able to communicate with one another in the dark and both the symbols and the terminology of their guild were derived, in the main, from the elements of architecture.

While stigmatized as pagans by reason of their philosophic principles, it is noteworthy that these Dionysiac craftsmen were almost universally employed in the erection of early Christian abbeys and cathedrals, whose stones even to this very day bear distinguishing marks and symbols cut into their surfaces by these illustrious builders. Among the ornate carvings upon the fronts of great churches of the Old World are frequently found representations of compasses, squares, rules, mallets, and clusters of builders' tools skillfully incorporated into mural decorations and even placed in the hands of the effigies of saints and prophets standing in exalted niches. A great mystery was contained in the ancient portals of the Cathedral of Notre Dame which were destroyed during the French Revolution, for among their carvings were numerous Rosicrucian and Masonic emblems; and according to the records preserved by alchemists who studied their bas-reliefs, the secret processes for metallic transmutation were set forth in their grotesque yet most significant figures.

The checkerboard floor upon which the modern Freemasonic lodge stands is the old tracing board of the Dionysiac Architects, and while the modern organization is no longer limited to workmen's guilds it still preserves in its symbols the metaphysical doctrines of the ancient society of which it is presumably the outgrowth. The investigator of the origin of Freemasonic symbolism who desires to trace the development of the order through the ages will find a practical suggestion in the following statement of Charles W. Heckethorn:

"But considering that Freemasonry is a tree the roots of which spread through so many soils, it follows that traces thereof must be found in its fruit; that its language and ritual should retain much of the various sects and institutions it has passed through before arriving at their present state, and in Masonry we meet with Indian, Egyptian, Jewish, and Christian ideas, terms, and symbols." (See *The Secret Societies of All Ages and Countries*.)

The Roman *Collegia* of skilled architects were apparently a subdivision of the greater Ionian body, their principles and organization being practically identical with the older Ionian institution. It has been suspected that the Dionysians also profoundly influenced early Islamic culture, for part of their symbolism found its way into the Mysteries of the dervishes. At one time the Dionysians referred to themselves as Sons of Solomon, and one of the most important of their symbols was the Seal of Solomon—two interlaced triangles. This motif is frequently seen in conspicuous parts of Mohammedan mosques. The Knights Templars—who were suspected of anything and everything—are believed to have contacted these Dionsyiac artificers and to have introduced many of their symbols and doctrines into mediæval Europe. But Freemasonry most of all owes to the Dionysiac cult the great mass of its symbols and rituals which are related to the science of architecture. From these ancient and illustrious artisans it also received the legacy of the unfinished Temple of Civilization—that vast, invisible structure upon which these initiated builders have labored continuously since the inception of their fraternity. This mighty edifice, which has fallen and been rebuilt time after time but whose foundations remain unmoved, is the true Everlasting House of which the temple on the brow of Mount Moriah was but an impermanent symbol.

Aside from the operative aspect of their order, the Dionysiac Architects had a speculative philosophic code. Human society they considered as a rough and untrued ashlar but lately chiseled from the quarry of elemental Nature. This crude block was the true object upon which these skilled craftsmen labored— polishing it, squaring it, and with the aid of fine carvings transforming it into a miracle of beauty. While mystics released their souls from the bondage of matter by meditation and philosophers found their keenest joy in the profundities of thought, these master workmen achieved liberation from the Wheel of Life and Death by learning to swing their hammers with the same rhythm that moves the swirling forces of Cosmos. They venerated the Deity under the guise of a Great Architect and Master Craftsman who was ever gouging rough ashlars from the fields of space and truing them into universes. The Dionysians affirmed constructiveness to be the supreme expression of the soul, and attuning themselves with the ever-visible constructive natural processes going on around them, believed immortality could be achieved by thus becoming a part of the creative agencies of Nature.

Solomon, the Personification of Universal Wisdom

The name *Solomon* may be divided into three syllables, *SOL-OM-ON,* symbolizing light, glory, and truth collectively and respectively. The Temple of Solomon is, therefore, first of all "the House of Everlasting Light," its earthly symbol being the temple of stone on the brow of Mount Moriah. According to the Mystery teachings, there are three Temples of Solomon—as there are three Grand Masters, three Witnesses, and three Tabernacles of the Transfiguration. The first temple is the Grand House of the Universe, in the midst of which sits the sun (SOL) upon his golden throne. The twelve signs of the zodiac as Fellow-Craftsmen gather around their shining lord. Three lights—the stellar, the solar, and the lunar—illuminate this Cosmic Temple. Accompanied by his retinue of planets, moons, and asteroids, this Divine King (SOLomon), whose glory no earthly monarch shall ever equal, passes in stately pomp down the avenues of space. Whereas *CHiram* represents the active physical light of the sun, SOLomon signifies its invisible but all-powerful, spiritual and intellectual effulgency.

The second symbolic temple is the human body—the Little House made in the image of the Great Universal House. "Know ye not," asked the Apostle Paul, "that ye are the temple of God, and that the Spirit of God dwelleth in you?" Freemasonry within a temple of stone cannot be other than speculative, but Freemasonry within the living temple of the body is operative. The third symbolic temple is the *Soul*ar House, an invisible structure, the comprehension of which is a supreme Freemasonic arcanum. The mystery of this intangible edifice is concealed under the allegory of the *Soma Psuchicon,* or Wedding Garment described by St. Paul, the Robes of Glory of the High Priest of Israel, the Yellow Robe of the Buddhist monk, and the Robe of Blue and Gold to which Albert Pike refers in his *Symbolism.* The soul, constructed from an invisible fiery substance, a flaming golden metal, is cast by the Master Workman, CHiram Abiff, into the mold of clay (the physical body) and is called the Molten Sea. The temple of the human soul is built by three Master Masons personifying Wisdom, Love, and Service, and when constructed according to the Law of Life the spirit of God dwells in the Holy Place thereof. The *Sola*r Temple is the true Everlasting House, and he who can *raise* or *cast* it is a Master Mason *indeed!* The best-informed Masonic writers have realized that Solomon's Temple is a representation in miniature of the Universal Temple. Concerning this point, A. E. Waite, in *A New Encyclopædia of Freemasonry,* writes: "It is macrocosmic in character, so that the Temple is a symbol of the universe, a type of manifestation itself."

Solomon, the Spirit of Universal Illumination—mental, spiritual, moral, and physical—is personified in the king of an earthly nation. While a great ruler by that name may have built a temple, he who considers the story solely from its historical angle will never clear away the *rubbish* that covers the secret vaults. The rubbish is interpolated matter in the form of superficial symbols, allegories, and degrees which have no legitimate part in the original Freemasonic Mysteries. Concerning the loss of the true esoteric key to Masonic secrets, Albert Pike writes:

"No one journeys now 'from the high place of Cabaon to the threshing floor of Oman the Yebusite,' nor has seen, 'his Master, clothed in blue and gold;' nor are apprentices and Fellow-crafts any longer paid at their respective Columns; nor is the Master's working tool the Tracing Board, nor does he use in his work 'Chalk, Charcoal, and an Earthen Vessel,' nor does the Apprentice, becoming a Fellow Craft, pass from the square to the compass; for the meanings of these phrases as symbols have long been lost."

According to the ancient Rabbins, Solomon was an initiate of the Mystery schools and the temple which he built was actually a house of initiation containing a mass of pagan philosophic and phallic emblems. The pomegranates, the palm-headed columns, the pillars before the door, the Babylonian cherubim, and the arrangement of the chambers and draperies all indicate the temple to have been patterned after the sanctuaries of Egypt and Atlantis. Isaac Myer, in *The Qabbalah,* makes the following observation:

"The pseudo-Clement of Rome, writes: 'God made man male and female. The male is Christ: the female, the Church.' The Qabbalists called the Holy Spirit, the mother, and the Church of Israel, the Daughter. Solomon engraved on the walls of his Temple, likenesses of the male and female principles, to adumbrate this mystery; such, it is said, were the figures of the cherubim. This was, however, not in obedience to the words of the Thorah. They were symbolical of the Upper, the spiritual, the former or maker, positive or male, and the Lower, the passive, the negative or female, formed or made by the first."

Masonry came to Northern Africa and Asia Minor from the lost continent of Atlantis, not under its present name but rather under the general designation Sun and Fire Worship. The ancient Mysteries did not cease to exist when Christianity became the world's most powerful religion. Great Pan did not die! Freemasonry is the proof of his survival. The pre-Christian Mysteries simply assumed the symbolism of the new faith, perpetuating through its emblems and allegories the same truths which had been the property of the wise since the beginning of the world. There is no true explanation, therefore, for Christian symbols save that which is concealed within pagan philosophy. Without the mysterious *keys* carried by the hierophants of the Egyptian, Brahmin, and Persian cults the gates of Wisdom cannot be opened. Consider with reverent spirit, therefore, the sublime allegory of the Temple and its Builders, realizing that beneath its literal interpretation lies hidden a Royal Secret.

According to the Talmudic legends, Solomon understood the mysteries of the Qabbalah. He was also an alchemist and a necromancer, being able to control the dæmons, and from them and other inhabitants of the invisible worlds he secured much of his wisdom. In his translation of *Clavicula Solomonis,* or *The Key of Solomon the King,* a work presumably setting forth the magical secrets gathered by Solomon and used by him in the conjuration of spirits and which, according to Frank C. Higgins, contains many sidelights on Masonic initiatory rituals, S. L. MacGregor-Mathers recognizes the probability that King Solomon was a magician in the fullest sense of that word. "I see no reason to doubt," he affirms, "the tradition which assigns the authorship of the 'Key' to King Solomon, for among others Josephus, the Jewish historian, especially mentions the magical works attributed to that monarch; this is confirmed by many Eastern traditions, and his magical skill is frequently mentioned in the Arabian Nights."

Concerning Solomon's supernatural powers, Josephus writes in his *Eighth Book of the Antiquities of the Jews:*

"Now the sagacity and wisdom which God had bestowed on Solomon was so great that he exceeded the ancients, in so much that he was no way inferior to the Egyptians, who are said to have been beyond all men in understanding; * * * God also enabled him to learn that skill which expelled demons, which is a science useful and sanative to him. He composed such incantations also by which distempers are alleviated. And he left behind him the manner of using exorcisms, by which they drive away demons, so that they never return; and this method of cure is of great force unto this day."

The mediæval alchemists were convinced that King Solomon understood the secret processes of Hermes by means of which it was possible to multiply metals. Dr. Bacstrom writes that the *Universal Spirit* (CHiram) assisted King Solomon to build his temple, because Solomon being wise in the wisdom of alchemy knew how to control this incorporeal essence and, setting it to work for him, caused the invisible universe to supply him with vast amounts of gold and silver which most people believed were mined by natural methods.

The mysteries of the Islamic faith are now in the keeping of the dervishes—men who, renouncing worldliness, have withstood the test of a thousand and one days of temptation. Jelal-ud-din, the great Persian Sufic poet and philosopher, is accredited with having founded the Order of Mevlevi, or the "dancing dervishes," whose movements exoterically signify the motions of the celestial bodies and esoterically result in the establishment of a rhythm which stimulates the centers of spiritual consciousness within the dancer's body.

"According to the mystical canon, there are always on earth a certain number of holy men who are admitted to intimate communion with the Deity. The one who occupies the highest position among his contemporaries is called the 'Axis' (Qūtb) or 'Pole' of his time. * * * Subordinate to the Qūtb are two holy beings who bear the title of 'The Faithful Ones,' and are assigned places on his right and left respectively. Below these is a quartette of 'Intermediate Ones' (Evtād); and on successively lower planes are five 'Lights' (Envār), and seven 'Very Good' (Akhyār). The next rank is filled by forty 'Absent Ones' (Rijal-i-ghaib), also termed 'Martyrs' (Shuheda). When an 'Axis' quits this earthly existence, he is succeeded by the 'Faithful One' who has occupied the place at his right hand. * * * For to these holy men, who also bear the collective titles of 'Lords of Souls,' and 'Directors,' is committed a spiritual supremacy over mankind far exceeding the temporal authority of earthly rulers." (See *Mysticism and Magic in Turkey,* by L. M. J. Garnett.)

The *Axis* is a mysterious individual who, unknown and unsuspected, mingles with mankind and who, according to tradition, has his favorite seat upon the roof of the Caaba. J. P. Brown, in *The Dervishes,* gives a description of these "Master Souls."

Freemasonry's Priceless Heritage

The *sanctum sanctorum* of Freemasonry is ornamented with the gnostic jewels of a thousand ages; its rituals ring with the divinely inspired words of seers and sages. A hundred religions have brought their gifts of wisdom to its altar; arts and sciences unnumbered have contributed to its symbolism. Freemasonry is a world-wide university, teaching the liberal arts and sciences of the soul to all who will hearken to its words. Its chairs are seats of learning and its pillars uphold an arch of universal education. Its trestleboards are inscribed with the eternal verities of all ages and upon those who comprehend its sacred depths has dawned the realization that within the Freemasonic Mysteries lie hidden the long-lost arcana sought by all peoples since the genesis of human reason.

The philosophic power of Freemasonry lies in its symbols—its priceless heritage from the Mystery schools of antiquity. In a letter to Robert Freke Gould, Albert Pike writes:

"It began to shape itself to my intellectual vision into something more imposing and majestic, solemnly mysterious and grand. It seemed to me like the Pyramids in their loneliness, in whose yet undiscovered chambers may be hidden, for the enlightenment of coming generations, the sacred books of the Egyptians, so long lost to the world; like the Sphinx half buried in the desert. In its symbolism, which and its spirit of brotherhood are its essence, Freemasonry is more ancient than any of the world's living religions. It has the symbols and doctrines which, older than himself, Zarathustra inculcated; and it seemed to me a spectacle sublime, yet pitiful—the ancient Faith of our ancestors holding out to the world its symbols once so eloquent, and mutely and in vain asking for an interpreter. And so I came at last to see that the true greatness and majesty of Freemasonry consist in its proprietorship of that and its other symbols; and that its symbolism is its soul."

Though the temples of Thebes and Karnak be now but majestic heaps of broken and time-battered stone, the spirit of Egyptian philosophy still marches triumphant through the centuries. Though the rock-hewn sanctuaries of the ancient Brahmins be now deserted and their carvings crumbled into dust, still the wisdom of the Vedas endures. Through the oracles be silenced and the House of the Mysteries be now but rows of ghostly columns, still shines the spiritual glory of Hellas with luster undiminished. Though Zoroaster, Hermes, Pythagoras, Plato, and Aristotle are now but dim memories in a world once rocked by the transcendency of their intellectual genius, still in the mystic temple of Freemasonry these god-men live again in their words and symbols; and the candidate, passing through the initiations, feels himself face-to-face with these illumined hierophants of days long past.

XLI

Mystic Christianity

he true story of the life of Jesus of Nazareth has never been unfolded to the world, either in the accepted Gospels or in the Apocrypha, although a few stray hints may be found in some of the commentaries written by the ante-Nicene Fathers. The facts concerning His identity and mission are among the priceless mysteries preserved to this day in the secret vaults beneath the "Houses of the Brethren." To a few of the Knights Templars, who were initiated into the arcana of the Druses, Nazarenes, Essenes, Johannites, and other sects still inhabiting the remote and inaccessible fastnesses of the Holy Land, part of the strange story was told. The knowledge of the Templars concerning the early history of Christianity was undoubtedly one of the main reasons for their persecution and final annihilation. The discrepancies in the writings of the early Church Fathers not only are irreconcilable, but demonstrate beyond question that even during the first five centuries after Christ these learned men had for the basis of their writings little more substantial than folklore and hearsay. To the easy believer everything is possible and there are no problems. The unemotional person in search of facts, however, is confronted by a host of problems with uncertain factors, of which the following are typical:

According to popular conception, Jesus was crucified during the thirty-third year of His life and in the third year of His ministry following His baptism. About A.D. 180, St. Irenæus, Bishop of Lyons, one of the most eminent of the ante-Nicene theologians, wrote *Against Heresies,* an attack on the doctrines of the Gnostics. In this work Irenæus declared upon the authority of the Apostles themselves that Jesus lived to old age. To quote: "They, however, that they may establish their false opinion regarding that which is written, 'to proclaim the acceptable year of the Lord,' maintain that He preached for one year only, and then suffered in the twelfth month. [In speaking thus], they are forgetful of their

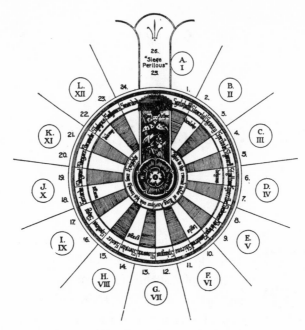

FROM JENNINGS' *THE ROSICRUCIANS, THEIR RITES AND MYSTERIES.*

THE ROUND TABLE OF KING ARTHUR.

According to tradition, Arthur, when a boy of fifteen, was crowned King of Britain, in A.D. 516. Soon after his ascension to the throne he founded the Order of the Knights of the Round Table at Windsor. Thereafter the Knights met annually at Carleon, Winchester, or at Camelot, to celebrate Pentecost. From all parts of Europe came the brave and the bold, seeking admission into this noble order of British knighthood. Nobility, virtue, and valor were its requirements, and those possessing these qualities to a marked degree were welcomed to King Arthur's court at Camelot. Having gathered the bravest and noblest Knights of Europe about him, King Arthur chose twenty-four who excelled all the others in daring and integrity and formed of them his Circle of the Round Table. According to legend, each of these Knights was so great in dignity and power that none could occupy a more exalted seat than another, so when they gathered at the table to celebrate the anniversary of their foundation it was necessary to use a round table that all might occupy chairs of equal importance.

While it is probable that the Order of the Round Table had its distinctive rituals and symbols, the knowledge of them has not survived the ages. Elias Ashmole, in his volume on the Order of the Garter, inserted a double-page plate showing the insignia of all the orders of knighthood, the block set aside for the symbol of the Round Table being left blank. The chief reason for the loss of the symbolism of the Round Table was the untimely death of King Arthur upon the field of Kamblan (A.D. 542) in the forty-first year of his life. While he destroyed his bitter enemy, Mordred, in this famous battle, it cost him not only his own life but the lives of nearly all his Knights of the Round Table, who died defending their commander.

own disadvantage, destroying His whole work, and robbing Him of that age which is both more necessary and more honourable than any other; that more advanced age, I mean, during which also as a teacher He excelled all others. For how could He have had His disciples, if He did not teach? And how could He have taught, unless He had reached the age of a Master? For when He came to be baptised, He had not yet completed His thirtieth year, but was beginning to be about thirty years of age (for thus Luke, who has mentioned His years, has expressed it: 'Now Jesus was, as it were, beginning to be thirty years old,' when He came to receive baptism); and, (according to these men,) He preached only one year reckoning from His baptism. On completing His thirtieth year He suffered, being in fact still a young man, and who had by no means attained to advanced age. Now, that the first stage of early life embraces thirty years, and that this extends onward to the fortieth year, every one will admit; but from the fourtieth and fiftieth year a man begins to decline towards old age, *which Our Lord possessed while He still fulfilled the office of a Teacher, even as the Gospel and all the elders testify;* those who were conversant in Asia with John, the disciple of the Lord, (affirming) that John conveyed to them that information. And he remained among them up to the time of Trajan. Some of them, moreover, saw not only John, but the other apostles also, and heard the very same account from them, and bear testimony as to the (validity of) the statement. Whom then should we rather believe? Whether such men as these, or Ptolemæus, who never saw the apostles, and who never even in his dreams attained to the slightest trace of an apostle?"

Commenting on the foregoing passage, Godfrey Higgins remarks that it has fortunately escaped the hands of those destroyers who have attempted to render the Gospel narratives consistent by deleting all such statements. He also notes that the doctrine of the crucifixion was a *vexata questio* among Christians even during the second century. "The evidence of Irenæus," he says, "cannot be touched. On every principle of sound criticism, and of the doctrine of probabilities, it is unimpeachable."

It should further be noted that Irenæus prepared this statement to contradict another apparently current in his time to the effect that the ministry of Jesus lasted but *one* year. Of all the early Fathers, Irenæus, writing within eighty years after the death of St. John the Evangelist, should have had reasonably accurate information. If the disciples themselves related that Jesus lived to advanced age in the body, why has the mysterious number 33 been arbitrarily chosen to symbolize the duration of His life? Were the incidents in the life of Jesus purposely altered so that His actions would fit more closely into the pattern established by the numerous Savior-Gods who preceded Him? That these analogies were recognized and used as a leverage in converting the Greeks and Romans is evident from a perusal of the writings of Justin Martyr, another second-century authority. In his *Apology*, Justin addresses the pagans thus:

"And when we say also that the Word, who is the first-birth of God, was produced without sexual union, and that He, Jesus Christ, our Teacher, was crucified and died, and rose again, and ascended into heaven, we propound nothing different from what you believe regarding those whom you esteem sons of Jupiter. * * * And if we assert that the Word of God was born of God in a peculiar manner, different from ordinary generation, let this, as said above, be no extraordinary thing to you, who say that Mercury is the angelic word of God. But if any one objects that He was crucified, in this also He is on a par with those reputed sons of Jupiter of yours, who suffered as we have now enumerated."

From this it is evident that the first missionaries of the Christian Church were far more willing to admit the other similarities between their faith and the faiths of the pagans than were their successors in later centuries.

In an effort to solve some of the problems arising from any attempt to chronicle accurately the life of Jesus, it has been suggested that there may have lived in Syria at that time two or more religious teachers bearing the name *Jesus, Jehoshua* or *Joshua,* and that the lives of these men may have been confused in the Gospel stories. In his *Secret Sects of Syria and the Lebanon,* Bernard H. Springett, a Masonic author, quotes from an early book, the name of which he was not at liberty to disclose because of its connection with the ritual of a sect. The last part of his quotation is germane to the subject at hand:

"But Jehovah prospered the seed of the Essenians, in holiness and love, for many generations. Then came the chief of the angels, according to the commandment of GOD, to raise up an heir to the Voice of Jehovah. And, in four generations more, an heir was born, and named Joshua, and he was the child of Joseph and Mara, devout worshippers of Jehovah, who stood aloof from all other people save the Essenians. And this Joshua, in Nazareth, reestablished Jehovah, and restored many of the lost rites and ceremonies. In the thirty-sixth year of his age he was stoned to death in Jerusalem * * *."

Within the last century several books have been published to supplement the meager descriptions in the Gospels of Jesus and His ministry. In some instances these narratives claim to be founded upon early manuscripts recently discovered; in others, upon direct spiritual revelation. Some of these writings are highly plausible, while others are incredible. There are persistent rumors that Jesus visited and studied in both Greece and India, and that a coin struck in His honor in India during the first century has been discovered. Early Christian records are known to exist in Tibet, and the monks of a Buddhist monastery in Ceylon still preserve a record which indicates that Jesus sojourned with them and became conversant with their philosophy.

Although early Christianity shows every evidence of Oriental influence, this is a subject the modern church declines to discuss. If it is ever established beyond question that Jesus was an initiate of the pagan Greek or Asiatic Mysteries, the effect upon the more conservative members of the Christian faith is likely to be cataclysmic. If Jesus was God incarnate, as the solemn councils of the church discovered, why is He referred to in the New Testament as "called of

God an high priest after the order of Melchizedek"? The words "after the order" make Jesus one of a line or order of which there must have been others of equal or even superior dignity. If the "Melchizedeks" were the divine or priestly rulers of the nations of the earth before the inauguration of the system of temporal rulers, then the statements attributed to St. Paul would indicate that Jesus either was one of these "philosophic elect" or was attempting to reestablish their system of government. It will be remembered that Melchizedek also performed the same ceremony of the drinking of wine and the breaking of bread as did Jesus at the Last Supper.

George Faber declares the original name of Jesus was Jescua Hammassiah. Godfrey Higgins has discovered two references, one in the *Midrashjoheleth* and the other in the *Abodazara* (early Jewish commentaries on the Scriptures), to the effect that the surname of Joseph's family was *Panther,* for in both of these works it is stated that a man was healed "in the name of Jesus ben Panther." The name *Panther* establishes a direct connection between Jesus and Bacchus—who was nursed by panthers and is sometimes depicted riding either on one of these animals or in a chariot drawn by them. The skin of the panther was also sacred in certain of the Egyptian initiatory ceremonials. The monogram *IHS,* now interpreted to mean *Iesus Hominum Salvator* (Jesus Savior of Men), is another direct link between the Christian and the Bacchic rites. *IHS* is derived from the Greek ΥΗΣ, which, as its numerical value (608) signifies, is emblematic of the sun and constituted the sacred and concealed name of Bacchus. (See *The Celtic Druids* by Godfrey Higgins.) The question arises, Was early Roman Christianity confused with the worship of Bacchus because of the numerous parallelisms in the two faiths? If the affirmative can be proved, many hitherto incomprehensible enigmas of the New Testament will be solved.

It is by no means improbable that Jesus Himself originally propounded as allegories the cosmic activities which were later confused with His own life. That the Χριστός, *Christos,* represents the solar power reverenced by every nation of antiquity cannot be controverted. If Jesus revealed the nature and purpose of this solar power under the name and personality of *Christos,* thereby giving to this abstract power the attributes of a god-man, He but followed a precedent set by all previous World-Teachers. This god-man, thus endowed with all the qualities of Deity, signifies the latent divinity in every man. Mortal man achieves deification only through at-one-ment with this divine Self. Union with the immortal Self is therefore "saved." This *Christos,* or divine man in man, is man's real hope of salvation—the living Mediator between abstract Deity and mortal humankind. As Atys, Adonis, Bacchus, and Orpheus in all likelihood were originally illumined men who later were confused with the symbolic personages whom they created as personifications of this divine power, so Jesus has been confused with the *Christos,* or god-man, whose wonders He preached. Since the *Christos* was the god-man imprisoned in every creature, it was the first duty of the initiate to liberate, or "resurrect," this Eternal One within himself. He who attained reunion with his *Christos* was consequently termed a *Christian,* or *Christened,* man.

One of the most profound doctrines of the pagan philosophers concerned the Universal Savior-God who lifted the souls of regenerated men to heaven through His own nature. This concept was unquestionably the inspiration for the words attributed to Jesus: "I am the way, the truth, and the life: no man cometh unto the Father but by me." In an effort to make a single person out of Jesus and His *Christos,* Christian writers have patched together a doctrine which must be resolved back into its original constituents if the true meaning of Christianity is to be rediscovered. In the Gospel narratives the *Christos* represents the perfect man who, having passed through the various stages of the "World Mystery" symbolized by the thirty-three years, ascends to the heaven sphere where he is reunited with his Eternal Father. The story of Jesus as now preserved is—like the Masonic story of Hiram Abiff—part of a secret initiatory ritualism belonging to the early Christian and pagan Mysteries.

During the centuries just prior to the Christian Era, the secrets of the pagan Mysteries had gradually fallen into the hands of the profane. To the student of comparative religion it is evident that these secrets, gathered by a small group of faithful philosophers and mystics, were reclothed in new symbolical garments and thus preserved for several centuries under the name of *Mystic Christianity.* It is generally supposed that the Essenes were the custodians of this knowledge and also the initiators and educators of Jesus. If so, Jesus was undoubtedly initiated in the same temple of Melchizedek where Pythagoras had studied six centuries before.

The Essenes—the most prominent of the early Syrian sects—were an order of pious men and women who lived lives of asceticism, spending their days in simple labor and their evenings in prayer. Josephus, the great Jewish historian, speaks of them in the highest terms. "They teach the immortality of the soul," he says, "and esteem that the rewards of righteousness are to be earnestly striven for." In another place he adds, "Yet is their course of life better than that of other men and they entirely addict themselves to husbandry." The name *Essenes* is supposed to be derived from an ancient Syrian word meaning "physician," and these kindly folk are believed to have held as their purpose of existence the healing of the sick in mind, soul, and body. According to Edouard Schuré, they had two principal communities, or centers, one in Egypt on the banks of Lake Maoris, the other in Palestine at Engaddi, near the Dead Sea. Some authorities trace the Essenes back to the schools of Samuel the Prophet, but most agree on either an Egyptian or Oriental origin. Their methods of prayer, meditation, and fasting were not unlike those of the holy men of the Far East. Membership in the Essene Order was possible only after a year of probation. This Mystery school, like so many others, had three degrees, and only a few candidates passed successfully through all. The Essenes were divided into two distinct communities, one consisting of celibates and the other of members who were married.

The Essenes never became merchants or entered into the commercial life of cities, but maintained themselves by agriculture and the raising of sheep for wool; also by such crafts as pottery and carpentry. In the Gospels and Apocrypha, Joseph, the father of Jesus, is referred to as both a carpenter and a potter. In the Apocryphal Gospel of Thomas and also that of Pseudo-Matthew, the child Jesus is described as making sparrows out of clay which came to life and flew away when he clapped his hands. The Essenes were regarded as among the better educated class of Jews and there are accounts of their having been chosen as tutors for the children of Roman officers stationed in Syria. The fact that so many artificers were listed among their number is responsible for the order's being considered as a progenitor of modern Freemasonry. The symbols of the Essenes include a number of builders' tools, and they were secretly engaged in the erection of a spiritual and philosophical temple to serve as a dwelling place for the living God.

Like the Gnostics, the Essenes were emanationists. One of their chief objects was the reinterpretation of the Mosaic Law according to certain secret spiritual keys preserved by them from the time of the founding of their order. It would thus follow that the Essenes were Qabbalists and, like several other contemporary sects flourishing in Syria, were awaiting the advent of the *Messiah* promised in the early Biblical writings. Joseph and Mary, the parents of Jesus, are believed to have been members of the Essene Order. Joseph was many years the senior of Mary. According to *The Protevangelium,* he was a widower with grown sons, and in the *Gospel of Pseudo-Matthew* he refers to Mary as a little child less in age than his own grandchildren. In her infancy Mary was dedicated to the Lord, and the Apocryphal writings contain many accounts of miracles associated with her early childhood. When she was twelve years old, the priests held counsel as to the future of this child who had dedicated herself to the Lord, and the Jewish high priest, bearing the breastplate, entered into the Holy of

Holies, where an angel appeared to him, saying, "Zacharias, go forth and summon the widowers of the people and let them take a rod apiece and she shall be the wife of him to whom the Lord shall show a sign." Going forth to meet the priests at the head of the widowers, Joseph collected the rods of all the other men and gave them into the keeping of the priests. Now Joseph's rod was but half as long as the others, and the priests on returning the rods to the widowers paid no attention to Joseph's but left it behind in the Holy of Holies. When all the other widowers had received back their wands, the priests awaited a sign from heaven, but none came. Joseph, because of his advanced age, did not ask for the return of his rod, for to him it was inconceivable that he should be chosen. But an angel appeared to the high priest, ordering him to give back the short rod which lay unnoticed in the Holy of Holies. As the high priest handed the rod to Joseph, a white dove flew from the end of it and rested upon the head of the aged carpenter, and to him was given the child.

The editor of *The Sacred Books and Early Literature of the East* calls attention to the peculiar spirit with which the childhood of Jesus is treated in most of the Apocryphal books of the New Testament, particularly in one work attributed to the doubting Thomas, the earliest known Greek version of which dates from about A.D. 200: "The child Christ is represented almost as an imp, cursing and destroying those who annoy him." This Apocryphal work, calculated to inspire its readers with fear and trembling, was popular during the Middle Ages because it was in full accord with the cruel and persecuting spirit of mediæval Christianity. Like many other early sacred books, the book of Thomas was fabricated for two closely allied purposes: first, to outshine the pagans in miracle working; second, to inspire all unbelievers with the "fear of the Lord." Apocryphal writings of this sort have no possible basis in fact. At one time an asset, the "miracles" of Christianity have become its greatest liability. Supernatural phenomena, in a credulous age interpolated to impress the ignorant, in this century have only achieved the alienation of the intelligent.

In *The Greek Gospel of Nicodemus* it is declared that when Jesus was brought into the presence of Pilate the standards borne by the Roman guards bowed their tops in homage to him in spite of every effort made by the soldiers to prevent it. In *The Letters of Pilate* the statement also appears that Cæsar, being wroth at Pilate for executing a just man, ordered him to be decapitated. Praying for forgiveness, Pilate was visited by an angel of the Lord, who reassured the Roman governor by promising him that all Christendom should remember his name and that when Christ came the second time to judge His people he (Pilate) should come before Him as His witness.

Stories like the foregoing represent the incrustations that have attached themselves to the body of Christianity during the centuries. The popular mind itself has been the self-appointed guardian and perpetuator of these legends, bitterly opposing every effort to divest the faith of these questionable accumulations. While popular tradition often contains certain basic elements of truth, these elements are usually distorted out of all proportion. Thus, while the generalities of the story may be fundamentally true, the details are hopelessly erroneous. Of truth as of beauty it may be said that it is most adorned when unadorned. Through the mist of fantastic accounts which obscure the true foundation of the Christian faith is faintly visible to the discerning few a great and noble doctrine communicated to the world by a great and noble soul. Joseph and Mary, two devout and holy-minded souls, consecrated to the service of God and dreaming of the coming of a Messiah to serve Israel, obeyed the injunctions of the high priest of the Essenes to prepare a body for the coming of a great soul. Thus of an immaculate conception Jesus was born. By *immaculate* is meant clean, rather than supernatural.

Jesus was reared and educated by the Essenes and later initiated into the most profound of their Mysteries. Like all great initiates, He must travel in an easterly direction, and the silent years of His life no doubt were spent in familiarizing Himself with that secret teaching later to be communicated by Him to the world. Having consummated the ascetic practices of His order, He attained to the *Christening*. Having thus reunited Himself with His own spiritual source, He then went forth in the name of the One who has been crucified since before the worlds were and, gathering about Him disciples and apostles, He instructed them in that secret teaching which had been lost—in part, at least—from the doctrines of Israel. His fate is unknown, but in all probability He suffered that persecution which is the lot of those who seek to reconstruct the ethical, philosophical, or religious systems of their day.

To the multitudes Jesus spoke in parables; to His disciples He also spoke in parables, though of a more exalted and philosophic nature. Voltaire said that Plato should have been canonized by the Christian Church, for, being the first propounder of the *Christos* mystery, he contributed more to its fundamental doctrines than any other single individual. Jesus disclosed to His disciples that the lower world is under the control of a great spiritual being which had fashioned it according to the will of the Eternal Father. The mind of this great angel was both the mind of the world and also the worldly mind. So that men should not die of worldliness the Eternal Father sent unto creation the eldest and most exalted of His powers—the Divine Mind. This Divine Mind offered Itself as a living sacrifice and was broken up and eaten by the world. Having given Its spirit and Its body at a secret and sacred supper to the twelve manners of rational creatures, this Divine Mind became a part of every living thing. Man was thereby enabled to use this power as a bridge across which he might pass and attain immortality. He who lifted up his soul to this Divine Mind and served It was righteous and, having attained righteousness, liberated this Divine Mind, which thereupon returned again in glory to Its own divine source. And because He had brought to them this knowledge, the disciples said one to another: "Lo, He is Himself this Mind personified!"

The Arthurian Cycle and Legend of the Holy Grail

According to legend, the body of the *Christos* (the Spiritual Law) was given into the keeping of two men, of whom the Gospels make but brief mention. These were Nicodemus and Joseph of Arimathea, both devout men who, though not listed among the disciples or apostles of the *Christos,* were of all men chosen to be custodians of His sacred remains. Joseph of Arimathea was one of the initiated brethren and is called by A. E. Waite, in his *A New Encyclopædia of Freemasonry,* "the first bishop of Christendom." Just as the temporal (or visible) power of the Holy See was established by St. Peter(?), so the spiritual (or invisible) body of the faith was entrusted to the "Secret Church of the Holy Grail" through apostolic succession from Joseph of Arimathea, into whose keeping had been given the perpetual symbols of the covenant—the ever-flowing cup and the bleeding spear.

Presumably obeying instructions of St. Philip, Joseph of Arimathea, carrying the sacred relics, reached Britain after passing through many and varied hardships. Here a site was allotted to him for the erection of a church, and in this manner Glastonbury Abbey was founded. Joseph planted his staff in the earth and it took root, becoming a miraculous thorn bush which blossomed twice a year and which is now called the Glastonbury thorn. The end of the life of Joseph of Arimathea is unknown. By some it is believed that, like Enoch, he was translated; by others, that he was buried in Glastonbury Abbey. Repeated attempts have been made to find the Holy Grail, which many believe to have been hidden in a crypt beneath the ancient abbey. The Glastonbury chalice recently discovered and by the devout supposed to be the original Sangreal can scarcely be accepted as genuine by the critical investigator. Beyond its inherent interest as a relic, like the famous Antioch chalice it actually proves nothing when it is realized that practically little more was known about the Christian Mysteries eighteen centuries ago than can be discovered today.

The origin of the Grail myth, as of nearly every other element in the great drama, is curiously elusive. Sufficient foundation for it may be found in the folklore of the British Isles, which contains many accounts of magic cauldrons, kettles, cups, and drinking horns. The earliest Grail legends describe the cup as a veritable horn of plenty. Its contents were inexhaustible and those who served it never hungered or thirsted. One account states that no matter how desperately ill a person might be he could not die within eight days of beholding the cup. Some authorities believe the Holy Grail to be the perpetuation of the holy cup used in the rites of Adonis and Atys. A communion cup or chalice was used in several of the ancient Mysteries, and the god Bacchus is frequently symbolized in the form of a vase, cup, or urn. In Nature worship the ever-flowing Grail signifies the bounty of the harvest by which the life of man is sustained; like Mercury's bottomless pitcher, it is the inexhaustible fountain of natural resource. From the evidence at hand it would indeed be erroneous to ascribe a purely Christian origin to the Grail symbolism.

In the Arthurian Cycle appears a strange and mysterious figure—Merlin, the magician. In one of the legends concerning him it is declared that when Jesus was sent to liberate the world from the bondage of evil, the Adversary determined to send an Antichrist to undo His labors. The Devil therefore in the form of a horrible dragon overshadowed a young woman who had taken refuge in sanctuary to escape the evil which had destroyed her family. When Merlin, her child, was born he partook of the characteristics of his human mother and demon father. Merlin, however, did not serve the powers of darkness but, being converted to the true light, retained only two of the supernatural powers inherited from his father: prophecy and miracle working. The story of Merlin's infernal father must really be considered as an allegorical allusion to the fact that he was a "philosophical son" of the serpent or dragon, a title applied to all initiates of the Mysteries, who thus acknowledge Nature as their mortal mother and wisdom in the form of the serpent or dragon as their immortal father. Confusion of the dragon and serpent with the powers of evil has resulted as an inevitable consequence from misinterpretation of the early chapters of Genesis.

Arthur while an infant was given into the keeping of Merlin, the Mage, and in his youth instructed by him in the secret doctrine and probably initiated into the deepest secrets of natural magic. With Merlin's assistance, Arthur became the leading general of Britain, a degree of dignity which has been confused with kingship. After Arthur had drawn the sword of Branstock from the anvil and thus established his divine right to leadership, Merlin further assisted him to secure from the Lady of the Lake the sacred sword *Excalibur*. After the establishment of the Round Table, having fulfilled his duty, Merlin disappeared, according to one account vanishing into the air, where he still exists as a shadow communicating at will with mortals; according to another, retiring of his own accord into a great stone vault which he sealed from within.

It is reasonably certain that many legends regarding Charlemagne were later associated with Arthur, who is most famous for establishing the Order of the Round Table at Winchester. Reliable information is not to be had concerning the ceremonies and initiatory rituals of the "Table Round." In one story the Table was endowed with the powers of expansion and contraction so that fifteen or fifteen hundred could be seated around it, according to whatever need might arise. The most common accounts fix the number of knights who could be seated at one time at the Round Table at either twelve or twenty-four. The twelve signified the signs of the zodiac and also the apostles of Jesus. The knights' names and also their heraldic arms were emblazoned upon their chairs. When twenty-four are shown seated at the Table, each of the twelve signs of the zodiac is divided into two parts—a light and a dark half—to signify the nocturnal and diurnal phases of each sign. As each sign of the zodiac is ascending for two hours every day, so the twenty-four knights represent the hours, the twenty-four elders before the throne in *Revelation,* and twenty-four Persian deities who represent the spirits of the divisions of the day. In the center of the Table was the symbolic rose of the Passion of Our Lord Jesus Christ, the symbol of resurrection in that He "rose" from the dead. There was also a mysterious empty seat called the *Siege Perilous* in which none might sit except he who was successful in his quest for the Holy Grail.

In the personality of Arthur is to be found a new form of the ever-recurrent cosmic myth. The prince of Britain is the sun, his knights are the zodiac, and his flashing sword may be the sun's ray with which he fights and vanquishes the dragons of darkness or it may represent the earth's axis. Arthur's Round Table is the universe; the *Siege Perilous* the throne of the perfect man. In its terrestrial sense, Arthur was the Grand Master of a secret Christian-Masonic brotherhood of philosophic mystics who termed themselves *Knights.* Arthur received the exalted position of Grand Master of these Knights because he had faithfully accomplished the withdrawal of the sword (spirit) from the anvil of the base metals (his lower nature). As invariably happens, the historical Arthur soon was confused with the allegories and myths of his order until now the two are inseparable. After Arthur's death on the field of Kamblan his Mysteries ceased, and esoterically he was borne away on a black barge, as is so beautifully described by Tennyson in his *Morte d'Arthur.* The great sword *Excalibur* was also cast back into the waters of eternity—all of which is a vivid portrayal of the descent of cosmic night at the end of the Day of Universal Manifestation. The body of the historical Arthur was probably interred at Glastonbury Abbey, a building closely identified with the mystic rites of both the Grail and the Arthurian Cycle.

The mediæval Rosicrucians were undoubtedly in possession of the true secret of the Arthurian Cycle and the Grail legend, much of their symbolism having been incorporated into that order. Though the most obvious of all keys to the *Christos* mystery, the Grail legend has received the least consideration.

XLII

The Cross and the Crucifixion
In Pagan and Christian Mysticism

ne of the most interesting legends concerning the cross is that preserved in *Aurea Legenda,* by Jacobus de Vorgaine. The story is to the effect that Adam, feeling the end of his life was near, entreated his son Seth to make a pilgrimage to the Garden of Eden and secure from the angel on guard at the entrance the *Oil of Mercy* which God had promised mankind. Seth did not know the way; but his father told him it was in an eastward direction, and the path would be easy to follow, for when Adam and Eve were banished from the Garden of the Lord, upon the path which their feet had trod the grass had never grown.

Seth, following the directions of his father, discovered the Garden of Eden without difficulty. The angel who guarded the gate permitted him to enter, and in the midst of the garden Seth beheld a great tree, the branches of which reached up to heaven. The tree was in the form of a cross, and stood on the brink of a precipice which led downward into the depths of hell. Among the roots of the tree he saw the body of his brother Cain, held prisoner by the entwining limbs. The angel refused to give Seth the *Oil of Mercy,* but presented him instead with three seeds from the Tree of Life (some say the Tree of Knowledge). With these Seth returned to his father, who was so overjoyed that he did not desire to live longer. Three days later he died, and the three seeds were buried in his mouth, as the angel had instructed. The seeds became a sapling with three trunks in one, which absorbed into itself the blood of Adam, so that the life of Adam was in the tree. Noah dug up this tree by the roots and took it with him into the Ark. After the waters subsided, he buried the skull of Adam under Mount Calvary, and planted the tree on the summit of Mount Lebanon.

HISTORY OF THE HOLY CROSS.

(1) Adam directing Seth how to reach the Garden of Eden. (2) Seth placing the three seeds from the Tree of Life under the tongue of the dead Adam. (3) The Queen of Sheba, refusing to place her feet upon the sacred tree, forded the stream. (4) Placing the sacred tree over the door of Solomon's Temple. (5) The crucifixion of Christ upon a cross made from the wood of the holy tree. (6) Distinguishing the true cross from the other two by testing its power to raise a corpse to life.

Moses beheld a visionary being in the midst of this tree (the burning bush) and from it cut the magical rod with which he was able to bring water out of a stone. But because he failed to call upon the Lord the second time he struck the rock he was not permitted to carry the sacred staff into the Promised Land; so he planted it in the hills of Moab. After much searching, King David discovered the tree; and his son, Solomon, tried to use it for a pillar in his Temple, but his carpenters could not cut it so that it would fit; it was always either too long or too short. At last, disgusted, they cast it aside and used it for a bridge to connect Jerusalem with the surrounding hills. When the Queen of Sheba came to visit King Solomon she was expected to walk across this bridge. Instead, when she beheld the tree, she refused to put her foot upon it, but, after kneeling and praying, removed her sandals and forded the stream. This so impressed

King Solomon that he ordered the log to be overlaid with golden plates and placed above the door of his Temple. There it remained until his covetous grandson stole the gold, and buried the tree so that the crime would not be discovered.

From the ground where the tree was buried there immediately bubbled forth a spring of water, which became known as *Bethesda*. To it the sick from all Syria came to be healed. The angel of the pool became the guardian of the tree, and it remained undisturbed for many years. Eventually the log floated to the surface and was used as a bridge again, this time between Calvary and Jerusalem; and over it Jesus passed to be crucified. There was no wood on Calvary; so the tree was cut into two parts to serve as the cross upon which the Son of Man was crucified. The cross was set up at the very spot where the skull of Adam had been buried. Later, when the cross was discovered by the Empress Helena, the wood was found to be of four different varieties contained in one tree (representing the elements), and thereafter the cross continued to heal all the sick who were permitted to touch it.

The prevalent idea that the reverence for the cross is limited to the Christian world is disproved by even the most superficial investigation of its place in religious symbolism. The early Christians used every means possible to conceal the pagan origin of their symbols, doctrines, and rituals. They either destroyed the sacred books of other peoples among whom they settled, or made them inaccessible to students of comparative philosophy, apparently believing that in this way they could stamp out all record of the pre-Christian origin of their doctrines. In some cases the writings of various ancient authors were tampered with, passages of a compromising nature being removed or foreign material interpolated. The supposedly spurious passage in Josephus concerning Jesus is an example adduced to illustrate this proclivity.

The Lost Libraries of Alexandria

Prior to the Christian Era seven hundred thousand of the most valuable books, written upon parchment, papyrus, vellum, and wax, and also tablets of stone, terra cotta, and wood, were gathered from all parts of the ancient world and housed in Alexandria, in buildings specially prepared for the purpose. This magnificent repository of knowledge was destroyed by a series of three fires. The parts that escaped the conflagration lighted by Cæsar to destroy the fleet in the harbor were destroyed about A.D. 389 by the Christians in obedience to the edict of Theodosius, who had ordered the destruction of the Serapeum, a building sacred to Serapis in which the volumes were kept. This conflagration is supposed to have destroyed the library that Marcus Antonius had presented to Cleopatra to compensate in part for that burned in the fire of the year 51.

Concerning this, H. P. Blavatsky, in *Isis Unveiled,* has written: "They [the Rabbis of Palestine and the wise men] say that not all the rolls and manuscripts, reported in history to have been burned by Cæsar, by the Christian mob, in 389, and by the Arab General Amru, perished as it is commonly believed; and the story they tell is the following: At the time of the contest for the throne, in 51 B.C., between Cleopatra and her brother Dionysius Ptolemy, the Bruckion, which contained over seven hundred thousand rolls all bound in wood and fire-proof parchment, was undergoing repairs and a great portion of the original manuscripts, considered among the most precious, and which were not duplicated, were stored away in the home of one of the librarians. * * * Several hours passed between the burning of the fleet, set on fire by Cæsar's order, and the moment when the first buildings situated near the harbor caught fire in their turn; and * * * the librarians, aided by several hundred slaves attached to the museum, succeeded in saving the most precious of the rolls." In all probability, the books which were saved lie buried either in Egypt or in India, and until they are discovered the modern world must remain in ignorance concerning many great philosophical and mystical truths. The ancient world more clearly understood these *missing links*—the continuity of the pagan Mysteries in Christianity.

The Cross in Pagan Symbolism

In his article on the *Cross and Crucifixion* in the *Encyclopædia Britannica,* Thomas Macall Fallow casts much light on the antiquity of this ideograph. "The use of the cross as a religious symbol in pre-Christian times, and among non-Christian peoples, may probably be regarded as almost universal, and in very many cases it was connected with some form of nature worship."

Not only is the cross itself a familiar object in the art of all nations, but the veneration for it is an essential part of the religious life of the greater part of humanity. It is a common symbol among the American Indians—North, Central, and South. William W. Seymour states: "The Aztec goddess of rain bore a cross in her hand, and the Toltecs claimed that their deity, Quetzalcoatl, taught them the sign and ritual of the cross, hence his staff, or sceptre of power, resembled a crosier, and his mantle was covered with red crosses." (*The Cross in Tradition, History and Art.*)

The cross is also highly revered by the Japanese and Chinese. To the Pythagoreans the most sacred of all numbers was the 10, the symbol of which is an X, or cross. In both the Japanese and Chinese languages the character of the number 10 is a cross. The Buddhist wheel of life is composed of two crosses superimposed, and its eight points are still preserved to Christendom in the peculiarly formed cross of the Knights Templars, which is essentially Buddhistic. India has preserved the cross, not only in its carvings and paintings, but also in its architectonics; a great number of its temples—like the churches and cathedrals of Christendom—are raised from cruciform foundations.

On the *mandalas* of the Tibetans, heaven is laid out in the form of a cross, with a demon king at each of the four gates. A remarkable cross of great antiquity was discovered in the island caves of Elephanta in the harbor of Bombay. Crosses of various kinds were favorite motifs in the art of Chaldea, Phœnicia, Egypt, and Assyria. The initiates of the Eleusinian Mysteries of Greece were given a cross which they suspended about their necks on a chain, or cord, at the time of initiation. To the Rosicrucians, Alchemists, and Illuminati, the cross was the symbol of light, because each of the three letters L V X is derived from some part of the cross.

The Tau Cross

There are three distinct forms of the cross. The first is called the TAU (more correctly the TAV). It closely resembles the modern letter T, consisting of a horizontal bar resting on a vertical column, the two arms being of equal length. An oak tree cut off some feet above the ground and its upper part laid across the lower in this form was the symbol of the Druid god *Hu*. It is suspected that this

symbol originated among the Egyptians from the spread of the horns of a bull or ram (Taurus or Aries) and the vertical line of its face. This is sometimes designated as the *hammer* cross, because if held by its vertical base it is not unlike a mallet or gavel. In one of the Qabbalistic Masonic legends, CHiram Abiff is given a hammer in the form of a TAU by his ancestor, Tubal-cain. The TAU cross is preserved to modern Masonry under the symbol of the T square. This appears to be the oldest form of the cross extant.

THE TAU CROSS.

The TAU Cross was the sign which the Lord told the people of Jerusalem to mark upon their foreheads, as related by the Prophet Ezekiel. It was also placed as a symbol of liberation upon those charged with crimes but acquitted.

The TAU cross was inscribed on the forehead of every person admitted into the Mysteries of Mithras. When a king was initiated into the Egyptian Mysteries, the TAU was placed against his lips. It was tattooed upon the bodies of the candidates in some of the American Indian Mysteries. To the Qabbalist, the TAU stood for heaven and the Pythagorean *tetractys*. The *Caduceus* of Hermes was an outgrowth of the TAU cross. (See Albert Pike.)

The Crux Ansata

The second type was that of a T, or TAU, cross surmounted by a circle, often foreshortened to the form of an upright oval. This was called by the ancients the *Crux Ansata,* or the cross of life. It was the key to the Mysteries of antiquity and it probably gave rise to the more modern story of St. Peter's golden key to heaven. In the Mysteries of Egypt the candidate passed through all forms of actual imaginary dangers, holding above his head the Crux Ansata, before which the powers of darkness fell back abashed. The student is reminded of the words *In hoc signo vinces.* The TAU form of the cross is not unlike the seal of Venus, as Richard Payne Knight has noted. He states: "The cross in this form is sometimes observable on coins, and several of them were found in a temple of Serapis [the Serapeum], demolished at the general destruction of those edifices by the Emperor Theodosius, and were said by the Christian antiquaries of that time to signify the future life."

THE CRUX ANSATA.

Both the cross and the circle were phallic symbols, for the ancient world venerated the generative powers of Nature as being expressive of the creative attributes of the Deity. The Crux Ansata, by combining the masculine TAU with the feminine oval, exemplified the principles of generation.

Augustus Le Plongeon, in his *Sacred Mysteries Among the Mayas and Quiches,* notes that the Crux Ansata, which he calls *The Key to the Nile* and the *Symbol of Symbols,* either in its complete form or as a simple TAU, was to be seen adorning the breasts of statues and bas-reliefs at Palenque, Copan, and throughout Central America. He notes that it was always associated with water; that among the Babylonians it was the emblem of the water gods; among the Scandinavians, of heaven and immortality; and among the Mayas, of rejuvenation and freedom from physical suffering.

Concerning the association of this symbol with the *waters of life,* Count Goblet d'Alviella, in his *Migration of Symbols,* calls attention to the fact that an instrument resembling the Crux Ansata and called the *Nilometer* was used by the ancient Egyptians for measuring and regulating the inundations of the river

Nile. It is probable that this relationship to the Nile caused it to be considered the symbol of life, for Egypt depended entirely upon the inundations of this river for the irrigation necessary to insure sufficient crops. In the papyrus scrolls the Crux Ansata is shown issuing from the mouths of Egyptian kings when they pardoned enemies, and it was buried with them to signify the immortality of the soul. It was carried by many of the gods and goddesses and apparently signified their divine benevolence and life-giving power. The Cairo Museum contains a magnificent collection of crosses of many shapes, sizes, and designs, proving that they were a common symbol among the Egyptians.

The Roman and Greek Catholic Crosses

The third form of the cross is the familiar Roman or Greek type, which is closely associated with the crucifixion of Jesus Christ, although it is improbable that the cross used resembled its more familiar modern form. There are unlimited subvarieties of crosses, differing in the relative proportions of their vertical and horizontal sections. Among the secret orders of different generations we find compounded crosses, such as the triple TAU in the Royal Arch of Freemasonry and the double and triple crosses of both Masonic and Roman Catholic symbolism.

To the Christian the cross has a twofold significance. First, it is the symbol of the death of his Redeemer, through whose martyrdom he feels that he partakes of the glory of God; secondly, it is the symbol of humility, patience, and the burden of life. It is interesting that the cross should be both a symbol of life and a symbol of death. Many nations deeply considered the astronomical aspect of religion, and it is probable that the Persians, Greeks, and Hindus looked upon the cross as a symbol of the equinoxes and the solstices, in the belief that at certain seasons of the year the sun was symbolically crucified upon these imaginary celestial angles.

The fact that so many nations have regarded their Savior as a personification of the sun globe is convincing evidence that the cross must exist as an astronomical element in pagan allegory. Augustus Le Plongeon believed that the veneration for the cross was partly due to the rising of a constellation called the *Southern Cross,* which immediately preceded the annual rains, and as the natives of those latitudes relied wholly upon these rains to raise their crops, they viewed the cross as an annual promise of the approaching storms, which to them meant life.

There are four basic elements (according to both ancient philosophy and modern science), and the ancients represented them by the four arms of the cross, placing at the end of each arm a mysterious Qabbalistic creature to symbolize the power of one of these elements. Thus, they symbolized the element of earth by a bull; water by a scorpion, a serpent, or an eagle; fire by a lion; and air by a human head surrounded by wings. It is significant that the four letters inscribed upon parchment (some say wood) and fastened to the top of the cross at the time of the crucifixion should be the first letters of four Hebrew words which stand for the four elements: "*Iammin,* the sea or water; *Nour,* fire; *Rouach,* the air; and *Iebeschah,* the dry earth." (See *Morals and Dogma,* by Albert Pike.)

That a cross can be formed by opening or unfolding the surfaces of a cube has caused that symbol to be associated with the earth. Though a cross within a circle has long been regarded as a sign of the planet Earth, it should really be considered as the symbol of the composite element earth, since it is composed of the four triangles of the elements. For thousands of years the cross has been identified with the plan of salvation for humanity. The elements—salt, sulphur, mercury, and Azoth—used in making the Philosopher's Stone in Alchemy, were often symbolized by a cross. The cross of the four cardinal angles also had its secret significance, and Masonic parties of three still go forth to the four cardinal points of the compass in search of the Lost Word.

The material of which the cross was formed was looked upon as being an essential element in its symbolism. Thus, a golden cross symbolized illumination; a silver cross, purification; a cross of base metals, humiliation; a cross of wood, aspiration. The fact that among many nations it was customary to spread the arms in prayer has influenced the symbolism of the cross, which, because of its shape, has come to be regarded as emblematic of the human body. The four major divisions of the human structure—bones, muscles, nerves, and arteries—are considered to have contributed to the symbolism of the cross. This is especially due to the fact that the spinal nerves *cross* at the base of the spine, and is a reminder that "Our Lord was crucified also in Egypt."

Man has four vehicles (or mediums) of expression by means of which the spiritual Ego contacts the external universe: the physical nature, the vital nature, the emotional nature, and the mental nature. Each of these partakes in principle of one of the primary elements, and the four creatures assigned to them by the Qabbalists caused the cross to be symbolic of the compound nature of man.

The Crucifixion—A Cosmic Allegory

Saviors unnumbered have died for the sins of man and by the hands of man, and through their deaths have interceded in heaven for the souls of their executioners. The martyrdom of the *God-Man* and the redemption of the world through

His blood has been an essential tenet of many great religions. Nearly all these stories can be traced to sun worship, for the glorious orb of day is the Savior who dies annually for every creature within his universe, but year after year rises again victorious from the tomb of winter. Without doubt the doctrine of the crucifixion is based upon the secret traditions of the Ancient Wisdom; it is a constant reminder that the divine nature of man is perpetually crucified upon the animal organism. Certain of the pagan Mysteries included in the ceremony of initiation the crucifixion of the candidate upon a cross, or the laying of his body upon a cruciform altar. It has been claimed that Apollonius of Tyana (the Antichrist) was initiated into the Arcanum of Egypt in the Great Pyramid, where he hung upon a cross until unconscious and was then laid in the tomb (the coffer) for three days. While his body was unconscious, his soul was thought to pass into the realms of the immortals (the place of death). After it had vanquished death (by recognizing that life is eternal) it returned again to the body, which then rose from the coffer, after which he was hailed as a brother by the priests, who believed that he had returned from the land of the dead. This concept was, in substance, the teaching of the Mysteries.

The Crucified Saviors

The list of the deathless mortals who *suffered* for man that he might receive the boon of eternal life is an imposing one. Among those connected historically or allegorically with a crucifixion are Prometheus, Adonis, Apollo, Atys, Bacchus, Buddha, Christna, Horus, Indra, Ixion, Mithras, Osiris, Pythagoras, Quetzalcoatl, Semiramis, and Jupiter. According to the fragramentary accounts extant, all these heroes gave their lives to the service of humanity and, with one or two exceptions, died as martyrs for the cause of human progress. In many mysterious ways the manner of their death has been designedly concealed, but it is possible that most of them were crucified upon a cross or tree. The first friend of man, the immortal Prometheus, was crucified on the pinnacle of Mount Caucasus, and a vulture was placed over his liver to torment him throughout eternity by clawing and rending his flesh with its talons. Prometheus disobeyed the edict of Zeus by bringing fire and immortality to man, so for man he suffered until the coming of Hercules released him from his ages of torment.

Concerning the crucifixion of the Persian Mithras, J. P. Lundy has written: "Dupuis tells us that Mithra was put to death by crucifixion, and rose again on the 25th of March. In the Persian Mysteries the body of a young man, apparently dead, was exhibited, which was feigned to be restored to life. By his sufferings he was believed to have worked their salvation, and on this account he was called their Savior. His priests watched his tomb to the midnight of the vigil of the 25th of March, with loud cries, and in darkness; when all at once the light burst forth from all parts, the priest cried, Rejoice, O sacred initiated, your God is risen. His death, his pains, and sufferings, have worked your salvation." (See *Monumental Christianity.*)

In some cases, as in that of the Buddha, the crucifixion *mythos* must be taken in an allegorical rather than a literal sense, for the manner of his death has been recorded by his own disciples in the *Book of the Great Decease.* However, the mere fact that the symbolic reference to death upon a tree has been associated with these heroes is sufficient to prove the universality of the crucifixion story.

The East Indian equivalent of Christ is the immortal Christna, who, sitting in the forest playing his flute, charmed the birds and beasts by his music. It is supposed that this divinely inspired Savior of humanity was crucified upon a tree by his enemies, but great care has been taken to destroy any evidence pointing in that direction. Louis Jacolliot, in his book *The Bible in India,* thus describes the death of Christna: "Christna understood that the hour had come for him to quit the earth, and return to the bosom of him who had sent him. Forbidding his disciples to follow him, he went, one day, to make his ablutions on the banks of the Ganges * * *. Arriving at the sacred river, he plunged himself three times therein, then, kneeling, and looking to heaven, he prayed, expecting death. In this position he was pierced with arrows by one of those whose crimes he had unveiled, and who, hearing of his journey to the Ganges, had, with a strong troop, followed with the design of assassinating him * * *. The body of the God-man was suspended to the branches of a tree by his murderer, that it might become the prey of vultures. News of the death having spread, the people came in a crowd conducted by Ardjouna, the dearest of the disciples of Christna, to recover his sacred remains. But the mortal frame of the redeemer had disappeared—no doubt it had regained the celestial abodes * * * and the tree to which it had been attached had become suddenly covered with great red flowers and diffused around it the sweetest perfume." Other accounts of the death of Christna declare that he was tied to a cross-shaped tree before the arrows were aimed at him.

The existence in Moor's *The Hindu Pantheon* of a plate of Christna with nail wounds in his hands and feet, and a plate in Inman's *Ancient Faiths* showing an Oriental deity with what might well be a nail hole in one of his feet, should be sufficient motive for further investigation of this subject by those of unbiased minds. Concerning the startling discoveries which can be made along these lines, J. P. Lundy in his *Monumental Christianity* presents the following information: "Where did the Persians get their notion of this prophecy as thus interpreted respecting Christ, and His saving mercy and love displayed on the cross? Both by symbol and actual crucifix we see it on all their monuments. If it came from India, how did it get there, except from the one common and original centre of all primitive and pure religion? There is a most extraordinary plate, illustrative of the whole subject, which representation I believe to be anterior to Christianity. It is copied from Moor's *Hindu Pantheon,* not as a curiosity, but as a most singular monument of the crucifixion. I do not venture to give it a name, other than that of a *crucifixion in space.* * * * Can it be the Victim-Man, or the Priest and Victim both in one, of the Hindu mythology, who offered himself a sacrifice before the worlds were? Can it be Plato's second God who impressed himself on the universe in the form of the cross? Or is it his divine man who would be scourged, tormented, fettered, have his eyes burnt out; and lastly, having suffered all manner of evils, would be *crucified?* Plato learned his theology in Egypt and the East, and must have known of the crucifixion of Krishna, Buddha, Mithra [*et al*]. At any rate, the religion of India had its mythical crucified victim long anterior to Christianity, as a type of the real one [*Pro Deo et Ecclesia!*], and I am inclined to think that we have it in this remarkable plate."

The modern world has been misled in its attitude towards the so-called pagan deities, and has come to view them in a light entirely different from their true characters and meanings. The ridicule and slander heaped by Christendom upon Christna and Bacchus are excellent examples of the persecution of immortal principles by those who have utterly failed to sense the secret meaning of the allegories. Who was the crucified man of Greece, concerning whom vague rumors have been afloat? Higgins thinks it was Pythagoras, the true story of whose death was suppressed by early Christian authors because it conflicted with their teachings. Was it true also that the Roman legionaries carried on the field of battle standards upon which were crosses bearing the crucified Sun Man?

The Crucifixion of Quetzalcoatl

One of the most remarkable of the crucified World Saviors is the Central American god of the winds, or the Sun, Quetzalcoatl, concerning whose activities great secrecy was maintained by the Indian priests of Mexico and Central America. This strange immortal, whose name means *feathered snake,* appears to have come out of the sea, bringing with him a mysterious cross. On his garments were embellished clouds and red crosses. In his honor, great serpents carved from stone were placed in different parts of Mexico.

FROM KINGSBOROUGH'S *ANTIQUITIES OF MEXICO.*

THE CRUCIFIXION OF QUETZALCOATL.
(FROM THE CODEX BORGIANUS.)

Lord Kingsborough writes: "May we not refer to the seventy-third page of the Borgian MS., which represents Quexalcoatl both cruci-fied, and as it were cut in pieces for the cauldron, and with equal reason demand, whether anyone can help thinking that the Jews of the New World [Lord Kingsborough sought to prove that the Mexicans were descendants of the Jews] applied to their Messiah not only all the prophecies contained in the Old Testament relating to Christ, but likewise many of the incidents recorded of him in the Gospels."

The cross of Quetzalcoatl became a sacred symbol among the Mayas, and according to available records the Maya Indian angels had crosses of various pigments painted on their foreheads. Similar crosses were placed over the eyes of those initiated into their Mysteries. When Cortez arrived in Mexico, he brought with him the cross. Recognizing this, the natives believed that he was Quetzalcoatl returned, for the latter had promised to come back in the infinite future and redeem his people.

In *Anacalypsis,* Godfrey Higgins throws some light on the cross and its symbolism in America: "The Incas had a cross of very fine marble, or beautiful jasper, highly polished, of one piece, three-fourths of an ell in length, and three fingers in width and thickness. It was kept in a sacred chamber of a palace, and held in great veneration. The Spaniards enriched this cross with gold and jewels, and placed it in the cathedral of Cuzco. Mexican temples are in the form of a cross, and face the four cardinal points. Quexalcoatl is represented in the paintings of the Codex Borgianus nailed to the cross. Sometimes even the two thieves are there crucified with him. In Vol. II. plate 75, the God is crucified in the Heavens, in a circle of nineteen figures, the number of the Metonic cycle. A serpent is depriving him of the organs of generation. In the Codex Borgianus, (pp. 4, 72, 73, 75,) the Mexican God is represented crucified and nailed to the cross, and in another place hanging to it, with a cross in his hands. And in one instance, where the figure is not merely outlined, the cross is red, the clothes are coloured, and the face and hands quite black. If this was the Christianity of the German Nestorius, how came he to teach that the crucified Savior was black? The name of the God who was crucified was Quexalcoatl."

The crucifixion of the Word in space, the crucifixion of the dove often seen in religious symbolism—both of these are reminders of pagan overshadowing. The fact that a cross is formed by the spread wings of a bird in relation to its body is no doubt one of the reasons why the Egyptians used a bird to symbolize the immortal nature of man, and often show it hovering over the mummified body of the dead and carrying in one of its claws the sign of life and in the other the sign of breath.

The Nails of the Passion

The three nails of the Passion have found their way into the symbolism of many races and faiths. There are many legends concerning these nails. One of these is to the effect that originally there were four nails, but one was dematerialized by a Hebrew Qabbalist and magician just as they were about to drive it through the foot of the Master. Hence it was necessary to cross the feet. Another legend relates that one of the nails was hammered into a crown and that it still exists as the imperial diadem of a European house. Still another story has it that the bit on the bridle of Constantine's horse was a Passion nail. It is improbable, however, that the nails were made of iron, for at that time it was customary to use sharpened wooden pegs. Hargrave Jennings, in his *Rosicrucians, Their Rites and Mysteries,* calls attention to the fact that the mark or sign used in England to designate royal property and called the *broad arrow* is nothing more nor less than the three nails of the crucifixion grouped together, and that by placing them point to point the ancient symbol of the Egyptian TAU cross is formed.

In his *Ancient Freemasonry,* Frank C. Higgins reproduces the Masonic apron of a colossal stone figure at Quirigua, Guatemala. The central ornament of the apron is the three Passion nails, arranged exactly like the British broad arrow. That three nails should be used to crucify the Christ, three murderers to kill CHiram Abiff, and three wounds to slay Prince Coh, the Mexican Indian Osiris, is significant.

C. W. King, in his *Gnostics and Their Remains,* thus describes a Gnostic gem: "The Gnostic Pleroma, or combination of all the Æons [is] expressed by the outline of a man holding a scroll * * *. The left hand is formed like *three bent spikes or nails;* unmistakably the same symbol that Belus often holds in his extended hand on the Babylonian cylinders, afterwards discovered by the Jewish Cabalists in the points of the letter *Shin,* and by the mediæval mystics in the Three Nails of the Cross." From this point Hargrave Jennings continues King's speculations, noting the resemblance of the nail to an obelisk, or pillar, and that the Qabbalistic value of the Hebrew letter *Shin,* or *Sin,* is 300, namely, 100 for each spike.

The Passion nails are highly important symbols, especially when it is realized that, according to the esoteric systems of culture, there are certain secret centers of force in the palms of the hands and in the soles of the feet.

The driving of the nails and the flow of blood and water from the wounds were symbolic of certain secret philosophic practices of the Temple. Many of the Oriental deities have mysterious symbols on the hands and feet. The so-called footprints of Buddha are usually embellished with a magnificent sunburst at the point where the nail pierced the foot of Christ.

In his notes on the theology of Jakob Böhme, Dr. Franz Hartmann thus sums up the mystic symbolism of the crucifixion: "The cross represents terrestrial life, and the crown of thorns the sufferings of the soul within the elementary body, but also the victory of the spirit over the elements of darkness. The body is naked, to indicate that the candidate for immortality must divest himself of all claims for terrestrial things. The figure is nailed to the cross, which symbolizes the death and surrender of the self-will, and that it should not attempt to accomplish anything by its own power, but merely serve as an instrument wherein the Divine will is executed. Above the head are inscribed the letters: I. N. R. J. whose most important meaning is: In Nobis Regnat Jesus (Within ourselves reigns Jesus). But this signification of this inscription can be practically known only to those who have actually died relatively to the world of desires, and risen above the temptation for personal existence; or, to express it in other words, those who have become alive in Christ, and in whom thus the kingdom of Jesus (the holy love-will issuing from the heart of God) has been established." One of the most interesting interpretations of the crucifixion allegory is that which identifies the man Jesus with the personal consciousness of the individual. It is this personal consciousness that conceives of and dwells in the sense of separateness, and before the aspiring soul can be reunited with the ever-present and all-pervading Father this personality must be sacrificed that the Universal Consciousness may be liberated.

XLIII

The Mystery of
the Apocalypse

he presence of the Temple of Diana at Ephesus marked that city as sacred to the Mystery religion, for the Seven Wonders of the ancient world were erected to indicate the repositories of recondite knowledge. Of Ephesus, H. P. Blavatsky writes:

"It was a focus of the universal 'secret' doctrines; the weird laboratory whence, fashioned in elegant Grecian phraseology, sprang the quintessence of Buddhistic, Zoroastrian, and Chaldean philosophy. Artemis, the gigantic concrete symbol of theosophico-pantheistic abstractions, the great mother Multimamma, androgyne and patroness of the 'Ephesian writings,' was conquered by Paul; but although the zealous converts of the apostles pretended to burn all their books on 'curious arts,' τα περιεργα, enough of these remained for them to study when their first zeal had cooled off." (See *Isis Unveiled.*)

Being a great center of pagan learning, Ephesus has been the locale for many early Christian myths. The assertion has been made that it was the last domicile of the Virgin Mary; also that the tomb of St. John the Divine was located there. According to legend, St. John did not depart from this life in the usual manner but, selecting his vault, entered it while still alive, and closing the entrance behind him, vanished forever from mortal sight. A rumor was current in ancient Ephesus that St. John would sleep in his tomb until the return of the Savior, and that when the apostle turned over on his sepulchral couch the earth above moved like the coverlets of a bed.

Subjected to more criticism than any other book now incorporated in the New Testament, the Apocalypse—popularly accredited to St. John the Divine—is by far the most important but least understood of the Gnostic Christian

FROM JACOB BEHMEN'S WORKS.

THE THRONE OF GOD AND OF THE LAMB.

Before the throne of God was the crystal sea representing the Schamayim, or the living waters which are above the heavens. Before the throne also were four creatures—a bull, a lion, an eagle, and a man. These represented the four corners of creation, and the multitude of eyes with which they were covered are the stars of the firmament. The twenty-four elders have the same significance as the priests gathered around the statue of Ceres in the Greater Eleusinian Rite and also the Persian Genii, or gods of the hours of the day, who, casting away their crowns, glorify the Holy One. As symbolic of the divisions of time, the elders adore the timeless and enduring Spirit in the midst of them.

writings. Though Justin Martyr declared the Book of Revelation to have been written by "John, one of Christ's apostles," its authorship was disputed as early as the second century after Christ. In the third century these contentions became acute and even Dionysius of Alexandria and Eusebius attacked the Johannine theory, declaring that both the Book of Revelation and the Gospel according to St. John were written by one Cerinthus, who borrowed the name of the great apostle the better to foist his own doctrines upon the Christians. Later Jerome questioned the authorship of the Apocalypse and during the Reformation his objections were revived by Luther and Erasmus. The once generally accepted notion that the Book of Revelation was the actual record of a "mystical experience" occurring to St. John while that seer was an exile *in* the Isle of Patmos is now regarded with disfavor by more critical scholars. Other explanations have therefore been advanced to account for the symbolism permeating the volume and the original motive for its writing. The more reasonable of these theories may be summed up as follows:

First, upon the weight of evidence furnished by its own contents the Book of Revelation may well be pronounced a pagan writing—one of the sacred books of the Eleusinian or Phyrgian Mysteries. As a corollary, the real author of a work setting forth the profundities of Egyptian and Greek mysticism must have been an initiate himself and consequently obligated to write only in the symbolic language of the Mysteries.

Second, it is possible that the Book of Revelation was written to reconcile the seeming discrepancies between the early Christian and pagan religious philosophies. When the zealots of the primitive Christian Church sought to Christianize pagandom, the pagan initiates retorted with a powerful effort to paganize Christianity. The Christians failed but the pagans succeeded. With the decline of paganism the initiated pagan hierophants transferred their base of operations to the new vehicle of primitive Christianity, adopting the symbols of the new cult to conceal those eternal verities which are ever the priceless possession of the wise. The Apocalypse shows clearly the resultant fusion of pagan and Christian symbolism and thus bears irrefutable evidence of the activities of these initiated minds operating through early Christianity.

Third, the theory has been advanced that the Book of Revelation represents the attempt made by the unscrupulous members of a certain religious order to undermine the Christian Mysteries by satirizing their philosophy. This nefarious end they hoped to attain by showing the new faith to be merely a restatement of the ancient pagan doctrines, by heaping ridicule upon Christianity, and by using its own symbols toward its disparagement. For example, the star which fell to earth (Rev. viii. 10–11) could be construed to mean the Star of Bethlehem, and the bitterness of that star (called *Wormwood* and which poisoned mankind) could signify the "false" teachings of the Christian Church. While the last theory has gained a certain measure of popularity, the profundity of the Apocalypse leads the discerning reader to the inevitable conclusion that this is the least plausible of the three hypotheses. To those able to pierce the veil of its symbolism, the inspired source of the document requires no further corroborative evidence.

In the final analysis, true philosophy can be limited by neither creed nor faction; in fact it is incompatible with every artificial limitation of human thought. The question of the pagan or Christian origin of the Book of Revelation is, consequently, of little importance. The intrinsic value of the book lies in its magnificent epitome of the Universal Mystery—an observation which led

St. Jerome to declare that it is susceptible of seven entirely different interpretations. Untrained in the reaches of ancient thought, the modern theologian cannot possibly cope with the complexities of the Apocalypse, for to him this mystic writing is but a phantasmagoria the divine inspiration of which he is sorely tempted to question. In the limited space here available it is possible to sketch but briefly a few of the salient features of the vision of the seer of Patmos. A careful consideration of the various pagan Mysteries will assist materially also in filling the inevitable gaps in this abridgment.

In the opening chapter of the Apocalypse, St. John describes the *Alpha and Omega* who stood in the midst of the seven golden candlesticks. Surrounded by his flaming planetary regents, this Sublime One thus epitomizes in one impressive and mysterious figure the entire sweep of humanity's evolutionary growth—past, present, and future.

"The first stages of man's earthly development," writes Dr. Rudolph Steiner, "ran their course at a period when the earth was still 'fiery'; and the first human incarnations were formed out of the element of fire; at the end of his earthly career man will himself radiate his inner being outwards creatively by the force of the element of fire. This continuous development from the beginning to the end of the earth reveals itself to the 'seer,' when he sees on the astral plane the archetype of evolving man. * * * The beginning of the earthly evolution stands forth in the fiery feet, its end in the fiery countenance, and the complete power of the 'creative word,' to be finally won, is seen in the fiery source coming out of the mouth." (See *Occult Seals and Columns.*)

In his *Restored New Testament,* James Morgan Pryse traces the relationship of the various parts of the Alpha and Omega to the seven sacred planets of the ancients. To quote:

"The Logos-figure described is a composite picture of the seven sacred planets: he has the snowy-white hair of Kronos ('Father Time'), the blazing eyes of 'wide-seeing' Zeus, the sword of Ares, the shining face of Helios, and the *chiton* and girdle of Aphrodite; his feet are of mercury, the metal sacred to Hermes, and his voice is like the murmur of the ocean's waves (the 'many waters'), alluding to Selene, the Moon-Goddess of the four seasons and of the waters."

The seven stars carried by this immense Being in his right hand are the Governors of the world; the flaming sword issuing from his mouth is the Creative Fiat, or Word of Power, by which the illusion of material permanence is slain. Here also is represented, in all his symbolic splendor, the hierophant of the Phrygian Mysteries, his various insignia emblematic of his divine attributes. Seven priests bearing lamps are his attendants and the stars carried in his hand are the seven schools of the Mysteries whose power he administers. As one *born again* out of spiritual darkness into perfect wisdom, this archimagus is made to say: "I am he that liveth, and was dead; and, behold, I am alive forever more, Amen; and have the keys of hell and of death."

In the second and third chapters St. John delivers to the "seven churches which are in Asia" the injunctions received by him from the Alpha and Omega. The churches are here analogous to the rungs of a *Mithraic* ladder, and John, being "in the spirit," ascended through the orbits of the seven sacred planets until he reached the inner surface of the Empyrean.

"After the soul of the prophet," writes the anonymous author of *Mankind: Their Origin and Destiny,* "in his ecstatic state has passed in its rapid flight through the seven spheres, from the sphere of the moon to that of Saturn, or from the planet which corresponds to Cancer, the gate of men, to that of Capricorn, which is the gate of the gods, a new gate opens to him in the highest heaven, and in the zodiac, beneath which the seven planets revolve; in a word, in the firmament, or that which the ancients called crystallinum primum, or the crystal heaven."

When related to the Eastern system of metaphysics, these churches represent the *chakras,* or nerve ganglia, along the human spine, the "door in heaven" being the *brahmarandra,* or point in the crown of the skull (Golgotha), through which the spinal spirit fire passes to liberation. The church of Ephesus corresponds to the *muladhara,* or sacral ganglion, and the other churches to the higher ganglia according to the order given in Revelation. Dr. Steiner discovers a relationship between the seven churches and the divisions of the Aryan race. Thus, the church of Ephesus stands for the Arch-Indian branch; the church of Smyrna, the Arch-Persians; the church of Pergamos, the Chaldean-Egyptian-Semitic; the church of Thyatira, the Grecian-Latin-Roman; the church of Sardis, the Teuton-Anglo-Saxon; the church of Philadelphia, the Slavic; and the church of Laodicea, the Manichæan. The seven churches also signify the Greek vowels, of which *Alpha* and *Omega* are the first and the last. A difference of opinion exists as to the order in which the seven planets should be related to the churches. Some proceed from the hypothesis that Saturn represents the church of Ephesus; but from the fact that this city was sacred to the moon goddess and also that the sphere of the moon is the first above that of the earth, the planets obviously should ascend in their ancient order from the moon to Saturn. From Saturn the soul would naturally ascend through the door in the Empyrean.

In the fourth and fifth chapters St. John describes the throne of God upon which sat the Holy One "which was and is, and is to come." About the throne were twenty-four lesser seats upon which sat twenty-four elders arrayed in white garments and wearing crowns of gold. "And out of the throne proceeded lightnings and thunderings and voices: and there were seven lamps of fire burning before the throne, which are the seven Spirits of God." He who sat upon the

FROM KLAUBER'S *HISTORIAE BIBLICAE VETERIS ET NOVI TESTAMENTI.*

JOHN'S VISION OF THE NEW JERUSALEM.

In the upper left-hand corner is shown the destruction of Babylon, also the angel which cast the great millstone into the sea, saying, "Thus with violence shall that great city Babylon be thrown down and shall be found no more at all." Below is the horseman, called Faithful and True, casting the beast into the bottomless pit. At the lower right is the angel with the key to the bottomless pit, who with a great chain binds Satan for a thousand years. In the heavens above is represented one like unto the Son of Man, who carries a great sickle with which he reaps the harvests of the world. In the center is the Holy City, the New Jerusalem, with its twelve gates and the mountain of the Lamb rising in the midst thereof. From the throne of the Lamb pours the great river of crystal, or living water, signifying the spiritual doctrine: upon all who discover and drink of its waters is conferred immortality. Kneeling upon a high cliff, St. John gazes down upon the mystic city, the archetype of the perfect civilization yet to be. Above the New Jerusalem, in a great sunburst of glory, is the throne of the Ancient One, which is the light of those who dwell in the matchless empire of the spirit. Beyond the recognition of the uninitiated world is an ever-increasing aggregation composed of the spiritual elect. Though they walk the earth as ordinary mortals, they are of a world apart and through their ceaseless efforts the kingdom of God is being slowly but surely established upon earth. These illumined souls are the builders of the New Jerusalem, and their bodies are the living stones in its walls. Lighted by the torch of truth they carry on their work; through their activities the *golden age* will return to the earth and the power of sin and death will be destroyed. For this reason the wise declare that virtuous and illumined men, instead of ascending to heaven, will bring heaven down and establish it in the midst of earth itself.

throne held in His right hand a book sealed with seven seals which no man in heaven or earth had been found worthy to open. Then appeared a Lamb (Aries, the first and chief of the zodiacal signs) which had been slain, having seven horns (rays) and seven eyes (lights). The Lamb took the book from the right hand of Him that sat upon the throne and the four beasts and all the elders fell down and worshiped God and the Lamb. During the early centuries of the Christian Church the lamb was universally recognized as the symbol of Christ, and not until after the fifth synod of Constantinople (the "Quinisext Synod," A.D. 692) was the figure of the crucified man substituted for that of *Agnus Dei.*

As shrewdly noted by one writer on the subject, the use of a lamb is indicative of the Persian origin of Christianity, for the Persians were the only people to symbolize the first sign of the zodiac by a lamb.

Because a lamb was the sin offering of the ancient pagans, the early mystic Christians considered this animal as an appropriate emblem of Christ, whom they regarded as the sin offering of the world. The Greeks and the Egyptians highly venerated the lamb or ram, often placing its horns upon the foreheads of their gods. The Scandinavian god Thor carried a hammer made from a pair of ram's horns. The lamb is used in preference to the ram apparently because of its purity and gentleness; also, since the Creator Himself was symbolized by Aries, His Son would consequently be the little Ram or Lamb. The lambskin apron worn by the Freemasons over that part of the body symbolized by Typhon or Judas represents that purification of the generative processes which is a prerequisite to true spirituality. In this allegory the Lamb signifies the purified candidate, its seven horns representing the divisions of illuminated reason and in seven eyes the *chakras*, or perfected sense-perceptions.

The sixth to eleventh chapters inclusive are devoted to an account of the opening of the seven seals on the book held by the Lamb. When the first seal was broken, there rode forth a man on a white horse wearing a crown and holding in his hand a bow. When the second seal was broken, there rode forth a man upon a red horse and in his hand was a great sword. When the third seal was broken there rode forth a man upon a black horse and with a pair of balances in his hand. And when the fourth seal was broken there rode forth Death upon a pale horse and hell followed after him. The four horsemen of the Apocalypse may be interpreted to signify the four main divisions of human life. *Birth* is represented by the rider on the white horse who comes forth conquering and to conquer; the impetuosity of *youth* by the rider on the red horse who took peace from the earth; *maturity* by the rider on the black horse who weighs all things in the scales of reason; and *death* by the rider on the pale horse who was given power over a fourth part of the earth. In the Eastern philosophy these horsemen signify the four *yugas*, or ages, of the world which, riding forth at their appointed times, become for a certain span the rulers of creation.

Commenting on the twenty-fourth allocution of Chrysostom, in *The Origin of all Religious Worship*, Dupuis notes that each of the four elements was represented by a horse bearing the name of the god "who is set over the element." The first horse, signifying the fire ether, was called Jupiter and occupied the highest place in the order of the elements. This horse was winged, very fleet, and, describing the largest circle, encompassed all the others. It shone with the purest light, and on its body were the images of the sun, the moon, the stars, and all the bodies in the ethereal regions. The second horse, signifying the element of air, was Juno. It was inferior to the horse of Jupiter and described a smaller circle; in color was black but that part exposed to the sun became luminous, thus signifying the diurnal and nocturnal conditions of air. The third horse, symbolizing the element of water, was sacred to Neptune. It was of heavy gait and described a very small circle. The fourth horse, signifying the static element of earth, described as immovable and champing its bit, was the steed of Vesta. Despite their differences in temperature, these four horses lived harmoniously together, which is in accord with the principles of the philosophers, who declared the world to be preserved by the concord and harmony of its elements. In time, however, the racing horse of Jupiter burned the mane of the horse of earth; the thundering steed of Neptune also became covered with sweat, which overflowed the immovable horse of Vesta and resulted in the deluge of Deucalion. At last the fiery horse of Jupiter will consume the rest, when the three inferior elements—purified by reabsorption in the fiery ether—will come forth renewed, constituting "a new heaven and a new earth."

When the fifth seal was opened St. John beheld those who had died for the word of God. When the sixth seal was broken there was a great earthquake, the sun being darkened and the moon becoming like blood. The angels of the winds came forth and also another angel, who sealed upon their foreheads 144,000 of the children of Israel that they should be preserved against the awful day of tribulation. By adding the digits together according to the Pythagorean system of numerical philosophy, the number 144,000 is reduced to 9, the mystic symbol of man and also the number of initiation, for he who passes through the nine degrees of the Mysteries receives the sign of the cross as emblematic of his regeneration and liberation from the bondage of his own infernal, or inferior, nature. The addition of the three ciphers to the original sacred number 144 indicates the elevation of the mystery to the third sphere.

When the seventh seal was broken there was silence for the space of half an hour. Then came forth seven angels and to each was given a trumpet. When the seven angels sounded their trumpets—intoned the seven-lettered Name of the Logos—great catastrophes ensued. A star, which was called Wormwood, fell from heaven, thereby signifying that the secret doctrine of the ancients had been given to men who had profaned it and caused the wisdom of God to become a destructive agency. And another star—symbolizing the false light of human reason as distinguished from the divine reason of the initiate—fell from heaven and to it (materialistic reason) was given the key to the bottomless pit (Nature), which it opened, causing all manner of evil creatures to issue forth. And there came also a mighty angel who was clothed in a cloud, whose face was as the sun and his feet and legs as pillars of fire, and one foot was upon the waters and the other upon the land (the Hermetic *Anthropos*). This celestial being gave St. John a little book, bidding him eat it, which the seer did. The book is representative of the secret doctrine—that spiritual food which is the nourishment of the spirit. And St. John, being "in the spirit," ate his fill of the wisdom of God and the hunger of his soul was appeased.

The twelfth chapter treats of a great wonder appearing in the heavens: a woman clothed with the sun, the moon under her feet, and upon her head a crown of twelve stars. This woman represents the constellation of Virgo and also the Egyptian Isis, who, about to be delivered of her son Horus, is attacked by Typhon, the latter attempting to destroy the child predestined by the gods to slay the Spirit of Evil. The war in heaven relates to the destruction of the planet Ragnarok and to the fall of the angels. The virgin can be interpreted to signify the secret doctrine itself and her son the initiate born out of the "womb of the Mysteries." The Spirit of Evil thus personified in the great dragon attempted to control mankind by destroying the mother of those illumined souls who have labored unceasingly for the salvation of the world. Wings were given to the Mysteries (the virgin) and they flew into the wilderness; and the evil dragon tried to destroy them with a flood (of false doctrine) but the earth (oblivion) swallowed up the false doctrines and the Mysteries endured.

The thirteenth chapter describes a great beast which rose out of the sea, having seven heads and ten horns. Faber sees in this amphibious monster the Demiurgus, or Creator of the world, rising out of the Ocean of Chaos. While most interpreters of the Apocalypse consider the various beasts described therein as typical of evil agencies, this viewpoint is the inevitable result of unfamiliarity with the ancient doctrines from which the symbolism of the book is derived. Astronomically, the great monster rising out of the Sea is the constellation of Cetus (the whale). Because religious ascetics looked upon the universe itself as an evil and ensnaring fabrication, they also came to regard its very Creator as a weaver of delusions. Thus the great sea monster (the world) and its Maker (the Demiurgus), whose strength is derived from the Dragon of Cosmic Power, came to be personified as a beast of horror and destruction, seeking to swallow up the immortal part of human nature. The Seven heads of the monster represent the seven stars (spirits) composing the constellation of the Great Dipper, called by the Hindus *Rishis,* or Cosmic Creative Spirits. The ten horns Faber relates to the ten primordial patriarchs. These may also denote the ancient zodiac of ten signs.

The number of the beast (666) is an interesting example of the use of Qabbalism in the New Testament and among early Christian mystics. In the following table Kircher shows that the names of Antichrist as given by Iranæus all have 666 as their numerical equivalent.

T	300	Λ	30	A	1	Λ	30
∈	5	α	1	ν	50	α	1
ι	10	μ	40	τ	300	τ	300
τ	300	π	80	∈	5	∈	5
α	1	∈	5	μ	40	ι	10
ν	50	τ	300	ο	70	ν	50
		ι	10	ς	200	ο	70
		ς	200			ς	200
	___		___		___		___
	666		666		666		666

James Morgan Pryse also notes that according to this method of figuring, the Greek term ἡφρην, which signifies the lower mind, has 666 as its numerical equivalent. It is also well known to Qabbalists that 'Ιησους, Jesus, has for its numerical value another sacred and secret number—888. Adding the digits of the number 666 and again adding the digits of the sum gives the sacred number 9—the symbol of man in his unregenerate state and also the path of his resurrection.

The fourteenth chapter opens with the Lamb standing on Mount Zion (the eastern horizon), about Him gathered the 144,000 with the name of God written in their foreheads. An angel thereupon announces the fall of Babylon—the city of confusion or worldliness. Those perish who do not overcome worldliness and enter into the realization that spirit—and not matter—is enduring; for, having no interests other than those which are material, they are swept to destruction with the material world. And St. John beheld One like unto the Son of Man (Perseus) riding upon a cloud (the substances of the invisible world) and bearing in his hand a sharp sickle, and with the sickle the Shining One reaped the earth. This is a symbol of the Initiator releasing into the sphere of reality the higher natures of those who, symbolized by ripened grain, have reached the point of liberation. And there came another angel (Boötes)—Death—also with a sickle (Karma), who reaped the vines of the earth (those who have lived by the false light) and cast them into the winepress of the wrath of God (the purgatorial spheres).

The fifteenth to eighteenth chapters inclusive contain an account of seven angels (the Pleiades) who pour their vials upon the earth. The contents of their vials (the loosened energy of the Cosmic Bull) are called the seven last plagues. Here also is introduced a symbolic figure, termed "the harlot of Babylon," which is described as a woman seated upon a scarlet-colored beast having seven heads and ten horns. The woman was arrayed in purple and scarlet and bedecked with gold, precious stones, and pearls, having in her hand a golden cup full of abominations. This figure may be an effort (probably interpolated) to vilify Cybele, or Artemis, the Great Mother goddess of antiquity. Because the pagans venerated the *Mater Deorum* through symbols appropriate to the feminine generative principle they were accused by the early Christians of worshiping a courtesan. As nearly all the ancient Mysteries included a test of the neophyte's moral character, the temptress (the animal soul) is here portrayed as a pagan goddess.

In the nineteenth and twentieth chapters is set forth the preparation of that mystical sacrament called the marriage of the Lamb. The bride is the soul of the neophyte, which attains conscious immortality by uniting itself to its own spiritual source. The heavens opened once more and St. John saw a white horse, and the rider (the illumined mind) which sat upon it was called *Faithful and True*. Out of his mouth issued a sharp sword and the armies of heaven followed after him. Upon the plains of heaven was fought the mystic Armageddon—the last great war between light and darkness. The forces of evil under the Persian Ahriman battled against the forces of good under Ahura-Mazda. Evil was vanquished and the beast and the false prophet cast into a lake of fiery brimstone. Satan was bound for a thousand years. Then followed the last judgment; the books were opened, including the book of life. The dead were judged according to their works and those whose names were not in the book of life were cast into a sea of fire. To the neophyte, Armageddon represents the last struggle between the flesh and the spirit when, finally overcoming the world, the illumined soul rises to union with its spiritual Self. The judgment signifies the weighing of the soul and was borrowed from the Mysteries of Osiris. The rising of the dead from their graves and from the sea of illusion represents the consummation of the process of human regeneration. The sea of fire into which those are cast who fail in the ordeal of initiation signifies the fiery sphere of the animal world.

In the twenty-first and twenty-second chapters are pictured the new heaven and the new earth to be established at the close of Ahriman's reign. St. John, carried in the spirit to a great and high mountain (the brain), beheld the New Jerusalem descending as a bride adorned for her husband. The Holy City represents the regenerated and perfected world, the trued *ashlar* of the Mason, for the city was a perfect cube, it being written, "the length and the breadth and the height of it are equal." The foundation of the Holy City consisted of a hundred and forty-four stones in twelve rows, from which it is evident that the New Jerusalem represents the *microcosm,* patterned after the greater universe in which it stands. The twelve gates of this symbolic dodecahedron are the signs of the zodiac through which the celestial impulses descend into the inferior world; the jewels are the precious stones of the zodiacal signs; and the transparent golden streets are the streams of spiritual light along which the initiate passes on his path towards the sun. There is no material temple in that city, for God and the Lamb are the temple; and there is neither sun nor moon, for God and the Lamb are the light. The glorified and spiritualized initiate is here depicted as a city. This city will ultimately be united with the spirit of God and absorbed into the Divine Effulgency.

And St. John beheld a river, the Water of Life, which proceeded out of the throne of the Lamb. The river represents the stream pouring from the First Logos, which is the life of all things and the active cause of all creation. There also was the Tree of Life (the spirit) bearing twelve manner of fruit, whose leaves were for the healing of the nations. By the tree is also represented the year, which every month yields some good for the maintenance of existing creatures. Jesus then tells St. John that He is the root and the offspring of David and the bright and morning star (Venus). St. John concludes with the words, "The grace of our Lord Jesus Christ be with you all. Amen."

XLIV

The Faith of Islam

R epresentative of the attitude of Christendom toward Islam, till recent years at least, is Alexander Ross's postscript to the Anglicized version, published in 1649, of Sieur Du Ryer's French translation of the *Koran*. The author of the postscript directs the following invective against Mohammed and the Koran:

"Good Reader, the great Arabian Impostor now at last after a thousand years, is by the way of France arrived in England, and his Alcoran, or gallimaufry of errors, (a brat as deformed as the parent, and as full of heresies as his scald head was of scurvy) hath learned to speak English. * * * If you will take a brief view of the Alcoran, you shall find it a hodgepodge made up of these four ingredients: 1. Of Contradictions. 2. Of Blasphemy. 3. Of ridiculous Fables. 4. Of Lies."

The accusation of blasphemy is emphasized against Mohammed because he affirmed that God, being unmarried, was incapable of having a Son! The fallacy of this argument, however, is apparent from the Prophet's own views of the nature of God as contained in the second *sura* of the Koran:

"To Allah [God] belongeth the east and the west; therefore, whithersoever ye turn yourselves to pray, there is the face of Allah; for Allah is omnipresent and omniscient. They say, Allah hath begotten children: Allah forbid! To him belongeth whatever is in heaven, and on earth; all is possessed by him, the Creator of heaven and earth; and when he decreeth a thing, he only saith unto it, Be, and it is." In other words, the God of Islam has but to desire and the object of that desire at once comes into being, whereas the God of Alexander Ross must proceed in accord with the laws of human generation!

Mohammed, Prophet of Islam, "the desired of all nations," was born in Mecca, A.D. 570 (?) and died in Medina, A.D. 632, or in the eleventh year after

MOHAMMED'S NIGHT JOURNEY TO HEAVEN.

In the seventeenth *sura* of the Koran it is written that upon a certain night Mohammed was transported from the temple at Mecca to that of Jerusalem, but no details are given of the strange journey. In the *Mishkātu 'l-Masabih,* Mohammed is made to describe his ascent through the seven heavens into the icy presence of the many-veiled God and his subsequent return to his own bed, all in a single night. Mohammed was awakened in the night by the Angel Gabriel, who, after removing the Prophet's heart, washed the cavity with *Zamzam* water and filled the heart itself with faith and science. A strange creature, called *Alborak,* or the *lightning bolt,* was brought for the conveyance of the Prophet. Alborak is described as a white animal of the shape and size of a mule, with the head of a woman and the tail of a peacock. According to some versions, Mohammed merely rode Alborak to Jerusalem, where, dismounting upon Mount Moriah, he caught hold of the lower rung of a golden ladder lowered from heaven and, accompanied by Gabriel, ascended through the seven spheres separating the earth from the inner surface of the empyrean. At the gate of each sphere stood one of the patriarchs, whom Mohammed saluted as he entered the various planes. At the gate of the first heaven stood Adam; at the gate of the second, John and Jesus (sisters' sons); at the third, Joseph; at the fourth, Enoch; at the fifth, Aaron; at the sixth, Moses; and at the seventh, Abraham. Another order of the patriarchs and prophets is given which places Jesus at the gate of the seventh heaven, and upon reaching this point Mohammed is said to have requested Jesus to intercede for him before the throne of God.

the *Hegira*. Washington Irving thus describes the signs and wonders accompanying the birth of the Prophet:

"His mother suffered none of the pangs of travail. At the moment of his coming into the world a celestial light illumined the surrounding country, and the newborn child, raising his eyes to heaven, exclaimed: 'God is great! There is no God but God, and I am his prophet!' Heaven and earth, we are assured, were agitated at his advent. The Lake Sawa shrank back to its secret springs, leaving its borders dry; while the Tigris, bursting its bounds, overflowed the neighboring lands. The palace of Khosru the king of Persia shook on its foundations, and several of its towers were toppled to the earth. * * * In the same eventful night the sacred fire of Zoroaster, which, guarded by the Magi, had burned without interruption for upward of a thousand years, was suddenly extinguished, and all the idols in the world fell down." (See *Mahomet and His Successors*.)

While the Prophet was still but a toddling babe, the Angel Gabriel with seventy wings came to him, and cutting open the child, withdrew the heart. This Gabriel cleansed of the black drop of original sin which is in every human heart because of the perfidy of Adam and then returned the organ to its proper place in the Prophet's body. (See footnote in E. H. Palmer's translation of the *Qur'an*.)

In his youth Mohammed traveled with the Meccan caravans, on one occasion acted as armor-bearer for his uncle, and spent a considerable time among the Bedouins, from whom he learned many of the religious and philosophic traditions of ancient Arabia. While traveling with his uncle, Abu Taleb, Mohammed contacted the Nestorian Christians, having encamped on a certain night near one of their monasteries. Here the young Prophet-to-be secured much of his information concerning the origin and doctrines of the Christian faith.

With the passing years Mohammed attained marked success in business and when about twenty-six years old married one of his employers, a wealthy widow nearly fifteen years his senior. The widow, Khadijah by name, was apparently somewhat mercenary, for, finding her young business manager most efficient, she resolved to retain him in that capacity for life! Khadijah was a woman of exceptional mentality and to her integrity and devotion must be ascribed the early success of the Islamic cause. By his marriage Mohammed was elevated from a position of comparative poverty to one of great wealth and power, and so exemplary was his conduct that he became known throughout Mecca as "the faithful and true."

Mohammed would have lived and died an honored and respected Meccan had he not unhesitatingly sacrificed both his wealth and social position in the

service of the God whose voice he heard while meditating in the cavern on
Mount Hira in the month of Ramadan. Year after year Mohammed climbed the
rocky and desolate slopes of Mount Hira (since called *Jebel Nur,* "the mountain
of light") and here in his loneliness cried out to God to reveal anew the pure religion of Adam, that spiritual doctrine lost to mankind through the dissensions
of religious factions. Khadijah, solicitous over her husband's ascetic practices
which were impairing his physical health, sometimes accompanied him in his
weary vigil, and with womanly intuition sensed the travail of his soul. At last one
night in his fortieth year as he lay upon the floor of the cavern, enveloped in his
cloak, a great light burst upon him. Overcome with a sense of perfect peace and
understanding in the blessedness of the celestial presence, he lost consciousness. When he came to himself again the Angel Gabriel stood before him,
exhibiting a silken shawl with mysterious characters traced upon it. From these
characters Mohammed gained the basic doctrines later embodied in the Koran.
Then Gabriel spoke in a clear and wonderful voice, declaring Mohammed to be
the Prophet of the living God.

In awe and trembling, Mohammed hastened to Khadijah, fearing the vision
to have been inspired by the same evil spirits who served the pagan magicians so
greatly despised by him. Khadijah assured him that his own virtuous life would
be his protection and that he need fear no evil. Thus reassured, the Prophet
awaited further visitations from Gabriel. When these did not come, however,
such a despair filled his soul that he attempted self-destruction, only to be
stopped in the very act of casting himself over a cliff by the sudden reappearance
of Gabriel, who again assured the Prophet that the revelations needed by his
people would be given to him as necessity arose.

Possibly as a result of his lonely periods of meditation, Mohammed seemingly was subject to ecstatic swoons. On the occasions when the various *suras* of
the Koran were dictated he is said to have fallen unconscious, and, regardless of
the chill of the surrounding air, to have been covered with beads of perspiration.
Often these attacks came without warning; at other times he would sit wrapped
in a blanket to prevent a chill from the copious perspiration, and while apparently unconscious would dictate the various passages which a small circle of
trusted friends would either commit to memory or reduce to writing. On one
occasion in later life when Abu Bekr referred to the gray hairs in his beard,
Mohammed, lifting the end of his beard and looking at it, declared its whiteness
to be due to the physical agony attendant upon his periods of inspiration.

If the writings attributed to Mohammed be considered as merely the hal-
lucinations of an epileptic—and for that reason discounted—his Christian

detractors should beware lest with the doctrines of the Prophet they also undermine the very teachings which they themselves affirm, for many of the disciples, apostles, and saints of the early church are known to have been subject to nervous disorders. Mohammed's first convert was his own wife, Khadijah, who was followed by other members of his immediate family, a circumstance which moved Sir William Muir to note:

"It is strongly corroborative of Mohammed's sincerity that the earliest converts to Islam were not only of upright character, but his own bosom friends and people of his household; who, intimately acquainted with his private life, could not fail otherwise to have detected those discrepancies which ever more or less exist between the professions of the hypocritical deceiver abroad and his actions at home." (See *The Life of Mohammad.*)

Among the first to accept the faith of Islam was Abu Bekr, who became Mohammed's closest and most faithful friend, in fact his *alter ego.* Abu Bekr, a man of brilliant attainments, contributed materially to the success of the Prophet's enterprise, and in accord with the express wish of the Prophet became the leader of the faithful after Mohammed's death. A'isha, the daughter of Abu Bekr, later became the wife of Mohammed, thus still further cementing the bond of fraternity between the two men. Quietly, but industriously, Mohammed promulgated his doctrines among a small circle of powerful friends. When the enthusiasm of his followers finally forced his hand and he publicly announced his mission, he was already the leader of a strong and well-organized faction. Fearing Mohammed's growing prestige, the people of Mecca, waiving the time-honored tradition that blood could not be spilt within the holy city, decided to exterminate Islam by assassinating the Prophet. All the different groups combined in this undertaking so that the guilt for the crime might thereby be more evenly distributed. Discovering the danger in time, Mohammed left his friend Ali in his bed and fled with Abu Bekr from the city, and after adroitly eluding the Meccans, joined the main body of his followers that had preceded him to Yathrib (afterwards called Medina). Upon this incident—called the *Hegira* or "flight"—is based the Islamic chronological system.

Dating from the Hegira the power of the Prophet steadily grew until in the eighth year Mohammed entered Mecca after practically a bloodless victory and established it as the spiritual center of his faith. Planting his standard to the north of Mecca, he rode into the city, and after circling seven times the sacred *Caaba,* ordered the 360 images within its precincts to be hewn down. He then entered the Caaba itself, cleansed it of its idolatrous associations, and rededicated the structure to Allah, the monotheistic God of Islam. Mohammed next granted amnesty to all his enemies for their attempts to destroy him. Under his protection Mecca increased in power and glory, becoming the focal point of a great annual pilgrimage, which even to this day winds across the desert in the months of pilgrimage and numbers over threescore thousand in its train.

In the tenth year after the Hegira, Mohammed led the valedictory pilgrimage and for the last time rode at the head of the faithful along the sacred way leading to Mecca and the Black Stone. As the premonition of death was strong upon him, he desired this pilgrimage to be the perfect model for all the thousands that would follow.

"Conscious that life was waning away within him," writes Washington Irving, "Mahomet, during this last sojourn in the sacred city of his faith, sought to engrave his doctrines deeply in the minds and hearts of his followers. For this purpose he preached frequently in the Caaba from the pulpit, or in the open air from the back of his camel. 'Listen to my words,' would he say, 'for I know not whether, after this year, we shall ever meet here again. Oh, my hearers, I am but a man like yourselves; the angel of death may at any time appear, and I must obey his summons.'" While thus preaching, the very heavens are said to have opened and the voice of God spoke, saying: "This day I have perfected your religion, and accomplished in you my grace." When these words were uttered the multitude fell down in adoration and even Mohammed's camel knelt. (See *Mahomet and His Successors.*) Having completed the valedictory pilgrimage, Mohammed returned to Medina.

In the seventh year after the Hegira (A.H. 7) an attempt was made at Kheibar to poison the Prophet. As Mohammed took the first mouthful of the poisoned food, the evil design was revealed to him either by the taste of the meat or, as the faithful believe, by divine intercession. He had already swallowed a small portion of the food, however, and for the remainder of his life he suffered almost constantly from the effects of the poison. In A.H. 11, when his final illness came upon him, Mohammed insisted that the subtle effects of the poison were the indirect cause of his approaching end. It is related that during his last sickness he rose one night and visited a burial ground on the outskirts of Medina, evidently believing that he, too, would soon be numbered with the dead. At this time he told an attendant that the choice had been offered him of continuing his physical life or going to his Lord, and that he had chosen to meet his Maker.

Mohammed suffered greatly with his head and side and also from fever, but on June 8th seemed convalescent. He joined his followers in prayer and, seating himself in the courtyard, delivered a lecture to the faithful in a clear and powerful voice. Apparently he overtaxed his strength, for it was necessary to assist him into the house of A'isha, which opened into the court of the mosque. Here upon a rough pallet laid on the bare floor the prophet of Islam spent his last two hours on earth. When she saw that her aged husband was suffering intense pain, A'isha—then but a girl of twenty—lifting the gray head of the man she had known from infancy and who must have seemed more like a father than a husband, supported him in her arms until the end. Feeling that death was upon him, Mohammed prayed: "O Lord, I beseech Thee, assist me in the agonies of death." Then almost in a whisper he repeated three times: "Gabriel, come close unto me." (For details consult *The Life of Mohammad* by Sir William Muir.) In *The Hero as Prophet*, Thomas Carlyle writes thus of the death of Mohammed: "His last words were a prayer, broken ejaculations of a heart struggling-up in trembling hope towards its Maker."

Mohammed was buried under the floor of the apartment in which he died. The present condition of the grave is thus described:

"Above the Hujrah is a green dome, surmounted by a large gilt crescent, springing from a series of globes. Within the building are the tombs of Muhammad, Abū Bakr, and 'Umar, with a space reserved for the grave of our Lord Jesus Christ, who Muslims say will again visit the earth, and die and be buried at al-Madīnah. The grave of Fātimah, the Prophet's daughter, is supposed to be in a separate part of the building, although some say she was buried in Baqī'. The Prophet's body is said to be stretched full length on the right side, with the right palm supporting the right cheek, the face fronting Makkah. Close behind him is placed Abū Bakr, whose face fronts Muhammad's shoulder, and then 'Umar, who occupies the same position with respect to his predecessor. Amongst Christian historians there is a popular story to the effect that Muhammadans believed the coffin of their Prophet to be suspended in the air, which has no foundation whatever in Muslim literature, and Niebuhr thinks the story must have arisen from the rude pictures sold to strangers." (See *A Dictionary of Islam*.)

Concerning the character of Mohammed there have been the grossest misconceptions. No evidence exists to support the charges of extreme cruelty and licentiousness laid at his door. On the other hand, the more closely the life of Mohammed is scrutinized by dispassionate investigators, the more apparent become the finer qualities of his nature. In the words of Carlyle:

"Mahomet himself, after all that can be said about him, was not a sensual man. We so err widely if we consider this man as a common voluptuary, intent mainly on base enjoyments—nay, on enjoyments of any kind. His household was of the frugalest, his common diet barley bread and water. Sometimes for months there was not a fire once lighted on his hearth. * * * A poor, hard-working, ill-provided man; careless of what vulgar man toiled for. * * * They called him a Prophet, you say? Why, he stood there face to face with them; there, not enshrined in any mystery, visibly clouting his own cloak, cobbling his own shoes, fighting, counselling, ordering in the midst of them, they must have seen what kind of man he was, let him be called what you like! No emperor with his tiaras was obeyed as this man in a cloak of his own clouting."

Confused by the apparently hopeless task of reconciling the life of the Prophet with the absurd statements long accepted as authentic, Washington Irving weighs him in the scales of fairness.

"His military triumphs awakened no pride nor vainglory, as they would have done had they been effected for selfish purposes. In the time of his greatest power, he maintained the same simplicity of manners and appearances as in the days of his adversity. * * * It is this perfect abnegation of self, connected with this apparent heart-felt piety, running throughout the various phases of his fortune, which perplex one in forming a just estimate of Mahomet's character. * * * When he hung over the death-bed of his infant son Ibrahim, resignation to the will of God was exhibited in his conduct under this keenest of afflictions; and the hope of soon rejoining his child in Paradise was his consolation." (See *Mahomet and His Successors.*)

A'isha, questioned after the death of the Prophet concerning his habits, replied that he mended his own clothes, cobbled his own shoes, and helped her in the household duties. How far removed from Western concepts of Mohammed's sanguinary character is A'isha's simple admission that he loved most of all to sew! He also accepted the invitations of slaves and sat at meals with servants, declaring himself to be a servant. Of all vices he hated lying the most. Before his death he freed all his slaves. He never permitted his family to use for personal ends any of the alms or tithe money given by his people. He was fond of sweetmeats and used rain water for drinking purposes. His time he divided into three parts, namely: the first he gave to God, the second to his family, and the third to himself. The latter portion, however, he later sacrificed to the service of his people. He dressed chiefly in white but also wore red, yellow, and green. Mohammed entered Mecca wearing a black turban and bearing a black standard. He wore only the plainest of garments, declaring that rich and conspicuous raiment did not become the pious, and did not remove his shoes at prayer. He was particularly concerned with the cleanliness of his teeth and at the time of his death, when too weak to speak, indicated his desire for a toothpick. When fearful of forgetting something, the Prophet tied a thread to his ring. He once

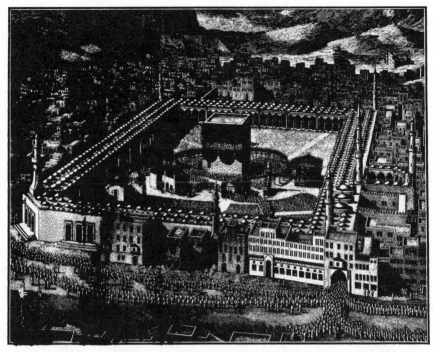

SECTION FROM PANORAMA OF MECCA IN D'OHSSON'S *TABLEAU GÉNÉRAL DE L'EMPIRE OTHOMAN.*

THE CAABA, THE HOLY PLACE OF ISLAM.

The *Caaba,* or cube-shaped bulding in the midst of the great court of the mosque at Mecca, is the most holy spot in the Islamic world. Toward it the followers of the Prophet must face five times a day at the appointed hours of prayer. Like the devotees of nearly all other faiths, the Mussulman originally faced the East while in prayer, but by a later decree he was ordered to turn his face toward Mecca.

Little is known of the history of the Caaba prior to its rededication as a Mohammedan mosque, other than that the building was a pagan temple. At the time the Prophet captured Mecca, the Caaba and surrounding court contained 360 idols, which were destroyed by Mohammed before he actually gained access to the shrine itself. The "Ancient House," as the Caaba is called, is an irregular cube measuring about 38 feet in length, 35 feet in height, and 30 feet in width. The length of each side wall varies slightly and that of the end walls over a foot. In the southeast corner of the wall at a convenient distance above the ground (about five feet) is embedded the sacred and mysterious black stone or aerolite of Abraham. When first given to that patriarch by the Angel Gabriel this stone was of such shining whiteness as to be visible from every part of the earth, but later it became black because of the sins of men. This black stone, oval in shape and about seven inches in diameter, was broken in the seventh century and is now held together by a silver mounting.

According to tradition, 2,000 years before the creation of the world the Caaba was first constructed in heaven, where a model of it still remains. Adam erected the Caaba on earth exactly below the spot in heaven occupied by the original, and selected the stones from the five sacred mountains: Sinai, al-Judī, Hirā, Olivet, and Lebanon. Ten thousand angels were appointed to guard the structure. At the time of the Deluge the sacred house was destroyed, but afterward was rebuilt by Abraham and his son Ishmael. (For details see *A Dictionary of Islam*). It is probable that the site of the Caaba was originally occupied by a prehistoric stone altar or ring of uncut monoliths similar to those of Stonehenge. Like the temple at Jerusalem, the Caaba has undergone many vicissitudes, and the present structure does not antedate the seventeenth century of the Christian Era. When Mecca was sacked in A.D. 930, the famous black stone was captured by the Carmathians, in whose possession it remained over twenty years, and it is a moot question whether the stone finally returned by them in exchange for a princely ransom was actually the original block or a substitute.

On the north side of the Caaba are the supposed graves of Hagar and Ishmael, and near the door (which is about seven feet above the ground) is the stone upon which Abraham stood while rebuilding the Caaba. Various coverings have always been thrown over the cube-shaped structure; the present drape, which is replaced annually, is a black brocade embroidered in gold. Small pieces of the old drape are cherished by pilgrims as holy relics.

Entrance to the Caaba is effected by a movable flight of steps. The interior is lined with varicolored marble, silver, and gilt. Although the building is generally conceived to be windowless, this point is disputed. Access to the roof is had through a silver-plated door. In addition to the sacred books the Caaba contains thirteen lamps. The great courtyard around the building contains a number of holy objects, and is bounded by a colonnade which originally consisted of 360 pillars. Opening into the courtyard are nineteen gates, the sacred and significant number of the Metonic Cycle and also the number of stones in the inner ring of Stonehenge. Seven great minarets tower above the Caaba, and one of the sacred ceremonials in connection with the building includes seven circumambulations about the central Caaba in an apparent effort to portray the motion of the celestial bodies.

had a very fine gold ring but, noting that his followers had taken to wearing similar rings in emulation of him, he removed his own and threw it away lest his followers form an evil habit. (See *The Life of Mohammad*.)

The most frequent, and apparently the most damaging, accusation brought against Mohammed is that of polygamy. Those who sincerely believe the harem to be irreconcilable with spirituality should with consistency move for the expurgation of the Psalms of David and the Proverbs of Solomon from the list of inspired writings, for the harem of Islam's Prophet was insignificant compared with that maintained by Israel's wisest king and the reputed favorite of the Most High! The popular conception that Mohammed taught that woman had no soul and could attain heaven only through marriage is not substantiated by the words and attitude of the Prophet during his lifetime. In a paper entitled *The Influence of Islam on Social Conditions*, read at the World's Parliament of Religions held in Chicago, in 1893, Mohammed Webb states the charge and answers it thus:

"It has been said that Mohammed and the Koran denied a soul to woman and ranked her with the animals. The Koran places her on a perfect and complete equality with man, and the Prophet's teachings often place her in a position superior to the male in some respects." Mr. Webb justifies his stand by quoting from the thirty-fifth verse of the thirty-third *sura* of the Koran:

"Verily the Moslems of either sex, and the true believers of either sex, and the devout men, and the devout women, and the men of veracity, and the women of veracity, and the patient men, and the patient women, and the humble men, and the humble women, and the alms-givers of either sex, and the men who fast, and the women who fast, and the chaste men, and the chaste women, and those of either sex who remember Allah frequently: for them hath Allah prepared forgiveness and a great reward." Here the attainment of heaven is clearly set forth as a problem whose only solution is that of individual merit.

On the day of his death Mohammed told Fatima, his beloved daughter, and Safiya, his aunt: "Work ye out that which shall gain acceptance for you with the Lord: for I verily have no power with Him to save you in any wise." The Prophet did not advise either woman to rely upon the virtues of her husband nor in any manner did he indicate woman's salvation to be dependent upon the human frailty of her spouse.

Everything to the contrary notwithstanding, Mohammed is not responsible for the contradictions and inconsistencies in the Koran, for the volume was not compiled and did not assume its present form until over twenty years after his death. In its present state the Koran is, for the major part, a jumble of hearsay through which occasionally shines forth an example of true inspiration. From what is known of the man Mohammed, it is reasonable to suppose that these nobler and finer portions represent the actual doctrines of the Prophet; the remainder are obvious interpolations, some arising from misunderstanding and others direct forgeries calculated to satisfy the temporal ambitions of conquering Islam. On this subject, Godfrey Higgins speaks with his usual perspicacity:

"Here we have the Koran of Mohammed and the first four sincere and zealous patriarchs, and the Koran of the conquering and magnificent Saracens—puffed up with pride and vanity. The Koran of the eclectic philosopher was not likely to suit the conquerors of Asia. A new one must be grafted on the old, to find a justification for their enormities." (See *Anacalypsis.*)

To the discerning few it is evident that Mohammed had a knowledge of that secret doctrine which must needs constitute the core of every great philosophical, religious, or ethical institution. Through one of four possible avenues Mohammed may have contacted the ancient Mystery teachings: (1) through direct contact with the Great School in the invisible world; (2) through the Nestorian Christian monks; (3) through the mysterious holy man who appeared and disappeared at frequent intervals during the period in which the *suras* of the Koran were revealed; (4) through a decadent school already existing in Arabia, which school in spite of its lapse into idolatry still retained the secrets of the Ancient Wisdom cult. The arcana of Islam may yet be demonstrated to have been directly founded upon the ancient pagan Mysteries performed at the Caaba centuries before the birth of the Prophet; in fact it is generally admitted that many of the ceremonials now embodied in the Islamic Mysteries are survivals of pagan Arabia.

The feminine principle is repeatedly emphasized in Islamic symbolism. For example, Friday, which is sacred to the planet Venus, is the Moslem's holy day; green is the color of the Prophet and, being symbolic of verdure, is inevitably associated with the World Mother; and both the Islamic crescent and the scimitar may be interpreted to signify the crescent shape of either the moon or Venus.

"The famous 'Stone of Cabar,' Kaaba, Cabir, or Kebir, at Mecca," says Jennings, "which is so devoutly kissed by the Faithful, is a Talisman. It is said that the figure of Venus is seen to this day engraved upon it with a crescent. This very Caaba itself was at first an idolatrous temple, where the Arabians worshipped Al-Uzza (God and Issa), that is Venus." (See Kenealy's *Enoch, The Second Messenger of God.*)

"The Mussulmans," writes Sir William Jones, "are already a sort of heterodox Christians: they are Christians, if Locke reasons justly, because they firmly believe the immaculate conception, divine character, and miracles of the MES-

SIAH; but they are heterodox, in denying vehemently his character of Son, and his equality, as God, with the Father, of whose unity and attributes they entertain and express the most awful ideas; while they consider our doctrine as perfect blasphemy, and insist that our copies of the Scriptures have been corrupted both by Jews and Christians."

The following lines are declared by the followers of the Prophet to have been deleted from the Christian Gospels: "And when Jesus, the Son of Mary, said, O children of Israel, verily I am the apostle of God sent unto you, confirming the law which was delivered before me, and bringing good tidings of an apostle who shall come after me, and whose name shall be AHMED." In the present text containing the prophecy of Jesus concerning a comforter to come after Him, it is further claimed that the word *comforter* should be translated *illustrious* and that it had a direct reference to Mohammed; also that the tongues of flame that descended upon the apostles on the day of Pentecost in no way could be interpreted as signifying the promised comforter. When asked, however, for definite proof that the original Gospels contained these so-called expurgated references to Mohammed, the Moslems make a counter-demand for production of the original documents upon which Christianity is founded. Until such writings are discovered, the point under dispute must remain a source of controversy.

To ignore the heritage of culture received from Islam would be an unpardonable oversight, for when the crescent triumphed over the cross in Southern Europe it was the harbinger of a civilization which had no equal in its day. In *Studies in a Mosque,* Stanley Lane-Poole writes:

"For nearly eight centuries under her Mohammedan rulers Spain set to all Europe a shining example of a civilized and enlightened state. * * * Art, literature and science prospered as they then prospered nowhere else in Europe. Students flocked from France and Germany and England to drink from the fountains of learning which flowed only in the cities of the Moors. The surgeons and doctors of Andalusia were in the van of science; women were encouraged to devote themselves to serious study, and a lady doctor was not unknown among the people of Cordova. Mathematics, astronomy and botany, history, philosophy and jurisprudence, were to be mastered in Spain and in Spain alone."

The *Library of Original Sources* thus sums up the effects of Islam:

"The results of Mohammedism have been greatly underestimated. In the century after Mohammed's death it wrested Asia Minor, Africa, and Spain from Christianity, more than half of the civilized world, and established a civilization, the highest in the world during the Dark Ages. It brought the Arabian race to their highest development, raised the position of women in the East, though it retained polygamy, was intensively monotheistic, and until the Turks gained control for the most part encouraged progress."

In the same work, among the great Islamic scientists and philosophers who have made substantial contributions to human knowledge are listed Gerber, or Djafer, who in the ninth century laid the foundations for modern chemistry; Ben Musa, who in the tenth century introduced the theory of algebra; Alhaze, who in the eleventh century made a profound study of optics and discovered the magnifying power of convex lenses; and in the eleventh century also, both Avicenna, or Ibn Sina, whose medical encyclopedia was the standard of his age, and the great Qabbalist Avicebron, or Ibn Gebirol.

"Looking back upon the science of the Mohammedans," resumes the authority just quoted, "it will be seen that they laid the first foundations of chemistry, and made important advances in mathematics and optics. Their discoveries never had the influence they should have had upon the course of European civilization, but this was because Europe itself was not enlightened enough to grasp and make use of them. Gerber's observation that oxidized iron weighs heavier than before oxidation had to be made over again. So had some of their work in optics, and many of their geographical discoveries. They had rounded Africa long before Vasco da Gama. The composition of gunpowder came into Northern Europe from them. We must never forget that the dark ages in Christian Europe were the bright ones of the Mohammedan world. In the field of philosophy the Arabs started by adopting the neo-Platonism they found in Europe, and gradually working back to Aristotle."

What means the subtle mystery of the phœnix reborn every six hundred years? Faintly from within the sanctuary of the World Mysteries is whispered the answer. Six hundred years before Christ the phœnix of wisdom (Pythagoras?) spread its wings and died upon the altar of humanity, consumed by the sacrificial fire. In Nazareth the bird was again reborn from its own ashes, only to die upon the tree which had its roots in Adam's skull. In A.D. 600 appeared *Ahmed* (Mohammed). Again the phœnix suffered, this time from the poison of Kheibar, and from its charred ashes rose to spread its wings across the face of Mongolia, where in the twelfth century Genghis Khan established the rule of wisdom. Circling the mighty desert of Gobi, the phœnix again gave up its form, which now lies buried in a glass sarcophagus under a pyramid bearing upon it the ineffable figures of the Mysteries. After the lapse of six hundred years from the death of Genghis Khan did Napoleon Bonaparte—who believed himself to be the man of destiny—contact in his wanderings this strange legend of the continual periodic rebirth of wisdom? Did he feel the spreading wings of the phœnix within himself and did he believe the hope of the world had taken flesh in him? The eagle on his standard may well have been the phœnix. This would explain why he was moved to believe himself predestined to establish the kingdom of Christ on earth and is, perhaps, the clue to his little-understood friendliness toward the Moslem.

American Indian Symbolism

he North American Indian is by nature a symbolist, a mystic, and a philosopher. Like most aboriginal peoples, his soul was *en rapport* with the cosmic agencies manifesting about him. Not only did his *Manidos* control creation from their exalted seats above the clouds, but they also descended into the world of men and mingled with their red children. The gray clouds hanging over the horizon were the smoke from the *calumets* of the gods, who could build fires of petrified wood and use a comet for a flame. The American Indian peopled the forests, rivers, and sky with myriads of superphysical and invisible beings. There are legends of entire tribes of Indians who lived in lake bottoms; of races who were never seen in the daytime but who, coming forth from their hidden caves, roamed the earth at night and waylaid unwary travelers; also of Bat Indians, with human bodies and batlike wings, who lived in gloomy forests and inaccessible cliffs and who slept hanging head downward from great branches and outcroppings of rock. The red man's philosophy of elemental creatures is apparently the outcome of his intimate contact with Nature, whose inexplicable wonders become the generating cause of such metaphysical speculations.

In common with the early Scandinavians, the Indians of North America considered the earth (the Great Mother) to be an intermediate plane, bounded above by a heavenly sphere (the dwelling place of the Great Spirit) and below by a dark and terrifying subterranean world (the abode of shadows and of submundane powers). Like the Chaldeans, they divided the interval between the surface of earth and heaven into various strata, one consisting of clouds, another of the paths of the heavenly bodies, and so on. The underworld was similarly divided and like the Greek system represented to the initiated the House of the Lesser Mysteries. Those creatures capable of functioning in two or more elements were

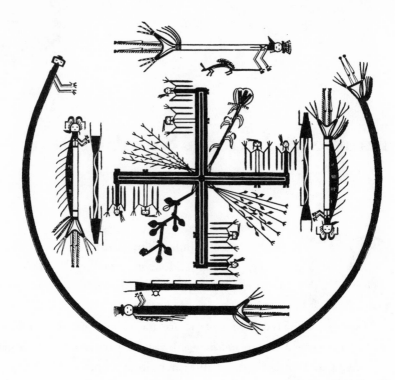

NAVAHO SAND PAINTING.

The Navaho dry or sand paintings are made by sprinkling varicolored ground pigment upon a base of smooth sand. The one here reproduced is encircled by the rainbow goddess, and portrays an episode from the Navaho cosmogony myth. According to Hasteen Klah, the Navaho sand priest who designed this painting, the Navahos do not believe in idolatry; hence they make no images of their gods, but perpetuate only the mental concept of them. Just as the gods draw pictures upon the moving clouds, so the priests make paintings on the sand, and when the purpose of the drawing has been fulfilled it is effaced by a sweep of the hand. According to this informant, the Zuni, Hopi, and Navaho nations had a common genesis; they all came out of the earth and then separated into three nations.

The Navahos first emerged about 3,000 years ago at a point now called La Platte Mountain in Colorado. The four mountains sacred to the Navahos are La Platte Mountain, Mount Taylor, Navaho Mountain, and San Francisco Mountain. While these three nations were under the earth four mountain ranges were below with them. The eastern mountains were white, the southern blue, the western yellow, and the northern black. The rise and fall of these mountains caused the alternation of day and night. When the white mountains rose it was day under the earth; when the yellow ones rose, twilight; the black mountains brought night, and the blue, dawn. Seven major deities were recognized by the Navahos, but Hasteen Klah was unable to say whether the Indians related these deities to the planets. Bakochiddy, one of these seven major gods, was white in color with light reddish hair and gray eyes. His father was the sun ray and his mother the daylight. He ascended to heaven and in some respects his life parallels that of Christ. To avenge the kidnaping of his child, Kahothsode, a fish god, caused a great flood to arise. To escape destruction, the Zunis, Hopis, and Navahos ascended to the surface of the earth.

The sand painting here reproduced is part of the medicine series prepared for the healing of disease. In the healing ceremony the patient is placed upon the drawing, which is made in a consecrated *hogan,* and all outsiders excluded. The sacred swastika in the center of the drawing is perhaps the most nearly universal of religious emblems and represents the four corners of the world. The two hunchback gods at the right and left assume their appearance by reason of the great clouds borne upon their backs. In Navaho religious art, male divinities are always shown with circular heads and female divinities with square heads.

considered as messengers between the spirits of these various planes. The abode of the dead was presumed to be in a distant place: in the heavens above, the earth below, the distant corners of the world, or across wide seas. Sometimes a river flows between the world of the dead and that of the living, in this respect paralleling Egyptian, Greek, and Christian theology. To the Indian the number four has a peculiar sanctity, presumably because the Great Spirit created His universe in a square frame. This is suggestive of the veneration accorded the *tetrad* by the Pythagoreans, who held it to be a fitting symbol of the Creator. The legendary narratives of the strange adventures of intrepid heroes who while in the physical body penetrated the realms of the dead prove beyond question the presence of Mystery cults among the North American red men. Wherever the Mysteries were established they were recognized as the philosophic equivalents of death, for those passing through the rituals experienced all after-death conditions while still in the physical body. At the consummation of the ritual the initiate actually gained the ability to pass in and out of his physical body at will. This is the philosophic foundation for the allegories of adventures in the Indian Shadow Land, or World of Ghosts.

"From coast to coast," writes Hartley Burr Alexander, "the sacred Calumet is the Indian's altar, and its smoke is the proper offering to Heaven." (See *Mythology of All Races.*) In the *Notes* on the same work is given the following description of the pipe ceremony:

"The master of ceremonies, again rising to his feet, filled and lighted the pipe of peace from his own fire. Drawing three whiffs, one after the other, he blew the first towards the zenith, the second towards the ground, and the third towards the Sun. By the first act he returned thanks to the Great Spirit for the preservation of his life during the past year, and for being permitted to be present at this council. By the second, he returned thanks to his Mother, the Earth, for her various productions which had ministered to his sustenance. And by the third, he returned thanks to the Sun for his never-failing light, ever shining upon all."

It was necessary for the Indian to secure the red stone for his *calumet* from the pipestone quarry where in some remote past the Great Spirit had come and, after fashioning with His own hands a great pipe, had smoked it toward the four corners of creation and thus instituted this most sacred ceremony. Scores of Indian tribes—some of them traveling thousands of miles—secured the sacred stone from this single quarry, where the mandate of the Great Spirit had decreed that eternal peace should reign.

The Indian does not worship the sun; he rather regards this shining orb as an appropriate symbol of the Great and Good Spirit who forever radiates life to his red children. In Indian symbolism the serpent—especially the Great Serpent—corroborates other evidence pointing to the presence of the Mysteries on the North American Continent. The flying serpent is the Atlantean token of the initiate; the seven-headed snake represents the seven great Atlantean islands (the cities of Chibola?) and also the seven great prehistoric schools of esoteric phi-losophy. Moreover, who can doubt the presence of the secret doctrine in the Americas when he gazes upon the great serpent mound in Adams County, Ohio, where the huge reptile is represented as disgorging the Egg of Existence? Many American Indian tribes are reincarnationists, some are transmigrationists. They even called their children by the names supposed to have borne by them in a former life. There is an account of an instance where a parent by inadver-tence had given his infant the wrong name, whereupon the babe cried inces-santly until the mistake had been rectified! The belief in reincarnation is also prevalent among the Eskimos. Aged Eskimos not infrequently kill themselves in order to reincarnate in the family of some newly married loved one.

The American Indians recognize the difference between the ghost and the actual soul of a dead person, a knowledge restricted to initiates of the Mysteries. In common with the Platonists they also understood the principles of an arche-typal sphere wherein exist the patterns of all forms manifesting in the earth plane. The theory of Group, or Elder, Souls having supervision over the animal species is also shared by them. The red man's belief in guardian spirits would have warmed the heart of Paracelsus. When they attain the importance of being protectors of entire clans or tribes, these guardians are called *totems.* In some tribes impressive ceremonies mark the occasion when the young men are sent out into the forest to fast and pray and there remain until their guardian spirit manifests to them. Whatever creature appears thereupon becomes their peculiar genius, to whom they appeal in time of trouble.

The outstanding hero of North American Indian folklore is Hiawatha, a name which, according to Lewis Spence, signifies "he who seeks the wampum-belt." Hiawatha enjoys the distinction of anticipating by several centuries the late Woodrow Wilson's cherished dream of a League of Nations. Following in the footsteps of Schoolcraft, Longfellow confused the historical Hiawatha of the Iroquois with Manabozho, a mythological hero of the Algonquins and Ojibwas. Hiawatha, a chief of the Iroquois, after many reverses and disappointments, succeeded in uniting the five great nations of the Iroquois into the "League of the Five Nations." The original purpose of the league—to abolish war by substituting councils of arbitration—was not wholly successful, but the power of the "Silver Chain" conferred upon the Iroquois a solidarity attained by no other confederacy of North American Indians. Hiawatha, however, met the same opposition which has confronted every great idealist, irrespective of time or race. The *shamans* turned their magic against him and, according to one legend, created an evil bird which, swooping down from heaven, tore his only daughter to pieces before his eyes. When Hiawatha, after accomplishing his mission, had sailed away in his self-propelled canoe along the path of the sunset, his people realized the true greatness of their benefactor and elevated him to the dignity of a demigod. In Longfellow's *Song of Hiawatha* the poet has cast the great Indian statesman in a charming setting of magic and enchantment; yet through the maze of symbol and allegory is ever faintly visible the figure of Hiawatha the initiate—the very personification of the red man and his philosophy.

The *Popol Vuh*

No other sacred book sets forth so completely as the *Popol Vuh* the initiatory rituals of a great school of mystical philosophy. This volume alone is sufficient to establish incontestably the philosophical excellence of the red race.

"The Red 'Children of the Sun,'" writes James Morgan Pryse, "do not worship the One God. For them that One God is absolutely impersonal, and all the Forces emanated from that One God are personal. This is the exact reverse of the popular western conception of a personal God and impersonal working forces in nature. Decide for yourself which of these beliefs is the more philosophical. These Children of the Sun adore the Plumèd Serpent, who is the messenger of the Sun. He was the God Quetzalcoatl in Mexico, Gucumatz in Quiché; and in Peru he was called Amaru. From the latter name comes our word America. *Amaruca* is, literally translated, 'Land of the Plumèd Serpent.' The priests of this God of Peace, from their chief centre in the Cordilleras, once ruled both Americas. All the Red men who have remained true to the ancient religion are still under their sway. One of their strong centres was in Guatemala, and of their Order was the author of the book called *Popol Vuh*. In the Quiché tongue Gucumatz is the exact equivalent of Quetzalcoatl in the Nahuatl language; *quetzal*, the bird of Paradise; *coatl*, serpent—'the Serpent veiled in plumes of the paradise-bird'!"

The *Popol Vuh* was discovered by Father Ximinez in the seventeenth century. It was translated into French by Brasseur de Bourbourg and published in 1861. The only complete English translation is that by Kenneth Sylvan Guthrie, which ran through the early files of *The Word* magazine and which is used as the basis of this article. A portion of the *Popol Vuh* was translated into English, with extremely valuable commentaries, by James Morgan Pryse, but unfortunately his translation was never completed. The second book of the *Popol Vuh* is largely devoted to the initiatory rituals of the Quiché nation. These ceremonials are of first importance to students of Masonic symbolism and mystical philosophy, since they establish beyond doubt the existence of ancient and divinely instituted Mystery schools on the American Continent.

Lewis Spence, in describing the *Popol Vuh,* gives a number of translations of the title of the manuscript itself. Passing over the renditions, "The Book of the Mat" and "The Record of the Community," he considers it likely that the correct title is "The Collection of Written Leaves," *Popol* signifying the "prepared bark" and *Vuh,* "paper" or "book" from the verb *uoch,* to write. Dr. Guthrie interprets the words *Popol Vuh* to mean "The Senate Book," or "The Book of the Holy Assembly"; Brasseur de Bourbourg calls it "The Sacred Book"; and Father Ximinez designates the volume "The National Book." In his articles on the *Popol Vuh* appearing in the fifteenth volume of *Lucifer,* James Morgan Pryse, approaching the subject from the standpoint of the mystic, calls this work "The Book of the Azure Veil." In the *Popol Vuh* itself the ancient records from which the Christianized Indian who compiled it derived his material are referred to as "The Tale of Human Existence in the Land of Shadows, and, How Man Saw Light and Life."

The meager available native records contain abundant evidence that the later civilizations of Central and South America were hopelessly dominated by the black arts of their priestcrafts. In the convexities of their magnetized mirrors the Indian sorcerers captured the intelligences of elemental beings and, gazing into the depths of these abominable devices, eventually made the scepter subservient to the wand. Robed in garments of sable hue, the neophytes in their search for truth were led by their sinister guides through the confused passageways of necromancy. By the left-hand path they descended into the somber depths of the infernal world, where they learned to endow stones with the power of speech and to subtly ensnare the minds of men with their chants and fetishes. As typical of the perversion which prevailed, none could achieve to the greater Mysteries until a human being had suffered immolation at his hand and the bleeding heart of the victim had been elevated before the luring face of the stone idol fabricated by a priestcraft the members of which realized more fully than they dared to admit the true nature of the man-made demon. The sanguinary and indescribable rites practiced by many of the Central American Indians may represent remnants of the later Atlantean perversion of the ancient sun Mysteries. According to the secret tradition, it was during the later Atlantean epoch that black magic and sorcery dominated the esoteric schools, resulting in the bloody sacrificial rites and gruesome idolatry which ultimately overthrew the Atlantean empire and even penetrated the Aryan religious world.

The Mysteries of Xibalba

The princes of Xibalba (so the *Popol Vuh* recounts) sent their four owl messengers to Hunhun-ahpu and Vukub-hunhun-ahpu, ordering them to come at once to the place of initiation in the fastnesses of the Guatemalan mountains. Failing in the tests imposed by the princes of Xibalba, the two brothers—according to the ancient custom—paid with their lives for their shortcomings. Hunhun-ahpu and Vukub-hunhun-ahpu were buried together, but the head of Hunhun-ahpu was placed among the branches of the sacred calabash tree which grew in the middle of the road leading to the awful Mysteries of Xibalba. Immediately the calabash tree covered itself with fruit and the head of Hunhun-ahpu "showed itself no more; for it reunited itself with the other fruits of the calabash tree." Now Xquiq was the virgin daughter of prince Cuchumaquiq. From her father she had learned of the marvelous calabash tree, and desiring to possess some of its fruit, she journeyed alone to the somber place where it grew. When Xquiq put forth her hand to pick the fruit of the tree, some saliva from the mouth of Hunhun-ahpu fell into it and the head spoke to Xquiq, saying: "This saliva and froth is my posterity which I have just given you. Now my head will cease to speak, for it is only the head of a corpse, which has no more flesh."

Following the admonitions of Hunhun-ahpu, the young girl returned to her home. Her father, Cuchumaquiq, later discovering that she was about to become a mother, questioned her concerning the father of her child. Xquiq replied that the child was begotten while she was gazing upon the head of Hunhun-ahpu in the calabash tree and that she had known no man. Cuchumaquiq, refusing to believe her story, at the instigation of the princes of Xibalba, demanded her heart in an urn. Led away by her executioners, Xquiq pleaded with them to spare her life, which they agreed to do, substituting for her heart the fruit of a certain tree (rubber) whose sap was red and of the consistency of blood. When the princes of Xibalba placed the supposed heart upon the coals of the altar to be consumed, they were all amazed by the perfume which rose therefrom, for they did not know that they were burning the fruit of a fragrant plant.

Xquiq gave birth to twin sons, who were named Hunahpu and Xbalanque and whose lives were dedicated to avenging the deaths of Hunhun-ahpu and Vukub-hunhun-ahpu. The years passed, and the two boys grew up to manhood and great were their deeds. Especially did they excel in a certain game called tennis but somewhat resembling hockey. Hearing of the prowess of the youths, the princes of Xibalba asked: "Who, then, are those who now begin again to play over our heads, and who do not scruple to shake (the earth)? Are not Hun-hun-aphu and Vukub-hunhun-ahpu dead, who wished to exalt themselves before our face?" So the princes of Xibalba sent for the two youths, Hunahpu and Xbalanque, that they might destroy them also in the seven days of the Mysteries. Before departing, the two brothers bade farewell to their grandmother, each planting in the midst of the house a cane plant, saying that as long as the cane lived she would know that they were alive. "O, our grandmother, O, our mother, do not weep; behold the sign of our word which remains with you." Hunahpu and Xbalanque then departed, each with his *sabarcan* (blowpipe), and for many days they journeyed along the perilous trail, descending through tortuous ravines and along precipitous cliffs, past strange birds and boiling springs, towards the sanctuary of Xibalba.

The actual ordeals of the Xibalbian Mysteries were seven in number. As a preliminary the two adventurers crossed a river of mud and then a stream of blood, accomplishing these difficult feats by using their *sabarcans* as bridges. Continuing on their way, they reached a point where four roads converged—a black road, a white road, a red road, and a green road. Now Hunahpu and Xbalanque knew that their first test would consist of being able to discriminate between the princes of Xibalba and the wooden effigies robed to resemble them; also that they must call each of the princes by his correct name without having been given the information. To secure this information, Hunahpu pulled a hair from his leg, which hair then became a strange insect called *Xan;* buzzing along the black road, the Xan entered the council chamber of the princes of Xibalba and stung the leg of the figure nearest the door, which it discovered to be a manikin. By the same artifice the second figure was proved to be of wood, but upon stinging the third, there was an immediate response. By stinging each of the twelve assembled princes in turn the insect thus discovered each one's name, for the princes called each other by name in discussing the cause of the mysterious bites. Having secured the desired information in this novel manner, the insect then flew back to Hunahpu and Xbalanque, who thus fortified, fearlessly approached the threshold of Xibalba and presented themselves to the twelve assembled princes.

When told to adore the king, Hunahpu and Xbalanque laughed, for they knew that the figure pointed out to them was the lifeless manikin. The young adventurers thereupon addressed the twelve princes by name thus: "Hail, Hun-came; hail, Vukub-came; hail, Xiquiripat; hail, Cuchumaquiq; hail, Ahalpuh; hail, Ahalcana; hail, Chamiabak; hail, Chamiaholom; hail, Quiqxic; hail, Patan; hail Quiqre; hail, Quiqrixqaq." When invited by the Xibalbians to seat themselves upon a great stone bench, Hunahpu and Xbalanque declined to do so, declaring that they well knew the stone to be heated so that they would be burned to death if they sat upon it. The princes of Xibalba then ordered Hunahpu and Xbalanque to rest for the night in the House of the Shadows. This completed the first degree of the Xibalbian Mysteries.

COURTESY OF ALICE PALMER HENDERSON.

MIDEWIWIN RECORD ON BIRCH BARK.

The birch-bark roll is one of the most sacred possessions of an initiate of the *Midewiwin,* or Grand Medicine Society, of the Ojibwas. Concerning these rolls, Colonel Garrick Mallery writes: "To persons acquainted with secret societies, a good comparison for the Midewiwin charts would be what is called a trestleboard of a Masonic order, which is printed and published and publicly exposed without exhibiting any secrets of the order; yet it is not only significant, but useful to the esoteric in assistance to their memory as to the details of ceremony."

A most complete and trustworthy account of the Midewiwin is that given by W. J. Hoffman in the *Seventh Annual Report of the Bureau of Ethnology.* He writes: "The Midewiwin—Society of the Mide or Shamans—consists of an indefinite number of Mide of both sexes. The society is graded into four separate and distinct degrees, although there is a general impression prevailing even among certain members that any degree beyond the first is practically a mere repetition. The greater power attained by one in making advancement depends upon the fact of his having submitted to "being shot at with the medicine sacks' in the hands of the officiating priests. * * * It has always been customary for the Mide priests to preserve birch-bark records, bearing delicate incised lines to represent pictorially the ground plan of the number of degrees to which the owner is entitled. Such records or charts are sacred and are never exposed to the public view."

The two rectangular diagrams represent two degrees of the Mide lodge and the straight line through the center the spiritual path, or "straight and narrow way," running through the degrees. The lines running tangent to the central path signify temptations, and the faces at the termini of the lines are *manidos,* or powerful spirits. Writing of the Midewiwin, Schoolcraft, the great authority on the American Indian, says: "In the society of the Midewiwin the object is to teach the higher doctrines of spiritual existence, its nature and mode of existence, and the influence it exercises among men. It is an association of men who profess the highest knowledge known to the tribes."

According to legend, *Manabozho,* the Great Rabbit, who was a servant of *Dzhe Manido,* the Good Spirit, gazing down upon the progenitors of the Ojibwas and perceiving them to be without spiritual knowledge, instructed an otter in the mysteries of Midewiwin. *Manabozho* built a Midewigan and initiated the otter, shooting the sacred Migis (a small shell, the sacred symbol of the Mide) into the body of the otter. He then conferred immortality upon the animal, and entrusted to it the secrets of the Grand Medicine Society. The ceremony of initiation is preceded by sweat baths and consists chiefly of overcoming the influences of evil manidos. The initiate is also instructed in the art of healing and (judging from Plate III of Mr. Hoffman's article) a knowledge of directionalizing the forces moving through the vital centers of the human body. Though the cross is an important symbol in the Midewiwin rites, it is noteworthy that the Mide priests steadfastly refused to give up their religion and be converted to Christianity.

The second trial was given in the House of Shadows, where to each of the candidates was brought a pine torch and a cigar, with the injunction that both must be kept alight throughout the entire night and yet each must be returned the next morning unconsumed. Knowing that death was the alternative to failure in the test, the young men burnt aras-feathers in place of the pine splinters (which they closely resemble) and also put fireflies on the tips of the cigars. Seeing the lights, those who watched felt certain that Hunahpu and Xbalanque had fallen into the trap, but when morning came the torches and cigars were returned to the guards unconsumed and still burning. In amazement and awe, the princes of Xibalba gazed upon the unconsumed splinters and cigars, for never before had these been returned intact.

The third ordeal took place presumably in a cavern called the House of Spears. Here hour after hour the youths were forced to defend themselves against the strongest and most skillful warriors armed with spears. Hunahpu and Xbalanque pacified the spearmen, who thereupon ceased attacking them. They then turned their attention to the second and most difficult part of the test: the production of four vases of the rarest flowers but which they were not permitted to leave the temple to gather. Unable to pass the guards, the two young men secured the assistance of the ants. These tiny creatures, crawling into the gardens of the temple, brought back the blossoms so that by morning the vases were filled. When Hunahpu and Xbalanque presented the flowers to the twelve princes, the latter, in amazement, recognized the blossoms as having been filched from their own private gardens. In consternation, the princes of Xibalba then counseled together how they could destroy the intrepid neophytes and forthwith prepared for them the next ordeal.

For their fourth test, the two brothers were made to enter the House of Cold, where they remained for an entire night. The princes of Xibalba considered the chill of the icy cavern to be unbearable and it is described as "the abode of the frozen winds of the North." Hunahpu and Xbalanque, however, protected themselves from the deadening influence of the frozen air by building fires of pine cones, whose warmth caused the spirit of cold to leave the cavern so that the youths were not dead but full of life when day dawned. Even greater than before was the amazement of the princes of Xibalba when Hunahpu and Xbalanque again entered the Hall of Assembly in the custody of their guardians.

The fifth ordeal was also of a nocturnal nature. Hunahpu and Xbalanque were ushered into a great chamber which was immediately filled with ferocious tigers. Here they were forced to remain throughout the night. The young men tossed bones to the tigers, which they ground to pieces with their strong jaws. Gazing into the House of the Tigers, the princes of Xibalba beheld the animals chewing the bones and said one to the other: "They have at last learned (to know the power of Xibalba), and they have given themselves up to the beasts." But when at dawn Hunahpu and Xbalanque emerged from the House of the Tigers unharmed, the Xibalbians cried: "Of what race are those?" for they could not understand how any man could escape the tigers' fury. Then the princes of Xibalba prepared for the two brothers a new ordeal.

The sixth test consisted of remaining from sunset to sunrise in the House of Fire. Hunahpu and Xbalanque entered a large apartment arranged like a furnace. On every side the flames arose and the air was stifling; so great was the heat that those who entered this chamber could survive only a few moments. But at sunrise when the doors of the furnace were opened, Hunahpu and Xbalanque came forth unscorched by the fury of the flames. The princes of Xibalba, perceiving how the two intrepid youths had survived every ordeal prepared for their destruction, were filled with fear lest all the secrets of Xibalba should fall into the hands of Hunahpu and Xbalanque. So they prepared the last ordeal, an ordeal yet more terrible than any which had gone before, certain that the youths could not withstand this crucial test.

The seventh ordeal took place in the House of the Bats. Here in a dark subterranean labyrinth lurked many strange and odious creatures of destruction. Huge bats fluttered dismally through the corridors and hung with folded wings from the carvings on the walls and ceilings. Here also dwelt Camazotz, the God of Bats, a hideous monster with the body of a man and the wings and head of a bat. Camazotz carried a great sword and, soaring through the gloom, decapitated with a single sweep of his blade any unwary wanderers seeking to find their way through the terror-filled chambers. Xbalanque passed successfully through this horrifying test, but Hunahpu, caught off his guard, was beheaded by Camazotz.

Later, Hunahpu was restored to life by magic, and the two brothers, having thus foiled every attempt against their lives by the Xibalbians, in order to better avenge the murder of Hunhun-ahpu and Vukub-hunhun-ahpu, permitted themselves to be burned upon a funeral pyre. Their powdered bones were then cast into a river and immediately became two great man-fishes. Later taking upon themselves the forms of aged wanderers, they danced for the Xibalbians and wrought strange miracles. Thus one would cut the other to pieces and with a single word resurrect him, or they would burn houses by magic and then instantly rebuild them. The fame of the two dancers—who were in reality Hunahpu and Xbalanque—finally came to the notice of the twelve princes of Xibalba, who thereupon desired these two miracle-workers to perform their strange feats before them. After Hunahpu and Xbalanque had slain the dog of the princes and restored it to life, had burned the royal palace and instantly rebuilt it, and given other demonstrations of their magical powers, the monarch of the Xibalbians asked the magicians to destroy him and restore him also to life.

So Hunahpu and Xbalanque slew the princes of Xibalba but did not return them to life, thereby avenging the murder of Hunhun-ahpu and Vukub-hunhun-ahpu. These heroes later ascended to heaven, where they became the celestial lights.

Keys to the Mysteries of Xibalba

"Do not these initiations," writes Le Plongeon, "vividly recall to mind what Henoch said he saw in his visions? That blazing house of crystal, burning hot and icy cold—that place where were the bow of fire, the quiver of arrows, the sword of fire—that other where he had to cross the babbling stream, and the river of fire—and those extremities of the Earth full of all kinds of huge beasts and birds—or the habitation where appeared one of great glory sitting upon the orb of the sun—and, lastly, does not the tamarind tree in the midst of the earth, that he was told was the Tree of Knowledge, find its simile in the calabash tree, in the middle of the road where those of Xibalba placed the head of Hunhun Ahpu, after sacrificing him for having failed to support the first trial of the initiation? * * * These were the awful ordeals that the candidates for initiation into the sacred mysteries had to pass through in Xibalba. Do they not seem an exact counterpart of what happened in a milder form at the initiation into the Eleusinian mysteries? and also the greater mysteries of Egypt, from which these were copied? Does not the recital of what the candidates to the mysteries in Xibalba were required to know, before being admitted, * * * recall to mind the wonderful similar feats said to be performed by the Mahatmas, the Brothers in India, and of several of the passages of the book of Daniel, who had been initiated to the mysteries of the Chaldeans or Magi which, according to Eubulus, were divided into three classes or genera, the highest being the most learned?" (See *Sacred Mysteries among the Mayas and the Quiches*.)

In his introductory notes to the *Popol Vuh*, Dr. Guthrie presents a number of important parallelisms between this sacred book of the Quichés and the sacred writings of other great civilizations. In the tests through which Hunahpu and Xbalanque are forced to pass he finds the following analogy with the signs of the zodiac as employed in the Mysteries of the Egyptians, Chaldeans, and Greeks:

"Aries, crossing the river of mud. Taurus, crossing the river of blood. Gemini, detecting the two dummy kings. Cancer, the House of Darkness. Leo, the House of Spears. Virgo, the House of Cold (the usual trip to Hell). Libra, the House of Tigers (feline poise). Scorpio, the House of Fire. Sagittarius, the

House of Bats, where the God Camazotz decapitates one of the heroes. Capricorn, the burning on the scaffold (the dual Phœnix). Aquarius, their ashes being scattered in a river. Pisces their ashes turning into *man-fishes,* and later back into human form."

It would seem more appropriate to assign the river of blood to Aries and that of mud to Taurus, and it is not at all improbable that in the ancient form of the legend the order of the rivers was reversed. Dr. Guthrie's most astonishing conclusion is his effort to identify Xibalba with the ancient continent of Atlantis. He sees in the twelve princes of Xibalba the rulers of the Atlantean empire, and in the destruction of these princes by the magic of Hunahpu and Xbalanque an allegorical depiction of the tragic end of Atlantis. To the initiated, however, it is evident that Atlantis is simply a symbolic figure in which is set forth the mystery of origins.

Concerned primarily with the problems of mystical anatomy, Mr. Pryse relates the various symbols described in the *Popol Vuh* to the occult centers of consciousness in the human body. Accordingly, he sees in the elastic ball the pineal gland and in Hunahpu and Xbalanque the dual electric current directed along the spinal column. Unfortunately, Mr. Pryse did not translate that portion of the *Popol Vuh* dealing directly with the initiatory ceremonial. Xibalba he considers to be the shadowy or etheric sphere which, according to the Mystery teachings, was located within the body of the planet itself. The fourth book of the *Popol Vuh* concludes with an account of the erection of a majestic temple, all white, where was preserved a secret black divining stone, cubical in shape. Gucumatz (or Quetzalcoatl) partakes of many of the attributes of King Solomon: the account of the temple building in the *Popol Vuh* is a reminder of the story of Solomon's Temple, and undoubtedly has a similar significance. Brasseur de Bourbourg was first attracted to the study of religious parallelisms in the *Popol Vuh* by the fact that the temple, together with the black stone which it contained, was named the *Caabaha,* a name astonishingly similar to that of the Temple, or *Caaba,* which contains the sacred black stone of Islam.

The exploits of Hunahpu and Xbalanque take place before the actual creation of the human race and therefore are to be considered essentially as spiritual mysteries. Xibalba doubtless signifies the inferior universe of Chaldean and Pythagorean philosophy; the princes of Xibalba are the twelve Governors of the lower universe; and the two dummies or manikins in their midst may be interpreted as the two false signs of the ancient zodiac inserted in the heavens to make the astronomical Mysteries incomprehensible to the profane. The descent of Hunahpu and Xbalanque into the subterranean kingdom of Xibalba by crossing over the rivers on bridges made from their blowguns has a subtle analogy to the descent of the spiritual nature of man into the physical body through certain superphysical channels that may be likened to the blowguns or tubes. The *sabarcan* is also an appropriate emblem of the spinal cord and the power resident within its tiny central opening. The two youths are invited to play the "Game of Life" with the Gods of Death, and only with the aid of supernatural power imparted to them by the "Sages" can they triumph over these gloomy lords. The tests represent the soul wandering through the sub-zodiacal realms of the created universe; their final victory over the Lords of Death represents the ascension of the spiritual and illumined consciousness from the lower nature which has been wholly consumed by the fire of spiritual purification.

That the Quichés possessed the keys to the mystery of regeneration is evident from an analysis of the symbols appearing upon the images of their priests and gods. In Vol. II of the *Anales del Museo Nacional de México* is reproduced the head of an image generally considered to represent Quetzalcoatl. The sculpturing is distinctly Oriental in character and on the crown of the head appear both the thousand-petaled sunburst of spiritual illumination and the serpent of the liberated spinal fire. The Hindu *chakra* is unmistakable and it frequently appears in the religious art of the three Americas. One of the carved monoliths of Central America is adorned with the heads of two elephants with their drivers. No such animals have existed in the Western Hemisphere since prehistoric times and it is evident that the carvings are the result of contact with the distant continent of Asia. Among the Mysteries of the Central American Indians is a remarkable doctrine concerning the consecrated mantles or, as they were called in Europe, magic capes. Because their glory was fatal to mortal vision, the gods, when appearing to the initiated priests, robed themselves in these mantles. Allegory and fable likewise are the mantles with which the secret doctrine is ever enveloped. Such a magic cape of concealment is the *Popol Vuh,* and deep within its folds sits the god of Quiché philosophy. The massive pyramids, temples, and monoliths of Central America may be likened also to the feet of gods, whose upper parts are enshrouded in magic mantles of invisibility.

XLVI

The Mysteries and Their Emissaries

D id that divine knowledge which constituted the supreme possession of the pagan priestcrafts survive the destruction of their temples? Is it yet accessible to mankind, or does it lie buried beneath the rubbish of ages, entombed within the very sanctuaries that were once illuminated by its splendor? "In Egypt," writes Origen, "the philosophers have a sublime and secret knowledge respecting the nature of God." What did Julian imply when he spoke of the secret initiations into the sacred Mysteries of the Seven-Rayed God who lifted souls to salvation through His own nature? Who were the blessed theurgists who understood these profundities concerning which Julian dared not speak? If this inner doctrine were always concealed from the masses, for whom a simpler code had been devised, is it not highly probable that the exponents of every aspect of modern civilization—philosophic, ethical, religious, and scientific— are ignorant of the true meaning of the very theories and tenets on which their beliefs are founded? Do the arts and sciences that the race has inherited from older nations conceal beneath their *fair exterior* a mystery so great that only the most illumined intellect can grasp its import? *Such is undoubtedly the case.*

Albert Pike, who has gathered ample evidence of the excellence of the doctrines promulgated by the Mysteries, supports his assertions by quoting from the writings of Clement of Alexandria, Plato, Epictetus, Proclus, Aristophanes, and Cicero, all of whom unite in lauding the high ideals of these institutions. From the unqualified testimony of such reputable authorities no reasonable doubt can exist that the initiates of Greece, Egypt, and other ancient countries possessed the correct solution to those great cultural, intellectual, moral, and social problems which in an unsolved state confront the humanity of the twenti-

FROM VÆNIUS' *THEATRO MORAL DE LA VIDA HUMANA.*

THE TABLE OF CEBES.

There is a legend to the effect that the *Tablet of Cebes,* a dialogue between Cebes and Gerundio, was based upon an ancient table set up in the Temple of Kronos at Athens or Thebes, which depicted the entire progress of human life. The author of the *Tablet of Cebes* was a disciple of Socrates and lived about 390 B.C. The world is represented as a great mountain. Out of the earth at the base of it come the myriads of human creatures who climb upward in search of truth and immortality. Above the clouds which conceal the summit of the mountain is the goal of human attainment—true happiness. The figures and groups are arranged as follows: (1) the door of the wall of life; (2) the Genius or Intelligence; (3) deceit; (4) opinions, desires, and pleasures; (5) fortune; (6) the strong; (7) incontinence, venery, insatiability, flattery; (8) sorrow; (9) sadness; (10) misery; (11) grief; (12) rage or despair; (13) the house of misfortune; (14) penitence; (15) true opinion; (16) false opinion; (17) false doctrine; (18) poets, orators, geometers, et al.; (19) incontinence, sexual indulgence, and opinion; (20) the road of the true doctrine; (21) continence and patience; (22) the true doctrine; (23) truth and persuasion; (24) science and the virtues; (25) happiness; (26) the highest (first) pleasure of the wise man; (27) the lazy and the strays.

eth century. The reader must not interpret this statement to mean that antiquity had foreseen and analyzed every complexity of this generation, but rather that the Mysteries had evolved a method whereby the mind was so trained in the fundamental verities of life that it was able to cope intelligently with any emergency which might arise. Thus the reasoning faculties were organized by a simple process of mental culture, for it was asserted that where reason reigns supreme, inconsistency cannot exist. Wisdom, it was maintained, lifts man to the condition of Godhood, a fact which explains the enigmatical statement that the Mysteries transformed "roaring beasts into divinities."

The preeminence of any philosophical system can be determined only by the excellence of its products. The Mysteries have demonstrated the superiority of their culture by giving to the world minds of such overwhelming greatness, souls of such beatific vision, and lives of such outstanding impeccability that even after the lapse of ages the teachings of these individuals constitute the present spiritual, intellectual, and ethical standards of the race. The initiates of the various Mystery schools of past ages form a veritable golden chain of supermen and superwomen connecting heaven and earth. They are the links of that Homeric "golden chain" with which Zeus boasted he could bind the several parts of the universe to the pinnacle of Olympus. The sons and daughters of Isis are indeed an illustrious line—founders of sciences and philosophies, patrons of arts and crafts, supporting by the transcendency of their divinely given power the structures of world religions erected to do them homage. Founders of doctrines which have molded the lives of uncounted generations, these Initiate-Teachers bear witness to that spiritual culture which has always existed—and always will exist—as a divine institution in the world of men.

Those who represent an ideal beyond the comprehension of the masses must face the persecution of the unthinking multitude who are without that divine idealism which inspires progress and those rational faculties which unerringly sift truth from falsehood. The lot of the Initiate-Teacher is therefore almost invariably an unhappy one. Pythagoras, crucified and his university burned; Hypatia, torn from her chariot and rended limb from limb; Jacques de Molay, whose memory survives the consuming flame; Savonarola, burned in the square of Florence; Galileo, forced to recant upon bended knee; Giordano Bruno, burned by the Inquisition; Roger Bacon, compelled to carry on his experiments in the secrecy of his cell and leave his knowledge hidden under cipher; Dante Alighieri, dying in exile from his beloved city; Francis Bacon, patient under the burden of persecution; Cagliostro, the most vilified man of modern times—all this illustrious line bear unending witness of man's inhumanity to man. The world has ever been prone to heap plaudits upon its fools and calumny upon its thinkers. Here and there notable exceptions occur, as in the case of the Comte de St.-Germain, a philosopher who survived his inquisitors and through the sheer transcendency of his genius won a position of comparative immunity. But even the illustrious Comte—whose illumined intellect merited the homage of the world—could not escape being branded an impostor, a charlatan, and an adventurer. From this long list of immortal men and women who have represented the Ancient Wisdom before the world, three have been chosen as outstanding examples for more detailed consideration: the first the most eminent woman philosopher of all ages; the second the more maligned and persecuted man since the beginning of Christian Era; the third the most brilliant and the most successful modern exponent of this Ancient Wisdom.

Hypatia

Sitting in the chair of philosophy previously occupied by her father, Theon the mathematician, the immortal Hypatia was for many years the central figure in the Alexandrian School of Neo-Platonism. Famed alike for the depth of her learning and the charm of her person, beloved by the citizens of Alexandria, and frequently consulted by the magistrates of that city, this noble woman stands out from the pages of history as the greatest of the pagan martyrs. A personal disciple of the magician Plutarch, and versed in the profundities of the Platonic School, Hypatia eclipsed in argument and public esteem every proponent of the Christian doctrines in Northern Egypt. While her writings perished at the time of the burning of the library of Alexandria by the Mohammedans, some hint of their nature may be gleaned from the statements of contemporaneous authors. Hypatia evidently wrote a commentary on the *Arithmetic* of Diophantus, another on the *Astronomical Canon* of Ptolemy, and a third on the *Conics* of Apollonius of Perga. Synesius, Bishop of Ptolemais, her devoted friend, wrote to Hypatia for assistance in the construction of an astrolabe and a hydroscope. Recognizing the transcendency of her intellect, the learned of many nations flocked to the academy where she lectured.

A number of writers have credited the teachings of Hypatia with being Christian in spirit; in fact she removed the veil of mystery in which the new cult had enshrouded itself, discoursing with such clarity upon its most involved principles that many newly converted to the Christian faith deserted it to become her disciples. Hypatia not only proved conclusively the pagan origin of the Christian faith but also exposed the purported miracles then advanced by the Christians as tokens of divine preference by demonstrating the natural laws controlling the phenomena.

At this time Cyril—later to be renowned as the founder of the doctrine of the

Christian Trinity and canonized for his zeal—was Bishop of Alexandria. Seeing in Hypatia a continual menace to the promulgation of the Christian faith, Cyril—indirectly at least—was the cause of her tragic end. Despite every later effort to exonerate him from the stigma of her murder, the incontrovertible fact remains that he made no effort to avert the foul and brutal crime. The only shred of excuse which might be offered in his defense is that, blinded by the spell of fanaticism, Cyril considered Hypatia to be a sorceress in league with the Devil. In contrast to the otherwise general excellence of the literary works of Charles Kingsley may be noted his puerile delineation of the character of Hypatia in his book by that name. Without exception, the meager historical references to this virgin philosopher attest her virtue, integrity, and absolute devotion to the principles of Truth and Right.

While it is true that the best minds of the Christianity of that period may readily be absolved from the charge of *participes criminis,* the implacable hatred of Cyril unquestionably communicated itself to the more fanatical members of his faith, particularly to a group of monks from the Nitrian desert. Led by Peter the Reader, a savage and illiterate man, they attacked Hypatia on the open street as she was passing from the academy to her home. Dragging the defenseless woman from her chariot, they took her to the Cæsarean Church. Tearing away her garments, they pounded her to death with clubs, after which they scraped the flesh from her bones with oyster shells and carried the mutilated remains to a place called Cindron, where they burned them to ashes.

Thus perished in A.D. 415 the greatest woman initiate of the ancient world, and with her fell also the Neo-Platonic School of Alexandria. The memory of Hypatia has probably been perpetuated in the hagiolatry of the Roman Catholic Church in the person of St. Catherine of Alexandria.

The Comte di Cagliostro

The "divine" Cagliostro, one moment the idol of Paris, the next a lonely prisoner in a dungeon of the Inquisition, passed like a meteor across the face of France. According to his memoirs written by him during his confinement in the Bastille, Alessandro Cagliostro was born in Malta of a noble but unknown family. He was reared and educated in Arabia under the tutelage of Altotas, a man well versed in several branches of philosophy and science and also a master of the transcendental arts. While Cagliostro's biographers generally ridicule this account, they utterly fail to advance in its stead any logical solution for the source of his magnificent store of arcane knowledge.

Branded as an impostor and a charlatan, his miracles declared to be leg-erdemain, and his very generosity suspected of an ulterior motive, the Comte di Cagliostro is undoubtedly the most calumniated man in modern history. "The mistrust," writes W.H.K. Trowbridge, "that mystery and magic always inspire made Cagliostro with his fantastic personality an easy target for calumny. After having been riddled with abuse till he was unrecognizable, prejudice, the foster child of calumny, proceeded to lynch him, so to speak. For over one hundred years his character has dangled on the gibbet of infamy, upon which the *sbirri* of tradition have inscribed a curse on any one who shall attempt to cut him down. His fate has been his fame. He is remembered in history, not so much for any-thing he did, as for what was done to him." (See *Cagliostro, the Splendour and Misery of a Master of Magic.*)

According to popular belief Cagliostro's real name was Giuseppe Balsamo, and he was a Sicilian by birth. Within recent years, however, doubts have arisen as to whether this belief is in accord with the facts. It may yet be proved that in part, at least, the tirades of abuse heaped upon the unfortunate Comte have been directed against the wrong man. Giuseppe Balsamo was born in 1743 of honest but humble parentage. From boyhood he exhibited selfish, worthless, and even criminal tendencies, and after a series of escapades disappeared. Trowbridge (*loc. cit.*) presents ample proof that Cagliostro was not Giuseppe Balsamo, thus disposing of the worst accusation against him. After six months' imprisonment in the Bastille, on his trial Cagliostro was exonerated from any implication in the theft of the famous "Queen's Necklace," and later the fact was established that he had actually warned Cardinal de Rohan of the intended crime. Despite the fact, however, that he was discharged as innocent by the French trial court, a deliberate effort to vilify Cagliostro was made by an artist—more talented than intelligent—who painted a picture showing him holding the fatal necklace in his hand. The trial of Cagliostro has been called the prologue of the French Revolu-tion. The smoldering animosity against Marie Antoinette and Louis XVI engen-dered by this trial later burst forth as the holocaust of the Reign of Terror. In his brochure, *Cagliostro and His Egyptian Rite of Freemasonry,* Henry R. Evans also ably defends this much persecuted man against the infamies so unjustly linked with his name.

Sincere investigators of the facts surrounding the life and mysterious "death" of Cagliostro are of the opinion that the stories circulated against him may be traced to the machinations of the Inquisition, which in this manner sought to justify his persecution. The basic charge against Cagliostro was that he had attempted to found a Masonic lodge in Rome—nothing more. All other accusations are of subsequent date. For some reason undisclosed, the Pope commuted Cagliostro's sentence of death to perpetual imprisonment. This act in itself showed the regard in which Cagliostro was held even by his enemies. While his death is believed to have occurred several years later in an Inquisitional dungeon in the castle of San Leo, it is highly improbable that such was the case. There are rumors that he escaped, and according to one very significant story Cagliostro fled to India, where his talents received the appreciation denied them in politics-ridden Europe.

After creating his Egyptian Rite, Cagliostro declared that since women had been admitted into the ancient Mysteries there was no reason why they should be excluded from the modern orders. The Princesse de Lamballe graciously accepted the dignity of Mistress of Honor in his secret society, and on the evening of her initiation the most important members of the French court were present. The brilliance of the affair attracted the attention of the Masonic lodges in Paris. Their representatives, in a sincere desire to understand the Masonic Mysteries, chose the learned orientalist Court de Gébelin as their spokesman, and invited Comte di Cagliostro to attend a conference to assist in clearing up a number of important questions concerning Masonic philosophy. The Comte accepted the invitation.

On May 10, 1785, Cagliostro attended the conference called for that purpose, and his power and simplicity immediately won for him the favorable opinion of the entire gathering. It took but a few words for the Court de Gébelin to discover that he was talking not only to a fellow scholar but to a man infinitely his superior. Cagliostro immediately presented an address, which was so unexpected, so totally different from anything ever heard before by those assembled, that all were speechless with amazement. Cagliostro declared the Rose-Cross to be the ancient and true symbol of the Mysteries and, after a brief description of its original symbolism, branched out into a consideration of the symbolic meaning of letters, predicting to the assembly the future of France in a graphic manner that left no room for doubt that the speaker was a man of insight and supernatural power. With a curious arrangement of the letters of the alphabet, Cagliostro foretold in detail the horrors of the coming revolution and the fall of the monarchy, describing minutely the fate of the various members of the royal family. He also prophesied the advent of Napoleon and the rise of the First Empire. All this he did to demonstrate that which can be accomplished by superior knowledge.

Later when arrested and sent to the Bastille, Cagliostro wrote on the wall of his cell the following cryptic message which, when interpreted, reads: "In 1789 the besieged Bastille will on July 14th be pulled down by you from top to bottom." Cagliostro was the mysterious agent of the Knights Templars, the Rosicrucian initiate whose magnificent store of learning is attested by the profundity of the Egyptian Rite of Freemasonry. Thus Comte di Cagliostro remains one of the strangest characters in history—believed by his friends to have lived forever and to have taken part in the marriage feast of Cana, and accused by his enemies of being the Devil incarnate! His powers of prophecy are ably described by Alexandre Dumas in *The Queen's Necklace*. The world he sought to serve in his own strange way received him not, but has followed with relentless persecution down through the centuries even the very memory of this illustrious adept who, unable to accomplish the great labor at hand, stepped aside in favor of his more successful compatriot, the Comte de St.-Germain.

The Comte de St.-Germain

During the early part of the eighteenth century there appeared in the diplomatic circles of Europe the most baffling personality of history—a man whose life was so near a synonym of mystery that the enigma of his true identity was as insolvable to his contemporaries as it has been to later investigators. The Comte de St.-Germain was recognized as the outstanding scholar and linguist of his day. His versatile accomplishments extended from chemistry and history to poetry and music. He played several musical instruments with great skill and among his numerous compositions was a short opera. He was also an artist of rare ability and the remarkably luminous effects which he created on canvas are believed to have been the result of his mixing powdered mother-of-pearl with his pigments. He gained worldwide distinction for his ability to reproduce in his paintings the original luster of the precious stones appearing upon the costumes of his subjects. His linguistic proficiency verged on the supernatural. He spoke German, English, Italian, Portuguese, Spanish, French with a Piedmontese accent, Greek, Latin, Sanskrit, Arabic, and Chinese with such fluency that in every land he visited he was accepted as a native. He was ambidextrous to such a degree that he could write the same article with both hands simultaneously. When the two pieces of paper were afterwards placed together with a light behind them, the writing on one sheet exactly covered, letter for letter, the writing on the other.

As a historian, the Comte de St.-Germain possessed uncanny knowledge of every occurrence of the preceding two thousand years, and in his reminiscences he described in intimate detail events of previous centuries in which he had

played important rôles. He assisted Mesmer in developing the theory of mesmerism, and in all probability was the actual discoverer of that science. His
knowledge of chemistry was so profound that he could remove flaws from diamonds and other precious stones—a feat which he actually performed at the
request of Louis XV in 1757. He was also recognized as an art critic without a
peer and was often consulted regarding paintings accredited to the great masters. His claim to the possession of the fabled *elixir of life* was borne witness to
by Madame de Pompadour, who discovered, she declared, that he had presented a lady of the court with a certain priceless liquid which had had the effect
of preserving her youthful vivacity and beauty for over twenty-five years beyond
the normal term.

The startling accuracy of his prophetic utterances gained for him no small
degree of fame. To Marie Antoinette he predicted the fall of the French monarchy, and he was also aware of the unhappy fate of the royal family years before
the Revolution actually took place. The crowning evidence, however, of the
Comte's genius was his penetrating grasp of the political situation of Europe
and the consummate skill with which he parried the thrusts of his diplomatic
adversaries. He was employed by a number of European governments, including the French, as a secret agent, and at all times bore credentials which gave him
entrée to the most exclusive circles.

In her excellent monograph, *The Comte de St.-Germain, the Secret of Kings,*
Mrs. Cooper-Oakley lists the most important names under which this amazing
person masqueraded between the years 1710 and 1822. "During this time," she
writes, "we have M. de St.-Germain as the Marquis de Montferrat, Comte Bella-
marre or Aymar at Venice, Chevalier Schoening at Pisa, Chevalier Weldon at
Milan and Leipzig, Comte Soltikoff at Genoa and Leghorn, Graf Tzarogy at
Schwalbach and Triesdorf, Prinz Ragoczy at Dresden, and Comte de St.-
Germain at Paris, The Hague, London, and St. Petersburg." It is evident that M. de
St.-Germain adopted these various names in the interests of the political secret
service work which historians have presumed to be the major mission of his life.

The Comte de St.-Germain has been described as of medium height, well
proportioned in body, and of regular and pleasing features. His complexion was
somewhat swarthy and his hair dark, though often shown powdered. He
dressed simply, usually in black, but his clothes were well fitting and of the best
quality. He had apparently a mania for diamonds, which he wore not only in
rings but also in his watch and chain, his snuff box, and upon his buckles. A jew-
eler once estimated the value of his shoe buckles at 200,000 francs. The Comte
is generally depicted as a man in middle life, entirely devoid of wrinkles and free

from any physical infirmity. He ate no meat and drank no wine, in fact seldom dined in the presence of any second person. Although he was looked upon as a charlatan and impostor by a few nobles at the French court, Louis XV severely reprimanded a courtier who made a disparaging remark concerning him. The grace and dignity that characterized his conduct, together with his perfect control of every situation, attested the innate refinement and culture of one "to the manner born." This remarkable person also had the surprising and impressive ability to divine, even to the most minute details, the questions of his inquisitors before they were asked. By something akin to telepathy he was also able to feel when his presence was needed in some distant city or state, and it has even been recorded of him that he had the astonishing habit not only of appearing in his own apartment and in those of friends without resorting to the conventionality of the door but also of departing therefrom in a similar manner.

M. de St.-Germain's travels covered many countries. During the reign of Peter III he was in Russia and between the years 1737 and 1742 in the court of the Shah of Persia as an honored guest. On the subject of his wanderings Una Birch writes: "The travels of the Comte de Saint-Germain covered a long period of years and a great range of countries. From Persia to France and from Calcutta to Rome he was known and respected. Horace Walpole spoke with him in London in 1745; Clive knew him in India in 1756; Madame d'Adhémar alleges that she met him in Paris in 1789, five years after his supposed death; while other persons pretended to have held conversations with him in the early nineteenth century. He was on familiar and intimate terms with the crowned heads of Europe and the honoured friend of many distinguished persons of all nationalities. He is even mentioned in the memoirs and letters of the day, and always as a man of mystery. Frederick the Great, Voltaire, Madame de Pompadour, Rousseau, Chatham, and Walpole, all of whom knew him personally, rivalled each other in curiosity as to his origin. During the many decades in which he was before the world, however, no one succeeded in discovering why he appeared as a Jacobite agent in London, as a conspirator in Petersburg, as an alchemist and connoisseur of pictures in Paris, or as a Russian general at Naples. * * * Now and again the curtain which shrouds his actions is drawn aside, and we are permitted to see him fiddling in the music room at Versailles, gossiping with Horace Walpole in London, sitting in Frederick the Great's library at Berlin, or conducting illuminist meetings in caverns by the Rhine." (See *The Nineteenth Century,* January, 1908.)

The Comte de St.-Germain has been generally regarded as an important figure in early activities of the Freemasons. Repeated efforts, however, probably with an ulterior motive, have been made to discredit his Masonic affiliations. An example of this is the account appearing in *The Secret Tradition in Freemasonry*, by Arthur Edward Waite. This author, after making several rather disparaging remarks on the subject, amplifies his article by reproducing an engraving of the *wrong* Comte de St.-Germain, apparently being unable to distinguish between the great illuminist and the French general. It will yet be established beyond all doubt that the Comte de St.-Germain was both a Mason and a Templar; in fact the memoirs of Cagliostro contain a direct statement of his initiation into the order of the Knights Templars at the hands of St.-Germain. Many of the illustrious personages with whom the Comte de St.-Germain associated were high Masons, and sufficient memoranda have been preserved concerning the discussions which they held to prove that he was a master of Freemasonic lore. It is also reasonably certain that he was connected with the Rosicrucians—possibly having been the actual head of that order.

The Comte de St.-Germain was thoroughly conversant with the principles of Oriental esotericism. He practiced the Eastern system of meditation and concentration, upon several occasions having been seen seated with his feet crossed and hands folded in the posture of a Hindu Buddha. He had a retreat in the heart of the Himalayas to which he retired periodically from the world. On one occasion he declared that he would remain in India for eighty-five years and then would return to the scene of his European labors. At various times he admitted that he was obeying the orders of a power higher and greater than himself. What he did not say was that this superior power was the Mystery school which had sent him into the world to accomplish a definite mission. The Comte de St.-Germain and Sir Francis Bacon are the two greatest emissaries sent into the world by the Secret Brotherhood in the last thousand years.

E. Francis Udny, a Theosophical writer, is of the belief that the Comte de St.-Germain was not the son of Prince Rákóczy of Transylvania, but because of his age could have been none other than the prince himself, who was known to be of a deep philosophic and mystic nature. The same writer believes the Comte de St.-Germain passed through the "philosophic death" as Francis Bacon in 1626, as Francois Rákóczy in 1735, and as Comte de St.-Germain in 1784. He also feels that the Comte de St.-Germain was the famous Comte de Gabalis, and as Count Hompesch was the last Grand Master of the Knights of Malta. It is well known that many members of the European secret societies have feigned death for various purposes. Marshal Ney, a member of the Society of Unknown Philosophers, escaped the firing squad and under the name of Peter Stuart Ney lived and taught school for over thirty years in North Carolina. On his deathbed, P. S. Ney told Doctor Locke, the attending physician, that he was Marshal Ney of France.

In concluding an article on the identity of the inscrutable Comte de St.-Germain, Andrew Lang writes: "Did Saint-Germain really die in the palace of Prince Charles of Hesse about 1780–85? Did he, on the other hand, escape from the French prison where Grosley thought he saw him, during the French Revolution? Was he known to Lord Lytton about 1860? * * * Is he the mysterious Muscovite adviser of the Dalai Lama? Who knows? He is a will-o'-the-wisp of the memoir-writers of the eighteenth century." (See *Historical Mysteries*.)

Episodes from American History

Many times the question has been asked, Was Francis Bacon's vision of the "New Atlantis" a prophetic dream of the great civilization which was so soon to rise upon the soil of the New World? It cannot be doubted that the secret societies of Europe conspired to establish upon the American continent "a new nation, conceived in liberty and dedicated to the proposition that all men are created equal." Two incidents in the early history of the United States evidence the influence of that *silent body* which has so long guided the destinies of peoples and religions. By them nations are created as vehicles for the promulgation of ideals, and while nations are true to these ideals they survive; when they vary from them they vanish like the Atlantis of old which had ceased to "know the gods."

In his admirable little treatise, *Our Flag*, Robert Allen Campbell revives the details of an obscure, but most important, episode of American history—the designing of the Colonial flag of 1775. The account involves a mysterious man concerning whom no information is available other than that he was on familiar terms with both General George Washington and Dr. Benjamin Franklin. The following description of him is taken from Campbell's treatise:

"Little seems to have been known concerning this old gentleman; and in the materials from which this account is compiled his name is not even once mentioned, for he is uniformly spoken of or referred to as 'the Professor.' He was evidently far beyond his threescore and ten years; and he often referred to historical events of more than a century previous just as if he had been a living witness of their occurrence; still he was erect, vigorous and active—hale, hearty, and clear-minded—as strong and energetic every way as in the prime of his life. He was tall, of fine figure, perfectly easy, and very dignified in his manners; being at once courteous, gracious and commanding. He was, for those times and considering the customs of the Colonists, very peculiar in his method of living; for he ate no flesh, fowl or fish; he never used for food any 'green thing,' any roots or anything unripe; he drank no liquor, wine or ale; but confined his diet to cereals and their products, fruits that were ripened on the stem in the sun, nuts, mild tea and the sweets of honey, sugar or molasses.

"He was well educated, highly cultivated, of extensive as well as varied information, and very studious. He spent considerable of his time in the patient and persistent conning of a number of very rare old books and ancient manuscripts which he seemed to be deciphering, translating or rewriting. These books and manuscripts, together with his own writings, he never showed to anyone; and he did not even mention them in his conversations with the family, except in the most casual way; and he always locked them up carefully in a large, old-fashioned, cubically shaped, iron-bound, heavy, oaken chest, whenever he left his room, even for his meals. He took long and frequent walks alone, sat on the brows of the neighboring hills, or mused in the midst of the green and flower-gemmed meadows. He was fairly liberal—but in no way lavish—in spending his money, with which he was well supplied. He was a quiet, though a very genial and very interesting, member of the family; and he was seemingly at home upon any and every topic coming up in conversation. He was, in short, one whom everyone would notice and respect, whom few would feel well acquainted with, and whom no one would presume to question concerning himself—as to whence he came, why he tarried, or whither he journeyed."

By something more than a mere coincidence the committee appointed by the Colonial Congress to design a flag accepted an invitation to be guests, while in Cambridge, of the same family with which the Professor was staying. It was here that General Washington joined them for the purpose of deciding upon a fitting emblem. By the signs which passed between them it was evident that both General Washington and Doctor Franklin recognized the Professor, and by unanimous approval he was invited to become an active member of the committee. During the proceedings which followed, the Professor was treated with the most profound respect and all of his suggestions immediately acted upon. He submitted a pattern which he considered symbolically appropriate for the new flag, and this was unhesitatingly accepted by the other six members of the committee, who voted that the arrangement suggested by the Professor be forthwith adopted. After the episode of the flag the Professor quietly vanished, and nothing further is known concerning him.

Did General Washington and Doctor Franklin recognize the Professor as an emissary of the Mystery school which has so long controlled the political destinies of this planet? Benjamin Franklin was a philosopher and a Freemason—possibly a Rosicrucian initiate. He and the Marquis de Lafayette—also a man of mystery—constitute two of the most important links in the chain of circumstance that culminated in the establishment of the original thirteen American Colonies as a free and independent nation. Doctor Franklin's philosophic attainments are well attested in *Poor Richard's Almanac,* published by him for many years under the name of Richard Saunders. His interest in the cause of Freemasonry is also shown by his republication of Anderson's *Constitutions of Freemasonry,* a rare and much disputed work on the subject.

It was during the evening of July 4, 1776, that the second of these mysterious episodes occurred. In the old State House in Philadelphia a group of men were gathered for the momentous task of severing the last tie between the old country and the new. It was a grave moment and not a few of those present feared that their lives would be the forfeit for their audacity. In the midst of the debate a fierce voice rang out. The debaters stopped and turned to look upon the stranger. Who was this man who had suddenly appeared in their midst and transfixed them with his oratory? They had never seen him before, none knew when he had entered, but his tall form and pale face filled them with awe. His voice ringing with a holy zeal, the stranger stirred them to their very souls. His closing words rang through the building: *"God has given America to be free!"* As the stranger sank into a chair exhausted, a wild enthusiasm burst forth. Name after name was placed upon the parchment: the Declaration of Independence was signed. But where was the man who had precipitated the accomplishment of this immortal task—who had lifted for a moment the veil from the eyes of the assemblage and revealed to them a part at least of the great purpose for which the new nation was conceived? He had disappeared, nor was he ever seen again or his identity established. This episode parallels others of a similar kind recorded by ancient historians attendant upon the founding of every new nation. Are they coincidences, or do they demonstrate that the divine wisdom of the ancient Mysteries still is present in the world, serving mankind as it did of old?

XLVII

Conclusion

hilip, King of Macedon, ambitious to obtain the teacher who would be most capable of imparting the higher branches of learning to his fourteen-year-old son, Alexander, and wishing the prince to have for his mentor the most famous and learned of the great philosophers, decided to communicate with Aristotle. He dispatched the following letter to the Greek sage: "PHILIP TO ARISTOTLE, HEALTH: Know that I have a son. I render the gods many thanks; *not so much for his birth, as that he was born in your time,* for I hope that being educated and instructed by you, he will become worthy of us both and the kingdom which he shall inherit." Accepting Philip's invitation, Aristotle journeyed to Macedon in the fourth year of the 108th Olympiad, and remained for eight years as the tutor of Alexander. The young prince's affection for his instructor became as great as that which he felt for his father. He said that his father had given him *being,* but that Aristotle had given him *well-being.*

The basic principles of the Ancient Wisdom were imparted to Alexander the Great by Aristotle, and at the philosopher's feet the Macedonian youth came to realize the transcendency of Greek learning as it was personified in Plato's immortal disciple. Elevated by his illumined teacher to the threshold of the philosophic sphere, he beheld the world of the sages—the world that fate and the limitations of his own soul decreed he should not conquer.

Aristotle in his leisure hours edited and annotated the *Iliad* of Homer and presented the finished volume to Alexander. This book the young conqueror so highly prized that he carried it with him on all his campaigns. At the time of his triumph over Darius, discovering among the spoils a magnificent, gem-studded casket of unguents, he dumped its contents upon the ground, declaring that at last he had found a case worthy of Aristotle's edition of the *Iliad!*

While on his Asiatic campaign, Alexander learned that Aristotle had published one of his most prized discourses, an occurrence which deeply grieved the young king. So to Aristotle, Conqueror of the Unknown, Alexander, Conqueor of the Known, sent his reproachful and pathetic admission of the insufficiency of worldly pomp and power: "ALEXANDER TO ARISTOTLE, HEALTH: You were wrong in publishing those branches of science hitherto not to be acquired except from oral instruction. In what shall I excel others if the more profound knowledge I gained from you be communicated to all? *For my part I had rather surpass the majority of mankind in the sublimer branches of learning, than in extent of power and dominion.* Farewell." The receipt of this amazing letter caused no ripple in the placid life of Aristotle, who replied that although the discourse had been communicated to the multitudes, none who had not heard him deliver the lecture (who lacked spiritual comprehension) could understand its true import.

A few short years and Alexander the Great went the way of all flesh, and with his body crumbled the structure of empire erected upon his personality. One year later Aristotle also passed into that greater world concerning whose mysteries he had so often discoursed with his disciples in the Lyceum. But, as Aristotle excelled Alexander in life, so he excelled him in death; for though his body moldered in an obscure tomb, the great philosopher continued to live in his intellectual achievements. Age after age paid him grateful tribute, generation after generation pondered over his theorems until by the sheer transcendency of his rational faculties Aristotle—"the master of those who know," as Dante has called him—became the actual conqueror of the very world which Alexander had sought to subdue with the sword.

Thus it is demonstrated that to capture a man it is not sufficient to enslave his body—it is necessary to enlist his reason; that to free a man it is not enough to strike the shackles from his limbs—his mind must be liberated from bondage to his own ignorance. Physical conquest must ever fail, for, generating hatred and dissension, it spurs the mind to the avenging of an outraged body; but all men are bound whether willingly or unwillingly to obey that intellect in which they recognize qualities and virtues superior to their own. That the philosophic culture of ancient Greece, Egypt, and India excelled that of the modern world must be admitted by all, even by the most confirmed of modernists. The golden era of Greek æsthetics, intellectualism, and ethics has never since been equaled. The true philosopher belongs to the most noble order of men: the nation or race which is blessed by possession of illumined thinkers is fortunate indeed, and its name shall be remembered for their sake. In the famous Pythagorean school at

Crotona, philosophy was regarded as indispensable to the life of man. He who did not comprehend the dignity of the reasoning power could not properly be said to live. Therefore, when through innate perverseness a member either voluntarily withdrew or was forcibly ejected from the philosophic fraternity, a headstone was set up for him in the community graveyard; for he who had forsaken intellectual and ethical pursuits to reenter the material sphere with its illusions of sense and false ambition was regarded as one dead to the sphere of Reality. The life represented by the thraldom of the senses the Pythagoreans conceived to be spiritual death, while they regarded death to the sense-world as spiritual life.

Philosophy bestows life in that it reveals the dignity and purpose of living. Materiality bestows death in that it benumbs or clouds those faculties of the human soul which should be responsive to the enlivening impulses of creative thought of ennobling virtue. How inferior to these standards of remote days are the laws by which men live in the twentieth century! Today man, a sublime creature with infinite capacity for self-improvement, in an effort to be true to false standards, turns from his birthright of understanding—without realizing the consequences—and plunges into the maelstrom of material illusion. The precious span of his earthly years he devotes to the pathetically futile effort to establish himself as an enduring power in a realm of unenduring things. Gradually the memory of his life as a spiritual being vanishes from his objective mind and he focuses all his partly awakened faculties upon the seething beehive of industry which he has come to consider the sole actuality. From the lofty heights of his *Self* hood he slowly sinks into the gloomy depths of ephemerality. He falls to the level of the beast, and in brutish fashion mumbles the problems arising from his all too insufficient knowledge of the Divine Plan. Here in the lurid turmoil of a great industrial, political, commercial inferno, men writhe in self-inflicted agony and, reaching out into the swirling mists, strive to clutch and hold the grotesque phantoms of success and power.

Ignorant of the cause of life, ignorant of the purpose of life, ignorant of what lies beyond the mystery of death, yet possessing within himself the answer to it all, man is willing to sacrifice the beautiful, the true, and the good within and without upon the blood-stained altar of worldly ambition. The world of philosophy—that beautiful garden of thought wherein the sages dwell in the bond of fraternity—fades from view. In its place rises an empire of stone, steel, smoke, and hate—a world in which millions of creatures potentially human scurry to and fro in the desperate effort to exist and at the same time maintain the vast institution which they have erected and which, like some mighty Juggernaut, is rumbling inevitably towards an unknown end. In this physical empire, which man erects in the vain belief that he can outshine the kingdom of the celestials, everything is changed to stone. Fascinated by the glitter of gain, man gazes at the Medusa-like face of greed and stands petrified.

In this commercial age science is concerned solely with the classification of physical knowledge and investigation of the temporal and illusionary parts of Nature. Its so-called practical discoveries bind man but more tightly with the bonds of physical limitation. Religion, too, has become materialistic: the beauty and dignity of faith is measured by huge piles of masonry, by tracts of real estate, or by the balance sheet. Philosophy which connects heaven and earth like a mighty ladder, up the rungs of which the illumined of all ages have climbed into the living presence of Reality—even philosophy has become a prosaic and heterogeneous mass of conflicting notions. Its beauty, its dignity, its transcendency are no more. Like other branches of human thought, it has been made materialistic—"practical"—and its activities so directionalized that they may also contribute their part to the erection of this modern world of stone and steel.

In the ranks of the so-called learned there is rising up a new order of thinkers, which may best be termed the *School of the Worldly Wise Men*. After arriving at the astounding conclusion that they are the intellectual salt of the earth, these gentlemen of letters have appointed themselves the final judges of all knowledge, both human and divine. This group affirms that all mystics *must* have been epileptic and most of the saints neurotic! It declares God to be a fabrication of primitive superstition; the universe to be intended for no particular purpose; immortality to be a figment of the imagination; and an outstanding individuality to be but a fortuitous combination of cells! Pythagoras is asserted to have suffered from a "bean complex"; Socrates was a notorious inebriate; St. Paul was subject to fits; Paracelsus was an infamous quack, the Comte di Cagliostro a mountebank, and the Comte de St.-Germain the outstanding crook of history!

What do the lofty concepts of the world's illumined saviors and sages have in common with these stunted, distorted products of the "realism" of this century? All over the world men and women ground down by the soulless cultural systems of today are crying out for the return of the banished age of beauty and enlightenment—for something *practical* in the highest sense of the word. A few are beginning to realize that so-called civilization in its present form is at the vanishing point; that coldness, heartlessness, commercialism, and material efficiency are *im*practical, and only that which offers opportunity for the expression of love and ideality is truly worth while. All the world is seeking happiness, but knows not in what direction to search. Men must learn that happiness crowns the soul's quest for understanding. Only through the realization of infinite goodness and infinite accomplishment can the peace of the inner Self be assured. In spite of man's geocentricism, there is something in the human mind that is reaching out to philosophy—not to this or that philosophic code, but simply to philosophy in the broadest and fullest sense.

The great philosophic institutions of the past must rise again, for these alone can rend the veil which divides the world of causes from that of effects. Only the Mysteries—those sacred Colleges of Wisdom—can reveal to struggling humanity that greater and more glorious universe which is the true home of the spiritual being called man. Modern philosophy has failed in that it has come to regard thinking as simply an *intellectual* process. Materialistic thought is as hopeless a code of life as commercialism itself. *The power to think true* is the savior of humanity. The mythological and historical Redeemers of every age were all personifications of that power. He who has a little more rationality than his neighbor is a little better than his neighbor. He who functions on a higher plane of rationality than the rest of the world is termed the greatest thinker. He who functions on a lower plane is regarded as a barbarian. Thus comparative rational development is the true gauge of the individual's evolutionary status.

Briefly stated, the true purpose of ancient philosophy was to discover a method whereby development of the rational nature could be accelerated instead of awaiting the slower processes of Nature. This supreme source of power, this attainment of knowledge, this unfolding of the god within, is concealed under the epigrammatic statement of the *philosophic life.* This was the key to the Great Work, the mystery of the Philosopher's Stone, for it meant that alchemical transmutation had been accomplished. Thus ancient philosophy was primarily the living of a life; secondarily, an intellectual method. He alone can become a philosopher in the highest sense who *lives the philosophic life.* What man lives he comes to *know.* Consequently, a great philosopher is one whose threefold life—physical, mental, and spiritual—is wholly devoted to and completely permeated by his rationality.

Man's physical, emotional, and mental natures provide environments of reciprocal benefit or detriment to each other. Since the physical nature is the immediate environment of the mental, only that mind is capable of rational thinking which is enthroned in a harmonious and highly refined material constitution. Hence *right action, right feeling,* and *right thinking* are prerequisites of *right knowing,* and the attainment of philosophic power is possible only to such as have harmonized their thinking with their living. The wise have therefore declared that none can attain to the highest in the science of knowing until first he has attained to the highest in the science of living. *Philosophic power is the natural outgrowth of the philosophic life.* Just as an intense physical existence emphasizes the importance of physical things, or just as the monastic metaphysical asceticism establishes the desirability of the ecstatic state, so complete philosophic absorption ushers the consciousness of the thinker into the most elevated and noble of all spheres—the pure philosophic, or rational, world.

In a civilization primarily concerned with the accomplishment of the extremes of temporal activity, the philosopher represents an equilibrating intellect capable of estimating and guiding the cultural growth. The establishment of the *philosophic rhythm* in the nature of an individual ordinarily requires from fifteen to twenty years. During that entire period the disciples of old were constantly subjected to the most severe discipline. Every activity of life was gradually disengaged from other interests and focalized upon the reasoning part. In the ancient world there was another and most vital factor which entered into the production of rational intellects and which is entirely beyond the comprehension of modern thinkers: namely, *initiation* into the philosophic Mysteries. A man who had demonstrated his peculiar mental and spiritual fitness was accepted into the *body of the learned* and to him was revealed that priceless heritage of arcane lore preserved from generation to generation. This heritage of philosophic truth is the matchless treasure of all ages, and each disciple admitted into these *brotherhoods of the wise* made, in turn, his individual contribution to this store of classified knowledge.

The one hope of the world is philosophy, for all the sorrows of modern life result from the lack of a proper philosophic code. Those who sense even in part the dignity of life cannot but realize the shallowness apparent in the activities of this age. Well has it been said that no individual can succeed until he has developed his philosophy of life. Neither can a race or nation attain true greatness until it has formulated an adequate philosophy and has dedicated its existence to a policy consistent with that philosophy. During the World War, when so-called civilization hurled one half of itself against the other in a frenzy of hate, men ruthlessly destroyed something more precious even than human life: they obliterated those records of human thought by which life can be intelligently directionalized. Truly did Mohammed declare the ink of philosophers to be more precious than the blood of martyrs. Priceless documents, invaluable records of achievement, knowledge founded on ages of patient observation and experimentation by the elect of the earth—all were destroyed with scarcely a qualm of regret. What was knowledge, what was truth, beauty, love, idealism, philosophy, or religion when compared to man's desire to control an infinitesimal spot in the fields of Cosmos for an inestimably minute fragment of time? Merely to satisfy some whim or urge of ambition man would uproot the universe, though well he knows that in a few short years he must depart, leaving all that he has seized to posterity as an old cause for fresh contention.

War—the irrefutable evidence of *ir*rationality—still smolders in the hearts of men; it cannot die until human selfishness is overcome. Armed with multifarious inventions and destructive agencies, civilization will continue its fratricidal strife through future ages. But upon the mind of man there is dawning a great fear—the fear that eventually civilization will destroy itself in one great cataclysmic struggle. Then must be reenacted the eternal drama of reconstruction. Out of the ruins of the civilization which died when its idealism died, some primitive people yet in the womb of destiny must build a new world. Foreseeing the needs of that day, the philosophers of the ages have desired that into the structure of this new world shall be incorporated the truest and finest of all that has gone before. It is a divine law that the sum of previous accomplishment shall be the foundation of each new order of things. The great philosophic treasures of humanity must be preserved. That which is superficial may be allowed to perish; that which is fundamental and essential must remain, regardless of cost.

Two fundamental forms of ignorance were recognized by the Platonists: *simple* ignorance and *complex* ignorance. Simple ignorance is merely lack of knowledge and is common to all creatures existing posterior to the First Cause, which alone has perfection of knowledge. Simple ignorance is an ever-active agent, urging the soul onward to the acquisition of knowledge. From this virginal state of unawareness grows the desire to become aware with its resultant improvement in the mental condition. The human intellect is ever surrounded by forms of existence beyond the estimation of its partly developed faculties. In this realm of objects not understood is a never-failing source of mental stimuli. Thus wisdom eventually results from the effort to cope rationally with the problem of the unknown.

In the last analysis, the Ultimate Cause alone can be denominated wise; in simpler words, only God is good. Socrates declared knowledge, virtue, and utility to be one with the innate nature of good. Knowledge is a condition of *knowing;* virtue a condition of *being;* utility a condition of *doing.* Considering wisdom as synonymous with mental completeness, it is evident that such a state can exist only in the Whole, for that which is less than the Whole cannot possess the fullness of the All. No part of creation is complete; hence each part is imperfect to the extent that it falls short of entirety. Where incompleteness is, it also follows that ignorance must be coexistent; for every part, while capable of knowing its own Self, cannot become aware of the Self in the other parts. Philosophically considered, growth from the standpoint of human evolution is a process proceeding from heterogeneity to homogeneity. In time, therefore, the isolated consciousness of the individual fragments is reunited to become the complete consciousness of the Whole. Then, and then only, is the condition of *all-knowing* an absolute reality.

Thus all creatures are relatively ignorant yet relatively wise; comparatively nothing yet comparatively all. The microscope reveals to man his significance; the telescope, his insignificance. Through the eternities of existence man is gradually increasing in both wisdom and understanding; his ever-expanding consciousness is including more of the external within the area of itself. Even in man's present state of imperfection it is dawning upon his realization that he can never be truly happy until he is perfect, and that of all the faculties contributing to his self-perfection none is equal in importance to the rational intellect. Through the labyrinth of diversity only the illumined mind can, and must, lead the soul into the perfect light of unity.

In addition to the simple ignorance which is the most potent factor in mental growth there exists another, which is of a far more dangerous and subtle type. This second form, called *twofold* or *complex* ignorance, may be briefly defined as *ignorance of ignorance.* Worshiping the sun, moon, and stars, and offering sacrifices to the winds, the primitive savage sought with crude fetishes to propitiate his unknown gods. He dwelt in a world filled with wonders which he did not understand. Now great cities stand where once roamed the Crookboned men. Humanity no longer regards itself as primitive or aboriginal. The spirit of wonder and awe has been succeeded by one of sophistication. Today man worships his own accomplishments, and either relegates the immensities of time and space to the background of his consciousness or disregards them entirely.

The twentieth century makes a fetish of civilization and is overwhelmed by its own fabrications; its gods are of its own fashioning. Humanity has forgotten how infinitesimal, how impermanent and how ignorant it actually is. Ptolemy has been ridiculed for conceiving the earth to be the center of the universe, yet modern civilization is seemingly founded upon the hypothesis that the planet earth is the most permanent and important of all the heavenly spheres, and that the gods from their starry thrones are fascinated by the monumental and epochal events taking place upon this spherical ant-hill in Chaos.

From age to age men ceaselessly toil to build cities that they may rule over them with pomp and power—as though a fillet of gold or ten million vassals could elevate man above the dignity of his own thoughts and make the glitter of his scepter visible to the distant stars. As this tiny planet rolls along its orbit in space, it carries with it some two billion human beings who live and die oblivious to that immeasurable existence lying beyond the lump on which they dwell. Measured by the infinities of time and space, what are the captains of industry or the lords of finance? If one of these plutocrats should rise until he ruled the earth itself, what would he be but a petty despot seated on a grain of Cosmic dust?

Philosophy reveals to man his kinship with the All. It shows him that he is a brother to the suns which dot the firmament; it lifts him from a taxpayer on a whirling atom to a citizen of Cosmos. It teaches him that while physically bound to earth (of which his blood and bones are part), there is nevertheless within him a spiritual power, a diviner Self, through which he is one with the symphony of the Whole. Ignorance of ignorance, then, is that self-satisfied state of unawareness in which man, knowing nothing outside the limited area of his physical senses, bumptiously declares there is nothing more to know! He who knows no life save the physical is merely ignorant; but he who declares physical life to be all-important and elevates it to the position of supreme reality—such a one is ignorant of his own ignorance.

If the Infinite had not desired man to become wise, He would not have bestowed upon him the faculty of knowing. If He had not intended man to become virtuous, He would not have sown within the human heart the seeds of virtue. If He had predestined man to be limited to his narrow physical life, He would not have equipped him with perceptions and sensibilities capable of grasping, in part at least, the immensity of the outer universe. The criers of philosophy call all men to a comradeship of the spirit: to a fraternity of thought: to a convocation of Selves. Philosophy invites man out of the vainness of selfishness; out of the sorrow of ignorance and the despair of worldliness; out of the travesty of ambition and the cruel clutches of greed; out of the red hell of hate and the cold tomb of dead idealism.

Philosophy would lead all men into the broad, calm vistas of truth, for the world of philosophy is a land of peace where those finer qualities pent up within each human soul are given opportunity for expression. Here men are taught the wonders of the blades of grass; each stick and stone is endowed with speech and tells the secret of its being. All life, bathed in the radiance of understanding, becomes a wonderful and beautiful reality. From the four corners of creation swells a mighty anthem of rejoicing, for here in the light of philosophy is revealed the purpose of existence; the wisdom and goodness permeating the

Whole become evident to even man's imperfect intellect. Here the yearning heart of humanity finds that companionship which draws forth from the inner-most recesses of the soul that great store of good which lies there like precious metal in some deep hidden vein.

Following the path pointed out by the wise, the seeker after truth ultimately attains to the summit of wisdom's mount, and gazing down, beholds the panorama of life spread out before him. The cities of the plains are but tiny specks and the horizon on every hand is obscured by the gray haze of the Unknown. Then the soul realizes that wisdom lies in breadth of vision; that it increases in comparison to the vista. Then as man's thoughts lift him heaven-ward, streets are lost in cities, cities in nations, nations in continents, continents in the earth, the earth in space, and space in an infinite eternity, until at last but two things remain: the Self and the goodness of God.

While man's physical body resides with him and mingles with the heedless throng, it is difficult to conceive of man as actually inhabiting a world of his own—a world which he has discovered by lifting himself into communion with the profundities of his own internal nature. Man may live two lives. One is a struggle from the womb to the tomb. Its span is measured by man's own cre-ation—time. Well may it be called the *unheeding* life. The other life is from real-ization to infinity. It begins with understanding, its duration is forever, and upon the plane of eternity it is consummated. This is called the *philosophic* life. Philosophers are not born nor do they die; for once having achieved the realiza-tion of immortality, they are immortal. Having once communed with Self, they realize that within there is an immortal foundation that will not pass away. Upon this living, vibrant base—Self—they erect a civilization which will endure after the sun, the moon, and the stars have ceased to be. The fool lives but for today; the philosopher lives forever.

When once the rational consciousness of man rolls away the stone and comes forth from its sepulcher, it dies no more; for to this second or philosophic birth there is no dissolution. By this should not be inferred physical immortality, but rather that the philosopher has learned that his physical body is no more his true Self than the physical earth is his true world. In the realization that he and his body are dissimilar—that though the form must perish the life will not fail—he achieves conscious immortality. This was the immortality to which Socrates referred when he said: "Anytus and Melitus may indeed put me to death, but they cannot injure me." To the wise, physical existence is but the outer room of the hall of life. Swinging open the doors of this antechamber, the illumined pass into the greater and more perfect existence. The ignorant dwell in a world bounded by time and space. To those, however, who grasp the import and dignity of Being, these are but phantom shapes, illusions of the senses—arbitrary limits imposed by man's ignorance upon the duration of Deity. The philosopher lives and thrills with the realization of this duration, for to him this infinite period has been designed by the All-Wise Cause as the time of all accomplishment.

Man is not the insignificant creature that he appears to be; his physical body is not the true measure of his real self. The invisible nature of man is as vast as his comprehension and as measureless as his thoughts. The fingers of his mind reach out and grasp the stars; his spirit mingles with the throbbing life of Cosmos itself. He who has attained to the state of understanding thereby has so increased his capacity to know that he gradually incorporates within himself the various elements of the universe. The unknown is merely that which is yet to be included within the consciousness of the seeker. Philosophy assists man to develop the sense of appreciation; for as it reveals the glory and the sufficiency of knowledge, it also unfolds those latent powers and faculties whereby man is enabled to master the secrets of the seven spheres.

From the world of physical pursuits the initiates of old called their disciples into the life of the mind and the spirit. Throughout the ages, the Mysteries have stood at the threshold of Reality—that hypothetical spot between *noumenon* and *phenomenon,* the Substance and the shadow. The gates of the Mysteries stand ever ajar and those who will may pass through into the spacious domicile of spirit. The world of philosophy lies neither to the right nor to the left, neither above nor below. Like a subtle essence permeating all space and all substance, it is everywhere; it penetrates the innermost and the outermost parts of all being. In every man and woman these two spheres are connected by a gate which leads from the not-self and its concerns to the Self and its realizations. In the mystic this gate is the heart, and through spiritualization of his emotions he contacts that more elevated plane which, once felt and known, becomes the sum of the worth-while. In the philosopher, reason is the gate between the outer and the inner worlds, the illumined mind bridging the chasm between the corporeal and the incorporeal. Thus godhood is born within the one who sees, and from the concerns of men he rises to the concerns of gods.

In this era of "practical" things men ridicule even the existence of God. They scoff at goodness while they ponder with befuddled minds the phantasmagoria of materiality. They have forgotten the path which leads beyond the stars. The great mystical institutions of antiquity which invited man to enter into his divine inheritance have crumbled, and institutions of human scheming now stand where once the ancient homes of learning rose a mystery of fluted columns and polished marble. The white-robed sages who gave to the world in ideals of culture and beauty have gathered their robes about them and departed from the sight of men. Nevertheless, this little earth is bathed as of old in the sunlight of its Providential Generator. Wide-eyed babes still face the mysteries of physical existence. Men continue to laugh and cry, to love and hate; some still dream of a nobler world, a fuller life, a more perfect realization. In both the heart and mind of man the gates which lead from mortality to immortality are still ajar. Virtue, love, and idealism are yet the regenerators of humanity. God continues to love and guide the destinies of His creation. The path still winds upward to accomplishment. The soul of man has not been deprived of its wings; they are merely folded under its garment of flesh. Philosophy is ever that magic power which, sundering the vessel of clay, releases the soul from its bondage to habit and perversion. Still as of old, the soul released can spread its wings and soar to the very source of itself.

The criers of the Mysteries speak again, bidding all men welcome to the House of Light. The great institution of materiality has failed. The false civilization built by man has turned, and like the monster of Frankenstein, is destroying its creator. Religion wanders aimlessly in the maze of theological speculation. Science batters itself impotently against the barriers of the unknown. Only transcendental philosophy knows the path. Only the illumined reason can carry the understanding part of man upward to the light. Only philosophy can teach man to be born well, to live well, to die well, and in perfect measure be born again. Into this band of the elect—those who have chosen the life of knowledge, of virtue, and of utility—the philosophers of the ages invite YOU.

Bibliography

Volumes Quoted from or Consulted in the Preparation of an Encyclopedic Outline of Masonic, Hermetic, Qabbalistic and Rosicrucian Symbolical Philosophy

ADAMS, W. MARSHAM
Book of the Master, The (New York and London, 1898)
House of the Hidden Places, The (London, 1895)

AGRIPPA, HENRY CORNELIUS
De Occulta Philosophia, Libri tres (——, 1551)
Magische Werke (Berlin, 1916)
Three Books of Occult Philosophy or Magic (Chicago, 1898)
Vanities of the Arts and Sciences, The (Paris?, 1537)
Works of Henry Cornelius Agrippa, The (Lugduni, circa 1531)

ALCIAT, ANDREÆ
Emblemata (Antwerp, 1608); do (Paris, 1618)

ALEXANDER, HARTLEY BURR
Mythology of All Races, The (Boston, 1916)

ANDERSON, JAMES
Constitutions of the Free-Masons, The (London, 1723)

ANDREÆ(?), JOHANN VALENTIN
Confessio Fraternitatis (Frankfort, 1615)
Fame, Fraternitatis (Frankfurt, 1615)

ANDREWS, W. S., AND CARUS, PAUL
Magic Squares and Cubes (Chicago, 1908)

ANONYMOUS
A Miscellaneous Metaphysical Essay (London, 1748)
An Enquiry into the Constitution, Discipline, Unity and Worship of the Primitive Church (London, 1713)
A Philosophicall Epitaph in Hierogliphicall Figures (London, 1673)
Book Sealed with Seven Seals, The (Manuscript in German, circa 1750)
Canon, The (London, 1897)
Codex: Nuttall. Facsimile of ancient Mexican Codex (Cambridge, 1902)
Complete Book of Magic Science (London, 1575). (Copy of British Museum Manuscript)
Freemasons Pocket Companion, The (Glasgow, 1771)
Goetia, the Lesser Key of Solomon (Chicago, ——)
Hermetical Triumph, The, To which is added The Ancient War of the Knights (London, 1723)
History of Friar Bacon (London, 1796)
Mysteries of the Rosie Cross (London, 1891)
On Mankind their Origin and Destiny (London, 1872)
Turbæ Philosophorum (Vienna, 1750)

AQUINAS, ST. THOMAS
Summa Theologica (London, 1912)

ASHMOLE, ELIAS
Institution, Laws & Ceremonies of the Most
Noble Order of the Garter, The (London,
1693)
Theatrum Chemicum Britannicum (London,
1652)

AUBREY, JOHN
Letters Written by Eminent Persons of the
Seventeenth and Eighteen Centuries
(London, 1813)

AUDSLEY, W. & G.
Handbook of Christian Symbolism (London,
1865)

AUGUSTINE, ST.
City of God, The (London, 1609?)
Homilies on the Gospel according to St. John
(Oxford, 1849)

AVALON, ARTHUR
Serpent Power, The (Madras, 1924)

BABBITT, EDWIN D.
Principles of Light and Color, The (London,
1878)

BACON, SIR FRANCIS
Advancement of Learning, The (London,
1640); do, Latin (Amsterdam, 1694);
do, First Edition, two sections (London,
1605)
Essayes or Counsels, Civill and Morall, The
(London, 1639)
Historia Regni Henrici Septimi (Amsterdam,
1695)
Historia Vitæ et Mortis (Amsterdam, 1663);
do, English (London, 1638)
History of the Reign of King Henry the Sev-
enth, The (London, 1641)
History of Winds, The (London, 1671)
Novum Organum Scientiarum (Amsterdam,
1694)
Opuscula Historico-Politica (Amsterdam,
1695)
Resuscitatio, etc. (London, 1661)
Scripta In Naturali et Universali Philosophia
(Amsterdam, 1653)
Sermones Fideles (Amsterdam, 1685)
Sylva Sylvarum, and the New Atlantis
(London, 1627)
Sylva Sylvarum, Sive Hist. Naturalis, et Nova
Atlantis (Amsterdam, 1661)

BACSTROM'S (DR. SIGISMUND)
COLLECTION OF ALCHEMICAL
MANUSCRIPTS
18 volumes of manuscript copies from rare alchemical writings, and a number of original manuscripts bound in. At least part are
from the original Bacstrom Collection
mentioned by A. E. Waite in his "Brotherhood of the Rosy Cross," pages 549–560.

Volume 1
The Great Work of the Lapis Sophorum
according to Lambspring's Process.
The Work of the Jewish Rabbi, by Rabbi Isaac
Calvo of Jerusalem.
The Work with Wolfram, by a Venetian Noble-
man.
Three Processes for Obtaining The Tincture,
by Baron de Welling.
A Treatise Concerning the Tincture of Anti-
mony, communicated to his friend
Theodore in 1536, by Theophrastus
Paracelsus.
Of the Tincture of Antimony, by Roger Bacon.
(Printed pages inserted.)
A Process for Obtaining the Tincture from
Urine, by an American Clergyman, with
remarks by Dr. Bacstrom.
The Process of the American Adept. (Manu-
script in German.)

Volume 2
The Work of Philope Ponia for accomplishing
the Elixer, copied from Manuscript dated
1587.
The Process of Philip Pony for accomplishing
the Tincture, as practised by Quercitan's
Daughter.
The Work of Neptis, communicated by him to
Quercitanus.
The Theory and Practice of the Philosopher's
Store, described by Quercitan's Daughter.

Volume 3
Count Bernardus Trevisan on the Transmuta-
tion of Metals.
A Treatise of Bernard Earl of Trevisan of the
Philosophers Stone. Printed copy with
note by Dr. Bacstrom.
The Answer of Bernardus Trevisanus to the
Epistle of Thomas of Bononia, Physician
to King Charles the Eighth. Printed copy
with many notes by Dr. Bacstrom.

Volume 4

The Way to Operate the Elixir, copied from an Original Manuscript without any date or signature.

Some Curious Processes extracted from an old manuscript entitled The Loving Mite, with remarks by Dr. Bacstrom.

The Work with the Butter of Antimony, as communicated verbally to Mr. Hand by a possessor.

Curious practical experiments on some metals.

An Ancient Manuscript.

Volume 5

A Short Process Indicated, translated from the German.

On a Short Process for Regenerating Metals.

Extracts from Paracelsus.

Remarks on the Work entitled Zoroaster's Cave, and also on Astromagus's Magical Gold.

The Process of Alexis Piemontese.

Alchemical Aphorisms.

Several Ancient Manuscripts.

Volume 6

The Chemist's Key, by Henry Nollius.

Monsr. de la Brie's Process for accomplishing the Tincture, translated from the French.

Remarks on the above, by Dr. Bacstrom.

Another Process for accomplishing the same, copied from a manuscript of Dr. Bacstrom.

Some Thoughts on a Hint Given by Basil Valentine of a Via Sicca Regenereationis Principiorum, by Dr. Bacstrom.

Copy of an Anonymous Letter sent to Mr. Ford, concerning the Lapis Philosophorum.

Process for the Lapis with Nitre and Gold.

Thoughts on Nynsicht's Letter to Hartman, from the Latin.

Anonymous Letter sent to Dr. Bacstrom in 1788, Original Letter with Envelope.

Volume 7

Fifty-five Letters of Michael Sendivogius to the Rosey-Crucian Society, with a description of their Seal. From old Manuscript.

Volume 8

Remarks on the Fountain of Bernhard, by Albert Beyer.

On the Lapis Philosophorum, copied from a Manuscript.

Extracts from Metallurgia, or the Generation of Metals, translated from the German.

The Process of Leona Constantia, Abbess, from the German work, The Sun-flower of the Wise.

Multum in Parvo. From a Latin Manuscript.

Opus Maximum, the Science of Alchemy.

Volume 9

The Archbishop of Roane's Questions on Alchemy answered by William de Cones, copied from a manuscript dated 1216.

The Practice of Philosophers.

Lully's Theory of the Philosophers Fires explained by Ripley.

An Alchemical Dialogue between a Disciple and His Master.

A Process by the aid of which a Woman supported her Family.

The Work of the Great Elixir.

The Science of Alchimy.

Copy of an Act by William and Mary permitting the multiplying of Metals.

An Original ancient Manuscript entitled The Book of Alchemy.

Volume 10

The Processes of Mr. John Yardley of Worcester.

The Work of St. Dunstan.

The Work of Johannes Gier.

Dedication prefixed to the German Edition of Trevisan's Works.

Aphorisms Respecting the Philosophical Metallic Work.

The Philosophical Processes of Charas Stella.

A Process upon Lead.

Letter of Dr. Dippelius concerning the Sophic Tincture.

Curious Anecdote Copied from the French Expedition to Egypt.

The Pontic, or Mercurial Water of the Wise, by Chrysogonus de Puris Uranapolita.

Remarks on Pontanus.

Extract from Metallurgia.

Concordantia Philosophorum.

Explanation of the Allegorical Description of the Principles of the Great Work in D'Espagret's Hermetic Secrets.

A Letter from Dr. Bacstrom
Another Letter from Dr. Bacstrom.

Volume 11
A Treatise of the Animal Stone, by Samuel
Norton.
Fundamental Doctrine concerning the First
Root of the Philosopher's Stone, by Frier
Vincentius Koffsky.
Gloria Mundi, A Collection of Wisdom from
Ancient Philosophers.
A Process, by Baron de Welling.
A Treatise of Aristotle the Alchemist, to
Alexander Magnus, concerning the Stone
of the Philosophers.
Extracts from An Ancient Treatise on the
Lapis Philosophorum by Ali Puli, trans-
lated from the Arabic.
The Philosophical Legacy.
Chrisostomi Ferdinandi de Sabot, Practica
Naturae Vera.
Extracts from the Key to the Hermetic Sci-
ences. From the French.

Volume 12
Letters to the Curious, Discovering Secrets
of Great Moment, by Joel Langelotus,
M.D.
Coelum Philosophorum, or Faithful Direc-
tions how to obtain the Hermetical
Treasure.
Archidoxorum, seu de Secretis Natura Libri
decemitem Manualia, by Paracelsus.
The Canons or Aphorisms of Alexander von
Suchten.
Instructions respecting Antimonial Labours
for the Sophic Mercury, by von Suchten,
M.D.
An Ancient Manuscript concerning Avicene
on the First Matter.
Observation collected from the conversation
of Dr. Helvetus and the Brass-founder who
turned lead into gold.
Remarks on the Second Book of Henry von
Batsdorff, called Filum Ariadnes. By Dr.
Bacstrom.

Volume 13
The Golden Chain of Homer. (Aurea Cantena
Homeri.)
Instructions respecting the Art of Transmut-
ing and Ameliorating the Metals, by
William Baron von Shroeder, F.R.S.

Johannis de Monte Raphaim, the forerunner
of Aurora.
Aphorisms concerning the Universal Salt.
A True Revelation of the Manual Operation
for the Universal Medicine, by the Philosopher of Leyden.
Two short manuscripts in the form of notes.

Volume 14
The Hermetical Signification of the Symbols
and Attributes of Isis.
Egyptian Hieroglyphics from the most remote
Antiquity.
The Hermetical Signification of the Hiero-
glyphical Symbols cut in stone over the
Doors of Notre Dame at Paris.
The Mineral Gluten, by Dorothea Juliana Wal-
lachin, a female Adept.
The Mysteries Contained in Sendivogius, ex-
plained, copied from a rare manuscript.
Extracts from Letters supposed to be by
Sendivogius, from a rare manuscript.
The Practice of William Blomefeeld of the
Noble Science of Alchemy.
Two Ancient Manuscripts.

Volume 15
Chemical Moon-Shine, by a Lover of Truth.
From the German.
Philosophical consideration of the Cold Fire.
Experiments by Modestin Fachsen, Director
of the Mint at Leipzig.
Particular Processes of David Beuther M.D.,
written while he was in Prison.
On the Sphaera Saturni by Paracelsus.
Sal Alembrot or Aqua Mercurii of Paracelsus.
The War of the Knights, by John Sternhals
Bishop of Bamberg.
The Key of Alchemy, by Samuel Norton,
1577.

Volume 16
The Emerald Table, with notes by Dr.
Bacstrom.
The Allegory of King Solomon's Navigations
and King Hiram's Ships explained by Dr.
Bacstrom.
Processes from John Gottfried Jugels' Experi-
mental Chemistry.
Neuman on the Nature and Difference of Salt-
Petre.
Sir Kenelm Digby's Sal Enixum and Abbé
Rousseau's Primum Ens Salis.

Extracts from Seventy-Nine Wonders of a Certain Subject.

Extracts from the Concordantia Chymica, by John Joachim Becker.

A Particular Process on Silver from Bacon Kunkel von Lowenstern.

The Epistle of Arnoldus de Villa Nove to the King of Naples, and Myriam's Instructions to King Aros.

Schroeder's Hint, respecting the Spirit of Mercury, also the work of Leona Constantia.

Ancient Manuscript.

Another ancient Manuscript.

Volume 17

Alchemy—A select collection of Testimonies respecting the Doctrines and Practices of the ancient Alchemists. In several parts.

Volume 18

Collection of Manuscripts on Magic, the Qabbalah, etc.

BALLARD, ROBERT
Solution of the Pyramid Problem, The (New York, 1883)

BANIER (ABBÉ)
Mythology and Fables of the Ancients, The (London, 1739)

BARCLAY, JOHN
Loves of Polyarchus & Argenis, The (London, 1636)
Satyricon (Hackiana, 1674)

BARRETT, FRANCIS
Magus, The, or Celestial Intelligencer (London, 1801)

BATCHELOR, H. CROUCH
Francis Bacon Wrote Shakespeare (London, 1912)

BAULDWIN, WILLIAM
A Treatise of Moral Philosophy (London, 1651)

BAYLEY, HAROLD
A New Light on the Renaissance (London, 1909)
Lost Language of Symbolism, The (London, 1912)
Shakespeare Symphony, The (London, 1906)

BEAUMONT, JOHN
Gleanings of Antiquities (London, 1724)

BELZONI, G.
Narrative of the Operation and Recent Discoveries in Egypt and Nubia (London, 1820)

BENN, ALPHRED WILLIAM
Greek Philosophers, The (London, 1882)

BERGERAC, CYRANO
Comical History of the States and Empires of the World of the Moon, The (London, 1687)

BESANT, MRS. ANNIE (WOOD)
Ancient Wisdom (London, 1922)
A Study in Consciousness (London, 1907)

BLAKE, WILLIAM
Marriage of Heaven and Hell, The. (Hand-colored copy from original in British Museum.)

BLAVATSKY, HELENE PETROVNA
Esoteric Instructions of The Theosophical Society, The Isis Unveiled (New York, 1877)
Secret Doctrine, The (London, 1888)

BLOCH, STELLA
Astronomy for All (London, 1911)

BÖHME, JAKOB
Von der Menschwerdung Jesus Christi (Amsterdam, 1682)
XL Questions Concerning the Soule (London, 1647)
Theosophia Revelata (Hamburg, 1715)
Works of Jacob Behmen, The, The Teutonic Theosopher (London, 1764)

BOND, FREDERICK BLIGH, AND LEA, THOMAS SIMCOX
Cabala contained in the Coptic Gnostic Books, The (Oxford, 1917)

BONUS OF FERRARIA
New Pearl of Great Price, The (London, 1894)

BOOTH, WILLIAM STONE
Some Acrostic Signatures of Francis Bacon (Boston, 1909)

BOUTELLE, CLARENCE MILES
Man of Mt. Moriah, The (Chicago, 1898)

BOYLAN, PATRICK
Thoth, the Hermes of Egypt (London, 1922)

BOYSE, SAMUEL
New Pantheon, The (Dublin, 1786)

BREITHAUPT, CHRISTIANUS
Ars Decifratoria sive scientia occultas Scrip-
    turas Solvendi et Legendi preamissa est
    disquisitio historica de variis modis Oc-
    culte Scribendi. (Helmstadii, 1737)

BROWN, JAMES CAMPBELL
A History of Chemistry (Philadelphia, 1920)

BROWN, JOHN P.
Dervishes, The (Philadelphia, 1868)

BROWN, ROBERT HEWITT
Stellar Theology and Masonic Astronomy
    (New York, 1882)

BROWN II, SANGER
Sex Worship and Symbolism (Boston, 1922)

BRYANT, JACOB
A New System, or, an Analysis of Ancient
    Mythology (London, 1774)

BUDGE, E. A. WALLIS
Book of the Dead, The (London, 1913)
Gods of the Egyptians, The (London, 1904)
Oris and the Egyptian Resurrection (London
    and New York, 1911)

BURTON, ROBERT
Anatomy of Melancholy, The (Oxford, 1628);
    do (London, 1660)

CALCOTT, WELLINS
A Candid Disquisition of the Principles and
    Practices of the most Ancient and Hon-
    ourable Society of Free and Accepted
    Masons (London, 1769)

CALMET
Dictionary of the Holy Bible, The (London,
    1800)

CAMDEN, WILLIAM
Remaines Concerning Britain (London, 1657)

CAMPBELL, ROBERT ALLEN
Our Flag (Chicago, 1890)

CARDANUS, HIERONYMUS
In Cl. Ptolemaei de Astrorum Iudiciis (Basil,
    1578)

CARLYLE, THOMAS
Hero as Prophet, The (Boston, 1901)

CARTARI, VINCENZO
Le Imaigini degli Dei degli Antichi (Venezia,
    1609)
Le Imagini degli Del degli Antichi (Padova,
    1626)

CARUS, PAUL
History of the Devil and the Idea of Evil, The
    (Chicago, 1900)

CASSOU, CHARLES
Religions de la Perse, de la Chaldée et de
    l'Égypte

CAUSEUS, MICHAEL ANGELUS
Romanum Museum (Rome, 1746)

CAWDRY, ROBERT
Treasurie or Storehouse of Similes, The
    (London, 1609)

CHARLETON, WALTER
A Ternary of Paradoxes (London, 1650)

CHATTO, WILLIAM ANDREW
Facts and Speculations on the Origin and His-
    tory of Playing Cards (London, 1848)

CHRISTIAN, P.
Histoire de la Magie (Paris, 1876)

CHRISTIE, JAMES
Disquisitions upon the Painted Greek Vases
    (London, 1825)

CHURCHWARD, ALBERT
Arcana of Freemasonry, The (London, 1915)
Signs and Symbols of Primordial Man, The
    (London, 1910)

CLARKE, JAMES FREEMAN
Ten Great Religions (Boston and New York,
    1883)

CLARKE, NATALIE RICE
Bacon's Dial in Shakespeare (Cincinnati,
    1922)

CLEMENT OF ALEXANDRIA
Writings contained in The Ante-Nicene
    Fathers (New York, 1926)

COLE, JOHN
A Treatise on the Circular Zodiac of Tentyra
    (London, 1824)

COLUMNA, FRANCESCO
Hypnerotomachia, ubi humana omnia non nisi
    Somnium esse ostendit, atque obiter
    plurima scitu sane quam digna commemo-
    rat (Venice, 1499)

COOK, ARTHUR BERNARD
Zeus, A Study in Ancient Reilgion (Cam-
    bridge, 1925)

CORNFORD, FRANCIS MACDONALD
From Religion to Philosophy (London, 1912)

CORY, ALEXANDER TURNER
Hieroglyphics of Horapollo Nilous, The
    (London, 1840)

CORY, ISAAC PRESTON
Ancient Fragments (London, 1832)

CRAVEN, J. B.
Doctor Robert Fludd the English Rosicrucian
    (Kirkwall, 1902)

CROLLI, OSWALD
Basilica Chymica.

CROSS, R. W. JEREMY L.
True Masonic Chart, The, or Hieroglyphic
    Monitor (New York, 1854)

CULLEN, CHARLES
History of Mexico, The (Philadelphia, 1804)

CUMONT, FRANZ
Astrology and Religion among the Greeks and
    Romans (New York and London, 1912)
Mysteries of Mithra, The (Chicago, 1910)

CULPEPER, NICHOLAS
Complete Herbal, The (London, 1835)
Semeiotica Uranica (London, ——)

CUNINGHAM, GRANVILLE
Bacon's Secret Disclosed in Contemporary
    Books (London, 1911)

D'ALVIELLA, COUNT GOBLET
Migration of Symbols, The (Westminster,
    1894)

DANTE ALIGHIERI
La Divina Commedia (Torino, 1891)
La Vita Nuova (New York, 1901)

DAVIDSON, D., AND ALDERSMITH, H.
Great Pyramid, Its Divine Message, The
    (London, 1925)

DAVIDSON, P.
Mistletoe and Its Philosophy, The (Glasgow,
    1892)

DAVIES, EDWARD
Mythology and Rites of the British Druids,
    The (London, 1809)

DEANE, JOHN BATHURST
Worship of the Serpent, The (London, 1830)

DE BOURBOURG, L'ABBÉ BRASSEUR
(TRANSLATOR)
Popol Vuh (Paris, 1861)

DEE, A.
Chemical Collection, The (London, 1629)

DE MONTE-SNYDERS
Metamorphosis Planetarum

DE QUINCEY, THOMAS
Historico-Critical Inquiry into the Origin of
    the Rosicrucians and the Freemasons
    (London, 1886)

DERMOTT, LAU.
True Ahiman Rezon, The (New York, 1805)

DE VIGENERE, BLAISE
Les Images ou Tableaux de platte peinture des
    deux Philostrates sophists Grecs et les stat-
    ues de Callistarte (Paris, 1637)

DIGBY, SIR KENELM
Of Bodies, and of Mans Soul (London, 1669)

DINSMORE, CHARLES ALLEN
Teachings of Dance, The (Boston and New
    York, 1910)

D'OHSSON, DE M
Tableau Général de l'Empire Othoman (Paris,
    1787)

D'OLIVET, FABRE
Hebrew Tongue Restored, The (New York,
    1921)

DONNELLY, IGNATIUS
Atlantis, the Antediluvian World (New York
    and London, 1882)
Cipher in the Plays and on the Tombstone,
    The (Minneapolis, 1899)
Great Cryptogram, The (Chicago, New York,
    and London, 1888)
Ragnarok: The Age of Fire and Gravel (New
    York, 1886)

DOYLE, SIR ARTHUR CONAN
Coming of the Fairies, The (New York, 1922)

DRUMMOND, HENRY
Natural Law in the Spiritual World (New York, 1883)

DRUMMOND, SIR W.
Œdipus Judaicus, The (London, 1866)

DUMAS, ALEXANDRE
Queen's Necklace, The (Boston, 1890)
Joseph Balsamo (Boston, 1890)

DUNLAP, S. F.
Sod, The Mysteries of Adoni (London, 1861)

DUPUIS, CHARLES FRANÇOIS
Origin of Religious Worship, The (New Orleans, 1872)

DURANT, W. J.
Story of Philosophy, The (New York, 1926)

DURNING-LAWRENCE, SIR EDWIN
Bacon is Shake-Speare (New York, 1910)
Shakespeare Myth, The (London, 1912)

DU RYER, SIEUR
Alcoran of Mahomet, The (London, 1649)

DWIGHT, M. A.
Grecian and Roman Mythology (New York, 1849)

ECKARTSHAUSEN, KARL VON
Cloud upon the Sanctuary, The (London, 1919)

EDGAR, JOHN AND MORTON
Great Pyramid Passages and Chambers, The (Glasgow, 1923)

EDWARDS, CHILPERIC
Hammurabi Code, The (London, 1921)

ERMAN, ADOLF
A Handbook of Egyptian Religion (London, 1907)

EVANS, HENRY R.
Cagliostro and his Egyptian Rite of Freemasonry (Washington, 1919)

EVERARD, DR. (TRANSLATOR)
Divine Pymander of Hermes Mercurius Trismegistus, The (London, 1650)

Divine Pymander, The. Bath reprint with introduction by Hargrave Jennings (London, 1884)

FABER, GEORGE STANLEY
Origin of Pagan Idolatry, The (London, 1816)

FABRICIUS, JO. ALBERTUS
Codex Pseudepigraphus Veteris Testamenti (Hamburg, 1722)

FAIRHOLT, W. F.
Gog and Magog, The Giants of Guildhall (London, 1859)

FALCONER, JOHN
Cryptomenysis Patefacta, or the Art of Secret Information disclosed without a Key (London, 1685)

FALLOWS, SAMUEL
Popular and Critical Bible Encyclopaedia, The (Chicago, 1919)

FANCOURT, CHARLES ST. JOHN
History of Yucatan, The (London, 1854)

FARNELL, LEWIS R.
Greece and Babylon (Edinburgh, 1911)

FAXARDO, DON DIEGO SAAVEDRA
Idea de Un Principe Politico Christiano (Amsterdam, 1659)

FELLOWS, JOHN
Mysteries of Freemasonry, The (London, 1877)

FIGULUS, BENEDICTUS
Golden and Blessed Casket of Nature's Marvels, The (London, 1893)

FLAMMEL, NICHOLAS
Hieroglyphical Figures, and Theory and Practise of the Philosophers Stone (London, 1624)

FLUDD, ROBERT
Collectio Operum (Oppenhemi, 1617)
Philosophia Moysaica (Goudae, 1638)
Responsum ad Hoplocrisma-Spongum (Goudae, 1638)

FERGUSSON, JAMES
Tree and Serpent Worship (London, 1873)

FOSBROKE, THOMAS DUDLEY
Encyclopaedia of Antiquities (London, 1825)

FRANCK, ADOLPH
Kabbalah, The (New York, 1926)

FRAZER, SIR JAMES GEORGE
Golden Bough, The (London, 1917)

FREUND, ALFRED
Das Bild des Speershüttlers die Lösung des
Shakespeare-Rätsels (Hamburg, 1921)

GAFFAREL JAMES
Unheard-of Curiosities (London, 1650)

GALLUP, MRS. ELIZABETH WELLS
Bi-literal Cypher of Sir Francis Bacon, The
(London, 1900); do (Detroit, 1910)

GARDNER, JAMES
Faiths of the World, The (London, 1858–60)

GARDNER, F. LEIGH
Bibliotheca Rosicruciana (London, 1903)

GARNETT, LUCY M. J.
Mysticism and Magic in Turkey (London,
1912)

GARVER, W. L.
Brother of the Third Degree, The (Chicago,
1894)

GASKELL, G. A.
Dictionary of the Sacred Language of All
Scriptures and Myths (London, 1923)

GAYLEY, CHARLES MILLS
Classic Myths, The (New York, 1911)

GÉBELIN, M. COURT DE
Monde Primitif, Analysé et Comparé avec le
Monde Moderne (Paris, 1776)

GICHTEL, JOHANN GEORG
Theosophia Practica (———, 1736)

GINSBURG, CHRISTIAN D.
Kabbalah, The (London, 1920)

GLAUBER, JOHN RUDOLPH
Works of the Highly Experienced and Famous
Chymist (London, 1689)

GODWIN, WILLIAM
Lives of the Necromancers (London, 1834)

GOLDSMITH, ELIZABETH E.
Life Symbols as Related to Sex Symbolism
(New York, 1924)

GORHAM, A.
Indian Masons' Marks, of the Moghul Dynasty
(London, 1911)

GOULD, ROBERT FREKE
A Concise History of Freemasonry (London,
1904)

GREEN, HENRY
Shakespeare and The Emblem Writers
(London, 1870)

GREGORY (SAINT AND POPE)
Morals on the Book of Job (Oxford, 1850)

GRIMM, JACOB
Teutonic Mythology (London, 1882)

GUERBER, H. A.
Myths of Northern Lands (New York, 1895)

HAECKEL, ERNST
Riddle of the Universe, The (New York,
1900)

HALL, FRANCIS
An Explication of the Diall Sett Up in the
Kings Garden at London, an. 1669 (Liège,
1673)

HAMILTON, SIR WILLIAM
Lectures on Metaphysics and Logic (Boston,
1865)

HARTMANN, FRANZ
In the Pronaos of the Temple of Wisdom
(London, 1890)
Life and Doctrines of Jacob Boehme, The
(London, 1891)
Occult Science in Medicine (London, 1893)
Paracelsus and The Substance of His Teach-
ings (London, 1887)
Secret Symbols of The Rosicrucians, The
(Boston, 1888)

HASTING, JAMES
A Dictionary of the Bible (Edinburgh, 1899)
Encyclopaedia of Religion and Ethics (New
York and Edinburgh, 1915)

HAVEN, DR. MARC
Le Maître Inconnu Cagliostro (Paris, 1912)

HEAD, R.
Life and Death of Mother Shipton, The
(London, 1687)

HECKETHORN, CHARLES WILLIAM
Secret Societies of All Ages and Countries,
The (London, 1897)

HEINDEL, MAX
Freemasonry and Catholicism (Oceanside,
1919)
Rosicrucian Cosmo-Conception, The
(Seattle, 1909)
Unpublished manuscripts (Courtesy of Mrs.
Heindel)

HEINDEL, MAX AND AUGUSTA FOSS
Message of the Stars, The (Mount Ecclesia,
1922)

HELMONT, JOHANNIS BAPTISTAE VON
Ausgang der Artznen-Kunst (Sulzbach, 1683)

HELMHOLTZ, HERMANN L. F. VON
Sensations of Tone (London, 1912)

HESIOD
Compositions from the Works and Days and
Theogony of Hesiod (London, 1817)

HEYDON, JOHN
English Physicians Guide: or a Holy Guide,
The (London, 1662)
Wise Mans Crown; or The Glory of the Rosie-
Cross, The (London, 1664)

HEYWOOD, THOMAS
Gynaikeion (London, 1624)
Hierarchie of the Blessed Angells, The
(London, 1635)

HICKSON, S.A.E.
Prince of Poets, The (London, 1926)

HIEROCLES
Upon the Golden Verses of Pythagoras
(London, 1682)

HIGGINS, FRANK C.
Ancient Freemasonry (New York, 1923)
A. U. M., The Lost Word (New York, 1914)
Cross of the Magi, The (New York, 1912)

HIGGINS, GODFREY
Anacalypsis (London, 1836)
Celtic Druids, The (London, 1827)
Horæ Sabbaticæ (New York, 1893)
Mahomet, The Illustrious (London, 1829)

HOISINGTON, H. R.
Oriental Astronomer, The (Jaffna, 1848)

HOMER
Odyssey, The (———, 1525)

HONE, WILLIAM
Ancient Mysteries Described (London, 1823)

HORT, W. JILLARD
New Pantheon, The (London, 1829)

HUGHES, THOMAS PATRICK
A Dictionary of Islam (London, 1895)

HUNT, GAILLIARD
History of the Seal of the United States, The
(Washington, 1909)

INMAN, THOMAS
Ancient Faiths Embodied in Ancient Names
(London, 1872)
Ancient Pagan and Modern Christian Symbol-
ism (New York, 1874)

IRELAND, SAMUEL
Miscellaneous Papers and Legal Instruments
under the Hand and Seal of William
Shakespeare (London, 1796). (Joseph
Haslewood's copy containing 25 examples
of W. H. Ireland's forgeries mounted with
explanatory notes.)

IRENÆUS AND JUSTIN MARTYR
Writings contained in The Ante-Nicene
Fathers (New York, 1926)

IRVING, WASHINGTON
Mahomet and his Successors (New York,
1854)

JACKSON, SAMUEL MACAULEY (EDITOR)
New Schaff-Herzog Encyclopedia of Religious
Knowledge, The (London and New York,
1909)

JACOLLIOT, LOUIS
Bible in India, The (New York, ———)

JAMES, WILLIAM
Pragmatism (New York, 1909)

JENNINGS, HARGRAVE
Indian Religions, The (London, 1890)
Letters of Hargrave Jennings, The (Bach,
1895)
Live Lights or Dead Lights (London, 1873)
Phallicism (London, 1884)
Rosicrucians, Their Rites and Mysteries, The
(London, 1887)

JOHNSON, MELVIN M.
Beginnings of Freemasonry in America, The
(New York, 1924)

JONES, SIR WILLIAM
Works of Sir William Jones, The (London,
1799)

JOSEPHUS, FLAVIUS
Works of Flavius Josephus, The (Oxford,
1839)

JOVIUS, PAULUS
Vitae Illustrium Virorum (Basil, 1578)

JOWETT, B.
Dialogues of Plato, The (New York, 1905)

KALISCH, ISIDOR
Sepher Yezirah, a Book on Creation (New
York, 1877)

KARAKA, DOSABHAI FRAMJI
History of the Parsis (London, 1884)

KEIGHTLEY, THOMAS
Mythology of Ancient Greece and Italy, The
(London, 1831)
Secret Societies of the Middle Ages (London,
1887)

KELLY, EDWARD
Alchemical Writings of Edward Kelly, The
(London, 1893)

KENEALY, E. Y.
Book of Enoch, The (London, ———)
Book of FO, The (London, 1878)

KHUNRATH, HENRICI
Amphitheatrum Sapientiae, etc. (Hanover,
1609)

KILNER, WALTER J.
Human Atmosphere, The (London, 1920)

KING, C. W.
Gnostics and Their Remains, The (London,
1864)

KINGSBOROUGH, LORD
Antiquities of Mexico (London, 1848)

KINGSFORD, ANNA
Astrology Theologized (London, 1886)
Virgin of the World, The (London, 1885)

KINGSLEY, CHARLES
Hypatia (London, 1920)

KIRCHER, ATHANASIUS
Ars Magna Sciendi (Amsterdam, 1669)
Magnes sive de Arte Magnetica Opus Triparti-
tum (———, 1643)
Œdipus Ægyptiacus (Rome, 1652)
Sphinx Mystagoga (Amsterdam, 1676)

KLAUBER, JOSEPHO AND JOANNE
Historiæ Biblicæ Veteris a Novi Testamenti
(———, 1640?)

KNIGHT, RICHARD PAYNE
A Discourse on the Worship of Priapus
(London, 1894)
Symbolical Language of Ancient Art and
Mythology, The (New York, 1876)

KUNOW, AMELIE DEVENTER VON
Francis Bacon, The Last of the Tudors (New
York, 1924)

LAERTIUS, DIOGENES
De Vitis, Dogmatibus, etc. (Amstelaedami,
1692)

LANE-POOLE, STANLEY
Studies in a Mosque (London, 1883)

LANG, ANDREW
Historical Mysteries (London, 1905)

LAWRENCE, BASIL E.
Notes on the Authorship of The Shakespeare
Plays and Poems (London, 1925)

LENOIR, ALEXANDRE
La Franche-Maconnerie (Paris, 1814)
Nouvel Essai sur la Table Isiaque (Paris, 1809)

LENORMANT, FRANÇOIS
Chaldean Magic: Its Origin and Development
(London, 1877)

LE PLONGEON, AUGUSTUS
Queen Moo and The Egyptian Sphinx (New
York, 1900)
Sacred Mysteries among the Mayas and the
Quiches (New York, 1909)

LEVI, ELIPHAS
Dogme et Rituel de la Haute Magie (Paris, 1894)
History of Magic, The (London, 1922)
Le Livre des Splendeurs (Paris, 1894)
Les Mystères de la Kabbale (Paris, 1920)
Magical Ritual of the Sanctum Regnum, The
(London, 1896)
Transcendental Magic (Chicago, 1910)

LEWIS, WILLIAM
A Course of Practical Chemistry (London, 1746)

LILLY, WILLIAM
An Astrological Prediction of the Occurrences in England (London, 1648)
Anima Astrologieae: or a Guide for Astrologers (London, 1676)
Astrology Modestly Treated of in three Books (London, 1647)
Merlin Reviv'd (London, 1615)

LLOYD, JOHN URI
Etidorhpa (Cincinnati, 1896)

LUNDY, JOHN P.
Monumental Christianity (New York, 1876)

LYCOSTHENES, CONRADUS
Prodigiorum ac Ostentorum Chronicon (Basle, 1557)

LYTTON, LORD BULWER-
Zanoni (London, 1843)

MAACK, FERDINAND (EDITOR)
Chymische Hochzeit: Christiani Rosencreutz, Anno 1459 (Berlin, 1913)

MACGOWAN, KENNETH, AND ROSSE, HERMAN
Masks and Demons (New York, 1923)

MACGREGOR-MATHERS, S. L.
Book of the Sacred Magic of Abra-Melin the Mage, The (New York, 1905)
Kabbalah Unveiled, The (New York, 1912)
Key of Solomon the King, The (London, 1889)

MACKENZIE, DONALD
Ancient Man in Britain (London, 1902)
Migration of Symbols, The (New York, 1926)

MACKEY, SAMPSON ARNOLD
Mythological Astronomy of the Ancients Demonstrated, The (Norwich, 1824)

MACOY, ROBERT
General History, Cyclopedia and Dictionary of Freemasonry (New York, 1870)

MAIER, MICHAEL
Scrutinium Chyrnicum (Frankfort, 1687)
Viatorium (Rothomagi, 1651)

MAIMONIDES, MOSES
Guide for the Perplexed, The (London, 1919)

MALCOLM, J. COOPER
"Tau," The (Brochure, 1901)

MANNHART, W.
Zauberglaube und Geheimwissen (Berlin, 1920)

MARTYN, JOHN
Bucolicks of Virgil, The (London, 1749)

MASSEY, GERALD
A Book of the Beginnings (London, 1881)
Natural Genesis, The (London, 1883)

MATHER, JR., FRANK JEWETT
Portraits of Dante, The (Princeton, 1921)

MAURICE, THOMAS
Indian Antiquities (London, 1800)

McCARTY, LOUIS P.
Great Pyramid Jeezeh, The (San Francisco, 1907)

MEAD, G.R.S.
Apollonius of Tyana (London and Benares, 1901)
Fragments of a Faith Forgotten (London, 1900)
Hymn of the Robe of Glory, The (London, 1908)
Orpheus (London, 1896)
Pistis Sophia (London, 1921)
Simon Magus, An Essay (London, 1892)
Thrice Great Hermes, The (London, 1906)

MERLIN, R.
Origine des Cartes à Jouer (Paris, 1869)

MEYRICK, SAMUEL, AND SMITH, CHARLES
Costume of the Original Inhabitants of The British Islands, The (London, 1815)

MILLS, L. H.
A Study in the Five Zarathushtrian Gàthàs (Oxford, 1892)

MINSHEU, JOHN
Minsheu's Guide into the Tongues, with their agreement and consent with one another in nine languages (London, 1626)

MONTFAUCON
Antiquity Explained by Montfaucon (London, 1721)
Morufauconii Antiquitates Graecae et Romanae (Nürnberg, 1757)

MOORE, EDWARD
Hindu Pantheon, The (London, 1810)

MOORE, GEORGE FOOTE
Judaism (Cambridge, 1927)

MORELL, J. D.
An Historical and Critical View of the Speculative Philosophy of Europe in the Nineteenth Century (New York, 1872)

MORLEY, HENRY
Life of Henry Cornelius Agrippa, The
(London, 1856)

MORLEY, SYLVANUS GRISWOLD
Inscriptions at Copan (Washington, 1920)

MUIR, SIR WILLIAM
Life of Mohammad, The (Edinburgh, 1912)

MULHALL, MARION MCMURROUGH
Beginnings or Glimpses of Vanished Civilizations (London, 1911)

MÜLLER, F. MAX
Natural Religion (London, 1889)

MYER, ISAAC
Qabbalah, The Philosophical Writings of
Avicebron (Philadelphia, 1888)
Scarabs (New York, 1894)

NAUMANN, EMIL
History of Music, The (London, ——)

NAXAGARAS, JOHANN
Concordantia Philosophorum (Breslau, 1712)

NEWBERRY, THOMAS
Tabernacle and the Temple (London, 1887)

NOSTRADAMUS, MICHAEL
True Prophecies of Michael Nostradamus,
The (London, 1685)

NOVI, CLAUDIUS DE DOMINICO
CELENTANO VALLIS
Rosicrucian, Hermetic and Alchemical Manuscript, written and illustrated in the year
1606 in Naples.

OAKLEY, I. COOPER-
Comte de St.-Germain, The (Milan, 1912)
Tracts of a Hidden Tradition in Masonry and
Mediæval Mysticism (London, 1900)

O'BRIEN, HENRY
Round Towers of Ireland, The (London, 1834)

OLIVER, GEORGE
Signs and Symbols, Twelve Lectures on
Freemasonry (New York, 1906)

O'NEILL, JOHN
Night of the Gods, The (London, 1893)

ORR, JAMES (EDITOR)
International Standard Bible Dictionary, The
(Chicago, 1915)

OUVAROFF, M.
Essay on the Mysteries of Eleusis (London,
1817)

OWEN, CHARLES
An Essay Towards a Natural History of
Serpents (London, 1742)

OXON, F. H.
Paracelsus, His Auroa, & Treasure of the
Philosophers As also The Water-Stone of
The Wise Men (London, 165-?)

PALMER, E. H. (EDITOR)
Qur'ân, The (Oxford, 1880)

PAPUS
Tarot of the Bohemians, The (London, 1919)

PARACELSUS
Complete Writings of Paracelsus of Hohen-
heim, The (Strasbourg, 1616)
Hermetic and Alchemical Writings of Aureo-
lus Philippus Theophrastus Bombast of
Hohenheim called Paracelsus the Great,
The (London, 1894). Edited by Arthur
Edward Waite.

PARADIN, CLAUDE
Symbola Heroica (Leiden, 1600)

PARSONS, ALBERT ROSS
New Light on the Great Pyramid (New York,
1893)

PAYNE, JOHN (TRANSLATOR)
Book of the Thousand Nights and One Night,
The (London, 1884)
Tales from the Arabic (London, 1884)

PECK, HARRY THURSTON
Harper's Dictionary of Classical Literature
and Antiquities (New York, 1897)

PEMBERTON, JR., HENRY
Shakespere and Sir Walter Ralegh (Philadelphia and London, 1914)

PERRY, RALPH BARTON
Present Philosophical Tendencies (New York, 1916)

PERRY, W. J.
Children of the Sun, The (New York, 1923)

PHANEG, G.
Cinquante Merveilleux Secrets d'Alchimie (Paris, 1912)

PHILALETHES, EIRENAEUS
Ripley Reviv'd (London, 1678)

PHILALETHES, EUGENIUS
Anthroposophia Theomagica (London, 1650)
Euphrates, Or the Waters of the East (London, 1655)
Lumen de Lumine: or a New Magicall Light (London, 1651)
Second Wash, The (London, 1651)

PHILO JUDÆUS
Works of, The (London, 1854)

PHILPOT, (MRS.) J. H.
Sacred Tree or The Tree in Religion and Myth, The (London, 1897)

PICART, BERNARD
Religious Ceremonies and Customs of the several Nations of the World (London, 1731)

PIETRO DI ABANO
Gli Elementi Magica (Manuscript on vellum, early 17th century)

PIGNORIUS, LAURENTIUS
Mensæ Isiacæ Expositio (Frankfort, 1608)

PIKE, ALBERT
Albert Pike Centenary Souvenir of His Birth (Washington, 1909) (By several eminent Masons)
Ancient and Accepted Scottish Rite of Freemasonry. The Constitutions and Regulations of 1762. (New York, A.M. 5664)
Ex Corde Locutiones (Washington, 1897)
Irano-Aryan Faith and Doctrine (Louisville, 1924)
Letter (The) "Human Genus" of the Pope, Leo XIII, and the Reply for the Ancient and Accepted Scottish Rite of Freemasonry (Charleston, 1884)

Liturgy of the Ancient and Accepted Scottish Rite of Freemasonry (A.M. 5638)
Masonic Symbolism
Morals and Dogma of the Ancient and Accepted Scottish Rite of Freemasonry (Charleston, A.M. 5641)
Sephar H'Debarim (The Book of the Words) (A.M. 5638)

PISTOR, JOHN
Book of the Cabalistick Art (Undated manuscript copy)

PLUNKET, EMMELINE M.
Ancient Calendars and Constellations (London, 1903)

POE, EDGAR ALLAN
Works of Edgar Allan Poe, The (New York, 1904)

PORTA, GIOVANNI BATTISTA DELLA
De Occultis Literarum Notis (Montisbeligardi, 1593)
Magiæ Naturalis, Libri Viginti (Frankfort, 1591)

POTT, (MRS.) HENRY
Francis Bacon and His Secret Society (London, 1891)

POTTENGER, MILTON
Symbolism (Sacramento, 1905)

PRASAD, RAMA
Nature's Finer Forces (London, 1911)

PRETON, WILLIAM
Illustrations of Masonry (London, circa 1801)

PRICHARD, J. C.
An Analysis of the Egyptian Mythology (London, 1819)

PRYSE, JAMES MORGAN
Book of the Azure Veil, The ("Lucifer" Magazine, 1894–1895)
Restored New Testament, The (New York, 1916)

PTOLEMY
Ptolemy's Tetrabiblos (London, 1822)

QUARLES, FRANCIS
Emblems, Divine and Moral (London, 1824)

RALEGH, SIR WALTER
History of the World, The (London, 1614)

RAMSAY, CHARLES A.
Tacheographia seu Ars Celeriter & compen-
diose quaelibet inter perorandum verba, ut
ne unum quidem excidat, describendi
(Paris, 1683)

RAND, BENJAMIN
Modern Classical Philosophers (Boston and
New York, 1908)

RAPHAEL
Astrologer of the Nineteenth Century, The
(London, 1825)

REDGROVE, H. STANLEY
Alchemy: Ancient and Modern (London,
1911)
Bygone Beliefs (London, 1920)

RENOUF, SIR P. LE PAGE
(TRANSLATOR)
Egyptian Book of the Dead, The (London,
1904). (Contains many notes in autograph
of Gerald Massey.)

RENSSELAER, (MRS.) JOHN KING VAN
Devil's Picture Books, A History of Playing
Cards, The (London, 1892)
Prophetical, Educational and Playing Cards
(Philadelphia, 1912)

RHIND, W. C.
High Priest of Israel, The (London, 1868)

RICHARDSON, J.
Works of Mr. Jonathan Richardson, The
(London, 1773)

RICHEPIN, JEAN
Nouvelle Mythologie Illustrée (Paris, 1920)

ROBERTS, SAMUEL
Gypsies, The (London, 1842)

ROBERTSON, JOHN M.
Philosophical Works of Francis Bacon, The
(London, 1915)

ROSENROTH, KORR VON
Kabbala Denudata (Francofurti, 1677)

ROSS, ALEXANDER
Mystagogus Poeticus (London, 1648)

SAINT-MARTIN, LOUIS CLAUDE DE
Man: His True Nature and Ministry (London,
1864)

SALMON, WILLIAM
Compleat English Physician, The (London,
1693)

SALVERTE, EUSEBE
Occult Sciences and The Philosophy of
Magic, The (London, 1846)

SANDIVOGIUIS, MICHEEL
A New Light of Alchymie (London, 1650)

SANTEE, M.D., HARRIS E.
Anatomy of the Brain and Spinal Cord
(Philadelphia, 1915)

SCHEIBLE, J.
Theoretical and Practical Teaching Concerning the Book of Thot, The (Stuttgart, 1857)

SCHERER, VALENTIN
Dürer, Des Meisters Gemalde Kupferstiche
und Holzschnitte (Stuttgart, 1908)

SCHOEFFER, IOANNIS
Collectanea Antiquitatum in Urbe atque Agro
Moguntino Repertarum (Mainz, 1520)

SCHOOLCRAFT, HENRY R.
Indian Tribes of the United States, The.
Edited by Francis S. Drake. (Philadelphia,
1884)

SCHOTTO, GASPARE
Physica Curiosa (Herbipoli, 1697)

SCHURÉ, EDOUARD
Great Initiates, The (London, 1920)

SCOTT, WALTER
Hermetica (Oxford, 1924, 1925, and 1926)

SEINGALT, JACQUES CASANOVA DE
Memoirs (Boston, 1903)

SELENUS, GUSTAVUS
Cryptomenytices, et Cryptographiæ, Libri IX
(Lunæburg, 1624)

SELER, DR. EDUARD (ELUCIDATED BY)
Codex Vaticanus No. 3773 (Berlin and London, 1902–1903)

SEPHARIAL
Kabala of Numbers, The (London, 1914)

SEYFFERT, OSKAR
A Dictionary of Classical Antiquities (London, 1904)

SEYMOUR, WILLIAM W.
Cross in Tradition, History and Art, The (New York, 1898)

SHAKESPEARE, WILLIAM
First Collected Edition of the Dramatic Works of William Shakespeare, The (London, 1623)
Second Collected Edition of the Dramatic Works of William Shakespeare, The (London, 1632)
Third Collected Edition of the Dramatic Works of William Shakespeare, The (London, 1663)
Fourth Collected Edition of the Dramatic Works of William Shakespeare, The (London, 1685)
Shakespeare (William) Works (London, 1880–1891). Quarto Facsimiles.

SHAW, CLEMENT B.
Frithiof's Saga (Chicago, 1908)

SIBLY, E.
A Key to Physic, and the Occult Sciences (London, 1787)
A New and Complete Astrology (London, 1785)

SICKELS, DANIEL
General Ahiman Rezon and Freemason's Guide, The (New York, 1920)

SICULUS, DIODORUS
Historia (Paris, 1513)

SIDNEY, SIR PHILIP
Countesse of Pembrokes Arcadia, The (London, 1633)

SINGER, JR., EDGAR A.
Modern Thinkers and Present Problems (New York, 1923)

SINGER, ISIDORE (EDITOR)
Jewish Encyclopedia, The (New York, 1903)

SINGER, SAMUEL WELLER
Researches into the History of Playing Cards (London, 1816)

SKINNER, J. RALSTON
Notes on the Cabbalah of the Old Testament (From "The Path," N.Y., 1887)
Source of Measures, The (Cincinnati, 1875)

SMEDLEY, WILLIAM T.
Mystery of Francis Bacon, The (London, 1912)

SMITH, DAVID EUGENE
History of Mathematics (Boston, 1925)

SMITH, GEORGE
Chaldean Account of Genesis, The (New York, 1876)

SMITH, ROBERT
Harmonics, or the Philosophy of Musical Sounds (London, 1759)

SMYTH, C. PIAZZI
Life and Work at the Great Pyramid (Edinburgh, 1867)
Our Inheritance in the Great Pyramid (London, 1874)

SPEED, JOHN
History of Great Britaine, The (London, 1627)

SPENCE, LEWIS
Myths and Legends of Babylonia and Assyria (London, 1916)
Myths of Mexico and Peru, The (New York, 1913)
Myths of the North American Indians (New York, 1914)

SPENSER, EDM.
Faerie Queene (The): The Shepheards Calendar: Together with other Works (London, 1617)

SPRINGETT, BERNARD H.
Secret Secrets of Syria and the Lebanon (London, 1922)

SQUIER, E. G.
Serpent Symbol, The (New York, 1851)

STANLEY, THOMAS
History of Philosophy, The (London, 1743); do (London, 1687)

STEFFEN, ALBERT
Hieram und Salomo (Dornach, 1925)

STEINER, DR. RUDOLF
Manuscript lectures on the Rosicrucians
Occult Seals and Columns (London, 1924)
Submerged Continents of Atlantis and
    Lemuria (Rajput Press, 1911)
Way of Initiation, The (New York, 1910)

STENGEL, GEORG
Emblems (Munich, 1635)

STENRING, KNUT
Book of Formation, The (London, 1923)

STEPHEN, HENRIE
A World of Wonders (London, 1607)

STEPHENS, JOHN L.
Incidents of Travel in Central America
    (London, 1841)

STILLMAN, JOHN MAXSON
Paracelsus, His Personality and Influence
    (Chicago, 1920)

STODDART, ANNA M.
Life of Paracelsus, The (Philadelphia, 1911)

SWANWICK, ANNA
Dramas of Æeschylus, The (London, 1873)

SWINBURNE, CHARLES
William Blake, A Critical Essay (London,
    1868)

SYLVESTER, JOSUAH
Du Bartas, His Divine Weekes and Workes
    (London, 1641)

TAYLOR, EDWARD S.
History of Playing Cards, The (London,
    1865)

TAYLOR, JOHN
Water Poet's Works, The (London, 1630)

TAYLOR, THOMAS
A Dissertation on the Eleusinian and Bacchic
    Mysteries (Amsterdam, ——)
An Answer to Dr. Gilles Supplement
    (London, 1804)
An Essay on the Beautiful by Plotinus
    (London, 1917)
Apuleius on the God of Socrates (London,
    1822)
Arguments of the Emperor Julian against the
    Christians (London, 1809)

Cratylus Phaedo, Parmenides and Timaeus of
    Plato (London, 1793)
Description of Greece, by Pausanias, The
    (London, 1794)
Eleusinian and Bacchic Mysteries (New York,
    1891)
Five Books of Plotinus (London, 1794)
Fragments of Proclus (London, 1825)
Iamblichus on The Mysteries (London,
    1895)
Life of Pythagoras, by Iamblichus (London,
    1818)
Metamorphosis, or Golden Ass of Apuleius
    (London, 1822)
Metaphysics of Aristotle (London, 1801)
Miscellanies in Prose and Verse (London,
    1805)
Mystical Hymns of Orpheus (London,
    1896)
Ocellus Lucanus on the Nature of the Uni-
    verse; etc. (London, 1831)
Phaedrus of Plato (London, 1792)
Philosophical and Mathematical Commen-
    taries of Proclus (London, 1788)
Political Fragments of Archytas, Charondas,
    Zaleucus and others (Chiswick, 1822)
Pythagoric Sentences of Demophilus (Lon-
    don, 1804)
Rhetoric, Poetic, and Nicomachean Ethics of
    Aristotle (London, 1818)
Sallust on The Gods and the World (London,
    1793)
Select Works of Plotinus (London, 1817)
Select Works of Porphyry (London, 1823)
Six Books of Proclus on the Theology of Plato
    (London, 1816)
Theoretic Arithmetic (London, 1816)
Treatises of Fictions on Suicide London,
    1834)
Two Orations of the Emperor Julian (London,
    1793)
Two Treatises of Proclus (London, 1833)
Works of Plato, The (London, 1804)

TEMPLE, RONALD
Message from the King's Coffer, The
    (Sausalito, 1920)

THOMAS, WILLIAM, AND PAVITT, KATE
Book of Talismans, Amulets and Zodiacal
    Gems, The (Philadelphia, circa 1914)

THOMASSIN, SIMON
Recueil des Figures, Groupes, Thermes,
    Fontaines, Vases et autres Ornements
    (Paris?, circa 1689)

TOY, CRAWFORD HOWELL
Judaism and Christianity (Boston, 1902)

TRISMOSIN, SOLOMON
Splendor Solis (Reprint of Manuscript dated
    1582, in British Museum)

TRITHEMIUS, JOHN
Liber Octo Quaestionum (Frankfort, 1550)
Steganographiæ nec non Claviculæ Salomonis
    (Cologne, 1635)

TROWBRIDGE, W.R.H.
Cagliostro, the Splendour and Misery of a
    Master of Magic (New York, 1910)

TULANE UNIVERSITY OF LOUISIANA,
THE (PUBLISHER)
Tribes and Temples (New Orleans, 1927)

TURPIN, M.
Histoire de la Vie de Mahomet (Paris, 1773)

ULLAH, MEAMET
History of the Afgans, The (London, 1829)

UPHAM, EDWARD
History and Doctrine of Budhism, The
    (London, 1829)

VÆNIUS, OTHO
Theatro Moral de la Vida Humana (Amberes,
    1733)

VAIL, CHARLES H.
Ancient Mysteries and Modern Masonry, The
    (New York, 1909)

VALENTINE, BASIL
Last Will and Testament of Basil Valentine,
    The (London, 1671)
Triumphant Chariot of Antimony, with Anno-
    tations of Theodore Kirkringius, M. D.,
    The (London, 1678)

VERSTEGAN, RICHARD
Restitution of Decayed Intelligence, The
    (London, 1628)

VIBERT, LIONEL
Rare Books of Freemasonry, The (London,
    1923)

VILLARS, ABBÉ N. DE MONTFAUCON DE
Comte de Gabalis (Paterson, 1914); do, origi-
    nal in French (Cologne, 1684)
Sub-Mundanes; or, The Elementaries of the
    Cabala (Bath, 1886)

VITRUVIUS
Cesariano's Edition of Vitruvius (Como,
    1521)
Di Lucio Vitruvio Pollione de Architectura
    Libri Dece (Venice, 1524)
Ten Books on Architecture, The (Cambridge,
    1914). Translated by Morris Hicky
    Morgan.

VOLNEY, M.
Ruins of Empires, The (London, 1792)

WAITE, ARTHUR EDWARD
A New Encyclopaedia of Freemasonry
    (London, 1921)
Book of Ceremonial Magic, The (London,
    1911)
Brotherhood of the Rosy Cross, The
    (London, 1924)
Doctrine and Literature of the Kabalah
    (London, 1902)
False Monarchy of Demons, The (Original
    Manuscript)
Lives of Alchemystical Philosophers (London,
    1888)
Occult Sciences, The (London, 1891)
Real History of the Rosicrucians, The
    (London, 1887)
Secret Doctrine in Israel, The (Boston,
    1914)
Secret Tradition in Freemasonry, The
    (London, 1911)
Works of Thomas Vaughan, The (London,
    1919)

WEEMES, JOHN
Observations, Natural and Moral (London,
    1636)

WEIDENFIELD JOHANNES SEGERUS
Secrets of the Adepts, The (London, 1685)

WEISSE, JOHN A.
Obelisk in Freemasonry, The (New York,
    1880)

WELLCOME, HENRY S.
Ancient Cymric Medicine (London, 1903)

WELLING, GEORGIUS VON
Salt, Sulphur and Mercury (Frankfort and
Leipzig, 1760)

WELLS, H. G.
Outline of History (London, 1920)

WESTCOTT, WILLIAM WYNN
A Recent Spiritual Development (London,
1917)
An Essay upon The Constitution of Man:
Spirit, Soul, Body (London,——)
An Introduction to the Study of the Kabalah
(London, 1910)
Data of the History of the Rosicrucians
(London, 1916)
Hermetic Arcanum (London, 1893)
Isiac Tablet of Cardinal Bembo, The (Bath,
1887)
Magic Roll, The (London, 1903)
Notes on a Curious Certificate and Seal
(London, 1906)
Numbers, Their Occult Power and Mystic
Virtues (London, 1911)
Origin and History of Astrology, The
(London, 1902)
Religion, Philosophy and Occult Science of
China, The (London, 1911)
Rosicrucians (The), Past and Present, at
Home and Abroad (London, ——)
Rosicrucian Thoughts on the Ever-Burning
Lamps of the Ancients (London, 1885)
Sepher Yetzirah (London, 1911)
Somnium Scipionis (London, 1894)
Star Lore of the Bible, The (London, 1912)

WESTROPP, HODDER M., AND WAKE, C.
STANILAND
Ancient Symbol Worship (New York, 1875)

WIGSTON, W.F.C.
Columbus of Literature, The (Chicago, 1892)
Francis Bacon versus Phantom Captain
Shakespeare (London, 1891)
Hermes Stella (London, 1890)

WILDER, ALEXANDER
Philosophy and Ethics of the Zoroasters
(——, 1885)

WILKINSON, J. G.
Manners and Customs of the Ancient Egyp-
tians (London, 1837) First Series; do
(London, 1841) Second Series.

WILLIAMS, JOHN
Life and Actions of Alexander the Great, The
(London, 1829)

WILLIS, WILLIAM
Shakespeare-Bacon Controversy, The. A Re-
port of the Trial of an Issue in Westminster
Hall, 1627. (London, 1903)

WILSON, H. H.
Vishnu Purana, The (London, 1840)

WILSON, JAMES
A Complete Dictionary of Astrology (London,
1819)

WILSON, THOMAS
Swastika, The (Washington, 1896)

WINDELBAND, DR. W.
History of Philosophy (London, 1898)

WITHER, GEORGE
A Collection of Emblemes, Ancient and Moderne (London, 1635)

WOLFIUS, HIERONYMUS
Epicteti Enchiridion, item Cebetis Thebani
Tabula (Basle, 1561)

WOODWARD, FRANK
Francis Bacon's Cipher Signatures (London,
1923)

WOODWARD, PARKER
Early Life of Lord Bacon, The (London,
1902)

WRIGHT, DUDLEY
Druidism, the Ancient Faith of Britain
(London, 1924)

WRIGHT, ROBERT C.
Indian Masonry (Ann Arbor, Michigan,
1907)

WULKER, RICHARD
Geschichte der Englishchen Litteratur
(Leipzig und Wien, 1896)

Y-WORTH, W.
Chymicus Rationalis; or, The Fundamental
Grounds of the Chymical Art (London,
1692)

MISCELLANEOUS
Anales del Museo Nacional de México
(Mexico, 1882)

Annual Report of the Board of Regents of the Smithsonian Institution for the year ending June 30th, 1915. (Washington, 1916)

Ancient Gems (London, ———). From Collections of Earl Percy, Hon. C. T. Greville, T. M. Slade.

Biblische Figuren des Alten Testaments ganz kunstlich gerissen durch den weit berühmten Vergilium Solis, Maler und Kunstecher zu Nürnberg.

Catholic Encyclopedia, The (New York, 1909)

Collectanea Chemica (London, 1893). By several authors.

Dictionnaire Mytho-Hermétique (Paris, 1758). By Antoine-Joseph Pernety.

Egyptian Magic (London, 1896). By S.S.D.D.

Encyclopædia Britannica, The (New York, 1911), Eleventh Edition.

English Hexapla, The (London, 1841). Being six English translations of the New Testament.

Geheime Figuren der Rosenkreuzer (Ultona, 1785)

Hermetic Museum (The), Restored and Enlarged (London, 1893); do (Frankfort, 1678)

History of the Holy Cross, The (London, 1863)

Household Words, A Weekly Journal (New York). Conducted by Charles Dickens.

Koran (The): commonly called The Alcoran of Mohammed (London, 1734). Translated by George Sale from the Arabic.

La Biblia Que Es, Los Sacros Libros del Vieio y Nuevo Testamento (1569). The "Bear Bible," first Protestant Spanish Bible.

Library of Original Sources, The (Milwaukee, 1915)

Margarita Philosophica (Basil, 1508). First Encyclopaedia printed in Europe.

Mosaize Historic der Hebreeuwse Kerke (Amsterdam, 1700)

Nuremberg Chronicle, The (Nuremberg, 1493)

Phenix, The (New York, 1835). By several authors.

Reprints from Ars Quatuor Coronatorum (Margate from 1892 to 1903). By several authors.

Review of Reviews (New York, 1921)

Sacred Books and Early Literature of the East, The (London and New York, 1911). Edited by Prof. Charles F. Horne.

Sammlung der Groessten Geheimnisse Ausserordentlicher Menschen in alter Zeit (Koeln, 1725). By several authors.

Smithsonian Institution, Bureau of Ethnology (Washington, 1904). Bull. 28.

Third Annual Report of the Bureau of Ethnology (Washington, 1884)

Fifth Annual Report of the Bureau of Ethnology (Washington, 1887)

Sixth Annual Report of the Bureau of Ethnology (Washington, 1888)

Eighth Annual Report of the Bureau of Ethnology (Washington, 1891)

Ninth Annual Report of the Bureau of Ethnology (Washington, 1892)

Fourteenth Annual Report of the Bureau of Ethnology (Washington, 1896)

Nineteenth Report of the American Bureau of Ethnology (Washington, 1900)

Twenty-First Annual Report of the Bureau of American Ethnology (Washington, 1903)

Twenty-Third Annual Report of the Bureau of American Ethnology (Washington, 1904)

Twenty-Fifth Annual Report of the Bureau of American Ethnology (Washington, 1903–04)

World Almanac and Book of Facts, The (New York, 1925). Edited by Robert Hunt Lyman.

Index

A

Abba, the Great Father, constitution of in the Sephirothic Tree 389

Abracadabra declared by Mackey to be ancient recognition of alternation of poles 151

Abraxas declared by Mackey to be ancient recognition of alternation of poles 151

Abraxas, description of the image of 56

Abraxas, numerical value of 56, 208

Abraxas, peculiar concept of the Deity formulated by Basilides 56

Abraxas usually symbolized as a composite creature 56

Absolute, The (See also AIN SOPH)
(See also God)

Absolute, The, realization of made possible through intellectual intuition 29

Absolute, The, teachings of Fichte and Schelling regarding 29

Acacia an emblem of immortality 298

Acacia an emblem of purity 298

Acacia an emblem of regeneration 298

Acacia an emblem of vernal equinox 298

Academic school of philosophy instituted by Plato 20

Academia, definition of 22

Acoustic properties of temples of initiation 256

Acroamatic cipher, definition of 560

Acroamatic cipher, examples of 560

Acroamatic cipher the most subtle form 561

Acrostic signatures a form of literal cipher 559

Acrostic signatures, examples found in Shakespearian writings 546

Acthnici one of the most important subdivisions of salamanders 338

Action, right, a prerequisite of right knowing 665

Action, right, one of three channels for expression of Christ power 240

Activity the only part of God cognizable to lower senses 230

Adam a prototype of Christ 401

Adam a type of the Temple 404

Adam accredited with power of spiritual generation 404

Adam, analogy between Sephiroth and 387

Adam, analogy with CHiram 239

Adam, androgynal nature of 401

Adam, concept of according to Zohar 401

Adam, fall of into the World to Assiah 401

Adam Kadmon, analogy of with Sephirothic Tree 388

Adam Kadmon the personification of the ten roots of Tree of Life 375

Adam likened to Pythagorean monad 400

Adam likened by St. Augustine to Christ 406

Adam likened to the Macrocosm or Demiurgus 402

Adam likened to the Microcosm 402

Adam likened to the rational nature 405

Adam, philosophical meaning of Adam's banishment from Garden of Eden 400, 406

Adam, Qabbalistic conception of 387

Adam, Qabbalistic legend concerning Adam and the cross 592

Adam representative of full spiritual nature of man 402

Adam, restoration of to Garden of Eden 406

Adam (ADM), significance of according to Notarikon 403

Adam the Platonic *Idea* of humanity according to the Neo-Platonists 400

Adam the primitive Phallus 403

Adam, universal nature and constitution of 401

Adamites a Gnostic sect 58

Adams, four, of the four Qabbalistic worlds 401

ADM, significance of 402

ADM, significance of according to Notarikon 403

Adepts, powers of 512

Adepts, true secrets of transmutation and multiplication possessed by 511

Adonai a personification of the sun 134

Adonai, Mysteries of the esoteric teachings of Judaism 397

Adonian Mysteries, Pythagoras initiated into 192

Adonis a solar deity 88, 134

Adonis, Atys considered synonymous with 88

Adonis (Adonai), Mysteries of 88

Adonis one of the crucified Saviors of humanity 600

Adonis, sun worshiped under name of 64

Adonis the exoteric name of the Jewish God 87

Adversary, the, power of evil inherent in matter 378

Aeons (Angels) product of the six emanations united with the Eternal Flame 55

Æsthetics, effect of upon human life 245

Æsthetics one of the six disciplines of philosophy 14

Aethalides one of the incarnations of Pythagoras 198

Æther symbolized by the brain 229

"Age" a paramount factor in determining form of religious worship 154

B

C

Ɛ

G

H

Ỉ

K

m

n

O

P

Q

R

U

V

W

X

Y

Z

About the Author

MANLY P. HALL (1901–1990) was the founder of the Philosophical Research Society. In over seventy-five years of dynamic public activity, he delivered more than 8,000 lectures in the United States and abroad, and authored countless books, essays, and articles. In his lectures and writings, Manly Hall always emphasized the practical aspects of philosophy and religion as they applied to daily living. He restated for modern man those spiritual and ethical doctrines which have given humanity its noblest ideals and most adequate codes of conduct. Believing that philosophy is a working tool to help the individual in building a solid foundation for his dreams and purposes, Manly Hall steadfastly sought recognition of the belief that world civilization can be perfected only when human beings meet on a common ground of intelligence, cooperation, and worthy purpose.

THE PHILOSOPHICAL RESEARCH SOCIETY (www.prs.org) is a nonprofit organization founded in 1934 for the purpose of assisting thoughtful persons to live more graciously and constructively in a confused and troubled world. The Society is entirely free from educational, political, or ecclesiastical control. Dedicated to an idealistic approach to the solution of human problems, the Society's program stresses the need for the integration of religion, philosophy, and the science of psychology into one system of instruction. The goal of this instruction is to enable the individual to develop a mature philosophy of life, to recognize his proper responsibilities and opportunities, and to understand and appreciate his place in the unfolding universal pattern.

Manly P. Hall's legacy includes the nation's premier educational institution dedicated solely to the wisdom traditions and cutting-edge consciousness studies. THE UNIVERSITY OF PHILOSOPHICAL RESEARCH (www.uprs.edu) in Los Angeles offers state-approved master's degree programs in consciousness studies and transformational psychology.

Lectures on Ancient Philosophy

COMPANION TO

The Secret Teachings of All Ages

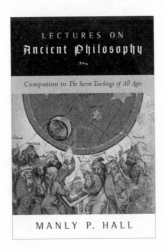

In *Lectures on Ancient Philosophy*, Manly P. Hall expands on the philosophical, metaphysical, and cosmological themes introduced in his classic work, *The Secret Teachings of All Ages.*

Hall wrote this volume as a reader's companion to his earlier work, intending it for those wishing to delve more deeply into the esoteric philosophies and ideas that undergird the *Secret Teachings.*

Particular attention is paid to Neoplatonism; ancient christianity; Rosicrucian and Freemasonic traditions; ancient mysteries; pagan rites and symbols; and Pythagorean mathematics.

First published in 1929 —the year after the publication of Hall's magnum opus—this new edition of *Lectures on Ancient Philosophy* includes the author's original subject index, twenty diagrams prepared under his supervision for the volume, and Hall's 1984 preface to frame the book for the contemporary reader.

Lectures on Ancient Philosophy: ISBN 1-58542-432-3 (trade paperback)